LABOR
AND
EMPLOYMENT
LAW DESK BOOK

LABOR
AND
EMPLOYMENT
LAW DESK BOOK

Gordon E. Jackson

Prentice-Hall, Inc.
Englewood Cliffs, New Jersey

Prentice-Hall International, Inc., *London*
Prentice-Hall of Australia, Pty. Ltd., *Sydney*
Prentice-Hall Canada, Inc., *Toronto*
Prentice-Hall of India Private Ltd., *New Delhi*
Prentice-Hall of Japan, Inc., *Tokyo*
Prentice-Hall of Southeast Asia Pte. Ltd., *Singapore*
Whitehall Books, Ltd., *Wellington, New Zealand*
Editora Prentice-Hall do Brasil Ltda., *Rio de Janeiro*
Prentice-Hall Hispanoamericana, S.A., *Mexico*

© 1986 *by*

Gordon E. Jackson

This publication is designed to provide accurate and authoritative information in regard to the subject matter covered. It is sold with the
understanding that the publisher is not engaged in rendering legal,
accounting, or other professional service. If legal advice or other expert assistance is required, the services of a competent professional
person should be sought.

*. . . From the Declaration of Principles jointly adopted by a Committee of the
American Bar Association and a Committee of Publishers and Associations.*

10   9   8   7   6

Library of Congress Cataloging-in-Publication Data

Jackson, Gordon E.
    The labor and employment law desk book.

    Includes index.
    1. Labor laws and legislation—United States.
I. Title.
KF3319.J33 1986   344.73′01   86-5034
                       347.3041

ISBN 0-13-517848-7

PRINTED IN THE UNITED STATES OF AMERICA

To
Sandy

for love—
and patience

About the Author

GORDON E. JACKSON is a nationally renowned author and speaker on the subject of labor relations. He is the author of *When Labor Trouble Strikes: An Action Handbook, Unlawful Terminations and Employment-at-Will, The Law of Employer and Employee Rights Case Manual* and *How to Stay Union Free,* the standard reference guide to union prevention.

Gordon Jackson is a frequent speaker and lecturer at Labor Relations Seminars and Conferences throughout the nation. He handles labor and employment law matters for a variety of industries, businesses, health-care facilities, and other employers, from his headquarters in Memphis, Tennessee, where he is the senior partner in the law firm of Jackson, Yeiser, Forman, and Allen.

Gordon Jackson is a member of the Lawyer-to-Lawyer Consultation Panel, the Labor and Employment Law Section of the American Bar Association, and a member of the American Academy of Hospital Attorneys of the American Hospital Association.

Preface

The *LABOR AND EMPLOYMENT LAW DESK BOOK* is a one-volume reference guide to the entire spectrum of federal and state labor and employment laws.

It provides attorneys, personnel professionals, executives, and labor representatives quick access to a comprehensive, yet succinct, discussion of a given legal issue within the scope of the labor law field.

This is a reference book, as distinguished from a treatise. It gets you quickly into the applicable law, rather than belaboring the historical and social developments.

The *LABOR AND EMPLOYMENT LAW DESK BOOK* is unique. It is the only one-volume reference guide to both federal and state substantive and procedural laws pertaining to labor relations. It is, indeed, the one book that a labor relations attorney, personnel professional, or labor representative should have within his or her immediate possession while in the office, "on the road," or in a court room, as the case may be.

You'll find this book to be a simplified tool to use in research matters. Researching a labor or employment question in the book is downright pleasurable in comparison with the more typical experience of trying to find answers from a host of other sources, sometimes involving multiple volumes or services.

The *LABOR AND EMPLOYMENT LAW DESK BOOK* addresses the procedural guidelines of each law and informs you how to process a particular claim, charge, or lawsuit. It also discusses the various defenses available to a given subject matter, as well. The book, therefore, is not only a ready reference guide, it is also a "how to" source.

The book is divided into six major parts so that each specific area of labor and employment law can be discussed in a systematic manner.

Part I covers the National Labor Relations Act, as amended, and related laws pertaining to collective bargaining rights. The Labor Management Relations Act, and its enforcement through the National Labor Relations Board, has created volumes of judicial precedent through the years. Part I is, therefore, an exercise in reducing this plethora of judicial precedent to an abbreviated, yet comprehensible form.

Part II covers Federal Anti-Discrimination laws, such as Title VII of the Civil Rights Act of 1964, another labor law that has generated an extremely large body of precedent since its inception. The Age Discrimination in Employment Act, the Equal Pay Act, the Rehabilitation Act and the Veterans Reemployment Act are also discussed in Part II of the book.

Part III discusses the Federal Wage and Hour laws, including an analysis of the Fair Labor Standards Act, the Walsh-Healy Act, the Davis-Bacon Act, and so forth.

Part IV discusses the Federal Safety and Health laws, including the Federal Occupational Safety and Health Act, the Federal Mine Safety and Health Act, and miscellaneous health and environmental statutes.

Part V addresses Federal Retirement, Welfare and Privacy laws, including a rather comprehensive discussion of the Pension Reform Act.

Part VI of the book addresses state statutory labor laws. Each state and its various labor laws are discussed separately for ease of reference and comprehension, thus providing the reader and researcher with a state-by-state analysis of the subject matter.

The last section of the book, Part VI, also addresses recent common law trends such as the continuing erosion of the employment-at-will doctrine and developments of employee rights such as the right to privacy, access to records, and protection against ''whistle-blowing.''

The *LABOR AND EMPLOYMENT LAW DESK BOOK* is a veritable one-volume labor law library. To that end, the book is dedicated to each and every labor relations attorney, personnel professional, and labor representative who needs rapid access and answers to labor law problems.

Gordon E. Jackson

Acknowledgments

Gratitude is expressed to my law partners, Ted M. Yeiser, Jr., Michael R. Forman, and Richard H. Allen, Jr., for their assistance and support toward the completion of this publication.

Special thanks are also expressed to my secretarial staff, Marcelle Browder, Pat Woods, Barbara Talley, Benita Caldwell, and Judy Warhurst for their cooperative spirit, encouraging comments, and professional dedication in the typing and coordination of various drafts and revisions in the preparation of this book.

Gratitude is also expressed to Jim Holt and Doug Gosden, who have most ably assisted me in research. Equal gratitude is extended to James M. Conlin, Jr., whose comments and suggestions have been most helpful throughout the course of this project.

Many thanks are also expressed to Geraldine Kyle, who performed the final editing and proofing of this desk book in keeping with her commendable writing talents.

Last, but not least, love and thanks are expressed to my wife, Sandy, and children, Angela, Celeste, Eric, and Amanda for their patience, understanding, and support.

Contents

ix

Part II
FEDERAL
ANTI-DISCRIMINATION LAWS
AND EXECUTIVE ORDERS   209

Part III
FEDERAL WAGE AND HOUR LAWS 315

Part IV
FEDERAL SAFETY AND HEALTH LAWS 369

Part V
FEDERAL RETIREMENT,
WELFARE, AND PRIVACY LAWS 403

Part VI
STATE LABOR LAWS   459

LABOR
AND
EMPLOYMENT
LAW DESK BOOK

PART I

NATIONAL LABOR
RELATIONS ACT
AND RELATED LAWS

1

Introduction to the Labor Management Relations Act

The present federal labor relations law is founded on four major statutes: The forerunner was the Norris-LaGuardia Act, which was passed in 1932; followed shortly thereafter by the National Labor Relations Act (NLRA), also known as the Wagner Act, in 1935; the NLRA was amended in 1947 by the passage of the Labor Management Relations Act (LMRA), also known as the Taft-Hartley Act; and, in 1959, the NLRA was amended for the second time with the enactment of the Labor-Management Reporting and Disclosure Act (LMRDA), also known as the Landrum-Griffin Act.

The Norris-LaGuardia Act will be discussed in Chapter 29 and the more specific provisions of the Labor-Management Reporting and Disclosure Act will be discussed in Chapter 25.

[1.01]   HISTORICAL DEVELOPMENT

The National Labor Relations Act was spawned by the Great Depression and the New Deal philosophy of the Roosevelt administration.

Although the Clayton Act of 1914, and especially the injunction prohibitions of the Norris-LaGuardia provisions of 1932, had curbed anti-labor decisions of the courts to some degree, by 1934 Congress perceived a need for additional legislation to protect the rights of employees in the private sector to unionize. As a result, U.S. Senator Robert Wagner urged his senatorial and congressional colleagues to pass his National Labor Relations bill.[1]

Although Senator Wagner was unsuccessful in his 1934 efforts, he proposed a similar bill in 1935, which, with the endorsement of the Roosevelt administration, successfully passed the Senate and the House and correspondingly became known as the National Labor Relations Act (The Wagner Act).

The 1935 Wagner Act addressed only employee protection against employers. Employers were given no protection against union misconduct, nor were employees given protection against union abuse.

In the late 1930s, and especially during the World War II period, much criticism was focused against the one-sidedness of the Wagner Act. The power of unions during this period and some unpopular work stoppages during the war years fostered the passage of the 1947 amendments to the NLRA. These amendments, which formulated the Labor Management Relations Act of 1947 (Taft-Hartley), attempted to balance the federal labor policy by adding restrictions on unions and guaranteeing certain freedoms of speech and conduct to employers and employees.[2]

Immediately after the passage of the Wagner Act, substantial criticism surfaced concerning its validity under the Federal Constitution. In 1936, the U.S. Supreme Court questioned the constitutionality of the NLRA without fully deciding the issue,[3] but in 1937, the court upheld the constitutionality of the Wagner Act.[4]

The Supreme Court held that it was a proper exercise and constitutional prerogative of Congress to regulate interstate and foreign commerce upon the rationale that strikes and other labor disturbances involving industries engaged in interstate commerce, so proximately obstruct and burden such commerce, as to bring labor relations of such industries within the regulatory powers of Congress.[5]

[1.02] SCOPE AND LIMITATIONS

The cornerstone of both the Wagner Act and the Labor Management Relations Act (hereinafter referred to as the LMRA and/or the Act)[6] is Section 7, which provides that protected employees shall have the right to form unions, join unions, and bargain collectively, as well as to engage in concerted activities for their mutual aid or protection. The LMRA amendments to Section 7 provide that employees shall also have the right to refrain from unions unless already represented by a union and subject to a union shop provision. Consequently, most of the provisions that follow Section 7 within the Act are designed to enforce and protect these rights of employees.

Section 8 of the Act addresses what actions (or inactions) will constitute an unfair labor practice on the part of employers as well as unions. (The original Act provided only for employer type unfair labor practices.)

Section 9 establishes the process of elections—conducted by the NLRB—to determine the representational desires of employees.

Section 10 of the Act outlines the powers of the National Labor Relations Board in the enforcement of the Act. Sections 11 and 13 set forth the respective investigatory responsibilities and limitations of the Board, and Section 12 establishes criminal sanctions for any individual interfering with the NLRB processes.

The LMRA has been held to be remedial in nature, rather than punitive.[7] The LMRA does not confer a private right to an employee, but was enacted to maintain industrial peace for the benefit of the public.[8]

The NLRB does not have self-enforcing powers and must enforce its decisions and injunctions through the federal courts. Nonetheless, substantial latitude and discretion is given the NLRB in its interpretation of the Act.[9]

The Labor Management Relations Act does not interfere with the rights of individuals to process claims under other federal and state statutes. For example, an aggrieved party may file simultaneous claims seeking relief under Title VII of the Civil Rights Act of 1964 and the LMRA.[10]

Similarly, the Fair Labor Standards Act, the Age Discrimination in Employment Act, and the Equal Pay Act, the Social Security Act, the Motor

Carriers Act, the Interstate Commerce Act, the Maritime Laws, the Federal Communications Act, and the Vietnam Era Veteran's Readjustment Assistance Act operate within their own spheres and in no way affect the scope of the LMRA.

[1.03] THE NATIONAL LABOR RELATIONS BOARD (NLRB)

The Wagner Act established the National Labor Relations Board (hereinafter referred to as the NLRB and/or the Board) to administer and enforce the provisions of the Act. The Wagner Act provided little guidance as to the structure and administration of the agency. Consequently, much criticism was directed at the agency for appointing itself as prosecutor, judge, and jury. To overcome this criticism, Congress restructured the agency to some degree with the 1947 Labor Management Relations Act amendments. For one change, the LMRA enlarged the Board from three members to five members. More significantly, the LMRA amendments divided the authority of the agency into two independent units—the five member Board and the office of the General Counsel.

The Labor Management Relations Act amendments removed the investigation and prosecution of unfair labor practice charges from the five-member Board. Therefore, since 1947, the primary function of the Board has been judicial. Although it is limited in its powers over the initial investigation and prosecution of such charges, it has the responsibility of adjudicating unfair labor practice charges once prosecution is commenced.

The Board has complete authority over representation matters pursuant to Section 9 of the Act. It delegated much of this power to the regional directors in 1961, but retained the right to review their decisions.

In addition to its responsibilities in unfair labor practice and representation matters, the LMRA also charges the Board with the duty to determine jurisdictional disputes[11] and to poll employees on their employer's last offer in "national emergency" situations.[12]

Members of the Board are appointed for five-year terms by the president with Senate approval. The Board is authorized to delegate its judicial powers to any three members. The Board members are located in Washington, D.C. along with their staffs, and the offices of Executive Secretary, Solicitor, Director of Information, and Division of Judges.

[1.04] STRUCTURE OF THE AGENCY

General counsel: The Office of the General Counsel has absolute authority over the issuing of an unfair labor practice complaint, as well as the scope of the complaint. Although the Board does have veto power over requests for Section 10(j) discretionary injunctions prior to the institution of court proceedings by General Counsel, the Board does not have the authority to overturn a refusal by the General Counsel to process other unfair practice allegations.

Also, pursuant to Section 3(d) of the Act, the General Counsel "shall exercise general supervision over all attorneys employed by the Board (other than administrative law judges and legal assistants to Board members) and over the officers and employees in the regional offices." In addition, the Board has further delegated to the office of General Counsel, supervisory responsibility over all nonlawyer personnel in the Washington, D.C. offices who are engaged in various administrative functions.[13]

The office of the General Counsel is located in Washington, D.C., along with its four divisions: (1) Division of Advice; (2) Division of Enforcement Litigation; (3) Division of Administration; and (4) Division of Operations-Management.

Administrative law judges: Formal hearings on unfair labor practice complaints are conducted by administrative law judges (originally called "trial examiners").

Administrative law judges are to serve independently of the Board and the General Counsel, are subject to the rules of the Civil Service Commission, and are removable only after a hearing before the Commission.

Administrative law judges, not unlike federal district court judges, are effectively appointed for life. They have the judicial function of hearing witnesses, ruling on the admissibility of evidence, and making findings and recommendations in unfair labor practice cases. Their initial decision, if excepted to by any party of interest, may be appealed to the Board. Otherwise, their decisions are final.[14]

Administrative law judges are based in such cities as Washington, D.C., New York City, Atlanta, and San Francisco, but conduct unfair labor practice trials in the area in which the alleged conduct was committed.

Executive secretary: The Executive Secretary has a multitude of duties, including planning and directing the functions of the Board's decision-making process; ruling upon procedural questions; determining priorities in case handling; assigning cases to staffs of individual Board members; and, conferring on behalf of the Board members with representatives of employers, employees, and unions, appearing as parties to cases. The Executive Secretary is considered the chief administrative officer of the Board.

Regional directors: There are thirty-three regional offices and several subregional offices located throughout the nation. A regional director is in charge of each regional office and is assisted by a regional attorney, field examiners, field attorneys, and other support personnel.

Unfair labor practice charges and representation petitions originate in regional offices and are investigated and processed by the staffs of the respective regional director.

[1.05]   RULE-MAKING POWERS OF THE NLRB

Section 6 of the National Labor Relations Act, as amended, empowers the Board to issue rules and regulations and implement procedures necessary to carry out the purposes of the Act. Pursuant to this authority and the Administrative Procedure Act (APA), the Board has subsequently published its rules and regulations pertaining to procedures in the processing of unfair labor practices and representation matters.

In addition, the Board has promulgated rules of general applicability by the process of adjudication, rather than by the rule-making formalities of the Administrative Procedure Act.[15] Much criticism was directed at the Board for this indulgence. In 1969, the U.S. Supreme Court chastised the Board for failure to comply with the APA;[16] however, in 1974, it retreated and held that the "choice between rule-making and adjudication lies within the Board's jurisdiction."[17]

NOTES TO CHAPTER 1

1. See generally: Charles J. Morris, *The Developing Labor Law,* 2nd ed. (Washington, D.C.: The Bureau of National Affairs, Inc., 1983), 3–34.

2. J. Warren Madden, "The Origin and Early History of the National Labor Relations Act," *George Washington Law Review* 29 (1960): 234–238.

3. *United States v. Butler,* 297 U.S. 1 (1936).

4. *Jones v. Laughlin Steel Corp.,* 301 U.S. 1 (1937).

5. *Washington v. Virginia & Maryland Coach Co.,* 301 U.S. 142 (1937).

6. The author chooses to use LMRA and/or the Act as a reference to the National Labor Relations Act, as amended by the Labor Management Relations Act of 1947 and the Labor Management Reporting and Disclosure Act of 1959, for simplicity and to avoid awkwardness, in contrast to using such terms as the NLRA, as amended.

7. *NLRB v. Brown Lumber Co.,* 336 F.2d 641 (CA-6, 1964).

8. *International Brotherhood of Teamsters, etc. v. NLRB,* 339 F.2d 795 (CA-2, 1964).

9. *Ford Motor Co. (Chicago Stamping Plant) v. NLRB,* 441 U.S. 488 (1979).

10. *Dobbins v. International Brotherhood of Electrical Workers,* 292 F.Supp. 413 (D.C. OH, 1968).

11. 29 U.S.C.A. §160(k).

12. 29 U.S.C.A. §179(b).

13. Kenneth McGuiness, *How to Take a Case Before the National Labor Relations Board* (Washington, D.C.: Bureau of National Affairs, Inc., 1967), 1–2.

14. NLRB Rules and Regulations §102.48(a).

15. See, for example: *Peerless Plywood Co.,* 107 NLRB 427 (1953).

16. *Wyman-Gordon v. NLRB,* 394 U.S. 759 (1969).

17. *NLRB v. Bell Aerospace Co., Div. of Textron, Inc.,* 416 U.S. 267 (1974).

2

Jurisdiction of the
National Labor Relations Board

[2.01] LABOR DISPUTE—ESSENTIAL ELEMENT

A "labor dispute" must exist to invoke NLRB jurisdiction.[1] The Act defines the term "labor dispute" as including any controversy concerning terms, tenure, or conditions of employment, or concerning the association or representation of persons in negotiating, fixing, maintaining, changing, or seeking to arrange terms or conditions of employment, regardless of whether the disputants stand in the proximate relation of employer and employee.[2]

[2.02] THE COMMERCE QUESTION

The second element necessary to establish jurisdiction of the Board is that the labor dispute affect commerce. The commerce nexus is not only essential as a jurisdictional requirement in the processing of unfair labor practice allegations, but it is also essential in the processing of representation matters.[3]

The Act defines "commerce" as trade, traffic, transportation, or communication among the several states, or between the District of Columbia or any territory of the United States as well as commerce among states, U.S. territories, the District of Columbia, and foreign countries.[4]

Much litigation has arisen over the term "affecting commerce." The NLRB and the courts have interpreted the term within the widest conceivable scope, meaning "acting upon," "working a change in," or "concerning."[5] Thus, the Act regulates labor relations to the fullest constitutional extent permissible under the commerce clause.[6]

The NLRB does not look solely at the quantitative effect of the activities before it, but rather, the existence of a relationship of an employer and its employees, which had led, or may tend to lead, to a labor dispute obstructing commerce.[7]

[2.03] NLRB STANDARDS FOR ASSERTING JURISDICTION

When, in the opinion of the Board, the effect of a labor dispute is so inconsequential as not to warrant the exercise of its powers, the Board may decline to assert jurisdiction.[8]

The NLRB has primarily limited its jurisdiction through the use of dollar-volume standards. For the purpose of determining these minimum-dollar standards, the Board usually looks at the last calendar year or the last twelve months.

In determining the dollar-volume standards, the Board takes into consideration both the direct sales of goods to consumers in other states and indirect sales through others across state lines (outflow), as well as the direct purchases of goods from suppliers in other states and indirect purchases through others across state lines (inflow). The Board will consider the total operations of the employer in applying these jurisdictional standards, even though the specific labor dispute may involve only a portion of its operations.[9]

As to general considerations in establishing minimum-dollar standards, the NLRB will assert jurisdiction in the following cases:

1. *Nonretail.* Gross outflow or inflow across state lines of at least $50,000, whether direct or indirect.[10]

2. *Retail.* Gross business volume of at least $500,000, including sales and excise taxes.[11]

3. *Combined establishments.* When an employer is both retail and nonretail, the nonretail minimum dollar test will be applied unless the affect of the nonretail portion is *de minimis.*[12]

4. *Multiemployer bargaining associations.* Where the annual business of all the associating employers total an amount that meets the respective retail or nonretail dollar-volume tests.[13]

5. *Multistate enterprises.* Where the annual business of all the enterprises total an amount that meets the respective retail or nonretail standards.[14]

6. *Nonprofit organizations.* Where the organization meets the respective minimum-dollar tests of retail or nonretail.[15]

7. *Apartment complexes.* Gross volume of at least $500,000 in annual revenue.[16]

8. *Communications enterprise.* Gross annual revenue of at least $100,000 from television, radio, telephone, or telegraph services.[17]

9. *Credit unions.* Where the lending of money appears to be retail in nature, the retail tests will apply; where the investing of money appears to be nonretail, the minimum-dollar tests for nonretail enterprises will prevail.[18]

10. *Hospital and health-care institutions.* Gross annual revenue of at least $100,000 is generated from nursing homes, visiting nurse associations, and related facilities; gross annual revenue of at least $250,000 is generated from profit, as well as nonprofit hospitals.[19] (Federal, state, and municipal health-care facilities are exempt from the coverage of the LMRA.)

11. *Hotels and motels.* Gross volume of at least $500,000 annual revenue is generated.[20]

12. *Newspapers.* Gross volume of at least $200,000 in annual revenue is

produced and some interstate commerce is shown, such as holding membership in or subscribing to interstate news services, advertising nationally sold products, and so on.[21]

13. *Office buildings, shopping centers, and parking lots.* Gross volume of at least $100,000 in annual revenue, of which at least $25,000 is produced from operations that meet any of the Board's minimum-dollar tests other than the nonretail standards.[22]

14. *Public utilities.* Gross annual revenue of at least $250,000 or in the alternative, an annual outflow or inflow across state lines of at least $50,000.[23] (Wholesale utilities are subject to the nonretail jurisdiction standards.)

15. *Transit companies.* Gross annual revenue of at least $250,000.[24] (Taxicab companies are classified as retail and fall within the retail minimum-dollar standards.)[25]

16. *Universities.* Gross annual revenue of at least $1 million, which may be compiled from all sources except for money derived from donors who designate that it is not available for operating costs.[26] (This test applies to all nongovernmental profit and nonprofit colleges, universities, and secondary schools.)

[2.04] MISCELLANEOUS JURISDICTIONAL GUIDELINES

Labor unions may be employers, in addition to their role as collective bargaining representatives; consequently, the NLRB has extended its coverage over labor unions, applying the nonretail tests to determine jurisdiction.[27]

Companies furnishing guard services to other employers are themselves subject to NLRB jurisdiction if the value of supplying such services satisfies one of the Board's dollar-volume standards.[28]

The Postal Service falls under the jurisdiction of the NLRB pursuant to the Postal Reorganization Act of 1970.[29] Likewise, national defense enterprises fall within the jurisdiction of the NLRB where a substantial impact on national defense can be shown, irrespective of whether the dollar-volume standards are met.[30]

The NLRB has asserted jurisdiction over day-care centers, using a gross annual dollar-volume test of at least $250,000.[31] The same $250,000 minimum-dollar jurisdictional test also applies to dental practices,[32] law firms,[33] and orphanages.[34] NLRB jurisdiction also has been extended to major league sports such as organized baseball.[35]

Irrespective of the tendency of the NLRB to extend periodically its jurisdiction into additional enterprises, there remain certain areas where, thus far, it has not asserted jurisdiction, such as race tracks,[36] real estate brokers,[37] and nonprofit institutions that are not engaged in commercial activities.[38]

Also, as a matter of policy the NLRB will refuse to assert jurisdiction when the labor dispute involves foreign commerce,[39] foreign shipping,[40] or political subdivisions.[41]

The NLRB's rules and regulations provide a procedure whereby parties to a dispute before a state court or agency may petition the Board for an advisory opinion on jurisdiction.[42] Also, the NLRB's rules and regulations permit the office of the General Counsel to petition the Board for a declaratory order disposing of certain jurisdictional issues.[43]

NOTES TO CHAPTER 2

1. 61 Stat. 136, Ch. 120 (June 23, 1947).
2. 29 U.S.C.A. §152(9).
3. 29 U.S.C.A. §159(c).
4. 29 U.S.C.A. §152(6).
5. *NLRB v. Suburban Lumber Co.*, 121 F.2d 829 (CA-3, 1941).
6. *NLRB v. Reliance Fuel Oil Corp.*, 371 U.S. 224 (1963).
7. *NLRB v. Fainblatt*, 306 U.S. 601 (1939).
8. 29 U.S.C.A. §164(c)(1). However, should the NLRB decline to assert jurisdiction over a labor dispute, such inaction permits state courts and agencies to assume jurisdiction over such a dispute.
9. *Siemons Mailing Service*, 122 NLRB No. 81, 43 LRRM 1056 (1958).
10. Ibid.
11. *Carolina Supplies and Cement Co.*, 122 NLRB No. 88 (1958).
12. *Appliance Supply Co.*, 127 NLRB 319 (1960).
13. See Note 9, *supra.*
14. *Ramada Inns, Inc.*, 171 NLRB 1060 (1968).
15. *Drexel Home*, 182 NLRB 1045 (1970).
16. *Adelsberg & Co.*, 225 NLRB 952 (1976).
17. *Raritan Valley Broadcasting System*, 122 NLRB No. 90 (1958).
18. *Federal Credit Union, East Div.*, 193 NLRB No. 103 (1971).
19. *Allegheny General Hospital*, 216 NLRB 1001 (1975).
20. *Penn-Keystone Realty Corp.*, 191 NLRB 800 (1971).
21. *Belleville Employing Printers*, 122 NLRB 350 (1958).
22. *Mistletoe Operating Co.*, 122 NLRB 1534 (1958).
23. *Sioux Valley Empire Electric Assn.*, 122 NLRB 92 (1958).
24. *Charleston Transit Co.*, 123 NLRB 1296 (1959).
25. *Union Taxi Corp.*, 130 NLRB 814 (1961).
26. 29 CFR §103.1.
27. *Chain Service Restaurant*, 132 NLRB 960 (1961).

28. *Burns Detective Agency,* 110 NLRB 995 (1954).
29. *United States Postal Service,* 208 NLRB No. 144 (1974).
30. *Ready Mixed Concrete & Materials, Inc.,* 122 NLRB 318 (1958).
31. *Salt & Pepper Nursery School & Kindergarten No. 2,* 222 NLRB 1295 (1976).
32. *Jack L. Williams,* 219 NLRB 1045 (1975).
33. *Camden Regional Legal Services, Inc.,* 231 NLRB No. 45 (1977).
34. *Roman Catholic Orphan Asylum of San Francisco,* 227 NLRB 404 (1976).
35. *American League of Professional Baseball Clubs,* 180 NLRB 190 (1969).
36. *Walter A. Kelley,* 139 NLRB 744 (1962).
37. *Seattle Real Estate Board,* 130 NLRB 608 (1961).
38. *Young Men's Christian Association of Portland, Oregon,* 146 NLRB 20 (1961).
39. *RCA OMS, Inc.,* 202 NLRB No. 42 (1973).
40. *Benz v. Compania Naviera Hidalgo,* 353 U.S. 138 (1957).
41. *City Public Service Board, San Antonio,* 197 NLRB No. 48 (1972).
42. NLRB Rules and Regulations, §102.98–102.104.
43. NLRB Rules and Regulations, §102.105–102.110.

3

LMRA Coverage

[3.01] EMPLOYER COVERAGE

Generally, only those "persons" who act as employers, and/or as their agents, come within the jurisdiction of the Labor Management Relations Act. Section 2(1) of the Act defines the term "person" to include any individual (or individuals), corporation, partnerships, associations, labor unions, legal representatives, trustees, trustees in bankruptcy, or receivers. The word "includes" has generally been held to be a term of enlargement rather than one of restriction.

Agency relationship: The term "employer" also includes any person acting as its agent, whether directly or indirectly. In determining if a person is acting as an agent of an employer, whether the specific acts performed were actually authorized, or later ratified, is not controlling.[1] Specific persons who are generally considered to be agents of their employers include

- *Corporate officials and managers,*[2]
- *Supervisors,*[3] and
- *Superintendents.*[4]

Although an employer may somewhat overcome the conduct of supervisory and management personnel through repudiation, or perhaps take reprisals against them for their action, the NLRB will normally find that an agency relationship exists even when "lower level" supervisors are involved in such conduct.[5] The agency relationship may also apply to a non-supervisory employee if it can be shown that the rank-and-file employee was acting in the employer's interest as a result of instigation, approval, or acquiescence.[6] In addition, the Board has extended the agency relationship to relatives,[7] local government officials,[8] and local businessmen,[9] where it was shown that the employer was responsible, directly or indirectly, for their conduct.

Single employers: Where two or more establishments have the same officials and directors, a centralized control over labor relations, and common ownership, the NLRB will regard the business relationship as a "single employer," even though the two firms may be separated in distance and do not interchange employees.[10]

Labor organizations: A labor union will be treated as an employer by the NLRB as to its own employees if it meets the nonretail jurisdictional standards.[11] The fact that a labor union serves in the capacity of a collective bargaining representative on behalf of other employees does not exempt it from being treated as an employer.[12] A welfare trust fund may be treated as an employer by the Board, even though it operates in a nonprofit capacity.[13]

[3.02] EXCLUDED EMPLOYERS

Although a given organization may satisfy all the prerequisites for "employer" status, it may nonetheless be excluded from the coverage of the LMRA. Those employers exempt from the coverage of the Act include the following.

Government agencies: Section 2(2) of the Act specifically excludes from its coverage, "the United States or any wholly owned government corporation, or any Federal Reserve Bank, or any State or political subdivision thereof. . . ." Consequently, such federal agencies as the Tennessee Valley Authority,[14] the Virgin Islands Port Authority,[15] and the Maritime Administration[16] have been held to be excluded from the coverage of the LMRA. However, this exclusion has not been extended to national banks[17] or mail contractors.[18]

On the basis of this governmental exclusion, local government agencies such as city governments, county governments, and state agencies are equally excluded from the coverage of the Act. This exclusion extends to public school boards,[19] school districts,[20] and state universities and colleges.[21] State, county, and municipal health-care facilities are also excluded from the coverage of the Act.[22]

Railroads and airlines: Section 2(3) of the Act also excludes "any person subject to the Railway Labor Act. . . ." The Railway Labor Act generally covers railroad[23] and airlines,[24] as well as related employers,[25] and, consequently, such employers are exempt from the Labor Management Relations Act.

The question frequently arises as to whether an employer falls within the coverage of the Railway Labor Act or the Labor Management Relations Act. When such a question arises, the NLRB generally will request the National Mediation Board, the primary agency that administers the Railway Labor Act, to decide the issue.[26] The National Mediation Board has determined that the following employers fall outside the coverage of the Railway Labor Act, and consequently, into the jurisdiction of the Labor Management Relations Act:

- Travel tour businesses not directly involved in air travel[27]
- Airline caterers[28]
- A fixed-based operation at a municipal airport[29]
- A motel owned by an airline and used to house airline flight crews[30]

[3.03] EMPLOYEE COVERAGE

Section 3(2) of the Labor Management Relations Act defines which "employees" fall within the coverage of the Act. In determining what constitutes an "employee," the courts have applied a rather broad and comprehensive interpretation, rather than one restricted to common-law standards.[31]

Some of the historical tests used by the NLRB to determine whether an individual is an "employee," instead of an "independent contractor," appear below:[32]

- Is the individual engaged in an independent business?
- Does another party have the right to hire or fire the individual?
- Does the individual furnish his or her own tools and materials by which to perform the job?
- Is the nature of the working relationship temporary or permanent?
- Is the individual to be paid traditional hourly wages as contrasted to a predetermined sum?
- What skills must the individual possess in the particular occupation?
- Does the individual stand to profit from the work done by others under his or her direction?
- Does the individual designate the place at which the work is to be performed and have control of such premises where the work is to be done?

Individuals who have been lawfully discharged, including permanently laid-off employees, will not be treated as "employees" within the protection of the Labor Management Relations Act.[33] However, individuals on temporary layoff status,[34] as well as injured employees who are recuperating, will be considered "employees" by the NLRB.[35] The NLRB will generally treat retired persons as nonemployees.[36]

[3.04] STRIKERS AS EMPLOYEES

Section 2(3) of the Labor Management Relations Act further defines an "employee" to include "any individual whose work has ceased as a consequence of, or in connection with, any current labor dispute or because of any unfair labor practice, and who has not obtained any other regular and substantially equivalent employment." As a result, unreplaced economic strikers retain their positions and status of employees during the period of an economic strike.[37]

Economic strikers may lose their status as "employees" should their positions be filled with economic strike replacements or should they later abandon their right to return to work pursuant to a preferential hiring list.[38]

Employees who engage in violent and unlawful conduct[39] and those who participate in illegal strikes[40] will generally lose their status as "employees" under the Act. However, only those employees actually participating in violence or unlawful conduct, their aiders and abettors, will be held to have severed their relationship with their employer.[41] Sit-down strikers lose their status as "employees" within the protection of the Act whenever they refuse to leave the premises at the request of an employer.[42]

[3.05] INDEPENDENT CONTRACTORS

Independent contractors are not considered "employees" by the NLRB, in keeping with the exclusions noted under Section 3(2) of the Act. In determining whether a person is an "independent contractor" or an "employee" within the meaning of the Act, the NLRB will resolve the matter on a case-by-case basis.[43] Although the NLRB will usually defer to the common-law test of right of control in its determination,[44] no single factor is determinative and the Board will consider all the surrounding circumstances in its decision.[45]

[3.06] EXCLUDED EMPLOYEES

Supervisors: Section 2(3) of the Act specifically excludes " . . . any individual employed as a supervisor" from the meaning of "employee." Section 2(11) of the Act defines "supervisor" as any individual having authority in the interest of the employer to (1) *hire,* (2) *transfer,* (3) *suspend,* (4) *lay-off,* (5) *recall,* (6) *promote,* (7) *discharge,* (8) *assign,* (9) *reward,* (10) *discipline other employees,* (11) *responsibly direct employees,* or (12) *adjust employees' grievances.*

The supervisory definition under Section 2(11) is extended to include individuals who effectively recommend any of the twelve criteria noted above. However, the same section includes the following condition:

> . . . [if] in connection with the foregoing, the exercise of such authority is not of a merely routine or clerical nature, but requires the use of independent judgment.

The NLRB has been given a large measure of discretion in determining whether an individual is a "supervisor,"[46] as distinguished from that of an "employee." Judicial resolution of supervisory status is generally regarded as a question of fact and will be determined on a case-by-case basis.[47] For example, an NLRB determination that an individual is a supervisor in a representation case is not necessarily controlling upon the Board in a later unfair labor practice case involving the same person.[48] Because the twelve previously noted criteria to establish supervisory status are set forth in the disjunctive, many courts have found the satisfaction of any one or two of them to be sufficient to meet the statutory definition of supervisor.[49] But the mere satisfaction of one of the aforementioned criteria is insufficient to satisfy the statutory definition if the individual does not utilize any independent judgment in carrying out the duties assigned to him or her.[50]

Consequently, group leaders, straw bosses, and other employees who possess only minor supervisory duties and are given authority only to lay out the work of others within a pre-established framework are usually considered mere conduits for transmitting orders and do not qualify as supervisors under the Act.[51]

The status of a person depends upon the existence of supervisory authority, not whether the authority has been exercised.[52] However, where an individual has never been informed of and has never exercised any supervisory powers, the Board has ruled that he or she is an employee, not a supervisor.[53]

Sporadic or infrequent duties as a supervisor will generally not be sufficient to classify an individual as a supervisor within the meaning of the Act.[54] However, a part-time supervisor or a seasonal supervisor may possess sufficient supervisory powers to fall within the statutory definition where an appreciable amount of his or her time is spent in carrying out supervisory functions.[55]

In addition to the twelve statutory tests discussed earlier which are used to determine supervisory status, the NLRB will frequently look at some secondary factors as well, such as[56]

- the ratio of employees to supervisors
- how much time is spent in manual labor
- the method of payment
- what supervisory benefits one is accorded
- what supervisory privileges one possesses
- what decisions are required on the job
- how the method of pay compares with the employees with whom one works
- how the method of pay is different from authentic supervisors
- what authority one possesses to pledge the employer's credit
- to what extent one's recommendation to fire, hire, promote, etc., is considered by higher management
- to what extent does one believe oneself to be a supervisor, and
- to what extent has he or she been informed that he or she has supervisory powers

Managerial employees: NLRB policy excludes managerial employees from the protection of the Act on the basis of their duties and responsibilities to the employer. Managerial employees are usually classified as those who formulate, effectuate, and administer management policies.[57]

Job titles and classifications are not controlling in determining whether an individual is a managerial employee. The NLRB will examine the exact duties, responsibilities, and authority of the individual in making its decision.[58]

Agricultural employees: Agricultural employees are specifically excluded from the definition of "employee" under Section 2(3) of the Act. In determining whether an individual falls outside the coverage of the Act because of this Agricultural exemption, the Board will defer to the definition contained in Section 3(f) of the Fair Labor Standards Act.[59] The Fair Labor Standards Act states, in substance, that agriculture includes all branches of farming in both a primary and a secondary sense.[60]

As a general rule, the determining factor in deciding whether an individual is an "agricultural laborer" will be the extent to which the work is confined to the produce of his or her employer as distinguished from the work being confined to the produce of someone other than his or her employer.[61]

Close relatives: A child or a spouse of an employer is generally excluded from the definition of "employee" and falls outside the coverage of the Act.[62] This exclusion extends to a partnership in which one of the partner's children is employed.[63]

However, this exclusion is generally limited to a parent/child or spousal relationship and would not extend to disavow coverage of the Act to such persons as godchildren[64] and daughters-in-law.[65]

Confidential employees: Confidential employees who are not members of any bargaining unit and who are closely aligned with management are generally excluded from the coverage of the LMRA.[66] However, the fact that a regular employee may obtain knowledge of some confidential matter in the course of his or her normal duties would not remove the employee from protection of the Act.[67]

NOTES TO CHAPTER 3

1. *NLRB v. United Insurance Co.,* 390 U.S. 254 (1968).
2. *United States v. Carter,* 311 F.2d 934 (CA-6, 1963).
3. *United Association of Journeymen, etc. v. NLRB,* 109 App. D.C. 315, 287 F.2d 354 (1961).
4. *NLRB v. Montgomery Ward & Co.,* 133 F.2d 676 (CA-9, 1943).
5. *NLRB v. Kaiser Agricultural Chemicals, Div. of Kaiser Aluminum & Chemical Corp.,* 473 F.2d 374 (CA-5, 1973).
6. *NLRB v. Dayton Motels, Inc.,* 474 F.2d 328 (CA-6, 1973).

7. *NLRB v. Taylor-Colquitt Co.*, 140 F.2d 92 (CA-4, 1943).

8. *Henry I. Siegel Co. v. NLRB*, 417 F.2d 1206 (CA-6, 1969).

9. *NLRB v. General Metals Product Co.*, 410 F.2d 473 (CA-6, 1969).

10. *V.I.P. Radio, Inc.*, 128 NLRB 113 (1960).

11. *Office Employees International Union*, 353 U.S. 313 (1957).

12. *Blassie v. Kroger Co.*, 345 F.2d 58 (CA-8, 1965).

13. *Chain Service Restaurant, Local 11*, 302 F.2d 167 (CA-2, 1962).

14. *Coleman v. Tennessee Valley Trades & Labor Council*, 396 F.Supp. 671 (D.C. Tenn., 1975).

15. *Virgin Islands Port Authority v. Siu de Puerto Rico*, 354 F.Supp. 312 (D.C. V.I., 1973).

16. *Douds v. Seafarers' International Union*, 148 F.Supp. 953 (D.C. N.Y., 1957).

17. *NLRB v. Bank of America National Trust & Savings Association*, 130 F.2d 624 (CA-9, 1942).

18. *NLRB v. Carroll*, 120 F.2d 457 (CA-1, 1941).

19. *Police Department of Chicago v. Mosely*, 408 U.S. 92 (1972).

20. *Children's Village, Inc.*, 197 NLRB 1218 (1972).

21. *Servomation Mathias Pa., Inc.*, 200 NLRB 1063 (1972).

22. *Board of Trustees v. NLRB*, 624 F.2d 177 (CA-10, 1980).

23. *International Brotherhood of Teamsters, etc. v. New York, N.H. and H.R. Co.*, 350 U.S. 155 (1956).

24. *Larsen v. American Airlines, Inc.*, 313 F.2d 599 (CA-2, 1963).

25. See, for example: *Mark Aero, Inc.*, 200 NLRB 304 (1972).

26. *Flight Safety, Inc.*, 171 NLRB 146 (1968).

27. *Arthur Frommer Enterprises, Inc.*, 241 NLRB 1189 (1979).

28. *Dobbs Houses, Inc. v. NLRB*, 443 F.2d 1066 (CA-6, 1971).

29. *Trans-East Air, Inc.*, 189 NLRB 185 (1971).

30. *Golden Nugget Motel*, 235 NLRB 1308 (1978).

31. *NLRB v. E.C. Alkins & Co.*, 331 U.S. 398 (1947).

32. See, for example: *National Van Lines, Inc. v. NLRB*, 273 F.2d 402 (CA-7, 1960); *NLRB v. Phoenix Mut. Life Ins. Co.*, 167 F.2d 983 (CA-7, 1948).

33. *NLRB v. Fansteel Metallurgical Corp.*, 306 U.S. 240 (1939).

34. *NLRB v. Atkinson Dredging Co.*, 329 F.2d 158 (CA-4, 1964).

35. *Palmer Asbestos & Rubber Corp.*, 160 NLRB 723 (1966).

36. *Allied Chemical & Alkali Workers v. Pittsburgh Plate Glass Co.*, 404 U.S. 157 (1971).

37. *NLRB v. Mackey Radio & Tel. Co.*, 304 U.S. 33 (1938).

38. *Textile Workers Union v. Arista Mills Co.*, 193 F.2d 529 (CA-4, 1951).

39. *NLRB v. Ohio Calcium Co.*, 133 F.2d 721 (CA-6, 1943).

40. *Southern S.S. Co. v. NLRB*, 316 U.S. 31 (1942).

41. *NLRB v. Ohio Calcium Co.*, supra.

42. *NLRB v. Fansteel Metallurgical Corp., supra.*
43. *SIDA of Hawaii, Inc. v. NLRB,* 512 F.2d 354 (CA-9, 1975).
44. *Aetna Freight Lines, Inc. v. NLRB,* 520 F.2d 928 (CA-6, 1975).
45. *NLRB v. A.S. Abell Co.,* 327 F.2d 1 (CA-4, 1964).
46. *NLRB v. Enid Stark,* 525 F.2d 422 (CA-2, 1975).
47. *NLRB v. Broyhill Co.,* 514 F.2d 655 (CA-8, 1975).
48. *Leonard Niederriter Co.,* 130 NLRB 13 (1961).
49. *Budd Mfg. Co.,* 169 F.2d 571 (CA-6, 1948).
50. *NLRB v. Broyhill, supra.*
51. *Southern Bleachery & Print Works, Inc.,* 115 NLRB 787 (1956).
52. *Ohio Power Co.,* 176 F.2d 385 (CA-6, 1949).
53. *Herald Tribune & Journal,* 111 NLRB 654 (1955).
54. *Illinois State Journal-Register, Inc. v. NLRB,* 412 F.2d 37 (CA-7, 1969).
55. *NLRB v. Crean,* 326 F.2d 391 (CA-7, 1964).
56. *Monarch Rubber Co.,* 129 NLRB 482 (1960).
57. *NLRB v. Bell Aerospace Co. Div. of Textron,* 416 U.S. 267 (1974).
58. Ibid.
59. *Re: Wayerhaeuser Co.,* 176 NLRB 913 (1969).
60. *Bayside Enterprises, Inc. v. NLRB,* 429 U.S. 298 (1977).
61. *NLRB v. Edinburg Citrus Asso.,* 147 F.2d 353 (CA-5, 1945).
62. *Foam Rubber City,* 167 NLRB 623 (1967).
63. *NLRB v. Hoffman,* 145 F.2d 679 (CA-3, 1945).
64. *Butchers' Union Amalgamated Meat Cutters & Butcher Workmen,* 160 NLRB 1465 (1966).
65. *Colonial Craft, Inc.,* 117 NLRB 1833 (1957).
66. *NLRB v. North Arkansas Electric Co-Op, Inc.,* 446 F.2d 602 (CA-8, 1971).
67. *NLRB v. Armour & Co.,* 154 F.2d 560 (CA-10, 1946).

4

LMRA—
Preemption
and Conflicts

[4.01] DOCTRINE OF PRIMARY JURISDICTION

The constitutional principles of preemption are purposely designed to avoid conflict among various official bodies which might have some authority over a matter in question.[1]

Labor attorneys and personnel professionals are frequently faced with the question of whether the LMRA preempts state and federal courts from asserting concurrent jurisdiction with the NLRB in a "labor dispute."

Whether or not the NLRB has exclusive jurisdiction over activities which are clearly or arguably subject to Sections 7 and 8 of the Act—sufficient to preempt state and federal courts from asserting concurrent jurisdiction—was answered affirmatively in *San Diego Building Trades Council v. Garmon.*[2]

If the NLRB asserts jurisdiction in a matter presently pending in a state or federal court, the respective court must yield jurisdiction to the NLRB.[3] Indeed, a state court must yield jurisdiction to the NLRB in any case where the question of possible NLRB jurisdiction is raised and it is not clear as to the state court's jurisdiction—even in cases where the NLRB might refuse to take jurisdiction.[4]

The Supreme Court has justified the preemption rationale upon the proposition that when Congress set forth its federal labor policy, it desired to alter materially the then prevailing substantive laws relating to management-labor relations, and did so by enacting the National Labor Relations Act, as amended, and creating the National Labor Relations Board, an expert administrative body whose purpose is to administer the new federal labor policy.[5]

[4.02] EXCEPTIONS—STATE COURTS AND AGENCIES

Even though the preemption doctrine is rigidly upheld in cases concerning employee rights protected by the Labor Management Relations Act, state courts do not necessarily yield jurisdiction in matters where the conduct in question touches local interests with such impact that one cannot infer that Congress has deprived the state of its power to act.[6] For example, states may enjoin conduct marked by violence and imminent threats to public order.[7] State jurisdiction prevails in such cases because the compelling state interest to maintain domestic peace is not overridden by the federal labor policy.[8]

The preemption doctrine does not preclude state courts jurisdiction over suits for malicious libel,[9] suits for damages as a consequence of violent or tortious conduct in a labor dispute,[10] matters affecting valuable property rights,[11] or suits for malicious interference with one's employment when such interference is unrelated to any possible legitimate union purpose.[12]

State courts may assert jurisdiction in cases where union members sue their unions to redress union interference with rights conferred upon them under a collective bargaining agreement.[13]

Although, as a general rule, state courts do not have proper jurisdiction to enjoin peaceful picketing which is arguably protected by the Act,[14] it may enjoin illegal picketing such as mass picketing or picketing by means of threats, force, or violence.[15] State labor boards may also assert jurisdiction where mass picketing and picketing by means of violence occurs,[16] even assuming the picketing constitutes an unfair labor practice under the Act.[17] Moreover, the NLRB preemption doctrine does not prevent a state court from granting injunctive relief in cases where

- the NLRB rules that workers, seeking to be organized by means of picketing, are not employees within the meaning of the Act, but rather, supervisors[18]
- such picketing is local in nature, causes irreparable harm, and the employer and/or the employees fall outside the jurisdiction of the LMRA[19]
- a union pickets for the purpose of compelling an employer to recognize it instead of another union which had been duly certified by the NLRB[20]
- a union pickets a retail store, not a party to a labor dispute between the union and a manufacturer of goods supplied to the store, for the purpose of inducing the retailer to cease doing business with the manufacturer[21]

The U.S. Supreme Court has held that a state court has proper jurisdiction to entertain an employer's action to enforce state trespass laws as long as the employer demands the union discontinue its trespass prior to initiating legal action.[22]

[4.03] "PERIPHERAL" MATTERS

The preemption doctrine does not deprive state courts and state labor boards of jurisdiction over matters of mere "peripheral concern" to the Labor Management Relations Act, such as

- state laws regulating payment of wages[23]
- state laws regulating payment of welfare benefits to striking union employees[24]
- state laws regulating conditions under which striking employees may draw unemployment compensation[25]
- resolution of disputes arising over internal union affairs that do not affect an employee's employment status[26]

Likewise, state fair employment laws prohibiting age discrimination,[27] sex discrimination, religious discrimination, and so forth, that do not conflict with the LMRA, are not preempted by the Act.[28]

Section 14(c) of the Act, as amended by a 1959 amendment, preserves the right of state and territorial courts and boards to assert jurisdiction over labor disputes in which the NLRB declines to assert jurisdiction. Whenever state courts or agencies assert jurisdiction in such cases, they are not bound by federal law, but may apply appropriate state law.[29]

[4.04] EXCEPTIONS—FEDERAL COURT ACTIONS

Although the preemption doctrine precludes federal district courts from asserting jurisdiction in labor dispute cases that arguably fall within the domain of the LMRA, they nevertheless maintain jurisdiction in certain labor-related cases. Two of the most prolific areas in which federal district courts maintain jurisdiction in labor-related matters involve what are commonly referred to as "Section 301 suits" and "Section 303 suits."

Section 301 Suits: Section 301 of the LMRA establishes jurisdiction in the federal district courts over "suits for violations of contracts between an employer and a labor organization representing employees in an industry affecting commerce as defined in this Act, or between any such labor organizations."

Section 301 suits are frequently filed to enforce arbitration provisions of collective bargaining contracts, the supportive facts and circumstances of which could also constitute an unfair labor practice in violation of Section 8 of the Act. In such cases the "authority of the Board to deal with an unfair labor practice which also violates a collective bargaining contract is not displaced by Section 301."[30]

Section 303 Suits: This section grants jurisdiction to federal district courts to entertain suits brought by business or property owners who are injured as a result of a labor union engaging in, inducing, or encouraging strikes or secondary boycotts prohibited by Section 8(b)(4) of the LMRA.

Both 301 and 303 actions may be brought in district courts without regard to the amount in controversy or the citizenship of the parties.[31]

[4.05] CONCURRENT JURISDICTION

There are many labor-related causes of action in which the federal and state courts have concurrent jurisdiction. For example, Section 301 suits and Section 303 suits may be brought in state courts as well as in federal courts.[32] However, state courts must apply federal law in such cases.[33] A state court has concurrent jurisdiction with a federal district court—and the NLRB—

over an employee's action against a union for failure to represent fairly the plaintiff in a discharge matter.[34]

Both federal and state courts may adjudicate a jurisdictional dispute between two unions to determine which union shall represent certain employees.[35] The employer also has the option of seeking an alternative remedy before the NLRB in such a jurisdictional dispute should it desire to exercise such option.[36]

Section 14(b) of the Act permits states to enact and enforce ''right-to-work'' statutes.[37] Such laws generally prohibit union security agreements[38] and forbid employers from discriminating against an employee for non-membership in a union.[39] Therefore, a state court as well as the NLRB may entertain a claim by an employee that he or she is being discriminated against by an employer and a union in violation of a ''right-to-work'' statute.[40] A state has no jurisdiction to enforce its ''right-to-work'' statute on a federal enclave or over employer/employee relationships that occur outside its borders.[41]

[4.06]   BANKRUPTCY PREEMPTION

A bankruptcy court may permit an employer to abrogate a collective bargaining agreement in a bankruptcy proceeding. However, before a bankruptcy court permits such abrogation, it must first find that the employer attempted to negotiate concessions from its employees, that such concessions were necessary to prevent a financial collapse of the employer, that the union in question rejected the employer's request for concessions without justification, and that the balance of the equities between the parties clearly favors a cancellation of the labor agreement.[42]

NOTES TO CHAPTER 4

1. *Amalgamated Assn. of Street, etc. v. Lockridge*, 403 U.S. 274 (1971).

2. 359 U.S. 236 (1959).

3. *Marine Engineers Beneficial Assn. v. Interlake S.S. Co.*, 360 U.S. 173 (1962).

4. *International Brotherhood of Boilermakers, etc. v. Hardeman*, 401 U.S. 233 (1971).

5. *Amalgamated Assn. of Street, etc. v. Lockridge*, supra.

6. *Linn v. United Plant Guard Workers*, 383 U.S. 53 (1966).

7. *San Diego Building Trades Council v. Garmon*, 359 U.S. 236 (1959).

8. *Teamsters, Chauffeurs & Helpers Union v. Morton*, 377 U.S. 252 (1964).

9. *Old Dominion Branch No. 496, etc. v. Austin*, 418 U.S. 264 (1974).

10. *Teamsters, Chauffeurs & Helpers Union v. Garmon*, supra.

11. *Art Steel Co. v. Velazquez*, 201 Misc. 141, 109 N.Y.S.2d 788 (1951).

12. *Davenport v. Terry*, 134 N.H.Super 88, 338 A 2d 815 (1975).

13. *Amalgamated Assn. of Street, etc. v. Lockridge, supra.*
14. *Weber v. Anheuser-Busch, Inc.,* 348 U.S. 468 (1955).
15. *International Union, United Auto, etc. v. Russell,* 356 U.S. 634 (1958).
16. *United Auto, etc. v. Wisconsin Employment Relations Board,* 351 U.S. 266 (1956).
17. *Art Steel Co. v. Velazquez, supra.*
18. *Hanna Mining Co. v. Marine Engineers Beneficial Assn.,* 82 U.S. 181 (1965).
19. *Montgomery Building & Construction Trades Council v. Ledbetter Erection Co.,* 256 Ala. 678, 57 So.2d 112 (1951).
20. *Pleasant Valley Packing Co. v. Talarico,* 5 N.Y.2d 40, 152 N.E.2d 505 (1958).
21. *Milwaukee Boston Store Co. v. American Federation of Hosiery Workers,* 269 Wis. 338, 69 N.W. 762 (1955).
22. *Sears, Roebuck & Co. v. San Diego County Dist. Council of Carpenters,* 436 U.S. 180 (1978).
23. *Chabot v. Prudential Ins. Co.,* 77 R.I. 396, 75 A 2d 317 (1950).
24. *ITT Lamp Div. International Tel. & Tel. Corp. v. Minter,* 318 F.Supp. 365 (D.C. Mass., 1970).
25. *Peak v. State Dept. of Industrial Relations,* 340 So.2d 796 (Ala. App., 1976).
26. *Megallanes v. Laborers' International Union,* 40 Cal. App. 809 (2d Dist., 1974).
27. *Walker Mfg. Co. v. Industrial Commission,* 27 Wis.2d 669, 135 N.W.2d 307 (1965).
28. *Goodyear Tire & Rubber Co. v. Department of Industry, Labor & Human Relations,* 87 Wis.2d 56, 273 N.W.2d 786 (1978).
29. *Kempf v. Carpenters & Joiners Local Union,* 376 P.2d 436 (1961).
30. *Smith v. Evening News,* 371 U.S. 195 (1962).
31. *Franchi Construction Co. v. International Hod Carriers, etc.,* 248 F.Supp. 131 (D.C. Mass., 1965).
32. 20 U.S.C.A. §§185, 187.
33. *Dowd Box Co. v. Courtney,* 368 U.S. 502 (1962).
34. *Amalgamated Assn. of Street, etc. v. Lockridge, supra.*
35. *Carey v. Westinghouse Electric Corp.,* 375 U.S. 261 (1964).
36. *Carey v. Westinghouse Electric Corp., supra.*
37. *Retail Clerks International Assn. v. Schermerhorn,* 375 U.S. 96 (1963).
38. *Minor v. Building and Constr. Trades Council,* 75 N.W.2d 139 (N.D., 1956).
39. *United Assn. of Journeymen and Apprentices, etc. v. Robertson,* 44 So.2d 899 (Fla., 1950).
40. *Retail Clerks International Assn. v. Schermerhorn, supra.*
41. *Vincent v. General Dynamics Corp.,* 427 F.Supp. 786 (D.C. Tex., 1977).
42. U.S. Bankruptcy Code, Section 541 of Subtitle J; 111 U.S.C. 113 (98 Cong. Rec. 7471, 7488) (1984).

5

Employer Interference with Protected Activities— Section 8(a)(1) Violations

[5.01] PROTECTED RIGHTS OF EMPLOYEES

Section 7 of the LMRA protects three specific rights of employees covered by the Act. First, it provides that employees shall have the right to "self-organization, to form, join, or assist labor organizations, to bargain collectively through representatives of their own choosing . . . ." This portion of the Act grants to employees the right to unionize, free of restraint, interference, and coercion. Second, Section 7 protects employees' activities for "other mutual aid or protection." This proviso has been invoked by the NLRB to protect concerted activities of employees unrelated to union organizational efforts.[1] Third, employees are also guaranteed the right to refrain from union or concerted activities. Employees may forfeit their right to refrain from union activity, however, when they are subject to a valid union security clause. Section 8(a)(3) of the Act specifically provides this exception.

[5.02] EMPLOYER INTERFERENCE WITH UNION ACTIVITY

Section 8(a)(1) of the Labor Management Relations Act makes it an unfair labor practice for an employer to "interfere with, restrain, or coerce employees in the exercise of the rights guaranteed in Section 7. . . . "

An employer may violate Section 8(a)(1) even though the employer acts in good faith.[2] Motive is not an essential element in proof of a Section 8(a)(1) violation.[3] Neither is the establishment of an anti-union bias necessary to prove a Section 8(a)(1) case.[4] In applying Section 8(a)(1) to a given case, the NLRB is not concerned with the employer's state of mind, but rather with the effect of the employer's conduct.[5]

Section 8(a)(1) prohibits favorable, as well as unfavorable, conduct of employer upon employees, if such favorable conduct is undertaken with the intent of infringing upon employees' freedom of choice as to a collective bargaining representative.[6]

An employer may refute a Section 8(a)(1) charge, however, if sufficient business justification can be established for the conduct.[7] For example, the LMRA does not preclude an employer the right to implement and administer rules of conduct and similar policies.[8]

Although the NLRB reserves the discretion to rule that a Section 8(a)(1) unfair labor practice does not necessarily constitute objectionable conduct on the employer's part in an NLRB election, the Board customarily equates one to the other. As will be discussed in chapter 23, whenever the NLRB determines that objectionable conduct has destroyed the "laboratory conditions'' necessary to maintain a fair election, it has the authority to void such an election and require a rerun.[9]

[5.03]   PROHIBITING EMPLOYEE SOLICITATION AND DISTRIBUTION

Section 7 of the Labor Management Relations Act guarantees the right of employees to discuss union-organizing matters among themselves and to solicit membership in support of a labor organization.[10] The right of employees to distribute union literature is equally protected by Section 7.[11]

Since working time is for work, an employer is not prohibited from promulgating and enforcing validly drafted no-solicitation and no-distribution rules relative to employee conduct during ''working time.'' Nonetheless, there are certain conditions and prerequisites necessary to effect a valid rule prohibiting employees from soliciting membership or distributing literature and information while on the employer's properties.

First, aside from special consideration given to retail stores and health-care facilities, an employer is prohibited from enforcing a rule which bars employees from engaging in union solicitation on the employer's premises during nonworking time,[12] or which prohibits distribution of union literature during nonworking time in nonworking areas,[13] unless the employer can show special circumstances which would make the application of the rule necessary to maintain proper discipline or efficiency.[14]

No-solicitation and no-distribution rules may not be enforced exclusively against union organizational activities.[15] Rather, they must be enforced consistently against all types of solicitation and distribution in working areas during working time.[16]

It is an unfair labor practice for an employer to implement a rule banning solicitation and distribution during working time if the rule is promulgated for the purpose of interfering with union activity, rather than for a legitimate purpose.[17]

Two exceptions exist as to the general doctrine banning rules that prohibit employee solicitation or distribution during nonworking time. The first exception relates to department stores and restaurants. Retail-related employers may prohibit all union solicitation and distribution within selling areas, even during an employee's nonworking time.[18] However, if a retail employer, having such a rule, makes anti-union speeches during working time on its premises to its employees, it must also grant a union's request to address employees during similar circumstances.[19] The second exception applies to health-care facilities which may properly ban solicitation and distribution during nonworking time in ''immediate patient care areas'' in order to preserve an atmosphere of tranquility.[20]

[5.04] NONEMPLOYEE SOLICITATION AND DISTRIBUTION RULES

As a general rule, an employer may validly post property against nonemployee distribution and solicitation, including distribution to and solicitation of employees on employer premises by outside union organizers.[21] However, if union organizers are not reasonably able to reach employees through other available channels of communications, an employer may not properly deny union representatives access to the premises for the purpose of soliciting union membership or distributing union literature to employees.[22] It has been held that employers may not ban outside union organizers from entering employer premises to solicit at such inaccessible places as an isolated lumber camp,[23] or a resort hotel at which employees live as well as work.[24]

Also, it is an unfair labor practice for an employer to limit union activity on its premises in favor of one union over a rival union.[25]

[5.05] INTERROGATION OF EMPLOYEES

Interrogation of employees as to their union sympathies is generally not viewed by the NLRB as "free speech" under Section 8(c) of the Act. Consequently, an employer who, through management and supervisory personnel, questions employees as to their union affiliation and activities will violate Section 8(a)(1) of the Act "because of its natural tendency to instill in the minds of employees, fear of discrimination on the basis of the information the employer has obtained."[26]

The NLRB does not consider each act of interrogation of employees as to union matters to be coercive. Whether it is coercive will depend upon the facts in a given case.[27] As stated in the *Blue Flash* case, the NLRB will find interrogation coercive and unlawful only in light of surrounding circumstances, considering "the time, the place, the personnel involved, the information sought, and . . . the employer's conceded preference . . . ."[28]

Casual or isolated inquiries may not give rise to a Section 8(a)(1) violation where they are free from coercion, threats, or promises.[29] Mere words of interrogation made in a nonthreatening manner by an employer free of anti-union background and not associated with a pattern of conduct adverse to unionism will generally be insufficient to support a finding of a Section 8(a)(1) violation.[30]

One exception to the general rule prohibiting interrogation of employees is an employer's right to question its employees in preparation of an NLRB hearing, provided the following conditions are met:[31]

• The employee should be told the purpose for the inquiry;

- The employee should be informed that his or her participation in the conference is strictly voluntary;
- The employee should be assured that no reprisals will be taken against him or her, whether or not he or she cooperates in the inquiry;
- The inquiries must be relevant to the preparation of the case;
- The questioning must be conducted in a noncoercive manner;
- The questioning must take place in an atmosphere free of anti-union hostility;
- The questioning should not attempt to probe the employee's subjective mind; and
- The questioning should not "otherwise interfere with the statutory [Section 7] rights of employees."

[5.06]   POLLING EMPLOYEES

Polling employees as to their union membership, support, or desires is a form of interrogation, and if conducted in a coercive manner, could also constitute a violation of Section 8(a)(1).[32] However, under certain conditions, an employer may conduct a reasonable poll of employees without violating the Act. According to the rules laid down in *Struksnes*,[33] the NLRB will consider an employer's poll of employees as to their union sympathies to be unlawful, unless

- the purpose of the poll is to determine the truth of a union's claim of majority;
- this purpose is communicated to the employees in question;
- the employees are given assurances against reprisal;
- the poll is conducted by a secret ballot; and
- the employer has not engaged in unfair labor practices or otherwise created a coercive atmosphere.

An employee opinion survey conducted by an employer to ascertain common complaints of employees just prior to a NLRB representation is not a violation per se of Section 8(a)(1); however, a violation is committed where the circumstances show that such a survey was used with an intent to solicit grievances and, in turn, promise to remedy the grievances as a means to undermine a union organizational drive.[34]

[5.07]   INVESTIGATORY INTERVIEWS

According to the NLRB, an employer violates Section 8(a)(1) of the Act when the employer denies an employee's request to have his or her union representative present at an investigatory interview in which the employee reasonably fears disciplinary action.[35]

The *Weingarten* rule applies only to an investigatory interview, not to a meeting held solely to inform the employee of a previously made disciplinary action.[36] Under the *Weingarten* principle, the employer is not obligated to inform an employee subject to an investigatory interview of his or her right to the presence of a union representative. Rather, the burden rests with the respective employee to so request such representation.[37] Should an employee request the presence of a union representative at an investigatory interview, the representative is limited in his or her role to assisting in the development of facts in the matter. The employer has no obligation to bargain with the union steward at such conference.[38]

The NLRB and the federal appellate courts have vacillated as to the application of the *Weingarten* rule to nonrepresented employees. At one point in time, the NLRB ruled that a nonunion employee had the protected right to the presence of a fellow employee in an interview that might lead to disciplinary action.[39] Later, the Board reversed itself and held that the *Weingarten* doctrine was not applicable to employees in a nonunionized facility.[40]

[5.08]   SPYING

Surveillance of employees' union activities by employers, whether through supervisors or outside agents, constitutes a violation of Section 8(a)(1) if such surveillance interferes with, restrains, or coerces employees in the exercise of their Section 7 rights.[41] For example, an employer violates Section 8(a)(1) of the Act by requesting employees to gather information about union organizational efforts and activities.[42]

To constitute a violation, it is not necessary to show that the surveillance was conducted by an employer's supervisors; rather, a violation of Section 8(a)(1) will occur so long as the surveillance was done by persons acting for, or on behalf of, the employer.[43] Likewise, it is not necessary to show that employees knew of the surveillance in order to establish a violation.[44] Attendance and/or surveillance of union meetings by supervisors will usually be found a violation of Section 8(a)(1) by the NLRB.[45]

As a general rule, an employer does not violate the Act by observing normal activities of employees carried on at its premises during working time.[46] However, when a supervisor purposely attempts to inhibit employees from using their coffee breaks for self-organization by sitting among the employees during their nonworking time, it may constitute illegal surveillance.[47]

Photographing employees or other participants in a union organizational campaign may also constitute surveillance sufficient to violate Section 8(a)(1) of the Act.[48]

A violation may also occur when an employer creates an impression that it is, or has been, spying upon union organizational activities.[49] Therefore, when a supervisor makes a statement to employees that he knew ''what was going on'' and that he ''knew how many people were attending those meetings and what was being done,'' the NLRB held that such conduct implied surveillance, and thus was a violation.[50]

[5.09]   THREATS AND REPRISALS

An employer commits a violation of Section 8(a)(1) of the Act when the employer makes a statement, either expressed or implied, in the nature of a threat as a means to coerce employees in the exercise of their self-organizational rights.[51]

The question frequently arises as to whether a certain statement by an employer constitutes a threat, or is merely an expression or opinion permitted under the ''free speech'' proviso of Section 8(c) of the Act. The test to decide such question is one of fact and turns on whether the statement would tend to have a threatening effect upon employees.[52]

Under Section 8(c) of the Act, an employer is free to make predictions concerning the effect of unionization on its operation and its employees if such predictions do not suggest a threat of reprisal.[53] Nonetheless, even when language appears predictive on surface, it may be deemed a threat of reprisal if employees could reasonably infer that the employer would use economic power to self-fulfill the prediction.[54]

For example, an employer goes beyond mere prediction, sufficient to reasonably infer a threat, when the employer suggests that unionization could adversely affect the employees' vacation pay,[55] insurance,[56] production standards,[57] etc. Similarly, a threat to withhold a planned pay increase during a union organizational drive has been held to constitute a violation of Section 8(a)(1).[58]

Threats to close down a plant[59] or to lay-off[60] employees, should a union be successful in its organizational efforts, will generally constitute an illegal threat, violative of Section 8(a)(1). Threats pertaining to discharge or discipline for supporting union activities will constitute a violation of Section 8(a)(1).[61] Suggesting that other employees have previously been discharged is equally violative of Section 7 rights.[62]

[5.10]   PROMISES AND GRANTING OF BENEFITS

A promise of benefit or financial inducement granted to employees for the purpose of preventing unionization will also constitute a violation of Section 8(a)(1) of the Act.[63]

The ''Free Speech'' provisions of Section 8(c) of the Act do not protect employers who promise or confer financial inducements prior to a NLRB Representation Election with the purpose of influencing employees against unionism.[64] The timing of a promise, or granting a benefit, is a significant factor in deciding whether Section 8(a)(1) is violated.

For example, a wage increase granted unilaterally by an employer to employees during a union organizational drive may well constitute a violation of the Act, absent reasonable justification by the employer.[65] However, the employer may be able to justify the action by showing the increase was consistent with past history and established policy,[66] was necessary due to economic considerations,[67] or was decided upon before the employer had knowledge of the campaign.

Employers may also violate Section 8(a)(1) when they imply that additional wages or benefits will be forthcoming only if the union is defeated in an upcoming NLRB Representation Election.[68]

Promises or inducements other than those tied to wages or benefits may also violate employees' Section 7 rights if they occur during a union organizational effort. Therefore, employer's promises of reduced working hours,[69] a revised seniority policy,[70] and improved promotional opportunities[71] to employees during a union campaign were held to be violations of Section 8(a)(1) of the Act.

[5.11] MISCELLANEOUS INTERFERENCES

The NLRB has also found Section 8(a)(1) violations to exist where

- an employer initiated and fostered a decertification petition[72]
- an employer prohibited the wearing of union insignia by employees,[73] absent special circumstances[74]
- an employer urged strikers to return to work accompanied by a promise to grant superior seniority to those who abandoned a strike[75]
- an employer stated to employees during a union drive that there are Communist elements in every union[76]
- an employer implied to employees that the selection of a union would be a "futile effort"[77]
- an employer implied that should the union be defeated in an NLRB election, the employer would preserve racial segregation in the plant[78]
- an employer's supervisor informed employees that they need not testify at an NLRB hearing and nobody could make them do so when the supervisor had knowledge that the employees had been subpoenaed to appear[79]
- an employer threatened to "blacklist" employees if they supported a union organizational campaign[80]
- an employer's application form required an applicant to divulge his previous union affiliation, especially if coupled with other interview questions concerning union sympathy[81]
- an employer's supervisors and managers visited employees' homes for the purpose of ascertaining their union support[82]

- an employer notified his or her employees that he or she intended to have a union representative arrested in the employees' presence for violating the company's no-solicitation policy[83]
- an employer interfered with union communications to employees by confiscating union literature previously distributed to employees[84]
- an employer threatened an employee with violence because of the employee's union activities[85]
- an employer threatened to move the plant operation to a different location because of anti-union motives[86]

NOTES TO CHAPTER 5

1. *Wall's Mfg. Co. v. NLRB*, 321 F.2d 753 (CA-DC, 1963).
2. *NLRB v. Burnup & Sims, Inc.*, 379 U.S. 21 (1964).
3. *Textile Workers Union v. Darlington Mfg. Co.*, 380 U.S. 263 (1965).
4. *NLRB v. Burnup & Sims, Inc., supra.*
5. *NLRB v. Litho Press of San Antonio*, 512 F.2d 73 (CA-5, 1975).
6. *NLRB v. Exchange Parts Co.*, 375 U.S. 405 (1964).
7. *National Cash Register Co. v. NLRB*, 466 F.2d 945 (CA-6, 1972).
8. *NLRB v. Mylan-Sparta Co.*, 166 F.2d 485 (CA-6, 1948).
9. See Chapter 22, *infra.*
10. *Central Hardware Co. v. NLRB*, 407 U.S. 539 (1972).
11. *Eastex, Inc. v. NLRB*, 437 U.S. 556 (1978).
12. *NLRB v. Walton Mfg. Co.*, 289 F.2d 177 (CA-5, 1961).
13. *Inland Steel Co.*, 238 NLRB 1204 (1978).
14. See, for example: *Goodyear Aircraft Corp.*, 57 NLRB 502 (1944).
15. *Hydraulics, Inc.*, 161 NLRB 1476 (1966).
16. *Walker Process Equipment, Inc.*, 163 NLRB 615 (1967).
17. *Time-O-Matic, Inc.*, 264 F.2d 96 (CA-7, 1959).
18. *Montgomery Ward & Co.*, 145 NLRB 846 (1964).
19. *Montgomery Ward & Co., supra.*
20. *Beth Israel Hospital v. NLRB*, 437 U.S. 483 (1977).
21. *NLRB v. Babcock & Wilcox Co.*, 351 U.S. 105 (1956).
22. *Central Hardware Co. v. NLRB*, 407 U.S. 539 (1972).
23. *NLRB v. Lake Superior Lumber Corp.*, 167 F.2d 147 (CA-6, 1948).
24. *NLRB v. S & H Grossinger's, Inc.*, 372 F.2d 26 (CA-2, 1967).
25. *NLRB v. Waterman S.S. Corp.*, 309 U.S. 206 (1940).
26. *NLRB v. West Coast Casket Co.*, 205 F.2d 902 (CA-9, 1953).
27. *Daniel Construction Company v. NLRB*, 341 F.2d 805 (CA-4, 1965).

28. *Blue Flash Express, Inc.,* 109 NLRB 591 (1954).
29. See, for example: *Beaver Valley Canning Co. v. NLRB,* 332 F.2d 429 (CA-8, 1964).
30. *NLRB v. Sellers,* 346 F.2d 625 (CA-9, 1965).
31. *Johnnie's Poultry Co.,* 146 NLRB 770 (1964).
32. *Daniel Construction Co. v. NLRB, supra.*
33. *Struksnes Construction Company,* 165 NLRB 1062 (1967).
34. *Herbert Kallen,* 228 NLRB 23 (1977).
35. *NLRB v. Weingarten, Inc.,* 420 U.S. 251 (1975).
36. *NLRB v. Certified Grocers of California, Ltd.,* 587 F.2d 449 (CA-9, 1978).
37. *NLRB v. Weingarten, Inc., supra.*
38. Ibid.
39. *Materials Research Corp.,* 262 NLRB No. 1010 (1982).
40. *Sears, Roebuck & Co.,* 274 NLRB No. 55 (1985).
41. *NLRB v. Purity Food Stores, Inc.,* 354 F.2d 926 (CA-1, 1965).
42. *Suburban Transit Corp. v. NLRB,* 499 F.2d 78 (CA-3, 1974).
43. *NLRB v. City Transportation Co.,* 303 F.2d 299 (CA-5, 1962).
44. *NLRB v. Grower-Shipper Vegetable Association,* 122 F.2d 368 (CA-9, 1941).
45. *NLRB v. City Transportation Co., supra.*
46. *NLRB v. R.C. Mahon Co.,* 269 F.2d 44 (CA-6, 1959).
47. *Kellwood Co., Hawthorn Co. Div.,* 166 NLRB 251 (1967).
48. *CBS Records Div. of CBS, Inc.,* 223 NLRB 709 (1976).
49. *Retail Store Employees Union, etc.,* 161 NLRB 1358 (1966).
50. *NLRB v. Tamper, Inc.,* 522 F.2d 781 (CA-4, 1975).
51. *NLRB v. General Shoe Corp.,* 207 F.2d 598 (CA-6, 1953).
52. *International Paper Co.,* 228 NLRB 1137 (1977).
53. *NLRB v. Gissel Packing Co.,* 395 U.S. 575 (1969).
54. *NLRB v. Hawthorn Co.,* 404 F.2d 1205 (CA-8, 1969).
55. *NLRB v. Frick,* 397 F.2d 956 (CA-3, 1968).
56. *Henry I. Siegel Co. v. NLRB,* 417 F.2d 1206 (CA-6, 1969).
57. *Continental Bus Systems, Inc.,* 229 NLRB 1262 (1977).
58. *Sta-Hi Div., Sun Chemical Corp. v. NLRB,* 560 F.2d 470 (CA-1, 1977).
59. *Textile Workers Union v. Darlington Mfg. Co.,* 380 U.S. 263 (1965).
60. *Multi-Medical Convalescent and Nursing Center v. NLRB,* 550 F.2d 974 (CA-4, 1977).
61. *Colson Corp. v. NLRB,* 347 F.2d 128 (CA-8, 1965).
62. *Jackson Packing Co.,* 170 NLRB 1361 (1968).
63. *NLRB v. Clearfield Cheese Co.,* 213 F.2d 70 (CA-3, 1954).
64. *NLRB v. Exchange Parts Co.,* 375 U.S. 405 (1964).
65. *NLRB v. Orleans Mfg. Co.,* 412 F.2d 94 (CA-2,1969).
66. *Advance Envelope Mfg. Co.,* 170 NLRB 1459 (1968).

67. *NLRB v. Newton Co.*, 236 F.2d 438 (CA-5, 1966).

68. *Offner Electronics, Inc.*, 134 NLRB 1064 (1961).

69. *Frito-Lay, Inc.*, 169 NLRB 903 (1968).

70. *Redcor Corp.*, 166 NLRB 1013 (1967).

71. *Great Atlantic & Pacific Tea Co.*, 167 NLRB 776 (1967).

72. *M & F Mfg. Co.*, 222 NLRB 105 (1975).

73. *Republic Aviation Corp. v. NLRB*, 324 U.S. 793 (1945).

74. See: *Campbell Soup Co.*, 159 NLRB 74 (1966) pertaining to sanitation; *Andrews Wire Corp.*, 189 NLRB 108 (1971) pertaining to safety.

75. *Swarco, Inc. v. NLRB*, 303 F.2d 668 (CA-6, 1962).

76. *NLRB v. Valley Broadcasting Co.*, 189 F.2d 582 (CA-6, 1951).

77. *NLRB v. Varo, Inc.*, 425 F.2d 293 (CA-5, 1970).

78. *NLRB v. Bush Hog, Inc.*, 405 F.2d 755 (CA-5, 1968).

79. *Amalgamated Clothing Workers v. NLRB*, 137 App. D.C. 93 420 F.2d 1296 (1969).

80. *Hertzka & Knowles v. NLRB*, 503 F.2d 625 (CA-9, 1974).

81. *Rochester Cadet Cleaners, Inc.*, 205 NLRB 773 (1973).

82. *J.P. Stevens & Co.*, 167 NLRB 266 (1967).

83. *Priced-Less Discount Foods, Inc.*, 162 NLRB 872 (1967).

84. *F.W. Woolworth Co.*, 216 NLRB 945 (1975).

85. *Casino Operations, Inc.*, 169 NLRB 328 (1968).

86. *NLRB v. Nina Dye Works Co.*, 203 F.2d 849 (CA-3, 1953).

6

Employer Domination and Retaliation— Sections 8(a)(2) and 8(a)(4) Violations

[6.01] ASSISTANCE IN FORMATION OF A UNION

A violation of Section 8(a)(2) of the Labor Management Relations act occurs when an employer dominates or interferes with the formation or administration of a union. An employer may violate Section 8(a)(2) in many ways. For example, an employer commits an unfair labor practice by actively participating in the organizational activities of a labor union.[1] An employer violates Section 8(a)(2) when he or she financially supports a union representing the employees, either directly or indirectly.[2] Indirect contributions to a union sufficient to constitute a Section 8(a)(2) violation may be evidenced by

- an employer's payments of its employees' union dues[3]
- an employer allowing a union to have profits from its vending machines[4]
- an employer allowing a union to profit from its concession stands[5]
- an employer paying a union's operating expenses[6]
- an employer paying for union expenditures incurred incident to its organizational campaign[7]
- an employer tendering gifts to union agents[8]

Whether payments to employees for time spent on union business constitute a Section 8(a)(2) violation is a question which frequently arises in NLRB cases. As a general rule, it is not a violation of Section 8(a)(2) for an employer to pay employee union representatives for the time spent in union-management meetings.[9] But, payments to such employees for time spent on union business outside union-management conferences will generally be held to violate Section 8(a)(2) of the Act.[10]

For instance, the Board has held it to be an unfair labor practice under Section 8(a)(2) for an employer to pay union representatives an amount above and beyond normal wages for time used in the reception and investigation of grievances.[11]

An employer does not commit a violation of Section 8(a)(2) by deducting union dues from wages of an employee and paying the deductions to the employee's collective bargaining representative, pursuant to the employee's written request, and in keeping with a check-off provision of a union contract. However, if the employer continues to deduct such union dues from an employee's wages subsequent to the employee's proper revocation of his check-off authorization, the employer violates Section 8(a)(2).[12]

Aside from rendering direct or indirect financial help to a union or its representatives, an employer may also "assist" a union in violation of Section 8(a)(2) by allowing union solicitation on company time, particularly if similar privileges are denied to other unions.[13]

[6.02] EVIDENCE OF DOMINATION

A variety of employer conduct may evidence ''domination'' of a union and constitute a Section 8(a)(2) violation. For example, when an employer suggests, instigates, and encourages employees to form a union to defeat a rival union, it will generally constitute an unfair labor practice.[14] Employer domination of a union may also be inferred when an employer prepares a union's bylaws and regulations;[15] allows a union the use of its facilities, office equipment, and clerical services;[16] and extends the services of its attorney to the union.[17]

Other factors that may demonstrate sufficient evidence to constitute a violation of Section 8(a)(2) of the Act would include the

- requirement of very small, if any, union dues from employees[18]
- union's lack of a constitution or bylaws[19]
- union meetings being held in the presence of the employer[20]
- employer's influence and control in the election of union officers[21]
- allowance of union organizational activities on company time[22]

[6.03] "GRIEVANCE COMMITTEES" AS EMPLOYER UNIONS

Employers are generally free to support employee entertainment committees, credit unions, and other nonlabor organizations without fear of a Section 8(a)(2) violation. However, when an employer sponsors an ''employee committee'' that deals with the employer concerning grievances, wages, rates of pay, hours, or other terms or conditions of employment, the committee may take on the responsibility of a labor organization, within the meaning of the Act, thereby causing the employer to violate Section 8(a)(2) of the LMRA.[23]

[6.04] IMPROPER RECOGNITION OF A UNION

When an employer grants exclusive recognition to a union representing only a minority of employees, the employer commits a violation of Section 8(a)(2) inasmuch as the recognized union is given preferential treatment over any other union in securing support of the employees.[24] Therefore, should a union demand recognition as the employees' collective bargaining representative from an employer, the employer would commit a violation of Section 8(a)(2) by recognizing the labor organization if it represented less than a majority of employees in the requested appropriate bargaining unit.

Similarly, an employer must permit the employees to make their own free choice as to which union they prefer, if any, when two or more unions are competing to gain representation of the employees.[25] Therefore, an employer violates Section 8(a)(2) when the employer discriminates against employees who refuse to join a preferred union or against employees who support a rival union.[26]

When an employer dominates or interferes with the formation or assistance of a union, as discussed above, it violates Section 8(a)(1) as well as Section 8(a)(2) of the Act because of the derivative nature of Section 8(a)(1).

[6.05] RETALIATION AGAINST EMPLOYEES

The NLRB attaches great significance to the right of employees to report matters to it and to use its processes, free from coercion or interference from anyone. It holds a special duty to protect employees who file unfair labor practice charges or become witnesses on its behalf from retaliation by employers.[27]

Consequently, an employer violates Section 8(a)(4) when the employer discharges or otherwise discriminates against an employee because the employee *has*

- given a written sworn statement to an NLRB agent[28]
- filed unfair labor practice charges against the employer[29]
- threatened to file an unfair labor practice charge against the employer[30]
- refused to withdraw charges previously filed[31]
- testified at an NLRB hearing as a subpoenaed witness[32]
- given evidence in a Representation hearing[33]
- threatened to seek NLRB assistance[34]

Retaliatory discrimination against employees for utilizing the NLRB processes or testifying on its behalf not only constitutes a violation of Section 8(a)(4) of the Act, it generally constitutes a violation of Section 8(a)(1) and 8(a)(3) as well.

NOTES TO CHAPTER 6

1. *Virginia Electric & Power Co. v. NLRB,* 319 U.S. 533 (1943).
2. *Kresge,* 77 NLRB 212 (1948).
3. *Dixie Bedding Mfg. Co. v. NLRB,* 268 F.2d 901 (CA-5, 1959).
4. *NLRB v. Thompson Ramo Wooldridge, Inc.,* 305 F.2d 807 (CA-7, 1962).
5. *NLRB v. Idaho Refining Co.,* 143 F.2d 246 (CA-9, 1944).
6. *Ampex Corp.,* 168 NLRB 742 (1967).

7. *NLRB v. Pennsylvania Greyhound Lines, Inc.,* 303 U.S. 261 (1938).
8. *Superior Engraving Co. v. NLRB,* 183 F.2d 783 (CA-1, 1957).
9. *Coppus Engineering Corp. v. NLRB,* 240 F.2d 564 (CA-1, 1957).
10. *Federal Mogul Co.,* 163 NLRB 927 (1967).
11. *Axelson Mfg. Co.,* 88 NLRB 761 (1950).
12. *NLRB v. Penn. Cork & Closures, Inc.,* 376 F.2d 52 (CA-2, 1967).
13. *NLRB v. Pick Mfg. Co.,* 135 F.2d 329 (CA-7, 1943).
14. *Coppus Engineering Corp. v. NLRB, supra.*
15. *NLRB v. Pennsylvania Greyhound Lines, Inc., supra.*
16. *Majestic Metal Specialties, Inc.,* 92 NLRB 1854 (1951).
17. *Watkins Furniture Co.,* 160 NLRB 188 (1966).
18. *NLRB v. Clapper's Mfg., Inc.,* 458 F.2d 414 (CA-3, 1972).
19. *Federal Mogul Corp., supra.*
20. *NLRB v. Erie Marine, Inc., Div. of Litton Industries,* 465 F. 2d 104 (CA-3, 1972).
21. *NLRB v. Employing Bricklayers' Assn.,* 292 F.2d 627 (CA-3, 1961).
22. *NLRB v. Bradford Dyeing Assn.,* 310 U.S. 318 (1940).
23. *NLRB v. James H. Matthews & Co.,* 156 F.2d 706 (CA-3, 1946).
24. *International Ladies' Garment Workers' Union v. NLRB,* 366 U.S. 731 (1961).
25. *NLRB v. Mark J. Gerry,* 355 F.2d 727 (CA-9, 1966).
26. *Virginia Electric & Power Co. v. NLRB, supra.*
27. 29 U.S.C.A. §158(a)(4).
28. *NLRB v. Scrivener,* 405 U.S. 117 (1972).
29. *First National Bank & Trust Company,* 209 NLRB 95 (1974).
30. *Hydraflow Valve & Mfg. Co.,* 158 NLRB 730 (1966).
31. *State Mechanical Constructors, Inc.,* 193 NLRB No. 80 (1971); *State Mechanical Constructors, Inc.,* 193 NLRB No. 547 (1971).
32. *Airlines Parking, Inc.,* 197 NLRB 762 (1972).
33. *G.K. Chevrolet, Inc.,* 176 NLRB 416 (1969).
34. *NLRB v. Retail Store Employees Union,* 570 F.2d 586 (CA-6, 1978).

7

Employer Discrimination and Discharge— Section 8(a)(3) Violations

[7.01] EMPLOYER DISCRIMINATION IN EMPLOYMENT

Section 8(a)(3) of the Labor Management Relations Act declares it an unfair labor practice for an employer to discriminate ''in regard to hire or tenure of employment or any term or condition of employment to encourage or discourage membership in any labor organization.''

Inasmuch as the Section 8(a)(3) proviso speaks of ''discrimination in regard to . . . any term or condition of employment,'' an employer's discriminatory conduct could be directed to a variety of work situations sufficient to constitute a violation other than typical discharge or disciplinary cases.

[7.02] REFUSAL TO HIRE

Although an employer may establish his or her own selection criteria and is free to hire his or her own employees, the employer may not refuse to hire an individual because of his or her previous union support or affiliation.[1] For instance, an employer has a right to deny employment to a known troublemaker, but cannot deny employment to such an applicant because of previous union activities, no matter how vociferous his or her former conduct might have been.[2]

Section 8(a)(3) also forbids an employer from encouraging unionism upon the applicant as a condition of employment unless the employer is subject to a valid union security clause within a collective bargaining agreement.[3]

[7.03] DISPARITY IN WAGES AND OTHER CONDITIONS OF EMPLOYMENT

Section 8(a)(3) of the Act forbids disparate wage treatment to employees based upon union activities,[4] whether the disparity is to discourage[5] or encourage[6] union affiliation and support.

Granting or denying benefits such as bonuses,[7] retirement,[8] insurance,[9] educational assistance,[10] holidays,[11] vacation,[12] profit-sharing[13] and so forth, to discourage or encourage union sympathies have been held to constitute violations of Section 8(a)(3) of the Act by the NLRB.

Disparity affecting other conditions of employment to encourage or discourage unionization upon employees may also constitute a violation of Section 8(a)(3), such as

- failure to promote an employee who was supporting a union[14]

47

- reduction of seniority[15] or awarding super seniority[16] without qualification
- transfer of a union supporter to a less desirable work area[17]
- demotion of a union shop steward in lieu of resignation[18]
- elimination of work break as a reprisal for union activities[19]
- denial of overtime work to an employee affiliated with a union[20]

[7.04]   DISCRIMINATORY DISCHARGE, DISCIPLINE, AND LAYOFF/RECALL

Section 8(a)(3) of the Labor Management Relations Act clearly prohibits an employer from discharging or disciplining an employee because of his or her union affiliation or activities[21] However, the jurisdiction of the Board in deciding whether an employee was discharged in violation of Section 8(a)(3) is limited to whether the discharge was for union activity or protected concerted activities,[22] not whether the discharge was just or unjust, merited or unmerited, drastic or mild.[23]

Where there is a discriminatory motive on the employer's part to discharge for union activity, the employer will not be able to evade a Section 8(a)(3) violation by attaching some pretextual reason as the ground for dismissal.[24]

An employer generally does not violate Section 8(a)(3) when an employee voluntarily quits or resigns from his or her employment. However, if the employee was induced or forced to resign because of his or her union activities, the employer commits an unfair labor practice under Section 8(a)(3) of the Act.[25] The NLRB refers to such action as a "constructive discharge." This same principle applies when an employer reduces its work force discriminatorily because of union activities.[26]

Although an employer may justifiably lay off and/or discharge employees for valid economic reasons,[27] lack of work,[28] shortage of materials,[29] etc., such reasons cannot be used as a pretext to circumvent Section 8(a)(3) of the Act.[30]

It is equally a violation to refuse to recall or reinstate an employee because of his or her union activity.[31]

[7.05]   RELOCATIONS, LOCKOUTS, AND SHUTDOWNS

An employer commits a violation of Section 8(a)(3) of the Act when he or she moves the operation to a new location as a means of frustrating union organizational efforts or collective bargaining.[32] However, the employer does not commit an unfair labor practice when he or she relocates for economic reasons or necessity, even though the employer might have harbored some animosity toward the union at the time of the move.[33]

It is also a violation of Section 8(a)(3) of the Act to lock out employees as a means to discourage union activity.[34] An employer may overcome a Section 8(a)(3) allegation, however, if the employer can demonstrate a substantial business justification and reason for the lock out.[35] Mere convenience is not sufficient.[36]

As a general rule, an employer may justify a lockout to protect its bargaining position, once an impasse is reached in negotiations.[37] Relocations and lockouts should be distinguished from permanent closure of a business. Unlike the law applying to the former, an employer may completely and permanently shut down the entire operation without violating the Act even though motivated by vindictiveness toward a union.[38] The Supreme Court justified its rationale for this rule by stating that the cessation of an entire business cannot yield future advantages to an employer as might result in discriminatory lockouts of "runaway" shops.[39]

On the other hand, where a partial closure occurs as a result of anti-union motivation, the NLRB may find a violation of Section 8(a)(3), as such action may be viewed as a means to discourage and "chill" unionization at other locations.[40]

Where a partial closure occurs as a result of economic considerations, it generally will not constitute a violation of Section 8(a)(3).[41] Economic reasons for such a closure must be honestly invoked and may not be used as a pretext for an anti-union motive.[42]

[7.06] STRIKER DISCRIMINATION

Whether an employer commits a violation of Section 8(a)(3) of the Act when he or she engages in conduct adverse to a striking employee depends upon the nature of the strike and the surrounding circumstances.

As a general rule, employees who participate in a strike for economic reasons are entitled to reinstatement upon an unconditional request until their jobs are filled by permanent replacements.[43] An employer's failure to honor such a request will constitute a violation of Section 8(a)(3) of the Act.[44] However, an economic striker's right of reinstatement does not prohibit an employer from permanently replacing him or her with another employee prior to an unconditional request to be reinstated.[45] Although an employer may lawfully replace an economic striker, he or she cannot permissibly discharge such a striker.[46]

Economic strikers retain their status as employees, even though they may have been permanently replaced, and are entitled to reinstatement upon the departure of their replacements, assuming they apply unconditionally to return to work and have not acquired regular and substantially equivalent employment elsewhere,[47] provided the striking employees have not engaged in unlawful conduct,[48] and the employer has no substantial business justification for refusal to reinstate them.[49]

Employees not part of a bargaining unit who are engaged in an economic strike also become economic strikers and are subject to the above discussed protection should they refuse to cross the economic strikers' picket line.[50] Therefore, an employer commits a Section 8(a)(3) violation by discharging an employee who refuses to cross his co-employees' picket line.[51]

An employer does not commit a violation of Section 8(a)(3) of the Act by discharging an employee for his or her participation in an unlawful strike,[52] or by discharging an employee who violates the terms of a collective bargaining contract by refusing to cross a picket line of a third party.[53] Also, as a general rule, employers are permitted to discharge wildcat strikers—employees striking in contravention of a ''no strike'' provision of a labor agreement—without committing a Section 8(a)(3) violation.[54]

An employer may also discharge employees for their participation in a ''sit-down'' strike without violating Section 8(a)(3) of the Act.[55]

An employer may not lawfully discharge employees for their participation in an unfair labor practice strike.[56] As distinguished from economic strikers, unfair labor practice strikers are entitled to reinstatement upon an unconditional request to return to work even though replacement employees may have been hired to fill their positions.[57]

Unlawful conduct on the part of unfair practice strikers may justify an employer's denial of their reinstatement rights. However, mere technical violations will generally be insufficient to deny them such rights.[58]

[7.07] HIRING HALLS

Although unions are more frequently the subject of unfair labor practices regarding improper hiring hall arrangements, an employer may also commit an unfair labor practice if the employer refuses to hire an applicant, having knowledge that a union had discriminatorily denied referral of the applicant.[59] However, where there is no evidence that an employer knew—or should have known—of a union's discriminatory refusal to defer an applicant from a hiring hall, the union's action will not cause the employer to violate Section 8(a)(3) of the Act.[60]

NOTES TO CHAPTER 7

1. *Phelps Dodge Corp. v. NLRB,* 313 U.S. 177 (1941).
2. *NLRB v. Aclang, Inc.,* 466 F.2d 558 (CA-5, 1972).
3. *NLRB v. Englander Co.,* 260 F.2d 67 (CA-9, 1958).
4. *Radio Officers' Union of Commercial Telegraphers Union v. NLRB,* 347 U.S. 17 (1954).
5. *McGraw-Edison Co. v. NLRB,* 419 F.2d 67 (CA-8, 1969).
6. *Rockaway News Supply Co.,* 94 NLRB 1056 (1951).

7. *NLRB v. Toffenetti Restaurant Co.*, 311 F.2d 219 (CA-2, 1962).

8. *Niagara Wires*, 240 NLRB No. 185 (1979).

9. *Prestige Bedding Co.*, 212 NLRB 690 (1974).

10. *Hollywood Brands, Inc.*, 169 NLRB 691 (1968).

11. *Tom's Monarch Laundry & Cleaning Co.*, 161 NLRB 740 (1966).

12. *Rockaway News Supply Co., supra.*

13. *Western Foundries, Inc.*, 233 NLRB 1033 (1977).

14. *J.W. Mortell Co.*, 168 NLRB 435 (1967).

15. *Miranda Fuel Co.*, 140 NLRB 181 (1962).

16. *Teamsters Local 20, etc. v. NLRB*, 198 App. DC 49, 610 F.2d 991 (1979).

17. *Packerland Packing Co.*, 203 NLRB 198 (1973).

18. *Cameron Iron Workers, Inc.*, 194 NLRB 168 (1971).

19. *Carbide Tools, Inc.*, 205 NLRB 318 (1973).

20. *J.P. Stevens & Co.*, 167 NLRB 266 (1967).

21. *NLRB v. Magnusen*, 523 F.2d 643 (CA-9, 1975).

22. Protected concerted activities are discussed in Chapter 11.

23. *P.G. Berland Paint City, Inc.*, 199 NLRB 927 (1972).

24. *NLRB v. Advanced Business Forms Corp.*, 474 F.2d 457 (CA-2, 1973).

25. *Lincoln Supply Co.*, 198 NLRB 932 (1972).

26. *NLRB v. Advanced Business Forms Corp., supra.*

27. *NLRB v. AAA Electric, Inc.*, 472 F.2d 444 (CA-6, 1973).

28. *Midtown Service Co.*, 171 NLRB 1306 (1968).

29. *NLRB v. Deena Products Co.*, 195 F.2d 330 (CA-7, 1952).

30. *River Togs, Inc.*, 160 NLRB 58 (1966).

31. *Victor Valley Hospital*, 227 NLRB No. 84 (1976).

32. *Local 57, International Ladies' Garment Workers Union v. NLRB*, 374 F.2d 295 (CA-DC, 1967).

33. *NLRB v. Adkins Transfer Co.*, 226 F.2d 324 (CA-6, 1955).

34. *Lane v. NLRB*, 135 App. DC 372, 418 F.2d 1208 (1969).

35. *Inland Trucking Co. v. NLRB*, 440 F.2d 562 (CA-7, 1971).

36. *Inland Trucking Co. v. NLRB, supra.*

37. *American Ship Bldg. Co. v. NLRB*, 380 U.S. 300 (1965).

38. *Textile Workers Union v. Darlington Mfg. Co.*, 380 U.S. 263 (1965).

39. Ibid.

40. *Textile Workers Union v. Darlington Mfg. Co., supra.*

41. *Thompson Transport Co.*, 165 NLRB 746 (1967).

42. *NLRB v. Savoy Laundry, Inc.*, 327 F.2d 370 (CA-2, 1964).

43. *NLRB v. Mackay Radio & Tel. Co.*, 304 U.S. 333 (1938).

44. *NLRB v. Fleetwood Trailer Co.*, 389 U.S. 375 (1967).

45. *NLRB v. Mackay Radio & Tel. Co., supra.*

46. *ABC Outdoor Advertising, Inc.,* 169 NLRB 113 (1968).

47. *Laidlaw Corp.,* 171 NLRB 1366 (1968).

48. *North Cambria Fuel Co., Inc.,* 247 NLRB 176 (1980).

49. *NLRB v. R.C. Can Co.,* 328 F.2d 974 (CA-5, 1964).

50. *NLRB v. Union Carbide Corp.,* 440 F.2d 54 (CA-4, 1971).

51. *Cooper Thermometer Co.,* 154 NLRB 502 (1965).

52. *NLRB v. Thayer Co.,* 213 F.2d 748 (CA-1, 1954).

53. *NLRB v. Rockaway News Supply Co.,* 345 U.S. 71 (1953).

54. *Food Fair Stores, Inc. v. NLRB,* 491 F.2d 388 (CA-3, 1974).

55. *NLRB v. Fansteel Metallurgical Corp.,* 306 U.S. 240 (1939).

56. *NLRB v. Comfort, Inc.,* 365 F.2d 867 (CA-8, 1966).

57. *Alba-Waldensian, Inc.,* 167 NLRB 695 (1967).

58. *Colonial Haven Nursing Home, Inc.,* 218 NLRB 1007 (1975).

59. *General Cinema Corp.,* 214 NLRB 1074 (1974).

60. *NLRB v. Master Stevedores Assn.,* 418 F.2d 140 (CA-5, 1969).

8

Protected Concerted Activities

[8.01] HISTORICAL ORIGIN OF "CONCERTED ACTIVITY"

"Concerted activities" derive from Section 7 of the Labor Management Relations Act and have been defined as any group action by employees to legitimately further their common interests relative to hours, wages, working conditions, and other terms and conditions of employment.[1]

"Concerted activities" are grounded in the "mutual aid or protection" provision of Section 7 of the Act and are not limited to organizational and collective bargaining rights of employees.[2] The purpose of the "mutual aid or protection" proviso of Section 7 is to assure the right of employees to act in concert, without having such activities being treated as an unlawful conspiracy.[3]

Concerted activities that fall within the protection of Section 7 of the LMRA are called "protected activities." Employers are forbidden by the LMRA to interfere with such "protected activities" of employees. An employer that disciplines or discharges employees who engage in "protected concerted activities" violates both Section 8(a)(1) and 8(a)(3) of the Act.[4]

[8.02] WHAT CONSTITUTES "CONCERTED ACTIVITIES"

Any number of employees, acting in concert for their mutual aid and protection, can constitute "concerted activities,"[5] whether the activities are engaged in, with, or on behalf of, other employees or themselves.[6]

Concerted activity is said to arise when a reasonable inference can be deduced from all the surrounding facts and circumstances that the persons acting together believed they had a grievance or complaint and, in turn, took it up with management personnel.[7] The fact that the protest or complaint lacks merit will not destroy the right of employees to engage in concerted activity to correct a condition, absent unusual circumstances.[8] The NLRB will normally consider that such a complaint was filed for a legitimate purpose, rather than for personal motives.

Frequently, the legal and personnel practitioner is faced with the question of whether a complaint or protest by a single employee constitutes protected concerted activity. As a general rule, where a single employee is protesting on his or her own behalf, the protestation is not regarded as "protected" under the LMRA. However, where a single employee complains or grieves as a means to enforce the terms of a collective bargaining agreement, the NLRB will deem the complaint or grievance "protected" under Section 7 of the Act.[9]

Similarly, the NLRB has held that protected concerted activity includes an individual employee's complaint relative to safety hazards, etc.

that might adversely affect other employees, if such complaint on behalf of such other employees is specifically authorized by them.[10]

[8.03] EXAMPLES OF "PROTECTED CONCERTED ACTIVITIES"

As a general rule, "protected concerted activity" must involve a work-related concern, gripe, grievance, or complaint, and must also seek some remedy in furtherance of some legitimate interest of a group or class of employees.[11] Accordingly, many types of employees' complaints or protests may constitute "concerted activity" protected by Section 7 of the Act.

Protests over wages and other conditions of employment: When employees present a grievance to management in protest of wages, hours or working conditions, the grievance falls within the protection of the Act and an employer is prohibited from taking adverse action against such employees for engaging in the protest.[12] A violation occurs whether a union is involved or not.[13]

Complaints over discriminatory hiring practices: An employer who takes disciplinary action against employees for protesting certain hiring practices of the employer will be deemed to have interfered with the protected concerted rights of the employees in question.[14]

Complaints about unsafe conditions: Employees not only have a right to complain or protest safety conditions, but should they in good faith withdraw their labor in the form of a work stoppage as a result of "abnormally dangerous conditions," such action would be deemed "protected" within the meaning of the LMRA.[15]

Filing complaints with government agents: Concerted action by employees who seek assistance from, or file complaints with, government agencies is protected by the "mutual aid and protection" proviso of Section 7 of the LMRA.[16] Thus, an employer is prohibited under Section 7 of the Act from taking adverse action against employees who file charges of discrimination with the U.S. Equal Employment Opportunity Commission against the employer,[17] or who file a complaint with the Occupational Safety and Health Administration regarding working conditions at the employer's facility.[18] Similarly, employees may appeal to public support in an effort to protest working conditions without interference from their employer.[19]

Circulation of petitions: An employer is prohibited from discharging, or otherwise taking adverse action, against employees who exercise their concerted rights in circulating petitions which express a desire for wage increases, additional overtime, etc.[20]

Processing grievances: Assisting in the preparation and presentation of grievances to management constitutes concerted activity protected by Section 7 of the Act, even though no union activities are involved.[21] Similarly, advising fellow employees of their right with respect to such matters as work assignments, vacation policies, holiday pay practices, etc., constitutes concerted activity under the Act sufficient to prohibit an employer from taking adverse action against the employees involved.[22]

Refusal to perform work of striking employees: An employer violates the Act by discharging an employee who refuses to do the work of a striking employee where such work is not generally performed by the subject employee.[23] The employer may, however, insist that the employee either perform the work or become a striker,[24] thus potentially subjecting the employee to being replaced permanently.

[8.04]   PROTEST OVER SUPERVISORS

The NLRB and the federal appellate courts do not always agree as to what constitutes "protected concerted activities" regarding employee protests on behalf of, or against, some supervisor or manager.

Change of supervisors: The NLRB has ruled that employees who protest the selection or dismissal of a supervisor are engaged in protected action and are not subject to discharge for resultant strike activity where the supervisor's identity and capability had a direct impact on their performance and job interests.[25]

Some federal courts disagree with the Board's extension of protected activities into the supervisory realm on the basis that the selection of supervisory personnel is strictly a management prerogative.[26] A few federal appellate courts have held that employees are protected in their protest over changes in supervision, as long as their protests do not evolve into a work stoppage, and is manifested in no more than "moderate conduct."[27]

Discharge of supervisors: Although employees may be protected from discharge for protesting a supervisor's dismissal under the *Dobbs House* doctrine, the supervisor has little, if any, redress against an employer under the provisions of the LMRA for such dismissal. Since supervisors do not enjoy protected rights to engage in concerted activities on behalf of a union, an employer does not necessarily commit an unfair labor practice charge when he or she discharges supervisors solely for their union activities or memberships.[28]

An employer may violate Section 8(a)(1) and 8(a)(3) of the Act should it discharge a supervisor for refusing to engage in an unfair labor practice on behalf of the employer or for giving unfavorable testimony at an NLRB arbitration hearing, since such a discharge would interfere with the Section 7 rights of the employees involved.[29]

The NLRB regards a dismissal of a supervisor for failure to engage in an unfair labor practice as having a "chilling" effect upon the union activities of the subject employees.[30] In such case, the NLRB will generally award reinstatement to the discharged supervisor, even though he or she is not technically protected by the Act.[31] Similarly, any employer discrimination against a supervisor for testifying before the NLRB will constitute a violation of the Act.[32]

[8.05] UNPROTECTED ACTIVITIES

The "mutual aid or protection" proviso of Section 7 of the Act does not protect all concerted activities of employees. As noted earlier, if a protest is for the singular and sole benefit of the protesting employee, it does not constitute "protected concerted activities."[33] Also, if the protests of a group do not relate to the furtherance of some common interests of the employees which is germane in some way to the employees' wages, hours, or other terms and conditions of employment, such protests will not generally rise to the protection of Section 7 of the Act.[34]

Abusive or insulting language: Section 7 of the Act does not protect employees who engage in abusive or threatening language, where such conduct disturbs the efficient operation of the employer's business.[35] For example, the NLRB refused to extend the protection of Section 7 to an employee who posted cartoons ridiculing a company official in an insulting and sarcastic manner where no furtherance of group action was shown.[36] The Board also refused to extend the Section 7 protection to an employee who defamed and disparaged other employees and company officials in the form of union campaign literature.[37]

Threatening fellow employees with violence: An employer does not violate Sections 8(a)(1) and 8(a)(3) of the Act when he or she discharges an employee who threatens a fellow employee with violence. Such activity is not protected under the Act.[38]

Voluntary terminations: An employee who voluntarily resigns or quits his or her job is not engaged in protected activities.[39]

Misconduct during strike: An employer does not violate an employee's protected rights under Section 7 by discharging him or her for engaging in serious misconduct during the course of a strike.[40]

Miscellaneous unprotected activity: Employees are not "protected" who *engage in:*

- recognitional picketing within twelve months of a valid NLRB election[41]
- gross insubordination or other breaches of established employer rules of conduct which have been administered in a nondisparate manner[42]

- violation of state laws[43]
- violence[44]
- distributing leaflets which disparage the quality of the employer's product in a manner calculated to harm the employer's reputation[45]

NOTES TO CHAPTER 8

1. *NLRB v. Phoenix Mutual Life Insurance Co.*, 167 F.2d 983 (CA-7, 1948).
2. *Salt River Valley Water Users' Assn. v. NLRB*, 206 F.2d 325 (CA-9, 1953).
3. *International Union, UAWA v. Wisconsin Employment Relations Board*, 336 U.S. 245 (1949).
4. *NLRB v. R.C. Can Co.*, 328 F.2d 974 (CA-5, 1964).
5. *NLRB v. Tex-Togs, Inc.*, 231 F.2d 310 (CA-5, 1956).
6. Ibid.
7. *NLRB v. Guernsey-Muskingum Electric Cooperative, Inc.*, 285 F.2d 8 (CA-6, 1960).
8. *Bob Henry Dodge, Inc.*, 203 NLRB 78 (1973).
9. *NLRB v. Interboro Contractors, Inc.*, 388 F.2d 495 (CA-2, 1967).
10. *Meyers Industries, Inc.*, 268 NLRB No. 73 (1984).
11. *Shelly & Anderson Furniture Mfg. Co. v. NLRB*, 497 F.2d 1200 (CA-9, 1974).
12. *Essex International, Inc.*, 213 NLRB 260 (1974).
13. *NLRB v. Sequoyah Mills, Inc.*, 409 F.2d 606 (CA-10, 1969).
14. *Frank Briscoe, Inc.*, 247 NLRB No. 6 (1980).
15. *NLRB v. Knight Morley Corp.*, 251 F.2d 753 (CA-6, 1957).
16. *Mercy Peninsula Ambulance Service, Inc.*, 217 NLRB 829 (1975).
17. *Frank Briscoe, Inc.*, 247 NLRB No. 6 (1980).
18. *Kiechler Mfg. Co.*, 238 NLRB No. 75 (1978).
19. *Community Hospital of Roanoke Valley, Inc.*, 220 NLRB 217 (1975).
20. *NLRB v. Schwartz*, 146 F.2d 773 (CA-5, 1945).
21. *NLRB v. Sequoyah Mills, Inc., supra.*
22. *Mushroom Transportation Co.*, 330 F.2d 683 (CA-3, 1964).
23. *General Tire & Rubber Co.*, 190 NLRB 227 (1971).
24. *Controls Div./Lexington, Ohio Plant*, 221 NLRB 742 (1975).
25. *Dobbs House, Inc.*, 135 NLRB 885 (1962).
26. See, for example: *Henning & Cheadle, Inc. v. NLRB*, 522 F.2d 1050 (CA-7, 1975).
27. *NLRB v. Guernsey-Muskingum Electric Co-Op, Inc., supra.*
28. *Beasley v. Food Fair of North Carolina, Inc.*, 416 U.S. 653 (1974). See also: *Parker-Robb Chevrolet, Inc.*, 262 NLRB No. 58 (1982).
29. *Parker-Robb Chevrolet, Inc., supra; NLRB v. Lowe*, 406 F.2d 1033 (CA-6, 1969).

30. *NLRB v. Miami Coca-Cola Bottling Co.*, 341 F.2d 524 (CA-5, 1965); *NLRB v. Lowe, supra.*

31. *Russell Stover Candies, Inc. v. NLRB*, 551 F.2d 204 (CA-8, 1977).

32. *Oil City Brass Works v. NLRB*, 357 F.2d 466 (CA-5, 1966).

33. *NLRB v. Bighorn Beverage*, 614 F.2d 1238 (CA-9, 1980).

34. *Indiana Gear Works v. NLRB*, 371 F.2d 273 (CA-7, 1967).

35. *NLRB v. Pepsi-Cola Co.*, 496 F.2d 226 (CA-4, 1974).

36. *Indiana Gear Works v. NLRB, supra.*

37. *Safeway Stores, Inc.*, NLRB Advice Memorandum Case No. 32-CA-1067 (1979).

38. *Corriveau & Routhier Cement Block, Inc.*, 410 F.2d 347 (CA-1, 1969).

39. *NLRB v. P.B. & S. Chemical Co.*, 567 F.2d 1263 (CA-4, 1977).

40. See, for example: *Kayser-Roth Hosiery Co. v. NLRB*, 447 F.2d 396 (CA-6, 1971).

41. *International Brotherhood of Teamsters*, 145 NLRB 263 (1963).

42. *NLRB v. Red Top, Inc.*, 455 F.2d 721 (CA-8, 1972).

43. *International Union, U.A.W.A. v. Wisconsin Employment Relations Board, supra.*

44. *Knitting Mills, Inc. v. NLRB*, 375 F.2d 385 (CA-4, 1967).

45. *NLRB v. International Brotherhood of Electrical Workers*, 346 U.S. 464 (1953).

9

Union Restraint
of Employee Rights—
Section 8(b)(1) Violations

[9.01] STANDARDS OF STATUTORY VIOLATION

The Labor Management Relations Act established provisions that prohibit labor organizations from interfering with employee rights guaranteed under Section 7 of the Act. The statutory prohibitions are typically referred to as Section 8(b) violations, referencing that portion of the Act which sets forth union unfair labor practices. The first of these prohibitions are reflected in Section 8(b)(1)(A) of the Act.

A union violates Section 8(b)(1)(A) when it restrains or coerces an employee in the exercise of his or her Section 7 rights. It is not necessary to show that the conduct of a union was successful, nor is it necessary that actual intent to coerce or restrain an employee be established in order to constitute a violation of this subsection.[1] It is sufficient if coercion can be shown to be the foreseeable consequence of the union's action or omission.[2]

Coercion and restraint of employees' Section 7 rights by labor organizations may be manifested in many ways, such as:

- *Threats of violence.*[3]
- *Threats of lost wages or benefits.*[4]
- *Mass picketing.* Mass picketing which prevents ingress and egress by employees to the employer's premises constitutes restraint and coercion in violation of Section 8(b)(1)(A) of the Act.[5] On the other hand, peaceful picketing does not.[6]
- *Coercing nonmembers to join.*[7]
- *Coercing strike participation.*[8] Section 7 of the Act guarantees an employee the right to refrain from engaging in concerted activities such as strikes. A union violates Section 8(b)(1)(A) when it interferes with an employee's right to refuse to participate in a strike.[9] However, verbal abuse such as calling employees "scabs" has been held permissible.[10]
- *Improper denial of membership.* A union violates Section 8(b)(1)(A) by denying union membership to individuals who cross picket lines or work during a strike.[11]
- *Support of rival union.* A union that threatens employees who support rival unions commits an unfair labor practice.[12]
- *Interference with employee statement to NLRB.* A union violates Section 8(b)(1)(A) when it threatens an employee with future job losses as a means to prevent the employee from giving an affidavit to the NLRB.[13]

[9.02] FAILURE TO REPRESENT EMPLOYEES FAIRLY

A union which becomes the exclusive collective bargaining representative of a unit of employees has a statutory duty to all of the employees in the unit—both nonunion members as well as members—to represent each and every one of them fairly.[14] The failure to comply with this statutory duty constitutes a violation of Section 8(b)(1)(A) of the Act.[15]

Unions breach their statutory duty of fair representation to a bargaining unit member only when their conduct is arbitrary, discriminatory, or in bad faith.[16]

A union may not capriciously sacrifice the rights of one employee, or a group of employees, within a bargaining unit for the benefit of other employees who possess more political clout within the union.[17] A union commits a violation of Section 8(b)(1)(A) when it discriminates against nonunion members within the bargaining unit.[18]

A union's duty of fair representation extends to proper grievance handling,[19] job assignment,[20] and control of seniority lists.[21]

[9.03] REPRESENTATION WITHOUT MAJORITY STATUS

It is a violation of Section 8(b)(1)(A) of the Act for a union to accept exclusive bargaining authority for an employer's employees at a time when it does not truly have the support of a majority of such employees.[22]

However, under Section 8(f) of the Act, it is not an unfair labor practice for an employer and a union to enter into a prehire agreement in the building and construction industry, even though the union may not represent a majority of the employer's employees at the time of the agreement.[23]

[9.04] DISCIPLINARY ACTION AGAINST MEMBERS

A union is free to administer its internal policies which reflect a legitimate union interest without violating Section 8(b)(1)(A) of the Act. For example, it is not an unfair labor practice for a union to impose reasonable fines on its members for crossing picket lines which were created as a result of an authorized strike.[24] It is not a violation of Section 8(b)(1)(A) for a union to enforce union rules which penalize its members for working with nonunion members.[25]

On the other hand, Section 8(b)(1)(A) forbids a union to use its internal rules as a means to interfere with an employee's Section 7 rights. For example, a union commits an unfair labor practice when it disciplines a member for crossing a picket line which was created to support a wildcat strike.[26] A union also violates Section 8(b)(1)(A) when it fines employees who resign from a union prior to crossing a picket line.[27] The U.S. Supreme Court has held that a union is prohibited from requiring an employee to give so many days' notice prior to resignation in such a situation.[28]

A union also violates Section 8(b)(1)(A) by fining a member for initiating, participating in, or encouraging the filing of a decertification petition where the fine's only effect is to punish the member, rather than to protect the legitimate interest of the union.[29] Fining members for filing unfair labor practice charges against a union has been held a violation of the Act.[30]

[9.05] UNION INTERFERENCE WITH EMPLOYER REPRESENTATIVE

Section 8(b)(1)(B) of the Act declares it an unfair labor practice for a union to restrain or coerce an employer in the selection of its representatives for the purposes of adjustment of grievances or collective bargaining. The NLRB generally regards all persons who are supervisors within the meaning of Section 2(11) of the Act as "representatives [of management] for the purposes of collective bargaining or the adjustment of grievances".[31]

The purpose of Section 8(b)(1)(B) is to assure employers of their right to select representatives who will be loyal and faithful to them and their desires in collective matters and grievance matters.[32] Therefore, a union that makes threats against an employer for failure to dismiss a certain foreman and replace him with an individual more supportive of the union violates Section 8(a)(1)(B) of the Act.[33]

Other examples of Section 8(b)(1)(B) violations include the following:

- *Refusal to bargain with employer representatives:* A union violates Section 8(b)(1)(B) by refusing to deal with an employer through its chosen representative.[34]

- *Discipline of supervisor members:* A union violates Section 8(b)(1)(B) by disciplining a supervisor (union member) when the disciplinary action may adversely affect the supervisor's conduct in his performance of adjusting grievances or collective bargaining.[35]

- *Supervisors working during strike:* A union violates Section 8(b)(1)(B) by disciplining supervisor members for working during a strike.[36] A fine against such a supervisor member is not violative of the Act if imposed for performing rank-and-file struck work.[37]

- *Refusal to deal with multi-employer association:* As a general rule, a union's refusal to bargain with the representative of an employer's association is violative of Section 8(b)(1)(B) of the Act where the union has no objection to negotiating with the association as a group but its refusal is motivated by an intent to destroy the association.[38]

NOTES TO CHAPTER 9

1. *NLRB v. Operative Plasterers & Cement Masons' International Assn.*, 606 F.2d 189 (CA-7, 1979).
2. *NLRB v. General Drivers, Chauffeurs & Helpers, etc.*, 264 F.2d 21 (CA-10, 1959).
3. *United Auto, etc. v. Wisconsin Employment Relations Board*, 351 U.S. 266 (1956).
4. See *Brewery Workers (Miller Brewing Co.)*, 195 NLRB 772 (1972).
5. *International Union of Operating Engineers v. NLRB*, 328 F.2d 850 (CA-3, 1964).
6. *Dayton Typographical Union v. NLRB*, 117 App. DC 91, 326 F.2d 634 (1963).
7. *Gimbel Bros., Inc. (Distributive, Processing & Office Workers, Local 2)*, 100 NLRB 870 (1952).
8. *Allen Bradley Co. v. NLRB*, 286 F.2d 442 (CA-7, 1961).
9. *Communications Workers of America v. NLRB*, 520 F.2d 411 (CA-2, 1975).
10. *International Longshoremen's & Warehousemen's Union*, 79 NLRB 1487 (1948).
11. *Communications Workers of America v. NLRB*, 520 F.2d 411 (CA-2, 1975).
12. See, for example: *General Truck Drivers, Chauffeurs, etc. v. NLRB*, 410 F.2d 1347 (CA-5, 1969).
13. *International Assn. of Bridge, etc. Workers*, 112 NLRB 1059 (1955).
14. *Vaca v. Sipes*, 386 U.S. 171 (1967).
15. *Miranda Fuel Co.*, 140 NLRB 181 (1962).
16. *Vaca v. Sipes, supra.*
17. *Truck Drivers & Helpers v. NLRB*, 126 App. DC 360, 379 F.2d 137 (1967).
18. *Branch 6000, National Assn. of Letter Carriers v. NLRB*, 194 App. DC 1, 595 F.2d 808 (1979).
19. *Vaca v. Sipes, supra.*
20. *Emmanual v. Omaha Carpenters Dist. Council*, 560 F.2d 382 (CA-8, 1977).
21. *United Steelworkers of America v. USWA*, 338 F.Supp. 1154 (WD Pa., 1972).
22. *International Ladies' Garment Workers' Union v. NLRB*, 366 U.S. 731 (1961).
23. *Hageman Underground Constr.*, 253 NLRB 60 (1980).
24. *NLRB v. Industrial Union of Marine & Shipbuilding Workers*, 391 U.S. 418 (1968).
25. *Glasser v. NLRB*, 395 F.2d 401 (CA-2, 1968).
26. *NLRB v. Retail Clerks Union, etc.*, 526 F.2d 142 (CA-9, 1975).
27. *Machinists Local Lodge 1414 (Neufeld Porsche-Audi)*, 270 NLRB No. 209 (1984).
28. *Pattern Makers' League v. NLRB*, 119 LRRM 2926 (S.Ct., 1985).
29. *Tool & Die Makers Lodge*, 207 NLRB 795 (1973).
30. *Electrical Workers, IBEW, Local 34 (Protection Alarms Inc.)*, 208 NLRB 639 (1974).
31. *Operating Engineers, Local 501*, 199 NLRB 551 (1972).
32. *International Brotherhood of Electrical Workers v. NLRB*, 159 App. DC 272, 487 F.2d 1143 (1973).
33. *McCally Co.*, 188 NLRB 951 (1971).

34. *International Brotherhood of Teamsters, etc.*, 191 NLRB 479 (1971).

35. *Florida Power & Light Co. v. International Brotherhood of Electrical Workers*, 417 U.S. 790 (1974).

36. *Laborers Local 322*, 229 NLRB No. 139 (1977).

37. *International Union of Elevator Constructors*, 213 NLRB 196 (1974).

38. *International Brotherhood of Teamsters, etc.*, 191 NLRB 479 (1971).

10

Coercion to Entice Employer Discrimination—Section 8(b)(2) Violations

[10.01]   RELATIONSHIP TO 8(a)(3) VIOLATIONS

Section 8(b)(2) of the Act declares it an unfair labor practice for a union to cause, or attempt to cause, an employer to discriminate against employees in violation of Section 8(a)(3). Thus, should a union be successful in such an attempt, it would cause both it and the employer to commit unfair labor practices.

As previously noted, Section 8(a)(3) forbids an employer to discriminate in regard to hire or tenure of employment or any term or condition of employment as a means "to encourage or discourage membership in any labor organization."

Section 8(a)(3) forbids an employer to discriminate against an employee to whom membership in such organization has been denied or terminated on some ground other than his or her failure to tender periodic dues and initiation fees uniformly required as a condition of acquiring or retaining membership.

In order to establish a violation of Section 8(b)(2), there must be some direct approach to an employer by a union representative, aimed at the employer for the purpose of causing it to discriminate against an employee.[1]

Not all attempts to cause discrimination by an employer against its employees constitute a violation of Section 8(b)(2) on the part of a union. For example, a union does not commit a violation of Section 8(b)(2) by attempting to cause an employer to demote, or promote, an employee as long as the union is acting on behalf of its membership as a whole.[2]

[10.02]   HIRING HALL DISCRIMINATION

A hiring hall agreement is a matter of negotiation between an employer and a union. An exclusive union hiring hall is a hiring process in which any person hired by the employer must have been referred to it by the union in question. Such hiring hall arrangements are legal as long as they are administered in a nondiscriminatory manner.[3]

A union has a statutory duty to refer nonunion workers as well as union workers from its hiring hall. To discriminate against a nonunion member in favor of a union member in its referral process is a violation of Section 8(b)(2).[4] Thus, a union commits an unfair labor practice where job applicants are furnished from an all-union assignment list.[5]

Similarly, a union violates Section 8(b)(2) of the Act where its hiring hall agreement specifically provides that an employer give preference to members of the contracting union.[6]

Also, a union commits an unfair labor practice when it refuses to accept a nonunion member's application for registration and referral in its hiring hall.[7]

Preferential treatment of certain employees in relation to referral from a union hiring hall over less favored employees may constitute a violation of Section 8(b)(2). For example, a union may commit an unfair labor practice when it discriminates against dissident workers,[8] suspended or expelled members,[9] or members of a different union or local[10] with regard to its hiring hall referrals.

Section 8(f) of the Act permits building and construction industry employers to enter into hiring hall agreements with unions that require such employers to notify the respective union of employment opportunities and to give the union an opportunity to refer qualified applicants for such employment.

Section 8(f)(4) further provides that such a hiring hall agreement may outline specified qualifications relating to training or experience, or provide for priority in employment, based on seniority with the employer, in the industry or in the particular geographical area.

[10.03] NONPAYMENT OF UNION DUES AND FEES

A union does not violate Section 8(b)(2) of the Act by causing an employer to discharge an employee for "his failure to tender the periodic dues and the initiation fees uniformly required as a condition of acquiring or retaining membership," pursuant to a valid union-security agreement.[11] However, a union's insistence that an employee pay union fees or dues in the absence of an obligation to do so would constitute an unfair labor practice.[12]

A union must first inform an employee of his or her obligation to pay such union fee or dues pursuant to a valid union security agreement prior to requesting an employer to discharge the employee for nonpayment in order for the request to be lawful.[13]

[10.04] NONPAYMENT OF UNION FINES OR ASSESSMENTS

Although a valid union security agreement may be invoked to bring about an employee's discharge for his or her failure to pay periodic dues and initiation fees, a union cannot lawfully request an employer to discharge an employee for failure to pay assessments, penalties or fines, as the payment of such items cannot be made a condition of continued employment.[14]

Section 302 of the LMRA permits an arrangement in a collective bargaining contract where periodic union dues may be "checked-off" from an employee's paycheck via a payroll deduction, if so authorized by an employee.

[10.05]   NONMEMBERSHIP IN UNION

Section 8(a)(3) of the Act permits union-security agreements requiring union membership as a condition of employment on or after the 30th day of employment, or the effective date of the agreement, whichever is later. Certain limitations apply to the use of such agreements, however, such as deference to right-to-work laws[15] and to persons whose religious convictions oppose union membership.[16]

Inasmuch as the LMRA, pursuant to its Section 8(a)(3), permits discharge of an employee only for failure to tender periodic union dues and fees, a union commits a violation of Section 8(b)(2) of the Act by requesting an employer to discharge an employee who refuses to apply for union membership as long as such employee continues to tender periodic dues and fees in accordance with an applicable union security provision.[17]

Consequently, the Act prevents the use of union security agreements for any purpose other than to compel the payment of periodic union dues and initiation fees.[18]

The legality of union security arrangements vary, depending upon the scope and nature of the agreement. The general rules applicable to such arrangements are as follows:

Closed shop agreements. A union which enters into a contract with an employer requiring a prospective employee to become a member of the union prior to hire violates Section 8(b)(2) of the Act, inasmuch as such agreement does not allow a thirty-day grace period to run as is required by Section 9(a)(3) of the Act.[19]

Union shop agreements. On the other hand, a union shop agreement which requires union membership ''on or after the thirtieth day following the beginning of such employment, or the effective date of such agreement, whichever is later'' constitutes a lawful arrangement, unless otherwise prohibited by conditions noted earlier.[20]

Agency shop arrangements. An agency shop arrangement is a union security agreement wherein the employee is required to pay a union service fee—usually equivalent to union dues and initiation fees—as a condition of employment, but is not required to become a union member. As a general rule, such arrangements do not violate Section 8(b)(2) of the Act.[21]

Maintenance of membership arrangements. A union security agreement which provides that employees who are union members on the date of the agreement, or who thereafter become members, must remain members as a condition of employment until they are promoted or transferred out of the bargaining unit, or the agreement is terminated, is also a lawful and permissible arrangement.[22]

Although a thirty-day grace period is usually required before an employee must become a union member (that is to say, before he or she may be required to pay periodic union dues and initiation fees) under a valid union security agreement as provided in Section 8(a)(3) of the Act, a special proviso in Section 8(f) of the Act specifies that membership in a union pursuant to a union shop arrangement may be required after a seven-day grace period in the building and construction industry.

[10.06]   MISCELLANEOUS DISCRIMINATION

Violating union rules: A union violates Section 8(b)(2) by causing an employer to discharge, discipline, or otherwise discriminate against an employee because of his or her failure to comply with some union rule or by-law,[23] irrespective of the validity or invalidity of the bylaw or rule.[24]

Failing job tests: Although an employer may, by agreement with a union, require a prospective employee to take and pass a union-administered job qualification test as a prerequisite to hire, a union may not lawfully cause an unwilling employer to discharge an employee for failure to take or pass a union-administered test not provided for in the collective bargaining agreement between the parties.[25]

Opposing a union official: As a general rule, a union violates Section 8(b)(2) by causing an employer to discriminate against an employee for his or her failure to accept the authority of a union official.[26]

Seniority provisions: A union violates Section 8(b)(2) by entering into a collective bargaining agreement which provides that the union will determine the seniority rights of the employees in question and will also settle any controversies that may arise over seniority disputes, inasmuch as such control over employee rights by a union might tend to improperly encourage membership in that union.[27] Although superseniority for union stewards may be lawful if limited to layoff or recall considerations, it usually becomes unlawful under Section 8(b)(2) of the Act when a union and employer agree to extend such superseniority to all contractual benefits in which seniority is a consideration.[28]

NOTES TO CHAPTER 10

1. *Associated Musicians of Greater New York,* 176 NLRB 365 (1969).
2. *Ohio Valley Carpenters Dist. Council,* 226 NLRB No. 144 (1976).
3. *NLRB v. Houston Chapter Associated General Contractors, Inc.,* 349 F.2d 449 (CA-5, 1965).
4. *Byrd v. International Brotherhood of Electrical Workers,* 375 F.Supp. 545 (DC Md., 1974).
5. *NLRB v. Philadelphia Iron Works, Inc.,* 211 F.2d 937 (CA-3, 1954).

6. *National Maritime Union,* 82 NLRB 1365 (1949).

7. *Utility & Industrial Constr. Co.,* 214 NLRB 1053 (1974).

8. *NLRB v. International Longshoremen's & Warehousemen's Union,* 514 F.2d 481 (CA-9, 1975).

9. *NLRB v. General Longshore Workers, etc.,* 212 F.2d 846 (CA-5, 1954).

10. *International Brotherhood of Boilermakers, etc.,* 206 NLRB 30 (1973).

11. *NLRB v. International Union of Operating Engineers,* 425 F.2d 17 (CA-7, 1970).

12. *NLRB v. Atlanta Printing Specialties & Paper Products Union,* 523 F.2d 783 (CA-5, 1975).

13. *Truck Drivers, Oil Drivers, etc.,* 222 NLRB 335 (1976).

14. *NLRB v. Spector Freight System, Inc.,* 273 F.2d 272 (CA-8, 1960).

15. 29 U.S.C.A. §164(b).

16. 29 U.S.C.A. §169.

17. *Union Starch & Refining Co. v. NLRB,* 186 F.2d 1008 (CA-7, 1951).

18. *Radio Officers' Union of Commercial Telegraphers Union v. NLRB,* 347 U.S. 17 (1954).

19. *NLRB v. Teamsters & Allied Workers, etc.,* 313 F.2d 655 (CA-9, 1963).

20. *Hammond v. United Papermakers & Papermakers Union,* 462 F.2d 174 (CA-6, 1972).

21. *Communications Workers of America v. NLRB,* 520 F.2d 411 (CA-2, 1975).

22. *Aluminum Co. of America v. NLRB,* 159 F.2d 523 (CA-7, 1946).

23. *Radio Officers' Union of Commercial Telegraphers Union v. NLRB, supra.*

24. *Associated Musicians of Greater New York,* 176 NLRB 365 (1969).

25. *NLRB v. Air Flow Sheet Metal, Inc.,* 396 F.2d 506 (CA-7, 1968).

26. *Lummus Co. v. NLRB,* 119 App. DC 229, 339 F.2d 728 (1964).

27. *NLRB v. International Brotherhood of Teamsters, etc.,* 225 F.2d 343 (CA-8, 1955).

28. *Dairylea Cooperative, Inc.,* 219 NLRB 656 (1975).

11

Secondary Boycotts—
Section 8(b)(4) (A), (B) and (C) Violations

[11.01] INTRODUCTION TO SECONDARY BOYCOTTS

Subsections 8(b)(4)(A), (B), and (C) of the LMRA are widely referred to as the "secondary boycott" provisions of the Act.

Section 8(b)(4)(A) prohibits a "hot cargo" arrangement in a collective bargaining agreement except in certain industries as discussed later in this chapter.

Section 8(b)(4)(B) prohibits economic action against a neutral employer as a means of bringing pressure against a primary employer.

Section 8(b)(4)(C) prohibits economic action to force an employer to bargain with a labor organization where another union has already been certified by the NLRB as the collective bargaining representative of its employees.

A secondary boycott can generally be defined as union pressure directed at a neutral employer to induce such employer to discontinue doing business with the employer with whom the union is engaged in a labor dispute.[1]

The preliminary investigation of an unfair labor practice charge alleging a violation of Sections 8(b)(4)(A), (B), or (C) must be given top priority by the NLRB. The Board will also seek an injunction in the appropriate federal district court to restrain the continuation of a union's conduct where it feels there is a reasonable cause to believe the charge has merit.[2]

Section 8(b)(4) contains a suffix "i" or "ii," which precedes the last letter "A", "B," or "C" as well as "D" (jurisdictional disputes as discussed in Chapter 12). The "i" suffix relates to a situation where a union engages, or induces and encourages, an "employee" to strike or refuse to handle products in violation of Section 8(b)(4). The "ii" suffix relates to a circumstance where a union threatens, coerces, or restrains "any person" in violation of the Section 8(b)(4) prohibitions.

[11.02] THE ALLY DOCTRINE

The central theme of the "secondary boycott" provisions of Section 8(b)(4) is to protect those neutral employers who are "wholly unconcerned" with the labor dispute in question.[3] However, where a secondary employer is associated with a primary employer in such a manner that it contributes some degree of control over the striking employees' fortunes, it will not be deemed one "wholly unconcerned," and the protection of Section 8(b)(4)(B) will not be extended to it.[4]

Two tests are used to determine whether an ally relationship exists. The "common control" test is one which examines whether the employers, though separate entities, are engaged in such closely integrated operations

73

that they should be regarded as a single employer for the purposes of Section 8(b)(4) of the Act.[5] This test usually involves a finding that some element of "common control" exists between the two employers in question.

The "struck work" test used by the NLRB to establish an ally relationship is one which evaluates whether the secondary employer is engaged in conduct inconsistent with its alleged neutrality.[6] This test usually involves a finding that the secondary employer is performing work which the primary employer can no longer do as a result of the strike against it.[7]

Where an ally relationship exists, the right to strike the primary employer also includes the right to strike its ally.[8]

[11.03]   COMMON-SITUS PICKETING

Another situation in which it is sometimes difficult to readily discern secondary activity is that of common-situs picketing. A common-situs situation occurs where two or more employers are performing separate tasks on common premises, such as at a construction project.

The difficulty of ascertaining whether the primary employer or the secondary employer at the common-situs project is the object of a union's picket has caused the NLRB to adopt certain tests or standards to resolve this question.

These tests are commonly referred to as the *Moore Dry Dock* standards, which have been approved by the courts. However, the U.S. Supreme Court has disapproved a pure mechanical application of them.[9] The *Moore Dry Dock* standards are employed as an evidentiary aid to determine whether common-situs picketing is unlawful secondary activity, absent more evidence of the union's intent.[10] Under the *Moore Dry Dock* standards, common-situs picketing will be determined "primary" by the NLRB, if it meets the following conditions:[11]

- The picketing is strictly limited to times when the situs of the dispute is located on the employer's premises;
- At the time of the picketing, the primary employer is engaged in normal business at the situs;
- The picketing is limited to places reasonably close to the location of the situs; and
- The picketing discloses clearly that the dispute is with the primary employer.

The *Moore Dry Dock* criteria are not absolute and if direct evidence exists to establish that the picket is directed at the neutral employer to achieve some effect over the primary employer, a violation will nonetheless be established.

[11.04] RESERVED–GATE PICKETING

The *Moore Dry Dock* criteria may be applied to establish unlawful picketing at a gate reserved solely for the use of employees, suppliers, and customers of a neutral employer on common-situs premises, without forbidding the union from picketing gates reserved for the employees, suppliers, and customers of the struck employer.[12]

A union's picketing of a reserved gate at the primary employer's premises is lawful primary activity unless the

- gate is a separate gate, marked and set apart from other gates;
- work performed by the personnel using it is unrelated to the primary employer's normal operations; and
- work performed by personnel who use the gate is of a kind that would not necessitate curtailing those operations, if performed when the primary employer was engaged in its regular operations.[13]

[11.05] CONSTRUCTION SITE PICKETING

Whether construction site picketing is unlawful secondary activity depends on whether the picketing union's object is to force neutrals to cease dealing with the primary employer. A union, in its dispute with a general contractor, violates Section 8(b)(4)(B) by picketing the job site for the purpose of inducing the employees of union subcontractors not to work on the project.[14]

On the other hand, a union does not engage in unlawful secondary activity by picketing the general contractor, although various suppliers may choose to respect the picket line and refuse to make deliveries.[15] The NLRB has held that a union does not violate Section 8(b)(4)(B) in picketing a construction site with the sole object of truthfully informing the public that some employer at the work site is operating under substandard working conditions.[16]

[11.06] CONSUMER PICKETING

The secondary boycott provisions of Section 8(b)(4) of the Act do not prohibit all peaceful consumer picketing at secondary sites, particularly when such picketing is limited in purpose to persuade customers not to buy a specific product from the picketed store.[17]

When consumer picketing exists, customers of a secondary employer may choose to honor the protest of such picketers or may continue to do business with the secondary employer, as the dispute, although extended, remains with the primary employer.[18]

However, in order for consumer picketing to be legal, the picketing must not appear to attempt to influence customers to completely cease all transactions with the neutral employer.[19] Also, it must not appear to force the neutral employer to cease doing business with the primary employer.[20]

[11.07] "HOT CARGO" PROVISION

Except for special provisions relating to the construction and apparel industry, Section 8(e) of the Act prohibits an agreement between a union and an employer in which the employer agrees to cease doing business with someone else. When such an arrangement occurs, both the union and the employer may be deemed to have violated the "Hot Cargo" prohibitions of the Act. Section 8(b)(4)(A) declares it to be an unfair labor practice for a union to force or require any employer to enter into any such "Hot Cargo" agreement.

While the construction industry exception to Section 8(e) of the Act permits clauses to be inserted in construction industry contracts which might otherwise be illegal, strikes and picketing to enforce such clauses are not sanctioned by this provision and may constitute a violation of Section 8(b)(4)(A).[21] However, in the garment industry, a union may lawfully use economic pressure to both enforce a "hot cargo" clause as well as to obtain it.[22]

[11.08] WORK PRESERVATION CLAUSES

A work preservation clause is an agreement between a union and an employer which provides that certain jobs are to be preserved to employees in a specific bargaining unit, is not a violation under either the "Hot Cargo" provision or the secondary boycott provision of the Act, as long as such agreement reserves only bargaining unit work that the bargaining unit has traditionally performed.[23]

NOTES TO CHAPTER 11

1. *NLRB v. Denver Building & Construction Trades Council*, 341 U.S. 675 (1951).
2. 29 U.S.C.A. §160(e).
3. *Newspaper Production Co. v. NLRB*, 503 F.2d 821 (CA-5, 1974).
4. *International Brotherhood of Teamsters, etc.*, 128 NLRB 916 (1960).
5. *Steelworkers (AFL-CIO) (United States Steel Corp.)*, 127 NLRB 823 (1960).
6. *National Woodwork Mfg. Assn. v. NLRB, supra.*
7. *Chemical Workers, Local 61 (Sterling Drug, Inc.)*, 189 NLRB 60 (1971).
8. *General Teamsters Local No. 324, International Brotherhood of Teamsters, etc.*, 122 NLRB 25 (1958).

9. *International Union of Electrical, etc. v. NLRB,* 366 U.S. 667 (1961), 6 L.Ed.2d 592, 81 S.Ct. 1285 (1961).

10. *Landstrom v. Chauffeurs, Teamsters, etc.,* 476 F.2d 1189 (CA-2, 1973).

11. *International Union of Electrical, etc. v. NLRB, supra.*

12. *International Union of Electrical, etc. v. NLRB, supra.*

13. *International Union of Electrical, etc. v. NLRB, supra.*

14. *Piezonki v. NLRB,* 219 F.2d 879 (CA-4, 1955).

15. *United Brotherhood of Carpenters & Joiners v. Markwell,* 305 F.2d 38 (CA-8, 1962).

16. *Centralia Bldg. & Constr. Trades Council v. NLRB,* 124 App. DC 212, 363 F.2d 699 (1966).

17. *NLRB v. Fruit & Vegetable Packers & Warehousemen,* 377 U.S. 58 (1964).

18. *NLRB v. Building Service Employees International Union,* 367 F.2d 227 (CA-10, 1966).

19. *Kaynard v. Independent Routemen's Association,* 479 F.2d 1070 (CA-2, 1973).

20. *Burr v. NLRB,* 321 F.2d 612 (CA-2, 1963).

21. *Building & Constr. Trades Council,* 218 NLRB 39 (1975).

22. *Danielson v. Joint Board of Coat S. & A.G. Workers' Union,* 494 F.2d 1230 (CA-2, 1974).

23. *National Woodwork,* 386 U.S. 612, 64 LRRM 2801 (1967).

12

Jurisdictional Disputes, Informational Picketing, and Other 8(b) Violations

[12.01] EXISTENCE OF WORK ASSIGNMENT DISPUTE

A work assignment dispute generally occurs when there is an active disagreement between two or more unions as to whose members should be entitled to the particular work.[1] Such work assignment disputes are frequently referred to as "jurisdictional disputes," and coercive activity designed to force an employer to assign work to one group exclusive of another may constitute a violation of Section 8(b)(4)(D) of the Act.[2]

[12.02] VOLUNTARY ADJUSTMENT

Although the NLRB and the courts favor voluntary adjustments of work assignment disputes, noting that Section 10(k) of the Act encourages voluntary settlement,[3] the NLRB will not defer to voluntary adjustments of a dispute if it conflicts with an NLRB certification,[4] or where an impartial arbitrator or umpire has based his or her decision on different criteria from that used by the Board to resolve work assignment controversies.[5] Moreover, the NLRB will not defer to a voluntary adjustment unless all parties, including the employer, have agreed to the method of settlement.[6]

Where an employer was not a party or signatory to the Impartial Jurisdictional Disputes Board (IJDB) of the Building and Construction Trades Department of the AFL–CIO, the NLRB refused to defer to this body for adjustment of a certain work assignment dispute.[7] Even where an employer is a party to such an agreement, it is released from its obligations thereunder if a work stoppage continues for more than forty-eight hours after the IJDB notifies the parties of its decision.[8] But, assuming all parties have agreed to be bound by the IJDB, the NLRB will generally defer to the IJDB decision.[9]

[12.03] NLRB CRITERIA TO RESOLVE JURISDICTIONAL DISPUTES

The NLRB has certain criteria to resolve work assignment disputes, although it has maintained that such judicial standards will not preclude it from deciding each case on its own merits.[10] Relevant factors to be considered by the NLRB in determining a jurisdictional dispute include the following:[11]

- NLRB certification
- Collective bargaining agreements
- Employer preference
- Efficiency of operation

- Labor-management tradition
- Inter-union agreements
- Third-party awards
- Safety[12]
- Employee job loss[13]
- Similarity to work previously performed by the competing groups[14]

An employer's preference and work assignment will normally be accorded substantial weight by the NLRB in determining a jurisdictional dispute.

[12.04]   SECTION 10(K) HEARINGS TO RESOLVE WORK ASSIGNMENT DISPUTES

The procedure for determining who shall be entitled to disputed work is set forth in Section 10(k) of the Act. When confronted with a jurisdictional dispute in which injunctive relief is sought under Section 10(l) of the Act, the NLRB will normally process the injunction with the utmost dispatch.[15] Section 10(j) injunctive relief may also be available to the NLRB in such cases.

Although Section 10(k) hearings are the most prevalent methods used to resolve jurisdictional disputes, other statutory provisions establish separate and distinct approaches to work assignment adjustments. Two independent causes of action would include

- a union-initiated lawsuit in federal court under Section 301 of the Act to compel an employer to comply with a work assignment made as part of an arbitration award;[16] and
- an employer-initiated lawsuit in federal court against a union under Section 301 of the Act for damages suffered because of a work assignment strike.[17]

If the local regional director of the NLRB finds reasonable cause to believe that a violation of Section 8(b)(4)(D) has occurred as a result of his or her investigation, the director will customarily serve a notice of a 10(k) hearing on all parties to the dispute.[18]

A Section 10(k) determination in and of itself does not dispose of the issue of whether a union (or other employee group) has committed a violation of Section 8(b)(4)(D). It determines merely which union or group should be awarded the work under the criteria noted before. A subsequent and separate hearing is required to determine whether an unfair labor practice has arisen under Section 8(b)(4)(D).[19]

[12.05] RECOGNITIONAL PICKETING

A union violates Section 8(b)(7) of the Act by picketing an employer where

- the employer has lawfully recognized another union and the picketing occurs at a time when a representation election is not appropriate—Section 8(b)(7)(A)

- a valid representation election has been conducted by the NLRB within the preceding twelve-month period—Section 8(b)(7)(B), or

- the picketing has been conducted for a period of time in excess of thirty days without a Representation Petition being filed with the NLRB—Section 8(b)(7)(C)

Picketing is not unlawful under Section 8(b)(7) unless an object thereof is: (1) to force or require an employer to recognize or bargain with a labor organization as the representative of his or her employees ("Recognitional" Picketing); or (2) to force or require the employees of an employer to accept or select such organization as their collective bargaining representative ("Organizational" Picketing).

Thus, the threshold question is whether the object of the union's picket is recognitional or organizational in scope. As a general rule, if the reasonably immediate object of the union's picketing is recognitional or organizational, the union violates Section 8(b)(7) of the Act.[20]

Whether a union's picketing has a recognitional or organizational object is a question of fact.[21] Some factors that evidence a union's recognitional or organizational objective would include

- organizational activities being conducted concurrently with the picketing[22]

- a picket sign legend stating that the employer does not employ the union's members[23]

- the picketing union's filing a refusal to bargain unfair labor practice charges against the employer concurrent with its picketing[24]

On the other hand, area standards picketing merely to inform the public that an employer does not offer wages or working conditions in keeping with union standards is not considered a violation of Section 8(b)(7) of the Act.[25]

[12.06] THIRTY–DAY LIMITATION RULE

Section 8(b)(7)(C) forbids recognitional or organizational picketing for more than a reasonable period, not to exceed thirty days, unless a representation petition is filed prior to the expiration of that period.[26] Should a timely petition be filed, it stays the thirty-day limitation and continued picketing is permitted, pending the processing of the representation petition.[27]

Although the NLRB will expedite a representation election where recognitional picketing occurs, such expedited elections will apply only when an unfair labor practice charge under Section 8(b)(7)(C) has been filed.[28] Absent such an unfair labor practice charge, a union will not be permitted an expedited election by merely filing a representation petition while continuing its recognitional or organizational picketing.[29]

[12.07]   INFORMATIONAL PICKETING EXCEPTION

A special provision to Section 8(b)(7)(C) declares that nothing in Subsection (C) prohibits any picketing or other publicity for the purpose of truthfully advising the public (including consumers) that an employer does not employ members of, or have a contract with, a labor organization, unless an effect of the picketing is to induce any individual employed by any other person in the course of his or her employment not to pick up, deliver, or transport any goods, or not to perform any services.

The informational picketing provision applies only to Section 8(b)(7)(C) cases and does not apply to Section 8(b)(7)(A) or (B) cases.[30]

[12.08]   EXCESSIVE OR DISCRIMINATORY UNION FEES

Section 8(b)(5) of the Act prohibits a union from imposing an excessive or discriminatory initiation fee against an employee where a union shop exists requiring union membership as a condition of employment.

This section is somewhat tempered by a provision which allows the Board to consider, ''among other relevant factors, the practices and customs of labor organizations in the particular industry, and the wages currently paid to the employees . . . '' prior to making an adverse finding against a union. An initiation fee may be found discriminatory even though not excessive by the NLRB.[31] In considering what constitutes an excessive or discriminatory fee, the NLRB will generally look at the context in which an increase in an initiation fee is made as well as the amount of the increase.[32]

[12.09]   ''FEATHERBEDDING'' PROHIBITION

Section 8(b)(6) of the Act declares it to be an unfair labor practice for a union to cause or attempt to cause an employer to pay for work which is not to be performed. This ''featherbedding'' provision has been interpreted very narrowly by the NLRB and the courts.[33] As a result of this strict construction, collective bargaining may properly determine what, if any, work—

including bona fide "make work"—shall be included within an agreement without violating this Section.[34]

NOTES TO CHAPTER 12

1. *Penello v. Sheet Metal Workers International Association,* 195 F.Supp. 458 (DC Del., 1961).
2. *Chicago Typographical Union No. 16,* 155 NLRB 963 (1963).
3. *William E. Arnold Co. v. Carpenters Dist. Council,* 417 U.S. 12 (1974).
4. *Graham v. Local 2247, United Brotherhood of Carpenters,* 34 CCH Lab. Case ¶71289 (DC Alaska, 1958).
5. *International Alliance of Theatrical, Stage Employees, etc.,* 222 NLRB No. 161 (1976).
6. *Bricklayers, Stone Masons, Marble Masons, Tile Setters and Terrazza Workers, etc.,* 188 NLRB 148 (1971).
7. *Local No. 17, Sheet Metal Workers,* 197 NLRB 1127 (1972).
8. *AFL–CIO, Bricklayers, etc., Local No. 7,* 199 NLRB 1256 (1972).
9. *Carpenters Dist. Council of Denver, Local Union No. 1,* 205 NLRB 155 (1973).
10. *International Association of Machinists, Lodge No. 1743,* 15 NLRB 1402 (1962).
11. *International Association of Machinists, Lodge No. 1743, supra.*
12. *Local 542, International Union of Operating Engineers,* 213 NLRB No. 24 (1974).
13. *NLRB v. International Longshoremen's Association,* 345 F.2d 4 (CA-3, 1965).
14. *NLRB v. International Longshoremen's Association,* 368 F.2d 107 (CA-3, 1966).
15. *NLRB Casehandling Manual,* Section 10200.
16. *NLRB v. Teamsters, Chauffeurs, Warehousemen and Helpers, etc.,* 403 F.2d 667 (CA-9, 1968).
17. *NLRB v. Radio & Television Broadcast Engineers Union,* 364 U.S. 573, 5 L.Ed.2d 302, 81 S.Ct. 330 (1961).
18. 29 CFR §102.90.
19. *NLRB v. Plasterers' Local Union No. 79,* 404 U.S. 116 (1971).
20. *NLRB v. Bakery & Confectionary Workers International Union,* 245 F.2d 542 (CA-2, 1957).
21. *Shell Chemical Co. v. NLRB,* 495 F.2d 1116 (CA-5, 1974).
22. *Retail Clerks International Association,* 140 NLRB 1258 (1963).
23. *Teamsters Local Union No. 5,* 171 NLRB 30 (1968).
24. *Retail, Wholesale & Department Store Union,* 141 NLRB 991 (1963).
25. *International Hod Carriers Bldg. and Common Laborers,* 135 NLRB 1153 (1962).
26. *Teamsters Local Union No. 115,* 157 NLRB 588 (1966).
27. *International Hod Carriers Bldg. and Common Laborers Union, supra.*
28. *NLRB v. Delsea Iron Works, Inc.,* 334 F.2d 67 (CA-3, 1964).

29. *International Hod Carriers Bldg. and Common Laborers Union, supra.*

30. *Retail Clerks International Association,* 136 NLRB 778 (1962).

31. *International Union, United Auto, Aircraft and Agricultural Workers,* 99 NLRB 1419 (1952).

32. *NLRB v. Television and Radio Broadcasting Studio Employees,* 315 F.2d 398 (CA-3, 1963).

33. *American Newspaper Publishers Assn. v. NLRB,* 345 U.S. 100 (1953).

34. Ibid.

13
Introduction to Collective Bargaining

[13.01] CONDITIONS PRECEDENT TO DUTY TO BARGAIN

Section 8(a)(5) of the Act declares it an unfair labor practice for an employer to refuse to bargain collectively with the representative of his or her employees, subject to the provisions of Section 9(a) of the Act.

Section 9(a) of the Act states that representatives designated or selected for the purposes of collective bargaining by the majority of the employees in the appropriate collective bargaining unit shall be the exclusive representatives of all of the employees in the unit for the purpose of collective bargaining in respect to rates of pay, wages, hours of employment, or other conditions of employment.

Section 9(a) of the Act also provides that such exclusive bargaining rights of the union are not intended to prevent an individual employee or a group of employees from presenting grievances directly to the employer, as long as an adjustment is not inconsistent with the terms of a collective bargaining agreement then in effect, and the bargaining representative has been given an opportunity to be present at the adjustment.

[13.02] GOOD FAITH REQUIREMENTS

Section 8(d) of the Act declares the duty to bargain collectively to include the mutual obligation of the employer and the collective bargaining representative of its employees to meet at reasonable times and confer in good faith with respect to wages, hours, and other terms and conditions of employment, and to execute a written contract incorporating any agreement reached if requested by either party. Section 8(d) also states that such obligation to bargain does not, however, compel either party to agree to a proposal or require either party to make a concession to the other.

[13.03] TERMINATION OR MODIFICATION OF CONTRACT

The duty to bargain collectively also requires either party who desires to terminate or modify an existing contract to do the following:

- Serve a written notice upon the other party of the proposed termination or modification sixty days prior to its expiration date, or in the event the contract does not express an expiration date, sixty days prior to the time it is proposed to make such termination or modification. (This time period is extended to ninety days where the collective bargaining agreement involves employees of a health-care institution.)[1]

- Offer to meet and confer with the other party for the purpose of negotiating a new contract or a contract containing the proposed modifications.[2]

- Notify the Federal Mediation and Conciliation Service within thirty days after such notice of the existence of a dispute, and simultaneously therewith notify any state or territorial agency established to mediate and conciliate disputes within the state or territory where the dispute occurs, provided no agreement has been reached by that time. (This time period is extended to sixty days where the collective bargaining agreement involves employees of a health care institution.)[3]

- Continue in full force and effect, without resorting to a strike or lockout, all the terms and conditions of the existing contract for a period of sixty days after such notice is given or until the expiration of such contract, whichever occurs later. (This time period is extended to ninety days where the collective bargaining involves employees of a health care institution.)[4]

[13.04] MAJORITY STATUS AS A BASIS TO BARGAIN

Should a union establish itself as the exclusive representative of certain employees, through obtaining majority status, the employer is required to bargain with such union or subject itself to a violation of Section 8(a)(5) of the Act.

A union may attain majority status through several means.

Certification as a result of election: The most prevalent method by which a union may establish majority status—so as to obligate the employer to bargain with it—is through the process of an NLRB-conducted election.

Voluntary recognition upon request: Another method used by unions to attempt to obligate an employer to bargain with it is to request recognition based upon an alleged authorization card majority. Although an employer may voluntarily recognize a union based upon a showing of an authorization card majority, it is not required to do so and may insist upon an election to establish majority status instead, unless the employer *has*

- engaged in unfair labor practices that impede the electoral process[5]

- agreed to utilize such method (card check) to determine majority status[6] or

- conducted a personal poll or interrogation disclosing that the union has attained a majority status[7]

However, once an employer voluntarily recognizes a union as the representative of its employees, the bargaining relationship is established and may not be withdrawn at will by the employer.[8]

Card-based bargaining order: Majority status may also be imposed upon an employer through the issuance of a bargaining order by the NLRB. A bargaining order by the NLRB, if upheld by the courts, compels the employer to bargain with a union even though the employer may have won the NLRB-conducted election held to determine majority status. The Supreme Court[9] has defined two categories of cases in which the NLRB may issue a bargaining order. These categories include[10]

1. Cases marked by "outrageous" and "pervasive" unfair labor practices by an employer which foreclose the possibility of holding a fair election, in which a bargaining order may issue, even without a showing that the union had obtained a card majority at any point in time;[11]
2. Cases marked by less pervasive unfair labor practices by an employer that, nonetheless, tend "to undermine majority strength and impede the election process." (Majority status is a condition precedent to the issuance of a bargaining order.) Less extensive unfair labor practices by an employer, which have only a minimal impact on the election process, are insufficient to warrant a bargaining order.[12]

[13.05] UNION'S LOSS OF MAJORITY STATUS

Although a union may later lose its majority status, there is a presumption by the NLRB that a union continues to enjoy majority support, a presumption which an employer must overcome if he or she wishes to withdraw recognition from the union.

Moreover, absent unusual circumstances, there is an irrebuttable presumption that a union has majority status for a one-year period following certification by the NLRB during which time an employer will not be permitted to withdraw from his or her bargaining duties with the union.[13]

An employer who voluntarily recognizes a union as the collective bargaining representative of his or her employees,[14] or with which he or she has been ordered to bargain by the NLRB,[15] is required to bargain with the union for a reasonable time during which period the NLRB will irrebuttably presume continued majority status.

An employer violates Section 8(a)(5) of the Act if he or she either unilaterally rescinds an existing collective bargaining contract[16] or bargains with another union during the period of the contract, even if the first union has been repudiated by a majority of the employer's employees.[17] However, absent the conditions and presumptions noted above, an employer who establishes that the union has in fact lost its majority status no longer has a duty to bargain with the union.[18]

NOTES TO CHAPTER 13

1. 29 U.S.C.A. §158(d)(1).

2. 29 U.S.C.A. §158(d)(2).

3. 29 U.S.C.A. §158(d)(3).

4. 29 U.S.C.A. §158(d)(4).

5. *NLRB v. Gissel Packing Co.*, 395 U.S. 575 (1969).

6. *Snow,* 134 NLRB 709 (1961).

7. *Sullivan Electric Co.,* 199 NLRB 809 (1972).

8. *NLRB v. A. Lasaponara and Sons, Inc.,* 541 F.2d 992 (CA-2, 1976).

9. *NLRB v. Gissel Packing Co., supra.*

10. *NLRB v. Armcor Industries, Inc.,* 535 F.2d 239 (CA-3, 1976).

11. Some circuit courts, as well as the NLRB, have taken the position that the Board does not have authority under Section 10(c) of the Act to issue a bargaining order unless majority status has been established. See *Conair Corp. v. NLRB,* 721 F.2d 1355 (CA-DC, 1983); *Gourmet Foods,* 270 NLRB No. 113 (1984).

12. *NLRB v. Gissel Packing Co., supra.*

13. *Brooks v. NLRB,* 348 U.S. 96 (1954).

14. *Brennan's Cadillac, Inc.,* 231 NLRB No. 34 (1977).

15. *NLRB v. Harris-Woodson Co.,* 179 F.2d 720 (CA-4, 1950).

16. *Shamrock Dairy, Inc.,* 124 NLRB 494 (1959).

17. *Harbor Carriers of Port of New York v. NLRB,* 306 F.2d 89 (CA-2, 1962).

18. *NLRB v. Newspapers, Inc.,* 515 F.2d 334 (CA-5, 1975).

14

Duty to Bargain:
Employer's Obligations

[14.01] REFUSAL TO NEGOTIATE MANDATORY BARGAINING SUBJECTS

An employer commits a violation of Section 8(a)(5) of the Act if he or she refuses to negotiate with a union representing his or her employees over mandatory bargaining subjects,[1] even though the employer desires to reach an agreement with the union and bargains in good faith toward that end.[2] If union proposals in negotiations deal with "wages, hours, and other terms and conditions of employment" within the meaning of Section 8(d) of the Act, they constitute mandatory bargaining subjects.[3]

Although an employer is required to bargain over mandatory bargaining subjects, he or she is free to bargain or not to bargain over nonmandatory (permissive) bargaining subjects.[4]

Whether a bargaining proposal constitutes a mandatory bargaining subject within the meaning of Section 8(d) of the Act depends upon the facts of each case.[5] The Fifth Circuit Court of Appeals has held that a proposal is a mandatory bargaining subject if it arises out of the employment relationship[6] and attempts to regulate the relationship between employer and employees or attempts to settle any term or condition of employment between the parties.[7]

However, a remote or incidental item is insufficient to render a proposal a mandatory subject of bargaining; rather, the proposal must materially or significantly affect the terms or conditions of employment.[8]

Some of the mandatory subjects of bargaining, about which an employer is required to negotiate, include the following:

- Wages and other pay (including noncompensatory emoluments of value furnished by the employer to the employees)[9]
- Hours[10] (including shift work)[11]
- Payment of wages for time spent in bargaining sessions by employee members[12]
- Vacations[13]
- Holidays[14]
- Insurance benefits[15]
- Sick benefits and sick leave[16]
- Pensions,[17] savings,[18] and retirement plans[19]
- Bonuses and gifts[20] (except for bonuses paid only intermittently)[21]
- Union trust funds[22] (e.g., health and welfare plans)
- Seniority[23]
- Promotions[24]

- Lay-offs[25]
- Transfers[26]
- Reinstatement of strikers[27]
- Work rules[28] (including safety rules)[29]
- Work schedules[30] and workloads[31]
- Food prices and services[32] (e.g., employer vending)
- Dues checkoff[33]
- Grievance procedure[34]
- Arbitration[35] and no-strike clauses[36]
- Lockout clauses[37]
- Management rights clauses[38]
- Contracting out work[39]
- Successor clauses[40]
- Union security clauses[41] (in states permitting such clauses)
- Union activity on employer property[42]
- Anti-discrimination clauses[43]
- Matters affecting new hires[44]
- ''Most Favored Nations'' clauses[45]
- ''Application of Contract'' clauses[46]
- Term of contract[47]

[14.02]   PERMISSIVE BARGAINING SUBJECTS

Although collective bargaining need not be limited to mandatory subjects of bargaining, insistence on the inclusion of a nonmandatory (permissive) bargaining subject in a collective bargaining contract as a condition to any agreement is an unfair labor practice.[48]

An employer may not legally bargain to impasse over a nonmandatory bargaining subject;[49] however, an employer may bargain to impasse over mandatory bargaining subjects without violating Section 8(a)(5) of the Act.[50]

[14.03]   SUCCESSOR EMPLOYERS: DUTY TO BARGAIN

As a general rule, if a transfer of assets and employees from one employer to another leaves substantial continuity in the identity of the employing enterprise, the duty to recognize and bargain with the incumbent union remains with the successor employer.[51]

Factors used by the NLRB in determining whether there remains a continuity in the identity of the employing enterprise would include:[52] supervision, working conditions, location, methods of production, machinery, equipment, product and the work force. The most substantial of these factors is that of a continuity of the work force.[53]

Successor employers are usually required to bargain with the incumbent union if a majority of the employees are former employees of the predecessor employer, irrespective of an absence of some of the other aforementioned factors.[54]

The NLRB makes a distinction between what it terms a "successor" employer and what it calls an "alter ego" employer. Successor employers are generally not bound by the terms of the predecessor's labor agreement, although required to bargain with the incumbent union.[55] Alter-ego employers are required to recognize and honor existing labor agreements as well as to bargain with the union as to future contracts.[56]

The NLRB and the courts look to such factors as (1) common ownership and financial control, (2) centralized control of labor relations, (3) common management and supervision, (4) interrelation of operations and equipment, (5) commonality of customers, and (6) similarity in business purpose in determining whether an alter-ego relationship exists.[57]

[14.04] MULTI-EMPLOYER BARGAINING

Employers may voluntarily bind themselves to multi-employer bargaining by indicating from the outset an unequivocal intention to be bound by a multi-employer collective bargaining agreement, assuming that the union representing their employees is notified of the formation and bargaining authority of the multi-employer group and agrees to negotiate with the group's representative.[58] However, once an employer commits itself to the multi-employer group, he or she violates Section 8(a)(5) of the Act by withdrawing from the group once negotiation with the union commences, barring "unusual circumstances"[59] such as the employer facing dire economic conditions.[60]

[14.05] BAD FAITH BARGAINING

Good faith bargaining requires a sincere effort to reach an agreement between the parties, although it does not require an agreement itself.[61]

The following were sufficient facts to support the NLRB's inference that the employer did not bargain in good faith:[62] An employer's shifting position, failure or refusal to furnish pertinent wage data, refusal to bargain on a union security proposal, failure to resume negotiations, failure to appear at a scheduled meeting during a strike, unilateral wage boost, and a statement that he or she intended to delay bargaining for a year and then seek decertification of the union.

Although an employer has a right to take a good faith, adamant bargaining position on a mandatory bargaining subject, the employer may not do so where his or her real purpose is to frustrate an agreement with the union[63] or to destroy or cripple the union.[64]

An employer's insistence upon the fulfillment of some unreasonable condition by the union prior to continuing negotiations may also constitute bad faith bargaining.[65]

[14.06] FAILURE TO FURNISH INFORMATION TO UNION

An employer's refusal to furnish information needed by the employees' representative for the proper performance of its duties,[66] including information in support of claims or assertions made at the bargaining table,[67] constitutes a violation of Section 8(a)(5) of the Act. However, an employer's duty to furnish information to a union is limited to information and data which are relevant to dealings between the employer and the union.[68]

[14.07] UNILATERAL ACTIONS

As a general rule, an employer commits a violation of Section 8(a)(5) of the Act by unilaterally altering the terms and conditions of employment of his or her employees without first giving notice to, and conferring with, the bargaining representative of the employees.[69] However, where the employer has bargained in good faith with the union and an impasse is reached, he or she may unilaterally grant a wage increase as long as the increase is no greater than that previously offered to the union as its last best offer.[70]

[14.08] BARGAINING DIRECTLY WITH EMPLOYEES

Once a duly authorized collective bargaining representative has been selected by the employees, an employer is not permitted to negotiate wages or other terms and conditions of employment with such individual workers.[71] Bargaining with individual employees constitutes a violation of Section 8(a)(5) of the Act, even in the absence of employer bad faith.[72] Moreover, inviting employees to disregard and bypass the union in seeking redress of their grievances has been held a violation of the duty to bargain in good faith on the part of an employer.[73]

[14.09] LOCKOUTS

An employer's right to lock out his or her employees has been considered a corollary to a union's right to strike.[74] Thus, the NLRB recognizes the validity of the lockout by an employer as a means of applying economic pressure on a union in support of the employer's bargaining position.[75]

Therefore, a lockout by an employer after impasse has been reached in negotiations does not constitute a violation of Section 8(a)(5) of the Act.[76]

[14.10] PLANT CLOSURES AND RELOCATIONS

The courts view partial closures of plant operations differently from complete closures with respect to bargaining obligations on the part of an employer. An employer is permitted to close his or her entire operations, even for anti-union reasons, without an obligation to bargain with a union over the employer's decision to close.[77] On the other hand, should an employer close part of his or her operations for noneconomic reasons and relocate elsewhere, a duty might arise to bargain over the "impact" of the decision as well as the "effects" of the decision.[78] Should the employer decide to close an operation and relocate elsewhere based on purely "economically motivated reasons," the employer may do so without an obligation to bargain over the "impact" of the decision, although an obligation may arise to bargain over the "effects" of the decision.[79]

NOTES TO CHAPTER 14

1. *NLRB v. Frontier Homes Corp.*, 371 F.2d 974 (CA-8, 1967).
2. *United Steelworkers of America v. NLRB*, 129 App. DC 80, 390 F.2d 846 (1967).
3. *United Electrical, etc. v. NLRB*, 133 App. DC 115, 409 F.2d 150 (1969).
4. *Fiberboard Paper Products Corp. v. NLRB*, 379 U.S. 203 (1964).
5. *Allis-Chalmers Mfg. Co. v. NLRB*, 213 F.2d 374 (CA-7, 1954).
6. *NLRB v. Bemis Bros. Bag Co.*, 206 F.2d 33 (CA-5, 1953).
7. *NLRB v. Houston Chapter, Associated General Contractors, Inc.*, 349 F.2d 449 (CA-5, 1965).
8. *Seattle First National Bank v. NLRB*, 444 F.2d 30 (CA-9, 1971).
9. *Weyerhaeuser Timber Co.*, 87 NLRB 672 (1949).
10. *Gallenkamp Stores Co. v. NLRB*, 402 F.2d 525 (CA-9, 1968).
11. *NLRB v. Laney & Duke Storage Warehouse Co.*, 369 F.2d 859 (CA-5, 1966).
12. *Axelson, Inc.*, 234 NLRB 414 (1978).
13. *NLRB v. Century Cement Mfg. Co.*, 208 F.2d 84 (CA-2, 1953).
14. *Singer Mfg. Co. v. NLRB*, 119 F.2d 131 (CA-7, 1941).
15. *Connecticut Light & Power Co. v. NLRB*, 476 F.2d 1079 (CA-2, 1973).
16. *Carlisle & Jacquelin*, 55 NLRB 678 (1944).
17. *Allied Chemical & Alkali Workers v. Pittsburgh Plate Glass Co.*, 404 U.S. 157 (1971).
18. *NL Industries, Inc.*, 220 NLRB 41 (1975).
19. *Inland Steel Co. v. NLRB*, 170 F.2d 247 (CA-7, 1948).
20. *NLRB v. Electric Steam Radiator Corp.*, 321 F.2d 733 (CA-6, 1963).

21. *NLRB v. Wonder State Mfg. Co.,* 344 F.2d 210 (CA-8, 1965).

22. *Hinson v. NLRB,* 428 F.2d 133 (CA-8, 1970).

23. *Ford Motor Co. v. Huffman,* 345 U.S. 330 (1953).

24. *Rapid Roller Co. v. NLRB,* 126 F.2d 452 (CA-7, 1942).

25. *NLRB v. Frontier Homes Corp.,* 371 F.2d 974 (CA-8, 1967).

26. *Rapid Roller Co. v. NLRB, supra.*

27. *Washougal Woolen Mills,* 23 NLRB 1 (1940).

28. *Gallenkamp Stores Co., supra.*

29. *NLRB v. Miller Brewing Co.,* 408 F.2d 12 (CA-9, 1969).

30. *Oughton v. NLRB,* 118 F.2d 486 (CA-3, 1941).

31. *Gallenkamp Stores Co. v. NLRB, supra.*

32. *Ford Motor Co. v. NLRB,* 441 U.S. 488 (1979).

33. *Caroline Farms Div. of Textron, Inc. v. NLRB,* 401 F.2d 205 (CA-4, 1968).

34. *NLRB v. Independent Stave Co.,* 591 F.2d 443 (CA-8, 1979).

35. *Washougal Woolen Mills, supra.*

36. *NLRB v. Wooster Div. of Borg-Warner Corp.,* 356 U.S. 342 (1958).

37. *NLRB v. Boss Mfg. Co.,* 118 F.2d 187 (CA-7, 1941).

38. *NLRB v. American National Ins. Co.,* 343 U.S. 395 (1952).

39. *Fiberboard Paper Products Co. v. NLRB, supra.*

40. *United Mine Workers of America,* 231 NLRB 573 (1977).

41. *NLRB v. Andrew Jergens Co.,* 175 F.2d 130 (CA-9, 1949).

42. *South Carolina Granite Co.,* 58 NLRB 1448 (1944).

43. *United Packinghouse, Food & Allied Workers International Union v. NLRB,* 135 App. DC 111, 416 F.2d 1126 (1969).

44. *NLRB v. Laney & Duke Storage Warehouse Co.,* 369 F.2d 859 (CA-5, 1966).

45. *Dolly Madison Industries, Inc.,* 182 NLRB 1027 (1970).

46. *United Mine Workers of America, supra.*

47. *Singer Mfg. Co., supra.*

48. *NLRB v. Wooster Div. of Borg-Warner Corp., supra.*

49. *Allis-Chalmers Mfg. Co. v. NLRB, supra.*

50. *NLRB v. Davison,* 318 F.2d 550 (CA-4, 1963).

51. *NLRB v. Burns International Security Services, Inc.,* 406 U.S. 272 (1972).

52. *W & W Steel Co.,* NLRB Advice Mem. Case No. 23-CA-6038 (1976), 1976–1977 CCH NLRB ¶20046.

53. *Nazareth Regional High School v. NLRB,* 549 F.2d 873 (CA-2, 1977).

54. *Pacific Hide & Fur Depot, Inc. v. NLRB,* 553 F.2d 609 (CA-9, 1977).

55. *Pinter Bros., Inc.,* 263 NLRB 723 (1982).

56. *Robert G. Shearer,* 262 NLRB 622 (1982).

57. *J.M. Tanaka Construction, Inc. v. NLRB,* 675 F.2d 1029 (CA-9, 1982); *Shellmaker, Inc.,* 265 NLRB 749 (1982).

58. *Komatz Constr., Inc. v. NLRB,* 458 F.2d 317 (CA-8, 1972).

59. *NLRB v. Beck Engraving Co.,* 522 F.2d 475 (CA-3, 1975).

60. *NLRB v. L.B. Priestor & Sons, Inc.,* 669 F.2d 335, 109 LRRM 3208 (CA-5, 1982).

61. *Jeffrey-DeWitt Insulator Co. v. NLRB,* 91 F.2d 134 (CA-4, 1937).

62. *NLRB v. Stanislaus Implement & Hardware Co.,* 226 F.2d 377 (CA-9, 1955).

63. *NLRB v. Acme Air Appliance Co.,* 117 F.2d 417 (CA-2, 1941).

64. *United Steelworkers of America v. NLRB,* 129 App. DC 80, 390 F.2d 846 (1968).

65. *NLRB v. Remington Rand, Inc.,* 94 F.2d 862 (CA-2, 1938).

66. *NLRB v. Truitt Mfg. Co.,* 351 U.S. 149 (1956).

67. *NLRB v. Truitt Mfg. Co., supra.*

68. *NLRB v. Item Co.,* 220 F.2d 956 (CA-5, 1955).

69. *Standard Oil Co.,* 174 NLRB 177 (1969).

70. *Holmes Typography, Inc.,* 218 NLRB 518 (1975).

71. *Medo Photo Supply Corp. v. NLRB,* 321 U.S. 678 (1944).

72. *NLRB v. Pepsi-Cola Bottling Co.,* 449 F.2d 824 (CA-5, 1971).

73. *Flambeau Plastics Corp. v. NLRB,* 401 F.2d 128 (CA-7, 1968).

74. *Morand Bros. Beverage Co. v. NLRB,* 190 F.2d 576 (CA-7, 1951).

75. *American Ship Building Co. v. NLRB,* 380 U.S. 300 (1965).

76. *American Ship Building Co. v. NLRB, supra.*

77. *Textile Workers Union v. Darlington Manufacturing Co.,* 380 U.S. 263 (1965).

78. *First National Maintenance Corp.,* 452 U.S. 666 (1981).

79. *First National Maintenance Corp., supra;* see, also: *Otis Elevator Co.,* 269 NLRB No. 162 (1984).

15

Collective Bargaining: Union's Obligations

[15.01] DUTY TO BARGAIN IN GOOD FAITH

Provided a union is the representative of certain employees pursuant to the provisions of Section 9(a) of the Act, the union violates Section 8(b)(3) of the Act if it refuses to bargain collectively with the employees' employer.

A union is required to meet and confer with management in good faith with a desire to reach an ultimate agreement in order to satisfy its bargaining duty.[1]

A union violates Section 8(b)(3) of the Act by entering negotiations with a fixed purpose of not reaching an agreement or signing a collective bargaining contract.[2]

A union also violates the Act by bargaining to an impasse over a nonmandatory bargaining subject[3] or insisting that the employer agree to a provision or take some action which is unlawful or inconsistent with the basic policy of the National Labor Relations Act.[4]

[15.02] INAPPROPRIATE UNIT

A union commits a violation of Section 8(b)(3) of the Act by demanding negotiation for an inappropriate unit.[5] It is also a violation of the Act for a union to insist that negotiations be concluded with respect to employees outside their bargaining unit as a condition prior to the execution of an agreed-upon collective bargaining contract.[6]

[15.03] REFUSAL TO BARGAIN WITH EMPLOYER'S REPRESENTATIVES

Both an employer and a union are prohibited, except by agreement relative thereto, from determining who shall represent the other for the purpose of negotiation or the consideration of grievances.[7] Therefore, a union generally violates Section 8(b)(3) of the Act by refusing to bargain with an employer's chosen representative in negotiations.[8]

[15.04] REFUSAL TO SIGN CONTRACT

Section 8(d) of the Act defines the collective bargaining duty of both the employer and the union to include "the execution of a written contract incorporating any agreement reached if requested by either party."

Thus, a union commits a violation of Section 8(b)(3) of the Act by refusing to sign a written collective bargaining agreement containing the terms, conditions, and provisions upon which the employer and the union have agreed.[9]

[15.05] IMPASSE OVER NONMANDATORY SUBJECTS OF BARGAINING

Section 8(d) of the Act requires an employer and the employees' representative to meet at reasonable times and confer in good faith with respect to such mandatory bargaining subjects as "wages, hours, and other terms and conditions of employment."

Therefore, a union that bargains to an impasse over nonmandatory subjects of bargaining—subjects that are outside the scope of "wages, hours, and other terms and conditions of employment"—commits a violation of Section 8(b)(3) of the Act.[10]

[15.06] STRIKE NOTICE REQUIREMENTS TO HEALTH-CARE INSTITUTIONS

Section 8(g) of the LMRA requires a union to notify a health-care institution in writing, as well as the Federal Mediation and Conciliation Service, of its intention to engage in any strike, picketing, or other concerted refusal to work with respect to such institution not less than ten days prior to such action.

The purpose of this ten-day notice requirement is to give health-care institutions advance notice of a work stoppage so as to permit them time to make arrangements for the continued care of their patients.[11]

NOTES TO CHAPTER 15

1. *NLRB v. Insurance Agents' International Union,* 361 U.S. 477 (1960).
2. *American Newspaper Publishers Association v. NLRB,* 193 F.2d 782 (CA-7, 1952).
3. *Brotherhood of Painters v. NLRB,* 110 App. DC 294, 293 F.2d 133 (1961).
4. *International Brotherhood of Electrical Workers,* 119 NLRB 1792 (1958).
5. *Utility Workers Union (Ohio Power Co.),* 203 NLRB 230 (1973).
6. *NLRB v. South Atlantic Gulf Coast Dist. International Longshoremen's Association,* 443 F.2d 218 (CA-5, 1971).
7. *NLRB v. Ross Gear & Tool Co.,* 158 F.2d 607 (CA-7, 1947).
8. *NLRB v. Ross Gear & Tool Co., supra.*
9. *Electrical Workers (IBEW) Local 1228,* 230 NLRB No. 45 (1977).
10. *Brotherhood of Painters v. NLRB, supra.*
11. *Senate Report,* 93–766, P.4.

16

How to Process
an Unfair Labor Practice Charge

[16.01]   FILING

Inasmuch as the NLRB cannot commence an unfair labor practice proceeding of its own initiative,[1] an unfair labor practice charge is necessary
to give the NLRB a preliminary basis to determine whether there is justification to investigate the charging party's allegation.[2] It serves merely as
the spark which sets the statutory machinery running.[3]

According to the NLRB rules, "any person," including a labor organization, an employer or an individual (with the exception of the NLRB
and its agents), may file an unfair labor practice charge.[4]

The unfair labor practice charge is to be filed with the NLRB regional
office in which area the alleged unfair labor practices have occurred.[5] An
unfair labor practice charge which alleges that illegal conduct has occurred
in two or more regions may be filed with the regional office within any of
such regions.[6]

[16.02]   TIME LIMITS FOR FILING

Section 10(b) of the Act requires that an unfair labor practice charge be
filed within six months of the alleged unfair labor practice. The unfair labor
practice charge should be filed with the Board's Regional Office along with
a copy of such charge to be served upon each of the parties against whom
the charge is alleged.[7] Although a regional director will customarily serve a
copy of the charge upon the charged party, it does not exonerate the charging party from directly serving the charged party should the regional director fail to do so.

[16.03]   CONTENTS OF THE CHARGE

Persons desiring to file unfair labor practice charges may obtain appropriate
forms on which to file such charges from any NLRB regional office. The
forms used for filing charges are broken down into three categories:

1. *Charge against employer* (NLRB Form-501). This form is used to process
   Section 8(a) cases, typically referred to as CA cases by the NLRB.
2. *Charge against labor organization or its agents* (NLRB Form-508). This form
   is used to process Section 8(b)(1), (2), (3), (5) or (6) cases—also known
   as CB cases, Section 8(b)(4)(A), (B) or (C) cases—also known as CC
   cases, Section 8(B)(4)(D) cases—also known as CD cases, Section
   8(b)(7) cases—also known as CP cases, and Section 8(g) cases—also
   known as CG cases.

3. *Charge alleging unfair labor practices under Section 8(e) of the Act* (NLRB Form-509). This form is used to process Section 8(e) cases—also known as DE cases.

Once the contents of the charge are completed on the form as instructed, the filing party should sign the declaration noted on the form that its contents are true to the best of his or her knowledge, or, in the alternative, the charge should be sworn to by the filing party before a notary public or a Board agent.[8]

[16.04]   AMENDED CHARGES

The NLRB recognizes that a charging party to an unfair labor practice may amend the original, or last amended, charge.[9] Such an amendment does not constitute a withdrawal of either the original or an earlier amended charge.[10]

Where an amended charge raises ''a new and separate cause of action,'' the amended charge must independently satisfy the six-month statute of limitation under Section 10(b) of the Act as to its filing and service.[11] However, the six-month limitation does not have to be met if the amended charge

- relates back to the original unfair labor practice allegations[12]
- is based on a like fact situation as contained in the original charge[13]
- clarifies the original charge and its allegations with particulars[14]
- defines more precisely the allegations contained in the earlier charges[15] or
- merely restates the original charge in some manner[16]

[16.05]   INVESTIGATION BY NLRB

Once an unfair labor practice charge is filed with an NLRB regional office, the NLRB is free to make a full investigation of the charging party's allegations. The initial investigation of the charge would consist of interviews and conferences with parties and witnesses by NLRB agents. Affidavits are normally requested from and are usually taken from supporting witnesses of the charging party. In addition, the NLRB agent assigned to the case customarily reviews copies of correspondence, records, and other documents that the charging party has filed with the regional office in support of his or her case.

After the initial investigation by an NLRB agent into the charging party's charge, and assuming some prima facie evidence exists in support of the charge, the NLRB agent will typically request the charged party to make witnesses available and submit a position statement in support of its defense to such charges.

The charged party is not required by law to cooperate with the NLRB agent in furnishing witnesses for the purpose of affidavits, but its failure to do so entitles the regional director to make a decision on whether to issue a complaint on the facts developed primarily from the charging party and his or her witnesses, whereas, countervailing evidence from the charged party may well convince the regional director that the charge is without merit and that a complaint in the matter is not to be issued.

[16.06]   DISPOSITION OF THE CHARGE

Withdrawal: A withdrawal of an unfair labor practice charge may be initiated by the charging party.[17] However, pursuant to the NLRB rules, "a charge may be withdrawn, prior to the hearing, only with the consent of the regional director with whom the charge was filed."[18]

Withdrawal is usually denied by the regional director where a private settlement between the parties does not remedy the unfair labor practice or where the public interest dictates that effective remedial action be taken for the alleged violation.[19] A withdrawal of a charge is often brought about at the request of the regional office. Where the investigation reveals that there has been no violation of the Act or the charging party's evidence is insufficient to support the issuance of a complaint, the NLRB agent will generally recommend to the charging party that the charge voluntarily be withdrawn.[20]

Dismissal and appeals: If the charging party refuses to withdraw the charge at the request of the regional office, the regional director will dismiss the charge.[21] The charging party may appeal the dismissal of his or her charge within ten days from the receipt of the regional director's letter informing the party of the dismissal. Such an appeal should be filed with the general counsel of the NLRB in Washington, D.C., with a copy of the appeal to the regional director.[22]

Appeals from dismissals of Section 8(b)(7) cases must be appealed to the general counsel of the NLRB within three days from the receipt of the notice of dismissal.

Settlement of the charge: Where the NLRB investigation reveals merit in the charge, the regional office will generally attempt to secure an informal settlement from the charged party prior to issuing a complaint and proceeding to litigation.[23]

Although the terms and conditions of an informal settlement are subject to the approval of the regional director, it is typically a stated agreement wherein the charged party undertakes to remedy the unfair labor practices alleged against it.

Complaint issued: If an unfair labor practice charge is not withdrawn, dismissed, or adjusted through an informal settlement agreement, the Board will then proceed to issue a complaint stating the charges in the matter and containing a notice of hearing before the NLRB.

NOTES TO CHAPTER 16

1. *Nash v. Florida Industrial Commission*, 389 U.S. 235 (1967).
2. *NLRB v. Kingston Cake Co.*, 191 F.2d 563 (CA-3, 1951).
3. *NLRB v. Fant Milling Co.*, 360 U.S. 301 (1959).
4. *NLRB Rules and Regulations*, §102.9.
5. *NLRB Rules and Regulations*, §102.10.
6. *NLRB Rules and Regulations*, §102.10.
7. *NLRB Rules and Regulations*, §102.14.
8. *NLRB Rules and Regulations*, §102.11.
9. *Brown Equipment & Mfg. Co.*, 1000 NLRB 801 (1952).
10. *NLRB v. Kobritz Co.*, 193 F.2d 8 (CA-1, 1951).
11. *McGraw-Edison Co.*, Speed Queen Div., 192 NLRB No. 142 (1971).
12. *NLRB v. R.H. Osbrink Mfg. Co.*, 218 F.2d 341 (CA-9, 1954).
13. *Mason-Rust*, 179 NLRB No. 71 (1969).
14. *NLRB v. Gaynor News Co.*, 197 F.2d 719 (CA-2, 1952).
15. *NLRB v. Gaynor News Co.*, *supra*.
16. *Mason & Hughes, Inc.*, 86 NLRB 848 (1949).
17. 29 CFR §101.5.
18. 29 CFR §102.9.
19. *NLRB v. Oertal Brewing Co.*, 197 F.2d 59 (CA-6, 1952).
20. 29 CFR §101.5.
21. 29 CFR §101.6.
22. 29 CFR §101.6.
23. Kenneth McGuiness, *How to Take a Case Before the National Labor Relations Board*, 4th Edition (Washington, D.C.: Bureau of National Affairs, Inc., 1976), 243 .

17

The Unfair Labor Practice Hearing

[17.01] COMPLAINT

The filing of a complaint, rather than the unfair labor practice charge, is the first formal pleading in an unfair labor practice proceeding and is designed to notify the charged party of the claims to be adjudicated.[1]

In drafting the complaint in an unfair labor practice proceeding, the NLRB has a wide discretion by which to include matters not included in the original unfair labor practice charge,[2] as long as the complaint does not go so far outside the charge as to be deemed an NLRB initiated proceeding on its own motion.[3]

The NLRB rules require the complaint to contain (1) a clear and concise statement of the facts upon which jurisdiction by the Board is predicated, and (2) a clear and concise description of the acts which are claimed to constitute unfair labor practices, including, where known, the approximate dates and places of such acts and the names of respondent's agents or other representatives by whom committed.[4]

The notice of hearing, usually a part of the formal complaint, specifies the time and place of the hearing.[5] The NLRB rules provide for a postponement of the hearing, if for ''good cause'' shown by the party requesting it.[6] Section 10(b) of the Act permits a complaint to be amended at any time prior to the issuance of an order relating to the complaint.[7]

[17.02] ANSWER TO COMPLAINT

The Labor Management Relations Act provides the party against whom the complaint is issued the right to file an answer to the complaint.[8] Such answer shall be filed within ten days of the service of the complaint.[9] The answer should respond to each and every allegation in the complaint by denial, admission, or explanation, unless the respondent is without knowledge, in which case the responding party should so state, such statement operating as a denial.[10]

The NLRB may treat unanswered complaints or unanswered allegations within a complaint as admissions of truth and judgment may be rendered on the complaint alone.[11] The responding party should file the original and four copies of the answer with the regional director who issued the complaint.[12]

[17.03] PREHEARING MATTERS

Settlement: The NLRB has had a long policy of encouraging compromises and settlements of alleged unfair labor practices as an alternative to litigation.[13] The fact that a complaint has been issued does not preclude a settlement of the alleged unfair labor practices in question.

Stipulations: Frequently, in NLRB unfair labor practice proceedings, the General Counsel will enter into stipulations of facts with the party against whom the complaint was filed, even though the charging party refuses to join in such stipulation.[14]

Subpoenas and petitions to revoke: NLRB rules provide that parties to an unfair labor practice hearing may secure the issuance of a subpoena by the administrative law judge.[15]

The party requesting the subpoena should submit an application in writing and indicate whether a *subpoena ad testificandum* (issued for the sole purpose of giving testimony) or a *subpoena duces tecum* (issued for the dual purpose of giving testimony and presenting certain documents and data listed in the subpoena) is desired.[16]

According to Section 102.31(a) of the Board's rules and regulations, the person against whom the subpoena is served has five days after the date of the service to petition the appointed administrative law judge to revoke the subpoena.

Depositions: Applications to take evidentiary depositions of witnesses in unfair labor practice proceedings are granted only if, in the exercise of his or her discretion, the administrative law judge has been shown "good cause" for the request.[17]

Although permission to take evidentiary depositions may be available when "good cause" is shown, such depositions may be used only as a means to preserve testimony inasmuch as the NLRB rules do not provide for the taking of depositions for the purpose of pre-trial discovery.[18]

Motions: Pre-trial motions are filed with the regional director, the chief administrative law judge, or the NLRB, depending on the type of motion.

Motions for postponement, extensions of time to file an answer, to intervene, or to take a deposition prior to the opening of the hearing are to be filed with the regional director.[19] Motions for summary judgment are to be filed with the NLRB.[20] All other motions prior to a hearing are to be filed with the chief administrative law judge in Washington, D.C., or with the associate chief administrative law judge in San Francisco, California, depending on the place of hearing.[21]

The original and seven copies of motions for summary judgment must be filed with the NLRB.[22] All other motions prior to transfer of the case to the NLRB shall be filed by the moving party in an original and four copies, and a copy thereof shall be immediately served on the other parties.[23]

Consolidation of cases: Consolidation of cases before the NLRB lies within the discretion of the general counsel or the Board.[24]

[17.04] HEARINGS—FUNCTIONS OF PARTIES

Unfair labor practice hearings are conducted in the region where the charge originated[25] and usually are open to the public.[26] A verbatim transcript is made by an official reporter of the proceedings; this transcript becomes the official record of the hearing.[27]

Function of the administrative law judge: The administrative law judge assigned to hear an unfair labor practice case is responsible for the orderly conduct of the hearing. He or she is also charged with the responsibility of seeing that a complete record is preserved and that all pertinent facts are elicited.[28]

Function of counsel for the general counsel: The office of the general counsel is responsible for presenting evidence to prove the allegations in the complaint. Therefore, the counsel for the general counsel has the burden of introducing evidence and presenting the case for the general counsel, including the burden of proving a violation of the statute.[29]

Although the counsel for the general counsel has the task of proving the allegations in the complaint, counsel for the charging party may also participate in the proceedings[30] and is entitled to present evidence and examine witnesses on his or her own behalf as long as this does not jeopardize or impede the counsel for the general counsel's efforts in the prosecution of the case.

Function of counsel for the charged party: Equally, the counsel representing the respondent, the charged party, is entitled to participate in the hearing to the fullest extent on behalf of his or her client.

[17.05] HEARINGS—EVIDENTIARY REQUIREMENTS

Under Section 10(b) of the Act, an unfair labor practice proceeding shall, so far as practicable, be conducted in accordance with the rules of evidence applicable in the federal district courts pursuant to the federal rules of civil procedure.

Although the federal rules of civil procedure are used by administrative law judges as a general guideline, the Act does not require a strict application of such rules inasmuch as each case is to be adjudicated upon its own set of facts and background.[31]

Sufficiency of evidence—burden of proof: The mere issuance of a complaint by the NLRB creates no presumption of a violation of the Act.[32] The burden of affirmatively proving allegations in the complaint rests upon the general counsel.[33]

Under the *Wright Line*[34] doctrine, the NLRB requires the general counsel to establish that employee conduct protected by the Act was a motivating factor in the employer's decision to take some adverse action against the employee. Once the General Counsel establishes this burden of proof, the burden then shifts to the respondent employer to show that it would have taken the same action against the employee under the circumstances, irrespective of the employee's protected activities. Thereafter, the general counsel is permitted to introduce any relevant evidence which might demonstrate that the employer's reasons for discharge were merely pretextual.[35]

Admissibility: All facts tending to prove or disprove allegations in the complaint are considered relevant evidence by the NLRB and are customarily admissible in an unfair labor practice proceeding.[36] However, if evidence is substantially contradicted by other evidence and the accompanying circumstances,[37] or if the evidence is merely cumulative,[38] the administrative law judge is not required to accept it.

All parties to an unfair labor practice proceeding have the right to introduce relevant documentary evidence into the record to the extent relevant and permitted by the administrative law judge.[39]

Furnishing documents to the opposing parties—limitations: The respondent in an unfair labor practice case is not, as a matter of right, entitled to "any files, documents, reports, memoranda, or records of the Board" without the written consent of the Board or the general counsel.[40]

However, the respondent in such a proceeding is entitled to inspect any written pretrial statement made by a witness of the general counsel, if such request is made after the general counsel's examination of the witness and prior to the respondent's cross-examination of the witness.[41] If after such request, the counsel for the general counsel refuses to furnish the statement to the respondent, the administrative law judge must strike the testimony of that witness from the record.[42]

Adverse inference rule: Where a party has relevant evidence within his control which he refuses to produce upon request or subpoena, the NLRB may properly hold that such refusal gives rise to an inference that he would have so produced had the evidence not been unfavorable to him.[43]

[17.06] HEARINGS—EXAMINATION AND CREDIBILITY OF WITNESSES

The administrative law judge in an unfair labor practice proceeding has the discretion of determining the extent of examination and cross-examination of witnesses.[44]

Rule 611 of the Federal Rules of Evidence permits the use of leading questions to adverse party witnesses as well as hostile witnesses.

Cross-examination of a witness in an unfair labor practice hearing may be limited where the matter to be inquired into is not material[45] or where the questions go beyond the scope of the matters covered upon direct or redirect examination.[46]

Inasmuch as an administrative law judge has an opportunity to observe the demeanor of witnesses during their testimony, the Administrative law judge has the province of determining their credibility.[47]

[17.07]   INTERVENTION AT HEARING

The NLRB rules provide that a regional director, before an unfair labor practice hearing commences, or an administrative law judge, after such an unfair labor practice hearing commences, may allow another person to intervene in a proceeding to such an extent and upon such terms as he or she deems appropriate.[48]

[17.08]   MISCONDUCT OF PARTIES

Misconduct by parties or counsel in an unfair labor practice hearing is sufficient grounds for summary exclusion from such hearing.[49] Moreover, counsel who engage in aggravated and contemptuous misconduct in a NLRB hearing are subject to suspension or debarment from further practice before the NLRB.[50] However, exclusion or disbarment of counsel or an attorney without specifying the particular basis for such action is violative of the Administrative Procedures Act.[51]

[17.09]   ORAL ARGUMENTS AND BRIEFS

Parties to an unfair labor practice proceeding are, upon request, entitled to present oral argument at the close of the NLRB hearing.[52] Additionally, or in the alternative, briefs may be filed upon request made prior to the closing of the hearing.[53] The administrative law judge prescribes time limits for the filings of briefs.[54]

NOTES TO CHAPTER 17

1. *Douds v. International Longshoremen's Association Independent,* 241 F.2d 278 (CA-2, 1957).
2. *NLRB v. W.R. Hall Distributor,* 341 F.2d 359 (CA-10, 1965).
3. *NLRB v. International Union of Operating Engineers,* 460 F.2d 589 (CA-5, 1972).
4. *NLRB Rules and Regulations,* §102.15.
5. *NLRB Rules and Regulations,* §102.15.
6. *NLRB Rules and Regulations,* §102.16.

7. *NLRB Rules and Regulations*, §102.17.

8. 29 U.S.C.A. §160(b).

9. *NLRB Rules and Regulations*, §102.20.

10. *NLRB Rules and Regulations*, §102.20.

11. *Liquid Carbonic Corp.*, 116 NLRB 795 (1956).

12. *NLRB Rules and Regulations*, §102.21.

13. *Wallace Corp. v. NLRB*, 323 U.S. 248 (1944).

14. Kenneth McGuiness, *How to Take a Case Before the National Labor Relations Board*, 4th Edition (Washington, D.C.: Bureau of National Affairs, Inc., 1976), 275.

15. *NLRB Rules and Regulations*, §102.31(a).

16. *NLRB Rules and Regulations*, §102.31.

17. *NLRB Rules and Regulations*, §102.30.

18. *NLRB v. Interboro Contractors, Inc.*, 432 F.2d 854 (CA-2, 1970).

19. *NLRB Casehandling Manual*, §102.90.

20. *NLRB Rules and Regulations*, §102.50.

21. *NLRB Casehandling Manual*, §102.90.

22. *NLRB Rules and Regulations*, §102.50.

23. *NLRB Casehandling Manual*, §102.90.

24. *NLRB v. Seamprufe, Inc.*, 186 F.2d 671 (CA-10, 1951).

25. 29 CFR §101.10(a).

26. *NLRB Rules and Regulations*, §102.34.

27. Kenneth McGuiness, *How to Take a Case Before the National Labor Relations Board*, 4th Edition (Washington, D.C.: Bureau of National Affairs, Inc., 1976), 266.

28. *NLRB Rules and Regulations*, §102.35.

29. *NLRB v. Miami Coca-Cola Bottling Co.*, 222 F.2d 341 (CA-5, 1955).

30. *Spector Freight Systems, Inc.*, 141 NLRB 1110 (1963).

31. *NLRB v. General Longshoremen Workers*, Local 1418, 212 F.2d 846 (CA-5, 1954).

32. *Boeing Airplane Co.*, 140 F.2d 423 (CA-10, 1944).

33. 29 CFR §101.10(b).

34. *Wright Line, Inc.*, 251 NLRB 1083 (1980).

35. *NLRB v. Transportation Mgmt. Corp.*, 462 U.S. 393 (1983).

36. *Jefferson Electric Co. v. NLRB*, 102 F.2d 949 (CA-7, 1939).

37. *NLRB v. Ford*, 170 F.2d 735 (CA-6, 1948).

38. *MPC Restaurant Corp. v. NLRB*, 481 F.2d 75 (CA-2, 1973).

39. *NLRB Rules and Regulations*, §102.38.

40. *NLRB Rules and Regulations*, §102.118.

41. *NLRB Rules and Regulations*, §102.118(b)(1).

42. *NLRB Rules and Regulations*, §102.118(b)(2).

43. *International Union, United Auto, etc. v. NLRB,* 148 App. D.C. 305, 459 F.2d 1329 (1972).

44. *NLRB v. Baltimore Paint & Chemical Corp.,* 308 F.2d 75 (CA-4, 1962).

45. *NLRB v. Ed Friedrich, Inc.,* 116 F.2d 888 (CA-5, 1940).

46. *Teamsters, Chauffeurs, Warehousemen & Helpers,* 167 NLRB 135 (1967).

47. *NLRB v. Rawac Plating Co.,* 422 F.2d 1259 (CA-6, 1970).

48. *NLRB Rules and Regulations,* §102.29.

49. *NLRB Rules and Regulations,* §102.44(a).

50. *NLRB Rules and Regulations,* §102.44(b).

51. *Great Lakes Screw Corporation v. NLRB,* 409 F.2d 375 (CA-7, 1969).

52. *NLRB Rules and Regulations,* §102.42.

53. *NLRB Rules and Regulations,* §102.42.

54. *NLRB Rules and Regulations,* §102.42.

18

Unfair Labor Practices: Post-Hearing Proceedings

[18.01] ADMINISTRATIVE LAW JUDGE'S DECISION

Following an unfair labor practice hearing, the administrative law judge shall prepare a decision, consisting of findings of fact and conclusions of law, as well as recommendations as to the disposition of the case.[1] The parties to the unfair labor practice proceeding may accept and comply with the administrative law judge's decision (recommendations), in which circumstance the recommendations will become the NLRB order regarding the case.[2]

Once an administrative law judge renders his or her decision in an unfair labor practice proceeding, copies of the decision are then filed with the NLRB in Washington, D.C. and served upon all parties to the case.[3] Upon receipt of the administrative law judge's decision, an order is entered transferring the case, along with the record, to the Board.[4]

[18.02] EXCEPTIONS TO THE ALJ'S DECISION

Any party, including general counsel, may file exceptions to an administrative law judge's decision, or to any other part of the record, including rulings upon motions or objections, if such exceptions are filed with the NLRB in Washington, D.C. within twenty days from the date of the service of the order transferring the case to the Board.[5] Each exception to the administrative law judge's decision shall

- set forth specifically the questions of procedure, fact, law, or policy to which exception is taken
- identify that part of the administrative law judge's decision to which objection is made
- designate by precise citation of page, the portions of the record relied upon
- state the grounds for the exceptions and include the citation of authorities unless set forth in a supporting brief[6]

Any exception that fails to comply with the foregoing requirements may be disregarded.[7] The NLRB rules provide that each party, as a matter of right, may file a brief in support of his or her exceptions.[8] Such a brief should be filed and served at the same time as the exceptions, but as a separate document.[9]

Briefs in support of exceptions should not contain matters not included within the scope of the exceptions noted. They must contain

- a concise statement of the case containing all that is material to the consideration of the question presented

- a specification of the questions involved and to be argued, and

- the argument, presenting clearly the points of fact and law relied upon in support of the position taken on each question, with specific reference to the transcript and the legal or other materials relied upon[10]

Briefs in support of exceptions must also contain an index if more than twenty pages in length.[11]

Any party may, within ten days from the filing of the exceptions, file an answering brief to the exceptions,[12] and/or file cross-exceptions relating to any portion of the administrative law judge's decision.[13] A brief may also be filed in support of cross-exceptions.[14]

It is within the NLRB's discretion whether or not to grant a request for oral argument in support of exceptions or cross-exceptions.[15] Parties desiring to argue orally before the NLRB must address a written request to the Board simultaneously with the filing of their exceptions or cross-exceptions.[16]

[18.03]   NLRB DECISION AND ORDER

An administrative law judge's recommended order is no more than a recommendation to the NLRB as to how the case should be disposed.[17] The Board may adopt, reject, or modify the findings, conclusions, and recommendations of the administrative law judge as it deems warranted.[18]

However, it is a Board policy not to overrule credibility findings of an administrative law judge unless a clear preponderance of the evidence convinces it that the findings are erroneous.[19]

Whenever exceptions are filed to the administrative law judge's decision, the Board makes its determination upon the entire record.[20]

Under Section 3(b) of the Labor Management Relations Act, the NLRB may delegate its powers to decide cases to a panel of three members.

[18.04]   REMEDIES FOR VIOLATIONS

Restrictive orders: Whenever the NLRB finds an unfair labor practice, the Board may issue a cease-and-desist order against the unlawful conduct.[21]

Aside from the cease-and-desist orders, the NLRB may impose other restrictive orders such as an order to withdraw union recognition[22] or an order to invalidate a collective bargaining agreement.[23]

Affirmative orders: In addition to a cease-and-desist order, the NLRB has wide discretion in ordering that affirmative action be taken by the guilty party.[24] For example, in formulating remedies for unfair labor practice violations the NLRB has ordered

- the resumption of a business and reinstatement of employees with back pay where an employer discriminatorily contracted out work[25]
- an employer to carry out the provisions of an agreement previously negotiated on its behalf[26]
- the hiring of certain applicants who were discriminatorily rejected from employment because of their union allegiance[27]
- an employer to furnish to the union a list of employees' names and addresses as a result of employer interference with a union-organizing campaign[28]
- reasonable access of company bulletin boards to union representatives as a result of unlawful interference of union organizational efforts by the employer[29]
- a union to refund money collected for work permits to employees[30]

Bargaining orders: The affirmative relief imposed by the Board may be in the nature of an order directing an employer to bargain collectively.[31] Such bargaining orders are typically imposed in two specific situations when[32]

- an employer commits such unfair labor practices that the holding of a fair and uncoerced election is unlikely, or
- an employer has been found guilty of Section 8(a)(5) of the Act for unlawful refusal to bargain

Reinstatement orders: Under Section 10(c) of the Act, the NLRB may issue a reinstatement order against an employer who has committed unfair labor practices, which orders customarily require immediate and full reinstatement of the employee to his or her former job, or, if the job no longer exists, to a substantially similar position.[33]

Reinstatement under such circumstance is without prejudice to the employee's seniority, and, if the employee would have received promotions, pay raises, or transfers to a more favorable work environment, but for the unlawful conduct of the employer, he or she will be entitled to such benefits upon reinstatement.[34]

Back-pay orders: Section 10(c) of the Act also provides that the NLRB may order an employer to pay back pay to an employee for the time lost as a result of the employer's unlawful discrimination against the employee. Back pay orders are typically used to restore the status quo to employees who have been discriminatorily discharged,[35] to strikers who have unlawfully been refused reinstatement[36] and to applicants who have been denied employment because of their union affiliation[37]

Notices: Board orders typically require postings of notices to employees which specify the action taken to remedy the unfair labor practices.[38]

Each notice is drafted to identify the particular unfair labor practice committed and is required to be posted for sixty consecutive days.[39]

[18.05]   ENFORCEMENT OF AN NLRB DECISION

Should the party against whom the NLRB order is issued fail or refuse to comply with the decision, the Board must close the case or petition the appropriate United States Court of Appeals for enforcement of its order[40] inasmuch as the decision and order of the Board are not self-enforcing.[41]

Moreover, Section 10(f) of the Act specifies that any person aggrieved by a final NLRB order may obtain a review of the order in any court in which the NLRB may seek enforcement.

Petitions to enforce or to review NLRB orders in the federal courts are governed by the Federal Rules of Appellate Procedure.[42]

Upon such review or enforcement proceeding, the appellate court is to review the record and the Board's findings and order and sustain them if they are in accordance with the requirements of the law.[43] The scope of judicial review of an NLRB decision and order by the appropriate federal court is limited to whether the record contains substantial evidence to support the NLRB's findings and conclusions.[44]

The court may enforce, modify or set aside in whole or in part the Board's findings and order, or it may remand the case to the Board for further proceedings as directed by the court.[45]

The Board's rules also provide that either the government or the private party aggrieved from an adverse decision by the federal court in a petition for enforcement or review of an NLRB order may petition the Supreme Court for review upon a writ of certiorari.[46]

[18.06]   BACK-PAY PROCEEDINGS

Following a court enforcement of an NLRB order rewarding back pay, the Board must then determine the precise amount of back wages due the respective employees.[47] The NLRB will generally attempt to settle the back-pay liability with the respondent on an informal basis.[48]

If the informal effort to settle out the back-pay liability with the respondent is unsuccessful, the regional director is then authorized to issue a "back-pay specification," setting forth computations showing gross and net back-pay due and other pertinent information.[49]

The respondent must file an answer to the back-pay specifications with the regional director within fifteen days from the date of service.[50]

Should the respondent fail to file an answer to the back-pay specification within the fifteen-day period, the NLRB may find the specification to be true and enter an appropriate order. Likewise, a failure to deny allegations within the specification permits the NLRB to consider the truth of the allegations admitted.[51]

A back-pay award resulting from a back-pay proceeding is not self-executing but must be enforced through an application for enforcement to the appropriate Federal Court of Appeals.[52]

NOTES TO CHAPTER 18

1. *NLRB Rules and Regulations,* §102.45.

2. 29 U.S.C.A. §160(c).

3. *NLRB Rules and Regulations,* §102.45.

4. *NLRB Rules and Regulations,* §102.45.

5. *NLRB Rules and Regulations,* §102.46(a).

6. *NLRB Rules and Regulations,* §102.46(b).

7. *NLRB Rules and Regulations,* §102.46(b).

8. *NLRB Rules and Regulations,* §102.46(a).

9. *NLRB Rules and Regulations,* §102.46(a).

10. *NLRB Rules and Regulations,* §102.46(c).

11. *NLRB Rules and Regulations,* §102.46(j).

12. *NLRB Rules and Regulations,* §102.46(d).

13. *NLRB Rules and Regulations,* §102.46(e).

14. *NLRB Rules and Regulations,* §102.46(e).

15. *NLRB Rules and Regulations,* §102.46(i).

16. *NLRB Rules and Regulations,* §102.46(i).

17. *NLRB v. Oregon Worsted Co.,* 94 F.2d 671 (CA-9, 1938).

18. *NLRB v. Oregon Worsted Co., supra.*

19. *Congdon Die Casting Co.,* 176 NLRB 482 (1969).

20. *NLRB Rules and Regulations,* §102.48(b).

21. *NLRB v. Express Publishing Co.,* 312 U.S. 426 (1941).

22. *NLRB v. Pennsylvania Greyhound Lines, Inc.,* 303 U.S. 261 (1938).

23. *International Association of Machinists v. NLRB,* 311 U.S. 72 (1940).

24. *Eichleay Corp. v. NLRB,* 206 F.2d 799 (CA-3, 1953).

25. *Fibreboard Paper Products Corp. v. NLRB,* 379 U.S. 203 (1964).

26. *NLRB v. Strong,* 393 U.S. 357 (1969).

27. *Phelps Dodge Corp. v. NLRB,* 313 U.S. 177 (1941).

28. *Florida Steel Corp.,* 231 NLRB No. 117 (1977).

29. *Decaturville Sportswear Co. v. NLRB,* 406 F.2d 886 (CA-6, 1969).

30. *NLRB v. Local 420, United Association of Journeymen and Apprentices of the Plumbing and Pipefitting Industry,* 239 F.2d 327 (CA-3, 1956).

31. See *NLRB v. Express Publishing Co., supra.*

32. *NLRB v. Gissel Packing Co.,* 395 U.S. 575 (1969).

33. *NLRB Casehandling Manual (Part III),* §10528.3.

34. *Mooney Aircraft, Inc.,* 164 NLRB 1102 (1967).

35. *NLRB v. Gullett Gin Co.,* 340 U.S. 361 (1951).

36. *NLRB v. J. H. Rutter-Rex Mfg. Co.,* 396 U.S. 258 (1969).

37. *NLRB v. Waumbec Mills, Inc.,* 114 F.2d 226 (CA-1, 1940).

38. Kenneth McGuiness, *How to Take a Case Before the National Labor Relations Board,* 4th Edition (Washington, D.C.: Bureau of National Affairs, 1976), 297.

39. Ibid.

40. 29 U.S.C.A. §160(e).

41. Re: *NLRB,* 304 U.S. 486 (1938).

42. Rule 1(a), *Federal Rules of Appellate Procedure.*

43. 29 CFR §101.14.

44. *NLRB V. Ogle Protection Service, Inc.,* 375 F.2d 497 (CA-6, 1967).

45. 29 CFR §101.14.

46. 29 CFR §101.14.

47. *Nathanson v. NLRB,* 344 U.S. 25 (1952).

48. 29 CFR §101.16(a).

49. 29 CFR §101.16(a).

50. *NLRB Rules and Regulations,* §102.54(c).

51. *NLRB Rules and Regulations,* §102.54(c).

52. Re: *NLRB, supra.*

19

Representation Petitions for Certification

[19.01] PURPOSE OF PETITIONS FOR CERTIFICATION

Section 9(a) of the Labor Management Relations Act provides that a labor organization designated by a majority of employees in an appropriate bargaining unit shall be the exclusive bargaining agent of such employees.

There are three methods used by the NLRB to ascertain whether a labor organization maintains majority status sufficient to represent employees within an appropriate bargaining unit:

1. Where an employer has no reasonable doubt as to the union's majority status and voluntarily recognizes a labor organization as the employees' collective bargaining representative;[1]
2. Where an employer engages in pervasive unfair labor practices during a union organizational drive which makes it impossible for employees to express a free and uncoerced choice in an NLRB conducted secret ballot election, and, as a result, the NLRB issues a bargaining order requiring the employer to recognize the union;[2] or
3. Where the NLRB election procedures are utilized, permitting employees an opportunity to vote in a secret ballot election as to their desire to be, or not to be, represented by a particular union.[3]

This chapter is concerned with the latter method of determining majority status via representation petitions for certification before the NLRB.

[19.02] TYPES OF PETITIONS FOR CERTIFICATIONS

"RC" petitions: A petition for certification filed by employees or a labor organization is referred to by the NLRB as an "RC" petition.

"RM" petitions: A petition for certification filed by an employer who alleges that one or more individuals or labor organizations have presented to it a claim to be recognized as the exclusive bargaining representative of his or her employees is termed an "RM" petition by the NLRB.

[19.03] FILING REQUIREMENTS

Section 9(c) of the Act specifies that a petition for certification of representatives may be filed by

• any individual, an employee, or a group of employees, acting on behalf of employees

- a labor organization acting on behalf of employees, or

- an employer, alleging that one or more employees, or labor organizations, have presented to him or her a claim to be recognized by a union[4]

Both "RC" and "RM" petitions must be filed with the NLRB regional office for the region wherein the proposed appropriate bargaining unit exists.[5] If the bargaining unit exists in two or more regions, the petition may be filed with the regional director for any of such regions.[6]

In exceptional cases, and as a means to avoid unnecessary costs or delays, the general counsel of the NLRB may permit a petition to be filed with his or her office in Washington, D.C.,[7] in which instance the general counsel assumes the powers and responsibilities granted to NLRB regional directors in representation matters.[8]

Certain information is required to be contained in the petition form prior to filing. Once the form is completed, the representative or person filing the petition is then to affix his or her signature at the bottom of the petition form, declaring that he or she has read the petition and that the statements within it are true to the best of his or her knowledge and belief.[9] In the alternative, the petition may be sworn to before a notary public, an NLRB agent, or other person duly authorized by law to administer oaths.[10]

[19.04] SHOWING OF INTEREST— 30 PERCENT REQUIREMENT

Whenever an "RC" petition is filed, it must be accompanied by evidence of representation—commonly called a showing of interest—that at least 30 percent of the employees in the appropriate unit desire the petitioning labor organization to be their bargaining representative or desire that the NLRB conduct an election to determine whether the labor organization should represent them.[11]

Although union authorization cards are typically used as evidence to establish the 30 percent showing of interest, the Act does not require any specific form of evidence necessary to fulfill this 30 percent rule.[12] The NLRB adopted the 30 percent showing of interest as an administrative guideline to facilitate the Board's decision as to whether circumstances justify the holding of an election.[13]

Consequently, the showing of interest data submitted to the Regional Office by a petitioning union is held in confidence by the NLRB[14] and no party has a right to question the adequacy of the petitioner's showing of interest,[15] authenticity of signatures,[16] or currency of dates reflected on the supporting documents.[17]

Furthermore, the Board's rules do not permit litigation of the showing of interest question in a representation proceeding.[18] Any party desiring to present evidence of forgeries of signatures on showing of interest documents, or evidence of fraud in the procurement of employees' signatures, must submit the evidence administratively to the attention of the regional director[19] or to the NLRB in Washington, D.C.[20]

[19.05] INVESTIGATION OF PETITION

Once a certification petition is filed with the regional office, the NLRB must investigate the petition to ascertain whether there is reasonable cause to believe that a question of representation exists.[21] The investigation of a petition for a certification election typically includes *whether*[22]

- the petitioner has satisfied the 30 percent showing of interest requirement
- there is an appropriate unit petitioned
- there exists a bona-fide question concerning representation within the meaning of the Act
- the election would affect the policies of the Act, and
- the Board has commerce jurisdiction over the employer and/or employees

[19.06] ELECTION BAR/CERTIFICATION BAR

A valid election conducted as a result of either an "RC" petition or an "RM" petition bars an election among employees in that unit for twelve months.[23] However, a petition for a subsequent election may be filed shortly before the twelve-month period, assuming there is no contract bar.[24]

In similar fashion, once a union is certified by the NLRB as the bargaining agent of a unit of employees, an election is barred for a one-year period during which time the union is irrevocably presumed to hold majority status.[25]

[19.07] CONTRACT BAR

Whenever a valid collective bargaining contract is for a definite duration for terms up to three years, it bars an NLRB conducted election for that entire period.[26] Contracts having fixed periods longer than three years are treated by the NLRB as three-year agreements and the contract bar rule applies only for the initial three-year period.[27] A collective bargaining agreement without a termination or automatic renewal date will not bar a representation petition.[28]

[19.08] JURISDICTIONAL DEFICIENCIES

The NLRB will not hold a representation election when it does not have jurisdiction over the parties sufficient to satisfy its interstate commerce guidelines as well as its jurisdictional standards.[29]

[19.09] WITHDRAWALS AND DISMISSALS

If an investigation of the petition reveals that an election cannot be held for some reason, the NLRB will usually request the petitioner to withdraw the petition.[30] If the petitioner refuses to withdraw the petition, after being requested to do so by the regional director, the regional director will then dismiss the petition, stating the grounds for the dismissal.

Most petitions are withdrawn or dismissed for the following reasons:

- The proposed unit is inappropriate;
- The petitioner has failed to establish an adequate showing of interest;
- There exists a valid outstanding contract that bars the petition;
- There is a pending unresolved unfair labor practice charge that blocks the holding of an election; or
- An election has been conducted within the previous twelve-month period.[31]

Also, the petitioner, for his or her own reasons and of his or her own initiative, may withdraw the petition.[32]

[19.10] AGREEMENTS FOR ELECTION

If a petition is not withdrawn or dismissed and the requirements for an election have been met, the investigating NLRB agent will attempt to persuade the parties to agree to an election in order to avoid a representation hearing and the ordering of an election by the regional director.[33]

There are two types of informal agreements for elections used by the NLRB.

Agreement for consent election: Whenever a petition has been duly filed, an employer and the petitioning union may enter into a consent election, agreeing to such issues as the appropriate unit; the place, date, and hours of balloting; and the payroll period to be used to establish eligibility of voters, etc.[34]

An agreement for a consent election also provides that the election will be held in accordance with the Act and the NLRB's rules, regulations, and policies, and, further, *that any rulings or determinations as to any question that may arise from the election by the regional director shall be final and binding on the parties.*[35]

Stipulation for certification upon consent election: Although a stipulation for certification upon consent election is similar to the agreement for consent election in that the parties agree to the time and place of election, the appropriate unit and the eligibility cutoff date, they do differ in a most important aspect: A consent election agreement provides that the regional director's rulings and determinations on questions affecting the election will be final; *a stipulation for certification provides that the parties reserve their rights to appeal any such adverse rulings or determinations by the regional director to the Board in Washington, D.C.*[36]

[19.11] EFFECT OF PENDING ULP CHARGES

As a general rule, the NLRB will not process a representation petition when there is an unfair labor practice charge pending against one of the parties.[37]

However, if the party who filed the unfair labor practice charge executes a "Request to Proceed," waiving his or her right to urge the allegedly illegal acts set forth in the charge as a basis for objections to any election, the NLRB will normally process the election to its completion.[38]

Whenever unfair labor practice charges allege Section 8(a)(2) violations (employer domination of a union) or Section 8(a)(5) violations (refusal to bargain), the NLRB will not honor a "Request to Proceed."[39]

NOTES TO CHAPTER 19

1. Kenneth McGuiness, *How to Take a Case Before the National Labor Relations Board,* 4th Edition (Washington, D.C.: Bureau of National Affairs, Inc., 1976), 47.
2. See *NLRB v. Gissel Packing Co.,* 395 U.S. 575 (1969).
3. 29 U.S.C.A. §159(c).
4. See Note 1, p. 49, *supra.*
5. 29 CFR §101.17.
6. *NLRB Rules and Regulations,* §10.60(a).
7. *NLRB Rules and Regulations,* §102.72(a).
8. *NLRB Rules and Regulations,* §102.72(b).
9. *NLRB Rules and Regulations,* §102.60(a).
10. *NLRB Rules and Regulations,* §102.60(a).
11. 29 CFR §101.18(a).
12. *Lebanon Steel Foundry v. NLRB,* 130 F.2d 404 (CA-D.C., 1942).
13. *NLRB v. Air Control Products, Inc.,* 335 F.2d 245 (CA-5, 1964).
14. *The Midvale Co.,* 114 NLRB 372 (1955).
15. *Morganton Full Fashioned Hosiery Co.,* 102 NLRB 134 (1953).
16. *Riviera Manor Nursing Home,* 200 NLRB No. 53 (1972).

17. *The Cleveland Cliffs Iron Co.,* 117 NLRB 668 (1957).
18. *Linden Lumber Div., Summer & Co. v. NLRB,* 419 U.S. 301 (1974).
19. *NLRB Casehandling Manual,* §11028.4.
20. *Globe Iron Foundry,* 112 NLRB 1200, (1955).
21. 29 U.S.C.A. §159(c)(1).
22. 29 CFR §101.18(a).
23. 29 U.S.C.A. §159(c)(3).
24. *Igleheart Bros. Div., General Foods Corp.,* 96 NLRB 1005 (1951).
25. *Mar-Jac Poultry Co.,* 136 NLRB 785 (1962).
26. *General Cable Corporation,* 139 NLRB 1123 (1962).
27. *Malco Theaters, Inc.,* 222 NLRB 81 (1976).
28. *Pacific Coast Assn. of Pulp & Paper Mfrs.,* 121 NLRB 990 (1958).
29. See Chapter 2 for a more complete discussion of jurisdictional standards.
30. 29 CFR §101.18(c).
31. 29 CFR §101.18(a).
32. 29 CFR §101.18(b).
33. *NLRB Rules and Regulations,* §102.6(a) and (b).
34. 29 CFR §101.19(a).
35. See Note 1, p. 97, *supra.*
36. See Note 1, p. 97, *supra.*

20

Pre-Election
Representation Hearings

[20.01] NATURE OF PROCEEDINGS

If the petition is not withdrawn or dismissed and the parties do not enter into a "consent" or "stipulated" election as discussed in Chapter 19, the regional director will schedule a representation hearing to resolve any pending issues relative to the proposed election.

The NLRB rules provide that a pre-election representation hearing must be conducted by a hearing officer.[1] The hearing officer, usually an NLRB agent attached to the respective regional office, has the duty of developing a full and complete record on all matters in issue.[2]

The NLRB considers a pre-election representation hearing to be investigatory in character, and the refusal of a hearing officer to permit an adversarial proceeding does not constitute a denial of due process.[3]

The NLRB rules provide that all motions in a pre-election representation hearing must be in writing or, if made at the hearing, stated on the record.[4] Any such motions should briefly state the order of relief sought and the grounds for such motion. An original and four copies of written motions must be filed, and a copy served immediately upon each of the other parties.[5]

Subpoenas are available to all parties in a representation hearing and may be obtained by filing an application with the regional director if made prior to the hearing, or with the hearing officer during the hearing.[6] An individual who does not intend to comply with a subpoena issued against him or her has five working days from the date of service within which to file a petition to revoke the subpoena.[7]

Inasmuch as pre-election representation hearings are considered nonadversary in character, the NLRB rules provide that the rules of evidence prevailing in the courts shall not be controlling.[8] Nonetheless, the NLRB encourages its agents and hearing officers in representation hearings to follow such rules of evidence to the extent possible.[9]

The hearing officer, as well as all parties, has the right to call, examine and cross-examine witnesses in a pre-election representation proceeding.[10]

[20.02] INTERVENTIONS

A party desiring to intervene in a representation proceeding must file a motion to intervene, stating the grounds upon which he or she claims to have an interest in the matter.[11] Intervention will be permitted by the regional director, and/or the hearing officer, to such extent and upon such terms as he or she deems proper.[12]

[20.03] THE EXPANDING UNIT QUESTION

Whether a particular petition is premature is sometimes an issue in a representation hearing. A petition for an election among an expanding or fluctuating work force may be dismissed as premature if it appears that the anticipated complement of employees has not yet been established.[13] Mere speculation as to the uncertainty of a future work force will not, however, be sufficient grounds to have a petition dismissed.[14]

[20.04] APPROPRIATE BARGAINING UNITS

One of the most prevalent issues arising in pre-election representative hearings is that of the appropriate unit. Section 9(c) of the Act mandates the NLRB to determine the unit appropriate for the purposes of collective bargaining so that employees may exercise their fullest freedom in choosing their bargaining representatives.[15]

Although the NLRB has broad discretion in making bargaining unit determinations,[16] the bargaining unit requested by a petitioning unit is presumptively appropriate.[17] The appropriate unit requested by the petitioner and/or determined by the NLRB does not have to be the "most" appropriate or "only" appropriate unit, as long as it is "an" appropriate unit.[18] However, Congress has mandated that there not be a proliferation of units in the health-care industry.

Community of interest standard: In determining appropriate units, the NLRB applies a community of interest test so as to "group together only employees who have a substantial mutual interest in wages, hours, and other conditions of employment."[19] Some of the community of interest factors to be considered by the NLRB in resolving bargaining unit issues include

- methods of payment of wages or compensation
- hours of work
- employment benefits
- supervision
- qualifications, training, and skills
- job functions
- amount of working time spent away from the employment situs
- infrequency or lack of contact with other employees
- lack of integration with the work functions of other employees
- the history of collective bargaining[20]

Self-determination (globe) elections: As a general rule, the NLRB does not delegate the selection of the unit question to employees.[21] However, where circumstances are such that certain employees could be properly included in either a craft (smaller) unit or a plant (larger) unit, and where either contention, if unopposed, would be adopted by the Board, the NLRB may hold a self-determination election, commonly referred to as a *Globe* election, in which the employees may decide for themselves which unit they desire.[22]

Accretion to existing units: The NLRB has authority to define an existing bargaining unit sufficiently broad to include new employees into it without holding an election, assuming the requisite community of interest is present and the inclusion would create a more efficient bargaining relationship.[23]

Factors considered by the NLRB in determining accretion issues include: (1) geographic proximity;[24] (2) degree of interchange among employees;[25] (3) functional integration of the business;[26] (4) centralization of management;[27] (5) similarity of working conditions;[28] (6) collective bargaining history;[29] (7) common control over labor relations;[30] (8) degree of local power to hire and fire;[31] and (9) size and number of employees in comparison with those in the existing facility.[32]

[20.05] APPROPRIATE UNIT RESTRICTIONS AND VOTER ELIGIBILITY

Another prevalent issue arising in NLRB representation hearings is whether or not certain employees are to be included in the proposed bargaining unit. The general rules applicable to individuals who are frequently the subject of such determinations appear below.

Professional employees: Section 9(b)(1) of the Act specifies that the Board shall not include both professional employees and nonprofessional employees into the same bargaining unit, unless a majority of the professional employees in question vote to be included in that unit.

This section of the Act requires the NLRB to conduct a self-determination (Globe) election to resolve whether the professional employees desire to be included into a mixed unit with nonprofessional personnel.[33]

Guards: Section 9(b)(3) of the Act prohibits the NLRB from including guards into a bargaining unit with other employees. The purpose of this prohibition is to insure an employer the availability of personnel to protect both persons and property during strikes or labor unrest involving other employees.[34]

Supervisors: Inasmuch as a bargaining unit is restricted to "employees" only,[35] supervisors, as well as managerial employees,[36] may not be included in bargaining units by the NLRB.[37]

Independent contractors: The NLRB may not properly include independent contractors into a bargaining unit as they are not "employees" within the meaning of the Act.[38]

Confidential employees: Confidential employees are also excluded from appropriate bargaining units.[39] The NLRB defines a confidential employee as one who assists and acts in a confidential capacity with respect to a member of management who formulates, determines, and effectuates management policies in the field of labor relations.[40]

An important factor in determining the confidential status of an employee is whether or not he or she has access to confidential labor relations matters and information.[41]

Relatives of management: Section 2(3) of the Act forbids the NLRB to include children or spouses of an employer into a bargaining unit. However, as to other relatives, the NLRB has held that exclusion from a bargaining unit cannot be based solely on the establishment of family relationship.[42]

Part-time, seasonal, and casual employees: Regular part-time employees are usually included in a bargaining unit if they have a sufficient community of interest with their fellow full-time employees.[43] The number of hours worked by a part-time employee, although not decisive in and of itself, is a highly relevant factor in determining whether a part-time employee should be included in a bargaining unit. Some of the other factors considered by the Board to determine inclusion or exclusion of a part-time employee would be: (1) regularity of work; (2) nature of work; and (3) similarity of pay scale.[44]

Part-time and casual employees who work on a sporadic, irregular, or temporary basis usually will be excluded from a bargaining unit by the NLRB.[45] On the other hand, seasonal employees who have a nearly certain expectation of reemployment from year to year and work with regular employees under the same supervision will normally be included in a bargaining unit with their fellow employees, even though they work less than the full year.[46]

Laid-off employees: Employees who have a reasonable expectation of returning to their jobs are usually included in a bargaining unit by the NLRB.[47] Therefore, temporarily laid-off employees,[48] as well as employees on leaves of absence,[49] are usually included in the respective bargaining units. On the other hand, where the prospect of an employee returning to work within a reasonable and foreseeable future is negligible, the NLRB will exclude the employee from the unit.[50]

Dual-function employees: Whenever an employee works for two or more employers, the question frequently arises as to whether that employee is includable in a bargaining unit with regular full-time employees.

Whether the employee has a sufficient interest in the unit's conditions of employment is the ultimate test in disposition of this issue.[51] Even assuming an employee devotes less than 51 percent of his or her time to unit work, he or she may nonetheless be included in a bargaining unit with other employees if he or she maintains a sufficient community of interest with them.[52]

Strikers and strike replacements: Economic strikers who have been permanently replaced in their jobs are includable into the bargaining unit up to twelve months from the commencement of the strike.[53]

Economic strikers who have not been replaced in their jobs remain eligible to vote even beyond the twelve-month period, and thus are included in the bargaining unit with other employees should there be a representation election conducted.[54] However, economic strikers have been found ineligible to vote—and excluded from the unit—where objective evidence convinces the NLRB that they have abandoned the struck job.[55]

Employees who engage in unlawful strikes are usually ineligible to vote and excluded from a bargaining unit.[56]

Permanent strike replacements are eligible to vote in a representation election and includable in a bargaining unit,[57] as long as they were hired prior to the eligibility cut-off date for such election.[58]

[20.06]   BRIEFS TO HEARING OFFICER

Once the parties to a representation hearing have presented their cases and the hearing officer has developed the pending issues and other matters to his or her satisfaction, the hearing is closed. The NLRB rules provide that a party to a representation hearing has a right to file a brief with the regional director or the NLRB, as the case may be, within seven days after the close of the hearing.[59]

[20.07]   REGIONAL DIRECTOR'S DECISION

After the close of hearing, the hearing officer usually submits his or her report, consisting of an analysis of the record, to the regional director.[60] Once the hearing officer's report is received, the regional director will determine whether a question concerning representatives exists, the appropriate unit, if any other pending issues exists, and either direct an election, dismiss the petition, or make some other disposition of the matter.[61]

Should the representation hearing raise questions that should be decided by the NLRB, the regional director may, as an alternative to his or her disposition of the case, issue an order to transfer the case to the Board in Washington, D.C. for its determination.[62]

[20.08]   APPEAL TO NLRB—REQUEST FOR REVIEW

Within ten days after service of the regional director's decision following the representation hearing, any party to the proceeding may file a request for review of the decision with the NLRB in Washington, D.C.[63]

The NLRB must review a request for review of a regional director's dismissal of a petition.[64] In all other cases, a request for review will be granted only when one or more of the following grounds are established:

- *That* a substantial question of law or policy is raised because of the absence or departure from officially reported Board precedent.
- *That* the regional director's decision on a substantial factual issue is clearly erroneous on the record and such error prejudicially affects the right of a party.
- *That* the conduct of the hearing or ruling made in connection with the proceeding has resulted in prejudicial error.
- *That* there are compelling reasons for reconsideration of an important Board rule or policy.[65]

On the granting of a request for review, the parties may file briefs in support of their respective positions with the NLRB, if such briefs are filed within seven days after issuance of the order granting review.[66] Unless otherwise ordered by the NLRB, a granting of a request for review will not stay the regional director's decision and order of election.[67]

Upon either the issuance of an order granting a request for review or the issuance of an order by the regional director transferring the case to the Board, the entire record of the representation hearing must be transmitted to the Board.[68] Once the case is transferred to the Board, whether by transfer from the regional director or by granting a request for review, the NLRB must either dismiss the petition, affirm or reverse the regional director's order in whole, or in part, direct a secret ballot election of the employees, or otherwise dispose of the matter as it deems appropriate.[69]

NOTES TO CHAPTER 20

1. *NLRB Rules and Regulations,* §102.64(a).
2. *NLRB Rules and Regulations,* §102.64(a).
3. *Livingston v. McLeod,* 209 F.Supp. 606 (DC NY, 1962).
4. *NLRB Rules and Regulations,* §102.65(a).
5. *NLRB Rules and Regulations,* §102.65(a).
6. *NLRB Rules and Regulations,* §102.66(c).
7. *NLRB Rules and Regulations,* §102.66(c).
8. *NLRB Rules and Regulations,* §102.66(a).

9. *NLRB Casehandling Manual,* §11216.

10. *NLRB Rules and Regulations,* §102.66(a).

11. *NLRB Rules and Regulations,* §102.65(b).

12. *NLRB Rules and Regulations,* §102.65(b).

13. *K-P Hydraulics Co.,* 219 NLRB 138 (1975).

14. *Whitteman Steel Mills, Inc.,* 253 NLRB 20 (1980).

15. *Pittsburgh Plate Glass Co. v. NLRB,* 313 U.S. 146 (1941).

16. *NLRB v. Wolverine World Wide, Inc.,* 477 F.2d 969 (CA-6, 1973).

17. *Grand Union Co.,* 176 NLRB 230 (1969).

18. *W.F. Hall Printing Co. v. NLRB,* 540 F.2d 873 (CA-7, 1976).

19. *Fifteenth Annual Report of the NLRB,* 39 (1950).

20. *Kalamazoo Paper Box Corporation,* 136 NLRB 134 (1962).

21. *Marshall Field Co. v. NLRB,* 135 F.2d 391 (CA-7, 1943).

22. *Boston Gas Co.,* 221 NLRB 628 (1975).

23. *Westinghouse Electric Corp. v. NLRB,* 440 F.2d 7 (CA-2, 1971).

24. *Sunset House,* 167 NLRB 870 (1967).

25. *Dura Corp.,* 153 NLRB 592 (1965).

26. *Beacon Photo Service, Inc.,* 163 NLRB 98 (1967).

27. *Masters-Lake Success, Inc.,* 124 NLRB 580 (1959).

28. *Fruehauf Trailer Co.,* 162 NLRB 195 (1966).

29. *Panda Terminals,* 161 NLRB 1215 (1966).

30. *Buy Low Supermarkets, Inc.,* 131 NLRB 23 (1961).

31. *NLRB v. R.L. Sweet Lumber Co.,* 515 F.2d 785 (CA-10, 1975).

32. *Buy Low Supermarkets, Inc., supra.*

33. *Lockheed Aircraft Corporation, Lockheed-California Co. Div.,* 202 NLRB 1140 (1973).

34. *McDonnell Aircraft Corporation,* 109 NLRB 967 (1954).

35. *Booth Broadcasting Co.,* 134 NLRB 817 (1961).

36. See *NLRB v. Bell Aerospace Co., Div. of Textron, Inc.,* 416 U.S. 267 (1974).

37. *NLRB v. Gold Spot Dairy, Inc.,* 432 F.2d 125 (CA-10, 1970).

38. See *NLRB v. Deaton, Inc.,* 502 F.2d 1221 (CA-5, 1974).

39. *Goodrich, B.F. (Oaks, Pa.),* 115 NLRB 722 (1956).

40. *Goodrich, B.F. (Oaks, Pa.), supra.*

41. *NLRB v. Hendricks County Rural Electric Membership Corporation,* 102 S.Ct. 216 (U.S., 1981).

42. *Pargas of Crescent City, Inc.,* 194 NLRB 616 (1971).

43. *Sears Roebuck & Co.,* 172 NLRB No. 132 (1968).

44. *NLRB v. Greenfield Components Corporation,* 317 F.2d 85 (CA-1, 1963).

45. *Bryant Chucking Grinder Co.,* 160 NLRB 1526 (1966).

46. *William J. Keller, Inc.,* 198 NLRB 1144 (1972).

47. *Sullivan Surplus Sales, Inc.,* 152 NLRB 132 (1965).

48. *Scobell Chemical Company,* 121 NLRB 1130 (1958).

49. *Kinkel, John & Son,* 157 NLRB 744 (1966).

50. *Pure Laboratories, Inc.,* 172 NLRB No. 13 (1968).

51. *NLRB v. Sunnyland Refining Co.,* 474 F.2d 407 (CA-5, 1973).

52. *Berea Publishing Co.,* 140 NLRB 516 (1963).

53. 29 U.S.C.A. §159(c)(3).

54. *Gulf States Paper Corporation, EZ Packing Division,* 219 NLRB 806 (1975).

55. *Q–T Tool Co.,* 199 NLRB 500 (1972).

56. *Mine Workers, UMW (McCoy Coal Co.),* 165 NLRB 592 (1967).

57. *Casey v. Glass, Inc.,* 219 NLRB 698 (1975).

58. *Greenspan Engraving Corp.,* 137 NLRB 1308 (1962).

59. *NLRB Rules and Regulations,* §102.67(a) and (i).

60. *NLRB Rules and Regulations,* §102.66(f).

61. *NLRB Rules and Regulations,* §102.67(a).

62. *NLRB Rules and Regulations,* §102.67(h).

63. *NLRB Rules and Regulations,* §102.67(b).

64. *NLRB Rules and Regulations,* §102.71.

65. *NLRB Rules and Regulations,* §102.67(c).

66. *NLRB Rules and Regulations,* §102.67(g).

67. *NLRB Rules and Regulations,* §102.67(g).

68. *NLRB Rules and Regulations,* §102.68.

69. *NLRB Rules and Regulations,* §102.67(j).

21

The NLRB Election Process

[21.01] "NOTICE OF ELECTION" POSTINGS

Once an election is ordered by the NLRB or agreed to by the parties through a "stipulated" or "consent" agreement, the NLRB will forward "Notice of Election" posters to the employer to be posted in a conspicuous place.[1] The "Notice of Election" poster usually contains such details as location of the polls, time and place of voting, voter eligibility rules and a reproduction of a sample ballot.[2]

An employer's failure to post such notices may result in the NLRB setting aside the election on the ground that the election was not properly publicized.[3]

[21.02] EXCELSIOR LIST REQUIREMENTS

Within seven days after the NLRB has directed a representation election, or after the regional director has approved a consent election agreement, the employer must file with the regional director an election eligibility list, commonly referred to as an *Excelsior* list, containing the names and addresses of all employees who are eligible to vote in the election.[4] The regional director will then make the list available to the petitioning union and all other parties in the case.[5]

Failure to comply with the *Excelsior* requirements may be grounds to set aside an election.[6] However, a representation election should not be set aside on this ground as long as the employer has acted in good faith and has not been grossly negligent.[7]

[21.03] ELECTION BALLOTS

Representation elections are conducted by the NLRB through the use of secret ballots.[8] In an effort to conduct a representation election within the Board's "laboratory conditions"[9] standard, no one will be permitted to handle a ballot before, during, or after an election, except an NLRB agent and the individual employee who casts the ballot.[10]

Balloting by mail, or absentee balloting, is generally limited to situations in which manual elections are not practical.[11] A representation election may include both manual and absentee ballots, but absentee ballots are made available only to employees who are assigned to duties that make it impossible, or impractical, for them to vote at the prescribed polling place.[12]

Mail ballots usually are not made available to employees who are on vacation or leave of absence due to their own decision to be away from the polling place, rather than their "employer's action."[13]

[21.04] TIME OF ELECTION

Although the regional director is given broad discretion in setting the date and hours of election,[14] an election may not be held sooner than ten days after the regional director has received the *Excelsior* list from the employer, with the exception that the ten-day period may be provisionally calculated from the date the *Excelsior* list is estimated to arrive at the regional director's office.[15]

Unless the right to file a request for review has been waived, a regional director should not direct an election prior to the twenty-fifth day following his or her decision.[16]

The NLRB is reluctant to schedule an election on days immediately preceding or following holidays or periods of time when many employees may be away from the employer's premises.[17]

[21.05] FUNCTIONS OF ELECTION OBSERVERS

The NLRB rules provide that any party in a representation election may be represented by observers of his or her own selection, subject to such limitations as the regional director may prescribe.[18] Also, as a general rule, each party may appoint an equal, preassigned number of observers to represent them at the polling place.[19]

Persons closely identified with the parties such as attorneys,[20] nonemployee union officials,[21] a company president's wife,[22] and supervisory personnel[23] are not permitted to serve as election observers, unless the parties agree otherwise.[24]

Election observers are prohibited from electioneering during the polling hours and are not permitted to carry on casual conversations with employees in the voting area.[25]

[21.06] VOTING MECHANICS

The actual polling of employees in a representation election is conducted under the supervision of NLRB agents.[26] The NLRB casehandling manual specifies that the Board Agent and the observers should assemble at the polling place from fifteen to forty-five minutes prior to the opening of the polls, and that the polls should be opened as scheduled.[27] NLRB agents are to arrange the polling place so that voters may enter, stop at the checking table, proceed to a voting booth, go to the ballot box, and then leave, all with as little confusion as possible.[28]

[21.07] THE CHALLENGED BALLOT

The NLRB rules provide that an authorized observer may challenge, for good cause, the eligibility of any person to vote in a representation election.

NLRB agents conducting an election also have a right to challenge the eligibility of prospective voters and are required to challenge anyone whose name does not appear on the eligibility list.[29] Although Board agents are required to challenge any voter they know or have reason to believe is ineligible to vote, they will not otherwise make challenges on behalf of the parties.[30]

Challenges must be made prior to the voter receiving the ballot.[31] Challenges will not be accepted by Board agents once the ballot is cast or after the close of the election.[32]

Once challenged, the voting employee will be given a ballot and instructed to enter the booth, mark the ballot, fold it so as to keep it secret, and return to the voting table. Upon the employee's return, he or she will be given a challenge ballot envelope and will be instructed to place his or her ballot into the envelope, seal it, and drop it into the ballot box along with the other ballots.[33]

[21.08] COUNTING AND TALLY OF BALLOTS

NLRB agents are instructed to count the ballots immediately after the closing of the polls.[34]

Ballots are opened and counted in the presence of the observers who may be asked to tally them by the Board agent.[35] Other parties, such as supervisors and executives, may also observe the count to the extent permitted by the physical facilities.[36]

In counting and determining the validity of disputed ballots, NLRB agents are governed by the following guidelines:

- An unmarked ballot will be voided and not counted.[37]
- A write-in vote will not be counted.[38]
- A ballot that identifies the voter will not be counted.[39]
- A ballot will be counted if the voter's intent is clearly indicated.[40]

Should a party disagree with the NLRB agent's ruling on whether a ballot should be counted or not, he or she may file timely objections after the count.[41]

Following the count and tabulation of the tallies, the election observers will be asked to sign a tally of ballots.[42] The tally of ballots, once signed by the observers, is then served upon each designated representative of the party.[43]

NOTES TO CHAPTER 21

1. *NLRB Casehandling Manual,* §11314.
2. 29 CFR §101.19(a)(1).
3. *F.H. Vahsling, Inc.,* 114 NLRB 1451 (1955).
4. *Excelsior Underwear, Inc.,* 156 NLRB 1236 (1966).
5. *Excelsior Underwear, Inc., supra.*
6. *Excelsior Underwear, Inc., supra.*
7. *Texas Christian University,* 220 NLRB 396 (1975).
8. 29 U.S.C.A. §§159(c)(1) and 159(e)(1).
9. *NLRB v. Urban Tel. Corp.,* 499 F.2d 239 (CA-7, 1974).
10. *NLRB Casehandling Manual,* §11306.
11. *NLRB Casehandling Manual,* §11336.
12. *NLRB Casehandling Manual,* §11336.1.
13. *NLRB Casehandling Manual,* §11336.1.
14. *Louis-Allis Co. v. NLRB,* 463 F.2d 512 (CA-7, 1972).
15. *NLRB Casehandling Manual,* §11302.1.
16. *NLRB Casehandling Manual,* §11302.1.
17. *NLRB Casehandling Manual,* §11302.1.
18. *NLRB Rules and Regulations,* §102.69(a).
19. *NLRB Casehandling Manual,* §11310.
20. *Peabody Engineering Co.,* 95 NLRB 952 (1951).
21. *Columbia Broadcasting System, Inc.,* 70 NLRB 1368 (1946).
22. *Wiley Mfg., Inc.,* 93 NLRB 1600 (1951).
23. *Mountain States Tel. & Tel. Co.,* 207 NLRB No. 87 (1973).
24. *NLRB Casehandling Manual,* §11310.
25. *NLRB Casehandling Manual,* §11326.2.
26. 29 CFR §101.19(a)(2).
27. *NLRB Casehandling Manual,* §11318 and §11320.
28. *NLRB Casehandling Manual,* §11316.
29. *NLRB Casehandling Manual,* §11338.
30. *NLRB Casehandling Manual,* §11338.
31. *NLRB Casehandling Manual,* §11338.3.
32. *NLRB v. A.J. Tower Co.,* 329 U.S. 324 (1946).
33. *NLRB Casehandling Manual,* §11338.1.
34. *NLRB Casehandling Manual,* §11340.1.
35. *NLRB Casehandling Manual,* §11340.2.
36. *NLRB Casehandling Manual,* §11340.2.

37. *Vulcan Furniture Mfg. Co.*, 214 F.2d 369 (CA-5, 1954).

38. *NLRB Casehandling Manual*, §11340.

39. *Eagle Iron Works*, 117 NLRB 1053 (1957).

40. *NLRB Casehandling Manual*, §11340.7.

41. *George K. Garrett Co., Inc.*, 120 NLRB 484 (1958).

42. *NLRB Casehandling Manual*, §11340.9.

43. 29 CFR §101.19(a)(3).

22

Interference with NLRB Elections

[22.01] THE "LABORATORY CONDITIONS" STANDARD

The NLRB has the responsibility of conducting a representation election in a fair and impartial manner.[1] In carrying out this responsibility, the Board has adopted a "laboratory conditions" test by which to evaluate the fairness of pre-election conduct.[2]

The "laboratory conditions" standard imposes upon the employer, the union, the NLRB agents, and other parties the responsibility of conducting themselves in such a manner that a free and untrammeled choice of representatives can be made by employees through the election process.[3]

Whenever the "laboratory conditions" standard is not met, the NLRB will set aside the election and conduct it over again.[4]

The NLRB does not necessarily apply the same criteria in evaluating misconduct sufficient to set aside an election as it applies in unfair labor practice cases.[5] Consequently, misconduct need not rise to the level of an unfair labor practice in order to have an election overturned.[6]

[22.02] THE CRITICAL PERIOD

As a general rule, the NLRB will look only to conduct of the parties that occurred between the date of the filing of the petition and the holding of the election in determining whether an election should be set aside.[7] This post-petition/pre-election period is commonly referred to as the "critical period."[8]

The NLRB may consider conduct occurring prior to the critical period if there is significant post-petition conduct continuing from pre-petition events.[9]

[22.03] FALSE OR MISLEADING STATEMENTS

Historically, the NLRB has taken varying positions on whether misrepresentative statements about material facts relating to an election would be grounds to set it aside.[10]

In 1962, the Board imposed the *Hollywood Ceramics*[11] standard, which specified an election should be set aside only where there is a misrepresentation of a material fact involving a substantial departure from the truth and uttered at a time that prevented an opportunity for reply and had a significant impact upon the free choice of employees to vote their convictions.[12] However, after reversing itself twice in the interim,[13] in 1982, the NLRB declared that it would no longer follow the *Hollywood Ceramics* standard and would set aside an election only where a party has used forged documents in its misleading propaganda.[14]

[22.04] THREATS AND COERCION

Although Section 8(c) of the Act provides that employers and unions have the right to express any views, arguments, or opinions, it nevertheless prohibits statements containing threats of reprisal or promises of benefit.

Consequently, pre-election campaign statements made by an employer regarding such matters as loss of jobs,[15] loss of business,[16] reductions in work force or closure,[17] or other possible harm caused as a consequence of unionization would generally be grounds for setting aside an election.[18]

In determining whether an employer's pre-election statement is permissible in such cases, the NLRB will usually consider such factors as

- whether the statement is demonstrably probable, rather than a mere prediction, and
- whether the employer has within itself the power to carry out the suggested consequence[19]

If an employer's suggestion of adverse consequences as a result of unionization is tied to anything other than economic necessity, the NLRB will most likely set aside the election upon timely objections being filed.[20]

An employers's pre-election campaign propaganda suggesting that unionization would be futile and could lead only to strikes, loss of income, and violence was held impermissible conduct sufficient to set aside an election.[21]

Also, an employer's repeated references to the inevitability of a strike if the union won the election was held impermissible conduct.[22]

Elections may also be set aside when union agents or representatives threaten employees with physical harm if they do not vote for the union.[23]

[22.05] PROMISES AND ECONOMIC INDUCEMENTS

An employer's promise of increased wages or benefits to employees as an inducement to vote against a union is impermissible conduct and grounds to set aside a representation election.[24] Thus, an employer's granting a wage increase prior to a representation election, as a means of influencing employees in their voting, is improper pre-election conduct.[25]

However, an employer does not commit objectionable conduct in a representation election by granting wage increases to employees in keeping with established policy and past practice.[26]

A union that offers to waive initiation fees only for employees who join the union prior to a representation election commits objectionable conduct sufficient to have an election overturned.[27] However, no ground for setting aside an election is established where a union's waiver of initiation fees is not conditioned upon the employee's support of the union prior to the election.[28]

Payments made to employees in excess of reimbursement for time lost in assisting a union may be grounds to set aside an election.[29] However, a union does not engage in objectionable conduct by serving complimentary drinks[30] or refreshments to employees during its pre-election campaign.[31]

[22.06]   INTERROGATION AND SURVEILLANCE

An employer's attempt to gain information about the union activities of employees through such means as interrogation[32] or surveillance[33] may constitute grounds to set aside an election. Similarly, meetings and interviews conducted with employees that have a tendency to subject a fear of discrimination in the minds of employees may constitute grounds to invalidate an election.[34]

In determining whether a particular meeting instills in the mind of an employee a fear of discrimination, the NLRB will evaluate both the location of the meeting as well as the number of employees in attendance.[35] For example, pre-election campaign meetings with employees in an isolated manager's office may constitute impermissible conduct on the part of an employer simply because of the location and atmosphere of the meeting, even in the absence of coercive statements.[36]

The NLRB also regards concerted visitations to employees' homes during the pre-election period by management members as objectionable conduct, irrespective of whether threatening or coercive remarks are made during the visit.[37]

[22.07]   PREJUDICIAL OR INFLAMMATORY PROPAGANDA

Whenever a party deliberately attempts to overstress and exacerbate racial feelings by irrelevant and inflammatory appeals in its pre-election propaganda, the NLRB will set aside the election.[38]

Other inflammatory statements may also constitute objectionable conduct such as a union's distribution of a handbill that referred to a company president as a "Hitler" and a "madman" and falsely accused him of stating that he would like to set female employees on fire.[39]

However, as a general rule, the Board will not invalidate an election for character attacks unless the other party can establish coercion, fraud, or campaign trickery that destroys the "laboratory conditions" standard.[40]

[22.08] ENFORCEMENT OF INVALID NO-SOLICITATION RULES

An election may be set aside should an employer enforce an unlawful "no-solicitation/no-distribution" rule,[41] or selectively invoke such a rule to prohibit pro-union activity during the pre-election period.[42]

[22.09] SPEECHES WITHIN TWENTY-FOUR HOURS

Captive audience speeches made to an assembly of employees on company time within twenty-four hours before the scheduled time for starting the election constitute objectionable conduct and will cause an election to be set aside whenever valid objections are filed.[43]

However, neither an employer nor a union is prohibited from making speeches on or off employer premises during this twenty-four hour period if the employees attend voluntarily during their own time.[44] The twenty-four hour rule does not prohibit the circulation of campaign literature during the otherwise prohibited period.[45]

[22.10] EMPLOYER FAVORITISM OF COMPETING UNION

Although an employer may state a preference of one union over another to the employees,[46] the employer commits objectionable conduct during the pre-election period if the employer supports one union in a more favorable manner, such as denying the competing union an equal opportunity to campaign to its employees[47] or suggesting that the employer would deal more favorably with one union than its competitor.[48]

[22.11] ABUSE OF THE NLRB PROCESS

The NLRB attempts to remain neutral in representation elections and will regard a physical alteration of its documents by either an employer or a union for partisan election use as impermissible conduct sufficient to invalidate an election.[49]

Also, a mischaracterization of a Board document, such as a misrepresentation of a settlement agreement between the NLRB and another party, if used for partisan election purposes, would constitute grounds for setting aside an election.[50]

The NLRB prohibits the reproduction of its official ballot unless the reproduction is an unaltered facsimile and clearly marked as a sample on its face.[51]

Unions and employers are prohibited from distributing or posting facsimiles of official sample ballots with an "X" marked in the "yes" or "no" box[52] inasmuch as the ballot might be used by the respective parties to suggest to employees NLRB endorsement. However, where a party distributes or posts a simulated ballot that does not have the appearance of an official ballot, the marking of an ''X'' in the ''yes'' or ''no'' box will not be grounds to set aside an election.[53]

The NLRB also regards its notice of election posters as official documents and may set aside an election where such posters are defaced in a manner that might suggest Board endorsement of one party over another.[54]

[22.12] MISCONDUCT IN OR NEAR POLLING AREAS

Prolonged conversation by representatives of either the employer or the union with voting employees in the polling area may constitute sufficient grounds to set aside a representation election.[55]

Electioneering in the voting place is forbidden and the mere presence of nonvoting union representatives within the vicinity of the polling area may constitute grounds to invalidate an election.[56] The presence of supervisors and managers at or near the polling area likewise is impermissible conduct and may constitute sufficient grounds to have an election set aside.[57]

[22.13] MISCONDUCT OF NLRB AGENTS

The conduct of Board agents must be beyond reproach in handling NLRB elections.[58] Accordingly, the NLRB has set certain standards by which Board agents should conduct themselves. When a Board agent gives the appearance of fraternizing with one party, suggesting partiality in the election process, the election may be set aside.[59]

An election may also be set aside where a Board agent fails to maintain custody of the ballot box sufficient to ensure the integrity of the ballots.[60] NLRB agents also are responsible for the accountability of election ballots and when such are mislaid or permanently lost, the election may be set aside and a new one ordered.[61]

An NLRB agent in charge of an election has the duty to ensure eligible voters their right to vote. When he or she denies an employee the right to vote through an abuse of discretion, the election may be set aside.[62]

[22.14] THIRD-PARTY INTERFERENCE

Whenever an election is held in such a general atmosphere of confusion and fear of reprisal as to render impossible the rational, uncoerced selection of a bargaining representative, an election may be set aside, and it is immaterial that the fear and confusion were created by someone other than the employer or the union.[63]

NOTES TO CHAPTER 22

1. *Collins & Aikman Corp. v. NLRB*, 383 F.2d 722 (CA-4, 1967).

2. *NLRB v. Urban Tel. Corp.*, 499 F.2d 239 (CA-7, 1974).

3. *Home Town Foods, Inc. v. NLRB*, 416 F.2d 392 (CA-5, 1969).

4. *NLRB v. Houston Chronical Publishing Co.*, 300 F.2d 273 (CA-5, 1962).

5. *Rosewood Mfg. Co.*, 263 NLRB 420 (1982).

6. *Independent, Inc. v. NLRB*, 406 F.2d 203 (CA-5, 1969).

7. *Ideal Electric & Mfg. Co.*, 134 NLRB 1275 (1961).

8. *NLRB v. Blades Mfg. Co.*, 344 F.2d 998 (CA-8, 1965).

9. See *Randall, Burkart/Randall Div., Inc. v. NLRB*, 638 F.2d 957 (CA-6, 1981).

10. See, for example: *Shopping Kart Food Market, Inc.*, 228 NLRB 1311 (1977) reversing *Hollywood Ceramics Co.*, 140 NLRB 221 (1962); *General Knit of California, Inc.*, 239 NLRB 619 (1978) reaffirming *Hollywood Ceramics Co., supra;* and *Midland Nat. Life Ins. Co.*, 263 NLRB No. 24 110 (1982) reversing again *Hollywood Ceramics Co., supra.*

11. *Hollywood Ceramics Co.*, 140 NLRB 221 (1962).

12. *Hollywood Ceramics Co., supra.*

13. See *Shopping Kart Food Market, Inc., supra;* and *General Knit of California, Inc., supra.*

14. *Midland Nat. Life Ins. Co., supra.*

15. *Vegas Village Shopping Corp.*, 229 NLRB 279 (1977).

16. *Whiting Mfg. Co., Inc.*, 258 NLRB No. 58 (1981).

17. *Anderson Cottonwood Concrete Products, Inc.*, 246 NLRB No. 172 (1979).

18. See, for example: *Rosewood Mfg. Co.*, 263 NLRB No. 55 (1982).

19. Kenneth McGuiness, *How to Take a Case Before the National Labor Relations Board,* 4th Edition (Washington, D.C.: Bureau of National Affairs, Inc., 1976), 165.

20. Ibid.

21. *Standard Forge & Axle Co.*, 170 NLRB 784 (1968).

22. *Boaz Spinning Co., Inc.*, 177 NLRB 788 (1969).

23. *Loose Leaf Hardware v. NLRB*, 666 F.2nd 1036 (CA-6, 1981).

24. *General Electric Co., Etc. v. NLRB*, 400 F.2d 713 (CA-5, 1968).

25. *General Electric Co., Etc. v. NLRB, supra.*

26. *Norfolk Carolina Tel. Co.*, 234 NLRB No. 197 (1978).

27. *NLRB v. Savair Mfg. Co.*, 414 U.S. 270 (1973).

28. *NLRB v. Con-Pac, Inc.*, 509 F.2d 270 (CA-5, 1975).

29. *Easco Tools, Inc.*, 248 NLRB 700 (1980).

30. *Labor Services, Inc.*, 259 NLRB No. 127 (1982).

31. *Labor Services, Inc., supra.*

32. *ITT Cannon Electric, Div. of ITT,* 172 NLRB 425 (1968).

33. *General Electronic Wiring Devices, Inc.,* 182 NLRB 876 (1970).

34. *NLRB v. West Coast Casket Co.,* 205 F.2d 902 (CA-9, 1953).

35. See Note 19, p. 167, *supra.*

36. *Marshall Durbin & Co.,* 179 NLRB 1027 (1969).

37. *Peoria Plastic Co.,* 117 NLRB 545 (1957).

38. *Sewell Mfg. Co.,* 138 NLRB 66 (1962).

39. *Schneider Mills, Inc. v. NLRB,* 390 F.2d 375 (CA-4, 1968).

40. *Georgia-Pacific Corporation,* 199 NLRB No. 43 (1972).

41. *Mallory, P.R. & Co. Capacitor Co. Div.,* 167 NLRB 647 (1967).

42. *Levi Strauss & Co., Inc.,* 256 NLRB No. 182 (1981).

43. *Peerless Plywood Co.,* 107 NLRB 427 (1953).

44. *Nebraska Consolidated Mills, Inc.,* 165 NLRB 639 (1967).

45. *Moody Nursing Home, Inc.,* 251 NLRB No. 22 (1980).

46. *LaPointe Machine Tool Co.,* 113 NLRB 171 (1955).

47. *LaPointe Machine Tool Co., supra.*

48. *Stevens Equipment Co.,* 174 NLRB 865 (1969).

49. *Dubie-Clark Co.,* 209 NLRB 217 (1974).

50. *Dubie-Clark Co., supra.*

51. *Building Leasing Corporation,* 239 NLRB No. 3 (1978).

52. *Modern Chevrolet Co.,* 169 NLRB 809 (1968).

53. *NLRB v. Clarytona Manor, Inc.,* 479 F.2d 976 (CA-7, 1973).

54. *Allied Electric Products, Inc.,* 109 NLRB 1270 (1954).

55. *Michelm, Inc.,* 170 NLRB No. 46 (1968).

56. *Pacific Maritime Assn.,* 112 NLRB 1280 (1955).

57. *Belk's Department Store of Savannah, Ga., Inc.,* 98 NLRB 280 (1952).

58. *New York Telephone Co.,* 109 NLRB 788 (1954).

59. *Athbro Precision Engineering Corporation,* 171 NLRB 21 (1968).

60. *Austill Waxed Paper Co.,* 169 NLRB 1109 (1968).

61. *New York Telephone Co., supra.*

62. See *NLRB v. Bata Shoe Co.,* 377 F.2d 821 (CA-4, 1967).

63. *Al Long, Inc.,* 173 NLRB 447 (1968).

23

Objections and Challenges to NLRB Elections

[23.01] FILING REQUIREMENTS

If a party desires to contest the outcome of a representation election, he or she must file objections to the conduct of the election, or conduct affecting the results of the election, within five working days after the tally of ballots has been furnished to him or her.[1] An original and five copies of the objections must be filed with the regional director within the five-day time limit.[2]

[23.02] RIGHT TO POST-ELECTION HEARING

Parties who have entered into an Agreement for a Consent Election have no right to a post-election hearing as they are bound by the regional director's decision and determination on objections.[3] Nonetheless, a regional director may conduct a hearing in such case if he or she so chooses.[4]

Parties to directed elections or who have entered into a Stipulation for Certification Upon Consent Election may be entitled to a hearing on their objections and/or challenges where it appears that substantial and material issues exist that can best be resolved through a hearing process.[5]

Whenever objections to an election and unfair labor practices cover the same ground, the regional director may consolidate the election objections and unfair labor practice complaint for the purpose of the hearing.[6]

[23.03] REGIONAL DIRECTOR'S REPORT

In an Agreement for Consent Election, the regional director's report on Objections and Challenges is final and binding on the parties.[7]

If objections are sustained in a consent election by the regional director, he may void the results of the election on his own volition; if the objections are not sustained, he may issue a certification of the results of the election, or certification of representative, as the case may be, which shall have the same force and effect as if issued by the NLRB.[8]

In a Stipulation for Certification Upon Consent Election, the regional director prepares a Report on Objections and/or Challenged Ballots and sends the report, along with his or her recommendations, and the tally of ballots, to the Board in Washington, D.C.[9] The regional director also serves his or her report and recommendation on the parties to the election.[10]

In an election directed by the NLRB, the regional director may

- issue a report on Objections and/or Challenges with specific recommendations as to their disposition (as in the case of stipulated elections), or

- exercise his or her authority to decide the case and issue a decision disposing of the issues and directing appropriate action or certifying the results of the election[11]

Whenever a regional director issues a decision in disposition of objections and/or challenges filed in a directed election, rather than a report, the rights of the parties are limited to a request for review of the decision conditioned upon the same ground rules as provided for appeals in pre-election hearings.[12]

[23.04] FILING EXCEPTIONS TO THE REGIONAL DIRECTOR'S REPORT

Parties desiring to file Exceptions to a Regional Director's Report on Objections or Challenges must file eight copies of their exceptions, and any accompanying supporting briefs, with the Board in Washington, D.C., within ten days from the date of issuance of the regional director's report.[13]

[23.05] NLRB REVIEW

If exceptions are filed and it appears to the Board that the exceptions raise substantial and material issues of fact, the Board may direct the regional director to order a hearing on the exceptions.[14]

If no exceptions are filed, or if filed, do not raise substantial or material factual issues, the Board has the discretion to decide the case forthwith, or dispose of it in any other manner it deems appropriate, without providing a hearing to the parties.[15]

[23.06] HEARINGS ON EXCEPTIONS TO REGIONAL DIRECTOR'S REPORT

Hearings on exceptions are conducted by either an NLRB agent from a regional office or an administrative law judge from Washington, D.C. If directed by NLRB order, the agent or judge conducting the hearing on exceptions to the regional director's report must prepare a report resolving credibility issues and containing findings of fact and make recommendations to the NLRB as to how the case should be disposed.[16]

A Hearing Officer's Report must also be served on the parties who may file exceptions to such report, accompanied by a supporting brief, if desired.[17]

[23.07] RERUN ELECTIONS

Should a regional director or the NLRB, as the case may be, set aside a representation election as a result of objectionable conduct or conduct affecting the results of the election, a new election—commonly referred to as a rerun election—may be ordered.[18]

The standard notice of election form may be modified in rerun elections to include a paragraph explaining why the original election was set aside.[19]

The voting procedures of a rerun election are the same as those of an original election except that the voting eligibility date of the rerun will be a current one and the certification will indicate the election is a rerun.[20]

[23.08] RUN-OFF ELECTIONS

The Board rules provide that, should a ballot in an original election contain three or more choices and no single choice receives a majority of the ballots cast, the regional director must conduct a run-off election.[21] The run-off election will be conducted for the two choices receiving the largest number of valid votes cast in the original election.[22]

Only employees who were eligible to vote in the original election and who are in an eligibility category on the date of the run-off election are eligible to vote in run-off elections.[23]

[23.09] CERTIFICATION

Where a majority of the employees have cast their ballots in favor of a specific union listed on the ballot form, the NLRB will issue a Certification of Representative,[24] indicating that such union shall be the exclusive collective bargaining agent of the employees in accordance with Section 9(a) of the Act.

If no union has received a majority of the valid ballots cast in a representation election, the NLRB will issue a Certification of Results of Election, indicating that a majority of the ballots were not cast for the union seeking to represent the employees.[25]

A certification may be corrected,[26] amended,[27] or revoked[28] by the NLRB. Petitions to amend certification are referred to as "AC" petitions. They may be processed by using the standard NLRB Petition Form and filed with the regional office in which the subject bargaining unit is located. As a general rule, the Board may not amend a certification if such amendment would lead to a significant difference in the kind of representation an employee might receive.[29] However, an amendment may be proper if there is merely a change in the name of the bargaining representative, and not a change in the representative itself.[30]

A certification may be revoked on a showing of good cause.[31] The failure of a particular union to represent fairly all employees in the bargaining unit has been the most prevalent grounds for revoking certifications.[32]

[23.10] COURT REVIEW OF CERTIFICATION

Unlike unfair labor practice proceedings, an NLRB certification of an election is not subject to direct review by the federal courts,[33] except in cases where

- a significant constitutional principle is involved[34]
- questions of great national interest are present[35]
- the Board has exceeded its authority in delegating powers[36]
- the Board has acted in an unlawful manner[37]
- the Board has acted contrary to a specified prohibition in the Act[38]

Although parties may not appeal NLRB certifications directly to the courts, certifications are reviewable as part of a review by the appropriate federal circuit court of a refusal to bargain order based upon such certification.[39]

NOTES TO CHAPTER 23

1. *NLRB Rules and Regulations,* §102.69(a).
2. *NLRB Rules and Regulations,* §102.69(a). (As revised on December 15, 1982.)
3. *NLRB v. Cadillac Steel Products Corporation,* 355 F.2d 191 (CA-9, 1966).
4. *NLRB Casehandling Manual,* §11396.1.
5. *NLRB v. Hale Mfg. Co.,* 602 F.2d 244 (CA-2, 1979).
6. *NLRB Casehandling Manual,* §11420.1.
7. *NLRB Casehandling Manual,* §11400.3.
8. *NLRB Rules and Regulations,* §102.62(a).
9. *NLRB Rules and Regulations,* §102.69(c).
10. *NLRB Rules and Regulations,* §102.69(c).
11. *NLRB Rules and Regulations,* §102.69(c).
12. *NLRB Rules and Regulations,* §102.69(d) and §102.67(c).
13. *NLRB Rules and Regulations,* §102.69(c) and §102.69(j).
14. *NLRB Rules and Regulations,* §102.69(f).
15. *NLRB Rules and Regulations,* §102.69(f).
16. *NLRB Rules and Regulations,* §102.69(f).
17. *NLRB Rules and Regulations,* §102.69(f).
18. *NLRB Casehandling Manual,* §11450.
19. *The Lufkin Rule Co.,* 147 NLRB 341 (1964).
20. *NLRB Casehandling Manual,* §11452 and §11454.
21. See 29 U.S.C.A. §159(c)(3).

22. *NLRB Rules and Regulations,* §102.70(c).

23. *NLRB Rules and Regulations,* §102.70(b).

24. *NLRB Casehandling Manual,* §11470.

25. *NLRB Casehandling Manual,* §11470.

26. *NLRB Casehandling Manual,* §11478.1.

27. *NLRB Casehandling Manual,* §11478.2.

28. *NLRB Casehandling Manual,* §11478.3.

29. *Cocker Saw Co. v. NLRB,* 446 F.2d 870 (CA-2, 1971).

30. *Cocker Saw Co. v. NLRB, supra.*

31. *International Brotherhood of Teamsters, Etc.,* 199 NLRB 994 (1972).

32. *United States Baking Co.,* 165 NLRB 951 (1967).

33. *American Federation of Labor v. NLRB,* 308 U.S. 401 (1940).

34. *Fay v. Douds,* 172 F.2d 720 (CA-2, 1949).

35. *McCulloch v. Sociedad National,* 372 U.S. 10 (1963).

36. *Leedom v. Kyne,* 358 U.S. 184 (1958).

37. *Inland Empire District Council, Lumber and Sawmill Workers Union v. Mills,* 325 U.S. 697 (1945).

38. *Leedom v. Kyne, supra.*

39. *Pittsburgh Plate Glass Co. v. NLRB,* 313 U.S. 146 (1941).

24

Decertification, Deauthorization, and Unit Clarification Petitions

Aside from the "RC" and "RM" petitions discussed in Chapter 19, the NLRB provides for the three other types of petitions, which include

- decertification ("RD")[1]
- deauthorization ("UD")[2]
- unit clarification ("UC")[3]

[24.01] THE DECERTIFICATION PETITION

An election to determine whether a currently recognized labor organization continues to represent a majority of employees within a certain bargaining unit is called a decertification election.[4]

Although decertification elections are also representation proceedings and are generally subject to the same rules as discussed in Chapters 19 through 23, they are discussed separately in this chapter due to some procedural distinctions.

[24.02] "RD" FILING REQUIREMENTS

The NLRB rules provide that a decertification petition may be filed by any individual, an employee, or group of employees acting on behalf of employees, or a labor organization acting on behalf of employees.[5]

An employer may not file a petition for decertification.[6] An employer who questions whether a union continues to represent a majority of his or her employees in a given bargaining unit must, instead, file an "RM" petition.[7]

As with other representation petitions, the "RD" petition should be filed at the NLRB regional office for the region wherein the bargaining unit is located.[8]

An "RD" petition may be filed not more than 90 days or less than 60 days prior to the expiration of an existing contract in nonhealth-care bargaining units;[9] and not more than 120 days nor less than 90 days in health-care bargaining units.[10]

In a decertification petition, the parties are not permitted to stipulate to a bargaining unit larger than the one covered in the last bargaining agreement.[11] Therefore, as a general rule, a decertification petition that seeks an election in a unit not coextensive with an existing or recognized unit will be dismissed.[12]

Whenever an "RD" petition is filed it should be accompanied by the petitioner's proof of interest that at least 30 percent of the employees in the bargaining unit desire a decertification election.[13]

[24.03] EMPLOYER ASSISTANCE PROHIBITED IN DECERTIFICATION PROCEEDINGS

Employers and their agents are prohibited from instigating and promoting a decertification proceeding or attempting to induce employees into signing some union-repudiating document in support of a decertification movement.[14]

[24.04] THE NLRB INVESTIGATION AND DECERTIFICATION HEARING

Both the NLRB investigation of the decertification petition and the conduct of the hearing in a decertification case are the same as those in other representation proceedings. (See [19.05] for a discussion of NLRB investigations of representation petitions. See Chapter 20 for a discussion of representation hearings.)

The hearing officer in a decertification hearing will not permit evidence that concerns "employer assistance" as such evidence should be presented through an unfair labor practice proceeding.[15] However, employer assistance may be the basis for objections to a decertification election, if timely filed.[16]

[24.05] SIGNIFICANCE OF THE RESULTS OF A DECERTIFICATION ELECTION

Should the currently certified or recognized union fail to receive a majority of the valid ballots cast in a decertification election, the NLRB regional director will issue a Certification of Results of Election to that effect.[17]

On the other hand, should the currently certified or recognized union receive a majority of the valid ballots cast, the NLRB or regional director will issue a Certification of Representative, indicating that the incumbent union will continue to be the employees' bargaining agent.[18]

[24.06] DEAUTHORIZATION PROCEEDINGS

Section 8(a)(3) of the Labor Management Relations Act permits a union shop clause in a collective bargaining agreement which typically requires union membership after thirty days[19] as a condition of obtaining or retaining employment unless such union security clauses are prohibited by state statute.

Although the Labor Management Relations Act permits a union security clause under the conditions noted above, Section 9(e)(1) of the Act accords employees subject to such arrangements the right to vote to rescind their bargaining agent's authority to enter into such agreements.

A petition to rescind the authority of a labor organization to enter into a union shop, agency shop, or some related union security arrangement with an employer in a collective bargaining agreement is commonly referred to as a union-shop deauthorization or a "UD" petition.[20]

[24.07] "UD" FILING REQUIREMENTS

The NLRB rules provide that a "UD" petition may be filed by

Thirty percent or more of the employees in the bargaining unit affected, or by an employee or group of employees acting on their behalf.[21]

Section 9(e)(2) of the Act prohibits the holding of a union-shop deauthorization election (referendum) in any bargaining unit in which a valid deauthorization election was held during the preceding twelve months. A deauthorization election may, however, be held within twelve months of a representation election.[22]

The regional director may direct a union-shop deauthorization election without a hearing.[23] Should a hearing be held, it is to be conducted in the same manner as in representation cases.

[24.08] SIGNIFICANCE OF THE RESULTS OF A DEAUTHORIZATION ELECTION

Unlike representation elections, a deauthorization election is determined by a majority of those eligible to vote in the election, not by a majority of those voting.[24] Consequently, the NLRB will not conduct a run-off of a deauthorization election.[25]

Should a majority of the employees eligible to vote in a deauthorization election cast their ballots to rescind the authority of their bargaining agent to enter into union-security clauses, any existing union-security clauses are invalidated[26] and the union is not permitted to enter into any other such agreement for a period of one year following the date of the certificate of results.[27]

[24.09] THE UNIT CLARIFICATION PETITION

Certifications are subject to clarification by the NLRB.[28] Whenever there is a certified or currently recognized bargaining agent and there exists no question of representation, a petition may be filed seeking clarification of the bargaining unit.[29] Such a petition is commonly referred to by the NLRB as a "UC" petition.[30]

A petition to clarify an existing unit may be filed by the currently recognized or certified bargaining agent of the employees or by the employer.[31]

A "UC" petition may not be used as a means to resolve work assignment disputes.[32] Neither may it be used as a method to add a classification of employees that had been deliberately omitted from the current bargaining unit.[33]

A "UC" petition is to be filed with the regional NLRB office in which the unit is located.[34] Clarification of an existing unit may be initiated by filing a petition on the standard NLRB petition form.

Once a "UC" petition has been filed, the regional director has wide discretion in how it is to be investigated and processed.[35] He or she may issue a notice of hearing on all parties, decide the matter without a hearing, or take any other action deemed appropriate.[36]

The regional director may also treat a certification petition as a petition to clarify an existing certification.[37] Should a hearing be ordered by the regional director, it should be conducted, as far as practical, in an identical manner as those conducted in representation proceedings.[38]

Should a petition to clarify a bargaining unit be dismissed, an order to that effect will be issued by the regional director, resulting in no change within the existing unit.[39]

Should a petition to clarify be granted, the regional director will issue an order stating the nature and extent of the clarification.[40]

NOTES TO CHAPTER 24

1. *NLRB Rules and Regulations,* §102.60(a).

2. *NLRB Rules and Regulations,* §102.83.

3. *NLRB Rules and Regulations,* §102.60(b).

4. *NLRB Casehandling Manual,* §11002.1.

5. *NLRB Casehandling Manual,* §11002.2.

6. *Sperry Gyroscope Co.,* 136 NLRB 294 (1962).

7. *NLRB Rules and Regulations,* §102.61(b).

8. *NLRB Casehandling Manual,* §11002.3.

9. *Bally Case & Cooler, Inc. v. NLRB,* 416 F.2d 902 (CA-6, 1969).

10. *Trinity Lutheran Hospital,* 218 NLRB 199 (1975).

11. *Brom Machine & Foundry Co. v. NLRB,* 569 F.2d 1042 (CA-8, 1978).

12. *Gem International, Inc.,* 202 NLRB 518 (1973).

13. *NLRB Casehandling Manual,* §11003.1.

14. See *NLRB v. Birmingham Publishing Co.,* 262 F.2d 2 (CA-5, 1958).

15. *Union Mfg. Co.,* 123 NLRB 1633 (1959).

16. *Sperry Gyroscope Co., supra.*

17. *NLRB Casehandling Manual,* §11470.

18. *NLRB Rules and Regulations,* §102.69(b).

19. Section 8(f) of the Act provides for a seven-day grace period in the building and construction industry.

20. See generally 29 U.S.C.A. §159(e)(1).

21. *NLRB Rules and Regulations,* §102.83.

22. *Monsanto Chemical Company,* 147 NLRB 49 (1964).

23. 29 CFR §101.29.

24. *NLRB Casehandling Manual,* §11512.

25. 29 CFR §101.29.

26. *Andor Co., Inc.,* 119 NLRB 925 (1957).

27. 29 U.S.C.A. §158(a)(3).

28. *The Bell Telephone Co. of Pennsylvania,* 118 NLRB 371 (1957).

29. 29 CFR §101.17.

30. *NLRB Casehandling Manual,* §11002.1(c).

31. *NLRB Casehandling Manual,* §11002.2(d).

32. *Ingersoll Products Division of the Borg-Warner Corporation,* 150 NLRB 912 (1965).

33. *Lufkin Foundry and Machine Co.,* 174 NLRB 556 (1968).

34. *NLRB Casehandling Manual,* §11002.3.

35. *NLRB Rules and Regulations,* §102.63(b).

36. *NLRB Rules and Regulations,* §102.63(b).

37. *United States Pipe & Foundry Co., Soil Pipe Div.,* 223 NLRB 1443 (1976).

38. *NLRB Rules and Regulations,* §102.63(b).

39. *NLRB Casehandling Manual,* §11496.1.

40. *NLRB Casehandling Manual,* §11496.3.

25

The Labor Management Reporting and Disclosure Act

[25.01] PURPOSE AND SCOPE

In 1959, Congress enacted the Labor Management Reporting and Disclosure Act, commonly referred to as the Landrum-Griffin Act, in reference to its legislative sponsors.[1]

The Labor Management Reporting and Disclosure Act (hereinafter referred to as the LMRDA) provides the machinery by which the internal affairs of labor organizations will be policed by the federal government.[2] Its primary purpose is to protect union members from union misconduct and to assure union members their right to fair and proper representation.[3]

[25.02] REPORTING REQUIREMENTS

Constitutions and bylaws: Under Title II of the LMRDA, every labor organization must adopt a constitution and bylaws and file a copy thereof with the Secretary of Labor within ninety days after the date on which the union first becomes subject to the Act.[4]

The report containing the union constitution and bylaws is entitled the ''Labor Organization Information Report'' and is to be filed on the United States Department of Labor Form LM-1.[5] Should there be changes in the information required in the Form LM-1 report, such changes must be reported to the Secretary of Labor at the time the union files its annual financial report.[6]

Financial reports: Every labor organization must file an annual financial report with the Secretary of Labor within ninety days after the end of its fiscal year.[7] This report should be prepared on Form LM-2 (revised) of the United States Department of labor and be signed by the president and treasurer (or corresponding principal officers) of the union. It is to be filed with the Secretary of Labor's Office in Washington, D.C. in accordance with the instructions accompanying the Form LM-2.

Labor organizations having less than $30,000 in gross annual receipts for its fiscal year, and not in trusteeship, may file their annual financial reports on the United States Department of Labor Form LM-3 (revised) in accordance with the instructions accompanying such form, subject to revocation of the privilege.[8]

Reports of union officers and employees: The LMRDA also provides that every union officer and employee (except clerks and custodians) must file with the Secretary of Labor a signed report listing and describing specific financial transactions with employers that occurred during the preceding fiscal year.[9] This report is to be filed on the United States Department of Labor Form LM-30, entitled "Labor Organization Officer and Employee Report."

Employer reports: The LMRDA also provides that every employer who makes a payment, loan, promise, or other agreement to any labor organization or an officer, agent, shop steward, or other representative of such union, must file a report to the Secretary of Labor listing pertinent details concerning such transaction.[10]

Payments of loans made by any national or state bank, credit union, insurance company, savings and loan associations, or other credit institutions and payments of the kind referred to in Section 302(c) of the Labor Management Relations Act are not required to be reported in the "Employer's Report."[11]

The "Employer's Report" should be filed on the United States Department of Labor Form LM-10 in accordance with the instructions contained therein, and forwarded in duplicate to the Department of Labor in Washington, D.C.[12]

Reports of persuaders and informers: The LMRDA requires every person who, pursuant to an arrangement or agreement with an employer, undertakes activities, the object of which is to persuade employees for, or against, unionism to file certain reports concerning such transactions with the Department of Labor in Washington, D.C.[13]

This report must also disclose information pertaining to any arrangement or agreement between an employer and a third party in which the third party undertakes to supply the employer with information concerning the activities of employees or a labor organization in connection with a labor dispute involving such employer, except where such information is used solely in conjunction with an administrative, arbitral, or judicial proceeding.[14] However, the LMRDA does not require individuals to file such reports *who*

- are not direct or indirect parties to such an agreement[15]
- are regular officers, supervisors or employees of an employer and payments to them are in compensation for services rendered by them in their respective position,[16] or
- are engaged by an employer merely to give advice to the employer or engaged to represent an employer before any court, administrative agency, or tribunal of arbitration, or engaged to assist the employer in collective bargaining[17]

Moreover, an attorney who is a member in good standing at the bar of any state is not required to report as persuader activities any information which was lawfully communicated to him or her by any of his or her clients in the course of a legitimate attorney-client relationship.[18] Although a licensed attorney need not report as "persuader activities" the giving of advice and the participation in labor-related legal proceedings, he or she must report activities which are directly persuasive, such as addressing employees during working time to dissuade them from joining a union.[19]

Trusteeship reports: The LMRDA also provides that every labor organization which assumes trusteeship over any subordinate labor organization must file with the Department of Labor in Washington, D.C., a report containing pertinent information concerning the trust relationship.[20] The trusteeship report is to be filed on the United States Department of Labor Form LM-15 in accordance with the instructions contained therein.

Surety company reports: The LMRDA also requires every surety company that issues any bond required by the LMRDA or the Employee Retirement Income Security Act (ERISA) to file an annual report with the Department of Labor.[21] This report is to be submitted on the United States Department of Labor Form LMSA S-1 and must describe the company's bond experience under the LMRDA and ERISA, including such pertinent information as premiums received, total claims paid, amounts received by subrogation, legal expenses, administrative fees, and related data.[22]

[25.03]   RETENTION AND USE OF REPORTS

Persons required to file any of the above mentioned reports must maintain sufficient records on the matters reported from which the Department of Labor may verify said reports.[23] Such records must be kept for examination for a period of not less than five years after the filing of the reports prepared from the information in such documents.[24]

The LMRDA requires every union required to submit any of the above discussed reports to make available to all of its members, the information contained in such reports.[25]

[25.04]   UNION MEMBERS' RIGHTS

Subject to reasonable rules and regulations, the LMRDA provides every union member an equal right within their union to

- nominate candidates for union office
- vote in elections or referenda
- attend membership meetings
- participate in the deliberations and vote upon matters arising in such meeting[26]

The "Bill of Rights" of union members is remedial in nature and, accordingly, should be liberally, yet reasonably, applied by the courts.[27]

The LMRDA provides that all union members shall have the right to "meet and assemble freely with other members"[28] and shall also have the right to express views, arguments, or opinions or their views upon union candidates or on any union business properly before the union meeting, subject to the union's established and reasonable rules pertaining to the conduct of such meeting.[29]

The LMRDA sets forth certain procedural safeguards that must be met before a local or an international union can increase dues, fees, or assessments payable by their members. In case of a local union, an increase must be approved by majority vote via secret ballot in either a special membership meeting or in a membership referendum.[30] In case of a national or international union (except federations of national or international unions), an increase must be approved by majority vote in a regular or special convention, by a secret ballot referendum of members in good standing, or by majority vote of the executive board, the latter to be effective only until the next regular convention.[31]

While a union member may be disciplined for violating his or her union's rules, no union member may be fined, suspended, expelled, or otherwise disciplined (except for nonpayment of dues) by his or her union, or its agents, unless he or she has been

- served with written notice of a specific charge against him or her
- given a reasonable time to prepare his defense, and
- accorded a full and fair hearing[32]

[25.05] UNION MEMBERS' RIGHT TO SUE

The LMRDA provides that no union may limit the right of its members to instigate a legal or administrative proceeding before a court of administrative agency irrespective of whether or not the union or its agents are named as defendants.[33] However, a union may require its members to exhaust reasonable hearing procedures within an organization prior to instituting legal or administrative action against it, although such requirement cannot exceed a four-month lapse of time.[34]

The four-month exhaustion period allows unions an opportunity to resolve complaints and conflicts internally without governmental intermeddling and to encourage the establishment and administration of responsive self-governing structures for resolving such disputes.[35] The exhaustion requirement may be excused if a union member's attempt to resort to union remedies would be futile.[36]

[25.06] UNION ELECTIONS

The LMRDA establishes certain requirements and safeguards that must be applied in conducting elections for union office.[37] The LMRDA requirements extend to the election of officers in local unions, national and international unions, and also intermediate bodies.[38] The LMRDA specifically excludes the election of officers of union federations from such requirements.[39]

The LMRDA requires that national and/or international union officers must be elected not less often than once every five years either by secret ballot among the members in good standing or at a convention of delegates chosen by secret ballot.[40]

It requires that every local union must elect officers not less often than once every three years by secret ballot among its members in good standing.[41]

Officers of intermediate bodies, such as general committees, joint boards, and joint councils, must be elected not less often than once every four years by secret ballot.[42] Although a union may conduct elections more frequently than required by law, they must be conducted in accordance with the statutory requirements.[43]

The LMRDA and related regulations specify certain campaign rights and restrictions in union elections, such as:

- Employer's funds may not be used to promote a union member's candidacy for union office;[44]
- No union funds received by way of dues, assessments, or similar levy may be used to promote the candidacy of any union member;[45]
- A union may not discriminate in favor of or against any candidate with respect to the use of membership lists;[46]
- In every secret ballot election, an election notice must be mailed to each member at least fifteen days before the election;[47]
- A union must comply with a candidate's reasonable request to distribute literature to its members in good standing at the candidate's expense;[48]
- Unions must treat candidates equally with respect to distribution of campaign literature;[49]
- All union members in good standing must be permitted to vote in legally required secret ballot elections;[50] and
- Union members who are candidates for union office have a right to have an observer at the polls and the counting of ballots.[51]

A union member who is a bona fide candidate for union office may institute a lawsuit in federal district court to enforce his or her equal access right to a union's membership list or to enforce his or her right to the distribution of campaign literature.[52]

In addition, the LMRDA provides a union member may file a complaint with the U.S. Secretary of Labor alleging a violation of any of his or her rights to a fair and impartial union election, including any contravention of the union's constitution and bylaws relative to the election or removal of union officers.[53]

The Secretary of Labor must investigate the complaint, and if he finds probable cause to believe that a violation of the law has occurred and has not been remedied, he must file suit in federal district court to obtain a new election.[54]

[25.07] UNION TRUSTEESHIPS

Union trusteeships, means by which international and national unions seek to control their subordinate bodies, are regulated by the LMRDA. Union trusteeships may be established and administered only for

- correcting corruption or financial malpractice
- assuring the performance of collective bargaining agreements or other duties of a bargaining representative
- restoring democratic procedures
- carrying out the legitimate objects of such labor organization[55]

[25.08] FIDUCIARY RESPONSIBILITIES OF UNION OFFICERS

The LMRDA provides that union officers, agents, shop stewards, and other representatives occupy positions of trust in relation to the organization and its members as a group.[56] Consequently, the statute imposes certain obligations upon such agents.

The LMRDA disqualifies an individual who has been convicted of certain crimes from serving in certain union offices and other positions for a prescribed period of time.[57]

Convictions which may bar individuals from holding union office include: robbery, bribery, extortion, embezzlement, grand larceny, burglary, arson, narcotics laws violation, murder, rape, assault with intent to kill, assault which inflicts grievous bodily injury, violations of reporting and disclosure requirements and trusteeships under the statute, or conspiracy to commit any such crimes.[58]

Except in unions whose property and financial receipts do not exceed $5,000 in value, the LMRDA requires the bonding of every union officer, agent, shop steward, or other representative or employee of any labor organization or trust in which a labor organization is interested.[59]

The LMRDA provides that union officers and agents be required to hold, invest, and expend the union's money and property solely for the benefit of the organization and its members and to refrain from dealing with its organization in any adverse manner.[60]

The statute forbids loans to union officers from any labor organization in excess of $2,000.[61]

In addition to prohibitions under the Federal Election Campaign Act, the LMRDA also forbids unions to make contributions or expenditures in connection with any

- election in which presidential and vice-presidential electors are to be determined
- election in which a Senator or Representative in Congress is to be determined, and
- election or political convention or caucus held to select candidates for any of the foregoing offices[62]

[25.09] DUTY OF FAIR REPRESENTATION

Inasmuch as Section 9(a) of the Labor Management Relations Act bestows upon a properly selected union the exclusive right to represent all employees in a bargaining unit, that union has a reciprocal duty to serve all the bargaining unit members in a fair and nondiscriminatory manner.[63]

The doctrine of fair representation requires a union to represent fairly the interests of all bargaining unit members during negotiations, administration, and enforcement of a collective bargaining agreement.[64]

A union breaches such duty when its conduct is arbitrary, discriminatory, or in bad faith.[65] For example, a union fails to represent fairly an employee when it arbitrarily ignores a meritorious grievance or processes it only in a perfunctory manner.[66] A failure of a labor organization to represent fairly employees in the respective bargaining unit causes the union to commit a violation of Section 8(b)(1) of the LMRA.

[25.10] JUDICIAL ENFORCEMENT OF THE LMRDA

The LMRDA provides that any person whose rights have been infringed by any violation of its ''Bill of Rights'' provisions may institute a civil action in federal district court for such relief as may be appropriate.[67]

Examples of cases in which federal courts have asserted jurisdiction under this provision include

- an action against union officials for improperly assessing and expending union funds[68]
- an action against a union and its representatives for refusing to furnish a copy of the applicable collective bargaining contract to a union member[69]
- an action alleging that an international union coerced and intimidated members of a local union to accept affiliation with another union[70]
- an action alleging that an international union wrongfully revoked a local's charter[71]

- an action against a union for refusing certain members the right to participate in union meetings[72]

NOTES TO CHAPTER 25

1. 29 U.S.C.A. §401, *et seq.*; see also: Benjamin Aaron, "The Labor-Management Reporting and Disclosure Act of 1959," *Harvard Law Review* 73 (1960): 851.
2. Howard J. Anderson, *Primer of Labor Relations,* 21st ed. (Washington, D.C.: The Bureau of National Affairs, Inc.), 89.
3. Benjamin J. Taylor and Fred Witney, *Labor Relations Law* (Englewood Cliffs, NJ: Prentice-Hall, Inc., 1971), 473.
4. 29 U.S.C.A. §431(a).
5. 29 CFR §402.2.
6. 29 U.S.C.A. §431(a).
7. 29 U.S.C.A. §431(b).
8. 29 CFR §403.4(a).
9. 29 U.S.C.A. §432(a).
10. 29 U.S.C.A. §433(a).
11. 29 U.S.C.A. §433(a).
12. 29 CFR §405.3.
13. 29 U.S.C.A. §433(b).
14. 29 U.S.C.A. §433(b).
15. 29 U.S.C.A. §433(d).
16. 29 U.S.C.A. §433(e).
17. 29 U.S.C.A. §433(c).
18. 29 U.S.C.A. §434.
19. *Wirtz v. Fowler,* 372 F.2d 315 (CA-5, 1966).
20. 29 U.S.C.A. §461.
21. 29 U.S.C.A. §441.
22. 29 U.S.C.A. §441.
23. 29 U.S.C.A. §436.
24. 29 U.S.C.A. §436.
25. 29 CFR §408.11.
26. 29 U.S.C.A. §411(a)(1).
27. *International Brotherhood of Boilermakers, Etc. v. Rafferty,* 348 F.2d 307 (CA-9, 1965).
28. 29 U.S.C.A. §411(a)(2).
29. 29 U.S.C.A. §411(a)(2).

30. 29 U.S.C.A. §411(a)(3).
31. 29 U.S.C.A. §411(a)(3).
32. 29 U.S.C.A. §411(a)(5).
33. 29 U.S.C.A. §411(a)(4).
34. 29 U.S.C.A. §411(a)(4).
35. *Brennan v. Amalgamated Clothing Workers,* 564 F.2d 657 (CA-3, 1977).
36. *Fulton Lodge No. 2 of the International Association of Machinists & Aerospace Workers v. Nix,* 415 F.2d 212 (CA-5, 1969).
37. 29 U.S.C.A. §481.
38. 29 U.S.C.A. §481.
39. 29 U.S.C.A. §481(d).
40. 29 U.S.C.A. §481(a).
41. 29 U.S.C.A. §481(b).
42. 29 U.S.C.A. §481(c).
43. 29 CFR §452.24.
44. 29 U.S.C.A. §481(g).
45. 29 U.S.C.A. §481(g).
46. 29 U.S.C.A. §481(c).
47. 29 U.S.C.A. §481(e).
48. 29 U.S.C.A. §481(c).
49. 29 U.S.C.A. §481(c).
50. 29 U.S.C.A. §481(e).
51. 29 U.S.C.A. §481(c)
52. 29 U.S.C.A. §481(c).
53. 29 U.S.C.A. §481(a).
54. 29 U.S.C.A. §481(b).
55. 29 U.S.C.A. §462.
56. 29 U.S.C.A. §501(a).
57. 29 U.S.C.A. §504(a).
58. 29 U.S.C.A. §504.
59. 29 U.S.C.A. §502(a).
60. 29 U.S.C.A. §502(a).
61. 29 U.S.C.A. §503(a).
62. 2 U.S.C.A. §441(b)(3)(A)
63. *United Rubber, Cork, Linoleum & Plastic Workers v. NLRB,* 368 F.2d 12 (CA-5, 1966).
64. *International Brotherhood of Electrical Workers v. Foust,* 442 U.S. 42 (1979).
65. *International Brotherhood of Electrical Workers v. Foust, supra.*
66. *Emmanuel v. Omaha Carpenters District Council,* 535 F.2d 420 (CA-8, 1976).

67. 29 U.S.C.A. §412.
68. *Clinton v. Hueston,* 308 F.2d 908 (CA-5, 1962).
69. *Forline v. Helpers Local No. 42,* 211 F.Supp. 315 (DC Pa., 1962).
70. *Safe Workers' Organization, Etc. v. Ballinger,* 389 F.Supp. 903 (SD Ohio, 1974).
71. *Parks v. International Brotherhood of Electrical Workers,* 314 F.2d 886 (CA-4, 1963).
72. *O'Brien v. Paddock,* 246 F.Supp. 809 (DC N.Y., 1965).

26

Labor Arbitration

[26.01] NATURE AND SCOPE OF THE ARBITRATION PROCESS

A grievance and arbitration procedure under a collective bargaining contract has been described as being "at the very heart of the system of industrial self-government."[1]

Inasmuch as arbitration is a preferred method to settle labor controversies, it is the federal policy to encourage the inclusion of grievance and arbitration clauses in a collective bargaining contract.[2]

The judicial policy favoring arbitration in the resolution of labor disputes was first outlined in three landmark decisions of the U.S. Supreme Court, frequently referred to as the *Steelworkers' Trilogy*.[3]

These decisions established the following propositions favoring court deferral to arbitration:

- The first function of the court should be a determination of whether the party seeking arbitration is making a claim which, on its face, is governed by a collective bargaining contract;[4]

- In making this determination, all doubts as to the coverage of an arbitration clause should be resolved in favor of arbitration;[5] and

- Courts are to uphold and enforce an arbitrator's award—resulting from an arbitrable issue under a collective bargaining contract—even though the court's interpretation of the contract would differ from that of the arbitrator's.[6]

[26.02] CONTRACTUAL OBLIGATIONS

The right to arbitrate a labor dispute arises solely from an agreement between the employer and the collective bargaining agent of the employees.[7] Therefore, neither an employer nor a union is required to submit to arbitration any labor dispute which it has not agreed to submit.[8]

Since arbitration is a contractual matter, neither party is required to arbitrate a dispute arising at a time when no collective bargaining agreement is in force.[9] However, if the dispute between the parties arose during the time the agreement was in force, the duty to arbitrate a grievance arising from the dispute does not expire at the termination of the collective bargaining, but continues thereafter.[10]

The contractual obligation to arbitrate a labor dispute will survive the merger of a corporate employer where there is a substantial continuity of identity in the business operation before and after the change in ownership.[11]

As a general rule, employees to a collective bargaining contract have no right to insist upon arbitration unless they can show that the union has failed to represent them fairly.[12]

[26.03] NLRB DEFERRAL TO ARBITRATION

The National Labor Relations Board does not favor the arbitral process in the resolution of labor disputes to the same degree as do the courts,[13] especially where the NLRB processes are necessary to protect public and employee interests as mandated by the Labor Management Relations Act.[14]

Although a collective bargaining agreement may provide a remedy through arbitration, it does not deprive the NLRB of jurisdiction to remedy an unfair labor practice involving the same or similar facts.[15]

Parties to a collective bargaining contract are prohibited from waiving NLRB jurisdiction by agreeing to submit labor disputes to arbitrators exclusively.[16] The NLRB may, however, defer its jurisdiction to the arbitral process in cases in which it feels the national labor policy of attaining industrial peace through the promotion of collective bargaining will be served.[17]

Speilberg Doctrine (Post-Arbitral Deferral): In deciding whether to process an unfair labor practice case or defer its jurisdiction to arbitration, the Board will frequently look to the arbitrator's award.[18]

Under this doctrine—commonly called the *Speilberg Doctrine*[19]—the NLRB will defer to an arbitrator's decision if such decision meets the following criteria:

- The arbitration proceedings appeared to have been "fair and regular";[20]
- All parties to the unfair labor practice charge had agreed to be bound by the arbitrator's decision;[21]
- The arbitrator's decision was not clearly repugnant to the purpose and policies of the Act;[22]
- The contractual issue in the arbitration proceeding was factually parallel to the unfair labor practice issue, and the arbitrator was presented generally with the facts relative to the unfair labor practice issue.[23]

The Collyer Doctrine (Pre-Arbitral Deferral): The doctrine of pre-arbitral deferral, the process of temporarily deferring the determination of unfair labor practice cases to the grievance and arbitration machinery by the NLRB, is commonly referred to as the *Collyer Doctrine.*[24]

Cases in which the NLRB has refused to invoke the *Collyer Doctrine*[25] on the grounds that it alone should resolve them include

- Section 8(a)(4) charges[26]
- alleged violations of Section 8(d) of the Act[27]

- an alleged refusal to comply with a previous board order[28]
- accretion to bargaining unit issues[29]
- questions on the validity or enforceability of a labor contract[30]
- questions on the scope of the statutory duty to bargain where the underlying dispute does not turn on the interpretation of an existing contract[31]

Moreover, the NLRB will not invoke the *Collyer Doctrine* and temporarily defer to the grievance and arbitration machinery unless the following conditions are met:

- There must exist a stable collective bargaining relationship.
- The respondent must be willing to arbitrate the issue involved.
- The contract and its meaning must be at the center of the dispute.[32]

The NLRB has also refused to invoke the *Collyer Doctrine* where the grievance and arbitration procedure did not culminate in binding and final arbitration,[33] and in cases in which it appeared that both the employer and the union were ''hostile'' to the interest of the employees involved.[34]

Should the NLRB invoke the *Collyer Doctrine* and temporarily defer its determination of pending charges to the grievance and arbitration machinery, once the final decision is rendered by an arbitrator, the Board will then determine if the final award meets the *Speilberg* standards, as discussed previously.[35]

The Dubo Doctrine (Interim-Arbitral Deferral): Prior to the NLRB's adoption of the *Collyer Doctrine,* it typically deferred its determination of unfair labor practice charges to arbitration whenever

- one of the parties had filed suit, or had secured a court order to compel arbitration of the particular dispute in question, or
- the parties had agreed to arbitrate the outstanding labor dispute and the matter was either set for, or in, arbitration[36]

The NLRB policy of deferring unfair labor practice cases to arbitration under these conditions is commonly referred to as the *Dubo Doctrine.*[37]

The *Collyer Doctrine* has somewhat displaced the *Dubo Doctrine* in that the NLRB will look to the *Collyer* criteria first in determining whether to defer its determination of a pending unfair labor practice charge to arbitration.[38] If grounds for deferral under the *Collyer* standards do not exist, the NLRB will then look to the *Dubo* criteria to decide whether deferral is appropriate.[39]

[26.04] FUNCTIONS AND LIMITATIONS OF ARBITRATORS

A labor arbitrator is usually chosen by the parties to a collective bargaining agreement under the grievance and arbitration provisions thereof.[40]

A labor arbitrator's source of law is not confined to the express provisions of the collective bargaining agreement, but involves the "industrial common law" as well.[41]

The authority of labor arbitrators is limited, however, to the power granted in the collective bargaining agreement.[42] Although an arbitrator has discretion in exercising his or her authority and wide latitude in fashioning an appropriate remedy, he or she must settle labor disputes in conformity with the provisions of the contract.[43] Collective bargaining parties do not inferentially bestow upon an arbitrator the power to dispense his or her own brand of industrial justice.[44]

[26.05] INTERPRETATION OF LABOR CONTRACTS

The determination of whether certain parties are bound by a collective bargaining agreement,[45] as well as the issue of arbitrability,[46] is an ultimate question for the courts, not arbitrators. However, once the courts determine that the parties are bound by the collective bargaining agreement and are contractually obligated to submit the dispute in question to arbitration, questions concerning whether a party failed to follow the procedural conditions specified in the contract are to be resolved by the arbitrator.[47] Likewise, the interpretation of a collective bargaining contract as to its meaning and application is a matter for the arbitrator instead of the courts.[48]

[26.06] ARBITRATION HEARINGS

Rules of evidence: As a general policy, arbitrators are not bound by the evidentiary rules applicable in federal and state courts, and therefore receive virtually any and all kinds of evidence offered to them in arbitration proceedings.[49] An arbitrator's award, nevertheless, must rest upon some relevant, competent, and material legal evidence sufficient to support the findings of the arbitrator to be valid and binding on the parties.[50]

Subpoenas: A party to an arbitration proceeding may request an arbitrator to issue a subpoena pursuant to state law or the Federal Arbitration Act, although there is some question as to whether the federal statute is applicable to collective bargaining agreements.[51] Arguably, an arbitrator's subpoena might be enforced through the courts pursuant to an arbitrator's power to compel production of material evidence under Section 301 of the Labor Management Relations Act.[52]

Production of documents: As a general rule, a party to a collective bargaining contract has a duty, under the Labor Management Relations Act, to supply relevant information and documents to the other party with respect to negotiations or the processing of a grievance through the grievance and arbitration procedures specified in the contract.[53]

Should either party fail to supply information requested that would be relevant to an arbitration proceeding, the other party may enforce its rights to such information by filing appropriate unfair labor practice charges with the National Labor Relations Board.[54]

Should a party to an arbitration proceeding refuse to furnish information requested, or should an individual refuse to honor an arbitrator's subpoena, an adverse inference may be drawn by the arbitrator against the party refusing to produce[55] or testify.[56]

Conduct of hearing: The conduct of an arbitration hearing is under the jurisdiction and control of the selected or appointed arbitrator.[57] No set standard of procedures apply in arbitration cases and hearings vary significantly depending upon such factors as the applicable law, administrative agency rules, specified agreements of the parties, and the opinions and views of the respective arbitrator.[58]

The *"Code of Professional Responsibility for Arbitrators of Labor-Management Disputes"*[59] provides some of the following guidelines to be used in the conduct of arbitration hearings:[60]

- An arbitrator may encourage stipulations of fact, restate the substance of issues or arguments to promote or verify understanding, question the parties' representatives or witnesses, and request that the parties submit additional evidence, either at the hearing or by subsequent filing.

- An arbitrator should not intrude into a party's presentation so as to prevent that party from putting forward its case fairly and adequately.

- An arbitrator must comply with mutual agreements in respect to the filing or nonfiling of post hearing briefs or submissions.

- An arbitrator's award should be definite, certain, and as concise as possible.

[26.07] LAWSUITS RELATIVE TO ARBITRATION

Four types of lawsuits may arise in labor arbitration matters. They include lawsuits (1) to compel arbitration, (2) to enjoin arbitration, (3) to enforce an arbitrator's award, or (4) to vacate an arbitrator's award.

Lawsuits to compel arbitration: The Labor Management Relations Act authorizes the federal courts to fashion a body of law for the enforcement of collective bargaining agreements.[61] The LMRA also confers original jurisdiction on federal courts to enforce a provision to arbitrate grievances as provided in a collective bargaining contract.[62] Therefore, pursuant to the LMRA, a party to a collective bargaining agreement containing an arbitration clause may process a federal suit to compel the other party to arbitrate a labor dispute arguably arising under the agreement.[63] In turn, the federal court may issue an order compelling the other party to arbitrate or, when such relief is warranted, grant injunctive relief in connection with such order.[64]

State courts are not deprived of jurisdiction to compel arbitration of claimed breaches of a collective bargaining contract; they have concurrent jurisdiction with federal courts in such suits.[65]

Lawsuits to enjoin arbitration: As in suits to compel arbitration, the LMRA also confers jurisdiction on federal courts to enjoin arbitration under a collective bargaining agreement in certain cases.[66]

In similar form, courts have authority to issue an order preventing a party from submitting an issue to arbitration,[67] as well as to enjoin a party from re-arbitrating a grievance previously decided in an arbitration proceeding.[68]

Lawsuits to enforce awards: Federal courts also have power to enforce an arbitration award, assuming the arbitrator's decision is final and binding under the terms of a valid and enforceable collective bargaining agreement.[69] However, in determining whether an arbitrator's award should be enforced, the court must give consideration to any NLRB ruling involving the dispute in question.[70]

Should a conflict arise between an arbitrator's award and an NLRB ruling, the NLRB order overrides the arbitrator's decision by operation of the supremacy doctrine and the court is to deny enforcement of the award.[71]

Lawsuits to vacate awards: Federal courts have jurisdiction to modify or vacate an arbitration award.[72] Some general grounds for vacating arbitrators' awards include the following:

- Fraud, corruption, partiality, duress, or similar misconduct on the part of an arbitrator;[73]
- The award violates public policy;[74]
- The arbitrator exceeded his authority in making his or her award;[75]
- The arbitrator exceeded his or her jurisdiction under the terms of the contract;[76] or
- The parties failed to arbitrate in accordance with the terms of the contract or stipulations.[77]

NOTES TO CHAPTER 26

1. *United Steelworkers of America v. Warrior & Gulf Navigation Co.*, 363 U.S. 574 (1960).

2. *International Assn. of Machinists, Etc. v. General Electric Co.*, 406 F.2d 1046 (CA-2, 1969).

3. *United Steelworkers of America v. American Mfg. Co.*, 363 U.S. 564 (1960); *United Steelworkers of America v. Warrior & Gulf Navigation Co., supra.*

4. *United Steelworkers of America v. American Mfg. Co., supra.*

5. *United Steelworkers v. Warrior & Gulf Navigation Co., supra.*

6. *United Steelworkers of America v. Enterprise Wheel & Car Corp.*, 363 U.S. 593 (1960).

7. *American Federation of Technical Engineers v. Western Electric Co.*, 508 F.2d 106 (CA-7, 1974).

8. *Gateway Coal Co. v. United Mine Workers*, 414 U.S. 368 (1974).

9. *Proctor & Gamble Independent Union v. Proctor & Gamble Mfg. Co.*, 312 F.2d 181 (CA-2, 1962).

10. *Minnesota Joint Board, Amalgamated Clothing Workers v. United Garment Mfg. Co.*, 338 F.2d 195 (CA-8, 1964).

11. *John Wiley & Sons, Inc. v. Livingston*, 376 U.S. 543 (1964).

12. *Anderson v. Grocers Supply Co.*, 483 F.Supp. 73 (SD Tex., 1979).

13. *NLRB v. Acme Industrial Co.*, 385 U.S. 432 (1967).

14. *NLRB v. Radio Officer's Union*, 196 F.2d 960 (CA-2, 1952).

15. *NLRB v. Wagner Iron Works*, 220 F.2d 126 (CA-7, 1955).

16. *NLRB v. Stone*, 125 F.2d 752 (CA-7, 1942).

17. *Carey v. Westinghouse Electric Corp.*, 375 U.S. 261 (1964).

18. *Speilberg Mfg. Co.*, 112 NLRB 1080 (1955).

19. *Speilberg Mfg. Co., supra.*

20. *Carey v. Westinghouse Electric Corp., supra; Speilberg Mfg. Co., supra.*

21. *Carey v. Westinghouse Electric Corp., supra; Speilberg Mfg. Co., supra.*

22. *Carey v. Westinghouse Electric Corp., supra; Speilberg Mgf. Co., supra.*

23. *Olin Corp.*, 268 NLRB No. 86 (1984).

24. *Collyer Insulated Wire*, 192 NLRB 837 (1971).

25. *Collyer Insulated Wire, supra.*

26. *McKinley Transport Limited*, 219 NLRB No. 184 (1975).

27. *IUE Local 742 (Randall Bearings, Inc.)*, 213 NLRB No. 119 (1974).

28. *Ernst Steel Corp.*, 217 NLRB No. 179 (1975).

29. *Hershey Foods Corp.*, 208 NLRB 452 (1974).

30. *Fenix & Scisson, Inc.*, 207 NLRB 752 (1973).

31. *Columbus Printing Pressmen (R.W. Page Co.)*, 219 NLRB No. 54 (1975).

32. *Collyer Insulated Wire, supra.*

33. *Evans Products Co.,* 171 NLRB 1002 (1968).

34. *Kansas Meat Packers,* 198 NLRB 543 (1972).

35. *Associated Press,* 199 NLRB 1110 (1972).

36. 1972 *NLRB Guidelines,* p. 18.

37. *Dubo Mfg. Co.,* 142 NLRB 431 (1963).

38. 1972 *NLRB Guidelines,* p. 17.

39. *Revised NLRB Guidelines,* p. 38.

40. Clarence M. Updegraff, *Arbitration and Labor Relations,* 3rd ed. (Washington, D.C.: The Bureau of National Affairs, Inc., 1970), 102–107.

41. *International Brotherhood of Electrical Workers v. Olin Corp.,* 471 F.2d 468 (CA-6, 1972).

42. *United Mine Workers v. Chris-Craft Corp.,* 385 F.2d 946 (CA-6, 1967).

43. *Schlesinger v. Building Service Employees International Union,* 367 F.Supp. 760 (ED Pa., 1973).

44. *Dallas Typographical Union v. A.H. Belo Corp.,* 372 F.2d 577 (CA-5, 1967).

45. *Pullman, Inc. v. International Brotherhood of Boilermakers, Etc.,* 354 F.Supp. 496 (ED Pa., 1972).

46. *John Wiley & Sons, Inc. v. Livingston,* 376 U.S. (1964).

47. *Amalgamated Clothing Workers v. Ironall Factories Co.,* 386 F.2d 586 (CA-6, 1967).

48. *United Steelworkers of America v. Enterprise Wheel & Car Corp., supra.*

49. See Frank Elkouri and Edna Aspar Elkouri, *How Arbitration Works* (Washington, D.C.: The Bureau of National Affairs, Inc., 1973), 252; see also: Rule 28 of the *Voluntary Labor Arbitration Rules of the American Arbitration Association* (as amended and in effect January 1, 1979).

50. *Frantz v. Inter-Insurance Exchange,* 229 Cal. App. 2d 269 (1964).

51. See Marvin Hill, Jr. and Anthony V. Sinicropi, *Evidence in Arbitration* (Washington, D.C.: The Bureau of National Affairs, Inc., 1980), 99, but see also the following cases where the Federal Arbitration Act was applied to enforce the arbitrator's subpoenas: *Great Scott Supermarkets v. Local 37,* 363 F.Supp. 1351 (ED Mich., 1973), *Local Lodge 176 v. United Aircraft Corp.,* 329 F.Supp. 283 (DC Conn., 1971).

52. Owen Fairweather, *Practice and Procedure in Labor Arbitration* (Washington, D.C.: The Bureau of National Affairs, Inc., 1973), 132.

53. Hill and Sinicropi, *Evidence in Arbitration,* 97-100.

54. Ibid.

55. Robben Wright Fleming, *The Labor Arbitration Process* (Urbana, Ill.: University of Illinois Press, 1965), 175.

56. *Brass-Craft Mfg. Co.,* 36 LA 1177, 1184 (Kahn, 1961).

57. Elkouri and Elkouri, *How Arbitration Works,* 182.

58. Ibid, 181.

59. The *Code of Professional Responsibility for Arbitrators of Labor-Management Disputes*

has been adopted by the National Academy of Arbitrators, the American Arbitration Association and the Federal Mediation and Conciliation Service.

60. See Rules V and VI of the *Code of Professional Responsibility for Arbitrators of Labor-Management Disputes.*

61. *Textile Workers Union v. Lincoln Mills of Alabama,* 353 U.S. 448 (1957).

62. *Textile Workers Union of Lincoln Mills of Alabama, supra.*

63. *General Electric Co. v. United Electrical, Radio & Machine Workers,* 353 U.S. 547 (1957).

64. *Edward L. Nezelek, Inc. v. Local Union No. 294,* 342 F.Supp. 507 (DC N.Y., 1972).

65. *Carey v. Westinghouse Electric Corp.,* 375 U.S. 261 (1964).

66. *Columbia Broadcasting System, Inc. v. American Recording & Broadcasting Assn.,* 414 F.2d 1326 (CA-2, 1969).

67. *Marine Engineers Beneficial Assn. v. Falcon Carriers, Inc.,* 374 F.Supp. 1342 (SD N.Y., 1974).

68. *Central Pennsylvania Motor Carriers Conference, Inc. v. International Brotherhood of Teamsters, Etc.,* 226 F.Supp. 795 (ED Pa., 1964).

69. *Buffalo Forge Co. v. United Steelworkers of America,* 428 U.S. 397 (1976).

70. *Smith Steel Workers v. A. O. Smith Corp.,* 420 F.2d 1 (CA-7, 1969).

71. *Smith Steel Workers v. A. O. Smith Corp., supra.*

72. *Amalgamated Meat Cutters & Butcher Workmen v. Cross Brothers Meat Packers, Inc.,* 518 F.2d 1113 (CA-3, 1975).

73. *Schlesinger v. Building Service Employees International Union, supra.*

74. *Botany Industries, Inc. v. New York Joint Board, Etc.,* 375 F.Supp. 485 (SD N.Y., 1974).

75. *Lee v. Olin Mathieson Chemical Corp.,* 271 F.Supp. 635 (WD Va., 1967).

76. *International Brotherhood of Teamsters v. Motor Freight Express, Inc.,* 56 F.Supp. 724 (WD Pa., 1973).

77. *International Hod Carriers, Etc. v. Sullivan,* 221 F.Supp. 696 (ED Ill., 1963).

27

Railway Labor Act

[27.01] ORIGIN AND PURPOSE

The Railway Labor Act[1] preceded the National Labor Relations Act by its enactment in 1926. The original Act applied to any express company, sleeping-car company, or railroad carrier subject to the Interstate Commerce Act.[2] The applicability of the Act was later extended to commercial airlines.[3]

The purpose of the Railway Labor Act is to protect the rights of employees to join labor unions and to bargain collectively through a union that a majority of the employees selects.[4] The statute was also enacted to promote the prompt and orderly settlement of labor disputes between interstate rail and airline carriers and their employees through the process of collective bargaining or arbitration.[5]

[27.02] JURISDICTION

Although the Railway Labor Act applies essentially to railroads and commercial airlines, there has been substantial litigation as to whether certain employers fall within the Railway Labor Act and are thereby exempt from the jurisdiction of the NLRB, or vice versa.[6]

As discussed briefly at [3.02], when an issue arises before the NLRB as to whether a certain employer falls within the coverage of the Railway Act, the NLRB will request the National Mediation Board, the agency having primary authority to determine the jurisdiction of the Railway Labor Act, to investigate the matter and decide the applicability of the Railway Labor Act to the subject employer.[7]

The provisions of the Railway Labor Act have been held to apply to

- air travel clubs[8]
- companies who provide freight handling services to commercial airlines[9]
- air carriers transporting U.S. mail[10]
- companies so engaged in the supply of air services that they fall within the jurisdictional definition of the Railway Labor Act[11]

However, not all companies fall within the jurisdiction of the Railway Labor Act by virtue of their relationship or association with the commercial airline industry. Companies that have been held to fall within the jurisdiction of the National Labor Relations Act, as amended, rather than within that of the Railway Labor Act, include

- an airline caterer supplying food services to commercial airlines[12]

- a company engaged in a fixed-base operation located at a municipal airport[13]
- an airline-owned motel used to house airline flight crews[14]
- a travel tour business not engaged in direct common carriage activities by air[15]
- an air shuttle service operating in intrastate commerce[16]

[27.03] EMPLOYEES' RIGHTS UNDER THE ACT

The Railway Labor Act states that employees who fall within the jurisdiction of its coverage shall have the right to organize and bargain collectively through representatives of their choosing.[17] (This proviso is not unlike the NLRA Section 7 rights guaranteed to employees who fall within the jurisdiction of the National Labor Relations Board.)[18]

The Railway Labor Act also provides that no carrier shall deny or in any way question or interfere with its employees' right to join, organize, or assist in organizing the labor organization of their choice; nor shall such carrier induce employees to join or remain or not to join or remain members of any union.[19] Railroad and airline employers are also forbidden to require any person seeking employment to sign any contract or agreement promising to join or not to join a labor organization.[20]

Carriers subject to the Act are required to notify their employees of these and other rights by posting appropriate printed notices in such form, and at such times and places, as may be specified by the National Mediation Board.[21]

[27.04] SELECTION OF EMPLOYEES' BARGAINING REPRESENTATIVE

The Railway Labor Act gives broad discretion to the National Mediation Board, the agency administering the Act, in determining representation questions and resolving disputes as to employee bargaining representatives.[22]

Upon request of either party to a representation dispute, the National Mediation Board is authorized to investigate the matter[23] through such methods and procedures as it considers desirable in each case.[24]

The rules and regulations of the National Mediation Board require that a petition for investigating a representation dispute be supported by authorization cards of at least 35 percent of the employees in a proposed class or craft if there is no bargaining agent currently representing such employees.[25] Such authorization cards must be signed and dated within one year of the filing of the petition.[26]

An employer need not be made a party to the procedure adopted by the National Mediation Board to define the scope and method of its investigation and may present his or her views on craft or class questions only at the permission of the Board.[27] The National Mediation Board is empowered to determine craft or class questions and is not required to hold a hearing prior to its determination.[28]

Once an investigation is completed by the National Mediation Board and a class or craft question is determined, the Board is to take a secret ballot of the employees involved—or utilize some similar method—in such a manner as to ensure their choice of bargaining representative is free from interference, influence, or coercion on the part of the employer.[30] In conducting a secret ballot election, the National Mediation Board is to designate who may participate in the election, or is to appoint a committee of three neutral persons who, after a hearing, shall, within ten days, designate the employees who may participate in the election.[31]

The Board shall have access to make copies of the books and records of the subject carrier and utilize such information as may be deemed necessary to carry out its function in the electorate process.[32]

The majority of the employees participating in such an election have the right to determine who shall be the bargaining representative of the class or craft, or whether they wish to remain free of union representation.[33]

[27.05] BARGAINING DUTIES AND AGREEMENTS

Once the National Mediation Board has certified the employees' representative, the carrier must recognize such representative as the bargaining agent of its employees.[34]

A labor organization so certified by the National Mediation Service becomes the bargaining representative of all the employees in the designated craft, whether such employees are members of the union or not.[35] All such employees are subject to the bargaining representative's efforts, and the union is under a duty to represent all employees within the designated craft fairly and non-discriminatorily.[36]

The Railway Labor Act provides that it is a duty of all carriers and employees to exert every reasonable effort to make and maintain collective bargaining agreements.[37]

[27.06] UNION SECURITY AND "CHECK-OFF" CLAUSES

A carrier and a union certified to represent employees may enter into an agreement requiring all employees to become members of such union within sixty days after the beginning of employment or the effective date of the bargaining agreement, whichever is later, as a condition of employment or as a condition of continued employment.[38]

The provisions of the Railway Labor Act permitting compulsory unionism in relation to railroad and airline employees[39] supersede state "right-to-work" statutes inasmuch as there are no parallel provisions of Section 14(b) of the LMRA within the Railway Labor Act.[40]

The Railway Labor Act also permits a carrier and a union to enter into an agreement providing for the deduction by a carrier from the wages of its employees, and the payment to the union of any dues, initiation fees, and assessments uniformly required as a condition of acquiring or retaining membership.[41]

[27.07] SETTLEMENT OF DISPUTES

The Railway Labor Act provides that it is a duty of all carriers and their employees to settle all disputes, whether arising out of the application of a collective bargaining agreement or otherwise, in order to avoid any interruption to commerce.[42]

The statute also provides that all disputes arising between a carrier and its employees must be expeditiously considered and, if possible, resolved in conference between representatives of both the carrier and the employees affected.[43]

"Minor" disputes: A labor dispute, arising out of grievances or out of the interpretation or application of collective bargaining agreements concerning rates of pay, hours, and other such terms and conditions of employment and not resolved in conference between representatives of the carrier and the employees affected, is to be referred to the appropriate adjustment board for determination on the petition of either party to the dispute.[44] Such a dispute is commonly termed a "minor" dispute inasmuch as it is concerned with a grievance arising out of the interpretation or application of an existing contract as distinguished from a dispute arising over a change or amendment in the agreement.[45] "Minor" disputes involving railroad carriers are referred to the National Railroad Adjustment Board for disposition.[46]

The statute does not specifically establish a national adjustment board in the case of air carriers, as it does in the case of railroads, for the disposition of "minor" disputes.[47] Notwithstanding, the National Mediation Board is empowered, should it deem appropriate, to direct air carriers and national employee unions to select and designate four representatives, equally divided between them, to constitute the "National Air Transport Adjustment Board." Such a board, once formulated, is empowered to act in the same manner and to the same extent as the National Railroad Adjustment Board.[48]

Once a "minor" dispute is submitted to an appropriate Adjustment Board, the board has exclusive jurisdiction over such dispute and is empowered to make its decision which shall be final and binding upon both the parties to the dispute.[49]

Should a carrier or employee be aggrieved by the terms of the Adjustment Board's decision, or should a carrier fail to comply with such decision, an action to obtain relief may be brought in federal district court.[50]

Judicial review of an adjustment board's decision is limited[51] and the court must accept the board's findings as final unless the board's order failed to conform or confine itself to matters within the scope of its jurisdiction, or where fraud or corruption is shown.[52]

"Major" disputes: Should a carrier and its employees fail to resolve a dispute concerning changes in rates of pay, rules, or working conditions through collective bargaining negotiations or other conferences, or in the case of any other "major" dispute, either party or both parties may request the services of the National Mediation Board to assist in the settlement of the controversy.[53] Upon such a request, the National Mediation Board must use its best efforts to mediate a settlement between the parties.[54]

Should the Mediation Board fail in its efforts to bring about a settlement, the board must endeavor to induce the parties to submit their controversy to arbitration.[55] If either party should refuse to submit the controversy to arbitration, the Mediation Board must immediately notify both parties in writing that its mediatory efforts have failed, and for thirty days thereafter, unless an emergency board is created under the Act or the parties agree to arbitration in the intervening period, no change may be made in the rates of pay, rules, or working conditions or established practices in effect prior to the time the dispute arose.[56]

Arbitration board: If a labor dispute between a carrier and its employees is not settled by conference, or by an Adjustment Board's decision, or as a result of mediation, the parties may agree to submit the dispute to an arbitration board consisting of three persons or of six persons, should the parties so stipulate.[57]

Although the submission of a labor dispute to an arbitration board is strictly voluntary on the part of the carrier and its employees, once the parties agree to arbitration the Railway Labor Act specifies the conditions under which the arbitration will be held.[58]

Some of the conditions required by the statute include a written agreement between the parties that the arbitration award will be valid and binding; that the award and the evidence of the proceedings, duly certified, will be filed in the designated district court; and, when so filed, shall be final and conclusive upon the parties as to the facts determined by the award and as to the merits of the dispute.[59]

An award so filed with the designated federal district court is conclusive on the parties, as agreed, and unless within ten days after the filing of the award a petition to impeach the award is filed with the district court, the court must enter judgment on the award.[60]

[27.08] EMERGENCY PROVISIONS

Should a carrier and its employees fail to resolve a labor dispute by conference, by an Adjustment Board's decision, by mediation, or by an arbitration board's award, and should the dispute threaten substantially to interrupt interstate commerce to a degree to deprive any section of the country of essential transportation service, the National Mediation Board is required to notify the President of the United States of such dispute and its potential consequences.[61]

In turn, the President, in his or her discretion, may create an Emergency Board who must investigate promptly the facts as to the dispute and submit a report to the President within thirty days from the date of its creation.[62]

After creation of such Emergency Board and for a period of thirty days after the board has made its report to the President, the parties to the controversy are prohibited from making any change—except by written agreement—in the conditions out of which the controversy arose.[63]

NOTES TO CHAPTER 27

1. 45 U.S.C.A. §§151–163.
2. See 45 U.S.C.A. §151; see also: *California v. Taylor,* 353 U.S. 553 (1957).
3. *International Assn. of Machinists v. Central Airlines, Inc.,* 372 U.S. 682 (1963).
4. Wesley M. Wilson, *Labor Law Handbook* (New York: The Bobbs-Merrill Company, Inc., 1963), 364.
5. See 45 U.S.C.A. §151(a).
6. *International Longshoremen's Assn. v. North Carolina Ports Authority,* 463 F.2d 1 (CA-4, 1972).
7. See, for example: *Northern Air Service, Inc.,* 219 NLRB 465 (1975); *Mark Aero, Inc.,* 200 NLRB 304 (1972); and *Air California,* 17 NLRB 18 (1968).
8. See, for example: *Voyager 1000 Corp.,* 202 NLRB 901 (1973).
9. See, for example: *Missouri-Illinois Cent. Industry, Ltd.,* 252 NLRB No. 143 (1980).
10. See 45 U.S.C.A. §181; see, also *NLRB v. Interior Enterprises, Inc.,* 298 F.2d 147 (CA-9, 1961).
11. See, for example: *Mark Aero, Inc., supra.*
12. *Dobbs Houses, Inc. v. NLRB,* 443 F.2d 1066 (CA-6, 1971).
13. *Trans-East Air, Inc.,* 189 NLRB 185 (1971).
14. *Golden Nugget Motel,* 235 NLRB 1348 (1978).

15. *Arthur Frommer Enterprises, Inc.,* 241 NLRB No. 191 (1979); but compare: *Voyager 1000 Corp., supra.*

16. See *Air California, supra.*

17. 45 U.S.C.A. §152 (Fourth).

18. See Chapter 5 at [5.01].

19. 45 U.S.C.A. §152 (Fourth).

20. 45 U.S.C.A. §152 (Fifth).

21. 45 U.S.C.A. §152 (Eighth).

22. See *Aeronautical Radio, Inc. v. National Mediation Board,* 127 App. DC 77, 380 F.2d 624 (1967).

23. See 45 U.S.C.A. §152 (Ninth).

24. *United States v. Feaster,* 376 F.2d 147 (CA-5, 1967).

25. Wilson, *Labor Law Handbook,* 367.

26. Ibid.

27. *Brotherhood of Railroad & S.S. Clerks, Etc. v. Assn. for Ben. of Non-Contract Employees,* 380 U.S. 650 (1965).

28. *Brotherhood of Railroad & S.S. Clerks, Etc. v. Assn. for Ben. of Non-Contract Employees, supra.*

29. *Brotherhood of Railroad & S.S. Clerks, Etc. v. Nashville C. & St. L. R. Co.,* 94 F.2d 97 (CA-6, 1937).

30. 45 U.S.C.A. §152 (Ninth).

31. 45 U.S.C.A. §152 (Ninth).

32. 45 U.S.C.A. §152 (Ninth).

33. 45 U.S.C.A. §152 (Fourth).

34. 45 U.S.C.A. §152 (Ninth).

35. *Brotherhood of Railroad & S.S. Clerks, Etc. v. Florida, E.C.R. Co.,* 384 U.S. 238 (1966).

36. *Conley v. Gibson,* 355 U.S. 41 (1957).

37. 45 U.S.C.A. §152 (First).

38. 45 U.S.C.A. §152 (Eleventh) (a).

39. 45 U.S.C.A. §152 (Eleventh) (a).

40. *Railway Employees' Dept. v. Hanson,* 351 U.S. 225 (1956).

41. 45 U.S.C.A. §152 (Eleventh) (b).

42. 45 U.S.C.A. §152 (First).

43. 45 U.S.C.A. §152 (Second).

44. 45 U.S.C.A. §152 (First)(a)-(i).

45. *Detroit & T.S.L.R. Co. v. United Transp. Union,* 357 F.2d 152 (CA-6, 1966).

46. 45 U.S.C.A. §153 (First)(a)-(i).

47. 48 Am. Jur. 2d *Labor and Labor Relations,* §1718.

48. Ibid.

49. 45 U.S.C.A. §153 (First)(m).

50. See 45 U.S.C.A. §153 (First)(p) and (q).

51. *Gunther v. San Diego & A.E.R. Co.*, 382 U.S. 257 (1965).

52. 45 U.S.C.A. §153 (p) and (q).

53. 45 U.S.C.A. §154.

54. 45 U.S.C.A. §153 (First) and §183.

55. 45 U.S.C.A. §153 (First) and §183.

56. 45 U.S.C.A. §155 (First).

57. 45 U.S.C.A. §157 (First).

58. 45 U.S.C.A. §158.

59. 45 U.S.C.A. §158.

60. 45 U.S.C.A. §159 (Second).

61. 45 U.S.C.A. §160.

62. 45 U.S.C.A. §160.

63. 45 U.S.C.A. §160.

28

Federal Service Labor-Management Relations Act

[28.01] ORIGIN

Title VII of the Civil Service Reform Act of 1978[1] codified into the federal statutes Executive Order 11491 which had accorded federal employees the right of self-organization, the right to join or form unions, or to refrain from such activities without fear of penalty or reprisal.[2]

Thus, Title VII of the Civil Service Reform Act, frequently referred to as the Federal Service Labor-Management Relations Act (hereinafter referred to as the Federal Labor Relations Statute—FLRS), was designed to prescribe certain collective bargaining rights and obligations of federal employees and to establish procedures necessary to meet the special requirements and needs of the government.[3]

[28.02] FEDERAL LABOR RELATIONS AUTHORITY

The Federal Labor Relations Statute also created the Federal Labor Relations Authority (FLRA), which is composed of three members, not more than two of whom may be adherents of the same political party.[4] Members of the Federal Labor Relations Authority are to be appointed by the President, with the advice of the United States Senate.[5]

The FLRA is charged with the responsibility of providing leadership in establishing policies and guidance pertaining to the administration of the Act.[6] The Federal Labor Relations Authority is also authorized by the statute to appoint an executive director and such regional directors, administrative law judges, and other individuals as may be necessary to carry out the purposes of the Act.[7]

The Authority may also delegate to officers and employees such powers as are necessary to fulfill their functions.[8] Particularly, the Act authorizes the Federal Labor Relations Authority to delegate to its regional directors its authority to

- determine appropriate unit questions
- conduct investigations and to provide for hearings
- determine whether a question of representation exists and to direct a representation election
- supervise or conduct secret ballot elections and certify the results thereof[9]

The Federal Labor Relations Authority, pursuant to its authorization under the Act, has promulgated operating regulations to govern the processing of unfair labor practice, representation, grievability/arbitrability, national consultation right cases and the processing of matters before the Federal Service Impasses Panel.[10]

[28.03] COVERAGE AND EXEMPTIONS

The coverage of the Federal Labor Relations Statute extends to all individuals employed in a federal agency or whose employment has ceased in a federal agency due to an unlawful discharge in violation of the prohibited practices section of the Act, except for the following:

- Aliens or other noncitizens of the United States who occupy a position outside the United States
- Members of the uniformed services
- Supervisory or management members of federal agencies
- Officers or employees in the Foreign Service of the United States employed in the Department of State, the Agency for International Development, or the International Communication Agency
- Persons who participate in strikes in violation of the Act[11]

In addition to the specific exceptions noted above, Executive Order No. 12171 exempts certain federal agencies and/or their subdivisions from the coverage of the Act due to their intelligence, counterintelligence, investigative or national security functions.[12]

[28.04] BARGAINING RIGHTS OF FEDERAL EMPLOYEES

Similar in scope and purpose to Section 7 of the Labor-Management Relations Act,[13] the Federal Labor Relations Statute provides that

> Each employee shall have the right to form, join, or assist any labor oganization, or to refrain from such activity, freely and without fear of penalty or reprisal, and each employee shall be protected in the exercise of such right.[14]

The FLRS also provides that an employee's right to assist a labor organization extends to participating in the management of the organization and acting for the organization in the capacity of representative, including the right to present his or her views to officials of the Executive Branch, the Congress, or other appropriate authorities and to engage in collective bargaining with respect to conditions of employment through representatives of his or her own choosing.[15]

[28.05]   UNFAIR LABOR PRACTICES

The Federal Labor Relations Statute prohibits certain conduct on the part of management agencies and labor organizations in order to more fully protect the rights accorded federal employees, as noted below.[16]

Agency management: The following conduct constitutes evidence of an unfair labor practice in violation of the FLRS on the part of a federal agency:

- Interference with, or restraint or coercion of, employees in the exercise of their rights under the Act
- Encouragement or discouragement of membership in a labor organization by discriminating against individuals covered under the Act in regard to hire, tenure, promotions, or other terms or conditions of employment
- Sponsorships, control, or assistance of a labor organization, except that an agency is permitted to furnish customary and routine services and facilities when consistent with the best interests of the agency, its employees, and the organization, and when furnished on an impartial basis to organizations having equivalent status
- Discrimination or discipline imposed against an employee by reason of his or her having filed a complaint or given testimony as protected by the Act
- Refusal to consult or negotiate in good faith with a labor organization as required by the statute
- Failure or refusal to cooperate in impasse procedures and impasse decisions as required by the statute
- Enforcement of any rule or regulation which is in conflict with any applicable collective bargaining agreement, except as specifically provided in the statute; or
- Failure or refusal, in some other manner, to comply with the requirements of the Act[17]

Labor Organizations: The Federal Labor Relations Statute prohibits the following conduct of labor unions, the violations of which constitute evidence of unfair labor practices:

- Interference with, restraint, or coercion of employees in the exercise of their rights under the statute
- Attempts to induce agency management to coerce an employee in the exercise of his or her rights under the statute
- Coercion, attempts to coerce, or discipline, fine, or take other eco-

nomic sanctions against a member of a labor organization as punishment or reprisal for the purpose of hindering or impeding his or her work performance, productivity, or the discharge of his or her duties as an officer or employee of the United States

- Discrimination against an employee with regard to the terms or conditions of membership in a labor organization because of race, color, creed, sex, age or national origin
- Refusal to consult or negotiate in good faith with an agency as required by the provisions of the statute
- Refusal or failure to cooperate in impasse decisions
- Calling for or engaging in a strike, work stoppage, or slowdown; picketing an agency in a labor-management dispute; or condoning any such activity by failing to take affirmative action to prevent or stop it
- Failing or refusing to comply with the Act in any other manner[18]

Labor organizations which are accorded exclusive recognition pursuant to the provisions of the Act are prohibited from denying membership to any employee in the appropriate unit except for the failure to meet reasonable occupational standards uniformly required for admission, or for the failure to tender initiation fees and dues uniformly required as a condition of acquiring and retaining membership.[19]

[28.06]　HOW TO PROCESS AN UNFAIR LABOR PRACTICE CHARGE

The Federal Labor Relations Authority rules and regulations provide that any person may file a charge against a federal agency or labor union alleging the commission of an unfair labor practice.[20] Unfair labor practice charges are to be submitted to the local regional director of the Federal Labor Relations Authority on forms prescribed by the Authority and shall contain pertinent information required on the appropriate form.

The regional director, on behalf of the general counsel of the Federal Labor Relations Authority, shall conduct such investigation of an unfair labor practice charge as deemed necessary and, as a result of his or her investigation (1) issue a complaint, (2) refuse to issue a complaint, (3) approve a request to withdraw the charge, (4) approve a written settlement agreement to dispose of the matter, (5) transfer the matter to the Federal Labor Relations Authority for a decision, upon agreement of all the parties, or (6) withdraw a complaint previously issued.[21]

The rules and regulations of the Federal Labor Relations Authority further provide for procedures to be used in conducting a hearing on unfair labor practice charges and processing of appeals therefrom.[22]

[28.07]   REPRESENTATION ELECTIONS

The Federal Labor Relations Statute specifies that a federal agency shall accord exclusive recognition to a labor organization if the organization has been selected as the representative by a majority of the employees in an appropriate unit who cast valid ballots pursuant to a secret ballot election.[23]

The rules and regulations of the Federal Labor Relations Authority specify, among other requirements, that a petition for an election shall contain the pertinent information required on the petition form,[24] and must be accompanied by a showing of interest of not less than 30 percent of the employees in the unit claimed to be appropriate, and an alphabetical list of names constituting such showing.[25]

The FLRS, and regulations pertaining to it, provide for other types of petitions, in addition to a petition for exclusive recognition, including a

- petition for an election to determine if a labor organization should cease to be the exclusive representative because it no longer represents a majority of employees in the existing unit
- petition seeking to clarify a matter relating to representation
- petition for clarification of an existing unit
- petition for determination of eligibility for dues allotment
- petition to consolidate existing recognized units[26]

The FLRA rules also provide hearings to resolve issues flowing from various petitions filed with the Authority,[27] as well as the procedures of conducting elections.[28]

[28.08]   DETERMINATION OF BARGAINING UNITS

The Federal Labor Relations Statute provides that the Federal Labor Relations Authority shall determine whether an appropriate unit should be established on an agency, plant, installation, functional or other basis.[29]

The Federal Labor Relations Authority is to assume that the appropriate unit also constitutes a clear and identifiable community of interest among the employees affected and that its structure will promote effective dealings with, and efficiency of, the operations of the agency involved.[30]

[28.09]   NATIONAL CONSULTATION RIGHTS

In lieu of bestowing exclusive recognition upon a labor organization as a result of a secret ballot election, a federal agency may accord national consultation rights to a labor union which is the exclusive representative of a substantial number of the employees of the agency, and which labor organization meets other criteria prescribed by the FLRA.[31]

[28.10] FEDERAL SERVICE IMPASSES PANEL

The Federal Labor Relations Statute also created the Federal Service Impasses Panel which is empowered to assist in the resolution of negotiation impasses.[32]

Whenever voluntary arrangements fail to resolve a negotiation impasse, either party may request assistance of the Panel.[33] In the alternative, the parties may agree to adopt a procedure for binding arbitration, but only if the procedure is approved by the Panel.[34] The Panel may make certain recommendations to the parties or take any other action it considers necessary to settle the impasse.[35]

If the parties do not arrive at a settlement after the assistance by the Panel, the Panel is authorized by the Act to hold hearings and take whatever action is necessary, not inconsistent with the Act, to resolve the impasse.[36]

Final action taken by the Federal Service Impasses Panel to resolve a negotiation impasse between an agency and a labor organization shall be final and binding on the parties, unless the parties come to a mutual agreement otherwise.[37]

[28.11] OTHER REQUIREMENTS OF THE FLRS

The Federal Labor Relations Statute also provides for certain standards of conduct for labor organizations as a condition to being recognized as exclusive representatives of federal employees.[38] Procedures for governing grievances and arbitration matters are likewise set forth in the statute.[39]

The Federal Labor Relations Statute provides additionally that the federal agencies falling within the coverage of its provisions shall retain basic management prerogatives, irrespective of their obligation to bargain in good faith with a labor organization recognized by the Federal Labor Relations Authority as the employees' exclusive bargaining representative.[40]

NOTES TO CHAPTER 28

1. 5 U.S.C.A. §7101, *et seq.*
2. See Executive Order No. 1491.
3. 5 U.S.C.A. §7101.
4. 5 U.S.C.A. §7104(a).
5. 5 U.S.C.A. §7104(b).
6. 5 U.S.C.A. §7105.
7. 5 U.S.C.A. §7105(d).
8. 5 U.S.C.A. §7105(d).
9. 5 U.S.C.A. §7105(e)(1)(A) through (D).

10. 5 CFR Part 2400.
11. 5 U.S.C.A. §7103(2)(A) and (B) (i) through (v).
12. Executive Order 12171.
13. See [5.01] for a discussion of Section 7 of the LMRA.
14. 5 U.S.C.A. §7102.
15. 5 U.S.C.A. §7102.
16. 5 U.S.C.A. §7116.
17. 5 U.S.C.A. §7116(a)(1) through (8).
18. 5 U.S.C.A. §7116(b)(1) through (8).
19. 5 U.S.C.A. §7116(c).
20. 5 CFR §2423.3.
21. 5 CFR §2423.9.
22. 5 CFR §2423.14 through §2423.31.
23. 5 U.S.C.A. §7111.
24. 5 CFR §2422.2.(a).
25. 5 CFR §2422.2(a)(9).
26. 5 U.S.C.A. §7111(b); 5 CFR §2422.1.
27. 5 CFR §2422.8 through 16.
28. 5 CFR §2422.17 through 22.
29. 5 U.S.C.A. §7112(a)(1).
30. 5 U.S.C.A. §7112(a)(1).
31. 5 U.S.C.A. §7113.
32. 5 U.S.C.A. §7119.
33. 5 U.S.C.A. §7119(b).
34. 5 U.S.C.A. §7119(b).
35. 5 U.S.C.A. §7119(b).
36. 5 U.S.C.A. §7119(b)(5)(B).
37. 5 U.S.C.A. §7119(b)(5)(C).
38. 5 U.S.C.A. §7120.
39. 5 U.S.C.A. §7121 and §7122.
40. 5 U.S.C.A. §7106.

29

Miscellaneous Labor Relations Laws

The Norris-LaGuardia Act, enacted in 1932, forbids federal courts from granting injunctive relief to prohibit a strike or work stoppage, unless within strict compliance with the provisions of the Act.[1]

The Norris-LaGuardia Act was adopted to reverse the earlier interpretation by the federal courts of Section 20 of the Clayton Act[2] in permitting injunctions against unions in various situations.[3] As a result, the Norris-LaGuardia Act largely displaces Section 20 of the Clayton Act as the limiting force in denying power to the federal courts to issue labor injunctions.[4]

One of the more noted features of the Norris-LaGuardia Act is the prohibition against "yellow-dog" contracts. In this connection, the statute provides that a federal court has no power to enforce or grant relief based upon a contract in which individuals agree that they will not join a union during their employment.[5]

Irrespective of the general prohibition against labor injunctions as provided by the Norris-LaGuardia Act, the Supreme Court has held that the statute does not prohibit federal courts from enjoining a strike which violates a no-strike clause in a collective bargaining contract, provided three prerequisites are met:

- The strike must be in breach of a no-strike clause under a valid and current collective bargaining agreement;
- The strike must be over an arbitrable issue;
- The no-strike clause in the collective bargaining contract must provide for mandatory arbitration of the particular dispute.[6]

The Norris-LaGuardia Act does permit labor injunctions in certain other situations, provided five jurisdictional or "procedural" conditions are met:

- That unlawful acts have been threatened and will be committed unless restrained or will continue unless restrained;[7]
- That the plaintiff's property will suffer substantial and irreparable injury;[8]
- That the plaintiff has no adequate remedy at law;[9]
- That greater injury will be inflicted upon the plaintiff by the denial of the relief than will be inflicted upon the defendant by the granting of it;[10]

• That police or other public officers are unable or unwilling to furnish adequate protection for plaintiff's property.[11]

[29.02]   FEDERAL MEDIATION AND CONCILIATION SERVICE

Title II of the Labor Management Relations Act provides for the creation of an independent mediation agency, known as the Federal Mediation and Conciliation Service.[12] This service is directed by the Federal Mediation and Conciliation Director, a presidential appointee.[13]

The Federal Mediation and Conciliation Service has the primary function of lending assistance in the settlement of labor disputes through the process of conciliation and mediation.[14]

The Federal Mediation and Conciliation Service may offer its services in any labor dispute in any industry affecting commerce on its own motion or on the request of one of the parties to the dispute.[15]

As a means to make available the services of the agency and attempt to avoid strikes that might cause a substantial interruption of commerce, Section 8(d) of the Labor Management Relations Act requires a party desiring termination or modification of a collective bargaining contract to give the Federal Mediation and Conciliation Service proper notice, as was previously discussed at [13.03].

If conciliation and mediation does not bring about an agreement within a reasonable time, the agency must seek to induce the parties voluntarily to seek other means of settling the dispute, including submission to the employees of the employer's last offer of settlement for approval or rejection in a secret ballot, as a means to avoid a strike, lockout, or other self-help on the part of the parties.[16]

However, since the utilization of the Federal Mediation and Conciliation Service is strictly voluntary, neither party to a labor dispute is required to agree to or accept the agency's recommendations or suggestions during the mediation and conciliation process.[17]

Another function provided by the Federal Mediation and Conciliation Service is its assistance in the selection of arbitrators to parties to a labor dispute. Arbitrators on the Federal Mediation and Conciliation Service roster are not employees of the federal government, but rather are independent arbitrators qualified and accepted under the agency's standards of ethics.[18]

National labor management panel: The Labor Management Relations Act, as part of the federal conciliation machinery, also created a National Labor-Management Panel, composed of six labor and six management representatives.

This panel has the duty, at the request of the Federal Mediation and Conciliation Service Director, to advise on the avoidance of industrial controversies and the manner in which mediation and voluntary adjustment is to be administered, especially with regard to controversies that might affect the general welfare of the nation.[19]

National emergency strikes: Ancillary to the provisions creating the Federal Mediation and Conciliation machinery is a provision of the Labor Management Relations Act which declares that the President of the United States may, whenever in his or her opinion a threatened or actual strike or lockout will imperil the national health or safety, appoint a Board of Inquiry to investigate the issues involved in the dispute and to make a written report to the President containing the board's recommendations.[20]

Upon reception of the Board of Inquiry's recommendations, the President may, through the U.S. Attorney General, petition a federal district court to enjoin the threatened or actual dispute for a period not in excess of eighty days.[21]

If an injunction is granted and the dispute is not settled within sixty days thereafter, the National Labor Relations Board must take a secret ballot within fifteen days to determine whether the employees wish to accept the employer's last offer.[22] Within five days after the election, the NLRB is to certify the results of the election to the Attorney General, who then has the duty of asking the court to dissolve the injunction.[23]

[29.03] TITLE III, LABOR MANAGEMENT RELATIONS ACT

Section 301 suits for breach of contract: Section 301 of the Labor Management Relations Act confers original jurisdiction on the federal district courts to entertain a lawsuit for the violation of a collective bargaining contract between an employer and a union representing employees in an industry affecting commerce.[24] Suits for violation of contracts between unions may also be brought in a federal district court pursuant to Section 301 of the LMRA.[25]

The NLRB's preemption doctrine[26] is usually irrelevant in a Section 301 suit for violation of a collective bargaining contract.[27] Should, in fact, a defendant's conduct constitute both a breach of a collective bargaining contract and an unfair labor practice, both federal district courts and the NLRB have jurisdiction to remedy the violation in their own respective forums.[28]

State courts have concurrent jurisdiction with federal district courts over actions brought for violations of collective bargaining agreements.[29]

Section 302 restrictions on payments to union representatives: Section 302 of the Labor Management Relations Act outlines certain criminal sanctions that may be imposed upon employees, unions, and individuals who violate guidelines restricting payments, agreements to make payments, or lending by employers or representatives of employers to a labor organization or any officer or employee of a labor organization.[30]

Section 303 suits for unlawful secondary boycotts: Section 303(a) of the Labor Management Relations Act provides that it shall be unlawful for any labor organization to engage in any of the secondary boycott activities defined as an unfair labor practice in Section 8(b)(4) of the Act.[31]

Section 303(b) of the LMRA provides that whoever is injured in his or her business or property by reason of such forbidden secondary boycott activities may sue therefor in any federal district court, subject to the limitations and provisions of Section 301 of the Act, without respect to the amount in controversy and shall recover the damages sustained and the cost of the suit.[32] State courts have concurrent jurisdiction with federal district courts over Section 303(b) actions, assuming the state court has jurisdiction of the parties.[33]

Although injunctive relief is typically accorded parties in 301 suits for breach of a collective bargaining contract,[34] federal and state courts are not permitted to enjoin secondary boycott activities in Section 303(b) actions in deference to the Norris-LaGuardia prohibitions against labor injunctions.[35] Individuals seeking injunctive relief against secondary boycotts may file an unfair labor practice charge with the NLRB and request the Board to apply for injunctive relief under its Section 10 provisions.[36]

Prohibition against strikes by government employees: Federal statutes provide that it shall be unlawful for any individual employed by the United States or any agency thereof to participate in any strike.[37] It further provides that any such employee who strikes shall be subject to immediate dismissal, shall forfeit his or her civil service status, and shall not be eligible for reemployment for three years by the federal government or any such agency.[38]

Section 313 prohibition against political contributions: Section 313 of the Labor Management Relations Act makes it a criminal offense for a corporation organized by authority of any law of Congress, a national bank, a labor organization, or any officer of a corporation or a union to make certain political contributions.

[29.04] POSTAL SERVICE LABOR RELATIONS

As a result of the Postal Reorganization Act of 1970, and to the extent not inconsistent with the provisions thereof, employee-management relations of the Postal Service are subject to the provisions of the Labor Management Relations Act.[39]

The Postal Reorganization Act specifies that the National Labor Relations Board will determine the appropriate units for collective bargaining, and set forth certain exclusions from bargaining units.[40]

The procedures for conducting and certifying the results of a secret ballot election of postal employees is not dissimilar from that used in other

NLRB elections.[41] Also, the unfair labor practice provisions of the National Labor Relations Act generally apply to Postal Service Labor relations.[42]

The Postal Reorganization Act provides that any collective bargaining agreements between the Postal Service and any recognized bargaining representative shall be effective for not less than two years.[43]

Collective bargaining agreements may provide for procedures for the resolution of disputes arising under the terms of such agreements, including procedures culminating in binding third-party arbitration.[44] The parties to such an agreement may also adopt procedures for the resolution of disputes or impasses arising in the negotiation of a collective bargaining agreement.[45]

Unresolved disputes must be resolved in some manner other than by self-help as the Postal Reorganization Act did not remove the ban against strikes which applies to all federal employees, including postal workers.[46]

[29.05] ANTI-RACKETEERING (HOBBS) ACT

The Anti-Racketeering Act, sometimes referred to as the Hobbs Act, makes it a felony to obstruct, delay, or affect commerce or the movement of any article or commodity by robbery or extortion.[47]

The Hobbs Act further provides that it is unlawful to conspire to do any of the above or to commit or threaten physical violence to any person or property in furtherance of any plan to commit such violation.[48] The Act is enforced through the U.S. Department of Justice.[49] Violators of the Act are subject to fines and imprisonment.[50]

Although the Act was enacted to punish interference with interstate commerce by extortion, robbery, or physical violence,[51] the U.S. Supreme Court has held that the Hobbs Act does not apply to strikers who damage an employer's property in an effort to obtain higher wages and other benefits since higher wages and benefits in return for genuine services of workers do not fall within the definition of "property" under the Act.[52]

[29.06] ANTI-STRIKEBREAKER'S (BYRNES) ACT

The Anti-Strikebreaker's Act, also known as the Byrnes Act, makes it a felony to transport in interstate commerce, any person employed for the purpose of interfering by force or threats with

- peaceful picketing by employees during any labor dispute, or
- the exercise of employees' rights of self-organization or collective bargaining.[53]

The Act applies to both strikebreakers who have knowledge of the purpose of their employment as well as to those persons willfully transporting them for strike-breaking purposes.[54] Violators are subject to fines and imprisonment and are prosecuted by the U.S. Attorney General.[55]

NOTES TO CHAPTER 29

1. 29 U.S.C.A. §§101–115.
2. 29 U.S.C.A. §52.
3. *Milk Wagon Drivers' Union v. Lake Valley Farm Products,* 22 U.S. 91 (1940).
4. *Wilson & Co. v. Birl,* 105 F.2d 948 (CA-3, 1939).
5. 29 U.S.C.A. §103.
6. *Boys Market, Inc. v. Retail Clerks Union,* 398 U.S. 235 (1970).
7. 29 U.S.C.A. §107(a).
8. 29 U.S.C.A. §107(b).
9. 29 U.S.C.A. §107(d).
10. 29 U.S.C.A. §107(c).
11. 29 U.S.C.A. §107(e).
12. 29 U.S.C.A. §172(a).
13. 29 U.S.C.A. §172(a).
14. 29 U.S.C.A. §173(a).
15. 29 U.S.C.A. §173(b).
16. 29 U.S.C.A. §173(c).
17. 29 U.S.C.A. §173(c).
18. 29 CFR §1404.2(a).
19. 29 U.S.C.A. §175.
20. 29 U.S.C.A. §§176–180
21. See 29 U.S.C.A. §178 and §179.
22. 29 U.S.C.A. §179(b).
23. 29 U.S.C.A. §179(b).
24. 29 U.S.C.A. §185.
25. 29 U.S.C.A. §185.
26. See Chapter 4 for a discussion on the Preemption Doctrine.
27. *Teamsters, Chauffeurs, Warehousemen & Helpers v. Lucas Flour Co.,* 69 U.S. 95 (1962).
28. See *Nuest v. Westinghouse Air Brake Co.,* 313 F.Supp. 1228 (SD Ill., 1970).
29. *Charles Dowd Box Co. v. Courtney,* 368 U.S. 502 (1962).
30. 29 U.S.C.A. §186.
31. 29 U.S.C.A. §187(a).
32. 29 U.S.C.A. §187(b).

33. *Teamsters, Chauffeurs & Helpers Union v. Morton,* 377 U.S. 252 (1964).

34. See for example: *Injunctions to Compel Arbitrators* (29–09).

35. *Sinclair Refining Co. v. Atkinson,* 370 U.S. 195 (1962).

36. See *Douglas v. International Brotherhood of Electrical Workers Union,* 136 F.Supp. 68 (DC Mich., 1955).

37. 5 U.S.C.A. §3333; 5 U.S.C.A. §7311.

38. 5 U.S.C.A. §3333; 5 U.S.C.A. §7311.

39. 39 U.S.C.A. §1209.

40. 39 U.S.C.A. §1202.

41. 39 U.S.C.A. §1204.

42. 39 U.S.C.A. §1209.

43. 39 U.S.C.A. §1206(a).

44. 39 U.S.C.A. §1206(b).

45. 39 U.S.C.A. §1206(c).

46. 39 U.S.C.A. §410(b).

47. 18 U.S.C.A. §1951.

48. 18 U.S.C.A. §1951.

49. 18 U.S.C.A. §1951.

50. 18 U.S.C.A. §1951.

51. *Stirone v. United States,* 361 U.S. 212 (1960).

52. *U.S. v. Emmons,* 410 U.S. 396 (1973).

53. 18 U.S.C.A. §1231.

54. 18 U.S.C.A. §1231.

55. 18 U.S.C.A. §1231.

PART II

FEDERAL ANTI-DISCRIMINATION LAWS AND EXECUTIVE ORDERS

30

Civil Rights Act of 1964, Title VII

[30.01] HISTORICAL DEVELOPMENT

Title VII of the Civil Rights Act of 1964[1] (hereinafter referred to as Title VII or the Act) forbids discrimination in all areas of the employer-employee relationship when based on race, color, sex, religion, or national origin.[2]

Title VII also prohibits employment agencies, unions, and joint labor-management training committees from discriminating on the basis of such protected characteristics.[3]

The purpose of Title VII is to require the removal of artificial, arbitrary, and unnecessary barriers to employment when such impediments operate invidiously to discriminate against individuals on the basis of racial or other impermissible classifications.[4]

Title VII of the Civil Rights of Act 1964 was amended in 1972 by the Equal Employment Opportunity Act.[5] The 1972 amendments extended coverage of the original Act to employees of state and local government, governmental agencies, political subdivisions, and departments and agencies of the District of Columbia, with certain exceptions.[6] The 1972 amendments also included special provisions which require the federal government to apply personnel actions without regard to race, color, sex, religion, or national origin.[7]

[30.02] ADMINISTRATION OF THE ACT

The Equal Employment Opportunity Commission (EEOC) is charged with the administration and enforcement of the Act.[8]

The EEOC is composed of five members who are appointed by the president by and with the advice and consent of the United States Senate.[9] The president designates one member to serve as chairman or chairwoman.[10] Each member is appointed to a five-year term.[11]

Inasmuch as the 1972 amendments to Title VII of the Civil Rights Act of 1964 empowered the EEOC to litigate as well as conciliate unfair employment practices, an office of the General Counsel was created to exercise that power.[12]

To assist in the administration and enforcement of Title VII, the EEOC has established district offices throughout the United States.

The EEOC has as its main function the processing of unfair employment practices and has been given the responsibility of

- receiving written charges of discrimination against employers, labor organizations, joint labor-management apprenticeship programs, and employment agencies[13]

- self-initiating charges of discrimination by members of the commission[14]

- investigating charges of unfair employment practices[15]

- instituting an action in federal district court for appropriate temporary or preliminary relief pending final disposition of a charge, should a preliminary investigation of a charge warrant such action[16]

- determining if there is reasonable cause to believe that a charge of discrimination is true following its investigation of the charge[17]

- attempting to eliminate the alleged unlawful practice through conciliation, should it find reasonable cause to believe the charge of discrimination is true[18]

- bringing an action in federal district court at the discretion of the members of the commission or, in the alternative, issuing a notice of right to sue to the charging party following the administrative processing of the unfair employment practice charge[19]

The EEOC publishes data on the employment status of minorities and women derived from six employment surveys[20] (EEO-1 through EEO-6). These reports cover employment practice data from employers, apprenticeship programs, labor organizations, state and local governments, elementary and secondary schools, and colleges and universities.[21]

In addition to its duty to administer and enforce Title VII of the Civil Rights Act of 1964, the EEOC has acquired enforcement powers relative to both the Equal Pay Act and the Age Discrimination in Employment Act as a result of the Presidential Reorganization Plan No. 1 of 1978.

[30.03]   TITLE VII COVERAGE

An *employer* falls under the jurisdiction of Title VII of the Civil Rights Act of 1964 if:

- He or she has fifteen or more employees;
- His or her employees have been employed for each working day in each of twenty or more calendar weeks in the current or preceding calendar year;
- He or she is engaged in an industry affecting commerce.[22]

Title VII defines *employee* as an individual employed by an employer covered by the Act, although it specifically excludes from coverage any individuals elected to public office in any state or political subdivison of any state by the qualified voters thereof, or immediate officers or advisors to such elected officials.[23] However, it is not necessary that a person be an employee in order to be protected by Title VII inasmuch as the Act prohibits discrimination not only by employers but by unions, employment agencies, apprenticeship programs, and even potential employers.[24]

Title VII regards an *employment agency* falling within its coverage as any person regularly undertaking, with or without compensation, to procure employees for an employer or to procure for employees the opportunities to work for an employer. It also includes an agent of such a person.[25]

Title VII defines a *labor union* falling within its coverage as any organization, agency, or employee representation committee, group, or association in which employees participate and which exists for the purpose of dealing with employees concerning grievances, labor disputes, wages, rates of pay, hours, or other terms or conditions of employment.

[30.04] DISCRIMINATION BY EMPLOYERS

Title VII provides that it is an unlawful employment practice for an *employer* to

- fail or refuse to hire or to discharge any individual, or otherwise to discriminate against any individual with respect to his or her compensation, terms, conditions, or privileges of employment, because of such individual's race, color, religion, sex, or national origin; or

- limit, segregate, or classify his or her employees or applicants for employment in any way which would deprive or tend to deprive any individual of employment opportunities or otherwise adversely affect his or her status as an employee, because of such individual's race, color, religion, sex, or national origin.[26]

[30.05] DISCRIMINATION BY LABOR UNIONS

Title VII specifies that it is an unlawful employment practice for a *labor union* to

- exclude or expel from its membership or otherwise to discriminate against, any individual because of his or her race, color, religion, sex, or national origin;

- limit, segregate, or classify its membership or applicants for membership, or to classify or to fail or refuse to refer for employment, any individual, in any way which would deprive or tend to deprive any individual of employment opportunities, or would limit such employment opportunities or otherwise adversely affect his or her status as an employee or as an applicant for employment, because of such individual's race, color, religion, sex, or national origin; or

- cause or attempt to cause an employer to discriminate against an individual in violation of Title VII.[27]

[30.06] DISCRIMINATION BY EMPLOYMENT AGENCIES

Title VII makes it an unlawful employment practice for an *Employment Agency* to

- fail or refuse to refer for employment, or otherwise to discriminate against any individual, because of his or her race, color, religion, sex, or national origin; or
- classify or refer for employment any individual on the basis of his or her race, color, religion, sex, or national origin.[28]

[30.07] DISCRIMINATION BY LABOR-MANAGEMENT TRAINING COMMITTEES

Title VII declares it be an unlawful employment practice for a *labor-man-agement training committee* to discriminate against any individual because of his or her race, color, religion, sex, or national origin in admission to, or employment in, any program established to provide apprenticeship or other training.[29] Unions and employers are likewise prohibited from such conduct.[30]

[30.08] RETALIATION PROHIBITED

Title VII also provides that it shall be an unlawful employment practice for an employer, employment agency, labor-management training committee or a labor union to discriminate against the respective employees, applicants, members, or other related individuals because of their opposition to an unlawful employment practice or because of their filing a charge, testifying, assisting, or participating in any manner in an investigation, proceeding, or hearing under the Act.[31]

[30.09] DISCRIMINATORY PUBLICATIONS PROHIBITED

Title VII declares it to be an unlawful employment practice for an employer, labor union, employment agency, or labor-management training committee to print or publish, or to cause to be printed or published, any notice or advertisement which indicates any preference, limitation, specification, or discrimination with respect to race, color, religion, sex, or national origin.[32]

However, a notice or advertisement which indicates a preference, limitation, specification, or discrimination based on religion, sex, or national origin may be permissible if religion, sex, or national origin is a bona fide occupational qualification for employment.[33]

[30.10]   DISPARATE IMPACT VERSUS DISPARATE TREATMENT

The EEOC distinguishes employer policies that are discriminatory "on their face" (disparate treatment) from rules or policies that are facially neutral but nonetheless have a disproportionate impact on minorities and other members of a protected group under the Act (disparate impact).

Employers who enforce policies and rules that adversely impact upon protected class employees or directly discriminate against protected class employees violate Title VII.

NOTES TO CHAPTER 30

1. 42 U.S.C.A. §2000E through 2000E-17.
2. See generally, 42 U.S.C.A. §2000e-2 and 3.
3. See generally, 42 U.S.C.A. §2000e-2 and 3.
4. *Griggs v. Duke Power Co.*, 401 U.S. 424 (1971).
5. P.L. 92-261 (Mar. 24, 1972) 86 Stat. 103.
6. 42 U.S.C.A. §2000e(a) and (b).
7. 42 U.S.C.A. §2000e-16(a).
8. 42 U.S.C.A. §2000e-4 and 5.
9. 42 U.S.C.A. §2000e-4(a).
10. 42 U.S.C.A. §2000e-4(a).
11. 42 U.S.C.A. §2000e-4(a).
12. 42 U.S.C.A. §2000-4(b).
13. 42 U.S.C.A. §2000e-4(f); 42 U.S.C.A. §2000-5(b).
14. 42 U.S.C.A. §2000e-5(b).
15. 42 U.S.C.A. §2000e-5(b).
16. 42 U.S.C.A. §2000e-5(f)(2).
17. 42 U.S.C.A. §2000e-5(b).
18. 42 U.S.C.A. §2000e-5(b).
19. 42 U.S.C.A. §2000e-5(f)(1).
20. *U.S. Government Manual*, 518 (1979-1980).
21. Ibid.
22. 42 U.S.C.A. §2000e(b).
23. 42 U.S.C.A. §2000e(f).
24. *Hackett v. McGuire Bros., Inc.*, 445 F.2d 442 (CA-3, 1971).
25. 42 U.S.C.A. §2000e(c).
26. 42 U.S.C.A. §2000e-2(a).
27. 42 U.S.C.A. §2000e-2(c).

28. 42 U.S.C.A. §2000e-2(b).
29. 42 U.S.C.A. §2000e-2(d).
30. 42 U.S.C.A. §2000e-2(d).
31. 42 U.S.C.A. §2000e-3(a).
32. 42 U.S.C.A. §2000e-2(a).
33. 42 U.S.C.A. §2000e-3(b).

31
Unfair
Employment Practices

[31.01] HIRING

Title VII of the Civil Rights Act of 1964 prohibits discrimination in recruiting and hiring based on race, color, sex, religion, or national origin.[1]

In 1978, the EEOC issued its Uniform Guidelines on Employee Selection Procedures. The focal point of the Uniform Guidelines is to eliminate hiring criteria that have an adverse or disparate impact upon members of a protected class under Title VII. The Uniform Guidelines specify that there is no adverse impact if the worst-performing group (the protected class in question) is achieving at a rate 80 percent as well as the best performing group. This is frequently referred to as the "80 percent" rule.

The Uniform Guidelines also adopt a "bottom line" approach to determine if adverse impact exists. The "bottom line" standard recognizes that whenever there exists a number of selection criteria for making a hiring decision, the investigating agency will look to the end result of all of them when assessing the "adverse impact" question.[2]

The federal courts have not placed the same reliance on the Uniform Guidelines as has the EEOC. For example, the "bottom line" test has been partially rejected in a decision by the Supreme Court.[3] Other federal courts have been even more unkind in their failure to rely upon the Uniform Guidelines.[4]

[31.02] JOB-RELATEDNESS STANDARD

Title VII prohibits job requirements that have a disparate impact on individuals as a result of their protected characteristics under the Act, unless the employer can show that the job requirement is job-related.

Some of the job qualifications that have been sources of EEOC litigation, not only with respect to hiring, but also with regard to other employment practices, include the following:

Education: As a general rule, the extent to which an employer may use education as a job requirement varies with the public's interest of health and safety in the performance of the job.[5] For example, a requirement of a high school diploma for employment may be unlawful if job relatedness is not shown and the use of such a job qualification has a disparate impact on groups of employees protected by the Act.[6]

Health requirements: An employer is permitted to reject a prospective employee who fails a physical examination for a particular job as long as the physical impairment or disability would prevent the applicant from performing the job functions.[7]

Strength requirement: An employer may reject an applicant who fails a strength test if strength is a bona fide, job-related qualification, since such a test is not used in the abstract but rather measures the individual for the job.[8]

Height or weight requirements: Height and weight specifications which deny equal employment opportunity to all groups of employees who are protected by Title VII are unlawful unless such qualifications are necessary to the performance of the job in question.[9]

Work experience: An employer may require previous work experience as a valid and relevant job requirement as long as it relates to the successful performance of the job in question[10] or is recognized as a business necessity.[11]

Appearance and dress requirements: As a general rule, an employer may not reject an applicant for employment because his or her appearance is typical of minority employees.[12] However, an employer's grooming regulations do not violate Title VII even though the prescribed dress standards may differ somewhat for male and female as long as the dress requirements are reasonably related to an employer's needs and find some justification in commonly accepted social norms.[13]

Hair requirements: Although there appear to be mixed rulings from the federal district courts on the issue, the EEOC generally considers it a violation of Title VII whenever an employer's grooming code requires men to have different hair styles from women.[14] However, the trend of the courts reflects a tendency to be less restrictive on such hair regulations if they have no significant effect on the employment opportunities of one sex in favor of the other.[15]

Credit requirements: The EEOC regards an employer's requirement that a job applicant have a good credit record unlawful as a job qualification unless business necessity is shown on the part of the employer, inasmuch as such a requirement has a disparate impact on minorities.[16]

Arrest and criminal records: Because of the disproportionate impact on blacks, the EEOC considers a requirement that applicants have no previous arrest records as an unlawful job qualification, unless it can be shown that such requirement is necessary to the operation of the employer's business.[17] Likewise, the refusal to hire an applicant on the basis that such applicant has been convicted of a crime may be unlawful unless the employer is able to show that he or she has first considered the circumstances surrounding the particular case and the employment of such applicant would be inconsistent with the safe and efficient operation of the business.[18]

Military record: An employer who disqualifies an applicant because he or she has received a less-than-honorable discharge from the military may be guilty of unlawful discrimination unless the employer can show that such rejection of the applicant is related to job performance.[19]

Alienage: The EEOC guidelines provide that citizenship requirements are unlawful job qualifications whenever they have the purpose or effect of discriminating against an individual on the basis of national origin.[20]

Language requirements: Proficiency in English as a job requirement may be unlawful as having an adverse impact with respect to national origin unless business necessity or job relatedness is shown.[21]

No-spouse requirements: Generally, an employer's policy against hiring the spouse of an employee has been held lawful under the Act.[22] However, such a rule must be neutral as to sex. An employer's policy forbidding the hiring of wives of employees but not forbidding the hiring of husbands has been held as unlawful.[23]

Marriage status: An employer's policy which prohibits the hiring of married women but does not forbid the employment of married men is unlawful under Title VII.[24]

Dependents' status: Generally, an employer may not lawfully refuse employment to a female applicant on the basis that she has children of preschool age when no such requirement exists for male applicants with preschool age children.[25] Also, it has been held unlawful for an employer to refuse to hire an applicant on the basis that she is an unwed mother, since such a requirement has no relation to job performance or business necessity and would disproportionately affect female applicants.[26]

Pregnancy: By virtue of an amendment to Title VII in 1978, an employer may not discriminate against women affected by pregnancy, childbirth, or related medical conditions, even in its hiring practices.[27]

Sex status: It is unlawful for an employer to limit a certain job to males only,[28] or to females only,[29] unless the employer can show that such requirement is a bona fide occupational qualification.[30]

National origin: An employer may not lawfully reject an applicant because of his or her national origin unless a bona fide occupational qualification is established.[31]

Religious convictions: An employer must make reasonable accommodations to the religious needs of prospective employees and may not reject them from employment because of their religious needs unless such accommodations would create an undue hardship on the conduct of the employer's business.[32]

Age requirements: Although employment discrimination on account of age between 40 and 70 violates the Age Discrimination in Employment Act, age restrictions in employment may also violate Title VII where such restrictions apply only to employees within a protected class under the Act.[33]

[31.03] METHODS OF RECRUITMENT

Recruiting practices that grant a preference to friends or relatives of current employees may constitute a violation of Title VII where minority employees are underrepresented in the employer's work force.[34] Similarly, the use of referrals from word-of-mouth recruiting may violate Title VII whenever the employer's work force is underrepresented with employees from the protected classifications within the Act.[35]

[31.04] TESTING

If a test or other selection procedure adversely affects a disproportionate number of persons protected by Title VII, it is an unlawful selection method unless

- the test or procedure is related to the successful peformance of the job in question, or
- its use is necessary to the operation of the employer's business.[36]

The EEOC requires a test or other selection procedure to be validated as a means to determine job relatedness when such test or procedure has an adverse impact on groups of employees protected by the Act.[37]

A test or other selection procedure will be regarded as having an adverse impact on persons protected by Title VII where its selection rate for any race, sex, or ethnic group is less than four-fifths of the rate for the group with the highest rate.[38]

The EEOC has accepted three methods of validating selection tests:[39]

- *Criterion-related validation.* This method compares identifiable criteria with successful job performance.[40]
- *Construct validation.* This method requires identification of general mental and psychological traits necessary to the successful performance of the job and the testing of applicants to determine if they possess such traits.[41]
- *Content validation.* This method uses tests which closely duplicate the actual duties to be performed on the job.[42]

[31.05] PRE-EMPLOYMENT INQUIRIES

Although Title VII does not expressly prohibit pre-employment inquiries into an applicant's race, color, sex, religion, or national origin, the utilization of such questions may constitute a violation of the Act unless business necessity or bona fide occupational qualification is shown.[43]

Pre-employment inquiries relating to credit ratings, arrest records, or military service and other criteria as discussed at [31.02], which have a disproportionate adverse impact on minorities, tend to have a "chilling effect" on the willingness of minorities to seek employment, and may violate Title VII unless job relatedness is shown.[44]

The EEOC does not require that all applicants be called in for an interview.[45] Nonetheless, an employer must conduct those interviews granted in a nondiscriminatory manner and in accordance with objective and standardized guidelines for evaluating the applicant's qualifications.[46]

[31.06] PREFERENTIAL TREATMENT

Assignments: An employer's assignment of minority employees to less desirable or low opportunity jobs while assigning white employees to high opportunity or more desirable jobs without regard to qualifications is an unlawful employment practice in violation of Title VII.[47] Sex-segregated job classifications, absent business necessity or bona fide occupational qualification, is likewise discriminatory under Title VII.[48]

Employers who assign employees on the basis of their customer's preference violate Title VII if such assignment would not have occurred but for the employee's race, color, sex, religion, or national origin.[49]

An employer also violates Title VII by denying overtime work to female employees while permitting male employees to work overtime.[50] Moreover, neither long working hours[51] nor jobs requiring heavy lifting[52] constitute bona fide occupational qualifications sufficient to justify exclusion of female employees from certain jobs.

Transfers and promotions: An employer who fails to give employees equal access to promotional opportunities[53] or transfer rights[54] violates Title VII if such action results in discrimination against a person protected by the Act and the employer has no business justification for his or her decision.

The failure to post job vacancies of high opportunity jobs may constitute a violation of Title VII, should such a failure preclude qualified minorities from receiving a potential promotion.[55]

Subjective criteria, such as adaptability, bearing, demeanor, verbal expression, maturity, drive, etc., may also indicate unlawful job-bias in the selection of employees for promotion or transfer.[56]

Compensation: An employer violates Title VII if he or she discriminates against any employee with respect to wages or benefits because of such employee's race, color, sex, religion, or national origin.[57]

Thus, it is a violation of Title VII for an employer to pay nonwhite employees less than white employees for work requiring substantially equal skill and responsibility.[58] It is also an unlawful employment practice for an employer to differentiate in the amount of call-in pay or Christmas bonus paid to minority employees.[59]

Seniority: An employer is permitted under Title VII to apply different standards of compensation or different terms, conditions, or privileges or employment pursuant to a bona fide seniority system, if such differences are not the result of an intention to discriminate against persons protected by the Act.[60]

A facially neutral seniority system which allows the continuation of pre-Title VII seniority rights, although discriminately applied during the pre-Act period, is not a *per se* violation of the Act, even absent a showing of business necessity.[61]

Departmental or craft seniority is permissible under Title VII provided the system is neutral in operation as to persons protected by the Act, is in accord with industry practice, and the distinction between the jobs in question is rational.[62]

The maintenance of a sex-segregated seniority system constitutes an unlawful employment practice absent a showing of a bona fide occupational qualification.[63] Similarly, dual lines of progression through which employees move up or down are unlawful when one line of progression is used for white employees and the other for black employees.[64]

It is improper for a court to override a bona fide seniority system in favor of affirmative action unless there is a judicial finding of discrimination.[65]

[31.07] DISCHARGE AND DISCIPLINE

An employer violates Title VII if he or she discharges an employee because of race, color, sex, religion, or national origin.[66] Thus, work rules which might otherwise justify discharge if applied equally to all employees become violative of Title VII when used pretextually to mask racial or ethnic discrimination.[67] However, the Act does not insulate persons protected by Title VII from discharge for just cause due to such factors as failure to carry out reasonable job assignments,[68] poor work performance,[69] excessive absenteeism,[70] or fighting on the job.[71]

An employer violates Title VII by making conditions of continued employment so intolerable toward an employee because of his or her race, color, sex, religion, or national origin that the individual quits the job.[72]

[31.08] BIAS-FREE WORK ATMOSPHERE

Employers subject to Title VII must maintain a working environment free of racial, sex, religious, or ethnic harassment.[73]

Although an employer may not be held strictly accountable for the bigotry or prejudice of employees, the employer is under a duty to take reasonable measures to attempt to control or eliminate overt expressions of harassment in the work place.[74]

Also, an employer is required under Title VII to treat persons protected by the Act on a basis equal to other employees relative to such working conditions as rest and break periods,[75] social and recreational activities provided for employees,[76] eating facilities,[77] restrooms,[78] and so forth.

[31.09] REVERSE DISCRIMINATION

Reverse discrimination is somewhat of a misnomer inasmuch as Title VII was designed to eliminate all discrimination in employment because of race, color, sex, religion, or national origin.[79] Indeed, federal courts have granted relief under Title VII to males, as well as to females,[80] and to whites, as well as blacks.[81]

However, judicial decisions have coined the term "reverse discrimination" and have generally defined the concept to be a policy or practice which favors or prefers females or minorities over males or nonminorities.[82]

Many lawsuits of "reverse discrimination" have attacked affirmative action policies that, in some manner, provide preferential treatment to females and blacks.[83] Notwithstanding, the U.S. Supreme Court has held that employers and unions in the private sector may voluntarily take affirmative action "to eliminate manifest racial imbalances in traditionally segregated job categories" without violating Title VII.[84]

[31.10] STATE PROTECTIVE STATUTES

State protective statutes typically prohibit or limit the employment of females in certain occupations such as in jobs requiring night work, overtime, lifting weights exceeding certain prescribed limits, and so forth.[85] Such state statutes, when in conflict with provisions or policies of the EEOC, are invalid and may not be used as a defense to Title VII claims.[86]

[31.11] UNLAWFUL UNION PRACTICES

A union can be guilty of committing an unlawful employment practice as well as an employer under Title VII.

For example, a union has an affirmative duty to ensure compliance with Title VII and its ratification or acquiescence in an employer's discriminatory employment practice is sufficient to render it liable under Title VII for a breach of such duty.[87]

A union must also be nondiscriminatory in its membership requirements and violates Title VII by suspending, expelling, or excluding an individual from membership because of race, color, religion, sex, or national origin.[88] A union also commits an unlawful employment practice under Title VII when it discriminates against individuals in the handling of grievances and arbitration cases because of their protected characteristics under the Act.[89]

A union violates Title VII when it discriminates in its recruitment practices,[90] job referrals,[91] or maintenance of segregated locals[92] because of race, color, sex, religion, or national origin.

A union is not permitted to waive or bargain away its members' rights guaranteed by Title VII in the negotiation of a collective bargaining contract.[93] Nor may unions require the payment of union dues by an employee pursuant to a union security clause in a collective bargaining contract if such requirement would violate the employee's religious convictions, although such an objecting employee may be required to pay a sum equal to the union's periodic dues to a nonreligious or nonlabor charity in lieu thereof.[94]

[31.12] UNLAWFUL APPRENTICESHIP PRACTICES

A union violates Title VII by refusing to accept females as apprentice trainees because of their sex,[95] or by refusing to accept black applicants into an apprenticeship program because of their race.[96]

It is a violation of Title VII for a union or joint apprenticeship committee to establish qualifications for membership in an apprenticeship program that do not bear a reasonable relationship to the skills required on the job if such qualifications have a disproportionate impact on groups protected by the Act.[97]

It is also an unlawful practice under Title VII for a union or joint apprenticeship committee to apply to minorities more stringent qualifications or standards than those applied to whites.[98]

NOTES TO CHAPTER 31

1. See 42 U.S.C.A. §2000e-2(a).
2. Kenneth J. McCullock, *Selecting Employees Safely Under the Law* (Englewood Cliffs, NJ: Prentice-Hall, Inc., 1981), 24–26.
3. *Connecticut v. Teal*, 457 U.S. 440 (1982).
4. See, for example: *Washington v. Kroger Co.*, 671 F.2d 1072 (CA-8,1982).
5. See *Townsend v. Nassau County Medical Center*, 558 F.2d 117 (CA-2, 1977).
6. *Griggs v. Duke Power Co.*. 401 U.S. 424 (1971).
7. See, for example: *Dorcus v. Westvaco Corp.*, 345 F.Supp. 1173 (DC VA., 1972).
8. *Dothard v. Rawlinson*, 433 U.S. 321 (1977).
9. *Davis v. County of Los Angeles*, 566 F.2d 1334 (CA-9, 1977).
10. *Griggs v. Duke Power Co.*, *supra*.
11. *Spurlock v. United Airlines, Inc.*, 475 F.2d 216 (CA-10, 1972).

12. See, for example: *EEOC Decision No. 70-90* (1969), *CCH EEOC Decisions Para. 6065.*

13. *Carroll v. Talman Federal Sav. & Loan Assoc.*, 604 F.2d 1028 (CA-7, 1979).

14. See, for example: *EEOC Decision No. 72-2179* (1972), *CCH EEOC Decisions Para. 6395.*

15. See, for example: *Rogers V. American Airlines, Inc.*, 527 F.Supp. 229 (SD NY, 1981).

16. See *EEOC Decision No. 74-02* (1973), *CCH EEOC Decisions Para. 6386.*

17. *Reynolds v. Sheet Metal Workers*, 498 F.Supp. 952 (DC Dist. Co., 1980).

18. *EEOC Decision No. 78-10* (1977).

19. *Dozier v. Chupka*, 395 F.Supp. 836 (DC Ohio, 1975).

20. See 29 CFR §1606.5.

21. *Berke v. Ohio Department of Public Welfare*, 628 F.2d 980 (CA-6, 1980).

22. *Harper v. T.W.A. Inc.*, 525 F.2d 409 (CA-8, 1975).

23. See *EEOC Decision No. 79-59* (1979).

24. *Sprogis v. United Air Lines, Inc.*, 444 F.2d 1194 (CA-7, 1971).

25. *Phillips v. Martin Marietta Corp.*, 400 U.S. 542 (1971).

26. *EEOC Decision No. 71-332* (1970), *CCH EEOC Decisions Para. 6164.*

27. See 42 U.S.C.A. §2000(e)(k) (as amended by Act of Oct. 31, 1978). See also [32.04] for a more comprehensive discussion of pregnancy rights under Title VII.

28. See, for example: *Krause v. Sacramento Inn*, 479 F.2d 988 (CA-9, 1973).

29. *Fesel v. Masonic Home of Delaware, Inc.*, 428 F.Supp. 573 (DC Del., 1977).

30. 29 CFR §1604.2(a)(1).

31. 42 U.S.C.A. §2000e-2(e).

32. 29 CFR §1605.2(b).

33. *EEOC Decision No. 70-38* (1969), *CCH EEOC Decisions Para. 6042.*

34. *EEOC v. Detroit Edison Co.*, 515 F.2d 301 (CA-6, 1975).

35. *United States v. Georgia Power Co.*, 474 F.2d 906 (CA-5, 1973).

36. *Griggs v. Duke Power Co.*, 401 U.S. 424 (1971).

37. 29 CFR §1607.3.

38. 29 CFR §1607.4D.

39. 29 CFR Part §1607.

40. 29 CFR §1607.7B and §1607.14B.

41. *Bridgeport Guardians, Inc. v. Members of Bridgeport Civil Service Commission*, 482 F.2d 1333 (CA-2, 1973).

42. *Bridgeport Guardians, Inc. v. Members of Bridgeport Civil Service Commission, supra.*

43. See EEOC *Pre-Hire Inquiries* Para. 4120.

44. *EEOC Decision No. 76-138* (1976).

45. See *EEOC v. American National Bank*, 21 EPD 30369 (DC Va., 1979).

46. *Jones v. First Federal Savings and Loan Assoc.*, 546 F.Supp. 762 (DC Md., 1982); *Tortorici v. Harris*, 610 F.2d 278 (CA-5, 1980).

47. *Stamps v. Detroit Edison Co.*, 365 F.Supp. 87 (DC Mich., 1973).

48. *Held v. Gulf Oil Co.*, 684 F.2d 427 (CA-6, 1982).

49. *Wigginess, Inc. v. Fruchtman*, 482 F.Supp. 681 (SD NY, 1979).

50. *Garneau v. Raytheon Co.*, 323 F.Supp. 391 (DC Mass., 1971).

51. *Chrapliwy v. Uniroyal, Inc.*, 458 F.Supp. 252 (ND, Ind., 1977).

52. *Weeks v. Southern Bell T & T Co.*, 408 F.2d 228 (CA-5, 1969).

53. *Young v. Edgecomb Steel Co.*, 499 F.2d 97 (CA-4, 1974).

54. *Abron V. Black & Decker*, 654 F.2d 951 (CA-4, 1981).

55. *Olson v. Philco-Ford*, 531 F.2d 474 (CA-10, 1976).

56. *Robinson v. Union Carbide Corp.*, 538 F.2d 652 (CA-5, 1976).

57. 42 U.S.C.A. §2000e-2(a)(1).

58. *Quarles v. Phillip Morris, Inc.*, 279 F.Supp. 505 (DC Va., 1968).

59. *EEOC Decision No. 71-32* (July 15, 1971), *CCH EEOC Decisions Para. 6205.*

60. 42. U.S.C.A. §2000e-2(h).

61. *International Brotherhood of Teamsters v. United States*, 431 U.S. 324 (1977).

62. *Internal Brotherhood of Teamsters v. U.S.*, *supra.*

63. *EEOC Decision No. 71-1103* (1971) *CCH EEOC Decisions Para. 6203.*

64. *Bush v. Lone Star Steel Co.*, 373 F.Supp. 526 (DC Tex., 1974).

65. *Memphis Firefighters v. Stotts*, 104 S.Ct. 2576 (1984).

66. 42 U.S.C.A. §2000e-2(a)(1).

67. *Seeking v. Ill. Bell Tel. Co.*, 476 F.Supp. 495 (ND Ill., 1978).

68. *Jack v. American Linen Supply Co.*, 498 F.2d 122 (CA-5, 1974).

69. *Alexander v. Gardner-Denver Co.*, 519 F.2d 503 (CA-10, 1975).

70. *Naraine v. Western Electric Co.*, 507 F.2d 590 (CA-8, 1974).

71. *EEOC Decision No. 70-007* (July 3, 1969), *CCH EEOC Decisions Para. 6143.*

72. *Muller v. United States Steel Corp.*, 509 F.2d 923 (CA-10, 1975).

73. See *Rogers v. EEOC*, 454 F.2d 234 (CA-5, 1971).

74. *EEOC Decisions No. 72-0957* (1972).

75. See, for example: *EEOC Decisions No. 68-6654* (1969); See also: EEOC, *Sex Discrimination Guidelines*, 29 CFR §1604.2(b)(4).

76. *EEOC Decision No. 72-0978* (1972).

77. *EEOC Decision No. 72-1845* (1972).

78. See, for example: *Johnson v. Shreveport Garment Co.*, 422 F.Supp. 526 (DC La., 1976).

79. See 44 *Fed. Reg.* 4422.

80. *Sibley Memorial Hospital v. Wilson*, 160 App. D.C. 14, 488 F.2d 1338 (1973).

81. *McDonald v. Santa Fe Trail Transp. Co.*, 427 U.S. 273 (1976).

82. See 15 Am. Jur. 2d Civil Rights §207.

83. See "Reverse Discrimination Developments Under Title VII, 15 *Houston Law Review*, Oct., 1977.

84. *United Steelworkers of America v. Weber*, 443 U.S. 193 (1979).

85. See *Annotation*: 46 ALR 3d. 369.

86. See 42 U.S.C.A. §2000e-7 and 2000h-4.

87. *Donnell v. General Motors Corp.*, 576 F.2d 1292 (CA-8, 1978).

88. *International Assoc. of Heat & Frost Insulators etc., v. Vogler*, 407 F.2d 1047 (CA-5, 1969).

89. See, for example: *EEOC Decision No. 75-174* (1975), *CCH EEOC Decision Para. 6549.*

90. *United States v. International Assoc. of Bridge, etc.*, 438 F.2d 679 (CA-7, 1971).

91. *EEOC Decision No. 77-41 (1978).*

92. See, for example: *Evans v. Sheraton Park Hotel*, 164 App. D.C. 86, 503 F.2d 177 (1974).

93. *Russell v. American Tobacco Co.*, 528 F.2d 357 (CA-4, 1975).

94. 29 U.S.C.A. §169.

95. See *EEOC Decision No. 76-676* (1970), *CCH EEOC Decision Para. 6144.*

96. *United States v. International Brotherhood of Electrical Workers*, 356 F.Supp. 104 (DC Nev., 1973).

97. *U.S. v. International Brotherhood of Electrical Workers*, supra.

98. *U.S. v. International Brotherhood of Electrical Workers*, supra.

32

Protected
Characteristics Discrimination

[32.01] RACE AND COLOR

Although Title VII is general in its application and extends protection to members of all races, including Caucasians and persons of other national origins, it has been directed most obviously to the members of the Negro race.[1]

The statutory prohibition against discrimination in employment because of color has not produced an abundance of claims in that the color of a person's skin would seemingly classify such person as a member of a particular race, and should he or she desire to file a claim of discrimination, a claim of racial discrimination would most likely be asserted.[2]

However, when the coloring of the members of a particular race varies and the employer selects an applicant who has the lightest complexion or the most distinct Caucasian features, but who is least qualified for the job, an unlawful employment practice might exist.[3]

[32.02] NATIONAL ORIGIN

One of the purposes of Title VII is an attempt to eliminate "widespread" practices of national origin discrimination.[4]

Some claims of national origin discrimination have been founded on an employer's requirement that an employee possess certain language skills as a condition of employment. Such language requirements are improper unless job relatedness is shown.[5] Similarly, an employer who prohibits employees of foreign descent to use their native language at work commits an unlawful employment practice if he or she is unable to show business necessity for such policy.[6]

The 1980 EEOC guidelines regarding national origin discrimination specify that employers have an affirmative duty to maintain a work environment free of harassment on the basis of national origin. The 1980 guidelines prohibit such conduct as ethnic jokes or other verbal or physical abuse which relate to an employee's national origin when such conduct occurs within the work place.[7]

[32.03] SEX DISCRIMINATION

Title VII bans all discrimination against any individual, male or female, on the basis of sex.[8] Nonetheless, the vast majority of sex-bias cases under Title VII have involved women. An employer violates Title VII when he or she imposes certain conditions or burdens on women that are not imposed upon men.[9]

231

An employer violates Title VII when he or she discriminates against women employees with regard to life insurance programs, retirement plans, profit sharing plans, bonus plans, sick pay, medical insurance coverage, and so forth.[10] The Supreme Court has held that it is a violation of Title VII for an employer to provide lower retirement benefits to female employees than to male employees, irrespective of mortality tables that show females have a longer life span than do males as a class.[11]

It is not necessary that discrimination in employment practices be directed at all members of a sex or focused on a characteristic unique to one sex in order to constitute unlawful sex bias. All that is required by the Act is that gender be a substantial factor in the job bias.[12]

[32.04] PREGNANCY DISCRIMINATION ACT

Under the Pregnancy Discrimination Act, an amendment to Title VII,[13] an employer may not discriminate against pregnant employees relative to employment practices. Thus, an employer's discriminatory exclusion of pregnant employees from such benefit programs as paid sick leave, disability insurance, or health insurance constitutes unlawful sex bias under Title VII.[14]

An employer may not lawfully deny a pregnant employee a leave of absence, or discriminate as to the duration or extension of such a leave, if leaves of absence are extended to male employees for other disabilities relating to sickness or health.[15]

An employer's requirement that maternity leave commence or terminate at predetermined times, without showing business or medical necessity, may be a violation of Title VII. For example, an employer's requirement that maternity leaves of absence terminate after six months was found unlawful when the employer had no such limitation applicable to male employees suffering temporary sicknesses or illnesses.[16] The Pregnancy Discrimination Act provides protection not only for female employees, but also for spouses of male employees.[17]

[32.05] SEXUAL HARASSMENT GUIDELINES

The EEOC places a special obligation on employers to see that supervisory personnel and other employees do not engage in unlawful sexual harassment.[18]

According to the Commission's Sexual Harassment Guidelines, any unwelcome sexual advance, request for sexual favor, or other verbal or physical conduct of a sexual nature will be treated as unlawful sexual harassment when response or reaction to the advances, or requests, will be permitted to affect on employment decision. An employer also violates the guidelines whenever a sexual advance or request for sexual favors within the work place has the purpose or effect of substantially interfering with an individual's work performance or creates an "intimidating, hostile, or offensive working environment".[19]

Although perhaps mitigating, an employer's policy which prohibits workers from engaging in sexual harassment does not necessarily protect such employer from liability for sexual harassment occurring in the work place as the EEOC infers absolute liability against employers for such conduct committed by their agents or supervisory personnel.[20] An employer may also be found liable for unlawful sexual harassment when it fails to immediately investigate claims of improper harassment.[21]

An employer may also violate Title VII by subjecting a female employee to sexual harassment even though the employee's response or resistance to such harassment does not result in her being deprived of a promotional opportunity or some other employment benefit.[22]

Vulgar and indecent language tolerated by management and directed toward female employees may constitute unlawful conduct on the part of the employer, even though some women affected may not resent or oppose the language used.[23]

[32.06] SEXUAL ORIENTATION

Title VII's ban on sex discrimination does not extend to the protection of sexual preferences or practices, but its applicability is limited to a prohibition of discrimination based on gender.[24] Courts have also held that Title VII does not protect transsexuals against job-bias discrimination.[25]

[32.07] THE COMPARABLE WORTH DOCTRINE

Comparable worth is usually defined as requiring equal pay for males and females doing dissimilar but comparable work. The courts have generally rejected the extension of Title VII to embrace the comparable worth doctrine distinguishing the concept of comparable worth from the guidelines of the Equal Pay Act which requires equal pay for similar work, rather than equal pay for dissimilar work.[26] (The Equal Pay Act is discussed in Chapter 39.)

However, the U.S. Supreme Court has held that even absent a showing of equal work, a cause of action can be brought under Title VII where there is evidence an employer intentionally depressed female employees' wages as a result of their sex.[27]

Although the *Gunther* decision opened the door in permitting an action to be brought under Title VII for intentionally discriminating against female employees with respect to wages, courts have narrowly construed its applicability, generally holding it is not up to the courts to evaluate the worth of jobs.[28]

[32.08] RELIGION

Whenever an employer requires an employee either to abandon a fundamental precept or to give up an employment opportunity, he or she will be liable for religious discrimination under Title VII.[29]

Title VII defines "religion" as including all aspects of religious observance, practice, and belief.[30] The EEOC has enlarged the definition to include moral and ethical beliefs not confined to theistic concepts or to traditional precepts but which, nonetheless, are sincerely held by an individual with the strength of traditional religious views.[31]

The Title VII ban on religious discrimination goes further than to require mere employer neutrality. It also places an affirmative action on an employer to reasonably accommodate an employee's religious observance or practice.[32]

How far an employer must go in accommodating an employee in his or her religious beliefs is measured against the hardship suffered by the employer and other employees.[33] The U.S. Supreme Court has held that only a minimum of additional costs need be incurred in order to satisfy the reasonable accommodation requirement; otherwise, the accommodation efforts on the part of the employer would result in an undue hardship on fellow employees.[34]

Undue hardship exists, sufficient to overcome the reasonable accommodation requirement, if an employer *has* to

- deny shift or job preference to other employees[35]
- take steps inconsistent with requirements in an otherwise valid collective bargaining contract[36]
- pay other employees at overtime rates when they substitute for the subject employee[37]
- move supervisors or employees from other areas to the vacant job at the expense and detriment of other functions[38]
- violate the seniority rights of other employees to accommodate the religious beliefs of another[39]
- bear more than a de minimus cost to effectuate such an accommodation[40]

An employee seeking to observe his or her religious beliefs also has a responsibility of properly notifying the employer as to the religious needs and doing everything possible to resolve conflicts between job duties and religious practices or observances.[41]

In addition to an employer's duty to reasonably accommodate the religious beliefs of his or her employees, an employer also is required to maintain a work environment free of religious bias. For example, an employer commits religious discrimination under Title VII when he or she permits a supervisor to espouse his or her religious convictions to employees while at work.[42]

An employer may also violate Title VII by requiring an applicant or employee to wear apparel other than that required by the employee's religious tenets.[43]

NOTES TO CHAPTER 32

1. 42 U.S.C.A. §2000e-2.
2. CCH *Employment Practices Guide* (1981) Para. 233.
3. *EEOC Decision No. 72-0454* (1971).
4. See EEOC *National Origin Discrimination Guidelines,* 29 CFR §1606.7.
5. *EEOC Decision No. 73-0377* (1972).
6. See, for example: *Saucedo v. Brothers Wells Service, Inc.,* 464 F. Supp. 919 (DC Tex., 1979).
7. Gordon E. Jackson, *Unlawful Terminations and Employment-at-Will* (Memphis, Tenn.: Executive Resources, Inc., 1985), 47–48.
8. See 42 U.S.C.A. §2000e-2.
9. *Nashville Gas Co. v. Satty,* 434 U.S. 136 (1977).
10. 29 CFR §1604.9.
11. *Arizona Governing Committee v. Norris,* 32 FEP Cases 233 (S.Ct., 1983).
12. *Munford v. James T. Barnes & Co.,* 441 F.Supp. 459 (DC Mich., 1977).
13. 42 U.S.C.A. §2000e(k) (as amended by Act, Oct. 31, 1978, P.L. 95–555, 92 Stat. 2076).
14. 42 U.S.C.A. §2000e(k).
15. 29 CFR §1604.10(b).
16. See *EEOC Decision No. 70-68* (1973), *CCH EEOC Decisions Para. 6422.*
17. *Newport News Shipbuilding & Dry Dock Co. v. EEOC,* 32 FEP 1 (S.Ct., 1983).
18. EEOC, *Sex Discrimination Guidelines,* 29 CFR §1604.11.
19. 29 CFR §1604.2 and §1604.11.
20. 29 CFR §1604.11.
21. *Kyriazi v. Western Electric Co.,* 461 F.Supp. 894 (DC Pa., 1978).
22. *Robson v. Eva's Super Market,* 538 F.Supp. 857 (ND Ohio, 1982).
23. *Morgan v. Hertz Corp.,* 542 F.Supp. 123 (WD Tenn., 1981).
24. *De Santi's v. Pacific Tel. & Tel. Co.,* 608 F.2d 327 (CA-9, 1979).
25. See, for example: *Halloway v. Arthur Anderson & Co.,* 566 F.2d 659 (CA-9, 1977); *Ulane v. Eastern Airlines,* 35 FEP Cases 1348 (CA-7, 1984).
26. *General Electric v. Gilbert,* 429 U.S. 125 (1976).
27. *County of Washington v. Gunther,* 101 S.Ct. 2242 (1981).

28. See, for example: *Plener v. Parson's Gilbane,* 713 F.2d 1127 (CA-5, 1983); *Spauldings v. University of Washington,* 36 FEP Cases 464 (CA-9, 1984).
29. 29 CFR §1605.2.
30. 42 U.S.C.A. §2000e(j).
31. 29 CFR §1605.1.
32. 42 U.S.C.A. §2000e(j); 29 CFR §1605.2.
33. *Trans World Airlines, Inc. v. Hardison,* 432 U.S. 63 (1977).
34. *Trans World Airlines, Inc. v. Hardison, supra.*
35. *Trans World Airlines, Inc. v. Hardison, supra.*
36. *Trans World Airlines, Inc. v. Hardison, supra.*
37. *Rohr v. Western Electric Co.,* 567 F.2d 579 (CA-3, 1977).
38. *Trans World Airlines, Inc. v. Hardison, supra.*
39. *Trans World Airlines, Inc. v. Hardison, supra.*
40. *Trans World Airlines, Inc. v. Hardison, supra.*
41. *Chrysler v. Mann,* 561 F.2d 1282 (CA-8, 1977).
42. See *EEOC Decision No. 72-1114,* (1972).
43. See *EEOC Decision No. 71-2620,* (1971).

33

How to Process
a Title VII Claim

[33.01] FILING AN EEOC CHARGE

Title VII provides that an EEOC charge may be filed by an "aggrieved" individual, by another party acting on behalf of an aggrieved individual, or by a member of the commission.[1]

Should an alleged unlawful unemployment practice occur in a state or locality that does not have its own anti-discrimination law, the "aggrieved" individual must file a charge with the local office of the Equal Employment Opportunity Commission within 180 days from the occurrence of the discriminatory act.[2] If a violation is continuing in nature, the 180-day time limitation is inapplicable.[3]

Whenever an alleged unlawful practice occurs in a state or locality with its own anti-discrimination law and enforcement agency, and the aggrieved party has filed an unlawful employment practice charge with such state or local agency, a charge must also be filed with the Equal Employment Opportunity Commission within 300 days after the alleged discriminatory practice occurred in order to be timely filed under Title VII, unless the charging party receives earlier notice that such agency has terminated its proceedings regarding the charge, in which case a charge with the EEOC must be filed within 30 days after such notification.[4]

An EEOC charge, in order to be valid, must be written, identifying the respondent against whom the allegation is directed, generally specifying the alleged unlawful conduct, and must be signed and verified.[5] Verification may be satisfied by the administration of an oath at the time the charge is filed.[6]

An EEOC charge may be filed at any EEOC district or area office, at the office of the commission in Washington, D.C., or with any designated representative of the commission.[7]

[33.02] INVESTIGATORY PROCESS

EEOC fact-finding conferences usually are held within a few weeks after a charge is filed, following the respondent's response to the EEOC's request for documents and data relative to the charge.[8] The conference is a face-to-face meeting between the charging party and representatives of the respondent.[9] A full record of the fact-finding conference is made by an EEOC employee to be used for settlement or determination purposes.

Although an attorney may attend EEOC fact-finding conferences on behalf of a client, his or her role is limited to advisory only and the attorney will not be permitted to speak on behalf of the client or cross-examine other parties.[10]

Another investigatory method used by EEOC agents is to make an on-

238

site investigation of the respondent's premises.[11] Such tours serve to educate EEOC investigators about the respondent's overall operation and how the job in question fits into the flow of work in a given situation.[12]

[33.03] FINDINGS AND DETERMINATIONS

Once the investigation of a charge is completed by EEOC agents, a determination is made by the commission on whether it believes the charge is true.[13] Although not mandatory,[14] Title VII suggests that such determination be made within 120 days from the filing of the charge.[15] There are two possible determinations by the EEOC:[16]

- reasonable cause determination
- no reasonable cause determination

A "no cause" determination signifies that the commission concludes that the alleged discrimination did not occur.[17] A "cause" determination indicates that the commission believes that the alleged discrimination did occur.[18]

Should the commission issue a "no cause" determination, it is required to send the charging party a "right-to-sue" notice and advise the charging party that the charge will be dismissed by the commission.[19] Notwithstanding the "no cause" determination by the commission, the "right-to-sue" notice informs the charging party that, should he or she desire to initiate a district court suit under Title VII, such suit must be filed within 90 days after receipt of the "right-to-sue" notice.[20]

Should the EEOC decide that there is reasonable cause to believe that discriminatory acts did occur, the commission will issue a determination letter to that effect and invite the parties to join in conciliation.[21]

The EEOC has a duty to notify a charging party of his or her right to sue. After 180 days have passed since the filing of a charge, the EEOC will promptly issue such a notice, upon written request.[22] Moreover, if the commission believes it improbable that it will complete its investigation and administrative processing within the 180-day period, it may issue a right-to-sue notification, upon written request, even prior to the expiration of 180 days from the date of filing.[23]

[33.04] CONCILIATION PROCESS

If a "cause" determination is found by the commission, the parties will be invited to participate in conciliation discussions.

If conciliation efforts between the parties are successful, the respondent and the charging party will enter into a written conciliation agreement.[24] This written agreement will be signed by all parties, including the EEOC conciliator.[25] If the agreement is approved by the conciliator's superiors, a fully executed copy of the agreement will be forwarded to each party, and a copy will also be filed with the commission's office in Washington, D.C.[26]

The EEOC insists that certain minimum conditions be contained in conciliation agreements.[27] As a result, there are specified standard clauses containing minimum requirements that the EEOC will attempt to insert in every conciliation agreement.[28] One such clause, for example, is that the charging party waives the right to sue the respondent with respect to matters covered under the agreement.[29]

Should the conciliation efforts fail between the parties, or should the respondent refuse to conciliate, thereby precluding conciliation, the EEOC will send the respondent written notification that it has terminated its efforts to conciliate and send the charging party notice of failure to conciliate as well as a "right-to-sue" notice.[30]

The EEOC has an obligation to review and assure compliance with conciliation agreements.[31] Compliance reviews of a conciliation agreement are to be accomplished not later than eighteen months after the agreement has been approved by the commission.[32]

[33.05]   EEO LITIGATION

Title VII provides that an aggrieved individual as well as the EEOC may bring an action in federal district court to vindicate Title VII rights, subject to certain conditions being met. Aggrieved individuals may seek Title VII relief through the federal courts in the following ways:

- *pursuant* to a right-to-sue notification, when no reasonable cause is found[33]

- *pursuant* to a right-to-sue notification issued upon request of the charging party despite the fact EEOC processing has not been concluded[34]

- *pursuant* to a right-to-sue notification issued upon failure of conciliations[35]

The EEOC at its discretion, may bring suits in an appropriate District Court under the following conditions:

- Whenever it reasonably believes a person or a group of persons is engaged in a pattern or practice of resistance to the full enjoyment of the rights accorded by Title VII and that such conduct is of such a nature and is intended to deny the full exercise of rights secured by the statute[36]

- On individual charges if, within thirty days after a charge is filed or within thirty days after the expiration of any deferral period, the EEOC has been unsuccessful in its efforts to secure from the respondent a conciliation agreement acceptable to the commission.[37]

- Whenever the commission concludes on the basis of its preliminary investigation that prompt judicial action is dictated, it may seek preliminary relief pending final disposition of the charge through its administrative processes.[38]

Although not considered a Title VII suit, *per se,* the EEOC also may seek to enforce a conciliation agreement in federal district court if it believes the respondent is not performing under its terms and conditions.[39]

[33.06] JURISDICTIONAL CONSIDERATION

Title VII provides that an action under its provisions may be brought in any judicial district in the state in which the unlawful employment practice is alleged to have been committed, in the judicial district in which the employment records relevant to such practice are maintained and administered, or in the judicial district in which the aggrieved person would have worked but for the alleged unlawful practice.[40] If the respondent is not found within any such district, such an action may be brought within the judicial district in which the respondent has its principal office.

There are certain statutory procedures that must be met as jurisdictional prerequisites to filing a Title VII suit in an appropriate federal district court, including the following:

- *The filing of a charge of discrimination with the EEOC.*[41]

- *The charge of discrimination filed within the statutory time limit provided by Title VII.*[42]

- *The EEOC's duty to attempt to conciliate before it institutes suit.*[43] (However, some courts require only minimal efforts on the part of EEOC to conciliate prior to filing suits,[44] and most courts agree that such failure on the part of the EEOC to attempt to conciliate does not destroy the right of the aggrieved party to file a private action under Title VII.[45])

- *The EEOC's duty to notify a respondent that conciliation efforts have failed.*[46] (This requirement is not likely to bar an EEOC Title VII suit where the respondent is unable to show any prejudice by the lack of notice.[47])

- *The receipt of a right-to-sue notice from the EEOC prior to filing a private suit under Title VII.*[48] (However, such a requirement usually will not bar a suit where the aggrieved party has requested such a notice prior to filing his Title VII action.[49])

- *The aggrieved party has ninety days from receipt of a right-to-sue notice to bring a private action under Title VII.*[50] (Nonetheless, several factors may toll this ninety-day time priod such as a motion for appointment of counsel,[51] or the filing of the right-to-sue notice with the court prior to formal suit.[52])

Title VII claimants are not restricted in their election of remedies. Title VII claims in federal courts are not destroyed by the fact that the aggrieved party has failed to seek available relief through some other procedure such as arbitration under a collective bargaining agreement.[53] Neither does a prior unsuccessful submission to the National Labor Relations Board, nor does some other administrative agency of the charging party's claim foreclose a subsequent lawsuit under Title VII.[54]

[33.07] CLASS ACTIONS UNDER TITLE VII

Class actions may be initiated in Title VII suits, assuming the requirements of Rule 23 of the Federal Rules of Civil Procedure are satisfied.

Membership in a Title VII class action is not limited to individuals who previously have filed charges of discrimination with the EEOC.[55] Individuals may fail to qualify as proper class members, however, when they fail to file their individual claims within the Title VII limitations period for filing charges.[56]

[33.08] SCOPE OF PLEADINGS AND DISCOVERY

As provided by the Federal Rules of Civil Procedure, Title VII suits, as other complaints in federal district court, must satisfy some basic drafting requirements, such as a

- statement of the court's jurisdictional grounds
- short and plain statement of plaintiff's claims
- demand for judgment for the relief to which the plaintiff deems entitled[57]

Aside from entering a timely answer to the complaint, a defendant to a Title VII suit may, under proper circumstances, utilize certain motions provided by the Federal Rules of Civil Procedure, such as a motion to dismiss.[58]

[33.09] TITLE VII TRIALS

A Title VII trial is a trial *de novo,* entirely separate and apart from the investigation and administrative disposition by the EEOC.[59] A Title VII suit is considered "equitable" in nature. Since its primary objective is to enjoin unlawful discriminatory employment practices, jury trials are not available in Title VII cases.[60]

Whether the EEOC's investigative report is admissible is a frequent issue in Title VII trials. Although Rule 803(8) of the Federal Rules of Evidence renders admissible the records, reports, statements, and data compilations of public offices or agencies, the admission and weight to be given to such evidence appears to be discretionary with the trial court.[61] An adverse ruling will not be overturned on appeal in the absence of a showing of abuse of such discretion.[62]

EEOC determinations,[63] as well as prior arbitration decisions[64] relative to the facts in question, have been held admissible by some courts in Title VII cases. However, evidence of EEOC conciliation efforts between the parties are strictly precluded as evidence absent written consent of the persons concerned.[65]

Appeals from judgments in "pattern-and-practice" cases go directly to the United States Supreme Court.[66] In all other Title VII suits, adverse judgments are appealed into the appropriate federal circuit courts.[67]

[33.10] REMEDIES

A federal district court may grant a preliminary injunction upon proper application by the EEOC, even prior to a final disposition of the matter by the EEOC,[68] assuming the commission has concluded that such action is necessary from its preliminary investigation, and upon proof of the existence of irreparable harm and the likelihood of ultimate success on the merits.[69]

Prohibitory injunctions,[70] as well as injunctions of an affirmative nature,[71] may be appropriate in Title VII cases. For example, a federal district court typically orders that the defendant offer reinstatement of employment to a discriminated individual who has been found victimized by a discriminatory refusal to hire.[72]

Title VII also grants authority to the federal district courts to award back pay to Title VII claimants for unlawful discrimination in appropriate cases.[73]

Back-pay awards are considered equitable and compensatory in nature, rather than punitive.[74] Therefore, as a general rule, punitive damages are not available in Title VII suits.[75] Also, since back pay is considered equitable in nature, it may be awarded even though a plaintiff does not request it as part of his or her claim for relief.[76]

Title VII empowers the court, in its discretion, to award a reasonable attorney's fee to the prevailing party in a Title VII suit, except that attorney's fees are not to be awarded to EEOC attorneys.[77]

Most courts have been very liberal in awarding attorney fees.[78] For example, the U.S. Supreme Court has ruled that attorney's fees are to be awarded to a prevailing plaintiff in all but "very unusual" cases on the theory that a plaintiff who brings a Title VII suit is acting as a private attorney general.[79]

Attorney's fees are to be awarded to defendants in Title VII cases when a court finds that the plaintiff's claim is frivolous, unreasonable, or groundless.[80]

NOTES TO CHAPTER 33

1. 42 U.S.C.A. §2000e-5(b).
2. 42 U.S.C.A. §2000e-5(e).
3. *Belt v. Johnson Motor Lines, Inc.,* 458 F.2d 443 (CA-5, 1972).
4. 42 U.S.C.A. §2000e-5(e).
5. 29 CFR §1601.9.
6. *EEOC Compliance Manual,* §2.4.
7. 29 CFR §1601.8.
8. *EEOC Compliance Manual,* §14.5.
9. *EEOC Compliance Manual,* §14.5.
10. *EEOC Compliance Manual,* §14.7.
11. *EEOC Compliance Manual,* §25.2.
12. *EEOC Compliance Manual,* §25.2(a).
13. See generally, *EEOC Compliance Manual,* §40.
14. *Stewart v. EEOC,* 611 F.2d 679 (CA-7, 1979).
15. 42 U.S.C.A. §2000e-5(b).
16. *EEOC Compliance Manual,* §40.
17. *EEOC Compliance Manual,* §40.
18. *EEOC Compliance Manual,* §40.
19. 42 U.S.C.A. §2000e-5(f)(1); 29 CFR §1601.19(f).
20. 29 CFR §1601.29(e).
21. 42 U.S.C.A. §2000e-5(b); see also: *EEOC Compliance Manual,* §40.8.
22. 29 CFR §1601.28(a)(1).
23. 29 CFR §1601.28(a)(2).
24. See 29 CFR §1601.24(a); *EEOC Compliance Manual,* §64.
25. *EEOC Compliance Manual,* §64.8(b).
26. *EEOC Compliance Manual,* §64.8(f).
27. *EEOC Compliance Manual,* ''Conciliation Standards,'' (Foreword).
28. Ibid.
29. *EEOC Compliance Manual,* §1102.3.
30. *EEOC Compliance Manual,* §66.4.
31. *EEOC Compliance Manual,* §80.2.
32. *EEOC Compliance Manual,* §80.3.
33. 42 U.S.C.A. §2000e-5(f)(1); 29 CFR §1601.19(f).
34. 29 CFR §1601.28(a)(1).
35. See *EEOC Compliance Manual,* §66.7.
36. 42 U.S.C.A. §2000e-6.
37. 42 U.S.C.A. §2000e-5(f)(1); 29 CFR §1601.27.

38. 42 U.S.C.A. §2000e-(f)(2); 29 CFR §1601.23(a).

39. *EEOC v. Contour Chair Lounge Co.,* 596 F.2d 809 (CA-8, 1979).

40. 42 U.S.C.A. §2000e-5(f)(3).

41. *McDonnell Douglas Corp. v. Green,* 411 U.S. 792 (1973).

42. *McDonnell Douglas Corp. v. Green, supra.*

43. *EEOC v. Sears Roebuck & Co.,* 650 F.2d 14 (CA-2, 1981).

44. *EEOC v. Firestone Tire & Rubber Co.,* 366 F.Supp. 273 (DC Md., 1973).

45. *Canavan v. Beneficial Finance Corp.,* 553 F.2d 860 (CA-3, 1977).

46. See 29 CFR §1601.25; *EEOC v. Hickey-Mitchell Co.,* 507 F.2d 944 (CA-8, 1974).

47. *EEOC v. Kimberly-Clark Corp.,* 511 F.2d 1352 (CA-6, 1975).

48. *McDonnell Douglas Corp. v. Green,* 411 U.S. 792 (1973).

49. *Pinkard v. Pullman-Standard, Div. of Pullman, Inc.,* 678 F.2d 1211 (CA-5, 1982).

50. *McDonnell Douglas Corp. v. Green, supra.*

51. *Huston v. General Motors Corp.,* 477 F.2d 1003 (CA-8, 1973).

52. *Metcalf v. Omaha Steel Castings Co.,* 476 F.Supp. 870 (DC Neb., 1979).

53. *Waters v. Wisconsin Steel Works of International Harvester Co.,* 502 F.2d 1309 (CA-7, 1974).

54. *United Rubber, Cork, Linoleum & Plastic Workers v. NLRB,* 368 F.2d 12 (CA-5, 1966).

55. *Albemarle Paper Co. v. Moody,* 422 U.S. 405 (1975).

56. *Wetzel v. Liberty Mut. Ins. Co.,* 508 F.2d 239 (CA-3, 1975).

57. See Rule 8(a), *Fed. Rules of Civ. Proc.*

58. See Rule 41(b), *Fed. Rules of Civ. Proc.*

59. *Alexander v. Gardner-Denver Co.,* 415 U.S. 36 (1974).

60. *Johnson v. Georgia Highway Express, Inc.,* 417 F.2d 1122 (CA-5, 1969).

61. *Dickerson v. Metropolitan Dade County,* 659 F.2d 574 (CA-5, 1981).

62. *Nulf v. International Paper Co.,* 656 F.2d 553 (CA-10, 1981).

63. *Georator Corp. v. EEOC,* 592 F.2d 765 (CA-4, 1979).

64. *Alexander v. Gardner-Denver Co., supra.*

65. 42 U.S.C.A. §2000e-5(b).

66. 42 U.S.C.A. §2000e-6(b).

67. 42 U.S.C.A. §2000e-5(i), 2000e-5(j).

68. 42 U.S.C.A. §2000d-5(f)(2).

69. *Faro v. New York University,* 502 F.2d 1229 (CA-2, 1974).

70. 42 U.S.C.A. §2000e-5(g) and 2000e-6(a).

71. 42 U.S.C.A. §2000-5(g).

72. *Franks v. Bowman Transp. Co.,* 424 U.S. 747 (1976).

73. 42 U.S.C.A. §2000e-5(g).

74. *Rogers v. EEOC,* 179 APP. DC 279, 551 F.2d 456 (1977).

75. *DeGrace v. Rumsfeld,* 614 F.2d 796 (CA-1, 1980).
76. *Robinson v. Lorillard,* 444 F.2d 791 (CA-4, 1971).
77. 42 U.S.C.A. §2000e-5(k).
78. *Reynolds v. Coomey,* 567 F.2d 1166 (CA-1, 1978).
79. *Christianburg Garmet Co. v. EEOC,* 434 U.S. 412 (1978).
80. *Christianburg Garment Co. v. EEOC, supra.*

34

Defenses to a
Title VII Claim

[34.01] BUSINESS NECESSITY

One of the most prevalent defenses used to counter a prima facie case in Title VII litigation is that of business necessity. Business necessity has been defined in various ways by the courts but may be best described as an overriding legitimate, nondiscriminatory business purpose.[1] Business necessity is not equated to management convenience,[2] but rather connotes an uncontrollable demand.[3]

In order to establish the doctrine of business necessity as a viable defense in a Title VII case, courts usually require the satisfaction of three elements:[4]

- There must exist an overriding legitimate business purpose such that the practice is necessary to the safe and efficient operation of the business;
- The challenged practice must effectively carry the business purpose it is alleged to serve; and
- There must exist no acceptable alternative policies or practices which would accomplish the business purpose advanced, or accomplish it equally well with lesser differential impact.

[34.02] BONA FIDE OCCUPATIONAL QUALIFICATION

Title VII permits selection of employees on the basis of religion, sex, or national origin in those certain instances in which such a characteristic is a bona fide occupational qualification, reasonably necessary to the normal operation of that particular business or enterprise.[5]

Since the bona fide occupational qualification exception is narrowly construed by the courts,[6] it is not widely used as a defense in Title VII cases. As a practical application, its use primarily is restricted to cases involving sex discrimination.[7] For example, sex has been held to be a bona fide occupational qualification for employment for such positions as an actor,[8] an actress,[9] and a salesperson employed in the foundations department of a retail store.[10]

[34.03] SENIORITY SYSTEMS

Bona fide seniority systems sometimes are used as a defense to Title VII actions. Title VII protects from challenge, different standards of compensation, or different terms, conditions, or privileges of employment, pursuant to a bona fide seniority system, if such differences are not the result of intentional discrimination with regard to race, color, religion, sex, or national origin.[11]

[34.04] TESTING

As discussed previously,[12] an employer has a duty to show that its testing requirements have a manifest relationship to the job in question. Thus, when pre-employment testing is an issue in a Title VII case, defendants may utilize validation as proper defense to plaintiff's claims.[13]

[34.05] JURISDICTIONAL DEFECTS

As discussed in Chapter 33, there are various jurisdictional prerequisites that should be satisfied in order to file a proper Title VII action in federal court, the absence of which might bar a successful claim.

Title VII defendants frequently check Title VII complaints to discern whether such prerequisites have been met. For example, should a defendant to a Title VII action determine that the plaintiff failed to institute suit within the statutory time limit provided by the statute, a motion to dismiss might be in order.[14]

Likewise, whenever a private plaintiff fails to file a Title VII action within ninety days from receipt of a right-to-sue notification, a defendant's motion to dismiss on that basis may be dictated.[15] Whenever an alleged defendant to a Title VII suit falls outside the coverage of the Act, the plaintiff's action may be dismissed upon proper motion of the defendant.[16]

[34.06] STATISTICAL DATA

Although statistical data are used widely by Title VII plaintiffs in attempting[17] to prove a prima facie case of discrimination, defendants to Title VII actions may likewise use statistical data as a defensive tool.[18]

While statistics may be an appropriate method of proving or rebutting a prima facie case of discrimination, the courts universally hold that such statistical data must be relevant, meaningful, and not segmented and particularized so as to obtain a desired result.[19]

[34.07] "FOR CAUSE" DEFENSE

A defendant may prevail in a Title VII action and overcome a plaintiff's prima facie case by showing the court that it had good cause or a legitimate nondiscriminatory reason for its action.[20]

For example, a defendant may demonstrate the absence of discrimination against an alleged dischargee by showing the court it had terminated the employee in question for failure to meet production standards.[21] Title VII defendants might overcome a prima facie case also, by showing the court that a minority applicant was legitimately rejected from employment because the job was awarded to another minority applicant.[22]

[34.08] MISCELLANEOUS DEFENSES

Defendants may use additional defenses in appropriate circumstances, such as:

Reasonable accommodation: A defendant may overcome a religious discrimination Title VII action by showing the court that he or she has attempted to make reasonable accommodations to the employee's religious needs or that an undue hardship renders unreasonable an employee's proposed accommodation of his or her religious needs.[23]

National security: A defendant does not violate Title VII for failure to hire an individual if the job in question is subject to certain requirements imposed in the interest of the national security of the United States and the alleged discriminatee does not fulfill the stated requirements.[24]

Reliance on EEOC opinion: A defendant who has, in good faith, relied upon a written interpretation or opinion of the EEOC for his or her alleged unlawful action or conduct may use such reliance as a proper defense in a Title VII suit.[25] However, the courts are divided on whether a Title VII defendant may use good faith reliance on a state protective statute as a proper defense in a Title VII case. Some courts have accepted this defense to some degree;[26] some have rejected it.[27]

Back-pay statute of limitation: A 1972 amendment to Title VII provides that back-pay liability in a Title VII action shall not accrue from a date more than two years prior to the filing of the charge of discrimination with the EEOC.[28] Therefore, as a general proposition, state statutes of limitation are inapplicable to Title VII actions in post-1972 cases with respect to back-pay issues.[29]

"Different location" defense: Section 703(h) of the Act provides that an employer may be justified in applying different practices or standards to employees who work in different locations, provided such differences are not the result of an intention to discriminate because of race, color, religion, sex, or national origin.

Preferential treatment for Indians: Title VII contains a special provision which permits any business or enterprise on or near an Indian reservation to provide preferential treatment to Indians living on or near such reservation without violating the Act.[30]

Religious preferences: Title VII provides that it shall not be unlawful for a school, college, university, or other educational institution to hire and employ individuals of a particular religion if such institution is, in whole or in substantial part, owned, supported, controlled, or managed by a particular religion or by a particular religious corporation, association, or society, or if the curriculum of such institution is directed toward the propagation of a particular religion.[31]

NOTES TO CHAPTER 34

1. *United Papermakers & Paperworkers v. United States,* 416 F.2d 980 (CA-5, 1969).
2. *United States v. Jacksonville Terminal Co.,* 451 F.2d 418 (CA-5, 1971).
3. *EEOC v. International Union of Operating Engineers,* 415 F.Supp. 1155 (DC NY, 1976).
4. *Robinson v. Lorillard Corp.,* 444 F.2d 791 (CA-4, 1971).
5. See 42 U.S.C.A. §20003-2(e).
6. *Dothard v. Rawlinson,* 433 U.S. 321 (1977).
7. Susan R. Agid, *Fair Employment Litigation,* 2nd Ed. (New York: Practicing Law Institute, 1979), 532.
8. *Utility Workers Union v. Southern California Edison Co.,* 320 F.Supp. 1262 (DC Cal., 1970).
9. *Utility Workers Union v. Southern California Edison Co., supra.*
10. *EEOC Decision No. 66-5759* (1968), *CCH Decisions Para. 6002.*
11. See 42 U.S.C.A. §20003-2(h).
12. See [31.04] for a discussion of validated tests.
13. *Moody v. Albermarle Paper Co.,* 474 F.2d 134 (CA-4, 1973).
14. See *McDonnell Douglas Corp. v. Green,* 411 U.S. 792 (1973).
15. *McDonnell Douglas Corp. v. Green, supra.*
16. See generally, 42 U.S.C.A. §20003-(b) through (3) for Title VII coverage.
17. See *Dothard v. Rawlinson,* 433 U.S. 321 (1977).
18. *Townsend v. Exxon Co., U.S.A.,* 420 F.Supp. 189 (DC Mass., 1976).
19. *EEOC v. Datapoint Corp.,* 570 F.2d 1264 (CA-5, 1978). See also: *International Brotherhood of Teamsters v. United States,* 431 U.S. 324 (1977).
20. *EEOC v. American Tel. & Tel. Co.,* 556 F.2d 167 (CA-3, 1977).
21. *Taylor v. Safeway Envelope Corp.,* 493 F.2d 191 (CA-5, 1975).
22. *United States v. N.L. Industries, Inc.,* 479 F.2d 354 (CA-8, 1973).
23. *Yott v. North American Rockwell Corp.,* 428 F.Supp. 763 (DC Cal., 1977).

24. 42 U.S.C.A. §2000e-2(g).
25. 42 U.S.C.A. §2000e-12(b).
26. *Kober v. Westinghouse Electric Corp.*, 480 F.2d 240 (CA-3, 1973).
27. *Stryker v. Register Publishing Co.*, 423 F.Supp. 476 (DC Conn., 1976).
28. 42 U.S.C.A. §2000e-5(g).
29. *Kirk v. Rockwell International Corp.*, 578 F.2d 814 (CA-9, 1978).
30. 42 U.S.C.A. §2000e-2(i).
31. 42 U.S.C.A. §2000e-2(e)(2).

35

Recordkeeping and Notice-Posting Requirements Under Title VII

[35.01] EMPLOYER REQUIREMENTS

Personnel records: The Equal Employment Opportunity Commission requires employers subject to Title VII to preserve personnel and employment records, including application forms, for a period of six months from the date of making the record or taking the personnel action involved, whichever occurs later.[1] Personnel records relevant to any charge of discrimination, such as personnel or employment records relating to the aggrieved person and to all other persons holding similar positions, must be maintained until final disposition of the charge or litigation.[2]

EEO-1 reports: The EEOC requires employers having 100 or more employees to file a report form known officially as Standard Form 100, but more commonly known as an ''EEO-1'' report.[3]

It is the obligation of all employers having an EEO-1 reporting responsibility to obtain necessary supplies of Form 100 and file its report prior to the annual filing date each year.[4] Copies of Standard Form 100 may be obtained from either the EEOC headquarters in Washington, D.C. or one of the EEOC district offices. It is also the responsibility of each employer to retain a copy of his or her most recent EEO-1 report for each reporting unit at its facility, or at its company or divisional headquarters, and to make available such copy to any officer, agent, or employee of the EEOC, upon request.[5]

[35.02] UNION REQUIREMENTS

Membership and referral records: The Equal Employment Opportunity Commission requires unions to preserve membership, referral, and application records for a period of six months from the date of making of the record.[6] In the event a charge of discrimination is filed against a union or a Title VII suit is instituted against it, such union must preserve all records and documents relevant to the charge or suit until final disposition of the matter.[7]

EEO-3 reports: Equal Employment Opportunity Commission regulations also provide that every union subject to Title VII and having 100 or more members at any time during the 12 months preceding the due date of the report, and either a local union or an independent or unaffiliated union, must file a copy of Local Union Equal Employment Opportunity Report EEO-3 with the commission or its delegate.[8]

Copies of EEO-3 reports may be obtained from the EEOC headquarters in Washington, D.C., or from any of the EEOC district offices. Copies of the most recent EEO-3 report must be maintained at all times by the subject union and made available to any EEOC agent, upon request.[9] Moreover, records kept solely for the purpose of completing the EEO-3 report must be preserved for a period of one year from the due date of the report.[10]

[35.03]   JOINT LABOR–MANAGEMENT APPRENTICESHIP COMMITTEES

EEO-2 reports: Joint labor-management apprenticeship committees having five or more apprentices enrolled in an apprenticeship program at any time during August and September of the reporting year, and representing at least one employer or union sponsor which are themselves subject to Title VII, must file an Apprenticeship Information Report EEO-2 with the commission.[11] A copy of the EEO-2 report must be maintained by the respective committee for inspection by EEOC agents, upon request.[12] Copies of EEO-2 reports may be obtained from the EEOC headquarters or its district offices.

Apprenticeship records: Records necessary for the completion of an EEO-2 report must be preserved for a period of one year from the due date of the report for which such records were used.[13] Other records relating to apprenticeship programs must be preserved for a period of at least two years from the date of making such record.[14] Records relevant to a Title VII charge of discrimination must be maintained until final disposition of the charge or disposition of litigation flowing from the charge.[15]

[35.04]   APPRENTICESHIP RECORDS RETENTION REQUIREMENTS

Every entity that controls an apprenticeship program must maintain a chronological list of names and addresses of all persons who have applied to participate in the program, including the dates on which their applications were received.[16]

The list must identify each applicant as to gender and note the applicant's identification as "White," "Black," "Hispanic," "Asian," "Pacific Islander," "American Indian," or "Alaskan Native."[17] In lieu of such a chronological list, written applications may suffice if they each contain a notation of the date the form was received, the address of the applicant, the sex, and the race, color, or national origin of each applicant.[18] Either the chronological list or proper written applications in lieu thereof must be maintained for a period of two years or for the period of a successful applicant's apprenticeship, whichever is longer.[19]

[35.05] ENFORCEMENT OF RECORDKEEPING REQUIREMENTS

EEOC regulations provide that legal sanctions may be imposed upon employers, unions, or joint labor-management committees who refuse or fail to comply with their EEOC recordkeeping and reporting responsibilities.[20]

Making willfully false statements in EEOC reports may subject violators to fines up to $10,000 or imprisonment up to five years, or both, pursuant to the United States Criminal Code.[21] Short of criminal sanctions, regulations provide that the EEOC may seek an order of a U.S. district court to compel compliance with its recordkeeping and reporting requirements.[22]

[35.06] EEOC NOTICE-POSTING

Title VII provides that every employer, employment agency, and union shall post and keep posted, in conspicuous places upon its premises, a notice prepared by the EEOC that sets forth pertinent provisions of the Act and information pertinent to the filing of a complaint.[23] EEOC regulations place this requirement upon joint labor-management committees as well.[24]

Some courts have held that the failure to post appropriate notices toll the 180- and 300-day limitation of action for filing EEOC claims.[25] Title VII also specifies that a willful failure or refusal to post such notice may subject the violator to a fine of not more than $100 for each separate offense.[26]

[35.07] AFFIRMATIVE ACTION PROGRAMS

The U.S. Supreme Court[27] has held that voluntary affirmative action plans are permissible and not violative of Title VII when such programs are used to "eliminate manifest racial imbalances in traditional segregated job categories."

The Equal Employment Opportunity Commission encourages employers as well as others subject to Title VII to develop and use voluntary affirmative action programs as a means to overcome the effect of past or present practices, policies, or other barriers to equal employment opportunity.[28]

The EEOC has issued *Guidelines on Affirmative Action*[29] as a means to clarify situations in which voluntary affirmative action plans should be undertaken. The main purpose of the *Guidelines on Affirmative Action* is to encourage voluntary adoption of affirmative action plans by providing employers with a defense to claims of reverse discrimination from males or Caucasians under Title VII.[30] Notwithstanding the permissibility of affirmative action programs, Title VII does not require an employer to adopt affirmative action plans in the absence of a showing of past or present discrimination on its part.[31]

NOTES TO CHAPTER 35

1. See 29 CFR §1602.14(a).
2. 29 CFR §1602.14(a).
3. 29 CFR §1602.7.
4. 29 CFR §1602.7.
5. 29 CFR §1602.7.
6. 29 CFR §1602.28(a).
7. 29 CFR §1602.28(a).
8. See 29 CFR §1602.22.
9. 29 CFR §1602.26.
10. 29 CFR §1602.28(a).
11. See 29 CFR §1602.15.
12. 29 CFR §1602.15.
13. 29 CFR §1602.21(a).
14. 29 CFR §1602.21(b).
15. 29 CFR §1602.21(b).
16. 29 CFR §1602.20(b).
17. 29 CFR §1602.20(b).
18. 29 CFR §1602.20(c).
19. 29 CFR §1602.21(a).
20. See 29 CFR §1602.8, 1602.16, and 1602.23.
21. 29 CFR §1602.8, 1602.16, and 1602.23; see also: 18 U.S.C.A. §1001.
22. 42 U.S.C.A. §2000e-8(c); see also: 29 CFR §1602.9, 1602.17 and 1602.24.
23. 42 U.S.C.A. §2000e-10(a).
24. 29 CFR §1601.30.
25. *Earnhardt v. Puerto Rico,* 691 F.2d 69 (CA-1, 1982).
26. 42 U.S.C.A. §2000e-10(b).
27. *United Steelworkers of America v. Weber,* 443 U.S. 193 (1979).
28. 29 CFR §1608; see also 44 *Fed. Reg.* 4422.
29. 29 CFR §1608.
30. 29 CFR §1608.1(d).
31. *EEOC Compliance Manual,* §156.

36

Related EEO Protective Laws

[36.01] CIVIL RIGHTS ACT OF 1866 (SECTION 1981 ACTIONS)

In addition to Title VII, litigants use other civil rights statutes by which to address discrimination in employment because of some protected characteristic. The Civil Rights Act of 1866 which evolved into 42 USCS Section 1981 (hereinafter referred to as Section 1981) is such an example.

Section 1981 states that all persons in the United States shall have the same right to make and enforce contracts, to sue, be parties, and give evidence, and to receive the full and equal benefit of all laws and proceedings for the security of persons and property, as is enjoyed by white citizens.[1] Section 1981 applies principally to racial discrimination.[2] However, the statute has been held to protect Caucasians as well as blacks.[3] Section 1981 has been used to redress racial discrimination against persons of Chinese[4] or Pakistani[5] descent. The statute has likewise been invoked to redress discrimination against Hispanic Americans but on the basis of racial rather than national origin status.[6] Section 1981 has been held not to apply to discrimination because of religion,[7] national origin,[8] sex,[9] or age.[10] The statute has been held to apply to public[11] as well as private acts[12] of discrimination in employment.

Section 1981 has no limitations of action specified. Consequently, federal courts apply the most applicable state statute of limitations.[13]

The limitation periods of Title VII do not apply to Section 1981 actions.[14] Thus, an action under Section 1981 may be maintained even though a Title VII suit may be barred for failure to comply with its prescriptive periods.[15] Moreover, filing of charges with the EEOC under Title VII does not toll the limitations period on a claim under Section 1981.[16]

[36.02] SECTION 1981 VERSUS TITLE VII

Plaintiffs who find obstacles under Title VII sometimes resort to Section 1981 for alternative relief to racial discrimination inasmuch as Section 1981 is broader in scope in some areas.[17] For example, an employer does not come within Title VII jurisdiction until he or she employs fifteen or more persons for a prescribed period.[18] Section 1981 has no such requirement. The term "employer" under Section 1981 appears to be much broader than when used in connection with Title VII actions.[19]

A racial discrimination claim may proceed directly to suit under Section 1981 without the necessity of processing a charge of discrimination through the EEOC as is required under Title VII.[20]

Since the filing of charges of discrimination with the EEOC is not a jurisdictional requirement to maintaining an action under Section 1981, a

259

party may be added to a Section 1981 suit, although not named in an original charge filed with the EEOC.[21]

Jury trials are available under Section 1982 and not under Title VII.[22] Punitive damages and compensatory damages, in addition to back pay (the Title VII remedy), are available in Section 1981 actions.[23]

It is not mandatory for a plaintiff to exhaust remedies before the EEOC prior to filing a Section 1981 action.[24] Neither is it a requirement that a plaintiff exhaust contractual remedies of a grievance/arbitration procedure as a prerequisite to filing a Section 1981 lawsuit.[25]

Although there may be some noted distinctions between a Section 1981 and Title VII action, several similarities exist as well. For example:

- Attorney fees may be available for the "prevailing party" in a Section 1981 action pursuant to the Civil Rights Attorney Fees Award Act of 1976.[26]
- The standards for determining attorney fees in Section 1981 actions are similar to those applied in Title VII cases.[27]
- Injunctive relief[28] is available in appropriate Section 1981 actions not unlike that available for Title VII plaintiffs. The courts may also look to the provisions of Title VII in fashioning a remedy in Section 1981 cases.[29]
- Both Section 1981[30] and Title VII cases are processed through federal district courts and allocations and orders of proof are basically the same.[31]
- The federal courts also look to many of the same standards used in deciding Title VII cases to determine Section 1981 suits. For example, disparate treatment may be used as a standard to establish proof of employment discrimination in Section 1981 cases as well as in Title VII actions.[32]

[36.03] CIVIL RIGHTS ACT OF 1871

A portion of the Civil Rights Act of 1871 provides that every person who, under color of statute, ordinance, regulation, custom, or usage, subjects or causes to be subjected, any person, within the jurisdiction of the United States, to the deprivation of any rights, privileges, or immunities secured by the Constitution and laws shall be held civilly liable for such actions.[33] This portion of the 1871 Civil Rights Act evolved into 42 USCS Section 1983 (hereinafter referred to as Section 1983).

The second part of the 1871 Civil Rights Act which evolved into 42 USCS Section 1985(3) (hereinafter referred to as Section 1985(3)) declares liable two or more persons who conspire for the purpose of depriving, either directly or indirectly, any person or class of persons of the equal protection of the law, or of equal privileges and immunities under the laws.[34]

Section 1983 is limited to state action by virtue of its reference to "color of statute."[35] Section 1985(3), however, applies to both private and public acts of discrimination.[36]

Both sections have had limited use in discrimination in employment actions. Section 1983 has been limited because it may be invoked only in public acts of discrimination.[37] Section 1985(3) has been limited in its application due to its purely remedial characteristics.

[36.04]   JURY SYSTEM IMPROVEMENT ACT

Another statute which provides some measure of protection against discrimination in employment is the Jury System Improvement Act of 1978.[38]

This statute makes it unlawful for an employer to discharge, threaten, or coerce any permanent employee because of the employee's jury service in any court of the United States.[39] An employer who violates this statute may be assessed damages for lost wages and benefits suffered by the aggrieved employee, enjoined from further violations, and ordered to offer reinstatement with restoration of full seniority rights to an aggrieved dischargee, and may also be subjected to a civil penalty of not more than $1,000.00 for each violation.[40]

[36.05]   FEDERAL ELECTION CAMPAIGN ACT

The Federal Election Campaign Act contains provisions that prohibit corporations and labor organizations from securing political contributions and expenditures from their respective employees and members by reason of threats of, or actual, job discrimination.[41] Willful violations of this statute could subject a guilty party to imprisonment up to a year and/or a maximum fine of $25,000.00.[42]

[36.06]   EMPLOYEE RIGHTS UNDER THE SHERMAN ANTI-TRUST ACT

Employees also may avail themselves of the federal anti-trust laws[43] to redress certain types of job discrimination.

For example, an agreement between two employers not to hire each other's former employees may constitute a violation of the Sherman Anti-Trust Act in that it would tend to restrain the employees' freedom of employment.[44] Similarly, when two or more employers conspire to blacklist an individual from employment, an action under the federal anti-trust laws may be invoked.[45]

NOTES TO CHAPTER 36

1. 42 U.S.C.A. §1981.

2. See *Veres v. County of Monroe*, 364 F.Supp. 1327 (DC Mich., 1973).

3. *Carter v. Gallagher*, 452 F.2d 315 (CA-8, 1971).

4. *London v. Coopers & Lybrand*, 644 F.2D 811(CA-9, 1981).

5. *Khawaja v. Wyatt*, 494 F.Supp. 302 (WD NY, 1980).

6. *Manzanares v. Safeway Stores, Inc.*, 593 F.2d 968 (CA-19, 1979).

7. *Runyon v. McCrary*, 427 U.S. 160, (1976).

8. *Vazquez v. Werner Continental, Inc.*, 429 F.Supp. 513 (DC Ill., 1977).

9. *Runyon v. McCrary, supra.*

10. *Kodish v. United Airlines, Inc.*, 463 F.Supp. 1245 (DC Colo., 1979).

11. *Guerra v. Manchester Terminal Corp.*, 498 F.2d, 641 (CA-5, 1974).

12. *Johnson v. Railway Express Agency, Inc.*, 421 U.S. 454 (1975).

13. *Griffin v. Pacific Maritime Assoc.*, 478 F.2d 1118 (CA-9, 1973).

15. *Long v. Ford Motor Co.*, 496 F.2d 500 (CA-6, 1974).

15. *Hackett v. McGuire Bros., Inc.*, 445 F.2d 442 (CA-3, 1971).

16. *Johnson v. Railway Express Agency, Inc., supra.*

17. *Watkins v. United Steel Workers*, 369 F.Supp. 1221 (DC La., 1974).

18. 42 U.S.C.A. §2000e(b).

19. *Young v. International Tel. & Tel. Co.*, 438 F.2d 757 (CA-3, 1971).

20. *Gresham v. Chambers*, 501 F.2d 687 (CA-2, 1974).

21. *Guerra v. Manchester Terminal Corp.*, 498 F.2d 641 (CA-5, 1974).

22. See, for example: *Setser v. Novak Inv. Co.*, 638 F.2d 1137 (8th Cir.) *cert. denied.* 454 U.S. 1064 (1981).

23. *Johnson v. Railway Express Agency, Inc., supra.*

24. *Waters v. Wisconsin Steel Works of International Harvester Co.*, 502 F.2d 1309 (CA-7, 1974).

25. *Waters v. Wisconsin Steel Works of Int'l Harvester Co., supra.*

26. 42 U.S.C.A. §1988.

27. *Brown v. Culpepper*, 559 F.2d 274 (CA-5, 1977).

28. *Young v. International Tel. & Tel. Co., supra.*

29. *Lee v. Southern Home Sites Corp.*, 444 F.2d 143 (CA-5, 1971).

30. 28 U.S.C.A. §1343(4).

31. *Long v. Ford Motor Co., supra.*

32. *Whatley v. Skaggs Cos.*, 502 F.Supp. 370 (DC Colo., 1980).

33. 42 U.S.C.A. §1983.

34. 42 U.S.C.A. §1985(3).

35. 42 U.S.C.A. §1983.

36. *Griffin v. Breckenridge,* 403 U.S. 88 (1971).

37. *Great American Federal Sav. & Loan Assoc. v. Novotny,* 442 U.S. 366 (1979).

38. 28 U.S.C.A. §1875.

39. 28 U.S.C.A. §1875(a).

40. 28 U.S.C.A. §1875(b).

41. 2 U.S.C.A. §431, *et seq.*

42. 2 U.S.C.A. §437 g(d)(1)(A)(B).

43. 15 U.S.C.A. §1 *et seq.*; 15 U.S.C.A. §12, *et seq.*

44. *Nichols v. Spencer International Press, Inc.,* 371 F.2d 332 (CA-7, 1967).

45. *Radovich v. National Football League,* 352 U.S. 445 (1957).

37

Federal Age Discrimination in Employment Act (ADEA)

[37.01] BACKGROUND AND COVERAGE

The Age Discrimination in Employment Act of 1967[1] (hereinafter referred to as the ADEA or the Act) was enacted with the purpose of promoting employment of older persons based on their ability rather than age and prohibiting arbitrary age discrimination in employment.[2] The Act forbids discharging or discriminating against employees who are between 40 and 70 because of their age.[3]

The ADEA generally extends to employers, employment agencies, and labor unions.[4]

The ADEA defines an "employer" as one engaged in an industry affecting commerce and having twenty or more employees for each working day in each of twenty or more calendar weeks during the current or preceding calendar year.[5] The term "employer" also includes a state or a political subdivision of a state,[6] as well as federal agencies, although federal employees are not entitled to a right to a jury trial under the Act.[7]

The Age Discrimination in Employment Act defines an "employment agency" as any person who regularly undertakes, with or without compensation, to procure employees for an employer.[8]

The ADEA defines a "labor organization" as an entity engaged in an industry affecting commerce in which employees participate and which exists for the purposes, in whole or in part, of dealing with employers concerning grievances, labor disputes, wages, rates of pay, hours, or other terms or conditions of employment, and any conference, general committee, joint or system board, or joint council so engaged that is subordinate to a national or international union.[9]

[37.02] PROHIBITED PRACTICES UNDER ADEA

Employers, unions, and employment agencies are prohibited from discriminating against their respective employees, members, referrals, and applicants as means of retaliation because such an employee, member, referral, or applicant made a charge, testified, assisted, or participated in any manner in an investigation, proceeding, or litigation under the act.[10]

Likewise, employers, unions, and employment agencies are prohibited from printing or publishing or causing to be printed or published, any notice or advertisement relating to employment or referral for employment which indicates any preference, limitation, specification, or discrimination based on age.[11]

In addition to these general prohibitions, the Age Discrimination in Employment Act outlines specific prohibited practices relating to employers, unions, and employment agencies.

Prohibited employer practices: The Age Discrimination in Employment Act declares it unlawful for an employer to

- fail or refuse to hire or to discharge any individual or otherwise discriminate against any individual with respect to his or her compensation, terms, conditions, or privileges of employment because of such individual's age

- limit, segregate, or classify his or her employees in any way which would deprive or tend to deprive any individual of employment opportunities or otherwise adversely affect the status of the employee because of age

- reduce the wage rate of any other employee or employees in order to comply with the Act[12]

Prohibited employment agency practices: The Age Discrimination in Employment Act provides that it shall be unlawful for an employment agency to fail or refuse to refer for employment, or otherwise discriminate against any individual because of such individual's age, or to classify or refer for employment any individual on the basis of such individual's age.[13]

Prohibited labor union practices: The Age Discrimination in Employment Act makes it unlawful for a labor organization to

- exclude or to expel from its membership, or otherwise discriminate against any individual because of his or her age

- limit, segregate, or classify its membership, or to classify or fail or refuse to refer for employment any individual, in a way which would tend to deprive that individual of employment opportunities, or which would limit such employment opportunities or otherwise adversely affect his status as an employee or as an applicant for employment, because of such individual's age

- cause or attempt to cause an employer to discriminate against an individual in violation of the Act.[14]

[37.03] ADMINISTRATION AND ENFORCEMENT

The Age Discrimination in Employment Act was originally administered by the Wage and Hour Division of the Department of Labor and utilized the Fair Labor Standards Act enforcement machinery and remedies rather than those provided by Title VII.[15]

However, pursuant to the Reorganization Plan No. 1 of 1978, the administration and enforcement of the ADEA was transferred from the Secretary of Labor, and its Wage and Hour Division, to the Equal Employment Opportunity Commission.[16]

Although the Equal Employment Opportunity Commission has established its own internal guidelines for investigating and conciliating ADEA cases,[17] the Act must be enforced through the prescribed procedures available under the Fair Labor Standards Act, rather than through procedures prescribed for Title VII claims.[18]

[37.04] EXCEPTIONS AND EXCLUSIONS

Employee benefit plan exception: The Age Discrimination in Employment Act provides than an employer, employment agency, or a union may adopt a bona fide employee benefit plan which provides lower benefits to older employees as long as such a plan is not a subterfuge to evade the purposes of the Act.[19]

Such a plan to fall within the employee benefit plan exception must be of the type or similar to the bona fide plans prescribed in the statute[20] (retirement plans, pension plans, or insurance plans) and must be justified by age-related cost considerations.[21] Moreover, the Tax Equity and Fiscal Responsibility Act of 1982 requires employers to provide employees between the ages of 65 and 70 and their dependents with the same group health plan benefits as employees under 65.[22]

Involuntary retirement exemption: Although the 1978 amendments to the Age Discrimination in Employment Act prohibit the involuntary retirement of any individual between the ages of 40 and 69 because of that individual's age, an exemption was preserved for the "bona fide executive".[23]

To qualify for the bona fide executive exception to the ban on mandatory retirements below age 70, the subject employee must have been employed in a bona fide executive or high policy-making position for the two-year period immediately preceding his or her retirement, must be entitled to an immediate nonforfeitable annual retirement of at least $44,000 exclusive of the employee's own contributions or contributions of other employees or social security, and must be between the ages of 65 and 69.[24]

[37.05] RECORDKEEPING REQUIREMENTS UNDER ADEA

Employers: The Equal Employment Opportunity Commission regulations require employers to keep records containing each employee's name, address, date of birth, occupation, and rate of pay and compensation earned each week for a period of three years.[25] The EEOC regulations also require that the following personnel records be maintained by the employer on each employee for a period of one year:

- Job applications, résumés, or other replies to job advertisements, including applications for temporary positions and records pertaining to failure to hire;

- Records pertaining to promotion, demotion, transfer, selection for training, lay-offs, recall, or discharge;
- Job orders submitted to an employment agency or union;
- Test papers in connection with employer-administered aptitude or employment tests or other employment tests;
- Records pertaining to the results of any physical examinations;
- Job advertisements or notices to employees regarding openings, promotions, training programs, or other opportunities for overtime work.[26]

Also, employers are required to maintain records pertaining to employee benefit plans, written seniority or merit rating systems for the full period of such plan or system and for at least one year following the termination of such plan or system.[27] Pre-employment records of applicants for temporary positions must be kept by employers for ninety days.[28]

Labor unions: The Equal Employment Opportunity Commission regulations require labor organizations covered by the Age Discrimination in Employment Act to maintain a current record identifying each of its members by name, address, and date of birth.[29] Such unions also are required to maintain for a period of one year, a record of the name, address, and age of any individual seeking membership in its organization.[30]

Employment agencies: The Equal Employment Opportunity Commission regulations require employment agencies covered by the Act to maintain, for one year, all records made, obtained, or used in the regular course of its business which relate to

- placements
- referrals relative to known or reasonably anticipated job openings
- job orders from employers
- job applications, résumés, or any other form of employment inquiry or record of any individual which identifies his or her qualifications for employment
- test papers completed by applicants for positions which disclose the results of any agency-administered aptitude or other employment tests considered by the agency in connection with such referrals
- any advertisements or other notices that relate to job openings[31]

Records pertaining to applicants for temporary positions must be kept by employment agencies for a period of ninety days.[32]

Records required to be maintained by employers, labor unions, and employment agencies also must be available for inspection by an authorized agent of the EEOC.[33] The EEOC may require that any record compelled to be maintained by employers, labor unions, or employment agencies which relates to an enforcement action be maintained until the final disposition thereof.[34]

[37.06] NOTICE-POSTING REQUIREMENT

The Equal Employment Opportunity Commission has prepared a standardized notice-poster which includes a brief discussion of the Age Discrimination in Employment Act, and the rights and remedies thereunder. All organizations covered by the Act are required to keep posted such poster in conspicuous places on their premises.[35]

The failure to post the EEOC notice-poster, as required by the regulations, might be used to toll the prescriptive period for filing an ADEA claim.[36]

NOTES TO CHAPTER 37

1. 29 U.S.C.A. §621, *et seq.*

2. 29 U.S.C.A. §621(b).

3. 29 U.S.C.A. §621, *et seq.*

4. 29 U.S.C.A. §623.

5. 29 U.S.C.A. §630(b).

6. 29 U.S.C.A. §630(b); *EEOC v. Wyoming*, 460 U.S. 226 (1983).

7. *Lehman v. Nakshain*, 453 U.S. 156 (1981).

8. 29 U.S.C.A. §630(c).

9. 29 U.S.C.A. §630(d).

10. 29 U.S.C.A. §623(d).

11. 29 U.S.C.A. §623(e).

12. 29 U.S.C.A. §623(a).

13. 29 U.S.C.A. §623(b).

14. 29 U.S.C.A. §623(c).

15. 29 U.S.C.A. §§211(b), 216(b) and (c), 217 and 626(e).

16. 43 *Fed. Reg.* 19807.

17. 29 U.S.C.A. §1625.1–1625.13.

18. *Allen v. Marshall Field & Co.*, 93 FRD 438 (ND Ill., 1982).

19. 29 U.S.C.A. §623(f)(2).

20. 29 U.S.C.A. §623(f)(2); See also: *Brennan v. Taft Broadcasting Co.*, 500 F.2d 212 (CA-5, 1974).

21. 29 U.S.C.A. §860.120(d).

22. See 29 U.S.C.A. §623(g)(1); §116(a) of P.L. 97-248, 96 Stat. 353, Sept. 3, 1982.

23. 29 U.S.C.A. §631(c).

24. 29 U.S.C.A. §631(c) (as amended).

25. 29 U.S.C.A. §1627.3.

26. 29 U.S.C.A. §1627.3(b)(1).

27. 29 U.S.C.A. §1627.3(b)(2).

28. 29 CFR §1627.3(b)(3).

29. 29 CFR §1627.5(a).

30. 29 CFR §1627.5(b).

31. 29 CFR §1627.4(a)(1).

32. 29 CFR §1627.4(a)(2).

33. 29 CFR §1627.6.

34. 29 CFR §§1627.3(b)(3), 1627.4(a)(3) and 1627.5(c).

35. 29 U.S.C.A. §627; 29 CFR §1627.10.

36. *Vance v. Whirlpool Corp.* 32 FEP Cases 1391 (CA-4, 1983).

38

How to Process
and Defend
an ADEA Claim

[38.01] ADMINISTRATIVE FILINGS

Individuals must file their age discrimination charges with the EEOC within 180 days of the alleged unlawful acts, unless the alleged misconduct occurred in a state which has an age anti-discrimination agency, in which case such charges should be filed within 300 days of the alleged unlawful practice or within 30 days after receipt of notice that the state proceedings have been terminated, whichever is earlier.[1]

The ADEA charge should be in writing, identify the potential defendant, and describe the alleged conduct believed in violation of the Act.[2]

[38.02] CONCILIATION

An individual must wait sixty days after filing his or her age discrimination charge before a lawsuit may be filed in federal district court.[3] The purpose of this jurisdictional prerequisite is to provide an opportunity for the Secretary of Labor (now the EEOC) to attempt to eliminate the alleged misconduct through conciliatory efforts.[4]

The Equal Employment Opportunity Commission's duty to attempt to resolve the alleged unlawful practice by informal methods of conciliation, conference, and persuasion has been held to be a mandatory prerequisite to any legal action in federal court by the EEOC.[5] However, the failure of the EEOC to attempt conciliation with a charged party will not bar an aggrieved charging party from initiating his or her own lawsuit under the provisions of ADEA.[6]

[38.03] RIGHT TO JURY TRIAL

The ADEA provides that an individual is entitled to a jury trial in ADEA actions seeking recovery of amounts owing as a result of unlawful practices under the Act, irrespective of whether equitable relief is sought in such action.[7] However, where an individual initiates a lawsuit under the ADEA solely for injunctive relief, a jury trial is not available.[8]

[38.04] STATUTE OF LIMITATIONS

Under Section 6 of the Portal-to-Portal Act,[9] which governs limitation of action periods for ADEA cases, an age discrimination lawsuit must be filed within two years from the date the cause of action accrued, except that a three-year limitation period is applied to cases of willful violations.[10] These prescriptive periods may be tolled up to one year during the time in which the Secretary of Labor (now the EEOC) attempts conciliation.[11]

[38.05] LITIGATION TO ENFORCE ADEA CLAIMS

Any person entitled to the protection of the ADEA may bring a civil action in any court of competent jurisdiction to seek redress for violations of the Act.[12] Nevertheless, several conditions must be met by the aggrieved party prior to filing a private action under the ADEA, including the requirement that the

- aggrieved party wait sixty days after filing the charge with the EEOC or a state deferral agency before initiating his or her private lawsuit[13]
- age discrimination charge be filed within the respective 180- to 300-day time limitations[14]
- lawsuit by the aggrieved individual be filed within the respective two- or three-year statute of limitation period.[15]

The right of an aggrieved individual to bring his or her private action under the Age Discrimination in Employment Act ceases once the EEOC commences its own civil action to enforce the rights of the aggrieved party.[16] ADEA actions may be brought in either federal or state courts of competent jurisdiction.[17]

The Secretary of Labor (now the EEOC) may bring a lawsuit in any court of competent jurisdiction to seek remedies for violations of ADEA.[18] The enforcement agency may also sue for liquidated damages in actions involving willful violations of the Act,[19] although liquidated damages are not available against government agencies.[20]

The EEOC must show that it attempted to resolve the alleged misconduct through informal methods of conciliation, conference, and persuasion,[21] and must file the suit within the two- or three-year limitation period as discussed earlier.[22]

[38.06] REMEDIES UNDER ADEA

Several types of relief are available to plaintiffs under the provisions of ADEA. Indeed, a court has jurisdiction to fashion such legal or equitable relief as it deems appropriate in ADEA cases, including without limitation: permanent injunctions, reinstatement or promotion, judgments compelling employment, and monetary damages for amounts owing to a person as a result of a violation of the Act.[23]

Where a willful violation is found in an ADEA lawsuit, liquidated damages are also available.[24] In such a case the defendant will be liable to the injured party in an amount double the latter's actual damages.[25] Liquidated damages are applicable to both individual and Secretary of Labor (now EEOC) actions.[26]

Attorney fees may also be awarded to a prevailing plaintiff in an ADEA case under the Equal Access to Justice Act[27] as well as under Section 16(b) of the Fair Labor[28] Standards Act, the latter of which has been incorporated by reference into the ADEA.[29]

[38.07] DEFENSES TO AN ADEA ACTION

Differentials based on reasonable factors other than age: One of the more common defenses to an ADEA lawsuit is that the defendant's decision which allegedly discriminated against the aggrieved party was based on some reasonable factor other than age. The "factor other than age" exemption reiterates the intent of Congress not to require the employment of anyone because of age, but rather to ensure that age, within the protected limits of the Act, would not be used as a determining factor in making an employment decision.[30]

The ADEA does not make it unlawful for an employer to discharge an employee within the 40-70 year age range when such dismissal is based on good cause.[31] Also, pre-employment physicals which are used by an employer in the screening process may be recognized as a reasonable factor other than age to qualify individuals for employment, provided such physical examinations are uniformly and equally applied to all applicants irrespective of their age.[32] The ADEA regulations likewise recognize such factors as production standards or certain minimal educational requirements as a permissible basis for differentiation where such factors are job related and applied uniformly to all employees, regardless of age.[33]

Bona fide occupational qualifications: Similar to the bona fide occupational qualification (BFOQ) defense available in Title VII cases,[34] the ADEA permits employers and other potential defendants to take certain discriminatory actions based upon age if such actions are reasonably necessary to the normal operation of a particular enterprise.[35] The ADEA regulations provide, however, that the bona fide occupational qualification exception will be narrowly construed and have limited applicability.[36]

Most ADEA cases which involve the bona fide occupational qualification defense relate to safety precautions taken by the employer.[37] Although public interest and safety considerations may justify a BFOQ exception, an assumption that most or even many employees of a given age no longer possess the qualifications for a certain job is an insufficient basis for disqualification.[38] In order to justify the exclusion of a certain age group under the BFOQ exception, the employer must show that it

- either has a factual basis for believing that all, or substantially all, members of the affected age group would be unable to perform the duties safely and efficiently; or

- that, because of physiological or psychological degeneration associated with some members of the age group, but not necessarily all, there is no practical way to deal with such affected members of the age group on an individual basis.[39]

Bona fide seniority system: The ADEA permits an employer and other potential defendants to ADEA actions to observe and maintain the terms of a bona fide seniority system, even though the effect of such system may discriminate against certain employees within the protected age group, as long as such a system is not used as a subterfuge to evade the purposes of the statute.[40] In order to be qualified as a bona fide seniority system, the seniority program must be based on length of service as its primary criterion.[41] Moreover, unless a seniority system is applied uniformly to all those affected, irrespective of age, and has been effectively communicated to the affected employees, the courts will most likely disqualify it as a bona fide system.[42]

Procedural and technical deficiencies: Defendants of ADEA actions may raise procedural and technical deficiencies as a defense to a claimant's lawsuit, such as the *failure* of the

- plaintiff to establish the interstate commerce connection and qualification;[43]
- plaintiff to show that a defendant is an employer who employs twenty or more employees for the period prescribed in the Act;[44]
- plaintiff to show a union defendant as one "affecting commerce" as required in the Act;[45]
- plaintiff to show a defendant as an employment agency who regularly undertakes to procure employees for an employer as required in the Act;[46]
- plaintiff to demonstrate that the alleged grievants were within the 40-70 year protected age class;[47]
- plaintiff to show that the age discrimination charge was filed timely with the appropriate agency;[48]
- Equal Employment Opportunity Commission to attempt to conciliate in accordance with its duty;[49]
- aggrieved party to wait sixty days after filing his or her initial charge before bringing the lawsuit;[50] and
- plaintiff to file suit within the applicable two- or three-year limitations period provided in the Act.[51]

Miscellaneous defenses: Some miscellaneous defenses to an ADEA lawsuit might include:

- A defendant's good faith reliance on an official written administrative regulation, order, ruling, approval, or interpretation, or an administrative practice or enforcement policy for his or her act or omission on which the complaint is based;[52] and

- The plaintiff's failure to establish a *prima facie* case.[53]

NOTES TO CHAPTER 38

1. 29 U.S.C.A. §626(d)(2); see also 43 *Fed. Reg.* 19807.
2. *Fulton v. NCR Corp.*, 472 F.Supp. 377 (WD Va., 1979).
3. 29 U.S.C.A. §626(d).
4. *Bishop v. Jelleff Associates, Inc.*, 398 F.Supp. 579 (DC D.C., 1974).
5. *Brennan v. Ace Hardware Corp.*, 495 F.2d 368 (CA-8, 1974).
6. See *Lundgren v. Continental Industries, Inc.*, 11 CCH EPD ¶10,778 (DC Okla., 1976).
7. 29 U.S.C.A. §626(c)(2).
8. See 29 U.S.C.A. §217 in conjunction with 29 U.S.C.S. §626(b).
9. See 29 U.S.C.A. §255.
10. 29 U.S.C.A. §255(a).
11. 29 U.S.C.A. §626(e).
12. 29 U.S.C.A. §626(c).
13. 29 U.S.C.A. §626(d); See also: *Rucker v. Great Scott Supermarkets*, 528 F.2d 393 (CA-6, 1976).
14. 29 U.S.C.A. §626(d)(2).
15. 29 U.S.C.A. §255(a).
16. 29 U.S.C.A. §626(c).
17. 29 U.S.C.A. §216(b).
18. 29 U.S.C.A. §216(c).
19. 29 U.S.C.A. §216(c).
20. *Lehman v. Nakshain*, 453 U.S. 156 (1981).
21. 29 U.S.C.A. §626(b).
22. 29 U.S.C.A. §255(a).
23. See generally: 29 U.S.C.A. §626(b).
24. 29 U.S.C.A. §216(b).
25. 29 U.S.C.A. §216(b).
26. 29 U.S.C.A. §216(b) and (c).
27. 28 U.S.C.A §2412.
28. 29 U.S.C.A. §216(b).
29. 29 U.S.C.A. §626(b).
30. 29 CFR §860.103(c).
31. 29 U.S.C.A. §623(f)(3).

32. 29 CFR §860.103(f)(1)(i).

33. 29 CFR §860.103(f)(2).

34. See [37.02].

35. 29 U.S.C.A. §623(f).

36. 29 CFR §860.102(b).

37. *Hodgson v. Greyhound Lines, Inc.*, 499 F.2d 859 (CA-7, 1974).

38. *Usery v. Tamiami Trail Tours, Inc.*, 531 F.2d 224 (CA-5, 1976).

39. *Houghton v. McDonnell Douglas Corp.*, 553 F.2d 561 (CA-8, 1977).

40. 29 U.S.C.A. §623(f)(2).

41. 29 CFR §860.105(a).

42. 29 CFR §860.105(c).

43. Discussed at [37.02].

44. Discussed at [37.02].

45. Discussed at [37.02].

46. Discussed at [37.02].

47. 29 U.S.C.A. §631(a).

48. 29 U.S.C.A. §626(d)(2) and 43 *Fed. Reg.* 19807.

49. Discussed at [38.02].

50. 29 U.S.C.A. §626(d); also discussed at [41.02].

51. Discussed at [38.02].

52. See 29 U.S.C.A. §626(e) and 29 U.S.C.A. §259.

53. See, for example: *Magruder v. Selling Areas Marketing, Inc.*, 439 F.Supp. 1155 (ND Ill., 1977).

39

Equal Pay Act

[39.01] BACKGROUND

The Equal Pay Act, an adjunct to the Fair Labor Standards Act, was enacted in 1963.[1] The statute provides that it is unlawful for any employer, subject to provisions, to discriminate on the basis of sex in the wage rates of male and female employees doing jobs which require equal skill, effort, and responsibility, and which are performed under similar working conditions, unless the wage differential is justified by statutory exceptions.[2]

The Equal Pay Act also prohibits a labor union or its agents to cause or attempt to cause such discrimination.[3] A union violates the Act whenever it demands any terms in a collective bargaining agreement that would cause a violation by the employer, or strikes or pickets an employer to induce such discrimination.[4]

The responsibility and authority for the administration and enforcement of the Equal Pay Act has been transferred from the Department of Labor to the Equal Employment Opportunity Commission (EEOC), pursuant to the Reorganization Plan No. 1 of 1978.

As a general rule, the Equal Pay Act applies to most employees subject to the Fair Labor Standards Act.[5] For example, bona fide executives, administrative, professional, and outside sales employees, who are exempt from the minimum wage and overtime pay provision of the FLSA, are nonetheless covered by the Equal Pay statute.[6]

[39.02] EQUAL PAY WORK STANDARDS

Although the Equal Pay Act uses the term "equal" in describing the appropriate work standard, the courts have interpreted the term to mean only substantially equal, rather than identical.[7] In determining whether an employer is in compliance with the Equal Pay Act, four work standards are considered: *skill; effort; responsibility;* and *working conditions.*

Equal skill: The equal pay work standard does not apply if the amount or degree of skill required to perform one job differs significantly from that required to perform another job.[8] In determining whether various jobs require equal skill, the EEOC and the courts usually consider such factors as *experience, training, education,* and *ability.* The mere possession of skill is irrelevant in determining equality of jobs under the Equal Pay Act. Rather, it is the performance requirements of the job that must be considered in measuring equality of skill.[9]

Equal effort: The equal pay work standard is inapplicable if the amount or degree of effort required to perform one job is substantially different from that required to perform another job.[10] In determining whether the performance of certain jobs requires equal effort, the EEOC and the courts will usually measure both the mental and the physical exertion needed to perform the job requirements.[11] The occasional or sporadic performance of work requiring additional mental and/or physical exertion will not make jobs unequal that are otherwise substantially equal.[12] Neither will different kinds of effort required in the performance of jobs make such jobs unequal if the amount or degree of effort exerted is substantially equal.[13]

Equal responsibility: The equal pay work standard does not apply if the amount or degree of responsibility required to perform one job is substantially greater than that required to perform another job.[14] The degree of accountability required in the performance of the job is the primary measurement used in determining equality of responsibility.[15] A minor or insignificant additional responsibility will not make one job unequal to another under the Equal Pay Act regulations.[16]

Similar working conditions: Wage differentials between male and female employees do not violate the Equal Pay Act where the jobs in question are performed under substantially different working conditions.[17] In determining whether the performance of certain jobs involve similar working conditions, the EEOC and the courts will usually consider whether the differences in conditions are the kind customarily taken into consideration in setting wage levels and whether the wage differentials are based upon bona fide job evaluation plans.[18]

[39.03]   WAGE DIFFERENTIAL EXCEPTIONS

The Equal Pay Act only forbids wage differentials based solely on sex.[19] The Act does not extend to wage variations based on factors other than sex such as the following:

Merit and incentive programs: Incentive payments, production bonuses, and performance raises do not violate the Equal Pay Act when applied without regard to sex distinction.[20] A merit system, whether written or unwritten, does not violate the Act if the system measures earnings based upon some predetermined criteria such as quality or quantity of production, and as long as the employees subject to the program are aware of its existence and the system is not based upon sex.[21]

Seniority systems: An employer does not violate the Equal Pay Act by paying wage differentials based upon seniority or longevity, when applied without distinction to employees of both sexes.[22]

Training programs: Bona fide training programs may also qualify as an exception to the equal pay work standards and be used as a basis to differentiate wages, when applied without regard to sex distinction.[23]

Shift differentials: As a general rule, shift differentials do not violate the Equal Pay Act as long as they are not based on sex distinction.[24]

Red circle rates for temporary assignments: Wage differentials may also be justified where an employee continues at his or her old wage rate after being transferred to a different job on temporary assignment.[25]

Miscellaneous exceptions: Other miscellaneous factors which may justify wage differentials based upon distinctions other than sex include:

- *Bona fide job classification programs;*
- *Probationary employee status;* and
- *Part-time employee status.*[26]

[39.04] COMPLIANCE THROUGH ADVERSE ACTION PROHIBITED

An employer who violates the Equal Pay Act by paying female employees less wages than male employees may not reduce the wages of the male employees in an effort to comply with the requirements of the Act.[27] Neither may an employer satisfy the requirements of the Equal Pay Act by transferring higher paid male employees into lower paying jobs previously held solely by female employees.[28]

[39.05] COMPARABLE WORTH

As discussed at [32.08], the federal courts have not extended the equal pay standards to embrace the comparable worth theory.

In keeping with the *Gunther* decision,[29] courts have generally failed to recognize the comparable worth theory either under the Equal Pay Act or Title VII, empahsizing the onerous task of attempting to evaluate the intrinsic worth of different jobs.[30]

[39.06] RECORDKEEPING REQUIREMENTS

Every employer subject to the Equal Pay Act must preserve and maintain records and documents that relate to the payment of wages, wage rates, job evaluations, merit and incentive systems, and seniority systems, including records of any practices that explain the basis for payment of wage differentials such as collective bargaining agreements.[31] Such records should be preserved and retained for a period of at least two years.[32]

[39.07] HOW TO PROCESS AN EQUAL PAY CLAIM

Although the Equal Employment Opportunity Commission (EEOC) has been delegated the responsibility of administering and enforcing the Equal Pay Act, complaints alleging violation of the Act may also be submitted to the Wage and Hour Division of the U.S. Department of Labor.[33]

Once a complaint is filed under the Equal Pay Act, the EEOC will conduct an investigation and gather necessary data such as records pertaining to wages, hours, and other conditions and practices of employment, to determine whether a violation of the Act has occurred.[34] The investigation might also include inspecting the employer's premises, conducting interviews with employees, and transcribing pertinent records and documents from the employer's files.[35]

A suit to redress equal pay violations may be filed in both state and federal courts of competent jurisdiction.[36]

An employee whose rights have been violated under the Equal Pay Act may bring action against his or her employer to seek a monetary award for back pay.[37] In addition, the EEOC may bring an action under the Equal Pay Act on behalf of employees to seek redress for alleged violations.[38]

The EEOC and employees affected by violations of the Equal Pay Act may also maintain class action type suits under 29 USCS Section 215(b), which statute also provides that no employee can become a party to such a plaintiff action without his or her express written consent.[39]

A plaintiff may be entitled to a jury trial in an Equal Pay suit if the action is brought to recover back pay and/or liquidated damages.[40] On the other hand, if an EEOC suit, grounded in equity, is filed to enforce the Act, the defending employer has no constitutional right to a jury trial.[41]

Both the EEOC and individuals bringing lawsuits under the Equal Pay Act have the burden of proving that a wage differential is based on sex.[42] Once the plaintiff to such an action establishes a prima facie case by showing that the defendant employer paid male employees higher wages than female employees for substantially equal work, the burden of proof shifts to the employer to justify such wage differential.[43]

[39.08] HOW TO DEFEND AN EQUAL PAY CASE

The defendant to an Equal Pay lawsuit may defend such action by showing the court that the wage differential at issue was justified by a seniority system, merit system, training program, or some factor other than sex. Should an employer establish any one of these affirmative defenses, it may not properly be held in violation of the Act.[44]

The defending employer may also defend an equal pay case by showing that his or her actions were based on a good-faith reliance on an interpretation of the Act by the EEOC.[45]

Applicable defenses available to defendants under other Fair Labor

Standard actions are discussed at [48.07] and may also be used to defend Equal Pay lawsuits.

The employer may also assert an affirmative defense that the Equal Pay action was not filed timely with the court, when applicable. In this connection, an action under the Equal Pay Act to recover unpaid wages must be brought within two years from the time the alleged violation occurred.[46] If the violation was willful, the suit must be commenced within three years from the time the cause of action accrued.[47] However, some courts have held that wage differentials based on sex constitute a continuing violation under the Equal Pay Act, and the two- and three-year prescriptive periods do not necessarily commence to run from the date the employer failed to pay proper wages.[48]

[39.09]   REMEDIES AVAILABLE IN AN EQUAL PAY ACTION

Under the Equal Pay Act, an employee adversely affected by violation of the Act is entitled to back pay for the wages not properly paid, as well as an amount equal to such back pay as liquidated damages.[49]

A successful plaintiff in an Equal Pay lawsuit may also be entitled to reasonable attorney's fee and costs of the action upon proper application to the court and subject to the court's discretion.[50]

The EEOC may seek injunctive relief for violations of the Equal Pay Act as well as damages for back-pay claims on behalf of affected employees.[51] As a general rule, however, injunctive relief in equal pay matters are not available to individual employees in private actions under the Act.[52]

An employer or a union that willfully violates the Equal Pay Act is subject to criminal prosecution, fines up to $10,000, and possible imprisonment.[53]

NOTES TO CHAPTER 39

1. 29 U.S.C.A. §206(d).
2. 29 U.S.C.A. §206(d).
3. 29 CFR §800.106.
4. See 29 CFR §800.106.
5. See Chapter 44 for a general discussion on coverage under the Fair Labor Standards Act.
6. 29 U.S.C.A. §213(a)(1).
7. *Shultz v. Wheaton Glass Co.,* 421 F.2d 259 (CA-3, 1970).
8. 29 CFR §800.125.
9. 29 CFR §800.125.
10. 29 CFR §800.127.
11. 29 CFR §800.127.

12. *Shultz v. Corning Glass Works*, 319 F.Supp. 1161 (DC NY, 1970).

13. *Usery v. Columbia University*, 568 F.2d 953 (CA-2, 1977).

14. 29 CFR §800.129.

15. 29 CFR §800.129.

16. 29 CFR §800.130.

17. 29 CFR §800.131.

18. *Corning Glass Works v. Brennan*, 417 U.S. 188 (1974).

19. 29 CFR §800.142.

20. 29 CFR §800.144.

21. *EEOC v. Aetna Ins. Co.*, 616 F.2d 719 (CA-4, 1980).

22. 29 CFR §800.145.

23. 29 CFR §800.148.

24. 29 CFR §800.145.

25. 29 CFR §800.146.

26. *Guidebook to Federal Wage-Hour Laws,* Para. 1105 (1978).

27. 29 U.S.C.A. §206(d)(1).

28. *Hodgson v. Miller Brewing Co.*, 456 F.2d 221 (CA-7, 1972).

29. *County of Washington v. Gunther*, 452 U.S. 161 (1981).

30. See, for example: *Power v. Barry County, Michigan*, 29 FEP Cases 559 (WD Mich.,
    1982).

31. 29 CFR §1620.21(b).

32. 29 CFR §1620.21(c).

33. 44 *Fed. Reg.* 38670.

34. 29 CFR §1620.19.

35. 29 CFR §1620.19.

36. 29 U.S.C.A. §216(b).

37. 29 U.S.C.A. §216(b).

38. 29 CFR §1620.19(b); 1620.22.

39. 29 U.S.C.A. §216(b).

40. *Altman v. Stevens Fashion Fabrics*, 441 F.Supp. 1318 (ND Cal., 1977).

41. *Brennan v. J. C. Penney Co.*, 61 FRD 66 (DC Ohio, 1973).

42. *Corning Glass Works v. Brennan*, 417 U.S. 188 (1974).

43. *Ammons v. Zia Co.*, 448 F.2d 117 (CA-10, 1971).

44. *Strecker v. Grand Forks County Social Service Board*, 640 F.2d 96 (CA-8, 1980).

45. 29 CFR §259.

46. *Hodgson v. Robert Hall Clothes, Inc.*, 326 F.Supp. 1264 (DC Del., 1971).

47. 29 U.S.C.A. §255.

48. *Hodgson v. Behrens Drug Co.*, 475 F.2d 1041 (CA-5, 1973).

49. 29 U.S.C.A. §216(b) and (c); see also: 29 CFR §1620.22.
50. 29 CFR §1620.22.
51. 29 U.S.C.A. §217.
52. *DeFigueiredo v. Trans World Airlines, Inc.*, 322 F.Supp. 1384 (DC NY, 1971).
53. 29 CFR §1620.22.

40

Veterans' Reemployment Rights

[40.01]   BACKGROUND AND COVERAGE

The veterans' reemployment laws, formally known as the Military Selective Service Act of 1967 (and its predecessor amendments), provide that a person who satisfactorily completes his or her military service and receives a certificate to that effect must, upon timely application, be restored to his or her previous position or a similar position, assuming the person is still qualified to perform the duties thereof.[1]

The veterans' reemployment laws extend not only to inductees, enlistees, and other military personnel whose service is full time, but such laws also protect reservists and National Guardsmen whose military service may vary in shorter time frames.[2] Employees applying for, as well as those rejected from, military service also have certain rights under the statute.[3]

[40.02]   ADMINISTRATION AND ENFORCEMENT

The veterans' reemployment laws are administered by the Office of Veterans' Reemployment Rights (OVRR), under the Labor Management Services Administration, which is a part of the U.S. Department of Labor.[4]

The Office of Veterans' Reemployment Rights has the responsibility of educating veterans and other interested parties as to the rights provided by the statute.[5] It also has the responsibility of processing, investigating, and conciliating veterans' cases that come before it.[6]

[40.03]   CONDITIONS TO REEMPLOYMENT

Although the preservice employer of a veteran generally is obligated by law to restore such individual to his or her previous or similar position upon completion of military service or training, certain conditions do attach to the right to enjoy reemployment benefits. Notwithstanding such conditions, however, a presumption does exist that a returning veteran is qualified to work for the preservice employer.[7] The burden is on the preservice employer to overcome this presumption and prove that the veteran is disqualified from returning to his or her previous or similar job, if such issue is raised.[8]

Some of the conditions that must be met by the returning veteran in order to qualify for reemployment are as follows:

Qualified to perform: One of the primary conditions that predispose a veteran returning to the former job is that he or she be qualified to perform the duties of the position or positions sought, in terms of physical and mental ability, performance standards, and so forth.[9]

Timely application: As a general rule, in order to be eligible for reemployment under the veterans' reemployment laws, a veteran must apply for reemployment with his or her preservice employer within ninety calendar days from the date on which he or she was unconditionally released from military service, unless hospitalized for a period continuing after discharge, in which case he or she must apply within one year.[10] However, where reservists or National Guardsmen are ordered to active duty to perform military training for not less than three months, they have thirty-one days from the date of their release after satisfactory service within which to apply for reemployment to their previous or similar jobs.[11] No applications for reemployment are required of reservists or National Guardsmen who are ordered to active duty for training for less then three months as a condition to their returning to work.[12]

Other than temporary position upon departure: Another condition to a veteran's reemployment right of return to a former position is that the previous employment must have been more than merely temporary in duration.[13] However, probationary period employees are protected under the statute if it can be shown that the employee would have continued indefinitely in the job had he or she satisfactorily completed the probationary period.[14]

Veteran's intent upon departure: Another condition for reemployment under the statute is that the veteran must have left the position with his or her preservice employer with the intent to perform military training or service, or to undergo a preinduction physical or other qualifying examination, rather than for some reason unrelated to military service.[15]

[40.04] VETERANS' RIGHTS UNDER THE LAWS

Should a veteran timely apply for reemployment and meet the conditions discussed above, he or she is entitled to the same benefits and wages as if he or she had remained employed during the period of military stay. The rights of qualifying veterans upon their return to previous or similar jobs usually include:

- *Seniority privileges.*[16] The veteran has the right to be restored to the same seniority rights and status which he or she would have enjoyed had the employment not been interrupted by military service or training.[17]

- *General wage increases.* Veterans are also entitled to be restored to the wage scale they would have enjoyed had they not entered military service;[18] however, pay increases granted as a result of an employee's merit, experience, or some similar criteria, does not inure to the returning veteran.[19]

- *Automatic promotions.*[20] Veterans are entitled, upon their return from

military service, to the promotional or progressive step they would have
occupied had their employment not been interrupted by military service, assuming that such promotions were rarely, if ever, denied regular employees.[21]

- *Sick leave credits.*[22] A returning veteran is entitled to sick leave credits
  customarily awarded employees on the basis of length of service with
  the employer.

- *Pension and retirement benefits.* A veteran's military service time must be
  counted as part of his or her continuous service with the employer for
  the purpose of determining eligibility for retirement and pension benefits.[23]

- *Severance pay;*[24] and usually

- *Holiday pay,*[25] *bonuses,*[26] *and insurance.*[27]

[40.05]   EMPLOYER OBLIGATIONS

As noted earlier, the primary responsibility of the preservice employer is to
reinstate the returning veteran to his or her previous, or similar job, without
loss of seniority. The employer's offer of reemployment must be in good
faith and remain open for 90 days.[28]

A preservice employer is excused from the obligation of reemploying
a returning veteran if the employer's circumstances have so changed as to
make it unreasonable to reinstate the previous employee.[29] Examples of
changed conditions which constitute reasonable grounds to deny reemployment to a returning veteran include such circumstances as abolition of the
veteran's old job,[30] or the sale of the employer's business.[31]

Reemployment obligations may be held to extend to a successor employer in the latter example.[32]

The preservice employer may not deny the returning veteran his or
her former job by pleading that the veteran's replacement is more experienced, or, in some other way, a better employee.[33]

Preservice employers are prohibited from discharging a returning veteran, without cause, within one year after reemployment.[34]

[40.06]   HOW TO PROCESS AND DEFEND VETERANS' CLAIMS

The Office of Veterans' Reemployment Rights (OVRR) has the function
of providing assistance to veterans, reservists, and other interested parties
who may have claims under the reemployment statute. Although the OVRR
has no power to issue rulings or decisions that would be binding upon either
an employee or the employer,[35] it has the obligation of attempting to settle
claims presented to it through informal voluntary compliance.[36]

Should a veteran's claim be unresolved through the efforts of the

OVRR or the grievance/arbitration provision of a collective bargaining contract,[37] if applicable, the veteran may apply to the local United States Attorney's Office[38] or secure private counsel[39] to prosecute his or her claim in federal district court. The United States District Court, for any district in which the complaining veteran's employer maintains a place of business, has the power to require such employer to comply with the reemployment laws.[40]

A defendant may raise several defenses to a veteran's action in federal district court, when applicable, such as

- the failure of the veteran to have filed his or her application timely[41]

- an assertion that the veteran's previous job was temporary[42]

- a claim that the veteran has not received a "satisfactory service" certificate[43]

- a claim that the veteran had left his or her previous job for some reason other than to enter military service[44]

- a showing that changed circumstances of the employer precluded reemployment of the veteran[45]

- an assertion that the veteran was not qualified to perform the duties in question upon his or her return from military service[46]

- a showing that no reasonable certainty existed by which the veteran should have obtained some promotion, etc.[47]

- an assertion that the veteran was discharged for "cause," although the discharge occurred within one year of his or her reemployment.[48]

NOTES TO CHAPTER 40

1. 38 U.S.C.A. §2021, *et seq.*

2. 38 U.S.C.A. §2024(c) and (d); See, also: *Monroe v. Standard Oil Co.,* 452 U.S. 549 (1981).

3. 38 U.S.C.A. §2024(e).

4. 38 U.S.C.A. §2025.

5. 38 U.S.C.A. §2021, *et seq.*

6. 38 U.S.C.A. §2021, *et seq.*

7. *McCoy v. Olin Mathieson Chemical Corp.,* 360 F.Supp. 1336 (DC Ill., 1973).

8. Ibid.

9. 38 U.S.C.A. §2021(a).

10. 38 U.S.C.A. §2021(a) and 2024(a) and (b)(1).

11. 38 U.S.C.A. §2024(c).

12. 38 U.S.C.A. §2024(d).

13. 38 U.S.C.A. §2021(a).

14. *Collins v. Weirton Steel Co.,* 398 F.2d 305 (CA-4, 1968).

15. 38 U.S.C.A. §2021(a) and 2024(e).

16. 38 U.S.C.A. §2021(a).

17. *Fishgold v. Sullivan Drydock & Repair Corp.,* 328 U.S. 275 (1946).

18. *Alfarone v. Fairchild Stratos Corp.,* 218 F.Supp. 446 (DC NY, 1963).

19. *Hatton v. The Tabard Press Corp.,* 406 F.2d 592 (CA-2, 1969).

20. *Brooks v. Missouri P.R. Co.,* 376 U.S. 182 (1964).

21. *Hatton v. Tabard Press Corp.* 406 F.2d 593 (CA-2, 1969).

22. See *Nichols v. Kansas City Power & Light Co.,* 391 F.Supp 833 (DC Mo., 1975).

23. *Davis v. Alabama Power Co.,* 383 F.Supp. 880 (DC Ala., 1974).

24. *Accardi v. Pennsylvania R. Co.,* 383 U.S. 225 (1966).

25. See *Eager v. Magma Copper Co.,* 389 U.S. 323 (1967).

26. Ibid.

27. *Dufner v. Penn. Central Transp. Co.,* 374 F.Supp. 979 (1974).

28. *Loeb v. Kivo,* 169 F.2d 346 (CA-2, 1948).

29. 38 U.S.C.A. §2021(a).

30. *Dyer v. Holston Mfg. Co.,* 237 F.Supp. 287 (DC Tenn., 1964).

31. *Hastings v. Reynolds Metals Co.,* 165 F.2d 484 (CA-7, 1947).

32. *Wimberly v. Mission Broadcasting Co.,* 523 F.2d 1260 (CA-10, 1975).

33. *Kay v. General Cable Corp.,* 144 F.2d 653 (CA-3, 1944).

34. See, generally, *Veteran's Re-employment Rights Handbook,* (Dept. of Labor, 1970). See also: 38 U.S.C.A. §2021.

35. See *Fishgold v. Sullivan Drydock & Repair Corp., supra.*

36. SR No. 93-907, 93rd Cong. 2nd Sess. 109, 113.

37. See Note 34, 127-128, *supra.*

38. 38 U.S.C.A. §2022.

39. See Note 34, P.129, *supra.*

40. 38 U.S.C.A. §2022.

41. See [40.03].

42. See [40.03].

43. 38 U.S.C.A. §2021(a).

44. 38 U.S.C.A. §2021(a) and 38 U.S.C.A. §2024(e).

45. 38 U.S.C.A. §2021(a).

46. 38 U.S.C.A. §2021(a).

47. *McKinney v. Missouri-Kansas-Texas R. Co.,* 357 U.S. 265 (1958).

48. *Larsen v. Air California,* 313 F.Supp. 218 (DC Cal., 1970).

41

The Rehabilitation Act of 1973 and Related Discrimination Bans in Federal Programs

[41.01] REHABILITATION ACT OF 1973 (SECTION 504)

Section 504 of the Rehabilitation Act of 1973 provides that recipients of federal financial assistance are prohibited from discriminating against otherwise qualified handicapped persons solely by reason of their handicap.[1]

Federal courts have generally ruled that a private right of action is available under Section 504 of the Handicapped Law.[2] The U.S. Supreme Court has held that Section 504 was intended to forbid employment discrimination against the handicapped even where the primary objective of the federal funding is not to promote employment.[3] However, the U.S. Supreme Court has also limited the applicability of Section 504, ruling that a state institution which denied employment to a handicapped individual could not be sued under the Section 504 provision inasmuch as the Eleventh Amendment to the U.S. Constitution bars suits against a state by private citizens.[4]

A "handicapped individual" has been defined as any individual who has a physical or mental impairment that substantially limits one or more major life activities and either has a record of such impairment or is regarded as having such an impairment.[5]

The term "handicapped individual" does not include alcoholics or drug abusers whose dependency upon alcohol or drugs prevents them from performing the duties of the job in question or constitutes a direct threat to property or the safety of others and themselves.[6] However, Section 504 has been held applicable to such disabilities as former drug addiction,[7] former mental illness,[8] epilepsy,[9] blindness,[10] congenital back problems,[11] and hypersensitivity to tobacco smoke.[12]

Recipients of federally assisted programs are prohibited from discriminating against handicapped individuals in such activities as recruitment and selection, advancement and promotions, transfer and recall, compensation, job assignments, leave and sick policy, benefit programs, social and recreational programs, job classifications, and other terms, conditions, or privileges of employment.[13]

Federally assisted recipients are also prohibited from denying any employment opportunity to a qualified handicapped applicant or employee on the basis that it would be necessary to make a reasonable accommodation to the physical or mental limitation of the applicant or employee.[14]

Violations of Section 504 trigger the same remedies as afforded by Title VII of the Civil Rights Act of 1964.[15]

[41.02]   REHABILITATION ACT OF 1973 (SECTION 503)

Section 503 of the Rehabilitation Act of 1973 requires federal contractors and subcontractors having contracts with the federal government, or any of its departments or agencies, in excess of $2,500, to take affirmative action to employ and advance in employment, qualified handicapped persons and otherwise treat qualified handicapped persons without discrimination based upon their physical or mental handicap in all employment practices.

The Office of Federal Contract Compliance Programs (OFCCP) has adopted Section 503 as part of its affirmative action requirements for governmental contractors and subcontractors holding contracts of $50,000 or more and having fifty or more employees.[16] Such contractors must file written affirmative action plans with the OFCCP, as directed in its regulations.[17]

The affirmative action requirements for handicapped workers provide that covered government contractors must invite all handicapped applicants and employees who believe themselves to be covered by the Rehabilitation Act of 1973, and who desire to be benefited under the affirmative action program, to identify themselves and communicate their interest to the contractor.[18]

Should an applicant or employee respond to the contractor's invitation, the OFCCP regulations specify that the contractor should seek the advice of the applicant or employee regarding proper placement and/or appropriate accomodation.[19]

The OFCCP regulations also require Section 503 contractors to maintain records regarding any complaints received from handicapped applicants and employees and what action, if any, was taken with respect to the complaints.[20] Such records are to be maintained for not less than one year.[21] The covered contractor must also maintain such other records as the director of the OFCCP may require.[22]

As with other affirmative action inspections and compliance reviews, Section 503 contractors must permit access to their places of business, books, records, and other documents for the purpose of complaint investigation relating to their compliance with affirmative action obligations to handicapped individuals.[23]

An aggrieved handicapped individual may file a complaint against a Section 503 contractor with the Department of Labor.[24] Should an investigation by the Department of Labor indicate a contractor violation of Section 503, an attempt will be made to conciliate the matter with the contractor.[25] Should conciliation fail, the director of the Office of Federal Contract Compliance Programs (OFCCP) may seek appropriate injunctive relief through a federal court, hold an administrative hearing to determine whether the contractor should be barred from receiving future contracts, or both of the above.[26]

[41.03]   REHABILITATION ACT OF 1973 (SECTION 501)

Section 501 of the Rehabilitation Act of 1973 provides a private right of action for federal government employees and applicants against federal agencies, departments, and instrumentalities whenever such federal entities discriminate against such employees or applicants because of their handicap or whenever such federal entities fail to provide affirmative action to accommodate the physical or mental impairment of the employees or applicants, as required by the statute.[27]

[41.04]   AFFIRMATIVE ACTION
FOR HANDICAPPED VETERANS

Section 402 of the Vietnam Era Veterans Readjustment Assistance Act of 1974 requires government contractors, with contracts in the amount of $10,000 or more, to take affirmative action to employ and advance in employment, qualified disabled veterans and veterans of the Vietnam era. Executive Order No. 11701 empowers the Secretary of Labor to administer and enforce affirmative action programs for disabled veterans.[28]

The Secretary of Labor has issued, through the Office of Federal Contract Compliance Programs, various rules and regulations pertaining to affirmative action programs for handicapped veterans.[29] The OFCCP regulations require each government contractor to agree to affirmative action clauses pertinent to disabled veterans and veterans of the Vietnam era.[30] These affirmative action clauses require covered contractors to agree to

- comply with nondiscrimination practices in the employment and advancement in employment of qualified veterans

- list suitable employment openings at local state employment service offices and provide certain reports regarding employment openings and hires as may be required

- comply with any rules, regulations, or relevant orders which the Secretary of Labor may issue pursuant to the federal statutes governing affirmative action

- post notices in conspicuous places of their nondiscrimination and affirmative action obligations regarding veterans

- notify each labor union or representative of workers with which they have collective bargaining agreements that they are bound by the nondiscrimination and affirmative action clauses of the Vietnam Era Veterans Readjustment Assistance Act

• include the affirmative action clause regarding veterans in every sub-contract or purchase order of $10,000 or more, and not otherwise exempted, so that such affirmative action obligations will be likewise binding upon subcontractors and vendors[31]

In addition, OFCCP regulations require a covered contractor to invite disabled veterans and veterans of the Vietnam era to register with it, any desire to seek employment or otherwise benefit under the contractor's affirmative action program.[32]

[41.05] TITLE VI OF THE CIVIL RIGHTS ACT OF 1964

Title VI of the Civil Rights Act of 1964 prohibits discrimination on the basis of race, color, or national origin in programs and activities receiving federal financial assistance.[33]

Title VI authorizes and directs each federal department and agency empowered to extend federal financial assistance to any program or activity, by way of grant, loan or contract, other than a contract of insurance or guaranty, to issue rules, regulations, or orders consistent with achieving the objectives of the statute authorizing such assistance and effectuating the provisions of Title VI.[34]

Except in certain continuing state programs, applications for federal financial assistance to carry out programs covered by Title VI regulations must contain assurances that such programs will comply with the Title VI requirements.[35] Contracts, subcontracts, agreements, or arrangements to carry out such programs must contain similar assurances of compliance with the Title VI requirements.[36]

Title VI provisions require covered recipients of federally assisted programs to post notices of its nondiscrimination commitments.[37]

[41.06] AGE DISCRIMINATION BAN IN FEDERAL CONTRACTS AND PROGRAMS

The Age Discrimination Act of 1975 forbids discrimination on the basis of age in programs receiving federal financial assistance.[38]

Executive Order No. 11141 prohibits contractors and subcontractors engaged in the performance of federal contracts from discriminating against persons because of their age in connection with the employment, advancement, discharge or other terms, conditions, or privileges of their employment, except upon the basis of a bona fide occupational qualification, pension plan, or statutory requirement.[39]

[41.07] DISCRIMINATION PROHIBITED IN REGISTERED APPRENTICESHIP PROGRAMS

Sponsors of apprenticeship programs registered with the United States Department of Labor or with recognized state apprenticeship agencies are prohibited from discriminating against individuals on the basis of race, color, religion, national origin, or sex in connection with the recruitment and selection of apprentices and in connection with other conditions of employment and training during apprenticeship.[40]

Sponsors of registered apprenticeship programs must also take affirmative action to provide equal opportunity with respect to apprenticeship programs.[41]

NOTES TO CHAPTER 41

1. 29 U.S.C.A. §794.
2. *Consolidated Rail Corp. v. Darrone,* 104 S.Ct. 1248 (1984).
3. Ibid.
4. *Atascadero State Hospital v. Scanlon,* 53 USLW 4985 (1985).
5. 29 U.S.C.A. §706(7); See also: 45 CFR §85.31(b)(1), (2), (3) & (4).
6. 29 U.S.C.A. §706(7).
7. *Davis v. Bucher,* 451 F.Supp. 791 (ED Pa., 1978).
8. *Doe v. Syracuse School District,* 508 F.Supp. 333 (ND NY, 1981).
9. *Drennon v. Philadelphia General Hospital,* 428 F.Supp. 809 (ED Pa., 1977).
10. *Gurmankin v. Costanzo,* 411 F.Supp. 982 (ED Pa., 1976).
11. *E. E. Black, Ltd. v. Marshall,* 497 F.Supp. 1088 (D. Hawaii, 1980).
12. *Vickers v. Veterans Administration,* 549 F.Supp. 85 (DC Wash., 1982).
13. See, for example: 13 CFR §113.3d; 45 CFR §84.11(b).
14. 49 CFR §27.33(d).
15. 29 U.S.C.A. §794.
16. 41 CFR §60-741.5(a).
17. 41 CFR §60-741.5(a).
18. 41 CFR §60-741.5(c)(1).
19. 41 CFR §60-741.5(c)(1).
20. See 41 CFR §60-741.52(a).
21. 41 CFR §60-741.52(a).
22. 41 CFR §60-741.52(a) and (b).
23. 41 CFR §60-741.53.
24. 41 CFR §741.26.

25. 41 CFR §741.26(g)(2).

26. 41 CFR §§60.741.28 and 60.741.29.

27. 29 U.S.C. §791; See also: 29 CFR §1613.701, *et seq.*

28. Executive Order No. 11701, Section 2.

29. 41 CFR §60-250.2.

30. 41 CFR §60-250.4.

31. 41 CFR §60-250.4.

32. 41 CFR §60-250.5(d) and 41 CFR §60-250, Appendix A.

33. 42 U.S.C.A. §2000d, *et seq.*

34. 42 U.S.C.A. §2000d, *et seq.*

35. 42 U.S.C.A. §2000d.

36. 29 CFR §31.6(b).

37. 28 CFR §42.405(c).

38. 42 U.S.C.A. §6101, *et seq.*

39. Executive Order No. 11141.

40. 29 U.S.C.A. §50; 29 CFR §30.1.

41. 29 CFR §30.1.

42

Federal Anti-Discrimination Executive Orders

[42.01]   EXECUTIVE ORDER NO. 11246

Executive Order No. 11246, as subsequently amended by Executive Order No. 11375 and Executive Order No. 12086, specifically prohibits job discrimination based on race, color, religion, sex, and national origin by government contractors and subcontractors.

Executive Order No. 11246 (hereinafter referred to as E.O. 11246) somewhat parallels the obligations imposed upon private sector employers who fall under the jurisdiction of Title VII of the Civil Rights Act of 1964.[1]

The Secretary of Labor is responsible for administering the nondiscrimination provisions of Executive Order 11246.[2] Much of the Secretary of Labor's responsibility has been delegated to the Office of Federal Contract Compliance Programs (hereinafter referred to as the OFCCP).[3] The OFCCP has developed a substantial body of regulations, the purpose of which is to achieve equal opportunity in federal contracting jobs without regard to race, color, religion, sex, or national origin.[4]

Federal contracting agencies, as well as federal contractors and subcontractors, are required to comply with OFCCP regulations and must furnish such information and data as the OFCCP may request.[5]

[42.02]   E.O. 11246 COVERAGE

All contractors and subcontractors operating under federal service, supply and construction contracts as well as contractors and subcontractors performing under federally aided construction contracts, who have contracts in excess of $10,000 with the federal government, must include within their government contracts an equal employment clause which, substantially, subjects such contractors to the Title VII equal employment opportunity requirements.[6]

Nonconstruction contractors and subcontractors with fifty or more employees who have prime contracts or subcontracts with the federal government in excess of $50,000 are forbidden by E.O. 11246 regulations to discriminate in employment on the basis of race, color, religion, sex, and national origin, and are further required to develop and implement written affirmative action programs, the purpose of which is to establish procedures, goal, and timetables for the increased employment and advancement of minorities and women.[7]

[42.03]   EQUAL EMPLOYMENT OPPORTUNITY CLAUSE

Unless otherwise exempted, a government contractor is required to execute an agreement with the federal contracting agency that it

- *will not* discriminate against any applicant or employee because of race, color, religion, sex, or national origin
- *will* take affirmative action to ensure that applicants are employed, and that employees are treated, during employment, without regard to their race, color, religion, sex, or national origin
- *will* post notices of the nondiscrimination provisions and requirements of E.O. 11246 in conspicuous places (such notices to be provided by the contracting agency)
- *will,* in all solicitations or advertisements for employment, state that all qualified applicants will receive consideration without regard to race, color, religion, sex, or national origin
- *will* send to each labor union or representative of employees with which it has a collective bargaining agreement or other contract or agreement, a notice advising the labor organization of the contractor's nondiscrimination commitment under E.O. 11246 and request the labor organization to post copies of such notices in conspicuous places available to employees and applicants for employment
- *will* comply with all nondiscrimination provisions and requirements of E.O. 11246 and of the rules, regulations, and relevant orders of the Secretary of Labor
- *will* furnish all information and reports required by the rules, regulations, and pertinent orders related to 11246
- *will* permit access to its books, records, and accounts by the administering agency and the Secretary of Labor for investigatory purposes to determine compliance[8]

OFCCP regulations provide that equal opportunity clauses in government contracts will also contain an agreement that, in the event of the contractor's noncompliance with the nondiscrimination clauses of the contract, or with any of the rules, regulations, and orders relating to E.O. 11246, the contracting agency or the Secretary of Labor may cancel, terminate, or suspend the contract, in whole or in part, and declare the contractor ineligible for further government contracts, and further, impose any other sanctions which may be imposed and remedies invoked as provided in E.O. 11246, or by any rules, regulations, or orders relating to it.[9]

Government contractors must also agree to include the equal employment opportunity clause in all subcontract and purchase orders so that such provisions will also be binding upon each subcontractor or vendor, unless otherwise exempted by rules, regulations, or orders of the Secretary of Labor issued pursuant to Section 204 of E.O. 11246.[10]

In addition, federally assisted construction contractors must agree that they will assist and cooperate actively with the administering agency and the Secretary of Labor in obtaining compliance of other contractors and subcontractors with the aforementioned clauses and rules, regulations, and pertinent orders relating to E.O. 11246, furnish such information as the administering agency or the Secretary of Labor may require for the supervision of such compliance, and otherwise assist the administering agency and the Secretary of Labor in its efforts to secure compliance therewith.[11]

[42.04]   EXEMPTIONS FROM EEO CLAUSES

The Secretary of Labor or the director of the OFCCP may exempt a contracting agency or a contractor or subcontractor from the requirement of including an equal opportunity clause in a federal contract whenever such exemption is deemed to be in the national interest.[12] The Secretary of Labor or the director of the OFCCP may also exempt contractors and contracting agencies from requiring the inclusion of an equal employment opportunity clause in a contract should either find it impracticable to require such where an exemption would better contribute to the administration of E.O. 11246,[13] or where OFCCP regulations specify exemptions.[14]

The director of the OFCCP is equally empowered to withdraw any exemptions from the E.O. 11246 requirements previously granted should he or she determine such withdrawal necessary or appropriate.[15]

[42.05]   PROHIBITED PRACTICES UNDER E.O. 11246

The Office of Federal Contract Compliance Programs, like the Equal Employment Opportunity Commission, has adopted the *Uniform Guidelines on Employee Selection Procedures*.[16]

Under OFCCP guidelines, covered federal contractors are required to review their employment practices to determine the extent of employment and utilization of minorities, females, and members of various religious and ethnic groups, particularly in higher and middle management positions, and to undertake appropriate outreach and positive recruitment activities to correct deficiencies reflected in such review.[17]

The Equal Opportunity Clause in federal and federally assisted construction contracts requires that employees may not be discriminated against because of their race, color, religion, sex, or national origin with respect to such terms and conditions of employment as:

- promotions and advancements
- transfers
- layoffs or terminations
- rates of pay or other forms of compensation
- selection for training[18]

Contractors falling under the coverage of E.O. 11246 must ensure that waiting rooms, work areas, lunch areas, time clocks, restrooms, washrooms, locker rooms, storage areas, parking lots, drinking fountains, recreational areas, transportation, housing, and other physical facilities for employees are provided in such a manner as to prevent segregation on the basis of race, color, religion, sex, or national origin.[19]

Covered government contractors must accommodate the religious observances of their employees unless they can demonstrate their inability to reasonably accommodate such observances without undue hardship on the conduct of their business.[20]

Federal contractors, subject to the OFCCP regulations governing E.O. 11246 contracts, may not penalize pregnant workers because they require time away from work on account of childbearing. Thus, should a female employee meet the equally applied minimum length of service requirements for sick or medical leave, she must be granted a reasonable leave on account of pregnancy, and the conditions applicable to her leave and to her return to employment must be consistent with the employer's sick or medical leave policy.[21]

[42.06] AFFIRMATIVE ACTION PROGRAMS UNDER E.O. 11246

As noted earlier, nonconstruction employers who have fifty or more employees with federal contracts or subcontracts in excess of $50,000 must develop and maintain written affirmative action programs.

An acceptable affirmative action program must contain a statement of the contractor's equal employment opportunity clauses.[22] Also, as a general requirement, an acceptable affirmative action program must contain a work force analysis, and an analysis of all major job groups at the contractor's facility, to determine the utilization of minorities and women in such areas.[23]

Where deficiencies exist in the utilization of minorities and women in certain job classifications or categories, the contractor must establish goals and timetables to correct the deficiences.[24] Should a government contractor fail to establish required goals or timetables to correct deficiencies, its affirmative action program must detail the reason for such failure.[25]

[42.07] INSPECTIONS, AUDITS, AND REVIEWS

The OFCCP regulations have established standardized procedures to evaluate government contractors in determining whether they have met their affirmative action commitments.[26] The OFCCP utilizes three different methods of evaluation:

- desk audits
- on-site reviews
- off-site reviews

The desk audit is a routine method of evaluation and requires a government contractor to submit its affirmative action program and supporting documentation to the OFCCP for inspection and review.[27] Unless an affirmative action program and its supporting documentation shows an unreasonable failure on the part of the government contractor to comply with the requirements of the OFCCP regulations, the OFCCP usually will schedule an on-site review of the contractor's facility following a desk audit of the aforementioned documents.[28]

OFCCP compliance officers have the authority to request certain data relevant to their investigation during the on-site review.[29] The regulations authorize OFCCP compliance officers to interview a reasonable number of employees as part of the on-site review.[30]

In addition to the desk audit and on-site review, the OFCCP compliance officer may choose, where necessary, to make a more thorough study and evaluation of the previously gathered information and data in an off-site analysis.[31]

Unless granted an extension of time by the director of the OFCCP within sixty days from the date the contractor's affirmative action program and supportive documentation are received, the compliance officer handling the review must either notify the contractor that it is in compliance or issue the contractor a thirty-day show cause notice of noncompliance.[32] Otherwise, the contractor is deemed to be in compliance with the requirements of the OFCCP regulations.[33]

[42.08] REPORTING, RECORDKEEPING, AND NOTICE-POSTING REQUIREMENTS

The OFCCP regulations provide that each government contracting agency shall require each bidder or prospective prime contractor or subcontractor to state the following information in its written bid:

- *Whether* it has on file an affirmative action program and supporting documentation as required by the OFCCP regulations;
- *Whether* it has participated in any previous government contract or subcontract subject to the E.O. 11246 requirements and its equal opportunity clause; and
- *Whether* it has filed all reports due under the applicable filing requirements.[34]

Such bidder is also required to submit such other information and data as requested by the director of the OFCCP.[35]

Prior to the award of any government contract or subcontract or federally assisted construction contract or subcontract, each contracting agency or applicant for federal assistance must require the prospective prime contractor (and, in turn, subcontractors) to submit a written certification that the contractor does not and will not maintain any facilities in a segregated manner.[36]

Once awarded a government contract, covered prime contractors and subcontractors must file a complete and accurate annual report on Standard Form 100 (EEO-1),[37] unless such contractors and subcontractors are otherwise exempt from such reporting requirements.[38]

Each covered prime contractor and subcontractor must permit access to their premises during normal business hours for the purpose of conducting on-site compliance evaluations.[39]

Government contractors must also permit compliance officers to copy such books, records, accounts, and other material as may be relevant to the on-site investigation.[40]

Under OFCCP regulations, government contractors are required to maintain records of any complaints received relating to veterans and handicapped employees, and the action taken on them, for at least one year.[41] Government contractors must also maintain such employment and other records as the Director of the OFCCP may require.[42]

Government contractors must post, in conspicuous places, notices to applicants and employees of their nondiscrimination policies.[43]

NOTES TO CHAPTER 42

1. Executive Order No. 11246 (§202) and 42 U.S.C.A. §2000(e), *et seq.*
2. Executive Order No. 11246 (§201).
3. See generally, 41 CFR Chapter 60.
4. See 41 CFR Parts 60-1, *et seq.*
5. Executive Order No. 11246 (§205).
6. 41 CFR §60-1.4(a) and (b).
7. 41 CFR §60-1.4(a).
8. See 41 CFR §60-1.4(a) and (b); see also, Executive Order No. 11246 (§202).
9. 41 CFR §60-1.4(a) and (b).
10. 41 CFR §60-1.4(a) and (b).
11. 41 CFR §60-1.4(b).
12. 41 CFR §60-1.5(b)(1).
13. 41 CFR §60-1.5(b)(1).
14. 41 CFR §60-1.5(a)(1), *et seq.*
15. 41 CFR §60-1.5(d).
16. See 41 CFR Part 60-3; see also: 43 *Fed. Reg.* 38290. (The Uniform Guidelines on Employee Selection Procedures are discussed at [31.01]).
17. See 41 CFR §60-50.2(b).
18. 41 CFR §60-1.4(a) and (b).

19. 41 CFR §60-1.8(a).
20. 42 CFR §60-50.3.
21. 41 CFR §60-20.3(g)(1).
22. 41 CFR §60-2.20(a).
23. 41 CFR §60-2.10.
24. 41 CFR §60-2.10 and 11.
25. See 41 CFR §60-2.12(k).
26. See 41 CFR §60-60.1.
27. 41 CFR §60-60.3.
28. 41 CFR §60-60.3(b).
29. 41 CFR §60-60.3(b)(1).
30. 41 CFR §60-60.5.
31. 41 CFR §60-60.3(c).
32. 41 CFR §60-60.7(a).
33. 41 CFR §60-60.7(b).
34. 41 CFR §60-1.4(b)(1).
35. 41 CFR §60-1.7(b)(2).
36. 41 CFR §60-1.8(b).
37. See 41 CFR §60-1.4(a)(1).
38. 41 CFR §60-1.7(a)(1).
39. 41 CFR §60-1.4(a) and (b).
40. 41 CFR §60-1.4(a) and (b).
41. 41 CFR §60-250.52(a).
42. 41 CFR §60-250.52(a) and 41 CFR §60-741.52(a).
43. 41 CFR §60-1.4(a) and (b); 41 CFR §60-1.42(b).

43

Enforcement of Executive Order 11246 and Related Laws

[43.01] OFCCP INVESTIGATIONS

The director of the Office of Federal Contract Compliance Programs (OFCCP) is authorized to investigate complaints against federal contractors for noncompliance with Executive Order No. 11246.[1] Complaints of noncompliance may be filed by contracting agencies, individuals, or whenever the director of the OFCCP considers an investigation necessary or appropriate.[2]

A complaint against a federal contractor alleging discrimination in violation of the E.O. 11246 equal employment opportunity clause must be filed with the OFCCP within 180 days from the date of the alleged occurrence, unless the time limitation is extended by the OFCCP upon a showing of good cause.[3]

Where there is an indication of a violation of the equal employment opportunity clause, OFCCP regulations provide that the matter should be resolved by informal means.[4] Where the matter is not resolved by informal means, the OFCCP director is required to refer the case to the Solicitor of Labor who, in turn, may issue an administrative complaint to be processed in accordance with the enforcement procedures of the OFCCP regulations.[5]

Should the accused contractor voluntarily comply with the recommendations or orders of the OFCCP director, under protest but without benefit of a hearing, he or she may file a request for a hearing and review of the case within ten days of such voluntary compliance.[6]

[43.02] OFCCP ADMINISTRATIVE PROCEEDINGS

An OFCCP administrative enforcement proceeding is instituted by the filing of an administrative complaint.[7]

The OFCCP regulations require the complaint to designate the Department of Labor (OFCCP) as the plaintiff and the alleged noncomplying contractor as the defendant.[8] Under OFCCP regulations, the defending contractor must file an answer to an administrative complaint issued against him or her within twenty days after service of the complaint.[9]

Should the defending contractor fail to file an answer, or admit all of the material allegations of fact contained in the complaint, he or she waives the right to a hearing and permits the administrative law judge assigned to the case to prepare a decision, adopting as his or her proposed findings of fact, the material facts alleged in the complaint, subject only to the right of the parties to file exceptions to the judge's decision.[10]

As a general proposition, OFCCP administrative proceedings are to be conducted in accordance with the Federal Rules of Civil Procedure.[11] Consequently, subject to time limitations and objections, parties to an

OFCCP administrative enforcement proceeding are entitled to rights of discovery.[12]

[43.03] OFCCP HEARINGS

The Office of Federal Contract Compliance Programs hearings are held before administrative law judges, as designated and assigned by the Chief Administrative Law Judge of the Department of Labor.[13]

The OFCCP regulations have given administrative law judges broad powers to conduct OFCCP hearings, including the power to

- hold pre-hearing and other conferences
- administer oaths
- rule on motions and other procedural matters
- regulate the course of the hearing and the conduct of parties and participants
- examine and cross-examine witnesses
- introduce documentary or other evidence into the record
- rule on evidentiary matters
- fix time limits for submission of written documents
- issue subpoenas
- take official notice of any material fact which is among the traditional matters of judicial notice
- impose appropriate sanctions against any person failing to obey an order under the OFCCP rules and regulations; and
- take any other action authorized by the rules [14]

Parties to OFCCP administrative enforcement hearings are not bound by formal rules of evidence, but rather, are bound by evidentiary principles designed to develop the most probative evidence available.[15]

An official transcript of testimony taken, together with any exhibits, briefs, memoranda, proposed findings, etc., must be filed with the administrative law judge prior to the close of the hearing.[16] Parties to OFCCP hearings have the right to file post-hearing briefs.[17]

The administrative law judge, after considering all the testimony, exhibits, memoranda, arguments and briefs, is required to make recommended findings, conclusions, and a decision to be certified to the Secretary of Labor for a final administrative order.[18] Within fourteen days after receipt of the administrative law judge's recommended findings, conclusions and decision, parties may submit exceptions with the Secretary of Labor.[19]

After the time for filing exceptions to the administrative law judge's recommendations has expired, the Secretary of Labor must make a final decision on the matter which, in turn, becomes the final administrative order in the case.[20]

Whenever the Secretary of Labor concludes, in his or her final administrative order, that the defending contractor has violated Executive Order No. 11246, the equal opportunity clause, or any other pertinent OFCCP rule or regulation, he or she is to enjoin the violations, require the contractor to provide appropriate remedies, and impose whatever sanctions he or she deems appropriate under the circumstances.[21]

[43.04]   JUDICIAL PROCEEDINGS

In addition to the administrative proceedings discussed above, the U.S. Department of Justice is authorized to institute a civil action in federal district court to temporarily restrain or permanently enjoin contractors attempting to avoid compliance with E.O. 11246.[22] Moreover, the U.S. Attorney General may conduct whatever investigation he or she deems appropriate to carry out the responsibilities in seeking equitable relief in federal district court.[23]

[43.05]   OFCCP SANCTIONS

Several sanctions may be taken against federal contractors who are found to be in noncompliance with E.O. 11246.[24] Possible sanctions for noncompliance with OFCCP nondiscrimination provisions include:

- Cancellation, termination, or suspension of any part, or the entirety, of any federal contract;[25]
- Debarment from participating in further contracts with the federal government[26] (although, as a general rule, no order for debarment is to be made against a contractor without affording the contractor an opportunity for a hearing);[27]
- Publication of the names of contractors and unions which have failed to comply with the nondiscrimination provisions of E.O. 11246;[28]
- Recommendation to the Department of Justice that action be instituted against the contractor to enforce the nondiscrimination provisions of E.O. 11246;[29] and
- Recommendation to the Equal Employment Opportunity Commission or the Department of Justice that appropriate action be brought against the contractor under the Civil Rights Act of 1964, Title VII.[30]

In addition, the Secretary of Labor may recommend to the Department of Justice that criminal action be brought against a contractor who furnishes false information in connection with the procurement of a federal contract.[31]

The Secretary of Labor is also empowered to take sanctions against applicants, for federal financial assistance in connection with construction contracts, who fail to comply with their undertakings under 11246.[32]

The OFCCP director may also invoke the above discussed sanctions against any prime contractor, subcontractor, or applicant who fails to take all necessary steps to ensure that no individual filing a complaint, furnishing information, or participating in an OFCCP investigation, compliance review, hearing, or other such proceeding related to the administration of E.O. 11246 is discriminated against, intimidated, threatened, or coerced for exercising such effort.[33]

[43.06]   ENFORCEMENT OF CLAIMS FROM HANDICAPPED AND VETERANS

The director of the OFCCP has the responsibility of evaluating the contract compliance of federal contractors to assure that their affirmative action obligations to handicapped individuals[34] and veterans have been met.[35] The director also has the responsibility of investigating complaints alleging a violation of affirmative action obligations to veterans[36] and handicapped individuals.[37]

Applicants for employment with federal contractors and employees of federal contractors, as well as authorized representatives of such employees, may file written complaints against federal contractors alleging a failure to meet the affirmative action obligations to handicapped individuals[38] and veterans.[39]

A complaint alleging a violation of affirmative obligations to veterans must be filed with the Veteran's Employment Service of the Department of Labor within 180 days from the date of the alleged violation.[40] The Veteran's Employment Service has the responsibility of then referring the complaint to the director of the OFCCP.[41]

Investigations of a complaint alleging a violation of affirmative action obligations to handicapped individuals and veterans follow the general procedures and guidelines prescribed for other OFCCP investigations[42], as discussed earlier in this chapter.

The procedure and rules of practice for administrative hearings to enforce the nondiscrimination provisions of E.O. 11246 are used to govern administrative proceedings to resolve handicapped and veteran complaints.[43]

Failure to comply with the affirmative action obligations to handicapped persons and veterans could subject the offending contractor to a variety of sanctions, depending on the nature of the violations, such as termination of existing contracts, withholding of progress payments on existing contracts, debarment from future contracts, placement on the government's ineligible list for future contracts, and judicial injunctions and mandates.[44]

[43.07] ENFORCEMENT OF FEDERALLY ASSISTED AND APPRENTICESHIP PROGRAMS

Title VI of the Civil Rights Act or 1964[45] is enforced through the U.S. Department of Justice.[46] Federal agencies that extend federal financial assistance have been given the responsibility of publishing guidelines for prompt processing and disposition of Title VI complaints.[47]

Judicial proceedings may be brought against applicants or recipients of federal assistance who fail to comply with the nondiscrimination provisions of Title VI.[48] Sanctions, such as termination of existing federal assistance or the refusal to grant an application for assistance, may be imposed against an applicant or recipient found in noncompliance with the Title VI requirements.[49] Persons aggrieved by a recipient's noncompliance with the Title VI nondiscrimination provisions may have a right of action to a private suit for violation of Title VI.[50]

Handicapped individuals or other persons aggrieved by any act or failure to act of any applicant or recipient of federal financial assistance under Section 504 of the Rehabilitation Act of 1973[51] are entitled to the same rights and remedies as provided in the Title VI violations.[52]

Apprentices or applicants for registered apprenticeship programs who have been discriminated against on the basis of race, color, religion, national origin, or sex may file a complaint of discrimination with the U.S. Department of Labor, or, in the alternative, with a private review body established to review such complaints.[53] Such complaints must be in writing and filed not later than 180 days from the date of the alleged discrimination.[54] The Department of Labor will customarily refer such complaints to a designated and approved review board, unless the complaint designates otherwise, to investigate the allegations of the complaint.[55]

Should a complaint be unresolved to the satisfaction of the Department of Labor within ninety days, the department will conduct its own investigation and, thereafter, take whatever steps it deems necessary to attempt to resolve the complaint.[56]

NOTES TO CHAPTER 43

1. 41 CFR §60-1.25.
2. 41 CFR §60-1.25; 41 CFR §60-1.21.
3. 41 CFR §60-1.21.
4. 41 CFR §60-1.24(c)(2).
5. See 41 CFR §60-1.26; See also 41 CFR Part 60-30.
6. 41 CFR §60-1.24(c)(4).
7. 41 CFR §60-30.5(a).
8. 41 CFR §60-30.5(a).

9. 41 CFR §60-30.6(a).
10. 41 CFR §60-30.6(c).
11. 41 CFR §60-30.1.
12. 41 CFR §60-30.9, 10 and 11.
13. 41 CFR §60-30.14.
14. 41 CFR §60-30.15.
15. See generally 41 CFR §60-30.18.
16. 41 CFR §60-30.22.
17. 41 CFR §60-30.25.
18. 51 CFR §60-30.27.
19. 41 CFR §60-30.28
20. 41 CFR §60-30.29.
21. 41 CFR §60-30.30.
22. 41 CFR §60-1.26(e).
23. 41 CFR §60-1.26(e).
24. Executive Order No. 11246, Section 209(a).
25. Executive Order No. 11246, Section 209(a).
26. 41 CFR §60-1.31.
27. 41 CFR §60-1.26(a)(2).
28. Executive Order No. 11246, Section 209(a).
29. Executive Order No. 11246, Section 209(a).
30. Executive Order No. 11246, Section 209(a).
31. Executive Order No. 11246, Section 209(a).
32. Executive Order No. 11246, Section 303(a) and (b).
33. 41 CFR §60-1.32.
34. 41 CFR §60-741.25.
35. 41 CFR §60-250.25.
36. 41 CFR §60-250.25.
37. 41 CFR §60-741.25.
38. 29 U.S.C.S. §793; 41 CFR §60-741.
39. 38 U.S.C.S. §2012; 41 CFR §60-250.
40. 41 CFR §60-250.26(a).
41, 41 CFR §60-250.26(a).
42. 41 CFR §60-741.26(e), (f) and (g).
43. See discussion of OFCCP Hearings at [72.02]; see also 41 CFR §60-741.29(a) and (b) (Handicapped); 41 CFR §60-250.29(a) and (b) (Veterans).
44. See generally: 41 CFR §60-250.28 (Veterans) and 41 CFR §60-741.28 (Handicapped).
45. Executive Order No. 11764, Section 1.

46. See a discussion of Title VI at [41.05].

47. See 28 CFR §42.404 through §42.408.

48. See generally 28 CFR §50.3.

49. 28 CFR §50.3.

50. *Cannon v. University of Chicago*, 99 S.Ct. 1946 (U.S., 1979).

51. 29 U.S.C.A. §794. (Section 504 of the Rehabilitation Act of 1973 was discussed more fully in Chapter 41.)

52. 29 U.S.C.A. §794(a)(2).

53. 29 CFR §30.11(a)(1). (Registered Apprenticeship Programs were discussed more fully in Chapter 41.)

54. 29 CFR §30.11(a)(2).

55. 29 CFR §30.11(b)(1).

56. 29 CFR §30.11(b)(1).

PART III

FEDERAL WAGE
AND HOUR LAWS

44

Introduction to the Fair Labor Standards Act

[44.01] BACKGROUND

The Fair Labor Standards Act (hereinafter referred to as the FLSA) was enacted by the U.S. Congress in 1938.[1] Since its enactment, the Fair Labor Standards Act has been amended several times.

The FLSA was amended in 1947 by the Portal-to-Portal Act[2] which, *inter alia*, relieved employers of the obligation of paying for time spent in nonproductive activities. A 1961 amendment to the FLSA subjected "enterprises" engaged in commerce or the production of goods for commerce to its jurisdiction.[3]

The Equal Pay Act of 1963 also amended the FLSA by forbidding employers and unions from differentiating wages and benefits on the basis of sex.[4]

The 1977 amendments to the FLSA tightened statutory exemptions from coverage, reduced maximum weekly hours, increased minimum hourly wages for many categories of employees, and generally attempted to equalize the coverage of the statute.[5]

[44.02] EMPLOYEES COVERED UNDER THE FLSA

The determination of whether an individual is an "employee" under the FLSA will not necessarily depend upon common-law employee categories.[6] Rather, the test appears to be whether an individual is dependent upon the employer's business as a means of livelihood.[7]

The test of whether an employee is "engaged in commerce" or "in the production of goods for commerce" within the coverage of the FLSA is determined primarily by the nature of the employee's employment activities, rather than the caracter of the employer's business.[8]

In order to satisfy the "engaged in commerce" provision of the FLSA, an employee's employment activities must be so closely related to interstate commerce as to be a part thereof.[9] An individual is not considered to be "engaged in commerce" when his or her job duties are so remotely connected with interstate commerce as to be regarded as merely local in nature.[10]

The test of whether an employee is engaged "in the production of goods for commerce" is rather comprehensive and encompasses both direct and indirect work related to the employer's production of goods.[11]

Several individuals, who may have previously fallen outside the coverage of the FLSA, are now considered employees and within the coverage of the statute. This group includes *domestic service employees*,[12] *homeworkers*,[13] *trainees*,[14] and *student workers*.[15]

[44.03] GOVERNMENT EMPLOYEES

A 1974 amendment to the FLSA extended its coverage to employees of federal, state, county, and municipal governments.[16]

Although the U.S. Supreme Court ruled initially that the extension of the Act to include state and municipal governments went beyond the bounds of the U.S. Constitution,[17] it later reversed itself and held that the provisions of the FLSA do not intrude upon "areas of traditional governmental functions," concluding that state and municipal employees are entitled to the prescriptions of the Act.[18]

[44.04] EMPLOYERS COVERED UNDER THE FLSA

The FLSA defines an "employer" as one who acts directly or indirectly in the interest of an employer.[19] The definition does not include a union or anyone acting in the capacity of officer or agent thereof, other than when acting as an employer.[20]

Enterprise test: The U.S. Congress adopted the "enterprise" coverage concept in 1961 to extend coverage to fellow employees of any employee who would have been protected by the original FLSA.[21] Three common types of "enterprise" exist: (1) the single establishment[22]; (2) the multi-unit business[23]; and (3) the complex business organization.[24]

Minimum dollar volume test: The FLSA provides that certain types of businesses must meet a specified dollar test relating to its yearly business volume before it will fall within the "enterprise" coverage of the statute.[25] The minimum dollar volume test is applied to two business activities, namely:

- An enterprise other than an enterprise that is comprised exclusively of retail or service establishments whose annual gross volume of sales or business produced is not less than $250,000, exclusive of retail excise taxes;[26] and
- An enterprise that is comprised exclusively of one or more retail or service establishments as defined in the Act[27] whose annual gross volume of sales made or business produced, exclusive of retail excise taxes, is not less than $362,500.[28]

Notwithstanding the minimum dollar volume test for certain business activities, the FLSA specifies four activities that fall within its "enterprise" coverage, irrespective of their dollar volume, namely an enterprise that is engaged in

- laundering, cleaning, or repairing fabrics or clothing[29]
- the business of construction or reconstruction, or both[30]

- the operation of a hospital, nursing home or school[31]
- an activity of a public agency[32]

Geographical test: The FLSA provisions apply to all fifty states and the District of Columbia.[33] It also applies to the territories and possessions of the United States.[34] Whenever an employer is located outside the geographical coverage of the FLSA, he or she is not subject to its provisions or requirements.

[44.05] EXEMPTIONS UNDER THE FLSA

Notwithstanding the pervasive coverage of the FLSA, there are several exemptions from both the minimum wage and overtime pay requirements of the Act.

The most frequently discussed FLSA exemptions are those referred to as the "white collar" exemptions, consisting of four major categories: (1) the *executive* exemption; (2) the *administrative* exemption; (3) the *professional* exemption; and (4) the *"outside salesperson"* exemption.

[44.06] EXECUTIVE EXEMPTION

"Short" test: An executive employee may be exempt from the minimum wage and overtime requirements of the FLSA, provided the following tests are satisfied:

- The employee is paid on a salary basis of not less than $250 per week ($200 per week if employed in Puerto Rico, the Virgin Islands, or American Samoa), exclusive of board, lodging, or other facilities;
- The employee customarily and regularly directs the work of two or more employees; and
- The employee's primary duty (generally 50 percent or more of his or her work time) consists of the management of an enterprise or department or subdivision thereof.[35]

General test: An executive employee may also be exempt from minimum wage and overtime requirements under the FLSA, even though he or she makes less than $250 per week, as long as the following conditions are met:

- The employee is paid on a salary basis of not less than $155 per week, ($130 per week if employed in Puerto Rico, the Virgin Islands, or American Samoa) exclusive of board, lodging, or other facilities;
- The employee customarily and regularly directs the work of two or more employees;

- The employee has the authority to hire and fire employees or make suggestions or recommendations in their employment status such as advancement or promotion;

- The employee customarily and regularly exercises discretionary powers; and

- The employee manages an enterprise, department, or subdivision thereof, of which not more than 20 percent of his or her weekly hours are spent performing nonexempt work in a nonretail or nonservice establishment, and of which not more than 40 percent of his or her weekly hours are spent performing nonexempt work in a retail or service establishment.[36]

An employee must meet *all* the above stated conditions in order to be exempt under the "executive" exemption guidelines.[37] The executive exemption is typically used to exempt supervisors and managers from overtime pay, assuming all the conditions and qualifications are met.

[44.07] ADMINISTRATIVE EXEMPTION

"**Short**" **test:** An administrative employee may be exempt from minimum wage and overtime requirements of the FLSA, provided the following conditions are met:

- The employee is paid on a salary basis of not less than $250 per week ($200 per week if employed in Puerto Rico, the Virgin Islands, or American Samoa), exclusive of board, lodging, or other facilities; and

- The employee exercises discretion and independent judgment; and

- The employee's primary duty (generally 50 percent or more of his or her time) consists of either the performance of office or nonmanual work relating to management policies, customer relations, or general business operations of his or her employer; or the performance of functions directly relating to academic administration, instruction, or training.[38]

General test: An employee may also be exempt from minimum wage and overtime requirements under the FLSA as an "administrative" employee, even though he or she makes less than $250 per week, provided the following conditions are satisfied:

- The employee is paid on a salary basis of not less than $155 per week ($130 per week if employed in Puerto Rico, the Virgin Islands, or American Samoa), exclusive of board, lodging, or other facilities;

- The employee customarily and regularly exercises discretionary powers and independent judgment;

- The employee's primary duty consists of either the performance of office or nonmanual work relating to management policies, customer relations, or general business operations of his or her employer; or the performance of functions directly relating to academic administration, instruction, or training;

- The nature of the employee's duties must include the regular and direct assistance to a proprietor, an executive, or another administrative employee; or the performance of work under only general supervision along specialized or technical lines, requiring special training, experience or knowledge; or the execution of special assignments and tasks under only general supervision; and

- The employee must not devote more than 20 percent of his or her workweek to activities that are not directly and closely related to his or her primary and related duties as described above (or no more than 40 percent in the case of a retail or service establishment).[39]

There are three types of employees that generaly qualify as an "administrative employee," assuming all of the aforementioned conditions are met.

One type of employee that typically qualifies as an "administrative employee" is an employee who assists a proprietor or some executive or administrative person.[40] Examples here include such positions as an assistant manager, executive secretary, assistant to the president, and so forth.[41]

Another type of employee that typically qualifies as an exempt employee under the administrative exemption category is an employee who works in a staff or support position within the management structure and performs specialized or technical work.[42] Examples here include such positions as personnel director, credit manager, tax specialist, comptroller, and so forth.[43]

A third type of employee that usually qualifies as an "administrative employee" is one who performs special assignments without close supervision, such as buyers, field representatives, advertising specialists, and so forth.[44]

All criteria in either the "short" test or the general test must be met in the three examples given above, however.

[44.08] PROFESSIONAL EXEMPTION

"Short" test: A professional employee may be exempt from the minimum wage and overtime requirements of the FLSA, provided the following conditions are met:

- The employee is paid on a salary or fee basis of not less than $250 per week ($200 per week if employed in Puerto Rico, the Virgin Islands, or American Samoa), exclusive of board, lodging, or other facilities;

- The employee's primary duty (generally 50 percent or more of his or her work time) consists of the performance of either work requiring scientific or specialized study, as distinguished from apprentice or on-the-job training; or work that is original and creative in character in a recognized field of artistic endeavor, depending primarily on the employee's talent, invention, or imagination; or teaching, tutoring, instructing, or lecturing in the activity of imparting knowledge by one who is employed and engaged in such activity as a teacher, certified or recognized as such, in a school or educational system;
- The employee consistently exercises discretionary powers and independent judgment with respect to scientific, specialized, or academic work and invention, imagination, and talent with respect to artistic endeavors.[45]

General test: An employee may also qualify as a "professional employee" and thus be exempt from the minimum wage and overtime requirements of the FLSA, even though he or she makes less than $250 per week, conditioned upon the following criteria being satisfied:

- The employee is compensated on a salary or fee basis of not less than $170 per week ($150 per week if employed in Puerto Rico, the Virgin Islands, or American Samoa), exlusive of board, lodging, or other facilities;
- The employee's primary duty consists of the performance of either work requiring scientific or specialized study, as distinguished from apprentice or on-the-job training; or work that is original and creative in character in a recognized field of artistic endeavor, depending primarily on the employee's talent, invention, or imagination; or teaching, tutoring, instructing, or lecturing in the activity of imparting knowledge by one who is employed and engaged in such activity as a teacher, certified or recognized as such, in a school or educational system;
- The employee performs work predominantly intellectual and varied in character that cannot be standardized in relation to a given point in time;
- The employee consistently exercises discretion and judgment in the performance of his or her work; and
- The employee does not devote more than 20 percent of his or her workweek to activities that are not an essential part of the duties described above.[46]

Unlike the "executive" and "administrative" exemption requirements, a professional employee may be paid either on a salary or fee basis in the satisfaction of the compensation requirement.[47] The salary or fee requirement noted in the general test ($170) does not apply to licensed attorneys, medical doctors, or teachers who are actually engaged in the practice of their respective professions.[48]

Not only must a professionally exempt employee be paid on a salaried (or fee) basis, he or she may not be docked pay for fractions of days of work missed and remain exempt.[49] (Neither may "executive" and "administrative" employees be docked pay for fractions of days missed and maintain the exemption.)[50]

[44.09] OUTSIDE SALESPERSON EXEMPTION

An outside salesperson may be exempt from the minimum wage and overtime requirement of the FLSA, assuming the following conditions are met:

- He or she is customarily and regularly engaged away from the employer's place of business in making sales of goods or services or in obtaining orders or contracts for services or for the use of facilities; and

- He or she does not devote more than 20 percent of the workweek to activities that are not directly or closely related to those described above.[51]

[44.10] AGRICULTURAL EMPLOYEE EXEMPTIONS

Various exemptions to the requirements of the FLSA exist for agricultural employees, depending upon their specific duties, nature of the work, size of the operation, age of the employee, family status, and so forth.[52]

The FLSA defines "agriculture" as farming in all its branches, including such activities as

- the cultivation and tillage of the soil
- dairying
- the production, cultivation, growing, and harvesting of agricultural or horticultural commodities
- the raising of livestock, bees, furbearing animals, or poultry[53]

The term "agriculture" as used in the FLSA also includes certain practices which are incidental to farming operations if such activities are performed either by a farmer or on a farm; performed in connection with the farming operations; and performed as an incident to, or in conjunction with, the farming operations.[54]

The following agricultural employees are exempt from both the minimum wage and overtime requirements of the FLSA:

- *Agricultural employees* whose employer did not use more that 500 workdays of agricultural labor in any calendar quarter of the preceding calendar year.

- *Agricultural employees* who are parents, spouses, children, or other members of the farmer's immediate family.

- *Agricultural employees* who are employed as hand harvest laborers on a piece-rate basis in an operation that is customarily and generally recognized as having been paid on a piece rate basis in the region of employment, commute daily from their permanent residence to the farm on which they are employed, and have been employed in agriculture less than thirteen weeks during the preceding calendar year.

- *Agricultural employees* who are principally engaged in the range production of livestock.

- *Agricultural employees* under 17 years old who are employed as hand harvesters on a piece-rate basis on the same farm as their parents and who are paid at the same piece rate as other employees 17 years or older.[55]

In addition to the above described agricultural exemptions from both the minimum wage and overtime requirements of the Act, the FLSA grants complete exemption from its overtime provisions to ''any employee employed in agriculture''.[56] However, it should be noted that some jobs, appearing to be agricultural in nature, do not qualify for the agricultural employee exemption.[57] For example, employees engaged in the production of mushroom compost were held not to be exempt agricultural employees, the court ruling that compost was ''nonsoil.''[58]

[44.11] RETAIL OR SERVICE ESTABLISHMENT EMPLOYEE EXEMPTION

Retail or service establishment employees are exempt from the minimum wage and overtime requirements of the FLSA if the following conditions are met:

- At least 75 percent of their employer's yearly dollar volume of sales or services, or of both, is not for resale and is recognized as retail sales or services in the particular industry;

- Over 50 percent of their employer's yearly dollar volume of sales or services is made within the state where the establishment is located;

- Their employer's establishment is not an enterprise engaged in commerce or in the production of goods for commerce; and

- Their employer's establishment is not engaged in laundering or dry cleaning or in the operation of a hospital, nursing home, or school.[59]

[44.12] MANUFACTURING OR PROCESSING RETAIL ESTABLISHMENT EMPLOYEE EXEMPTION

The FLSA provides a minimum wage and overtime pay exempton for employees of retail establishments that manufacture or process goods which they sell, subject to the following conditions being satisfied:

- The establishment qualifies as an exempt retail establishment under the conditions outlined under [44.11]; and

- More than 85 percent of such establishment's annual dollar volume of sales of goods that it makes or processes is made within the state in which the establishment is located; and

- The goods which the establishment makes or processes are sold at the same establishment.[60]

[44.13] SPECIAL EXEMPTIONS FOR PARTICULAR EMPLOYEES

The FLSA also provides for other special employee exemptions from either the minimum wage requirements, the overtime pay requirements, or both, including the following.

Babysitters: Employees who are employed to provide babysitting services on a casual basis in a domestic setting are exempt from both the minimum wage and overtime pay requirements of the FLSA.[61]

Domestic companions: Employees, who are employed to provide companionship services on a casual basis in a domestic setting for individuals unable to care for themselves due to age or infirmity, are exempt from the minimum wage and overtime pay requirements of the Act.[62]

Domestic live-ins: The FLSA provides that a domestic live-in household service employee is exempt from its overtime pay provisions, but is not exempt from its minimum wage requirements.[63]

Taxi drivers: The FLSA exempts any driver employed by an employer engaged in the business of operating taxicabs from its overtime pay requirements.[64]

Seamen: The FLSA also provides that any employee employed as a seaman on an American vessel is exempt from its overtime pay provisions.[65]

Railroad employees: The FLSA exempts any employee of an employer engaged in the operation of a common carrier by rail and subject to the provisions of Part I of the Interstate Commerce Act from its overtime pay requirements.[66]

Motor carrier's exemption: The FLSA exempts from its overtime pay provisions employees of interstate motor carriers whom the Secretary of Transportation has power to establish qualifications and maximum hours of service pursuant to the provisions of Section 204 of the Motor Carrier Act.[67]

Fishing or aquatic products employees: Employees employed in the catching, taking, propagating, harvesting, cultivating, or farming of any kind of fish or other aquatic forms of animal and vegetable life or in the first processing, canning, or packaging of such aquatic products at sea as an incident to, or in conjunction with, such fishing operations, are exempt from both the minimum wage and overtime pay provisions of the FLSA.[68]

Automobile and farm implement dealer's employees: Employees who are employed as salespeople, partsmen, or mechanics primarily engaged in selling or servicing automobiles, trucks, or farm implements to ultimate purchasers are exempt from the overtime pay provisions of the FLSA.[69]

Aircraft, boat, and trailer salespeople: Employees employed as salespeople primarily engaged in selling trailers, boats, or aircraft to ultimate purchasers are also exempt from the overtime pay requirements of the FLSA.[70]

Airline employees: An employee of an air carrier subject to the provisions of Title II of the Railway Labor Act[71] is exempt from the overtime pay provisions of the FLSA.[72] However, employees who are instructors or sales or service personnel at a fixed base operation may not be entitled to the exemption.[73]

Learners, apprentices, students, and handicapped workers: Employers of learners, apprentices, students, handicapped workers, and messengers employed primarily in delivering letters and messages may pay less than the required minimum wage requirement if a special certificate, issued under a regulation or order of the Secretary of Labor, has been obtained for their employment.[74] Such a permit may be issued conditional upon such factors as time, number, proportion, and length of service as the Secretary may require.[75]

[44.14] MISCELLANEOUS EXEMPTIONS

Other employees who may be exempt from minimum wage requirements, overtime pay requirements, or both, subject to certain conditions and limitations as noted in the statute and pertinent regulations include

- child actors [76]
- certain children employed in agriculture[77]
- amusement or recreational establishment employees[78]
- employees in foreign countries[79]

- employees in U.S. territories[80]
- drivers or driver helpers in local deliveries[81]
- forestry or lumbering employees[82]
- motion picture employees[83]
- newspaper employees of a small local[84]
- newspaper delivery employees[85]
- outside buyers of poultry or dairy products[86]
- news editors and chief engineers of radio or TV[87]
- tobacco services employees[88]
- switchboard operators (less than 750 stations)[89]

NOTES TO CHAPTER 44

1. See 29 U.S.C.A. §201 *et seq.*
2. 29 U.S.C.A. §251, *et seq.*
3. See P.L. 87-30, 75 Stat. 65 (May, 1961).
4. The Equal Pay Act is discussed in Chapter 39.
5. See P.L. 95-151, 91 Stat. 1245 (Nov., 1977).
6. *Walling v. Portland Terminal Co.*, 330 U.S. 148, (1947).
7. *Weisel v. Singapore Joint Venture Inc.*, 602 F.2d 1185 (CA-5, 1979).
8. *A.B. Kirschbaum Co. v. Walling*, 316 U.S. 517 (1942).
9. *Overstreet v. North Shore Corp.*, 318 U.S. 125 (1943)
10. *Batts v. Professional Bldg. Inc.*, 276 F.Supp. 356 (DC W.Va., 1967).
11. See 29 CFR §776.15(b) and 16 (b).
12. 29 U.S.C.A. §206(f).
13. *Goldberg v. Whitaker House Cooperative*, 366 U.S. 28 (1961).
14. 29 U.S.C.A. §214.
15. 29 U.S.C.A. §203(e).
16. 29 U.S.C.A. §203(5)(6).
17. *National League of Cities v. Usery*, 427 U.S. 833 (1976).
18. *Garcia v. San Antonio Metropolitan Transit Authority*, 26 W&H Cases 65 (S.Ct. 1985).
19. 29 U.S.C.A. §203(d).
20. 29 U.S.C.A. §203(d); see also 29 CFR §779.19, 783.7, 784.8.
21. *Maryland v. Wirtz*, 392 U.S. 183 (1968).
22. 29 CFR §779.203.
23. 29 CFR §779.203.

24. 29 CFR §779.203.

25. 29 U.S.C.A. §203(s)(1) and (2).

26. 29 U.S.C.A. §203(s)(1).

27. 29 U.S.C.A. §213(a)(2).

28. 29 U.S.C.A. §203(s)(2).

29. 29 U.S.C.A. §203(s)(3).

30. 29 U.S.C.A. §203(s)(4).

31. 29 U.S.C.A. §203(s)(5).

32. See 29 U.S.C.A. §203(s)(6).

33. 29 U.S.C.A. §202, 203(b); 29 CFR §776.7(a).

34. 29 U.S.C.A. §203(c); 29 CFR §776.7(a).

35. See generally 29 CFR §§541.1(f), 541.103 and 541.119. (Although the regulations have been revised by 46 *Fed. Reg.* 3010 to require higher salary requirements to qualify for this "upset" salary test for "executive" employees, the implementation of these revised rules have been postponed indefinitely pursuant to 46 *Fed. Reg.* 11972.)

36. See generally 29 CFR §§541.1(f), 541.119. (Revised regulations requiring higher salary requirements to qualify under this general test for "executive employees" have been postponed indefinitely pursuant to 46 *Fed. Reg.* 11972.)

37. *McReynolds v. Pocahontas Corp.*, 192 F.2d 301 (CA-4, 1951).

38. See generally 29 U.S.C.A. §213(a)(1) and 29 CFR §541.2(e)(2). (Revised regulations requiring higher salary requirements to qualify under this "upset" test for "administrative employees" have been postponed indefinitely pursuant to 46 *Fed. Reg.* 11972.)

39. See generally 29 CFR §541.2. (Revised regulations requiring higher salary requirements to qualify under this general test for "administrative employees" have been postponed indefinitely as pursuant to 46 *Fed. Reg.* 11972.)

40. See 29 CFR §541.201(a)(1).

41. 29 CFR §541.201(a)(1).

42. See 29 CFR §541.201(a)(2).

43. 29 CFR §541.201(a)(2).

44. See 29 CFR §541.201(a)(3).

45. See generally 29 CFR §§541.3(e) and 541.315. (Revised regulations requiring higher salary or fee requirements to qualify under this "upset" test for professional employees have been postponed indefinitely pursuant to 46 *Fed. Reg.* 11972.)

46. See 29 CFR §541.3. (Revised regulations requiring higher salary or fee requirements to qualify under this general test for "professional employees" have been postponed indefinitely pursuant to 46 *Fed. Reg.* 11972.)

47. 29 CFR §541.313(a).

48. 29 CFR §541.3(e).

49. *Donovan v. Carls Drug Co.*, 703 F.2d 650 (CA-2, 1983).

50. See, for example: *Donovan v. Whitehead's Investments*, 26 W&H Cases 759 (ND Tex., 1983)

51. Generally 29 CRF §541.5.

52. 29 U.S.C.A. §§203(f) and 213(a) through (g); see also 29 CFR §§780.403, 780.503, 780.802, 780.904, and 780.1003.

53. 29 U.S.C.A. §203(f).

54. 29 CFR §780.129.

55. 29 U.S.C.A. §213(a)(6)(A)-(E).

56. *Guidebook to Federal Wage-Hour Laws*, Para. 309.7 (1978); See also 29 U.S.C.A. §213(b)(12).

57. *Hodgson v. Wittenburg*, 464 F.2d 1219 (CA-5, 1972).

58. *Marshall v. Frezzo Brothers, Inc.*, 25 W&H Cases 462 (ED Pa., 1982).

59. 29 U.S.C.A. §203(s) and 29 U.S.C.A. §213(a)(2).

60. See 29 CFR §779.346; see also 29 U.S.C.A. §213(a)(4).

61. 29 U.S.C.A. §213(a)(15).

62. 29 U.S.C.A. §213(a)(15).

63. 29 CFR §552.102(a).

64. 29 U.S.C.A. §213(b)(17).

65. 29 U.S.C.A. §213(b)(6).

66. 29 U.S.C.A. §213(b)(2), as amended in 1974.

67. See 29 U.S.C.A. §213(b)(1); see also 49 U.S.C.A. §304.

68. 20 U.S.C.A. §213(a)(5); 29 CFR §784.102.

69. 29 U.S.C.A. §213(b)(10)(A).

70. 29 U.S.C.A. §213(b)(10)(B).

71. 45 U.S.C.A. §181-188.

72. 29 U.S.C.A. §213(b)(3).

73. See 29 U.S.C.A. §213(b)(3); see also *Wallace v. Tennessee Airmotive, Inc.*, 238 F.Supp. 206 (DC Tenn., 1965).

74. 29 U.S.C.A. §213(a)(7), 214(a).

75. 29 U.S.C.A. §214(a).

76. 29 U.S.C.A. §213(c)(3).

77. 29 U.S.C.A. §213(c)(1) and (2).

78. 29 U.S.C.A. §213(a)(3).

79. 29 U.S.C.A. §213(f).

80. 29 U.S.C.A. §213(f).

81. 29 U.S.C.A. §213(b)(11).

82. 29 U.S.C.A. §213(b)(28).

83. 29 U.S.C.A. §213(b)(27).

84. 29 U.S.C.A. §213(a)(8).

85. 29 U.S.C.A. §213(d)

86. 29 U.S.C.A. §213(b)(5).

87. 29 U.S.C.A. §213(b)(9).

88. 29 U.S.C.A. §207(m).

89. 29 U.S.C.A. §213(a)(10).

45

Minimum Wage Requirements Under the FLSA

[45.01] MINIMUM WAGE RATES

Although the Fair Labor Standards Act previously specified separate minimum wage rates for particular classes of employees,[1] the Act now provides a universal minimum wage schedule for all covered workers.[2]

Notwithstanding the minimum wage rate requirement, the FLSA permits a payment of less than the general rate to certain employees who are not fully experienced or industrialized.

For example, learners, apprentices, students, handicapped workers, and messengers employed primarily in delivering letters and messages may be paid less than the required minimum wage under the FLSA, provided their employer has obtained a special certificate, issued pursuant to an order or regulation of the Secretary of Labor, permitting such a lower wage payment.[3]

Determining what is, and what is not, minimum wage rates is not as simple as it might initially appear. This chapter deals with some of the complexities of the minimum wage requirements of the FLSA.

[45.02] "WORKING TIME" DEFINED

The Fair Labor Standards Act, as amended, generally requires the payment of specified minimum hourly wages[4] and "overtime" pay[5] for hours worked over forty in any one-week period. However, before a determination can be made as to whether "minimum wages" and "overtime pay" have been properly computed, it is first necessary to ascertain what constitutes "working time."

"Working time" is the time for which an employee is entitled to compensation under the Act.[6] As a general rule, "working time" includes all the time during which an employee covered by the Act is required to be on duty on the employer's premises or at a prescribed work place.[7]

[45.03] EXCLUSIONS FROM "WORKING TIME"

Portal-to-Portal exclusions: Congress specifically excluded "preliminary" and "postliminary" activities—those occurring either before or after an employee's "principal" activities—from the definition of "working time" by the enactment of the 1947 Portal-to-Portal Act.[8] The Portal-to-Portal Act was enacted as a result of the United States Supreme Court's ruling that activities occurring before or after a "shift change" could constitute compensable working time, irrespective of custom or collective bargaining contracts.[9]

333

The Portal-to-Portal provisions do not govern an employee's "principal" activities; thus time devoted to those duties to which an employee is "engaged to perform" is compensable.[10] Moreover, "preliminary" or "postliminary" time may be compensable if compensation is called for by a contract between an employer and the employee or his or her union, or pursuant to the employer's custom or practice.[11]

Clothes change and wash-up activities exclusion: The Fair Labor Standards Act specifically provides that time spent in changing clothes or washing at the beginning or end of a workday may be excluded from compensable "working time" if such exclusion is pursuant to the express terms of a bona fide collective bargaining agreement applicable to the particular employees.[12] Such activities may also be excluded from compensable "working time" if occurring before or after the end of the work shift, if they are unrelated to the employees "principal" activities.[13]

American seaman's off-duty exclusion: The Fair Labor Standards Act provides that an owner of an American vessel may contractually exclude from compensable "working time" the off-duty periods of its seamen.[14]

Live-in domestics' off-duty exclusion: An employer, pursuant to an employment agreement with its employee, may exclude from compensation those periods of time in which a live-in domestic employee has complete freedom from all duties and is free to leave the premises should he or she desire.[15]

De minimus activities exclusion: As a general proposition, activities which involve insignificant periods of time are not compensable, such as a brief span of two or three minutes.[16] On the other hand, working time worth one dollar or more will generally fall outside the *de minimus* rule and require compensation.[17]

[45.04]   COMPENSABLE WORKING TIME

Generally, all hours which an employee is required to give his or her employer are considered compensable working time.[18] One of the determining factors in deciding whether a particular activity should be considered "working time" is whether the activity undertaken is primarily for the benefit of the employer or the employee.[19]

Although, as a general rule, an employee must work with the knowledge and consent of his or her employer in order to be paid proper wages, an employer who "suffers or permits" his or her employees to work is nonetheless obligated to compensate the employee for such work performed.[20]

In addition, the following activities normally constitute compensable "working time":

- *Rest or meal periods* used to promote the efficiency of the employee and twenty minutes or less in duration.[21]
- *On-duty waiting time* which time an employee is unable to use effectively for his or her own purpose.[22]
- *On-call waiting time*, if such activity precludes the employee from effectively using the time for his or her own purpose.[23]
- *Reporting time* for the period of time during which an employee is required to remain at the work side.[24]
- *Sleeping time* where an employee is on duty at the employer's premises for twenty-four hours or more in duration and the use of sleeping facilities is primarily for the employer's benefit.[25] (However, by an employment agreement, a bona fide regularly scheduled sleeping period of not more than eight hours of the twenty-four hour period may be excluded from working time.[26]
- *Training time* designed to help the employee perform his or her job more effectively or prepare the employee for another job with the employer.[27]
- *Grievance adjustment time* between management and employees.[28]
- *Civic and charitable work* if done at the employer's request, or under the employer's direction, or while on the employer's premises.[29]
- *Homework* if performed at the employer's direction or done with the employer's knowledge.[30]
- *Fire and disaster drills*, whether voluntary or involuntary, are considered to be for the benefit of the employer.[31]
- *Travel time* away from home or from one work site to another during the employee's workday where such travel is connected to the employer's business.[32] (However, time spent in travel away from home, outside of regular work hours as a passenger on an airplane, train, boat, bus or car, may be excluded from compensable working time.)[33]

[45.05] NONCOMPENSABLE WORKING TIME

The administrator of the Wage and Hour Division of the Department of Labor has generally considered the following activities as noncompensable:

- *Pre-employment tests*[34]
- *Medical attention* outside working hours, or by personal physicians during regular working hours[35]

- *Bona fide meal periods* usually of at least twenty minutes in duration and where the employee is completely relieved of his or her duties during such period[36]

- *Bona fide rest periods* of greater duration than twenty minutes, especially where the employee is free to leave the employer's premises[37]

- *Training programs* if voluntarily attended outside the employee's regular working hours, unrelated to the employee's job, and during which time no productive work is performed[38]

- *Traveling time* to and from home[39]

- *Waiting time* during which the employee is completely relieved from duty and of sufficient duration to enable the employee to use the time effectively for his or her own purpose.[40]

- *On-call duty* where the employee is not restricted in his or her activities but merely leaves word with the employer where he or she may be reached[41]

- *Athletic events* if the employee's participation is strictly voluntary and performed outside his or her regular work hours[42]

- *Civic work* if voluntarily undertaken outside the employee's regular work hours[43]

- *Illnesses* resulting in absence from regular work hours[44]

- *Leaves of absence*[45]

- *Vacations*[46]

- *Holidays*[47]

[45.06] MINIMUM WAGE COMPUTATIONS FOR THE "WORKWEEK" STANDARD

The Administrator of the Wage and Hour Division of the Department of Labor has specified the "workweek" as the standard measurement of time to be used in determining compliance with the minimum wage regulations.[48] Thus, as a general rule, a "workweek" consists of seven consecutive days over which wages should be calculated for the purpose of the minimum wage requirements.[49]

An employer may properly ascertain whether he or she has complied with the minimum wage requirements under the FLSA by dividing the actual compensation received by the employee during the "workweek" by the total number of hours worked during the period.[50]

Minimum wages must be paid timely and usually no later than the regular payday for each workweek.[51] If the pay period covers more than a single week, minimum wages should be paid no later than the regular payday for the workweek in which the particular period ends.[52]

[45.07] NONCASH METHODS OF PAYMENT

Although the usual payment of wages is in the form of cash or by negotiable instrument,[53] the Wage and Hour Division will permit an employer to credit the "reasonable cost" of board, lodging, and other facilities toward the minimum wages it owes an employee, provided the facilities are not furnished for the employer's benefit, the employer derives no profit from the transaction, and the inclusion of such cost as wages is not excluded by the provisions of a collective bargaining contract.[54]

The employee also must voluntarily accept the facilities as creditable toward his or her wages and must receive the benefits therefrom in order for the employer to include the reasonable costs of such facilities as wages.[55]

In addition, the reasonable cost of such facilities may be included as wages only where such facilities are "customarily furnished" to employees, with a mutual obligation on the part of the employer to furnish such facilities and the affected employee to use them.[56]

[45.08] NONCASH ITEMS "INCLUDIBLE" IN WAGES

The Wage and Hour Administration has permitted the reasonable cost or fair value of certain noncash items to be included in wages for purposes of satisfying the minimum wage requirements imposed by the FLSA, provided the aforementioned qualifications have been met. The reasonable cost of the following noncash items has been permitted an inclusion in computing overall wages:

- *Meals* furnished for the benefit of the employee, rather than for the benefit of the employer.[57]
- *Lodging* where furnished primarily for the benefit of the employee.[58]
- *Merchandise* as long as both the employer and employee agree upon the purchase price and specify that its price may be deducted from wages—assuming the employer does not derive a profit from the transaction.[59]
- *Transportation* furnished employees between their homes and work.[60]
- *Tuition* furnished to student employees of a university.[61]
- *Savings bond* bought on behalf of an employee by an employer, if authorized by the employee.[62]
- *Insurance premiums* may be credited against minimum wages when paid by the employer upon request or approval by the employee and where the employer derives no benefit or profit in the transaction.[63]
- *Union dues* deducted from an employee's paycheck pursuant to an employee's direction and through the terms of a collective bargaining agreement, may be credited against minimum wages.[64]

- *Garnishments and wage* attachments pursuant to court proceedings.[65]
- *Charitable contributions* made by an employer at the employee's request or direction, assuming no profit inures to the employer from such contribution.[66]
- *Tips*—up to 40 percent of the tips received by an employee who qualifies as a "tipped employee" under the FLSA may be credited toward the employee's minimum wage.[67] (A "tipped employee" is one who is engaged in an occupation in which he or she customarily and regularly receives at least $30 or more a month in tips.)[68]

[45.09] PARTICULAR ARRANGEMENTS AS BASIS OF PAYMENT

Neither the FLSA nor the Wage and Hour Administration requires an employer to pay employees on a fixed hourly basis.[69]

In addition to a specified hourly wage, some of the more prevalent arrangements through which various employers pay their employees include:

- *Specified piece rate.* An employee paid on the basis of a specified piece rate must be paid sufficient average hourly earnings for the workweek to equal or exceed the minimum wage requirements under the Act.[70]
- *Fixed weekly wage.* An employee paid under the arrangement must be paid a sufficient weekly salary to equal or exceed minimum wage requirements under the Act when divided by the number of hours worked during a particular workweek.[71]
- *Fixed monthly or semimonthly wage.* An employee paid under a fixed monthly or semimonthly arrangement must receive a sufficient salary to, when converted into a weekly wage equivalent, satisfy the requirements of the fixed weekly rate, noted above.[72]

NOTES TO CHAPTER 45

1. 29 U.S.C.A. §207(a)(1) and (5); and 29 U.S.C.A. §206(b).
2. 29 U.S.C.A. §207(a)(1), as amended in 1977.
3. 29 U.S.C.A. §§213(a)(7), 214.
4. 29 U.S.C.A. §206.
5. 29 U.S.C.A. §207.
6. *Skidmore v. Swift & Co.*, 323 U.S. 134 (1944).
7. 29 CFR §778.223.
8. 29 U.S.C.A. §251, *et seq.*
9. *Anderson v. Mt. Clemens Pottery Co.*, 328 U.S. 680 (1946).
10. 29 CFR §790.4(a) through 790.8(a).

11. 29 U.S.C.A. §254.
12. 29 U.S.C.A. §203(o).
13. *Mitchell v. Southeastern Carbon Paper Co.*, 228 F.2d 934 (CA-5, 1955).
14. 29 U.S.C.A. §206(a)(4).
15. 29 CFR §552.102(a).
16. *Frank v. Wilson & Co.*, 172 F.2d 712 (CA-7, 1949).
17. *Addison v. Huron Stevedoring Corp.*, 204 F.2d 88 (CA-2, 1953).
18. *Armour & Co. v. Wantock*, 323 U.S. 126 (1944).
19. *Armour & Co. v. Wantock, supra.*
20. 29 U.S.C.A. §203(g); 29 CFR §778.223.
21. 29 CFR §785.18 and 19(a).
22. 29 CFR §785.15.
23. 29 CFR §785.17.
24. *Wage and Hour Field Operations Handbook*, Para. 31a00.
25. 29 CFR §785.22(a).
26. 29 CFR §785.22(a).
27. 29 CFR §785.27.
28. 29 CFR §785.42.
29. 29 CFR §785.44.
30. 29 CFR §785.12.
31. *Wage and Hour Field Operations Handbook*, Para. 31b15.
32. 29 CFR §785.
33. 29 CFR §785.39.
34. *Guidebook to Federal Wage-Hour Laws*, Para. 603.12 (1978).
35. *Ibid.*
36. 29 CFR §785.19(a) and (b).
37. See *Wage and Hour Field Operations Handbook*, Para. 31a01(b).
38. 29 CFR §785.27.
39. See generally 29 CFR §785.34 and 35; see also 29 CFR §790.7(c).
40. 29 CFR §785.16(a).
41. 29 CFR §785.17.
42. *Wage and Hour Field Operations Handbook,* Para. 31b05.
43. 29 CFR §785.44.
44. *Boll v. Federal Reserve Bank*, 365 F.Supp. 637 (DC Mo., 1973).
45. *Boll v. Federal Reserve Bank, supra.*
46. *Boll v. Federal Reserve Bank, supra.*
47. *Boll v. Federal Reserve Bank, supra.*
48. 29 CFR §783.43.
49. *Blankenship v. Thurston Motor Lines, Inc.*, 415 F.2d 1193 (CA-4, 1969).

50. *Fleming v. Knox*, 42 F.Supp. 948 (DC Ga., 1941).

51. *United States v. Klinghoffer Bros. Realty Corp.*, 285 F.2d 487 (CA-2, 1960).

52. *Wage and Hour Field Operations Handbook*, Para. 30c04.

53. 29 CFR §531.27(a).

54. 29 U.S.C.A. §203(m).

55. 29 CFR §531.30.

56. See *Brotherhood of Maintenance or Way Employees v. Nashville C & S.L. Ry.*, 56 F.Supp. 552 (DC Tenn., 1944).

57. 29 CFR §552.100(b) and (c).

58. *Schultz v. A-1 Ambulance Service, Inc.*, (DC Ark., 1970).

59. 29 CFR §531.32(a).

60. 29 CFR §531.32(a).

61. 29 CFR §531.32(a).

62. 29 CFR §531.40(c).

63. 29 CFR §531.40(c).

64. 29 CFR §531.40(c).

65. 29 CFR §531.39(a).

66. 29 CFR §531.40(c).

67. See 29 U.S.C.A. §203(m), as amended in 1977.

68. See 29 U.S.C.A. §203(t), as amended in 1977.

69. See note 34, Para. 701.5, *supra*.

70. See note 34, Para. 701.5, *supra*.

71. See note 34, Para. 701.5, *supra*.

72. See note 34, Para. 701.5, *supra*.

46

Overtime Pay Requirements Under the FLSA

[46.01] OVERTIME COMPENSATION REQUIREMENT

The Fair Labor Standards Act requires an employer to pay overtime to employees covered under the Act at the rate of one and one-half times the employee's "regular rate" for hours worked in excess of forty hours in any one "workweek."[1]

The Fair Labor Standards Act does not require an employee to be paid overtime compensation for hours worked in excess of eight hours per day or for work performed on holidays, Saturday, or Sunday.[2] The Act does not restrict or limit the number of hours an employee is required to work.[3] The "workweek" standard as defined at [45.06] is used as a means to compute hours worked for the purposes of calculating overtime payments.[4]

[46.02] COMPUTATION OF THE "REGULAR RATE"

The FLSA requires an employer to pay overtime compensation at a rate of not less than one and one-half times the employee's "regular rate" of pay.[5] A determination of the "regular rate" is essential in computing an employee's overtime pay.[6]

The "regular rate" has been interpreted as an hourly rate figured on a weekly basis. An employee might, however, be paid on some other basis such as on a piece rate, salary, commission, and so on.[7] When an employee is paid on some basis other than hourly, it is necessary to convert the pay to an hourly rate for purposes of determining the overtime compensation due.[8]

As a general proposition, the "regular rate" of pay is determined by dividing the employee's total renumeration for the workweek, with the exception of statutory exclusions, by the total number of hours worked in the particular workweek.[9]

[46.03] STATUTORY EXCLUSIONS FROM EARNINGS

The FLSA specifically authorizes employers to exclude certain payments from earnings when computing the "regular rate" of pay. The statutory exclusions consist of payments and remuneration to employees in the form of discretionary bonuses, gifts, holiday pay, reimbursed expenses incurred on the employer's behalf, profit sharing payments, savings plan payments, talent fees, insurance premiums, vacation pay, and pension plan contributions.[10]

In addition, overtime premiums paid to an employee for work in excess of some daily or weekly standard; for work performed on a Saturday, Sunday, holiday, or some other "special" day; or for work performed outside of clock-time periods as arranged through a collective bargaining or employment agreement are not required to be included in earnings for the purpose of computing the "regular rate."[11] Rather, the FLSA provides that such overtime premiums may be used to offset any overtime compensation owed to a particular employee.[12]

[46.04] COMPUTATION OF FIXED AND PIECE-RATE WAGES

As noted earlier, when employees are paid on the basis of a single hourly rate, the hourly rate is synonymous with the "regular rate" for computation of overtime premiums.[13] However, when employees are paid on some basis other than an hourly rate, it is necessary to convert their compensation into an hourly rate in order to ascertain the "regular rate."[14]

Piece rates: Absent other permitted arrangements under the Act, the "regular rate" for pieceworkers may be determined by adding the total earnings of the employee for the workweek, with the exception of statutory exclusions, and then dividing the total earnings by the total number of hours worked in the particular workweek.[15]

The employee then must be paid a sum equivalent to one half the "regular rate" multiplied by the number of overtime hours so as to comply with the overtime pay requirements of the Act.[16]

Fixed weekly salary: Whenever an employee covered by the FLSA is paid a fixed weekly salary as compensation for regular workweeks comprising a fixed number of working hours, the "regular rate" is figured by dividing the fixed salary by the fixed number of hours agreed upon as the regular workweek.[17]

If the fixed number of working hours are more than the statutory forty-hour straight-time workweek, only a sum equivalent ot one-half the "regular rate" need be paid for overtime hours worked up to the fixed number inasmuch as the fixed weekly wage would cover straight-time for those hours. However, one and one-half the computed "regular rate" must be paid for hours worked in excess of the fixed number of working hours.[18] In the event the fixed number of hours agreed upon amounted to the statutory forty-hour straight-time workweek or less, then one and one-half the computed "regular rate" is to be paid for all hours worked in excess of forty.[19]

[46.05] FLUCTUATING WORKWEEK FORMULA

Where an employee's work hours are somewhat irregular and fluctuate from week to week, the employer may work out an arrangement with the employee that a fixed weekly wage is to compensate the employee for all hours worked during any particular workweek.[20]

Under such an arrangement, the "regular rate" is to be figured by dividing the total number of hours worked during a particular workweek by the fixed weekly wages.[21] However, the following conditions must be met in order for an employer to take advantage of this method of compensation:

- The employee must receive a sum equivalent to not less than one-half his or her "regular rate" of pay for all hours worked in excess of forty during any one workweek;[22]
- The employee must clearly understand the arrangement;[23]
- The amount of salary must be sufficient to meet the minimum wage requirements for every hour worked in a workweek;[24]
- The employee's hours must be irregular and significantly fluctuate from week to week, both below and above forty hours;[25]
- The fixed weekly wage must be paid the employee even though the employee works less than forty hours during the workweek;[26] and
- The employer may not deduct absences of less than a week of duration from the fixed weekly wage since the fixed salary is to cover both short and long weekly work hours.[27]

The fact that the "regular rate" decreases as the number of hours increase under the fluctuating workweek formula was not found objectionable by the U.S. Supreme Court.[28]

Some courts have permitted the employee's "regular rate" to be computed by dividing the employee's weekly salary by the number of scheduled hours worked in the workweek with overtime to be assessed at a sum equivalent to one-half that regular rate for hours worked in excess of forty, even in the absence of an understanding or agreement between the employer and the employee to that affect.[29]

Except in Belo agreements, discussed below, a fluctuating workweek arrangement will not be permitted where an employer attempts to include in an employee's lump sum weekly salary both straight-time and overtime compensation without regard to the number of overtime hours worked in any workweek.[30]

[46.06] BELO CONTRACT ARRANGEMENT

The FLSA specifies that an employer may pay employees who work irregular hours a fixed wage intended to include payment for ovetime hours up to a limited number, providing certain conditions are met.[31] This plan is commonly referred to as a *Belo* contract and entails a guaranteed weekly wage to be paid an employee pursuant to a bona fide individual contract or a collective bargaining agreement.[32] Such contracts are valid under the FLSA if the following conditions are satisfied:

- The contract must specify a weekly guarantee of pay;[33]

- The employee's work hours must significantly fluctuate from week to week;[34]

- The contract must specify a sufficient rate of pay to satisfy the minimum wage requirements;[35]

- The weekly guarantee must cover no more than sixty hours in any one week based upon the rates so specified;[36] and

- The contract must specify compensation of at least one and one-half times such minimum rate for all hours worked in excess of the employee's maximum workweek.[37]

[46.07] MONTHLY AND SEMIMONTHLY PAY ARRANGEMENTS

Whenever an employee is paid on a fixed salary for a period longer than a workweek, the salary must first be reduced to its workweek equivalent before the "regular rate" can be figured.[38]

The accepted method of computing the "regular rate" for monthly salaried employees is to multiply the monthly salary by twelve to obtain the pay for the year, then divide the annual amount by fifty-two to obtain the pay for the week, and then divide the latter sum by the number of hours worked per week.[39]

In similar fashion, to ascertain the regular rate of pay for an employee compensated on a semimonthly basis, his or her salary should first be multiplied by twenty-four which sum should be divided by fifty-two, and the resulting sum further divided by the number of hours worked per week.[40]

Once the regular rate of pay has been established for either the monthly or semimonthly salaried employee, overtime compensation is computed at one and one-half the established regular rate for all hours worked in excess of forty in any one workweek.[41] However, if the employee has already been paid his or her regular rate of pay for the overtime hours, he or she is entitled to only an amount equivalent to one-half the regular rate for the overtime hours.[42]

Employees paid on a monthly or semimonthly basis may be paid overtime compensation pursuant to a fluctuating workweek formula provided all the requirements for such a plan are met.[43] However, they may not be paid pursuant to a Belo contract since such would permit averaging over more than one workweek.[44]

[46.08] GUARANTEED HOURS ARRANGEMENT

The FLSA provides that an employer who enters into a collective bargaining agreement with a bona fide bargaining agent of its employees, which agreement provides for a maximum of 1,040 employment hours during any twenty-six consecutive weeks, is not required to pay overtime for hours in excess of the applicable statutory maximum workweek as long as such employees receive compensation of at least one and one-half times their regular rate for all hours worked in excess of twelve in any one day or in excess of fifty-six in any one week.[45]

The FLSA also provides that an employer is not required to pay statutory overtime to an employee for hours under twelve in any one day or hours under fifty-six in any one week if such employee is governed by a bona fide collective bargaining agreement that specifies that the employee shall work a maximum of 2,240 hours, shall be guaranteed at least 1,840 hours but not more than 2,080, all within a period of fifty-two consecutive weeks, and shall be paid for hours in excess of 2,080 during such period at one and one-half times his or her regular rate.[46]

[46.09] OVERTIME PAY FOR COMMISSIONED EMPLOYEES

The Wage and Hour Division considers commissions as payments for hours worked that must be reflected in the "regular rate" and overtime pay.[47]

The "regular rate" of pay for a commissioned employee is computed by dividing the total weekly commissions by the number of hours worked in the week.[48] If the employee is paid both commissions and salary, both must be added and then divided by the number of hours worked in the workweek to determine the applicable "regular rate."[49]

Notwithstanding the general requirement that commissions must be includible in the "regular rate" for the purposes of computing overtime compensation, an employee of a retail or service establishment who is paid either partially or totally by commissions need not be paid overtime compensation for hours worked in excess of the standard statutory workweek, provided the following conditions are met:

- The employee's "regular rate" of pay is more than one and one-half times the current minimum hourly rate under the FLSA;[50]
- More than half of the employee's compensation for a representative period—not less than one month—must represent commissions on goods or service;[51] and
- The employer must qualify as a "retail or service establishment."[52]

[46.10] FOURTEEN-DAY WORK PERIOD FOR HEALTH-CARE EMPLOYEES

The FLSA permits health care employees to be employed during a period of fourteen consecutive days in lieu of the standard seven-day workweek for purposes of computing overtime, provided such employees are paid at the rate of at least one and one-half times their regular rate for all hours worked in excess of eight in a one-day period and in excess of eighty in a fourteen-day work period.[53]

Moreover, there must be an agreement or understanding to such pay arrangement between the Health-Care employer and the employees prior to the performance of the work under the arrangement.[54]

[46.11] PARTIAL OVERTIME EXEMPTIONS

The FLSA authorizes a partial overtime exemption for certain employers, provided specified conditions are met. Employers entitled to partial overtime exemptions include tobacco employers who employ workers to buy, strip, stem, sort, and generally handle specified green-leaf and cigar-leaf tobacco[55] and petroleum distributors.[56]

[46.12] WAGES INCLUDIBLE IN REGULAR RATE

The employer must include "all remuneration" given to an employee as compensation for his or her employment in the computation of his or her "regular rate,"[57] with the exception of statutory exclusions discussed at [46.03].

The statutory term "all remuneration" encompasses all payments received regularly during the workweek, whether in the form of wages or some other thing of value.[58] Some of the more common items required to be included in the "regular rate" are as follows:

- *Absence pay* for personal purposes;[59]
- *Attendance bonuses*;[60]
- *Board and lodging* qualifying as noncash wages under 29 USCS Section 203(m);[61]
- *Contest prizes* paid as an additional remuneration for quality, quantity, efficiency, attendance, etc.;[62]
- *Cost-of-living bonuses*;[63]
- *Incentive bonuses*;[64]
- *Merchandise* furnished free at company stores;[65]
- *Rest period premiums*;[66]
- *Shift differentials*;[67]
- *Tips*, up to an amount not exceeding 40 percent of the applicable minimum wage rate;[68]
- *Transportation* furnished by the employer for the employee's benefit and not an incident of employment;[69] and
- *Traveling expenses* of employee to and from work for the employee's benefit.[70]

NOTES TO CHAPTER 46

1. 29 U.S.C.A. §207(a)(1).

2. 29 CFR §778.102.

3. *Walling v. Helmerich & Payne, Inc.*, 323 U.S. 37 (1944).

4. 29 CFR §778.103; see also *Jewell Ridge Coal Co. v. United Mine Workers*, 325 U.S. 161 (1945).

5. 29 U.S.C.A. §107(a).

6. *Masters v. Maryland Management Co.*, 493 F.2d 1329 (CA-4, 1974).

7. 29 CFR §§778.108 and 778.109.

8. 29 CFR §778.109.

9. 29 CFR §§778.109 and 778.321.

10. 29 U.S.C.A. §207(e).

11. 29 U.S.C.A. §207(e).

12. 29 U.S.C.A. §207(h).

13. See [46.02].

14. 29 CFR §778.109.

15. *Walling v. Youngerman Reynolds Hardwood Co.*, 325 U.S. 419 (1945).

16. 29 CFR §778.111(a).

17. See *Guidebook to Federal Wage-Hour Laws*, Para. 803.3 (1978).

18. Ibid.

19. See Note 17, *supra*.

20. See 29 U.S.C.A. §207(f); see also 29 CFR §778.114.

21. *Overnight Motor Transp. Co. v. Missel*; 316 U.S. 572 (1942).

22. 29 CFR §778.114.(c).

23. 29 CFR §778.114.(c).

24. 29 CFR §778.114.(a) and (c).

25. *Donovan v. Brown Equipment & Service Tools, Inc.*, 666 F.2d 148 (CA-5, 1982).

26. 29 CFR §778.114(c).

27. 29 CFR §778.114(c).

28. *Overnight Motor Transp. Co. v. Missel, supra.*

29. *Mumbower v. Callicott*, 526 F.2d 1183 (CA-8, 1975).

30. *Overnight Motor Transp. Co. v. Missel, supra.*

31. 29 U.S.C.A. §207(f).

32. See 29 CFR §778.404; see also *Walling v. A.H. Belo Corp.*, 316 U.S. 624 (1942).

33. 29 U.S.C.A. §207(f).

34. 29 U.S.C.A. §207(f).

35. 29 U.S.C.A. §207(f).

36. 29 U.S.C.A. §207(f).

37. 29 U.S.C.A. §207(f).
38. 29 CFR §778.113(b).
39. 29 CFR §778.113(b)
40. 29 CFR §778.113(b).
41. 29 CFR §778.113(b).
42. *Triple "AAA" Co. v. Wirt*, 378 F.2d 884 (CA-10, 1967).
43. *General Electric Co. v. Porter*, 208 F.2d 805 (CA-9, 1953).
44. 29 CFR §778.410(a).
45. 29 U.S.C.A. §207(b)(1).
46. 29 U.S.C.A. §207(b)(2).
47. 29 CFR §778.117.
48. 29 CFR §778.117.
49. 29 CFR §778.117.
50. 29 U.S.C.A. §207(i).
51. 29 U.S.C.A. §207(i).
52. 29 CFR §779.411.
53. 29 U.S.C.A. §207(j).
54. 29 CFR §778.601(b).
55. 29 U.S.C.A. §207(m).
56. 29 U.S.C.A. §207(b)(3).
57. 29 CFR §778.201(c).
58. 29 CFR §778.330.
59. See Note 17, Para. 810.1, *supra*.
60. 29 CFR §778.211(c).
61. 29 CFR §778.116.
62. 29 CFR §778.331.
63. *Wage and Hour Field Operations Handbook*, Para. 32c00(b)(3).
64. 29 CFR §778.211(c).
65. 29 CFR §§531.37 and 778.116.
66. 29 CFR §778.218(b).
67. 29 CFR §778.207(b).
68. 29 CFR §531.60(a).
69. 29 CFR §778.217(d).
70. 29 CFR §778.217(d).

47

Child Labor Laws Under the FLSA

[47.01] BACKGROUND

The Fair Labor Standards Act restricts the use of child labor to certain age groups, depending on the type of employment and the degree of hazards unique to the particular job in question.[1]

The child labor provisions of the FLSA prohibit the shipment, in commerce, of any goods produced in an establishment in or about which oppressive child labor was employed within thirty days prior to the removal of such goods from the producing establishment.[2]

The FLSA also forbids covered employers[3] from employing any children at ages below those set by the statute or pertinent regulations for various types of occupations, unless otherwise exempt.[4]

[47.02] CHILD LABOR LAW EXEMPTIONS

The FLSA exempts several individuals from its child labor provisions. Here are some examples.

Family members: A parent, including persons standing in the place of a parent, may employ a child under the age of 16 years on a farm or in some similar nonhazardous occupation.[5]

Child actors: A child of any age may be employed as an actor or performer in motion pictures, television and radio productions, or in theatrical performances, without violating the child labor provisions of the FLSA.[6]

Newspaper carriers: The child labor provisions of the FLSA do not apply to newspaper carriers engaged in making deliveries to the homes of subscribers or other consumers or engaged in making street sales to consumers.[7]

Agricultural employees: The child labor provisions of the FLSA do not apply to any employee employed in agriculture outside of school hours for the school district in which the employee resides while he or she is so employed, so long as the Secretary of Labor has not classified the particular job in question to be particularly hazardous for the employment of children under 16 years of age, and provided the employee is either

- at least 14 years of age, or
- at least 12 or 13 years of age and the employment is with the consent of his parent or person standing in the place of his or her parent, or his or her parent or such other person is employed on the same farm as the child, or

- under 12 years of age, but nonetheless is employed by his or her parents or a person standing in the place of his or her parent on a farm owned or operated by such parent or such other person or is employed with the consent of his or her parent or such other person on a farm that is not covered by the FLSA because the employer did not use more than 500 workdays of agricultural labor during any calendar quarter during the preceding calendar year.[8]

[47.03]   18-YEAR MINIMUM AGE STANDARDS

The Secretary of Labor has determined certain occupations to be particularly hazardous to children and has prescribed a table of prohibited occupations for persons under particular age groups. The Secretary has declared the following occupations to be closed to children under 18 years of age:[9]

- Occupations in or about plants manufacturing or storing explosives or articles containing explosive components
- Operations of motor vehicles
- Coal mine operations and occupations relating to mining other than coal
- Logging and related occupations
- Occupations requiring the operation of power-driven woodworking machines
- Occupations exposing employees to radioactive substances
- Occupations requiring the operation of power-driven hoisting apparatus
- Occupations requiring the operation of power-driven metal forming, punching, and shearing machines
- Occupations involving the slaughter of animals and meat packing
- Occupations requiring the operation of power-bakery machines
- Occupations requiring the operation of power-driven paper products machines
- Occupations involving the manufacture of brick, tile, and kindred products
- Occupations requiring the operation of circular saws, bandsaws and guillotine shears
- Occupations in wrecking, demolition and shipbreaking operations
- Occupations in roofing operations
- Occupations in excavation operations

[47.04] 16–YEAR MINIMUM AGE STANDARDS

The Secretary of Labor has declared the following occupations to be closed to children under 16 years of ages:[10]

- Manufacturing, mining, or processing of goods, including occupations requiring any duties in work places where goods are manufactured, mined, or otherwise processed
- Occupations involving the use of hoisting apparatus or power-driven machinery other than office machines
- Operation of motor vehicles or helper service on such vehicles
- Public messenger service.
- Occupations (except for office or sales work) connected with transportation of persons or property by rail, highway, air, water, pipeline, or other means; warehousing and storage; communications and public utilities; and construction, including demolition and repair.

[47.05] 14–YEAR MINIMUM AGE STANDARDS

The Secretary of Labor has specifically authorized the employment of children who are at least 14 years of age in retail, food-service, and gasoline service establishments;[11] and in work experience and career exploration programs sponsored and supervised by local school officials.[12]

However, the employment of children in the 14- and 15-year category is subject to the following conditions:

- All work must be performed between 7:00 A.M. and 7:00 P.M., except during the summer months when the evening hour is extended to 9:00 P.M.;
- Employment must be outside of regular school hours (except EEOC programs);
- Employment is limited to a maximum of three hours on any school day and eight hours on any nonschool day;
- Employment is limited to a maximum of eighteen hours in any week when school is in session, and forty hours in other weeks.[13]

[47.06] AGE CERTIFICATES

The FLSA provides a method for employers to protect themselves against child labor violations.

An employer who has on file an officially executed age certificate has a complete defense to a claim that the employer has violated the child labor provisions of the FLSA, assuming the employer had no independent reason to suspect the child was actually below the required age.[14]

Age certificates are issued only upon application of the minor desiring employment or the prospective employer.[15]

[47.07] LEGAL PENALTIES FOR VIOLATIONS

An employer who violates the child labor provisions of the FLSA is subject to a civil penalty not to exceed $1,000 for each such violation.[16] Such an employer may also be enjoined from continuing to violate the child labor provisions, and held in contempt of court for failure to comply with the terms of any such injunction.[17]

An employer who willfully violates the child labor provisions of the FLSA may be subject to a fine up to $10,000 for a first violation, and imprisonment up to six months and/or a fine up to $10,000 for a second violation.[18]

[47.08] RELATED CHILD LABOR RESTRICTIONS

In addition to the child labor prohibitions set forth under the FLSA, other federal statutes also regulate child labor under specific conditions, such as

- *The Walsh-Healey Act* which applies to government contractors[19]
- *The Mining Land Leasing Act* which applies to mining operations on and leased from the federal government[20]
- *The Interstate Commerce Act* which limits the employment of children as drivers in interstate commerce[21]
- *The Sugar Act* which limits child labor in the sugar industry[22]

State laws may also limit the employment of children in certain occupations and such state laws may set standards higher than those required under the FLSA.[23]

NOTES TO CHAPTER 47

1. 29 U.S.C.A. §203.
2. 29 U.S.C.A. §212(a).
3. Refer to [44.04] for a discussion of employer coverage under the FLSA.
4. 29 U.S.C.A. §212(c).
5. See 29 U.S.C.A. §203(L)(1); 29 U.S.C.A. §213(c)(2).
6. 29 U.S.C.A. §213(c)(3).
7. 29 U.S.C.A. §213(d).
8. 29 U.S.C.A. §213(c)(1)(A),(B), and (C).

9. 29 CFR §570.120.
10. 29 CFR §570.119.
11. 29 CFR §570.34(a).
12. 29 CFR §570.35(a).
13. 29 CFR §570.35(a).
14. 29 CFR §570.5.
15. 29 CFR §570.7.
16. 29 U.S.C.A. §§215(a)(4) and 216(e).
17. 29 U.S.C.A. §217.
18. See 29 CFR §216(a).
19. 41 U.S.C.A. §35, *et seq.*
20. 30 U.S.C.A. §187, *et seq.*
21. 49 U.S.C.A. §304, *et seq.*
22. 7 U.S.C.A. §1131, *et seq.*
23. 29 U.S.C.A. §218(a).

48

FLSA Administration, Enforcement, and Recordkeeping

[48.01] GENERAL ADMINISTRATION

The FLSA is administered by the Wage and Hour Division of the U.S. Department of Labor.[1] The division is under the direction of an administrator whose office is located in Washington, D.C.[2]

The Wage and Hour Administrator is also responsible for the various regional and local wage and hour offices located throughout the United States.[3]

[48.02] RECORDKEEPING REQUIREMENTS

Every employer subject to the wage provisions of the FLSA is required to make, keep, and preserve records concerning the wages, hours, sex, occupations, and other terms and practices of employment regarding employees covered by the Act.[4] Recordkeeping under the wage and hour requirements is principally the responsibility of the employer.[5] The recordkeeping requirements of the wage and hour regulations are enforceable by injunctions.[6] A willful violation of the recordkeeping requirements is ground for criminal prosecution.[7]

Special and/or additional records must be maintained and preserved in accordance with the pertinent wage and hour regulations on seamen, commissioned individuals, students, "tipped" employees, etc.[8]

Records are also required to be maintained and preserved on employees covered by the Act but who are nonetheless exempt from minimum wage and overtime pay provisions.[9]

Basic records containing employee information, payrolls, individual contracts, collective bargaining agreements, sales and purchase records, and applicable certificates and notices listed or named in any regulations of the Wage and Hour Division must be preserved for at least three years from the last date of entry.[10]

Supplementary basic records must be maintained for at least two years, such as wage rate tables; work time schedules; orders, shipping and billing records; records of additions to or deductions from wages paid; documentation of basis for payment of any wage differential to employees of the opposite sex in the same establishment; and other basic employment and earnings records.[11]

[48.03] POSTER DISPLAY REQUIREMENTS

Every employer subject to the Act and who is not specifically exempt from both the minimum wage and overtime pay provisions of the Act must post and maintain notices prescribed and provided by the Wage and Hour Division in conspicuous places within the respective establishment.[12]

[48.04] INSPECTIONS AND INVESTIGATIONS

The FLSA provides that the Administrator of the Wage and Hour Division, or his or her representatives, may investigate and gather data relative to wages, hours, and other conditions and practices of employment of any employer subject to the Act.[13]

The Administrator and his or her representatives are empowered to inspect places and records, question employees, investigate facts, conditions, practices, or matters as are deemed necessary or appropriate to determine whether the Act has been violated.[14]

Should an employer refuse to permit an investigation by the Wage and Hour Division, the Administrator is empowered to subpoena production of documents, papers, tangible data, or other evidentiary evidence relating to any matter under investigation.[15]

[48.05] LITIGATION

Should a violation of the Act be discovered through a Wage and Hour investigation, or some other means, several civil actions are available to both the Secretary of Labor or to employees adversely affected. For example, an employee may file a civil action in any federal or state court of competent jurisdiction to recover unpaid overtime compensation, unpaid minimum wages, or both, as the case may be, and an additional equal amount as liquidated damages, plus a reasonable attorney's fee and the costs of the action.[16]

An action may also be filed in any federal or state court of competent jurisdiction by one or more employees for and on behalf of himself and/or other employees similarly situated, to recover unpaid overtime compensation, unpaid minimum wages, or both, as the case may be, and an additional equal amount as liquidated damages, plus a reasonable attorney's fee and costs of the action.[17]

In addition to employee suits, an action may also be brought by the U.S. Secretary of Labor in any court of competent jurisdiction to recover unpaid minimum wages, unpaid overtime compensation, or both, as the case may be, and an equal amount as liquidated damages.[18] The Secretary of Labor may also bring an injunctive action to restrain an employer from withholding payment of minimum wages or overtime compensation due to employees.[19]

[48.06]   LIMITATIONS OF ACTION

A cause of action for unpaid minimum wages or unpaid overtime compensation under the FLSA must be brought within two years after a cause of action accrues in the case of a nonwillful violation, and within three years after a cause of action accrues in the case of a willful violation.[20] The federal statute limiting actions to the two- or three-year period applies to actions brought in either state or federal courts.[21]

[48.07]   DEFENSES

In addition to pleading the applicable two- or three-year limitations of action provisions as an affirmative defense, other possible defenses in a wage and hour suit might include

- payment[22]
- exemptions from the Act[23]
- stopped because of employee deceit[24]
- discharge in bankruptcy[25]
- accord and satisfaction[26]
- good faith reliance on administrative rulings and regulations[27]

An employer may be excused from the payment of liquidated damages but not unpaid wages or unpaid overtime compensation, if he or she can show to the court's satisfaction that the action in failing to pay minimum wages and/or the appropriate overtime compensation was in good faith based upon reasonable grounds that his or her act or omission was not a violation of the FLSA.[28] However, this limited defense is a matter of court discretion.[29]

[48.08]   SUITS FOR RETALIATION

Under the FLSA, it is unlawful for an employer to discharge or in any other manner discriminatorily retaliate against any employee because that employee has filed a complaint or instituted a proceeding under the Act, or who appeared as a witness in such proceeding.[30]

In addition to being subjected to possible criminal sanctions, any employer who so retaliates against an employee may be ordered to reimburse the employee for lost wages[31] and reinstate the employee to his or her former job.[32]

NOTES TO CHAPTER 48

1. 29 U.S.C.A. §204(a).
2. 29 U.S.C.A. §204(a) and (c).
3. 29 U.S.C.A. §204(c).
4. See 29 U.S.C.A. §211(c) and 29 CFR Part 516.
5. *Wirtz v. Mississippi Publishers Corp.,* 364 F.2d 603 (CA-5, 1966).
6. 29 U.S.C.A. §217.
7. 29 U.S.C.A. §216(a).
8. 29 CFR §516.
9. 29 CFR §516.11.
10. 29 CFR §516.5(a)(b) and (c).
11. 29 CFR §516.6(a) through (d).
12. 29 CFR §516.4.
13. 29 U.S.C.A. §211(a).
14. 29 U.S.C.A. §211(a).
15. 29 U.S.C.A. §209 and 15 U.S.C.A. §§49 and 50.
16. 29 U.S.C.A. §216(b).
17. 29 U.S.C.A. §216(b).
18. 29 U.S.C.A. §216(b).
19. 29 U.S.C.A. §216(c).
20. 29 U.S.C.A. §255.
21. 29 U.S.C.A. §255.
22. *Caperna v. Williams - Bauer Corp.,* 47 NY/S/2d 328 (Sup. App., 1944); Rule 8(c), *Fed. Rules of Civ. Proc.*
23. *McCloskey & Co. v. Eckart,* 164 F.2d 257 (CA-5, 1947).
24. *Cotton v. Weyerhaeuser Timber Co.,* 29 Wash 2d 300, 147 P2d 299 (1944).
25. Rule 8(c), *Fed. Rules of Civ. Proc.*
26. Rule 8(c), *Fed. Rules of Civ. Proc.*
27. 29 U.S.C.A. §259.
28. 29 U.S.C.A. §260.
29. See *Thomas v. Louisiana,* 348 F.Supp. 792 (DC La., 1972).
30. 29 U.S.C.A. §215(a)(3).
31. *Mitchell v. Robert DeMario Jewelry Inc.,* 361 U.S. 288 (1960).
32. 29 U.S.C.A. §216(b).

49

Miscellaneous Federal Wage and Hour Laws

[49.01] WALSH-HEALEY ACT

The Walsh-Healey Act, which was enacted in 1936, requires the payment of minimum wages and overtime pay to employees who work on government contracts made and entered into by their employer and any agency or instrumentality of the United States for purchases or supplies exceeding $10,000, unless the employees are otherwise exempt under the statutory provisions.[1] In addition, employers who are covered by the Walsh-Healey provisions must post copies of all of the Walsh-Healey stipulations in conspicuous places at the work site[2] and keep certain records as required by the Act.[3]

Employees covered by the Walsh-Healey provisions must be paid not less than the minimum wages as established by the Secretary of Labor to be the prevailing minimum wages for persons employed on similar work within the particular industry.[4] Such employees must also be paid one and one-half times the applicable basic hourly rate for hours worked in excess of eight hours in any one day or in excess of forty hours worked in any one week.[5]

The Walsh-Healey Act, and other pertinent regulations, specify several exemptions to its coverage.

For example, a government contract for services, as distinguished from a contract for goods or products, is exempt from the Walsh-Healey provisions.[6] Likewise, a government contract for perishables is exempt from the Act.[7] The Walsh-Healey provisions do not apply to government purchases of materials, supplies, articles, or equipment that may customarily be bought in the open market.[8] To fall within Walsh-Healey coverage, an employer must be a manufacturer of, or a regular dealer in, materials, supplies, articles, or equipment to be manufactured or used as provided by the contract.[9] Government contracts of less than $10,000 are not covered by the Walsh-Healey Act.[10]

In addition, the Walsh-Healey Act does not apply to the following:

- stockpiles on hand that were produced prior to the award of the contract[11]
- foreign goods[12]
- newspapers, magazines, and related publications delivered by the publisher[13]
- rentals[14]
- transportation by common carriers[15]
- communications through radio, telephone, telegraph, or other establishments subject to the Federal Communications Act[16]

- general office employees, general maintenance workers, and other "indirect labor" employees[17]
- Executive, administrative, and professional employees[18]

The Walsh-Healey Act is administered and enforced by the United States Secretary of Labor, who is empowered to hold hearings and make findings of fact regarding violations of the Act.[19] The Secretary of Labor, through the office of the United States Attorney General, may enforce his or her findings of fact through actions in a federal court.[20] Employees covered by Walsh-Healey do not have a private right of action to recover unpaid wages and liquidated damages.[21]

Employers who violate the provisions of the Walsh-Healey Act may be required to pay all underpayment of wages and such sums of money may be withheld from any amounts due to the employers on the contract.[22] In addition, a violation of the Walsh-Healey Act might subject the employer to cancellation of the contract in question by the government agency.[23] The employer might also be blacklisted from receiving further contracts from the United States government.[24]

[49.02]   DAVIS-BACON ACT

The Davis-Bacon Act, which was enacted in 1931, requires the payment of minimum wages and fringe benefits to laborers and mechanics employed on federal public works contracts exceeding $2,000.[25] A public works contract does not fall within the coverage of the Davis-Bacon Act unless the contract provides for construction, alteration, and/or repair, including painting or decorating.[26] A public works contract must also involve the employment of mechanics or laborers to be covered by the Davis-Bacon provisions.[27] The Davis-Bacon Act generally applies to construction activity as distinguished from manufacturing or furnishing of materials, articles, supplies, or equipment.[28]

The Davis-Bacon Act requires employers covered by its provisions to pay their employees at least the minimum wages established by the Secretary of Labor to be prevailing for other laborers and mechanics employed on similar projects in the local area.[29] Davis-Bacon employers are also required to maintain and preserve certain employee records[30] as well as post notices concerning the scale of wages to be paid employees as determined by the Secretary of Labor.[31]

Employers who violate the Davis-Bacon provisions are liable for any unpaid wages. Funds due and owing the employer by the government may be withheld to compensate employees for the wages to which they are entitled.[32] In addition, the government may cancel an employer's contract because of Davis-Bacon violations and may also blacklist the employer from receiving future public works contracts.[33] Willful violations of the Davis-Bacon provisions are grounds for criminal prosecution.[34]

The Secretary of Labor is responsible for the administration and enforcement of the Davis-Bacon Act.[35]

[49.03] GOVERNMENT SERVICE CONTRACT ACT

The Service Contract Act provides that every contract entered into by the United States (including the District of Columbia) in excess of $2,500, the principal purpose of which is to furnish services through the use of service employees, must contain certain stipulations regarding minimum wages and fringe benefits, unless such contract is otherwise exempted.[36]

Employers subject to the Service Contract Act must pay their employees at least the minimum monetary wages and benefits established by the Secretary of Labor in accordance with prevailing rates and benefits for such employees in the local area.[37] The Service Contract Act further specifies the manner in which fringe benefits furnished shall be treated in computing overtime pay to which service employees are entitled under other federal laws.[38]

Employers covered by the provisions of the Service Contract Act must maintain and preserve certain employee records[39] and also post notice of the compensation required under the Act in a prominent place at the work site.[40]

Unpaid wages due employees by a Service Contract employer may be withheld from money owed the employer to compensate employees for the wages to which they are entitled.[41] The government may also cancel an employer's contract[42] and blacklist him or her from further government contracts as a result of such violations.[43]

The Secretary of Labor is responsible for the administration and enforcement of the Service Contract Act.[44]

[49.04] THE COPELAND ACT

The Copeland Act, sometimes referred to as the "Anti-kickback" Act, prohibits a government contractor or subcontractor from compelling or inducing an employee to give back part of his or her compensation to the employer.[45] The purpose of the Copeland Act is to ensure that workers on federal projects receive the full wages they have lawfully earned from their employer.[46]

Any employer who, by force, intimidation, or threat of discharge, or by any other manner whatsoever, induces any person covered by the provisions of the Act to give up any part of his or her compensation which he or she has earned and is entitled to receive, shall be subject to monetary fines up to $5,000 or imprisonment up to five years, or both.[47]

[49.05] THE MILLER ACT

The Miller Act provides that government contractors on public works contracts exceeding $2,000 must furnish a bond to protect the payment of wages to all employees employed on the project.[48]

[49.06] THE CONTRACT WORK HOURS AND SAFETY STANDARDS ACT

The Contract Work Hours and Safety Standards Act provides that employees covered by the Davis-Bacon Act or employed on construction projects financed by the federal government must be paid time and one-half for hours worked in excess of eight hours in any one day or forty hours in any one week.[49] The Act also requires employers covered by its provisions to provide safe and healthy working surroundings for their employees.[50]

The Service Contract Act, the Fair Labor Standards Act, and the Contract Work Hours and Safety Standards Act are considered to be mutually supplemental to each other in that an employee coming within the coverage of all three would be entitled to receive the highest pay of any provided within any of the statutes relative to minimum wage and/or overtime pay.[51]

[49.07] GARNISHMENT AND CREDIT LAWS

Title III of the Consumer Credit Protection Act sets restrictions on the amount of an individual's earnings that may be deducted in any one week as a result of garnishment proceedings.[52]

Specifically, the statute establishes that the maximum part of the aggregate disposable earnings of an individual be garnished no more than

- Twenty-five percent of such disposable earnings in any one week, or
- The amount by which the disposable earnings for that week exceeds thirty times the federal minimum hourly wage prescribed by Section 6(a)(1) of the Fair Labor Standards Act, except that such restrictions do not apply in any case of any order for the support of any person issued by a court of competent jurisdiction, any order of any court of bankruptcy under Chapter XIII of the Bankruptcy Act, or any debt due for the payment of any state or federal taxes.[53]

The Act further provides that no employer may discharge any employee by reason of the fact that his or her earnings have been subjected to garnishment for any one indebtedness.[54] The term "one indebtedness" refers to a single debt, regardless of the number of levies made or creditors seeking satisfaction.[55]

Whoever willfully violates the statute may be fined up to $1,000 or imprisoned for not more than one year, or both.[56]

NOTES TO CHAPTER 49

1. 41 U.S.C.A. §35.
2. 41 CFR §50-201.1(g).
3. 41 CFR §50-201.501.
4. 41 U.S.C.A. §35(b); 41 CFR §50-201.1(b).
5. 41 U.S.C.A. §35(c); 41 CFR §50-201.1(c).
6. 41 U.S.C.A. §35.
7. 41 U.S.C.A. §43.
8. 41 U.S.C.A. §43.
9. 41 U.S.C.A. §35(a).
10. 41 U.S.C.A. §35.
11. See *Walsh-Healey Act Rulings & Regulations No. 3* §24(a) and (b).
12. 41 CFR §50-201.603(b).
13. 41 CFR §50-201.603(d).
14. See Note 11, §17, *supra.*
15. 41 U.S.C.A. §43.
16. 41 U.S.C.A. §43.
17. 41 CFR §50-201.102.
18. See generally 41 CFR §50-201.102.
19. 41 U.S.C.A. §§38 and 39.
20. 41 U.S.C.A. §39.
21. *United States v. Lovknit Mfg.,* 189 F.2d 454 (CA-5, 1951).
22. 41 U.S.C.A. §36.
23. 41 U.S.C.A. §36.
24. 41 U.S.C.A. §37.
25. 40 U.S.C.A. §276a(a).
26. 40 U.S.C.A. §276a(a).
27. 40 U.S.C.A. §276a(a).
28. See 40 CFR §5.2(f).
29. 40 U.S.C.A. §276a(a).
30. 29 CFR §5.5(a)(3)(i).
31. 40 U.S.C.A. §276a(a).
32. 29 CFR §5.9.
33. 40 U.S.C.A. §276a-2(a).
34. See 29 CFR §5.10(b).
35. 29 CFR §1.1, 5.1.
36. 41 U.S.C.A. §351(a).
37. 41 U.S.C.A. §351(a)(1) and (2).

38. 29 CFR §4.180.

39. 29 CFR §4.6(g).

40. 29 CFR §4.6(e).

41. 41 U.S.C.A. §352(a).

42. 41 U.S.C.A. §352(c).

43. 41 U.S.C.A. §352(a).

44. 41 U.S.C.A. §353(a).

45. 18 U.S.C.A. §874.

46. *United States v. Carbone,* 327 U.S. 633 (1946).

47. 18 U.S.C.A. §874.

48. 40 U.S.C.A. §270a(a)(2); 32 CFR §10.101-10.

49. 40 U.S.C.A. §329.

50. 40 U.S.C.A. §329.

51. *Masters v. Maryland Management Co.,* 493 F.2d 1329 (CA-4, 1974).

52. 15 U.S.C.A. §1671, *et seq.*

53. 15 U.S.C.A. §1673.

54. 15 U.S.C.A. §1674.

55. 15 U.S.C.A. §1671, *et seq.*

56. 15 U.S.C.A. §1674.

PART IV

FEDERAL SAFETY
AND HEALTH LAWS

50

Introduction to the Federal Occupational Safety and Health Act

[50.01] BACKGROUND

The Occupational Safety and Health Act of 1970 (hereinafter referred to as OSHA or the Act) was made effective April 28, 1971.[1] The Act requires every employer engaged in interstate commerce to furnish employees "a place of employment . . . free from recognized hazards that are causing, or are likely to cause, death or serious harm to employees".[2]

OSHA generally applies to every employer engaged in business affecting commerce who has at least one employee in his or her employment.[3] However, OSHA's regulations exempt certain employers who have no more than ten employees from some of the requirements and penalties.[4]

The coverage of OSHA extends to employment performed in Puerto Rico, American Samoa, the Virgin Islands, Guam, the Trust Territory of the Pacific Islands, Wake Island, Outer Continental Shelf Lands, Johnson Island, the Coral Zone, and the District of Columbia.[5]

[50.02] RELATIONSHIP WITH OTHER LAWS

The safety and health standards promulgated under the Walsh-Healey Act,[6] the Service Contract Act,[7] the Construction Safety Act of 1969,[8] the Longshoremen's and Harbor Worker's Compensation Act,[9] and the National Foundation on Arts and Humanities Act of 1965[10] are superseded by OSHA standards.[11]

However, nothing in the Occupational Safety and Health Act supersedes or, in any other manner, affects the various worker's compensation laws, or other statutory or common law rights, duties, or liabilities of employers or employees regarding injuries, diseases, disabilities, or deaths of employees arising out of, or in the scope of, employment.[12]

[50.03] EXEMPTIONS UNDER OSHA

Standards and regulations of federal agencies that were adopted pursuant to statutory authority to regulate occupational safety and health preempt OSHA requirements.[13] However, where a federal agency, although empowered to regulate an aspect of public safety and health, fails to provide the protection intended by the statute, the requirements of the OSHA are not preempted.[14]

The Occupational Safety and Health Act's regulations exempt residential owners who employ persons for such ordinary domestic household tasks as cooking, housecleaning, and caring for children from its safety and health standards.[15]

State and local governments are not covered by the Occupational Safety and Health Act inasmuch as they are not considered to be employers under the statutory definitions.[16] Neither is the United States government an employer within the coverage of the Act.[17] The Occupational Safety and Health Act's requirements may not apply to business enterprises operated on Indian reservations if such application would violate Indian treaty rights.[18]

[50.04]   OSHA ADMINISTRATION

The Occupational Safety and Health Act is administered by the Occupational Safety and Health Administration of the United States Department of Labor.[19]

The Occupational Safety and Health Administration has the power to investigate, inspect, and issue citations as well as propose penalties for violations of the Act.[20]

The Act also established the Occupational Safety and Health Review Commission.[21] The commission, which is composed of three members appointed by the President, is empowered to issue orders, uphold, vacate, or modify OSHA citations and direct other relief and penalties as deemed appropriate.[22]

Notwithstanding the administration and enforcement of the Occupational Safety and Health Act through the U.S. Department of Labor and the Occupational Safety and Health Administration, the Act permits states to adopt and submit their own occupational safety and health standards, which, whenever approved by the U.S. Department of Labor, replace enforcement of federal standards in that state with respect to those matters covered by the state plan.[23]

[50.05]   OSHA RECORDKEEPING REQUIREMENTS

The Occupational Safety and Health Act directs the Secretary of Labor, in cooperation with the Secretary of Health and Human Services, to issue regulations which require employers to *maintain*

- accurate records of, and to make periodic reports on, work related deaths, injuries, and illnesses other than minor injuries
- accurate records of employee exposures to potentially toxic materials or harmful physical agents[24]

The Act also requires the Secretary of Labor to develop and maintain an effective program of collection, compilation, and analysis of statistics relating to occupational safety and health.[25]

The Occupational Safety and Health Act requires employers to compile and post an annual summary of occupational injuries and illnesses for each establishment.[26] The Act also requires each employer to maintain a log of occupational injuries and illnesses for his or her establishment.[27] The employer must enter each recordable injury and illness on the log as early as practicable, but no later than six working days after receiving information on the injury or illness.[28]

Each covered employer is required by the provisions of the Act to have available for inspection a supplementary record for each occupational injury or illness occurring at the establishment.[29] The supplementary record must be completed within six working days after receiving information that a recordable injury or illness has occurred.[30]

An employer must report the occurrence of an occupational accident which is fatal to one or more employees or which results in the hospitalization of five or more employees within forty-eight hours following such accident.[31] This report must be submitted either orally or in writing to the nearest area office of the Occupational Safety and Health Administration.[32]

The occupational injuries and illnesses log, the supplementary record, and an annual summary must be made available to any representative of the Secretary of Labor, or to a representative of the Secretary of Health and Human Services, for the purposes of inspection or copying upon proper request.[33]

A failure to maintain OSHA records or file OSHA reports in keeping with the requirements of the regulations may result in the issuance of a citation and the assessment of civil penalties.[34] An employer who knowingly falsifies a statement, representation, or certification in any document or report required to be maintained by OSHA regulations is subject to a fine of not more than $10,000, or imprisonment for not more than six months, or both, upon conviction.[35]

[50.06] NOTICE-POSTING REQUIREMENTS

An employer subject to the OSHA regulations is required to post, in conspicuous places, notices furnished to it by the Occupational Safety and Health Administration which inform employees of the Act and where employees may obtain assistance and additional information about the provisions of the Act.[36]

An employer who receives a citation resulting from a violation of the Act or its standards must immediately post such citation, or an unedited copy of it, at or near the place where the alleged violation occurred.[37]

An employer who violates any of the OSHA posting requirements may be assessed a civial penalty up to $1,000 for each violation.[38]

NOTES TO CHAPTER 50

1. 29 U.S.C.A. §651, *et seq.*
2. 29 U.S.C.A. §654(a)(1).

3. 29 CFR §1975.3(d).

4. See, for example: P.L. 95-480, 92 Stat. 1567; P.L. 96-86, 93 Stat. 656; P.L. 96-123, 93 Stat. 923, OSHA Instruction CPL 2.33 (April 6, 1979). See also 29 CFR §1904.15(b); P.L. 96-86, 93 Stat. 659; P.L. 96-123, 93 Stat. 925.

5. 29 U.S.C.A. §653(a).

6. 41 U.S.C.A. §35, *et seq.*

7. 41 U.S.C.A. §351, *et seq.*

8. 40 U.S.C.A. §333.

9. 33 U.S.C.A. §941.

10. 20 U.S.C.A. §951, *et seq.*

11. 29 U.S.C.A. §653(b)(2).

12. 29 U.S.C.A. §653(b)(4).

13. 29 U.S.C.A. §653(b)(1).

14. *Fineberg Packing Co.*, OSHRC Docket No. 61, CCH OSHD, para. 17518 (1973-1974).

15. 29 CFR §1975.6.

16. 29 U.S.C.A. §652(5).

17. 29 U.S.C.A. §652(5).

18. See *Navajo Forest Products Industries*, OSHRC Docket No. 76-5013, CCH OSHD, para. 24822.

19. 29 U.S.C.A. §656(a).

20. 29 U.S.C.A. §658(a) and 659(a); See also: 29 CFR §1903.

21. 29 U.S.C.A. §661.

22. 29 U.S.C.A. §659(c).

23. 29 U.S.C.A. §667; 29 CFR §1902.

24. 29 U.S.C.A. §657(c)(2) and (3).

25. 29 U.S.C.A. §673(a).

26. 29 CFR §1904.5(a).

27. 29 CFR §1904.12(c).

28. 29 CFR §1904.2(a).

29. 29 CFR §1904.4.

30. 29 CFR §1904.4.

31. See 29 CFR §1904.8.

32. 29 CFR §1904.8.

33. 29 CFR §1904.7(a).

34. 29 CFR §1904.9.

35. 29 U.S.C.A. §666(g).

36. 29 CFR §1903.2(a)(1).

37. 29 CFR §1903.16(a).

38. 29 U.S.C.A. §666(i).

51
OSHA Standards

[51.01] ESTABLISHMENT OF OSHA STANDARDS

The Occupational Safety and Health Act requires an employer to comply with specific occupational safety and health standards and all rules, regulations, and orders issued pursuant to the Act which apply to the work place.[1] The Act provides that the establishment of OSHA standards are to be based upon research, demonstrations, experiments, and other such information as may be appropriate.[2]

One court has held that the Secretary of Labor must consider the economic consequences upon an affected employer in promulgating OSHA standards.[3] Indeed, a presidential executive order requires the Secretary of Labor to prepare an analysis for significant OSHA regulations that may have major economic consequences for the general economy, individual industries, or geographic regions.[4]

[51.02] NATIONAL CONSENSUS STANDARDS

The Secretary of Labor was empowered by OSHA to promulgate national consensus standards for a two-year period following the effective date of the Act.[5] The Act defines a national consensus standard as any occupational safety and health standard or modification that

- has been adopted or promulgated by a nationally recognized standards-producing organization under procedures and within certain guidelines acceptable to the Secretary of Labor
- was formulated under conditions that allowed an opportunity to consider diverse views
- has been designated as a national consensus standard by the Secretary of Labor, after consultation with other appropriate federal agencies[6]

The Secretary of Labor also had the duty to adopt established federal standards in its promulgation of national consensus standards.[7] Established federal standards are defined as those operative occupational safety and health standards established by agencies of the United States government, or contained in any Act of Congress, in effect and in force on December 29, 1970.[8]

Whenever the Secretary of Labor proposes that a standard should be promulgated, modified, or revoked, he or she must publish the proposal in the Federal Register and must afford interested parties a period of thirty days after publication to submit written data or comments.[9]

Should objections be filed to the Secretary of Labor's proposed rule, and a hearing be requested, the Secretary is required to publish such information in the Federal Register as well as specify a time and place for a proper hearing.[10] Within sixty days after the expiration of the period provided by the Act for the submission of written data or comments, or within sixty days after the completion of any hearing, the Secretary of Labor is required to issue a rule promulgating, modifying, or revoking the OSHA standard in question.[11]

[51.03]   CHALLENGES TO OSHA STANDARDS

An employer may challenge the validity of an OSHA standard by filing a petition in a U.S. Court of Appeals within sixty days following its promulgation by the Secretary of Labor.[12] However, the standard, as established by the Secretary of Labor, will be upheld by the Appellate Court if the Secretary's determinations are supported by substantial evidence in the record considered as a whole.[13]

[51.04]   VARIANCES FROM OSHA STANDARDS

An employer may apply to the Secretary of Labor for a temporary variance from an OSHA standard provided it

- notifies employees of the application so they may be given a chance to participate in any hearing on the proposed variance
- demonstrates that it will provide employees with employment that is as safe and healthful as would prevail if he or she were to comply immediately with the standard[14]

Applications for temporary variances are to be filed with the Assistant Secretary for Occupational Safety and Health, U.S. Department of Labor, Washington, D.C. 20210.[15]

The Occupational Safety and Health Act also authorizes permanent variances under which an employer is fully exempted from OSHA standards provided the following conditions are met:[16]

- The employer must demonstrate by a preponderance of the evidence, how the conditions, practices, means, methods, operations, or processes used or proposed to be used by it would provide employment as safe and healthful as would be provided by complying with the standards.
- The employer must certify that the affected employees have been duly notified of the application for a permanent variance and informed of their right to petition and/or participate in a hearing on the proposed variance.
- The employer's application must meet the other technical requirements prescribed by the statute and its regulations.[17]

Applications for permanent variances are also to be filed with the Assistant Secretary for Occupational Safety and Health in Washington, D.C.[18]

[51.05] OSHA'S GENERAL DUTY STANDARD

The Occupational Safety and Health Act imposes upon employers the general duty to furnish to each of their employees, employment and places of employment which are free from recognized hazards that are causing or are likely to cause death or serious physical harm to their employees.[19]

Congress inserted the general duty clause into the OSHA legislation on the premise that precise standards to cover every conceivable situation would not always exist.[20] The general duty clause was designed to apply to only "recognized" hazards; the general duty clauses should not be applied whenever a duly promulgated occupational safety and health standard, a specific duty standard, is applicable to a condition or practice alleged to be a violation of the Act.[21]

[51.06] CODIFICATION OF OSHA STANDARDS

The Occupational Safety and Health Act standards are codified in the Code of Federal Regulations, along with all amendments, corrections, insertions, or deletions.

For example, the general industry standards are codified in 29 CFR Part 1910. The safety and health standards for construction are codified in 29 CFR Part 1926. In addition, safety and health standards for other industry are codified as follows:

- Ship Building Standards are codified in 29 CFR Part 1916.
- Ship Repairing Standards are codified in 29 CFR Part 1915.
- Ship Breaking Standards are codified in 29 CFR Part 1917.
- Longshoring Standards are codified in 29 CFR Part 1918.
- Agricultural Operations Standards are codified in 29 CFR Part 1928.
- Federal Service Contracts Standards are codified in 29 CFR Part 1925.
- Federal Supply Contracts Standards are codified in 41 CFR Part 50-204.

[51.07] DEFERRAL OF OSHA STANDARDS
TO STATE AGENCIES

The Occupational Safety and Health Act does not prohibit a state agency from enforcing its own occupational safety and health standards as long as such state statutes do not conflict with a federal OSHA standard.[22] On the contrary, the Occupational Safety and Health Act encourages states to assume the fullest responsibility in the administration and enforcement of their own state laws pertaining to the protection of employees from occupational diseases and injuries.[23]

The Occupational Safety and Health Act provides that states, desiring to assume responsibility for the establishment and enforcement of state developed occupational safety and health standards, may submit such plans to the U.S. Secretary of Labor for approval.[24]

Whenever such state standards are approved by the Secretary of Labor, the state plans then replace enforcement of federal OSHA standards with respect to those issues covered by the respective state plans.[25]

Once an initial approval is issued, a state is permitted to begin enforcement of its plan.[26] However, until the state plan receives a final approval, the Occupational Safety and Health Administration maintains concurrent enforcement authority.[27]

NOTES TO CHAPTER 51

1. 29 U.S.C.A. §654(a)(2) and (b).
2. 29 U.S.C.A. §655(b)(5).
3. *Industrial Union Dept. v. Hodgson*, 162 D.C. App. 331, 499 F.2d 467 (1974).
4. Executive Order No. 12044, §3.
5. 29 U.S.C.A. §655(a).
6. 29 U.S.C.A. §652(9).
7. *Usery v. Kennecott Copper Corp.*, 577 F.2d 1113 (CA-10, 1977).
8. 29 U.S.C.A. §652(10).
9. 29 U.S.C.A. §655(b)(2).
10. 29 U.S.C.A. §655(b)(3).
11. 29 U.S.C.A. §655(b)(4).
12. 29 U.S.C.A. §655(f).
13. 29 U.S.C.A. §655(f).
14. 29 CFR §1905.10(b).
15. 29 CFR §1905.10(a).
16. 29 U.S.C.A. §655(d).
17. 29 U.S.C.A. §655(d); 29 CFR §1905.11(b).
18. 29 CFR §1905.11(b).
19. 29 U.S.C.A. §654(a)(1).
20. SR No. 91-1282 (91st. Cong., 2d Sess.).
21. See *OSHA Field Operations Manual,* Chapter VIII-A; 29 CFR $1910.5.

22. See 29 U.S.C.A. §667(a).
23. 29 U.S.C.A. §651(b)(11).
24. 29 U.S.C.A. §667(b).
25. 29 U.S.C.A. §667(b); 29 CFR §1902.2.
26. 29 U.S.C.A. §667(e); 29 CFR §1902(c)(1).
27. 29 CFR §1902(c)(1).

52

OSHA Enforcement

[52.01] INSPECTION POWERS

The Occupational Safety and Health Act and its regulations empower the Secretary of Labor to make inspections of employer premises to determine whether OSHA standards are being met, subject to satisfying the search and seizure safeguards of the Fourth Amendment to the U.S. Constitution.[1]

OSHA inspections and investigations are to be conducted during working time, or at other reasonable times, and within a reasonable manner.[2]

[52.02] OBJECTIONS TO INSPECTIONS

If an employer objects to an OSHA inspection at his or her place of employment, the Secretary of Labor is required to obtain a warrant or other judicial process sufficient to satisfy the Fourth Amendment rights of the employer prior to proceeding with an inspection and investigation.[3]

Should an employer refuse to permit an OSHA inspection, the regulations provide that the OSHA investigator must attempt to ascertain the reason for the refusal.[4] He or she is then required to terminate the inspection and immediately report the refusal and the reason for the refusal to the area director of the Occupational Safety and Health Administration.[5]

An OSHA inspection warrant will generally not be issued without a showing that there is probable cause to believe that OSHA violations are occurring on the employer's premises or a showing that reasonable legislative or administrative standards for conducting an inspection are satisfied with respect to a given establishment.[6]

[52.03] EMPLOYEE COMPLAINTS OF OSHA VIOLATIONS

The Occupational Safety and Health Act entitles any employee or representative of employees the right to notify the Secretary of Labor of violations they believe exist which threaten physical harm or imminent danger and to request an OSHA inspection of the work place.[7]

Employee complaints of OSHA violations and requests for inspections must be in writing, state the grounds upon which the complaints are based, and be signed by the complaining party.[8] The employer is to be furnished an unsigned copy of the employee complaint before the time of inspection.[9]

Whenever the OSHA area director determines that an inspection is not warranted, he or she must furnish written notification of his or her determination to the complaining party.[10] The area director's determination that an employee's complaint is not warranted is reviewable by the OSHA assistant regional director, upon proper appeal by the complaining party.[11]

[52.04] INSPECTION PROCEDURE

As a general policy, no advance notice of OSHA inspections will be given the affected employer.[12] Any person who gives advance notice of an OSHA inspection, unless authorized by the Secretary of Labor or his or her designees, is subject to a fine of up to $1,000 and/or imprisonment for up to six months.[13]

However, should the OSHA area director determine that the giving of advance notice of an inspection would enhance the efficacy and thoroughness of the inspecton, enable an employer to abate an apparent imminent danger as quickly as possible, help prepare for special arrangements, or assure the presence of employees and/or their representative needed to aid in the inspection, advance notice to the employer may be given.[14]

An OSHA agent is required to present his or her credentials to the employer, explain the nature, purpose, and scope of the inspection, and specify the records and documents desired to be reviewed, prior to commencing an OSHA inspection.[15]

The Occupational Safety and Health Act specifies that a representative of the employer and a representative authorized by the employees must be given an opportunity to accompany the compliance officer during the OSHA inspection of the employer's work site.[16] An employer is not required to pay employees their regular wages for the time spent in accompanying the OSHA investigator during the "walkaround."[17] The representative of the employer must be an employee of the employer, rather than a third party.

The Occupational Safety and Health Act provides compliance officers the right to consult with employees concerning occupational safety and health matters, and also provides that employees shall have the right to bring OSHA violations to the attention of the OSHA investigator during an OSHA inspection.[18]

During an OSHA inspection, OSHA investigators are required to wear and use appropriate protective clothing and equipment.[19] They must also comply with the employer's safety and health rules while at the work site.[20]

OSHA investigators are required to conduct their inspections in such a manner as to avoid disruption of the employer's business operations.[21] They are also required to treat the employer's "trade secrets" as confidential.[22] They must also take reasonable precautions to ensure that their photography, or the taking of samples necessary to their inspection, do not create or cause hazardous conditions.[23]

OSHA regulations provide that OSHA investigators should, at the conclusion of their inspections, confer with the employer and inform him or her of any apparent safety and health violations detected or disclosed during the inspection and give the employer an opportunity to respond and explain his or her position regarding the alleged violations.[24]

[52.05] CITATIONS AND PROPOSED PENALTIES

If, upon inspection or investigation of an employer's work place, the OSHA agent believes that the employer has violated the Act, he or she must issue, with reasonable promptness, a citation to the employer.[25] The written citation must describe the nature of the violation and prescribe a reasonable time for abatement thereof.[26]

An employer may file a petition for modification of the abatement date when he or she has made a good faith effort to comply with the requirements of the citation but has been unable to abate the violative conditions due to factors beyond his or her reasonable control.[27]

Employees of the cited employer, or a representative of such employees, may contest, within fifteen working days after issuance of a citation, the period of time fixed for abatement of the violation as being unreasonably long.[28]

Within a reasonable time after a citation is issued, the employer will be notified of the proposed penalty to be assessed against him or her as a result of the violation.[29] Following receipt of this notice, the employer has fifteen working days to contest either the citation or the proposed penalty.[30]

If the employer fails to contest the citation or the proposed penalty and the affected employees fail to contest the reasonableness of the abatement period, the citation and the proposed penalty then become the final order of the Occupational Safety and Health Review Commission regarding the case.[31]

If an inspection reveals that an employer has failed to correct an alleged OSHA violation in the time prescribed in a citation, the OSHA area director will give notice to the employer of an additional proposed penalty by reason of such failure.[32] Unless the employer contests the notice of an additional proposed penalty within fifteen working days, the additional penalty likewise becomes final and not reviewable.[33]

[52.06] PENALTY LIMITS

An employer who receives a citation for a serious violation of the Occupational Safety and Health Act *will* be assessed a civil penalty of up to $1,000 for each violation.[34] Serious violations are considered to be those that create a substantial probability of death or serious physical harm of which the employer knew or should have known were present.[35]

An employer who receives a citation for a nonserious violation of the Occupational Safety and Health Act *may* be assessed a civil penalty of up to $1,000 for each violation.[36]

Imposition of a penalty for a nonserious violation is discretionary; imposition of a penalty for a serious violation is mandatory.[37]

An employer who fails to correct an OSHA violation within the prescribed abatement period may be assessed a penalty of not more than $1,000 for each day during which such failure or violation continues.[38]

Willful or repeated violations of the Act may carry a civil penalty of up to $10,000 for each violation.[39] Willful violations of the Act that cause death carry criminal penalties of up to $10,000 in fines and/or six months imprisonment for a first conviction and of up to $20,000 in fines and/or one-year imprisonment for a second conviction.[40]

Anyone who forcibly resists, opposes, impedes, intimidates, interferes with, or assaults a representative of the Secretary of Labor assigned to conduct an OSHA inspection or investigation, or some related function, while such representative is engaged in carrying out his or her official duties, is subject to a fine of $5,000 and/or imprisonment for not more than three years.[41] In case of the use of a deadly weapon in such an encounter, a fine of up to $10,000 and/or imprisonment up to ten years may be imposed against the offender.[42]

NOTES TO CHAPTER 52

1. 29 U.S.C.A. §657(a).
2. 29 U.S.C.A. §657(a).
3. *Marshall v. Barlow's, Inc.*, 436 U.S. 307 (1978).
4. 29 CFR §1903.4(a).
5. 29 CFR §1903.4(a).
6. *Marshall v. Barlow's, Inc.*, supra.
7. 29 U.S.C.A. §657(f)(1).
8. 29 CFR §1903.11(a).
9. 29 CFR §1903.11(a).
10. 29 CFR §1903.12(a).
11. 29 CFR §1903.12(a). (Employee appeals are discussed more fully in Chapter 53.)
12. 29 CFR §1903.6.
13. 29 U.S.C.A. §666(f).
14. 29 CFR §1903.6.
15. 29 CFR §1903.7(a).
16. 29 U.S.C.A. §657(e).
17. *Chamber of Commerce v. OSHA*, 636 F.2d 464 (CA-D.C., 1980).
18. 29 U.S.C.A. §657(a)(2); 29 CFR §1903.10.
19. 29 CFR §1903.7(c).

20. 29 CFR §1903.7(c).

21. 29 CFR §1903.7(d).

22. 29 U.S.C.A. §664.

23. 29 CFR §1903.7(c).

24. 29 CFR §1903.7(e).

25. 29 U.S.C.A. §658(a).

26. 29 U.S.C.A. §658(a); 29 CFR §1903.14(b).

27. 29 CFR §1903.14a(a).

28. 29 U.S.C.A. §659(c); 29 CFR §1903.17(b).

29. 29 U.S.C.A. §659(a).

30. 29 U.S.C.A. §659(a).

31. 29 U.S.C.A. §659(a).

32. 29 U.S.C.A. §659(b); 29 CFR §1903.18(a).

33. 29 U.S.C.A. §659(b); 29 CFR §1903.18(b) and (c).

34. 29 U.S.C.A. §666(b).

35. 29 U.S.C.A. §666; see also *Usery v. Hermitage Concrete Pipe Co.*, 584 F.2d 127 (CA-6, 1978).

36. 19 U.S.C.A. §666(c).

37. *Cam Industries, Inc.* (1974) OSHRC Docket No. 258, 1973-1974 CCH OSHD, para 17373.

38. 29 U.S.C.A. §666(d).

39. 29 U.S.C.A. §666(a).

40. 29 U.S.C.A. §666(e).

41. 18 U.S.C.A. §111.

42. 18 U.S.C.A. §111.

53

OSHA Hearings and Reviews

[53.01] EMPLOYER'S RIGHT TO HEARING

Upon receipt of an employer's notice to contest an OSHA citation or proposed penalty, the OSHA area director must notify the Occupational Safety and Health Review Commission of the notice of contest so that a hearing can be properly arranged.[1]

Within twenty days after receipt of an employer's notice to contest a citation or proposed penalty, the Secretary of Labor must file a complaint with the Occupational Safety and Health Review Commission setting forth all alleged violations and proposed penalties which are contested, stating the time, location, place, and circumstances of the alleged violation and specifying the considerations upon which the period for abatement and the proposed penalties are founded.[2]

The employer against whom the complaint is issued must file an answer to the complaint containing a short and plain statement denying those allegations in the complaint that he or she desires to contest.[3] The employer's answer must be filed with the Occupational Safety and Health Review Commission within fifteen days after service of the complaint.[4]

Employees of a cited employer who are exposed to the alleged hazard described in the citation and other such affected employees, or representatives of affected employees, must be provided an opportunity to participate in an OSHA hearing, upon proper petitions to intervene as parties of interest.[5]

The Occupational Safety and Health Review Commission has the authority to issue subpoenas requiring the attendance and testimony of witnesses and the production of documents upon proper application of any party to an OSHA proceeding.[6]

OSHA hearings are conducted before administrative law judges assigned by the chairman of the Occupational Safety and Health Review Commission. The administrative law judge assigned to an OSHA hearing may direct the parties to participate in a prehearing conference for the purpose of exploring settlement or simplifying the issues contested.[7]

[53.02] EMPLOYEE'S RIGHT TO HEARING

Upon receipt of an employee's notice to contest the reasonableness of the period of time for abatement of a cited violation, the employee's notice, or that of his or her representative, must be immediately transmitted by the OSHA area director to the Occupational Safety and Health Review Commission.[8] The Review Commission, in turn, must provide the employee, or his or her representative, with an OSHA hearing.[9]

[53.03] OSHA HEARINGS

OSHA hearings are governed by the rules of evidence applicable to the United States District Courts.[10] The Secretary of Labor has the burden of proof in a contest of a citation or proposed penalty.[11] All parties are entitled to a reasonable period of time for oral argument at the close of an OSHA hearing, upon proper request.[12] All parties are entitled, upon proper requests made before the close of the hearing, to file briefs in support of their respective contentions, as well as proposed findings of fact and conclusions of law.[13]

The Administrative Law Judge appointed to conduct an OSHA hearing is empowered to hear evidence and prepare a decision upon the completion of the proceedings.[14] The decision must contain findings of fact and conclusions of law, and the reasons therefor, on all the material issues of fact and law presented on the record and specify the appropriate rule, order, sanction, relief or denial thereof.[15]

[53.04] EMPLOYER'S DEFENSES AT AN OSHA HEARING

Once the Secretary of Labor has established a prima facie case that the citation issued to the employer is supported by the evidence, the employer has the burden to rebut the Secretary's prima facie case and may present contrary evidence or establish affirmative defenses to justify noncompliance with the Act.[16]

Several defenses avail for an employer who has been cited for an OSHA violation, such as contending

- the citation lacks sufficient particularity[17]
- compliance with the standard in question would render performance of the work impossible[18]
- compliance with the standard in question would subject employees to a greater hazard than the failure to comply[19]
- the employer is exempt from the coverage of the Act[20]
- the employer has been granted a variance from the standard in question[21]
- the employer has previously been granted a petition for modification of an abatement and has complied with the modifications[22]

[53.05] SIMPLIFIED PROCEEDING

In limited cases, the Occupational Safety and Health Review Commission will provide the parties to an OSHA contest a simplified proceeding in lieu of an OSHA hearing.

Simplified proceedings are designed to save time and expense.[23] For example, there are no complaints, answers, or other formal pleadings in an OSHA simplified proceeding.[24] In addition, the Federal Rules of Evidence are inapplicable. Interlocutory appeals are impermissible and discovery is not permitted in a simplified proceeding.[25]

Notwithstanding the absence of pleadings and adherence to traditional procedural requirements, the simplified proceeding is conducted by an administrative law judge who renders a written decision, unless the matter is mutually settled by the parties prior thereto.[26]

[53.06] PETITIONS FOR REVIEW OF ALJ DECISIONS

A party to an OSHA hearing or simplified proceeding who is aggrieved by a decision of an OSHA administrative law judge must file a petition for a discretionary review before the Occupational Safety and Health Review Commission on or before the twentieth day after the judge mails a copy of his or her decision to the parties.[27]

Should an aggrieved party fail to so appeal, the judge's decision becomes the final order of the Review Commission, assuming no commission member, on his or her own motion, directs review of the decision on or before the thirtieth day following the docket of the judge's report.[28]

A review by the Occupational Safety and Health Commission is discretionary, not a matter of right.[29]

An original and three copies of an employer's petition for review must be filed with the Review Commission's Executive Secretary within the twenty-day period noted above.[30] Statements in opposition to petitions for review may also be filed by an opposing party.[31] Briefs in support of the parties' contentions may also be filed with the Review Commission.[32]

The Review Commission is empowered to issue an order affirming, modifying, or vacating the citation and/or proposed penalty issued against the employer who has petitioned for relief.[33]

Although the Review Commission has authority to direct ''other appropriate relief'' upon reviewing an administrative law judge's decision, it does not have authority to award attorney's fees or assess costs against a party.[34]

The Review Commission is not bound by the administrative law judge's finding of fact in proceedings for review.[35] The Commission must, however, substantiate its contentions should it reject an administrative law judge's disposition of a case.[36]

[53.07] COURT REVIEW OF OSHA DECISIONS

Parties aggrieved or adversely affected by a decision and order of the Occupational Safety and Health Review Commission may obtain a review of such decision and order in an appropriate United States Court of Appeals.[37]

The Secretary of Labor may likewise obtain enforcement of a final order of the Review Commission, as well as obtain a review of a Commission's decision and order, in an appropriate U.S. Appellate Court.[38]

Parties who seek judicial review of an adverse decision and order of the Occupational Safety and Health Review Commission, must file their petitions for review with the appropriate federal court within sixty days following issuance of the commission's final order.[39]

Should an aggrieved party fail to file his or her petition for review within the sixty-day time limit, the Secretary of Labor may petition for enforcement of the Review Commission's order in an appropriate federal appellate court.[40]

Where an employer files a petition for review with an appropriate court of appeals, the Review Commission's final order is not automatically stayed as a result.[41] Rather, the aggrieved employer must file a motion for a stay of the Commission's order with the court to gain relief pending the appellate proceedings.[42]

The United States Circuit Courts of Appeal must apply the substantial evidence standard in reviewing the Review Commission's findings of fact.[43] Thus, if the Review Commission's findings of fact are supported by substantial evidence on the record considered as a whole, the Commission's findings are conclusive on the court.[44]

NOTES TO CHAPTER 53

1. 29 U.S.C.A. §659(c); 29 CFR §1903.17(a).
2. 29 CFR §2200.33(a)(1) and (2).
3. 29 CFR §2200.33(b)(2).
4. 29 CFR §2200.33(b)(1).
5. 29 U.S.C.A. §659(c); 29 CFR §2200.20(a) and (b).
6. 29 CFR §2200.55(a).
7. 29 CFR §2200.51(a).
8. 29 CFR §1903.17(b).
9. 29 U.S.C.A. §659(c).
10. 29 CFR §2200.72.
11. 29 CFR §2200.73(a).
12. 29 CFR §2200.76.
13. 29 CFR §2200.76.
14. 29 CFR §2200.66 and §2200.90(a).
15. 29 CFR §2200.90(a).
16. See 29 CFR §2200.90.
17. 29 U.S.C.A. §658(a); 29 CFR §1903.14(b).

18. *Taylor Building Associates* (1977) OSHRC Docket No. 3735, 1977–1978 CCH OSHD, para. 21592.

19. *Lumb Woodworking Co.* (1977) OSHRC Docket No. 76-470, 1977–1978 CCH OSHD, para. 22048.

20. See Chapter 50 for a discussion of OSHA coverage and exemptions.

21. See Chapter 51 for a discussion of temporary and permanent variances from OSHA standards.

22. See 29 CFR §1903.14a(a) .

23. 29 CFR §§2200.200 and 2200.202.

24. 29 CFR §§2200.200 and 2200.204.

25. 29 CFR §2200.200.

26. 29 CFR §2200.208.

27. 29 CFR §2200.91(b)(2).

28. 29 CFR §2200.90(b)(3).

29. 29 CFR §2200.92(a).

30. 29 CFR §2200.91(f).

31. 29 CFR §2200.91(e).

32. 29 CFR §2200.93.

33. 29 U.S.C.A. §659(c).

34. See *McGowan v. Marshall,* 604 F.2d 885 (CA-5, 1979).

35. See *Accu-Namics, Inc. v. OSHRC,* 515 F.2d 828 (CA-5, 1975).

36. *Brennan v. Gilles and Cotting, Inc.,* 504 F.2d 1255 (CA-4, 1974).

37. 29 U.S.C.A. §660(a).

38. 29 U.S.C.A. §660(b).

39. 29 U.S.C.A. §660(a).

40. 29 U.S.C.A. §660(b).

41. See 29 U.S.C.A. §660(a); 29 CFR §2200.94.

42. 29 CFR §2200.94(a).

43. See *Brennan v. OSHRC,* 487 F.2d 438 (CA-8, 1973).

44. 29 U.S.C.A. §660(a).

54

Federal Mine
Safety and Health Act
and Miscellaneous
Safety and Health Laws

[54.01] MSHA BACKGROUND

The Federal Mine Safety and Health Act of 1977[1] amended the Federal Coal Mine Health and Safety Act of 1969[2] and repealed the Federal Metal and Nonmetallic Act of 1966.[3] The Federal Mine Safety and Health Act, commonly referred to as MSHA, consolidated the safety and health provisions of the 1969 laws protecting coal miners and the safety and health provisions of the 1966 laws applicable to noncoal-mining facilities.[4]

The Federal Mine Safety and Health Act of 1977 (hereinafter referred to as MSHA) transferred the administration and enforcement of its provisions from the U.S. Department of Interior to the U.S. Department of Labor.[5]

It is the declared purpose of MSHA to establish improved and mandatory health and safety standards to protect the health and safety of the nation's miners, to require operators to comply with such standards and to improve and expand programs aimed at the prevention of mine accidents and occupationally caused diseases in the industry.[6]

The Federal Mine Safety and Health Act extends coverage to all mines that affect commerce,[7] and includes all underground and surface areas from which minerals are extracted, whether in liquid or nonliquid form.[8] The Act further defines "mines" to include milling of such minerals and work involved in the preparation of such coal or other minerals.[9] In addition, Title IV of the statute authorizes certain benefits to miners disabled or killed by pneumoconiosis (black lung).

The Federal Mine Safety and Health Act established a Mine Safety and Health Administration within the U.S. Department of Labor to administer and enforce its provisions.[10]

The Mine Safety and Health Administration is empowered to promulgate procedural rules and regulations covering such matters as record keeping, inspection practices, complaint procedures, and so forth.[11] The Mine Safety and Health Administration is also charged with the responsibility of conducting work-place inspections, issuing citations, proposing penalties for violations, issuing withdrawal orders, acting upon variance applications, and seeking injunctions and/or judicial enforcement of its orders.[12]

In addition to primary administration and enforcement of the Act falling under the Department of Labor, the Act also charges the Department of the Interior with the responsibility of conducting Mine Safety research.[13]

[54.02] MINER'S RIGHTS AND DUTIES UNDER MSHA

Mine employees (miners) who fall within the protection of the Federal Mine Safety and Health Act are entitled to receive appropriate training in mine safety practices and procedures.[14] Such training is to be provided by the employer during normal working hours and miners are to be paid their usual rate of compensation during the training sessions.[15] Mine operators are required to certify, on certificates supplied by the Secretary of Labor, that their employees have completed the required training in health and safety matters.[16]

Mine operators are required to post copies of the Mine Safety and Health Standards on their bulletin boards.[17] Copies of orders, citations, notices, and decisions directed at the respective mine operators must also be posted on the employer's bulletin board. Such postings must be clearly visible and protected from the weather and involuntary removal.[18]

A mine employee or his or her authorized representative may file a written notice with the Mine Safety and Health Administration requesting an immediate inspection, should such employee reasonably believe that a violation of a health or safety standard exists at the mine.[19]

Mine employees may also file written complaints of alleged safety and health violations directly with MSHA inspectors before or during a local government inspection.[20] Mine employees, or their representatives, may contest the issuance, modification, or termination of any order issued by the Mine Safety and Health Administration.[21] Mine employees, or their representatives, must be given an opportunity to accompany MSHA inspectors during an official inspection of a mine.[22]

Under certain conditions, mine employees may be entitled to compensation lost due to a government order withdrawing mine employees from a mine site.[23]

Mine employees are entitled to observe and examine records utilized by a mine operator in monitoring a miner's exposure to toxic materials or harmful physical agents as required by the mine safety and health standards.[24]

No mine operator or other person may discriminate against a miner, representative of miners, or applicants for employment who exercise their rights under the Federal Mine Safety and Health Act.[25] A mine employee who believes that he or she has been discriminated against in the exercise of his or her rights under the statute may file a complaint with the Department of Labor (MSHA) within sixty days of the alleged wrongdoing. Persons discriminating against a miner in violation of MSHA may be cited and fined up to $10,000.[26]

[54.03] MSHA INSPECTIONS AND INVESTIGATIONS

The Federal Mine Safety and Health Act provides that all underground mines must be inspected by the Department of Labor in their entirety at least four times a year to assure compliance with the mine safety and health standards.[27]

Surface mines must be inspected at least twice a year to assure compliance with the Act.[28]

Such inspections are conducted by agents of the Secretary of Labor.[29] The Secretary of Health, Education, and Welfare (now Health and Human Services) is also authorized to inspect mines, primarily in relation to miner health research reponsibilities.[30]

Records resulting from investigations of mine accidents must be maintained by mine operators and made available to the Secretary of Labor and other interested parties.[31]

[54.04] MSHA ENFORCEMENT

The Federal Mine Safety and Health Act is enforced initially through the issuance of a citation from the government inspector upon finding a violation of an MSHA safety and health standard, rule, order, or regulation.[32]

If the violation described in the citation is not remedied within the time period prescribed by the inspector, the Secretary of Labor may issue an order requiring the operator to remove certain persons from the mine area.[33]

Subsequent to the issuance of a citation, a notice of the proposed penalty for the cited violation will be mailed to the mine operator.[34]

Should the mine operator desire to contest the penalty or citation, he or she must notify the Secretary of Labor of the fact within thirty days of the receipt of the proposed penalty.[35] Failure to contest the citation or penalty within the thirty-day time period forecloses any further right of appeal.[36]

If an operator contests the citation and/or the amount of penalty proposed, the notice of contest is then referred to the Federal Mine Safety and Health Review Commission which, in turn, is required to schedule a hearing before an administrative law judge to conduct a proceeding on the merits of the case.[37] The administrative law judge's decision becomes the final disposition of the case and the final order of the Commission forty days after its issuance, unless directed for review.[38]

[54.05] JUDICIAL REVIEW OF MSHA DECISION

The Federal Mine Safety and Health Act provides that any person adversely affected by a decision of the Review Commission, including the Secretary of Labor, may obtain a review of the Commission's order by filing an appeal with any U.S. Court of Appeals for the circuit in which the violation is alleged to have occurred.[39] The petitioner seeking relief in the appellate court must file his or her appeal within thirty days of the issuance of the Review Commission's order.[40]

[54.06] MISCELLANEOUS SAFETY AND HEALTH LAWS

Aside from the Federal Occupational Safety and Health Act of 1970, and the Federal Mine Safety and Health Act of 1977, other federal statutes also provide certain protection to employees from unsafe and hazardous conditions within the work place.

Such statutes include: *The National Environmental Policy Act; The Federal Clean Air Act; The Federal Water Pollution Control Act; the Resource Conservation and Recovery Act; The Migrant and Seasonal Agricultural Worker Protection Act;* and *The Migrant Health Act.*

[54.07] NATIONAL ENVIRONMENTAL POLICY ACT

The National Environmental Policy Act [41] and related federal anti-pollution laws provide health safeguards not only to the general public but also to American workers.

The most essential function of the National Environmental Policy Act (hereinafter referred to as NEPA) is its requirement that federal agencies must consider ecological factors when dealing with activities that may have an impact on the environment. [42]

In keeping with the dictates of NEPA in 1970, the Environmental Protection Agency was created as an independent agency of the executive branch in an effort to coordinate major environmental pollution responsibilities of the federal government. [43]

Although NEPA does not create a private right of action for individuals, [44] plaintiffs with sufficient standing may bring an action to enforce a federal agency's obligation to comply with the Act. [45]

[54.08] FEDERAL CLEAN AIR ACT

The purpose of the Federal Clean Air Act is to protect and enhance the quality of the nation's air resources, to initiate and accelerate a national research and developmental program to achieve the prevention and control of air pollution, to provide technical and financial assistance to state governments in their efforts to prevent and control air pollution, and to encourage and assist the development and operation of regional air pollution control programs. [46] The Environmental Protection Agency is responsible for the administration of the Clean Air Act. [47]

Penalties may be assessed against those persons or entities who do not comply with the requirements of the Clean Air Act. [48] In addition, any individual may commence a civil action against any person or entity who is alleged to be in violation of an emission standard or limitation. [49]

Employees may also commence a proceeding for the enforcement of any requirement imposed under the Clean Air Act.[50] Employers are prohibited from discharging or taking other adverse actions against an employee because of his or her commencement of such a proceeding.[51]

[54.09] THE FEDERAL WATER POLLUTION CONTROL ACT

The Federal Water Pollution Control Act was enacted to restore and maintain the chemical, physical, and biological integrity of the nation's waters.[52]

The Act prohibits the discharge of any radiological, chemical, or biological warfare agent of high-level radioactive waste into navigable waters.[53]

It is unlawful for a person to discharge a pollutant into waterways without obtaining a National Pollutant Discharge Elimination System (NPDES) permit, and once obtained, full compliance of its terms must be met.[54]

Any interested person who has been denied a NPDES permit or otherwise adversely affected by a decision relating to its issuance or nonissuance may submit a request to the regional administrator of the Environmental Protection Agency, the federal agency responsible for administering the Act, for an evidentiary hearing to reconsider or contest the decision in question.[55] The initial decision of the presiding officer of such a hearing becomes final and binding after thirty days unless a party files a petition for review by the administrator, or the administrator files a notice that he or she will so review the decision of the presiding officer.[56]

The U.S. District Courts have jurisdiction of civil actions brought by citizen suits, or by the Environmental Protection Agency Administrator, to compel enforcement of the Act.[57]

[54.10] HAZARDOUS WASTE CONTROL LAWS (RCRA)

The Resource Conservation and Recovery Act of 1976 established a federal regulatory program to manage and control hazardous waste.[58]

The Act requires persons who generate, transport, treat, store, or dispose of materials or matters classified by the Environmental Protection Agency as hazardous wastes to comply with the hazardous waste permit requirements, the standards applicable to hazardous waste treatment, storage and disposal facilities, the standards applicable to generators and transporters of hazardous waste and the notification requirements of the Act.[59]

An employee is protected from adverse actions in employment by reason of his or her filing a proceeding against an employer related to the requirements of the Act.[60] Citizen civil actions against persons who violate the requirements of the Resource Conservation and Recovery Act are also permitted in U.S. District Courts under the provision of the Act.[61]

[54.11] MIGRANT AND SEASONAL AGRICULTURAL WORKER PROTECTION ACT OF 1983

This particular statute was enacted to remove restraints on commerce caused by activities detrimental to migrant and seasonal agricultural workers, to require farm labor contractors to procure certificates of registration, and to assure necessary protections for migrant and seasonal agricultural workers, agricultural associations, and agricultural employers.[62]

The Act specifically provides that no person shall engage in any farm labor contracting activity unless first applying for and receiving a certificate of registration from the U.S. Secretary of Labor.[63]

The statute prohibits a farm labor contractor from recruiting, hiring, employing, or using the services of any individual who is known by him or her to be an alien not lawfully admitted for permanent residence or who has not been authorized by the U.S. Attorney General's office to accept employment.[64]

Farm labor contractors, agricultural employers, and agricultural associations that recruit migratory agricultural workers must disclose certain information pertaining to the terms and conditions of their employment to such workers[65] and keep certain records of such disclosures.[66] Farm labor contractors, agricultural employers, and agricultural employees must also comply with specified safety standards whenever using motor vehicles to transport migrant or seasonal farm workers.[67]

[54.12] MIGRANT HEALTH ACT

The Migrant Health Act[68] was enacted to expand service to improve health care and health conditions for domestic agricultural migratory workers and their families.[69]

The Act makes provision for federal grants to public and other non-profit agencies to contribute to the cost of establishing and operating family health-service clinics, and other special projects to improve health services and conditions of domestic agricultural migratory workers.[70]

NOTES TO CHAPTER 54

1. 30 U.S.C.A. §801 *et seq.,* as amended.
2. P.L. 91-173.
3. P.L. 89-577.
4. *Federal Mine Safety & Health Act of 1977, Law & Explanation,* para. 101 (CCH, 1977).
5. Ibid., para. 102.
6. 30 U.S.C.A. §801.

7. 30 U.S.C.A. §803.

8. 30 U.S.C.A. §802.

9. 30 U.S.C.A. §802.

10. 30 U.S.C.A. §802.

11. See Note 4, para. 106, *supra*.

12. See Note 4, para. 106, *supra*.

13. 30 U.S.C.A. §812.

14. Section 115, *Federal Mine Safety & Health Act of 1977.*

15. Section 115(b), *Federal Mine Safety & Health Act of 1977.*

16. Section 115(c), *Federal Mine Safety & Health Act of 1977.*

17. Section 109, *Federal Mine Safety & Health Act of 1977.*

18. Section 109(a), *Federal Mine Safety & Health Act of 1977.*

19. Section 103(g), *Federal Mine Safety & Health Act of 1977.*

20. See Section 103(g)(2), *Federal Mine Safety & Health Act of 1977.*

21. See generally, Section 105, *Federal Mine Safety & Health Act of 1977.*

22. Section 103(f), *Federal Mine Safety & Health Act of 1977.*

23. Sections 104(g)(2) and 111, *Federal Mine Safety & Health Act of 1977.*

24. Section 101(a)(7), *Federal Mine Safety & Health Act of 1977.*

25. Section 105(c)(1), *Federal Mine Safety & Health Act of 1977.*

26. See Sections 105(c)(3) and 110(a), *Federal Mine Safety & Health Act of 1977.*

27. Section 103(a), *Federal Mine Safety & Health Act of 1977.*

28. Section 103(a), *Federal Mine Safety & Health Act of 1977.*

29. Section 103(a), *Federal Mine Safety & Health Act of 1977.*

30. Section 103(a), *Federal Mine Safety & Health Act of 1977.*

31. Section 103(d), *Federal Mine Safety & Health Act of 1977.*

32. Section 104(a), *Federal Mine Safety & Health Act of 1977.*

33. Section 104(b), *Federal Mine Safety & Health Act of 1977.*

34. Section 105(a), *Federal Mine Safety & Health Act of 1977.*

35. Section 105(a), *Federal Mine Safety & Health Act of 1977.*

36. Section 105(a), *Federal Mine Safety & Health Act of 1977.*

37. Section 105(d), *Federal Mine Safety & Health Act of 1977;* see also: Section 113, *Federal Mine Safety & Health Act of 1977.*

38. Section 113, *Federal Mine Safety & Health Act of 1977.*

39. Section 106(a), *Federal Mine Safety & Health Act of 1977.*

40. Section 106(a), *Federal Mine Safety & Health Act of 1977.*

41. 42 U.S.C.A. §4321, *et seq.*

42. J. Gordon Arbuckle, *Environmental Law Handbook,* Eighth Edition (Rockville, Md.: Government Institute, 1985), p.66.

43. 5 U.S.C.A. §903 and Reorganization Plan No. 3 (1970).

44. *Pye v. Department of Transportation,* 513 F.2d 290 (CA-5, 1977).

45. *United States v. Students Challenging Regulatory Agency Procedure (SCRAP),* 412 U.S. 669 (1979).

46. 42 U.S.C.A. §7401.

47. 42 U.S.C.A. §7402

48. 42 U.S.C.A. §7420.

49. 42 U.S.C.A. §7604(a)(1).

50. 42 U.S.C.A. §7622(a).

51. 42 U.S.C.A. §7622(a).

52. 33 U.S.C.A. §1251(a).

53. 33 U.S.C.A. §1311(f).

54. 33 U.S.C.A. §1342.

55. 40 CFR §124.76, *et seq.*

56. 40 CFR §124.89.

57. 33 U.S.C.A. §§1319(b) and 1365(a).

58. 42 U.S.C.A. §§6921-6931.

59. 42 U.S.C.A. §§6921, 6922, 6923, and 6924.

60. 42 U.S.C.A. §6971(a).

61. 42 U.S.C.A. §6972.

62. P.L. 97-470, signed on January 14, 1983.

63. P.L. 97-470, Section 101(a).

64. P.L. 97-470, Section 101(b).

65. P.L. 97-470, Section 201(a).

66. P.L. 97-470, Section 301(a).

67. P.L. 97-470, Section 401(a).

68. 42 U.S.C.A. §254b.

69. 42 U.S.C.A. §254b.

70. 42 U.S.C.A. §254b.

PART V

FEDERAL RETIREMENT, WELFARE, AND PRIVACY LAWS

55

Introduction to the Employee Retirement Income Security Act

[55.01] BACKGROUND

The Employee Retirement Income Security Act[1] (hereinafter referred to as ERISA) was enacted in 1974 by Congress. In 1980, ERISA was amended by the Multi-Employer Pension Plan Amendments Act[2] (hereinafter referred to as MPPAA). The original statute was further amended by the Retirement Equity Act of 1984.

The primary purpose of ERISA is to protect the interests of participants in employee benefit plans and their beneficiaries through

- disclosure and reporting requirements
- establishment of certain fiduciary standards of conduct, responsibility, and obligation
- authorization of appropriate penalties, sanctions, and ready access to the federal courts against employers, trustees, and other covered entities who fail to comply with the requirements of the ERISA provisions[3]

ERISA was also enacted to protect interstate commerce and the taxing powers of the federal government[4] as well as to encourage the growth and development of voluntary, private employer-financed benefit plans.[5]

[55.02] SUMMARY OF KEY ERISA PROVISIONS

The Employee Retirement Income Security Act is divided into four titles:

- *Title I* is administered by the U.S. Department of Labor and deals primarily with the protection of employee rights.[6]
- *Title II* is administered by the Internal Revenue Service and is composed of amendments to the Interal Revenue Code.[7]
- *Title III* specifies the division of responsibility among the Department of Labor, the Internal Revenue Service, and the Pension Benefit Guaranty Corporation relating to the jurisdiction, administration and enforcement of ERISA.[8]
- *Title IV* establishes a system for employee plan termination insurance, including special provisions for multi-employer plans, and also creates the Pension Benefit Guaranty Corporation.[9]

[55.03] TYPES OF ERISA BENEFIT PLANS

The Employee Retirement Income Security Act applies to two types of employee benefit plans:

- *PENSION PLANS*—Programs that provide retirement or deferral income to employees.[10] (Pension plans are divided into two main categories: *defined benefit plans,* in which retirement benefits are determined in advance but the amount of money contributed to the fund varies, and *defined contribution plans,* in which the contributions to the fund are fixed but the retirement benefits are unknown until retirement.)

- *WELFARE PLANS*[11]—Programs that provide benefits in the event of sickness, accident, hospitalization, death, disability, unemployment or vacation benefits, apprenticeship and other training programs, scholarship funds, prepaid legal services, day-care centers, or any related benefits described in the Labor Management Relations Act.[12]

[55.04] ERISA COVERAGE AND EXEMPTIONS

Except for those plans specifically exempted by the statute, the labor provisions of ERISA cover employee benefit plans established or maintained by any employer engaged in commerce or by any employee organization representing employees so engaged, or by both.[13]

The labor provisions of ERISA exempt the following employee benefit plans from its coverage:

- *Governmental plans*[14] (including Railroad Retirement Act plans and plans of certain international associations)[15]

- *Tax-exempt church plans*[16]

- *Plans maintained solely to comply with workers' compensation laws, unemployment compensation laws or disability insurance laws*[17]

- *Plans maintained outside the U.S. primarily for nonresident aliens*[18]

- *Excess benefit plans*[19] (programs that provide benefits or contributions in excess of those allowable for tax qualified plans)

[55.05] PENSION BENEFIT GUARANTY CORPORATION

As a means to partially ensure the vested pension benefits of employees and retirees under a defined benefit, single employer plan, ERISA established the Pension Benefit Guaranty Corporation (PBGC).[20] Within certain limits, the Pension Benefit Guaranty Corporation guarantees the payment of non-forfeitable benefits to participants should such a plan terminate without enough money to pay vested pension benefits.[21]

ERISA imposes upon each plan covered by its termination insurance provisions, a requirement that the plan pay certain insurance premiums into the PBGC.[22]

Upon termination, an employer may be liable to the Pension Benefit Guaranty Corporation for guaranteed basic benefits paid by the PBGC.[23]

ERISA provides that where an employer who maintains a single employer plan fails to pay contingent insurance premiums for each of the five-plan years immediately prior to the year the plan is terminated, such employer will be liable to the PBGC for any guaranteed basic benefits paid by the PBGC, up to certain specified limits. ERISA specifies that the employer's liability in such an event is the excess of the current value of the plan's benefits guaranteed by the PBGC on the date of termination above the current value of the plan's assets. The assets are allocable to those benefits on the date of termination of the plan but are not to exceed 30 percent of the employer's net worth, as determined by a given day within 120 days before termination by the PBGC.[24]

Whenever multi-employer pension plans are terminated, any employer maintaining the plan at its termination, or any employer making contributions under the plan at any time within the five years before its termination, will be liable to the PBGC for any guaranteed benefits by the PBGC on a basis similar to the liability of an employer who maintains a single employee plan, as discussed above.[25]

[55.06] MERGERS, CONSOLIDATION, AND TRANSFERS

ERISA requires that each "tax qualified" defined employee benefit plan must provide protection to its participants in the event of any merger or consolidation with, or transfer of assets or liabilities to, any other benefit plan.[26] The Act also provides that each such participant is entitled to benefits at least equal to those having accrued prior to a merger.[27]

[55.07] PROTECTION AGAINST ASSIGNMENTS

As a general rule, ERISA prohibits the assignment or alienation of benefits under a covered employee pension plan.[28] However, vested benefits may be used as collateral for reasonable loans from pension plans, assuming no fiduciary provisions of the law are violated.[29]

Participants may also make voluntary revocable assignments of up to 10 percent of their vested benefits as long as their benefits are in pay status and none of the assigned benefits are used to defray administrative costs of the plan.[30]

[55.08] SPOUSAL PROTECTION UNDER ERISA

ERISA requires that pension plans which provide that a participant may take retirement benefits in the form of an annuity must correspondingly provide for a joint and survivor annuity.[31] A qualified joint and survivor annuity is an annuity for the life of the participating employee with a survivor annuity for the life of the spouse.[32] The written consent of a spouse must be obtained before an employee may waive survivor benefits.[33] ERISA amendments also require that a spouse of an employee with vested rights in a pension plan be provided a pension in the event the employee dies before reaching retirement.[34] In the event of a divorce from a participant in a pension plan, the law empowers courts to award the spouse a share of the participant pension as a part of the settlement, without violating the nonassignability provisions of ERISA.[35]

[55.09] PROTECTION FROM HARASSMENT

ERISA provides that no plan participant or beneficiary shall be discharged, fined, suspended, expelled, disciplined, or discriminated against for exercising his or her rights under an employee welfare or benefit plan covered by its provisions.[36]

ERISA also makes it unlawful to retaliate or discriminate against any person because he or she has given information or testimony in any inquiry or proceeding relating to ERISA.[37]

Any person using or threatening force, fraud, or violence to restrain, coerce, or interfere with rights or prospective rights of plan participants or beneficiaries is punishable by a fine up to $10,000 and/or up to one year in prison.[38]

NOTES TO CHAPTER 55

1. 29 U.S.C.A. §1001, *et seq.*
2. Public Law 96-364, Sept. 26, 1980, 94 Stat. 1207.
3. 29 U.S.C.A. §1001(b).
4. 29 U.S.C.A. §1001(c).
5. *Altemose Construction Co. v. Building and Construction Trades Council,* 443 F.Supp. 492 (ED Pa., 1977).
6. See generally 29 U.S.C.A. §1001-1145.
7. 29 U.S.C.A. §401, *et seq.*
8. See generally 29 U.S.C.A. §1201-1242.
9. See generally 29 U.S.C.A. §1301-1461.
10. 29 U.S.C.A. §1002(2)(A).
11. 29 U.S.C.A. §1002(1)(A).
12. 29 U.S.C.A. §186(c).
13. 29 U.S.C.A. §1003(a).
14. 29 U.S.C.A. §1003(b)(1).
15. 29 U.S.C.A. §1002(32).

16. 29 U.S.C.A. §1002(b)(2).

17. 29 U.S.C.A. §1003(b)(3).

18. 29 U.S.C.A. §1003(b)(4).

19. 29 U.S.C.A. §1003(b)(5).

20. 29 U.S.C.A. §1302.

21. 29 U.S.C.A. §1322(a).

22. 29 U.S.C.A. §1307.

23. 29 U.S.C.A. §1362(a).

24. 29 U.S.C.A. §1362(a), (b), (c).

25. 29 U.S.C.A. §1364.

26. 26 U.S.C.A. §401(a)(12); 29 U.S.C.A. §1058.

27. 26 U.S.C.A. §401(a)(12); 29 U.S.C.A. §1058.

28. 26 U.S.C.A. §401(a)(13); 29 U.S.C.A. §1056(d)(1).

29. 26 U.S.C.A. §401(a)(13); 26 CFR §1.401(a)-13(d)(2).

30. 26 U.S.C.A. §401(a)(13); 29 U.S.C.A. §1056(d)(2).

31. 26 U.S.C.A. §401(a)(11)(A); 29 U.S.C.A. §1055(a).

32. 26 CFR §1.401(a)-11(b)(1).

33. 29 U.S.C.A. §1055(c)(2).

34. 29 U.S.C.A. §1055(a)(2), as amended.

35. 29 U.S.C.A. §1056(d)(3).

36. 29 U.S.C.A. §1140.

37. 29 U.S.C.A. §1140.

38. 29 U.S.C.A. §1141.

56

Participation, Vesting, and Funding Requirements Under ERISA

[56.01] ELIGIBILITY FOR PARTICIPATION

The participation requirements of the Employee Retirement Income Security Act generally apply to pension, profit sharing, stock bonus, and related employee pension benefit plans as defined by the Act.[1] The ERISA participation requirements do not apply, however, to employee welfare benefit plans, as defined earlier.[2]

ERISA establishes certain minimum participation standards relating to employee pension benefit plans.[3] For example, no pension plan covered by the Act may require, as a condition of participation, that an employee complete a period of service extending beyond the date on which he or she reaches 21 years of age, or the date on which he or she completes one year of service, whichever occurs later.[4] Should a pension benefit plan provide full and immediate vesting for all participants, the plan is permitted to require three years of service in addition to a minimum age limit of 21 years as a condition of participation.[5]

With certain exceptions, the ERISA regulations define a "year of service" to be at least 1000 hours of service during a twelve-month period.[6]

ERISA permits pension plans of tax-exempt educational institutions which provide for full and immediate vesting to require an employee to reach age 26 and complete one year of service before attaining eligibility to participate in the plan.[7]

A self-employed person may require his or her employees to complete three years of service in order to be eligible to participate in a Keogh pension plan, but age requirements are not permitted in such self-employed pension programs.[8]

Participation in a covered pension plan cannot ordinarily be denied an employee because he or she is too old.[9] However, plans defining benefits (rather than defining contributions) are permitted to exclude from pension plan participation any employee who commences employment within five years of the plan's normal retirement age.[10]

Once an employee has met the specified age and service requirements imposed by the plan, the employee must then commence to participate in the plan no later than the earlier of

- the first day of the first plan year, beginning after the date on which the employee satisfied the plan's requirements, or
- six months after the date on which the employee satisfied the plan's requirements.[11]

[56.02]   MINIMUM VESTING STANDARDS

ERISA provides that vesting occurs when a participant acquires a legal (nonforfeitable) right to receive his or her normal retirement benefits upon attaining normal reitrement age.[12]

Vesting occurs fully and immediately in accrued benefits derived from an employee's own contributions to a plan.[13] As to accrued benefits based on employer contributions, ERISA requires a pension plan to meet one of three minimum vesting standards:

- *Full vesting after ten years' service.* Under this vesting schedule, an employee who has at least ten years of service has a nonforfeitable right to 100 percent of his or her accrued benefit derived from the employer's contributions.[14]

- *Graded vesting.* This vesting schedule provides that an employee is to be at least 25 percent vested in his or her accrued benefit after five years of covered service, 5 percent additional vesting for each of the next five years, and 10 percent additional vesting for each year thereafter until 100 percent vesting is attained.[15]

- *The rule of 45.* This vesting schedule provides that each employee with five years or more of covered service must be at least 50 percent vested when the sum of his or her age and the years of covered service total forty-five, with at least 10 percent additional vesting for each year of covered service thereafter until 100 percent vesting is attained.[16]

In addition to the vesting schedules noted above, profit sharing, stock bonus, and money purchase type retirement plans, also known as "class-year" plans, in which each year's contributions vest separately, must provide for 100 percent vesting not later than the end of the fifth plan year, following the plan year for which the contributions are made.[17]

[56.03]   PERMISSIBLE FORFEITURES OF VESTED RIGHTS

Although an employee's vested rights to accrued benefits derived from his or her own contributions may not be forfeited,[18] accrued benefits based on employer contributions may be forfeited under certain conditions should the plan so prescribe.[19]

For example, ERISA permits a plan to provide that vested rights to an accrued benefit derived from employer contributions may be forfeited if the participant dies where no joint and survivor annuity exist.[20]

A plan is also permitted to provide that payment of benefits from employer contributions may be suspended for any period in which the employee is reemployed by the subject employer.[21]

ERISA also has established certain guidelines under which an employer-derived accrued benefit may be forfeited as a result of the participant's withdrawal of mandatory contributions to the plan.[22]

[56.04] ACCRUED BENEFIT FORMULAS

ERISA defines an "accrued benefit" in a defined benefit pension plan as the participant's rights to a retirement benefit according to the provisions of the plan.[23]

Accrued benefits relative to an individual account plan (a defined contribution plan) mean the balance of the individual's account.[24] Where a plan requires both employer and employee contributions, an employee's accrued benefit derived from his or her employer's contributions is the excess of the employee's accrued benefits derived from contributions made by the employee.[25]

A defined benefit pension plan must have a procedure for determining accrued benefits which satisfies one of three alternative accrued benefit formulas specified by ERISA.[26] They are:

- *3 Percent Rule.* Under this formula, each participant in a defined benefit pension plan must accrue at least 3 percent of the normal retirement benefit for each year of participation up to a maximum of thirty-three and one-third years.[27]

- *Fractional Test.* This formula gears the accrued benefit to an employee's proportionate time under the plan, so that, if an employee's maximum possible period of accrual would have been forty years from the date of beginning plan participation to the date of the plan's normal retirement age, an employee starting under the plan at age 25 and working to 60, for example, would be entitled to accrual benefits of 35/40 of the maximum credit toward a pension.[28]

- *133-⅓ Percent Rule.* Under this test, the ERISA requirements are met if the accrued benefit payable at the normal retirement age is equal to the normal retirement benefit, and if the accrued rate for any employee for any later plan period is not more than 133-⅓ percent of his or her accrual rate for the current year.[29]

Under any of the aforementioned tests, the accrual of benefits can become effective when the employee has two continuous years of service.[30]

[56.05] BREAK-IN-SERVICE RULES

ERISA has established certain guidelines to govern circumstances under which employee benefit plans are required to recognize prior service, should an employee return to his or her former employer.[31] ERISA generally forbids covered pension plans to recognize, as a break in service, breaks of employment which are less than one year in duration.[32] A one-year break in service is generally regarded as a calendar year, plan year, or other twelve-month period in which an employee does not complete more than 500 hours of service.[33]

ERISA amendments provide that employees with fewer than five years of service must be allowed to take up to five years off without incurring a "break in service" for pension accrual purposes.[34] ERISA amendments also provide that pension plans must allow up to a one-year maternity leave before counting the leave as a "break in service."[35] Otherwise, for any periods in excess of five years, an employer is still permitted to count as a break in service any break from employment that exceeds the number of years perviously worked.[36]

Pension plans may also require a one-year waiting period before pre-break and post-break service must be aggregated.[37]

[56.06] FUNDING REQUIREMENTS

ERISA provides that all covered pension plans must provide a procedure for establishing and administering the minimum funding requirements of its provisions.[38]

The two most important funding requirements under ERISA are

- the establishment and maintenance of a funding standard account[39]
- the utilization of acceptable actuarial methods in determining costs, past service liabilities, accrued liability, and previous gains and losses with regard to the plan[40]

The funding requirements imposed by ERISA are enforced under the provisions of the Internal Revenue Code.

Should a plan experience an "accumulated funding deficiency" that is not corrected within the taxable year, the employer administering the plan will be assessed a 5 percent excise tax on accumulated deficiencies.[41]

ERISA imposes its funding requirements to special pension plans irrespective of whether maintained under collective bargaining contracts,[42] multi-employer plans,[43] or controlled group plans.[44]

On the other hand, most welfare and related plans are not subjected to the ERISA funding requirements.

NOTES TO CHAPTER 56

1. 29 U.S.C.A. §1052.
2. 29 U.S.C.A. §1051(1).
3. 29 U.S.C.A. §1052.

4. 29 U.S.C.A. §1052(a)(1).

5. 29 U.S.C.A. §1052(a)(1)(B)(i); 26 CFR §1.410(a)-3(d).

6. 29 U.S.C.A. §1052(a)(3)(A).

7. 29 U.S.C.A. §1052(a)(1)(B)(ii); 26 CFR §1.410(a)-3(c).

8. *What You Should Know About the Pension and Welfare Law* (Washington, D.C.: U.S. Dept. of Labor, 1978), p. 15.

9. 29 U.S.C.A. §1052(a)(2); 26 CFR §1.410(a)-4(a)(1).

10. 29 U.S.C.A. §1052(a)(2); 26 CFR §1.410(a)-4(a)(1).

11. 26 CFR §1.410(a)-4(b)(1).

12. 29 U.S.C.A. §1053(a).

13. 29 U.S.C.A. §1053(a)(i).

14. 29 U.S.C.A. §1053(a)(2)(A); 26 CFR §1.411(a)-3(b).

15. 29 U.S.C.A. §1053(a)(2)(B); 26 CFR §1.411(a)-3(c).

16. 29 U.S.C.A. §1053(a)(2)(C)(i); 26 CFR §1.411(a)-3(d).

17. 29 U.S.C.A. §1053(c)(3); 25 CFR §1.411(d)-3(a)(1).

18. 29 U.S.C.A. §1053(a)(1).

19. 29 U.S.C.A. §1053(a)(3).

20. 29 U.S.C.A. §1053(a)(3)(A).

21. 29 U.S.C.A. §1053(a)(3)(B).

22. 29 U.S.C.A. §1053(a)(3)(D).

23. 29 U.S.C.A. §1002(23)(A).

24. 29 U.S.C.A. §1002(23)(B).

25. 29 U.S.C.A. §1054(c)(1).

26. 29 U.S.C.A. §1054(a).

27. 29 U.S.C.A. §1054(a), and 1054(b)(1).

28. 29 U.S.C.A. §1054(b)(1)(C); See also Note 7, p. 18, *supra*.

29. 29 U.S.C.A. §1054(a), (b)(1)(B).

30. 29 U.S.C.A. §1054(b)(1)(E).

31. 29 U.S.C.A. §1052(b).

32. 26 U.S.C.A. §1.410(a)-7(a)(3).

33. 29 U.S.C.A. §1053(b)(3)(A).

34. 29 U.S.C.A. §1053(b)(3)(C).

35. 29 U.S.C.A. §1053(b)(3)(E).

36. See generally 29 U.S.C.A. §§1052 and 1053, as amended.

37. Ibid.

38. 29 U.S.C.A. §1102(b)(1).

39. 29 U.S.C.A. §1082(b).

40. 29 U.S.C.A. §1082(c)(1).
41. 26 U.S.C.A. §4971(a).
42. 26 U.S.C.A. §413(b)(5).
43. 29 U.S.C.A. §§1060(a)(3).
44. 29. U.S.C.A. §1060(c).

57

Fiduciary Requirements
of ERISA

[57.01] GENERAL FIDUCIARY RESPONSIBILITIES

The Employee Retirement Income Security Act establishes guidelines and requirements to protect employee pension and welfare plans from financial losses caused by fiduciary mismanagement, misuse, or abuse of plan assets.[1]

ERISA defines a fiduciary of an employee benefit plan, and one subject to its fiduciary responsibility provisions, as anyone who exercises discretionary control or authority over plan management or assets, anyone with discretionary authority or responsibility in the administration of a plan, or anyone who has authority or responsibility to provide investment advice, or actually provides such advice, to a plan for compensation.[2]

The general fiduciary responsibility provisions of ERISA set forth

- the duties of plan fiduciaries[3]
- the prohibition of certain transactions by fiduciaries[4]
- a requirement that all persons who handle assets of a plan be bonded[5]
- a requirement that the assets of employee benefit plans be held in trust unless the assets consist of insurance or annuity contracts[6]
- a requirement that employee benefit plans be established and maintained under a written contract with proper designation of ''named fiduciaries'' to control and manage the plan[7]
- enrollment requirements of actuaries as well as the means of handling enrollment and suspension proceedings for actuaries[8]
- a requirement that persons convicted of certain crimes be prohibited from serving in specified positions with respect to employee benefit plans for a specified period of time.[9]

[57.02] SPECIFIC STANDARDS FOR PLAN FIDUCIARIES

Specifically, ERISA mandates that plan fiduciaries, in the discharge of their duties, must

- act exclusively for the purpose of providing plan benefits to participants and beneficiaries and defray the reasonable expenses of administering the plan[10]
- act with the care, skill, prudence, and diligence under the circumstances that a ''prudent man'' acting in like capacity and familiar with such matters would use in the conduct of an enterprise of a like character and like aims[11]
- diversify the investments of the plan so as to minimize the risk of large losses, unless it would clearly be prudent to do otherwise[12]

- act in accordance with the plan documents and instruments to the extent such documents and instruments are consistent with the ERISA provisions.[13]

[57.03]   PROHIBITED TRANSACTIONS UNDER ERISA

As a means to prevent conflicts of interest and self-dealing, ERISA prohibits a number of transactions and activities by plan fiduciaries. For example, a fiduciary to an employee benefit plan is barred from

- being paid for his or her services in the management or administration of the plan in the event he or she is already receiving full-time pay from an employer or union whose employees or members are participants[14]
- acting in any capacity involving a plan on behalf of a party whose interests are adverse to the interests of the plan[15]
- dealing with plan assets for his or her own account or in his or her own interest[16]
- permitting the investment of more than 10 percent of plan assets in employer securities or real property except in the case of profit sharing, stock bonus, thrift or savings or employee stock ownership plans, and certain money purchase plans[17]
- causing a plan to engage in a transaction with a party of interest if the transaction involves, either directly or indirectly, the sale, exchange, or lease of property; the lending of money or the extension of credit; the furnishing of goods or services or facilities; or the transfer of assets to, or the use of assets by or for the benefit of a party of interest[18]
- receiving any consideration for his or her personal account from any party dealing with the plan in connection with a transaction involving plan assets.[19]

[57.04]   PROHIBITED TRANSACTION EXEMPTIONS

ERISA provides some exemptions to the above discussed prohibited transactions by plan fiduciaries. For example, irrespective of the general prohibition against transactions between employee benefit plans and parties of interest, ERISA does permit loans by the plan to parties of interest who are participants or beneficiaries, if such loans are available on a nondiscriminatory basis, bear a reasonable rate of interest, are adequately secured, and are made in accordance with plan rules.[20]

ERISA also permits an employee benefit plan to reasonably compensate parties of interest for office space, or legal, accounting, or other services necessary for the establishment and management of the plan.[21]

ERISA permits parties of interest and plan fiduciaries to conduct the following transactions without violating its earlier discussed prohibitions:

- loans to Employee Stock Ownership Plans (ESOP), assuming the loan is used primarily for the benefit of plan participants and beneficiaries and is at a reasonable rate of interest[22]
- investments in deposits in banks, savings and loan associations, or credit unions where such institutions are the employers of the participants[23]
- purchase of life or health insurance, or annuities from an insurer, where the insurer is the employer maintaining the plan and the plan pays no more than adequate consideration for the insurance and the insurer is qualified to do business in the state[24]
- ancillary bank services, assuming the services are provided at reasonable rates, the bank has adopted adequate internal safeguards to assure sound banking and financial practices, and the services are not rendered in an excessive or unreasonable manner that would be inconsistent with the best interest of the plan participants and beneficiaries[25]
- distribution of plan assets, as long as the assets are distributed in accordance with the allocation rules of the termination insurance provisions applicable to defined benefit plans[26]
- conversion of employer securities if no less than adequate consideration is received under the conversion[27]
- transactions with pooled investment funds, if the bank or trust in question is paid no more than reasonable compensation for managing the fund and the purchase or sale of the funds is expressly permitted by the plan documents[28]

ERISA also exempts from its prohibited transactions provisions certain acquisitions and holdings of employer securities and real property, assuming no commission is charged with respect to the transaction, the transaction is for adequate consideration, and similar conditions are met.[29]

[57.05] LIABILITY OF FIDUCIARIES

A fiduciary who breaches his or her duties to an employee benefit plan is personally liable for any loss or damage suffered by the plan as a result of such breach, and is required by the Act to restore to the plan any profits made through improper use of plan assets.[30]

In addition, should a fiduciary conduct transactions that are prohibited under the ERISA provisions, and not otherwise exempted, he or she may be subjected to a special excise tax equal to 5 percent of the amount involved with respect to the prohibited transaction for each year, or part thereof, in the taxable period.[31] If the prohibited transaction is not corrected within a specified period, the fiduciary may thereafter be subjected to an additional tax of 100 percent of the amount involved in such transaction.[32] Other equitable and remedial relief may also be awarded by the court to a damaged employee benefit plan.[33]

NOTES TO CHAPTER 57

1. 29 U.S.C.A. §1101-1114.
2. 29 U.S.C.A. §1002(21).
3. 29 U.S.C.A. §1104(a)(1).
4. 29 U.S.C.A. §1106(a)(1).
5. 29 U.S.C.A. §1112.
6. 29 U.S.C.A. §1103.
7. 29 U.S.C.A. §1102.
8. 29 U.S.C.A. §1241 and §1242, and 20 CFR Part 900.
9. 29 U.S.C.A. §1111.
10. 29 U.S.C.A. §1104(a)(1)(A).
11. 29 U.S.C.A. §1104(a)(1)(B).
12. 29 U.S.C.A. §1104(a)(1)(C).
13. 29 U.S.C.A. §1104(a)(1)(D).
14. 29 U.S.C.A. §1108(c)(2).
15. 29 U.S.C.A. §1106(b)(2).
16. 29 U.S.C.A. §1106(b)(1).
17. 29 U.S.C.A. §1107(a)(2).
18. 29 U.S.C.A. §1106(a)(1)(A),(B),(C),(D) and (E).
19. 29 U.S.C.A. §1106(b)(3).
20. 29 U.S.C.A. §1108(b)(1).
21. 29 U.S.C.A. §1108(b)(2).
22. 29 U.S.C.A. §1108(b)(3).
23. 29 U.S.C.A. §1108(b)(4); 29 CFR §250, §408b-4.
24. 29 U.S.C.A. §1108(b)(5)(A).
25. 29 U.S.C.A. §1108(b)(6).
26. 29 U.S.C.A. §1109(b)(9).
27. 29 U.S.C.A. §1108(b)(7).
28. 29 U.S.C.A. §1108(b)(8).
29. 29 U.S.C.A. §1108(e).
30. 29 U.S.C.A. §1109(a).
31. 26 U.S.C.A. §503, §4975.
32. 26 U.S.C.A. §4975(b).
33. 29 U.S.C.A. §1109(a).

58

Multi-Employer Pension Plans

[58.01] DEFINITION

The term "Multi-Employer Plan" means an employee benefit plan to which more than one employer contributes, which is maintained pursuant to one or more collective bargaining agreements between one or more employee organizations and more than one employer, and which satisfies any other requirements prescribed by the Secretary of Labor's regulations.[1]

[58.02] PARTICIPATION AND VESTING STANDARDS

ERISA provides that service with any employer who is a member of a multi-employer plan is to be counted toward the satisfaction of its minimum participation standards.[2]

The minimum vesting and accrued benefit standards are likewise applied with respect to plans maintained by more than one employer, as though all employees of each of the employers who maintained the plan were employed by a single employer.[3] However, the application of any rules with respect to "break in service" in a multi-employer plan must be made under specific regulations.[4]

Moreover, a multi-employer plan may not disregard periods of service in which the employee's employer failed to make contributions to the plan in the determination of such employee's accrued benefits.[5]

[58.03] SUSPENSIONS AND FORFEITURES

ERISA provides that a multi-employer pension plan may suspend benefit payments when an employee-participant is reemployed in the same industry, the same trade or craft, and the same geographic area covered by the plan, as was the case before his or her benefits began.[6]

Multi-employer benefit payments may also be suspended when they exceed the resource benefit level and the plan is insolvent.[7]

The Multi-Employer Pension Plan Amendments Act (MPPAA) sets forth two types of forfeitures permitted with respect to multi-employer plans:

- MPPAA permits the forfeiture of benefits accrued as a result of service with an employer before that employer had an obligation to contribute to the multi-employer plan and that employer then ceases contributions to the plan.[8]
- MPPAA permits reductions of benefits as a result of certain amendments to a multi-employer plan.[9]

[58.04] MERGERS BETWEEN MULTI-EMPLOYER PLANS

The Pension Benefit Guaranty Corporation will generally permit a multi-employer plan to merge with one or more other multi-employer plans, or to engage in a transfer of assets or liabilities to or from another multi-employer plan, if the following conditions are met:[10]

- The PBGC is properly notified of the merger or transfer at least 120 days prior to the effective date of the merger or transfer.
- Accrued benefits of participants and beneficiaries are no lower after the merger or transfer than they were immediately prior to the effective date of such merger or transfer.
- The benefits of participants and beneficiaries are not reasonably expected to be subject to suspension under the ERISA insolvency provision.
- An actuarial valuation has been performed of assets and liabilities of each of the affected plans for the plan year prior to the effective date of the merger or transfer.

[58.05] MERGERS BETWEEN MULTI-EMPLOYER AND SINGLE EMPLOYER PLANS

ERISA permits a merger or a transfer of assets or liabilities between a multi-employer plan and a single employer plan provided no accrued benefit of a participant or beneficiary may be less immediately after the effective date of such a merger or transfer than the benefit immediately prior to that date.[11]

As a general rule, when a multi-employer plan transfers liabilities to a single employer plan, the multi-employer plan is liable to the Pension Benefit Guaranty Corporation if the single employer plan terminates within sixty months after the transfer.[12]

[58.06] CHANGE IN BARGAINING REPRESENTATIVE TRANSFERS

ERISA provides that whenever any employer completely or partially withdraws from a certain multi-employer pension plan as a result of a certified change of collective bargaining representative, and thereafter participates in another multi-employer plan as a result of such circumstances, the former plan must transfer assets and liabilities to the new plan in such a manner as to protect the employee-participants and their beneficiaries.[13]

[58.07] WITHDRAWAL LIABILITY

The Multi-Employer Pension Plan Amendments Act (MPPAA) requires an employer who totally or partially withdraws from a multi-employer plan to continue funding a proportionate share of the plan's unfunded vested benefits by making annual withdrawal liability payments to the plan.[14]

Whenever an employer withdraws from a multi-employer plan, the plan sponsor must determine the amount of the employer's withdrawal liability, notify the employer of the amount of the withdrawal liability, and collect the amount of the withdrawal liability from the employer.[15]

Whenever there is a demand against an employer in a multi-employer plan for withdrawal liability, it triggers a ninety-day period for requesting review by the plan of specific issues and disagreements.[16] Once a request for review is made, the employer is then required to file a timely demand for arbitration to preserve its right to raise defenses.[17] The time limits for filing a demand for arbitration is sixty days after the plan's response on review or 108 days after a request for review, whichever is the earliest.[18]

Most courts have held that if the above review procedures are not adhered to by the employer, the employer may not later raise any defenses relative to his or her position regarding denial or liability.[19]

The retroactivity imposition of the withdrawal liability provisions of the Multi-Employer Pension Plan Amendments Act has been attacked, constitutionally, in several cases. Although the U.S. Supreme Court upheld the retroactivity features of the Act,[20] the Tax Reform Act of 1984 eliminated the retroactivity impositions of MPPAA.[21]

As far as other constitutional questions surrounding the withdrawal liability provisions of MPPAA, most lower courts have upheld the statute.[22]

NOTES TO CHAPTER 58

1. 29 U.S.C.A. §1002(37)(A) (as amended by the Multi-Employer Pension Plan Amendments Act [MPPAA] of 1980).
2. 29 U.S.C.A. §1060(a)(1).
3. 29 U.S.C.A. §1060(a)(2).
4. 26 U.S.C.A. §413(b)(4); 29 U.S.C.A. §1060(a)(2).
5. See ERISA Opinion Letter No. 79–44 (1979).
6. See 29 U.S.C.A. §1053(a)(3)(B); see also 26 U.S.C.A. §411(a).
7. 29 U.S.C.A. §1426, §1441.
8. 29 U.S.C.A. §1053(a)(3)(E)(i).
9. See, for example: 29 U.S.C.A. §1425, §1441.
10. 29 U.S.C.A. §1411(a).
11. 29 U.S.C.A. §1412(b).
12. 29 U.S.C.A. §1412(c)(1).

13. 29 U.S.C.A. §1415(a).

14. 29 U.S.C.A. §1381, *et seq.*

15. 29 U.S.C.A. §1382.

16. ERISA §4219(b)(2)(A).

17. ERISA §4221(b)(1).

18. ERISA §4221(a)(1).

19. See, for example: *Speckmann v. Paddock Chrysler Plymouth,* 565 F.Supp. 469 (ED Mo., 1983). See *contra: IAM National Pension Fund v. Allied Corp.,* 97 F.R.D. 34 (D. D.C., 1983) in cases involving undisputed facts relied upon as defenses.

20. *Pension Benefit Guaranty Corp. v. R. A. Gray & Co.,* 52 U.S.L.W. 4810 (S.Ct. 1984).

21. Tax Reform Act of 1984 §558.

22. See, for example: *Terson Co. v. Bakery Drivers Local 194 Pension Fund,* 5 EBC 1729 (CA-3, 1984). See *contra: Keith Fulton & Sons Inc. v. New England Teamsters & Trucking Pension Fund,* 5 EBC 1761 (CA-1, 1984).

59

ERISA
Recordkeeping, Reporting, and Disclosure Requirements

[59.01] GENERAL REPORTING AND DISCLOSURE REQUIREMENTS

The Employee Retirement Income Security Act imposes upon plan administrators of employee benefit plans some of the most complex and comprehensive reporting and disclosure requirements found within the labor law spectrum.[1] Such reports must be complete and accurate.[2]

In addition, plan administrators have a duty under ERISA to disclose certain reports, documents, information, and materials to participants and beneficiaries of such employee benefit plans.[3]

Except for certain exemptions,[4] ERISA's reporting and disclosure requirements apply to all pension and welfare plans which are subject to the coverage of the Act.[5]

[59.02] SUMMARY PLAN DESCRIPTIONS

ERISA requires each plan administrator of a covered employee benefit plan to file a copy of the summary plan description with the Secretary of Labor within 120 days after the plan becomes subject to the reporting and disclosure requirements of the Act.[6] In addition, should a plan be materially modified, the plan administrator must file, with Secretary of Labor, a summary of such modifications and changes within 210 days after the end of the plan year in which the modification and changes were adopted.[7]

Updated plan descriptions may also be required to be filed with the Secretary of Labor, but no more frequently than once every five years, assuming no material modifications are made during the interim.[8]

ERISA also requires each plan administrator to furnish to each participant, as well as to each beneficiary receiving benefits under a plan, a copy of the summary plan description within 120 days after the plan becomes subject to its disclosure requirements,[9] or within 90 days after the recipient becomes a participant in the plan.[10] Also, copies of the plan description must be made available for participants to examine in the administrator's principal office or some alternatively designated place.[11] A copy of a plan description must be furnished upon the written request of any participant or beneficiary, subject to a reasonable charge for such copy.[12]

[59.03] ANNUAL REPORTS

ERISA provides that every employee benefit plan subject to its coverage must publish and file an annual report unless otherwise exempted.[13]

Inasmuch as the Department of Labor, the Internal Revenue Service, and the Pension Benefit Guaranty Corporation each require annual reports, annual reporting forms have been combined and unified into a 5500 series which meets the respective requirements of the three agencies.[14]

As a general rule, plan administrators are required to file an annual report with the Secretary of Labor within 210 days after the close of the plan year, or within such time as may be required by Department of Labor regulations to reduce duplicative filing.[15] Administrators must furnish participants and beneficiaries receiving benefits a summary annual report within nine months after the close of the plan year.[16]

[59.04]   NOTICE OF REPORTABLE EVENTS AND PLAN TERMINATION

ERISA requires an administrator of a plan covered by termination insurance to notify the Pension Benefit Guaranty Corporation within thirty days after he or she knows or has reason to know of the occurrence of a reportable event.[17] Conditions and circumstances that constitute reportable events include

- plan amendments that may decrease benefits[18]
- a determination by the Secretary of Labor that a plan is no longer in compliance with ERISA requirements[19]
- notice from the Treasury Department that a pension or annuity plan has ceased to be tax qualified[20]
- a determination by the Treasury Department that a plan has been terminated under the Internal Revenue Code's vesting provisions[21]
- the failure of a defined benefit plan to meet the minimum funding standards of the Internal Revenue Code or of the ERISA labor provisions[22]
- inability of an employee benefit plan to make a timely payment of benefits that are due to participants or beneficiaries[23]
- a merger, consolidation, or other transfer of assets to another plan[24]
- an alternative method of compliance with ERISA's reporting and disclosure requirements[25]
- a substantial decrease (20 percent or more) in the number of plan participants[26]
- a distribution of plan assets to a ''substantial owner'' under certain conditions[27]
- a determination by the Pension Benefit Guaranty Corporation that certain events indicate a need to terminate a particular plan[28]

ERISA also requires a plan administrator to file various reports to the Pension Benefit Guaranty Corporation regarding an intent to terminate a plan.[29] ERISA provides that special terminal reports must also be filed with the Secretary of Labor.[30]

[59.05] RETENTION OF RECORDS

ERISA requires all individuals who are responsible for filing the aforementioned and related reports to keep sufficiently detailed records so that information and data gathered from such documents can be verified and checked for accuracy and completeness.[31] As a general rule, such records must be retained for a period of six years.[32]

Employers who sponsor employee benefit plans must also maintain records with respect to each of their employees, sufficient to determine the benefits due, or that may become due, to an employee in the future.[33] ERISA also requires the plan's sponsor employer to furnish such records to the plan administrator.[34]

Organizations such as insurance carriers, banks, plan sponsors, actuaries, etc., who customarily supply information necessary to enable a plan administrator to comply with ERISA's labor provisions, are required to transmit and certify the accuracy of such information to the plan administrator within 120 days after the end of the plan year.[35]

The Employee Retirement Income Security Act also provides that the Secretary of Labor may prescribe alternative methods for satisfying ERISA's reporting and disclosure requirements.[36]

[59.06] REPORTING AND DISCLOSURE EXEMPTIONS

ERISA provides a full exemption from its reporting and disclosure requirements for governmental employee benefit plans, certain church plans, certain excess benefit plans that are unfunded, plans maintained solely for the purpose of complying with local worker's compensation and unemployment compensation laws as well as applicable disability insurance laws, and plans maintained outside the United States primarily for the benefit of persons substantially all of whom are nonresident aliens.[37]

The Secretary of Labor, either partially or fully, has exempted several other employee benefit plans from ERISA's reporting and disclosure requirements, including the following:

- welfare plans that cover 100 or more participants[38]
- certain group insurance arrangements[39]
- unfunded and certain insured plans[40]
- employee welfare benefit plans that provide solely for apprenticeship training benefits[41]
- day-care center plans[42]

- welfare plans for a select group of management or highly compensated employees[43]

[59.07] PENALTIES FOR FAILURE TO REPORT AND DISCLOSE

Both civil and criminal penalties may be imposed for failure to report or disclose information as required by ERISA.[44] For example, ERISA provides for a

- $50 penalty for each failure to furnish timely statements, or for furnishing false or fraudulent statements to a participant regarding annual registration information[45]
- $1,000 penalty for each failure to file a timely actuarial report[46]
- penalty of $1 per participant for each day of delinquency for failure to file a timely annual registration statement[47]
- $10 penalty for each day of delinquency for failure to file a timely annual information return required with respect to deferred compensation plans or the information return required in connection with certain trusts and annuity and bond purchase plans[48]
- $25 penalty per participant for failure to file information required in connection with retirement savings, multiplied by the number of years during which such failure continues[49]
- $1 penalty for each day of delinquency for failure to file a timely notification of change in status[50]

NOTES TO CHAPTER 59

1. *Reporting and Disclosure Guide for Employee Benefit Plans* (U.S. Dept. of Labor).
2. 29 CFR §2520.104a-1(a).
3. 29 CFR §2520.104b-1(a).
4. Discussed at [68.07].
5. See 29 U.S.C.A. §1003(a).
6. 29 U.S.C.A. §1024(a)(1)(C).
7. 29 CFR §2520.104a-4(b)(1) and §2520.104a-7.
8. See 29 U.S.C.A. §1024(a)(1)(B); see also 29 U.S.C.A. §1024(a)(1)(D) and 29 CFR §2520.104a-4(b)(1).
9. 29 U.S.C.A. §1024(b)(1)(B).
10. 29 U.S.C.A. §1024(b)(1)(A).
11. 29 U.S.C.A. §1024(b)(2).
12. 29 U.S.C.A. §1024(b)(4).
13. 29 U.S.C.A. §1021(b)(4) and §1023(a)(1)(A).

14. See 29 CFR §2611.3.(b).
15. 29 U.S.C.A. §1024(a)(1)(A): 29 CFR §2520.104a–5(a)(2).
16. 29 CFR §2520.104b-10(a).
17. 29 U.S.C.A. §1343(a).
18. 29 U.S.C.A. §1343(b)(2).
19. 29 U.S.C.A. §1343(b)(1).
20. 26 U.S.C.A. §401(a) and 404(A)(2); see also 29 U.S.C.A. §1343(b)(1).
21. 29 U.S.C.A. §1343(b)(4).
22. 29 U.S.C.A. §1343(b)(5).
23. 29 U.S.C.A. §1343(b)(6).
24. 29 U.S.C.A. §1343(b)(8).
25. 29 U.S.C.A. §1343(b)(8).
26. 29 U.S.C.A. §1343(b)(3).
27. 29 U.S.C.A. §1343(b)(6) and 29 U.S.C.A. §1343(b)(7).
28. 29 U.S.C.A. §1343(b)(9).
29. 29 U.S.C.A. §1341(a).
30. 29 U.S.C.A. §1021(b)(5).
31. 29 U.S.C.A. §1027.
32. 29 U.S.C.A. §1027.
33. 29 U.S.C.A. §1059(a)(1).
34. 29 U.S.C.A. §1059(a)(1).
35. 26 U.S.C.A. §1023(a)(2).
36. 29 U.S.C.A. §1030(a).
37. 29 U.S.C.A. §1003(b).
38. 29 CFR §2520.103-1(a)(2).
39. 29 CFR §2520.103-2.
40. 29 CFR §2520.104.44(a).
41. 29 CFR §2520.104-22.
42. 29 CFR §2520.104-25.
43. 29 CFR §2520.104-24.
44. See 26 U.S.C.A. §6652 and 26 U.S.C.A. §7201
45. 26 U.S.C.A. §6690.
46. 26 U.S.C.A. §6692.
47. 26 U.S.C.A. §6652(e)(1).
48. 26 U.S.C.A. §6652(f).
49. 26 U.S.C.A. §6652(h).
50. 26 U.S.C.A. §6652(e)(2).

60

ERISA Administration and Enforcement

[60.01] ADMINISTRATION

The ERISA labor provisions are administered and enforced primarily through the U.S. Department of Labor.[1] The Secretary of Labor has delegated the administration of the ERISA labor provisions to its Labor-Management Services Administration.[2] (The compliance to ERISA's tax provisions is through the U.S. Internal Revenue Service.)

[60.02] INVESTIGATIONS

ERISA has delegated to the Secretary of Labor broad powers to conduct investigations to determine if, and to what degree, violations of the Act have occurred.[3] The Secretary of Labor is authorized by ERISA to apply Sections 9 and 10 of the Federal Trade Commission Act[4] in connection with investigations of alleged violations of the labor provisions of the Act.[5] Pursuant to the application of Sections 9 and 10 of the Federal Trade Commission Act to ERISA investigations, the Secretary of Labor and his or her designated agents are empowered to examine and copy any documentary evidence of any person, partnership, or corporation being investigated, at any reasonable time.[6] These sections also empower the Secretary and his or her agents to require, by subpoena, the production of all documentary evidence and the attendance and testimony of witnesses relating to any matter under investigation.[7]

The Secretary is not required to show probable cause as a prerequisite to the issuance of such a subpoena.[8] However, Labor-Management Services Administration investigators must give a written justification with each request for a subpoena.[9] Subpoenas issued by the Secretary of Labor, or his or her designee, are enforceable through the federal district courts.[10] Failure to obey federal court orders compelling compliance with subpoenas may be punishable by contempt.[11]

Any person who willfully violates a subpoena authorized by Section 9 of the Federal Trade Commission Act may be guilty of a criminal offense, punishable by fines and/or imprisonment.[12]

In addition to the authority to issue subpoenas and compel production of documents in connection with an ERISA investigation, the Secretary, or his or her agent, is authorized to enter upon plan premises and, while there, inspect books and records and question such persons as deemed necessary as part of his or her investigatory efforts to determine the facts relative to the investigation, provided the agent has reasonable cause to believe a violation exists or such entry is permitted by the plan documents.[13]

435

[60.03]   HOW TO PROCESS CLAIMS FOR ERISA BENEFITS

Every employee benefit plan, with the exception of exempted and apprenticeship training plans, is required to establish and maintain a reasonable procedure relating to the filing of participant and beneficiary claims.[14]

The ERISA regulations governing the establishment and maintenance of a proper claims procedure provide that a participant or beneficiary claim is deemed filed whenever the requirements under the plan have been met, or in the absence of a reasonably established procedure for filing claims, whenever the claimant or his or her authorized representative makes a written or oral communication reasonably calculated to bring the claim to the attention of the person or organizational unit authorized to make a decision on the claim.[15]

Employee benefit plans must also provide a procedure for notifying claimants whenever a claim is denied.[16] Notification of denial of a claim is due the claimant within a reasonable time after receiving a claim, but in no event to exceed ninety days.[17] ERISA regulations require notices denying claims for benefits to be written in a clear and understandable manner and to include

- specific reasons for denial
- references to pertinent plan provisions on which the denial is based
- descriptions of any additional material or information necessary for the claimant to perfect his or her claim, if applicable, and any other information that might explain why the additional material or information is necessary
- information regarding the steps to be taken for a review of the denied claim[18]

[60.04]   RIGHT OF REVIEW OF DENIED BENEFIT

ERISA and its regulations require covered employee benefit plans to accord a reasonable opportunity to any participant whose claims for benefits have been denied a full and fair review of the denial.[19]

Review procedures must contain provisions that permit a claimant or his or her representative to

- make written application for a review
- examine pertinent documents relating to the denial of a claim
- submit issues and comments in support of a claimant's position[20]

The decision on review must be written in a clear and understandable manner and must include specific reasons and references to the pertinent plan provisions for the decision.[21]

[60.05] EXHAUSTION OF ADMINISTRATIVE REMEDIES

Although the Employee Retirement Income Security Act does not require a claimant to exhaust the claims procedures of an employee benefit plan as a prerequisite to filing a lawsuit to enforce his or her claims, such a requirement has been recognized by the courts.[22]

Where a resort to internal appeals procedures would be futile or where there is a wrongful denial of access to such procedure, however, the courts have not required a claimant to exhaust his or her administrative remedies as a prerequisite to filing an ERISA suit.[23]

[60.06] LAWSUITS TO ENFORCE ERISA PROVISIONS

ERISA grants exclusive jurisdiction to the U.S. District Courts of civil actions brought by the Secretary, plan participants, beneficiaries, or fiduciaries to enforce its labor provisions.[24]

ERISA grants concurrent jurisdiction to the federal district courts and state courts of civil actions brought by participants or beneficiaries to recover plan benefits, to enforce rights under the terms of an employee benefit plan, or to clarify rights to future benefits under the terms of an employee benefit plan.[25]

A civil action to enforce the labor provisions of ERISA may be appropriately filed in a U.S. District Court located where the plan is administered, where the breach which is the subject to the suit took place, or where a defendant resides.[26]

A civil action by a plan administrator, participant, beneficiary, or fiduciary to compel the Secretary of Labor to take action required by ERISA labor provisions, to restrain the Secretary from taking action adverse to the ERISA provisions, or to review a final order of the Secretary, may be brought in the federal district court for the district where the plan has its principal office or in the U.S. District Court for the District of Columbia.[27]

Civil actions brought to obtain relief for a breach of a fiduciary duty, or any violation of the fiduciary responsibility rules, must be commenced within

- six years after the date of the last action constituting a breach, or, in the case of an omission, the latest date by which the fiduciary could have cured the breach,[28] or

- three years after the earliest date on which the plaintiff had actual knowledge or should have known of the breach.[29]

[60.07] TYPES OF CIVIL ACTIONS

Various civil actions may be brought in the appropriate courts to enforce ERISA's labor provisions or to obtain relief for breach of fiduciary duties.

Plan participants and beneficiaries may commence lawsuits to

- recover benefits due them under the terms of their employee benefit plan[30]
- enforce rights accorded to them under the specific terms of their employee benefit plan[31]
- clarify their rights to future benefits under the terms of their employee benefit plan[32]
- enjoin any act or practice that violates the labor provisions of ERISA or the specific terms of their employee benefit plan[33]
- enforce ERISA labor provisions or the specific terms of their employee benefit plan[34]
- obtain relief against a plan fiduciary for breach of his or her responsibilities, obligations, or duties under the Act[35]
- redress the failure of a plan administrator to comply with a request for information[36]
- redress interference with protected rights against discrimination[37]
- review adverse actions taken by the Secretary of Labor[38]

The *Secretary of Labor* is authorized by the Employee Retirement Income Security Act to commence civil action to

- enjoin any act or practice that violates ERISA's labor provisions[39]
- enforce any of the labor provisions of ERISA[40]
- obtain relief for a breach of fiduciary duty[41]
- collect penalties against parties of interest for prohibited transactions[42]
- seek equitable relief for a violation of any of the participation, vesting and funding provisions of ERISA, provided he or she is requested to do so by the Treasury Secretary or one or more of the participants, beneficiaries, or fiduciaries of the plan[43]
- recover the expenses of an audit or actuarial evaluation required by the Secretary upon rejecting the filing of any required report[44]
- require the attendance and testimony of witnesses or the production of documents[45]

[60.08] CIVIL SANCTIONS AND CRIMINAL PENALTIES

Should judgment be rendered against a fiduciary for breach of duty to an employee benefit plan, the court may hold the fiduciary personally liable for losses resulting from his or her breach and require him or her to restore to the plan any profits he or she has made through the use of plan assets.[46] Further, the court may remove the fiduciary from his or her position.[47]

Should a plan administrator fail to comply properly and timely with the request of a participant or beneficiary for information to which such person is entitled, the court may hold the administrator personally liable in an amount not exceeding $100 per day from the date of his failure or refusal.[48]

Criminal prosecutions may be brought against persons who willfully violate the Act. For example, any person who willfully violates any of the reporting and disclosure requirements of ERISA labor provisions will, upon conviction, be subject to fines up to $5,000 and/or imprisonment up to one year.[49] Corporations committing such willful violations may be fined up to $100,000.[50]

Persons who willfully make false statements or misrepresentations of fact in any document required by ERISA[51] or who coercively interfere with rights of participants and beneficiaries;[52] engage in theft or embezzlement of plan assets;[53] or solicit, make, or offer kick-backs, bribes, or similar payments in relation to employee benefit plans;[54] may be subjected to fines up to $10,000 and/or imprisonment, upon conviction.

NOTES TO CHAPTER 60

1. See, generally, 29 U.S.C.A. §1134, *et seq.*
2. Order No. 9–77, 42 *Fed. Reg.* 49530, Para. 3.
3. 29 U.S.C.A. §1134(a).
4. 15 U.S.C.A. §49 and §50.
5. 29 U.S.C.A. §1134(c).
6. 15 U.S.C.A. §49.
7. 15 U.S.C.A. §49.
8. *Federal Trade Commission v. Scientific Living,* 150 F.Supp. 495 (DC Pa., 1957).
9. See *PWBP Compliance Manual,* Ch. 17, §13.
10. 15 U.S.C.A. §49.
11. 15 U.S.C.A. §49.
12. 15 U.S.C.A. §50.
13. 29 U.S.C.A. §1134(a)(2).
14. 29 U.S.C.A. §1133(a) and (2).
15. 29 CFR §2560.5003-1(d).
16. 29 CFR §2560.503-1(e).
17. 29 CFR §2560.503-1(e).
18. 29 CFR §2560.503-1(f).
19. 29 U.S.C.A. §1133(s) and 29 CFR §2560.503-1(g).
20. 29 CFR §2520.503(g)(1).
21. 29 CFR §2520.503-1(h).

22. *Amato v. Bernard,* 618 F.2d 559 (CA-9, 1980).

23. *Sample v. Monsanto Co.,* 485 F.Supp. 1018 (ED Mo., 1980).

24. 29 U.S.C.A. §1132(e)(1).

25. 29 U.S.C.A. §1132(e)(1).

26. 11 U.S.C.A. §1132(e)(2).

27. 29 U.S.C.A. §1132(k).

28. 29 U.S.C.A. §1113(a)(1)(A) and (B).

29. 29 U.S.C.A. §1113(a)(2)(A) and (B).

30. 29 U.S.C.A. §1132(a)(1)(B).

31. 29 U.S.C.A. §1132(a)(1)(B).

32. 29 U.S.C.A. §1132(a)(1)(B).

33. 29 U.S.C.A. §1132(a)(3)(A).

34. 29 U.S.C.A. §1132(a)(3)(B).

35. 29 U.S.C.A. §1132(a)(2).

36. 29 U.S.C.A. §1132(a)(1)(A) and (c).

37. 29 U.S.C.A. §1140.

38. See 5 U.S.C.A. §702 and 29 U.S.C.A. §1137(a).

39. 29 U.S.C.A. §1132(a)(5)(A).

40. 29 U.S.C.A. §1132(a)(5)(B).

41. 29 U.S.C.A. §1132(a)(2).

42. 29 U.S.C.A. §1132(a)(6).

43. 29 U.S.C.A. §1132(b)(1).

44. 29 U.S.C.A. §1024(a)(5).

45. 29 U.S.C.A. §1134.

46. 29 U.S.C.A. §1109(a).

47. 29 U.S.C.A. §1109(a).

48. 29 U.S.C.A. §1132(c).

49. 29 U.S.C.A. §1131.

50. 29 U.S.C.A. §1131.

51. 18 U.S.C.A. §1027.

52. 29 U.S.C.A. §1141.

53. 18 U.S.C.A. §664.

54. 18 U.S.C.A. §1954.

61

Federal Social Security
and Related Programs

[61.01] SOCIAL SECURITY ACT

The Social Security Act[1] provides for several nationwide systems of social insurance and assistance to protect American workers and their families against loss of income due to such circumstances as retirement, old age, disability, and death. Inasmuch as social security benefits are derived primarily as a result of the employer/employee relationship and from the money accruing therefrom, it is considered an appropriate subject of coverage within this reference book.

In order to be eligible for disability,[2] old age, and survivor insurance benefits under the Social Security Act,[3] an insured individual must have fulfilled certain work history and age requirements as provided in the statute and its regulations.

The government determines whether an individual has fullfilled the work history requirements of the statute by applying a "quarters of coverage" measurement.[4]

The amount of insurance benefits to which an individual or survivor is entitled involves a detailed process, including the use of computation charts and tables.[5] The amount of benefits derived from the computation process is referred to as the "primary insurance amount."[6]

Individuals who are "fully insured" and who have satisfied the age requirements established by the statute are entitled to old age benefits in a sum equal to their "primary insurance amount."[7]

Disability benefits are provided for insured individuals under the age of 65 who become unable to engage in any substantial gainful activity by reason of any medically determinable physical or mental impairment that can be expected to result in death, or that has lasted or can be expected to last for a continuous period of not less than one year.[8]

[61.02] HOW TO FILE A SOCIAL SECURITY CLAIM

Social security benefits are not paid automatically.[9] They are not payable to insured individuals unless an application is submitted to the Social Security Administration.[10]

Should the Social Security Administration disallow a social security claim, the claimant has a right under the regulations to submit a written request for reconsideration, provided the request is submitted no later than six months from the date the notice of the initial determination was mailed to the claimant.[11] Upon the filing of a proper request for reconsideration of an administrative determination, the Social Security Administration has the obligation to reconsider the findings of its initial determination, consider the entire evidence in the matter and to either affirm or revise, in whole or in part, the findings and recommendations in question.[12]

In the event a claimant disagrees with the reconsidered determination of the Administration, the claimant may ask for a hearing before a hearing examiner.[13] Otherwise, the reconsidered determination is dispositive of the claim and becomes final and binding upon all parties in question.[14]

[61.03] SOCIAL SECURITY HEARINGS AND APPEALS

A claimant who desires a hearing upon his or her social security claim must submit a written request for a hearing to the Social Security Administration no later than six months from the date of the reconsidered determination.[15]

Social security hearings are considered to be nonadversarial in nature.[16] For example, subject to limitations regarding evidence of earnings, evidence is admissible without rigid adherence to regular evidentiary or procedural rules.[17]

Hearing examiners are empowered to issue subpoenas for the production of books, records, papers, and other documents that may be relevant to any matter in issue at a hearing.[18]

Once a hearing is concluded, the hearing officer renders a written decision in the case, based on the relevant evidence submitted. This decision becomes final and binding on all parties to the hearing, unless reviewed or revised.[19] If a claimant disagrees with the hearing examiner's decision, he or she may submit a written request for review by the Appeals Council of the Bureau of Hearings and Appeals.[20] Requests for appeals to the Appeals Council must be submitted within sixty days of the date that the hearing examiner's decision is mailed.[21] A request for review may be dismissed, denied, or granted by the Appeals Council.[22]

If a claimant is dissatisfied with the Appeals Council decision he or she may file a civil suit in an appropriate U.S. District Court.[23] Civil suits to review social security rulings must be filed within sixty days of the date the notice of the Appeals Council decision was mailed to the claimant.[24]

[61.04] RAILROAD RETIREMENT ACT

The Railroad Retirement Act[25] provides for a nationwide system of social insurance for the protection of railroad industry employees and their families.[26]

The Railroad Retirement Act is administered by the Railroad Retirement Board, an independent federal agency.[27] The Railroad Retirement Act program is separate from the social security system, but is similar to it in concept and services.[28]

The retirement program provides for certain benefits to railroad employees who retire on account of old age or disability; it also provides certain survivor benefits to widows, children and parents, as well as certain annuities to wives of railroad employees.[29]

The Railroad Retirement Board also administers a Federal Health Insurance (Medicare) program for railroad employees and their families who are 65 years of age, or older.[30]

Employees, dependents, or survivors who are eligible for Railroad Retirement benefits must file their claims with the Railroad Retirement Board.[31]

Similar to the procedure provided in the Social Security Act,[32] claimants who receive unfavorable rulings on their benefit claims may appeal them to the Railroad Retirement Board's Office of Hearings and Appeals, where they are entitled to a hearing before a referee.[33]

Should a claimant disagree with a referee's decision, he or she may then appeal directly to the board itself,[34] and ultimately to the federal courts.[35]

[61.05] HEALTH MAINTENANCE ORGANIZATION ACT (HMO)

The Health Maintenance Organization Act of 1976, as amended, requires an employer to include in any health plan offered employees the option of membership in a qualified health maintenance organization (HMO) within the employer's geographical area.[36]

In offering an eligible employee the option of joining a qualified HMO, the employer must include the HMO option in the health benefits plan on terms no less favorable than what he or she had voluntarily contributed on behalf of the employee previously in other health benefit plans.[37]

However, the Act does not require that such an employer pay more for health benefits for his or her employees as a result of the HMO requirement than he or she would otherwise pay as required through a collective bargaining contract or other arrangement of health benefits.[38]

An employer that refuses or fails to comply with the requirements of the Health Maintenance Organization Act may be subjected to a civil penalty of up to $10,000 for an initial violation, and to a penalty in like amount for each additional month of noncompliance.[39]

NOTES TO CHAPTER 61

1. See generally 42 U.S.C.A. §301, *et seq.*
2. 42 U.S.C.A. §423(c).
3. 42 U.S.C.A. §414.
4. 42 U.S.C.A. §414.

5. 42 U.S.C.A. §415.

6. 42 U.S.C.A. §415.

7. 42 U.S.C.A. §402(a).

8. 42 U.S.C.A. §423(a)(1) and (d)(1)(A).

9. *Coy v. Folsom,* 228 F.2d 276 (CA-3, 1955).

10. 20 CFR §404.701.

11. 20 CFR §404.909, §405.1510 and §422.10.

12. 20 CFR §404.914, §405.1514 and §405.1515.

13. 20 CFR §404.917 and §404.1530.

14. 20 CFR §409.916 and §404.1517.

15. 20 CFR §404.917 and §405.1530.

16. See, for example: *Gold v. Secretary of Health, Education & Welfare* 463 F.2d 38 (CA-2, 1972).

17. 20 CFR §404.928 and §405.1546.

18. 20 CFR §404.926 and §405.1544.

19. See 20 CFR §404.939 and §404.940.

20. 20 CFR §404.945 and §404.950.

21. 20 CFR §404.945.

22. 20 CFR §404.943 and §404.949.

23. 42 U.S.C.A. §405(g).

24. 42 U.S.C.A. §405(g).

25. 45 U.S.C.A. §228, *et seq.*

26. See generally 42 U.S.C.A. §228(a) through §228(z).

27. 45 U.S.C.A. §228j.

28. See 42 U.S.C.A. §228q, and generally 45 U.S.C.A. §228(a) through §228(z).

29. 42 U.S.C.A. §228b.

30. 42 U.S.C.A. §228s-2.

31. 20 CFR §200.1.

32. See discussion of Social Security Appeals at [61.03].

33. 20 CFR §259.

34. 20 CFR §259 and §260.

35. 42 U.S.C.A. §228k.

36. See generally 42 U.S.C.A. §300e-9(a)(1).

37. 42 CFR §110.808(a).

38. 42 U.S.C.A. §300e-9(c).

39. 42 U.S.C.A. §300e-9(e)(1).

62

Federal Unemployment
and Worker's Compensation Laws

[62.01] UNEMPLOYMENT INSURANCE UNDER THE SOCIAL SECURITY ACT

The Federal Social Security Act established a nationwide federal-state system of insurance to protect workers and their families against loss of income due to unemployment.[1] As a result of this particular legislation, unemployment insurance is a joint federal-state program that incorporates certain basic standards specified in the Social Security Act[2] and the Federal Unemployment Tax Act.[3]

The Social Security Act provides that all money received in state unemployment funds are to be paid over to the U.S. Treasury Department to the credit of the federal "Unemployment Trust Funds."[4]

The Secretary of the Treasury is obligated to invest the money contributed from the various states in limited kinds of securities.[5] He or she is also obligated to keep proper records and accounts for each state contributing to the fund as well as being responsible for the proper and accurate disbursement of payments from the fund to each contributing state.[6]

The Secretary of the U.S. Department of Labor is prohibited from certifying any unemployment payments to a particular state until he or she determines that the state has met certain standards required by the Social Security Act.[7]

[62.02] THE FEDERAL UNEMPLOYMENT TAX ACT

The Federal Unemployment Tax Act, adjunct to and in support of the above mentioned social security provisions, was established to regulate the unemployment tax rates imposed on employers covered under the statute,[8] to specify what tax credits are available to covered employers,[9] to define conditions of additional credit allowance,[10] to set forth certain standards to approve state laws,[11] to specify what entities, organizations, and instrumentalities are to be included or excluded from its coverage,[12] and to provide for judicial review of any adverse decisions flowing from its provisions.[13] The Federal Unemployment Tax Act defines an "employer" subject to its provisions as any person who

- during any calendar quarter in the calendar year, or preceding calendar year, paid wages of $1,500 or more,
- on each of some twenty days during the current calendar year or during the preceding calendar year, each day being in a different calendar week, employed at least one individual in employment for some portion of that day[14]

447

The fifty states have enacted unemployment compensation laws that incorporate certain basic standards imposed by the Social Security Act and the Federal Unemployment Tax Act.

[62.03] UNEMPLOYMENT COMPENSATION FOR FEDERAL EMPLOYEES

Federal employees and veterans of the armed forces are eligible for unemployment compensation benefits provided they qualify for such benefits under the statute regulating the federal program.

The state unemployment insurance agencies serve as agents of the Secretary of the U.S. Department of Labor in processing claims and paying benefits to such individuals where such an arrangement has been worked out by the Secretary of Labor and a state agency.[15]

In the absence of such an agreement between the Secretary of Labor and the subject state agency, unemployment compensation benefits are payable to the eligible individual by the Secretary of Labor.[16] Irrespective of whether benefits are processed through the state agencies or directly with the Secretary of Labor, the benefits are paid by the federal government.[17]

Application for benefits processed in a state agency are disposed of in the same manner and to the same extent as are state claims determined under the state unemployment compensation statute.[18] Applications processed through the Secretary of Labor's office are determined in accordance with regulations prescribed by the Secretary.[19]

Veterans of the armed forces are ineligible for unemployment compensation benefits for the period they receive a veteran's subsistence or educational allowance under federal laws.[20]

[62.04] RAILROAD UNEMPLOYMENT INSURANCE ACT

The Railroad Unemployment Insurance Act established a nationwide system for the payment of unemployment and sickness benefits to qualified railroad employees.[21]

The statute is administered by the Railroad Retirement Board,[22] which also administers the Railroad Retirement Act.

Similar to the "Unemployment Trust Fund" established by Section 1101 of the Social Security Act, the Secretary of the Treasury is required to maintain an account known as the "Railroad Unemployment Insurance Account," contributions that are collected from railroads and other companies performing services in connection with the railroad transportation, and railway labor organizations.[23]

Benefit payments under the Act are based on earnings in the base year in accordance with specified tables and schedules.[24]

Employees may also be disqualified for sickness pay under the Railroad Unemployment Insurance Act.[25] As with the case of social security claimants, railroad employees who are denied claims of unemployment or sickness benefits under the Railroad Unemployment Insurance Act may appeal unfavorable or adverse decisions through the appellate procedures set forth in the Act, and as a final forum, to an appropriate U.S. Court of Appeals.[26]

[62.05]   FEDERAL EMPLOYEES' COMPENSATION ACT

The Federal Employees' Compensation Act provides workers' compensation coverage to civilian employees of the United States who die or become disabled due to personal injury sustained while in the performance of duty, or because of some occupational disease.[27]

The Federal Employees' Compensation Act, similar in concept to state workers' compensation laws, establishes certain criteria and standards to determine whether an individual is qualified to receive benefits under the program.[28] For example, workers' compensation benefits are not to be paid to federal employees if an injury or disease is caused by the willful misconduct of the employee or by the employee's intention to inflict injury or death on himself or another, or if intoxication is determined to be the proximate cause of the injury or death.[29]

Employees who qualify for workers' compensation benefits under the Federal Employees' Compensation Act are also entitled to the payment of all necessary medical and hospital care arising from the on-the-job injury, disease, or death.[30]

Benefits and payments are paid to employees in accordance with established schedules, the amounts and duration of which are dependent upon the gravity of the injury or disease and whether the disability is temporary or permanent and/or partial or total.[31]

Federal employees, or their survivors, are entitled to a hearing on their claims should they disagree with a final determination by the Office of Workers' Compensation Programs.[32]

Should an adverse determination result from such a hearing, the affected party may appeal the decision for an additional review to the Division of Hearings and Reviews, and, ultimately, to the Employees' Compensation Appeals Board in Washington, D.C., if so disposed.[33]

[62.06]   LONGSHOREMEN'S AND HARBOR WORKERS' COMPENSATION ACT

This particular act provides workers' compensation benefits for maritime employment on the navigable waters of the United States, including employment on dry docks,[34] but excludes compensation benefits to seamen and other crew members of vessels on such waters.[35]

In addition to providing workers' compensation benefits for longshore-men and ship repairmen while aboard a vessel on U.S. navigable waters,[36] the Act also extends coverage to all private employment in the service of contractors with the United States at military, air, or naval bases or on pub-lic works, if such employment is performed outside the United States.[37] Pri-vate employment in the District of Columbia is also covered by the Act,[38] as well as is certain employment on the outer continental shelf lands[39] and employment at post exchanges and other nonappropriated fund instrumen-talities of the armed forces.[40]

The Act provides for payment of benefits and medical services to cov-ered employees who suffer accidental injuries and diseases arising out of, and in the course of, their employment.[41]

[62.07]   THE JONES ACT

The Jones Act authorizes any seaman aboard vessels on U.S. navigable waters, who is injured in the course of his or her employment, to maintain an action for damages in an appropriate U.S. District Court.[42] Injured sea-men are entitled to jury trials in their causes of action against their em-ployers.[43] Certain benefits and medical expenses are paid to, or on behalf of, injured seamen under the same guidelines as paid to railroad employees who are similarly injured.[44]

NOTES TO CHAPTER 62

1. See generally 72 U.S.C.A. §501, *et seq.*
2. 42 U.S.C.A. §501, *et seq.*
3. 26 U.S.C.A. §3301, *et seq.*
4. 42 U.S.C.A. §1104.
5. 42 U.S.C.A. §1104.
6. 42 U.S.C.A. §1104.
7. 42 U.S.C.A. §503.
8. 26 U.S.C.A. §3301.
9. 26 U.S.C.A. §3302.
10. 26 U.S.C.A. §3303.
11. 26 U.S.C.A. §3304.
12. 26 U.S.C.A. §3305, §3308 and §3309.
13. 26 U.S.C.A. §3310.
14. 26 U.S.C.A. §3306(a).
15. 5 U.S.C.A. §8502 and §8521.
16. 5 U.S.C.A. §8503 and §8521.

17. 5 U.S.C.A. §8502 and §8505.

18. 5 U.S.C.A. §8502(d).

19. See generally 5 U.S.C.A. §8503.

20. 5 U.S.C.A. §8525(b).

21. See generally 45 U.S.C.A. §351, *et seq.*

22. 45 U.S.C.A. §362.

23. 45 U.S.C.A. §360 and §361.

24. 45 U.S.C.A. §352.

25. 45 U.S.C.A. §354.

26. See discussion of Social Security Appeals at [61.03].

27. 5 U.S.C.A. §8101, *et seq.*.

28. 5 U.S.C.A. §8102.

29. 5 U.S.C.A. §8102.

30. 5 U.S.C.A. §8103.

31. 5 U.S.C.A. §8107.

32. See 20 CFR §10.131 through §136.

33. 29 CFR §10.137.

34. See 33 U.S.C.A. §901, *et seq.*

35. 46 U.S.C.A. §688.

36. 33 U.S.C.A. §901.

37. 42 U.S.C.A. §1651, *et seq.*

38. See 36 D.C. Code, Section 501.

39. 43 U.S.C.A. §1333.

40. 5 U.S.C.A. §150k.

41. See generally 33 U.S.C.A. §906 through §910.

42. 46 U.S.C.A. §688, *et seq.*

43. 46 U.S.C.A. §688.

44. 46 U.S.C.A. §688.

63

Federal Privacy
and Related Laws

The Privacy Act was enacted in 1974 to safeguard an individual's rights of privacy from any unwarranted encroachment or invasion from federal agencies.[1] The Act generally requires federal agencies to maintain records of individuals in a current, accurate, and relevant manner;[2] to permit individuals to gain access to records and other information pertaining to them;[3] and to refuse to disclose records or information about individuals, except under limited conditions specified in the Act.[4]

The Act also requires each federal agency that maintains a system of records to permit an individual to request a correction to a record pertaining to him or her and, within a specified time period, either make whatever correction the individual requested or inform the individual of its refusal, the reason for the refusal, and the procedures established by the agency for the individual to request a review of the refusal.[5]

In addition, should a federal agency refuse to correct an individual's record pursuant to his or her request, it must permit the individual to request a review of such refusal and, not later than thirty days thereafter (excluding Saturdays, Sundays, and legal holidays) make a final determination pertaining to the request.[6]

Following an agency's final determination to refuse to correct an individual's records, the statute provides that the individual shall be advised of his or her right to seek judicial review of the agency's refusal.[7]

The Privacy Act of 1974 provides that a federal agency may disclose or release records of individuals, without their consent or request, under certain circumstances, such as to the Census Bureau, to satisfy the requirements of the Freedom of Information Act, etc.[8] Both civil remedies and criminal penalties may be invoked for violation of the Privacy Act.[9]

Civil actions may be brought in U.S. District Courts by individuals against federal agencies that improperly refuse to make corrections to records; fail to maintain records in an accurate, relevant, current and complete manner; or fail to comply with the disclosure prohibitions of the statute.[10]

The court may enjoin a federal agency from violating the requirements of the Act as well as assess reasonable attorney fees and litigation costs against the offending agency.[11]

Should the court find a federal agency to have acted in an intentional or willful manner in its failures to maintain appropriate records, the agency may be held liable for actual damages sustained by the individual and the costs of the action together with reasonable attorney fees.[12]

Any officer or employee of a federal agency, who by virtue of his or her position, has possession of, or access to, agency records and who willfully discloses such prohibited records to another person or agency, may be found guilty of a misdemeanor punishable by a fine of not more than $5,000.[13]

Likewise, an officer or employee of any federal agency who willfully maintains a system of records that does not meet the notice requirements for the Federal Register publication may be found guilty of a misdemeanor and subject to a fine of not more than $5,000.[14]

Any person who knowingly and willfully requests or obtains any record concerning an individual from a federal agancy under false pretenses shall be guilty of a misdemeanor and subject to a fine of not more than $5,000.[15]

[63.02]   THE FEDERAL SUNSHINE ACT

The Sunshine Act is a companion statute to the aforementioned Privacy Act and provides that meetings of federal agencies, headed by two or more persons appointed by the President, must be open to the public unless otherwise exempted.[16]

The purpose of the Sunshine Act is to provide the public with the "fullest practicable information regarding the decision-making processes of the federal government."[17]

The Sunshine Act specifically exempts certain federal agency meetings from the requirement that they be open to the public,[18] such as meetings which might disclose trade secrets, law enforcement records, classified material from the military, etc.[19]

Federal agencies are required by the Sunshine Act to promulgate regulations to implement the requirements of the statute.[20]

Should a federal agency fail or refuse to comply with the requirements of the Sunshine Act, an individual adversely affected thereby may bring an action in the appropriate U.S. District Court to seek enforcement of the requirements.[21]

[63.03]   FREEDOM OF INFORMATION ACT

The Freedom of Information Act requires federal agencies to make its rules, opinions, orders, records, and proceedings available to the general public.[22] In addition, each federal agency is required to publish certain information in the Federal Register for the guidance of the public, particularly those matters which might adversely affect members of the public,[23] including employers and employees.

Specifically, the Freedom of Information Act requires each federal agency to publish in the Federal Register:

- descriptions of its central and field organization and the established places at which, the employees from whom, and the methods whereby, the public may obtain information, make submittals or requests, or obtain decisions

- information concerning the general course and method by which its functions are channeled and determined, including the nature and requirements of all formal and informal procedures available

- procedural rules, descriptions of forms available or the places at which forms may be obtained, and instructions as to the scope and contents of all papers, reports, or examinations

- substantive rules of general applicability adopted as authorized by law, and related statements or interpretations of general policies

- amendments, revisions, or repeals of the above[24]

Federal agencies are also required by the provisions of the statute to make available for public inspections and copying, such information as final opinions and orders made in the adjudication of cases; statements of policies and interpretations that have been adopted by the agencies but not published in the Federal Register; administrative staff manuals and instructional materials that affect the public, unless such materials and information are promptly published and copies are offered for sale.[25]

Although federal agencies may be required to make certain materials and information available to the public for inspection or copying, agencies may charge a reasonable fee for document search and duplication.[26]

The Act provides that documents shall be furnished without charge, or at a reduced charge, where the agency determines that action is in the public interest.[27]

The Freedom of Information Act does not apply to personnel and medical records of an agency, geological, or geophysical information and other records, documents, and information as are similarly exempted under the Sunshine Act.[28]

Whenever a federal agency fails to comply with the provisions and requirements of the Freedom of Information Act, an action may be brought in the appropriate U.S. District Court to enforce compliance.[29]

[63.04] THE FAIR CREDIT REPORTING ACT

The Federal Fair Credit Reporting Act also provides certain rights to applicants and employees.[30] Under this particular statute an employer may not procure an investigative consumer report on an applicant for employment or an employee unless the employer

- delivers or mails a written notice to the applicant or employee that a consumer investigative report (including information as to his or her character, general reputation, personal characteristics, and mode of living) will be made, and

- provides a complete disclosure of the nature and scope of the investigation, upon request of the applicant or employee.[31]

The Act also provides that whenever employment is denied, either wholly or partly because of information contained in a consumer report from a consumer reporting agency, the employer shall so advise the applicant or employee against whom such adverse action has been taken and supply the name and address of the consumer reporting agency making the report.[32]

Any consumer reporting agency or employer using information obtained from such an agency that willfully or negligently fails to comply with the requirements of The Fair Credit Reporting Act may be held liable for damages to the suffering party through a cause of action in an appropriate U.S. District Court.[33]

[63.05] EQUAL ACCESS TO JUSTICE ACT

The Equal Access to Justice Act was enacted to diminish the deterrent effect of certain individuals, partnerships, corporations, and labor and other organizations from seeking review of, or defending against, governmental action by providing in specified situations an award of attorney fees, expert witness fees, and other costs against the United States.[34]

The Act requires federal agencies that conduct an adversary proceeding to award reasonable fees of expert witnesses, the reasonable cost of any study, analysis, engineering report, test, or project that is found by the agency to be necessary for the preparation of the party's case, and reasonable attorney or agent fees incurred in the preparation and defense of the proceedings to the prevailing party, unless the adjudicative officer of the agency finds that the position of the agency as a party to the proceedings was substantially justified or that special circumstances would make an award unjust.[35]

However, a party seeking an award of fees and other expenses must, within thirty days of a final disposition in the adversary adjudication, submit an application for such fees and expenses directly to the applicable agency in order to be eligible for such fees or expenses.[36]

Individuals whose net worth exceeds $1 million at the time the adversary adjudication is initiated, any sole owner or an unincorporated business, corporation, association or organization whose net worth exceeds $5 million at the time the adversary adjudication is initiated, or any sole owner of an entity having more than 500 employees at the time the adversary adjudication is initiated are not eligible recipients under the statute.[37]

[63.06] OMNIBUS CRIME CONTROL AND SAFE STREETS ACT

This statute prohibits deliberate interceptions of wire and oral communications between two individuals.[38] Thus, employers who intercept confidential information about an employee or employees, by or through such means, without proper consent, may violate the Act.[39]

A party who suffers adversely as a result of an employer's violation of the Act is entitled to a private cause of action against the offending employer for damages and cost.[40] However, courts have been reluctant to sustain damages against employers who demonstrate that the conversation monitored on the telephone was done in the ordinary course of the employer's business.[41]

[63.07] FEDERAL "WHISTLE-BLOWING" STATUTE

The Civil Service Reform Act of 1978 forbids, among other actions, federal officials to retaliate against an applicant for employment or an employee, for disclosing information he or she believes to be a violation of any law, rule, regulation, or mismanagement, a gross waste of funds, an abuse of authority, or a substantial danger to public health and safety.[42]

The statute, sometimes referred to as the federal "whistle-blowing" statute, empowers an Office of Special Counsel to investigate claims of reprisals taken against federal employees (or applicants) who report violations of federal laws and regulations, waste of public funds, and abuse of power by government officials.[43]

[63.08] EMPLOYMENT RIGHTS OF ALIENS

The Immigration and Nationality Act of 1972 was enacted to administer programs to the admission of immigrant aliens and temporary foreign workers for employment opportunities in the United States.[44] Admission is limited, however, and certification for alien employment is to be permitted only when there is a showing that American workers are not available for the work in question and, further, that the wages and working conditions in the job will not adversely affect similarly employed workers in the United States.[45]

NOTES TO CHAPTER 63

1. 5 U.S.C.A. §552a; 5 CFR §297.101.
2. 5 U.S.C.A. §552a(e).
3. 5 U.S.C.A. §552a(d).
4. 5 U.S.C.A. §552a(b).
5. 5 U.S.C.A. §552a(d)(2).
6. 5 U.S.C.A. §552a(d)(3).
7. 5 U.S.C.A. §552a(d)(3).
8. 5 U.S.C.A. §552a(b)(1) through (11).
9. 5 U.S.C.A. §552a(g) and (i).

10. See generally 5 U.S.C.A. §552a(g).
11. 5 U.S.C.A. §552a(g)(2) and (3).
12. 5 U.S.C.A. §552a(g)(4).
13. 5 U.S.C.A. §552a(i).
14. 5 U.S.C.A. §552a(i).
15. 5 U.S.C.A. §552a(i).
16. 5 U.S.C.A. §552b.
17. 5 U.S.C.A. §552b.
18. 5 U.S.C.A. §552b(c).
19. 5 U.S.C.A. §552b(c)(1) through (10).
20. 5 U.S.C.A. §552b(g).
21. 5 U.S.C.A. §552b(h).
22. See generally 5 U.S.C.A. §552.
23. 5 U.S.C.A. §552(a)(1).
24. 5 U.S.C.A. §552(a)(1)(A) through (E).
25. 5 U.S.C.A. §552(a)(2)(A), (B), and (C).
26. 5 U.S.C.A. §552(a)(4)(A).
27. 5 U.S.C.A. §552(a)(4)(A).
28. 5 U.S.C.A. §552(b)(1) through (9).
29. 5 U.S.C.A. §552(a)(4).
30. 15 U.S.C.A. §1681d.
31. 15 U.S.C.A. §1681d.
32. 15 U.S.C.A. §1681m.
33. 15 U.S.C.A. §1681n, 1681o and 1681p.
34. P.L. 96–481 (October 21, 1980); see also 5 U.S.C.A. §504.
35. 5 U.S.C.A. §504(a)(2).
36. 5 U.S.C.A. §504(a).
37. 5 U.S.C.A. §504b(a)(B).
38. 18 U.S.C.A. §2510, *et seq.*.
39. See generally 18 U.S.C.A. §2510, *et seq.*
40. 18 U.S.C.A. §2520.
41. See, for example: *Briggs v. American Air Filter Co., Inc.*, 630 F.2d 414 (CA-5, 1980).
42. See 5 U.S.C.A. §2302(b)(8).
43. See generally 5 U.S.C.A. §2301, *et seq.*
44. 8 U.S.C.A. §1104.
45. 8 U.S.C.A. §1104, *et seq.*

PART VI

STATE LABOR LAWS

64

Introduction to State Labor and Employment Laws

Both federal and state legislators have enacted a variety of laws designed to regulate labor relations and protect certain employee rights.

The federal labor laws have been previously discussed in Chapters 1 through 63; state labor laws are discussed in the remaining chapters.

Where both federal and state governments have enacted laws regulating the same subject matter, but which conflict with each other, a question arises as to which statute controls. Such question is basically determined by the supremacy clause (clause 2 of Article VI) of the U.S. Constitution, which provides that the laws of the United States shall be the supreme and controlling laws of the land, and state judges, as well as federal judges, shall be bound by such laws.

As a result of this constitutional provision, state legislators who desire to regulate labor and employment laws within their boundaries must ascertain to what extent federal laws govern the proposed legislation.

There are many areas pertaining to labor and employment matters that have not been addressed by federal statutes. It is within this remaining arena that state governments have promulgated labor and employment legislation confined in application to their own respective jurisdictions.

Therefore, labor attorneys and personnel practitioners who are faced with a given issue regarding labor and employment law should first look to the federal statutes, as discussed in Chapters 1 through 63, and then observe state statutes, as discussed in Chapters 66 through 116, for appropriate references and analysis.

Chapters 66 through 116 of this book are devoted to a discussion of state statutory laws that govern labor relations and protect employee and employer rights. Chapters 66 through 116 are subdivided into decimalized subheadings for ease of discussion and comprehension. These subheadings consist of the following.

[64.01] STATE LABOR RELATIONS LAWS

Collective bargaining laws: The ''.01'' subheadings of Chapters 66 through 116 are devoted to a discussion of various collective bargaining statutes relating to private and public sector employees within a given state. For example, several states have enacted collective bargaining statutes relating to agricultural employees, a group of employees unprotected by the Labor Management Relations Act. Other states have enacted little ''Taft-Hartley'' laws, patterned after the federal statute of the same name. Many states have also enacted collective bargaining laws which inure to the protection and interest of state and other public sector employees, such as teachers and firefighters.

Right-to-work: The ".01" subheadings also discuss the right-to-work posture of each state. For example, the remaining chapters reflect that some twenty-one of the fifty states have enacted right-to-work legislation, namely:

- Alabama
- Arizona
- Arkansas
- Florida
- Georgia
- Idaho
- Iowa
- Kansas
- Louisiana
- Mississippi
- Nebraska
- Nevada
- North Carolina
- North Dakota
- South Carolina
- South Dakota
- Tennessee
- Texas
- Utah
- Virginia
- Wyoming

The remaining twenty-nine states have not adopted right-to-work statutes pursuant to the authority of Section 14(b) of the National Labor Relations Act, and consequently, permit union security clauses in collective bargaining contracts. As noted earlier, the provisions of the Railway Labor Act, which permit compulsory unionism in relation to railroad and airline employees, supersede state "right-to-work" statutes by operation of the supremacy doctrine.

"Yellow-dog" contracts: Most states have enacted statutes which make it unlawful for anyone to coerce or compel any person to enter into an agreement not to join or become a member of any labor union as a condition of employment. These commonly referred to "yellow-dog" contracts and the state statutes that forbid them are likewise discussed under the ".01" decimalized subheading in the remaining chapters.

[64.02] STATE STRIKE, PICKETING, AND BOYCOTT LAWS

Striker replacements and strikebreakers: The ".02" subheadings of Chapters 66 through 116 are utilized to discuss various state laws relating to striker replacements and strikebreakers. For example, many state statutes require notification to prospective employees of the existence of a work stoppage or lockout.

Various states also forbid employers to utilize professional strikebreakers to replace employees who are participating in a strike or lockout.

Other statutes relating to *unlawful assembly, secondary boycotting, jurisdictional disputes, mass picketing, interference with lawful employment, picketing at res-*

idence or dwelling, and *anti-injunction laws* are also discussed under the ".02" subheadings in Chapters 66 through 116 as to those states having such laws.

[64.03] STATE MEDIATION AND ARBITRATION LAWS

Under subheading ".03," state statutes relating to mediation, conciliation, and arbitration are addressed. For example, several states have adopted the Uniform Arbitration Act recognizing any written agreement to submit an existing controversy to arbitration as valid, enforceable and irrevocable, excepting such grounds as exist at law or equity for the revocation of such agreements.

Other state statutes regulating the mediation duties of certain state officials are discussed under the ".03" subheadings.

[64.04] STATE STATUTES REGULATING UNION ACTIVITIES

The ".04" subheading of Chapters 66 through 116 is utilized to discuss state regulation or union activities. For example, many states have enacted statutes forbidding the forgery or misuse of union labels. Some state statutes require unions to register with certain state officials, while other state laws require labor unions to furnish certain financial statements to the state and/or to their members.

This subheading discusses these statutes as well as those state laws regulating the conduct of union officials, administration of welfare and pension funds, and the degree to which unions are permitted to restrain the shipment of goods through collective bargaining contracts. State laws relating to anti-trust provisions and the right of unions to incorporate are likewise discussed under this particular subheading in Chapters 66 through 116.

[64.05] STATE STATUTES REGULATING EMPLOYMENT PRACTICES

The ".05" subheadings of Chapters 66 through 116 provide a discussion of state statutes that regulate a host of employment practices. Some of the topics discussed under this subheading include:

- Anti-Discrimination Laws
- Access to Employment Records
- Arrest Records
- Blacklisting

- Credit Bureau Requirements
- Deceptive Advertising
- Disclosure of Consumer Reports
- Employment Under False Pretenses
- Employment of Illegal Aliens
- Electronic Surveillance Forbidden
- Fraudulent Receipt of Advancements
- Fingerprinting Restrictions
- Jury Service Requirements
- Importation of Migratory Farm Workers
- Lie Detector Limitations
- Medical Information Confidentiality Requirements
- Misrepresentation of Employment Opportunities
- Military Leaves of Absence
- Protection of Political Freedom and Voting Privileges
- Protection of Political Activities
- Protection of Railroad Employees
- Physical Examination Restrictions
- Rights of State Employees
- Selection of Physicians
- Service Letter Requirements
- Re-Employment Rights of Military Personnel
- Relocation of Severance Pay
- Shut-Down Requirements
- Successor Clauses
- Unlawful Enticement of Employees
- Use of Detectives as "Spotters"
- Union Dues Deduction
- "Whistle-Blowing" Protection
- Witness Protection

Obviously, some states have more statutes on the above topics than do others. Only those states that have enacted such legislation are discussed with respect to these topics in the following chapters. (As with other subheadings in Chapters 66 through 116, whenever there is no discussion as to a particular topic, it reflects that no statute had been implemented in the subject matter as of this writing.)

[64.06] STATE WAGE AND HOUR LAWS

The ''.06'' subheadings in Chapters 66 through 116 are devoted to a discussion of the wage and hour laws of the respective states. For example, state *child labor laws*, *equal pay*, *payment of wages*, and *payment upon termination* are all discussed within the ''.06'' subheading.

State statutes requiring employers to allow their employees *time off to vote*, *garnishment restrictions*, and *medical insurance continuance requirements* are also covered under this subheading.

[64.07] STATE SAFETY AND HEALTH LAWS

Subheading ''.07'' of Chapters 66 through 116 deals with a discussion of state safety and health laws. Most states have enacted some type of legislation that places a duty on employers within their boundaries to provide a safe work place for their employees. State legislation with respect to *toxic substances* are also discussed in this subheading.

Many state statutes typically require employers, as well as employees, to comply with prescribed occupational safety and health standards as provided in various regulations and orders issued in connection therewith.

[64.08] STATE UNEMPLOYMENT COMPENSATION LAWS

Subheading ''.08'' of Chapters 66 through 116 makes reference to state unemployment insurance laws. As discussed earlier, state unemployment insurance programs are governed by a dual system of federal and state laws. The federal system of unemployment insurance is governed by the Federal Unemployment Tax Act, a part of the Social Security Act and the Internal Revenue Code, the provisions of which impose certain eligibility and qualification requirements upon potential recipients of unemployment insurance benefits.[1]

State unemployment insurance statutes typically establish procedures for the distribution of unemployment funds within the state. Although state statutes customarily establish their own eligibility and qualifying criteria relative to their unemployment insurance programs, such statutes must defer to the federal guidelines when a conflict arises.

Most state unemployment insurance laws specify those employers and employees who are exempt from coverage of the statute's provisions.

[64.09] STATE WORKERS' COMPENSATION LAWS

The ''.09'' subheadings in Chapters 66 through 116 are devoted to a discussion of the state workers' compensation laws.

Unlike unemployment insurance laws, there is no dual system of legislation relating to workers' compensation benefits. Federal workers' compensation laws enacted for the benefit of various federal employees have been previously discussed.[2]

As to other private and public sector employees, the individual states have adopted a variety of workers' compensation legislation.

States typically enact workers' compensation statutes as an exclusive remedy to redress job-related injuries, deaths, and occupational illnesses. At common law, an employee had the burden of proving negligence or intentional misconduct on the part of his or her employer, as well as overcoming such defenses as contributory negligence, assumption of the risk, and the fellow servant doctrine, in order to establish a cause of action sufficient to recover damages for job-related injuries, deaths, or occupational illnesses.[3]

Workers' compensation statutes have been enacted to permit employees to recover regulated compensation for injuries, deaths, or occupational illnesses sustained during, arising out of, and in the course of the employees' employment without requiring a showing of fault on the part of the employer.

State workers' compensation statutes vary as to specific coverage. Some state statutes are elective in nature, granting to an employer and employee the right to accept or reject the provisions thereof. Most state workers' compensation laws are more compulsory in character.[4]

Many of the state workers' compensation laws permit ordinary remedies at law for an injury or death resulting to an employee because of some willful act or gross negligence on the part of an employer.[5] Also, many state workers' compensation statutes provide that recovery of benefits will be denied those employees who sustain on-the-job injuries due to their own serious and/or willful misconduct. Also frequently excluded from compensability are those injuries which are purposely self-inflicted or intentionally produced by the complaining employee.[6]

[64.10] EMPLOYMENT-AT-WILL DEVELOPMENTS

Subheading ''.10'' addresses judicial developments in the state courts with respect to employee rights and responsibilities in the work place.

In recent years, state courts have been most active in addressing employee rights and responsibilities through newly established legal precedent. The most noticeable trend of state courts has been the recognition of certain exceptions to the historic employment-at-will doctrine.

Chapter 65 is devoted to a discussion of the latest developments in the area of employment-at-will. Moreover, the ''.10'' subheadings in Chapters 66 through 116 are utilized to discuss the peculiar developments within each respective state as to the employment-at-will question, lending itself, in turn, to an overall state-by-state analysis of the subject matter.

NOTES TO CHAPTER 64

1. See Chapter 62 for a more complete discussion of Federal Unemployment Insurance Statutes.

2. See Chapter 62 for a more complete discussion of Federal Worker Compensation Statutes.

3. Robert H. Gibbs and Dan Siegel, *Guide to Labor Law* §6.02, 2d ed. (New York: Clark Boardman Company, Ltd., 1984).

4. 81 *Am. Jur.*2d, *Workmen's Compensation*, §39.

5. 81 *Am. Jur.*2d, *Workmen's Compensation*, §359.

6. 81 *Am. Jur.*2d, *Workmen's Compensation*, §231-235.

65

Employment-at-Will Developments

State courts are not only confronted with continuously increasing state statutory laws governing employee rights, but must also come to terms with similarly developing judicial trends regarding individual rights in the work place.

The most noticeable judicial trend in this area has been an emergence toward the protection of employees against unjust dismissals and a slow, but steady, erosion of the century-old employment-at-will doctrine.

[65.01]   HISTORICAL DOCTRINE

Since 1877, at least, the traditional common-law rule in the United States has been that an employee, without benefit of a contractual agreement to the contrary, or protected from such adverse action by federal or state statute, is considered to be employed at the will of his or her employer and may be terminated at any time, without notice and with or without just cause.[1]

By the latter part of the 19th century, the employment-at-will doctrine was firmly entrenched into the American judicial process and resoundingly echoed in such judicial comment as:[2]

> All [employers] may dismiss their employees at will, be they many or few, for good cause, for no cause, or even for cause morally wrong, without being thereby guilty of legal wrong.

The employment-at-will doctrine in the United States is seemingly founded upon the rationale that inasmuch as an employee, not under contract, may not be compelled to perform personal service, an employer should not be compelled to provide employment.[3]

[65.02]   STATUTORY EROSION OF THE AT-WILL DOCTRINE

Although the employment-at-will doctrine is yet judicially sound in some states, federal and state statutes have greatly eroded the right of an employer to discharge employees at his or her pleasure.

Some of the federal laws that limit the employment-at-will doctrine by prohibiting discrimination or retaliation, most of which have heretofore been discussed in preceding chapters, include

- Labor Management Relations Act;[4]
- Fair Labor Standards Act;[5]
- Title VII, Civil Rights Act of 1964;[6]
- Age Discrimination in Employment Act of 1967;[7]

- Rehabilitation Act of 1973;[8]
- Employee Retirement Income Security Act of 1974;[9]
- The Vietnam Era Veterans Readjustment Assistance Act;[10]
- Energy Reorganization Act of 1974;[11]
- Clean Air Act;[12]
- Civil Service Reform Act of 1978;[13]
- Consumer Credit Protection Act;[14]
- Federal Water Pollution Control Act;[15]
- Judiciary and Judicial Procedure Act;[16]
- Railway Labor Act;[17] and the
- Railroad Safety Act[18]

Various state statutes have also made substantial inroads into the historic employment-at-will doctrine, as will be more fully discussed in Chapters 66 through 116.

[65.03] PUBLIC POLICY EXCEPTIONS TO THE AT-WILL DOCTRINE

Several state courts have developed exceptions to the termination-at-will principle when employees are discharged in contravention of some substantial public policy principle.[19]

Most state court decisions that have modified the employment-at-will doctrine, based upon public policy considerations, involve discharge for one of the following:

- refusal to commit an unlawful act
- reporting violations of law
- exercising a statutory right or privilege
- performing a public obligation
- upholding the law

Discharge for refusal to commit an unlawful act: Some of the more active litigation involving public policy considerations relate to dismissals based upon a refusal to commit a crime or unlawful act. For example, a California Appellate Court reversed a lower court's dismissal of a case in which the plaintiff alleged he was discharged for refusing to testify falsely before a legislative committee.[20] In a later California case in which an employee alleged that his dismissal was based upon a refusal to participate in an illegal price-fixing scheme, the California Supreme Court ruled that an employer cannot condition continual employment on an employee's participation in unlawful conduct and held the employer liable for damages to the discharged employee.[21]

Similarly, the New York Appellate Division upheld a lower court's denial of an employer's motion to dismiss where the plaintiff had alleged wrongful discharge for having refused to participate with other employees and superiors in unspecified unlawful conduct.[22]

New Jersey Superior Court, in disregard of the termination at-will rule, held actionable a plaintiff's case alleging wrongful dismissal based upon an X-ray technician's refusal to perform a catheterization of a patient, a procedure permitted only by a licensed physician or nurse under state law.[23]

In Michigan, the State Court of Appeals ruled that a plaintiff who allegedly had been discharged for refusal to illegally manipulate and adjust sampling results for state pollution reports had a cause of action, and went on to cite that:

> [A]n employer-at-will is not free to discharge an employee when the reason for the discharge is an intention on the part of the employer to contravene the public policy of state.[24]

Discharge for reporting violations of law: Although several states have enacted "whistle-blowing" statutes to forbid discharges of employees who report or disclose alleged violations of law, many state courts have permitted such employees a right of action in common law as well. For example, the Illinois Supreme Court held actionable a case in which a plaintiff alleged his dismissal from employment was based on his supplying information to police about the suspected wrongdoing of a fellow employee.[25] The Connecticut Supreme Court sustained a plaintiff's cause of action in a case in which the plaintiff was discharged because he continually called to his employer's attention the employer's repeated violations of the Connecticut Uniform Food, Drug and Cosmetic Act.[26] The West Virginia Supreme Court of Appeals held actionable a case in which a plaintiff was discharged in retaliation for bringing to the attention of his employer a violation of the West Virginia Consumer Credit and Protection Act.[27]

Discharge for exercising a statutory right: As with various federal laws previously discussed, state laws frequently contain anti-reprisal provisions that are designed to protect employees in the exercise of their rights under such statutes. Some state courts have held, even in the absence of a statutorily imposed anti-reprisal provision, that employees are protected against retaliatory dismissals at common law. An example of a judicially imposed anti-reprisal sanction is found in a 1973 Indiana case in which the Indiana Supreme Court recognized a private cause of action for a plaintiff who had been discharged for having filed a wokers' compensation claim, even though the Indiana workers' compensation laws did not bar the employer from such action.[28]

Discharge for performing a public obligation or upholding a law:
Some state courts have also ruled that an employee who has been dismissed
for upholding a public law or performing a public obligation has a common
law cause of action, notwithstanding the employment-at-will doctrine. An
example of this modification to the termination-at-will rule is found in a
1975 Oregon case in which the Oregon Supreme Court held a plaintiff's
suit actionable wherein the plaintiff alleged she had been discharged after
making herself available for jury duty in contravention of her employer's
desires.[29]

[65.04]   IMPLIED COVENANTS OF GOOD FAITH
AND FAIR DEALINGS

Courts in a number of state jurisdictions have made exceptions to the traditional employment-at-will doctrine on the principle that an implied covenant of good faith and fair dealing exists in employment relationships,
the violation of which sustains a private right of action.[30]

An example of the implied covenant theory is reflected in a 1977 Massachusetts case in which a plaintiff, a commissioned salesperson with some
twenty-five years of seniority, was discharged from his employment as an
effort to avoid paying him a $92,000 bonus following his obtaining an un-
expected sales order in the amount of $5,000,000.[31] Holding that the dis-
charge violated an implied covenant of good faith and fair dealing in the
employment relationship with the employee, the Massachusetts Supreme
Judicial court sustained the plaintiff's cause of action.[32]

In a case decided in 1974 and prior to the sexual harassment regulations, the New Hampshire Supreme Court upheld a jury verdict in favor
of a plaintiff who had been discharged because she had refused to date her
supervisor.[33] Although the plaintiff had sued under tort theory claiming her
discharge was abusive and in bad faith, the court applied the implied covenant of good faith and fair dealing doctrine and ruled as follows:

> We hold that a termination by the employer of a contract of employment-
> at-will which is motivated in bad faith or malice or based on retaliation
> is not in the best interest of the economic system or the public good and
> constitutes a breach of the employment contract.[34]

[65.05]   "GOOD CAUSE" REQUIREMENTS
FOR TERMINATION

Although the implied covenant exception to the employment-at-will doctrine
was based initially on a judicial inference from the employment relationship
itself, later cases suggest that an implied covenant of good faith and fair
dealing may be inferred by an employer's own policies regarding such commitments.

A 1980 California case appears to be such an example.[35] In this particular case, the California Court of Appeals reversed a lower court's grant of summary judgment for the defendant and held that the plaintiff, who had been allegedly discharged without good cause after 18 years of service, was entitled to an implied covenant of good faith and fair dealing from the defendant-employer inasmuch as the employer had mandated such a covenant in the employer's own policies.[36]

In a 1981 California case, the California Court of Appeals held that employment contracts are terminable only for good cause if such contract was supported by consideration independent of services to be performed by the employee, or the parties agreed, expressly or impliedly, that good cause be required for termination.[37]

[65.06] IMPLIED CONDITIONS IN PERSONNEL MANUALS AND HANDBOOKS

The employment-at-will doctrine has been further eroded in recent years on the premise that an employer is subject to those employment conditions implied within his or her own personnel policy manuals and employee handbooks.

The most publicized case regarding this particular exception to the employment-at-will principle is a 1980 Michigan case in which the Michigan Supreme Court held that a provision in an employer's personnel policy manual or employee handbook which is unilaterally and voluntarily adopted by an employer, distributed to employees, and which provides that a discharge will only be for good cause, protects employees from discharge in the absence of a showing of good cause.[38]

This "implied-in-fact" contract theory has been adopted by several other state courts. For example, a 1982 New York case holds that an action may lie for a breach of contract against a former employer who discharges an employee without just and sufficient cause in contravention of statements made in the employer's handbook that employees may be discharged only for just cause.[39]

[65.07] THE PROMISSORY ESTOPPEL EXCEPTION

The promissory estoppel doctrine, in principle, forbids an individual to renege on a promise to another whenever the latter has reasonably relied upon the promise to his or her detriment.

This promissory estoppel principle of law has been used by several employees to attempt to convince courts that it is a proper exception to the at-will doctrine. In a 1981 Minnesota case,[40] for example, the Minnesota court ruled that the promissory estoppel doctrine was applicable as an exception to the at-will principle when the plaintiff was offered a position with the defendant, resigned his old position upon the reliance that he had the position, only to be informed later that the position was being abolished and he would need to find work elsewhere.

[65.08] THE TORTIOUS DISCHARGE EXCEPTION

A few courts have upheld wrongful discharge actions on the theory that the termination of an employee occurred under circumstances so outrageous that the dismissal gave rise to a cause of action for intentional infliction of emotional distress.[41]

Another court, finding that an employer had breached the employer's implied duty to conduct the plaintiff's performance evaluation in a timely and fair manner, held the defendant negligent in the defendant's duty to use ordinary or reasonable care in performing the plaintiff's review, and thereby liable in tort damages for the defendant's negligent discharge.[42]

[65.09] IMPACT OF THE DOCTRINE

Although the employment-at-will doctrine remains the basic rule of law in most states, there appears to be more exceptions to the rule than what remains of the rule. Given the trend in recent years to expand the exceptions further, one must assume that the doctrine will continue to lose in future years whatever impact it has left.

As noted earlier in Chapter 64, the subheading ".10" in the Chapters 66 through 116 will be utilized to discuss the employment-at-will developments as to each state.

NOTES TO CHAPTER 65

1. H. G. Wood, *Law of Master and Servant,* 2d ed., §134 (Albany, NY: J. D. Parsons, Jr., 1877), 272–273.

2. *Payne v. Western & Atlantic Railroad,* 81 Tenn. 507, 519–520 (1884).

3. *Adair v. United States,* 208 U.S. 161 (1908).

4. 29 U.S.C.A. §151, *et seq.*

5. 29 U.S.C.A. §215.

6. 42 U.S.C.A. §2000e-2 and §2000e-3(a).

7. 29 U.S.C.A. §621&734.

8. 29 U.S.C.A. §794.

9. 29 U.S.C.A. §1140, 1141.

10. 38 U.S.C.A. §2021(b)(1), 2024(c).

11. 42 U.S.C.A. §5851.

12. 42 U.S.C.A. §7622.

13. 5 U.S.C.A. §7513(a).

14. 15 U.S.C.A. §1674(c).

15. 33 U.S.C.A. §1367.

16. 28 U.S.C.A. §1875.

17. 45 U.S.C.A. §152 (3).

18. 45 U.S.C.A. §441(a) and (b)(1).

19. *Peterman v. International Brotherhood of Teamsters, Local 396*, 174 Cal. App. 2d 184, 344 P.2d 25 (1959).

20. *Peterman v. International Brotherhood of Teamsters, Local 396, supra.*

21. *Tameny v. Atlantic Richfield Co.*, 27 Cal. 3d 167, 610 P.2d 1330 (1980).

22. *McCullough v. Certain Teed Products Corp.*, 70 A.D. 2d 771, 417 N.Y.S. 2d 353 (4th Dep't 1979).

23. *O'Sullivan v. Mallon*, 160 N.J. Super. 416, 390 A.2d 149 (1978).

24. *Trombetta v. Detroit, Toledo & Ironton Railroad Co.*, 81 Mich. Appl 489, 265 N.W. 2d 385 (1978).

25. *Palamateer v. International Harvester Co.*, 85 Ill. 2d 124, 421 N.E. 2d 876 (1981).

26. *Sheets v. Teddy's Frosted Foods, Inc.*, 179 Conn. 471 (1980).

27. *Harless v. First National Bank in Fairmont*, 246 S.E. 2d 270 (Sup. Crt. Appl, W.Va. 1978).

28. *Frampton v. Central Indiana Gas Co.*, 260 Ind. 249, 297 N.E. 2d 425.

29. *Nees v. Hocks*, 272 Or. 210, 536 P.2d 512 (1975).

30. *Monge v. Beebe Rubber Co.*, 114 N.H. 130, 316 A.2d 549 (1974).

31. *Fortune v. National Cash Register Co.*, 363 Mass. 96, 364 N.E. 2d 1251 (1977).

32. *Fortune v. National Cash Register Co., supra.*

33. *Monge v. Beebe Rubber Co., supra.*

34. *Monge v. Beebe Rubber Co., supra.*

35. *Cleary v. American Airlines, Inc.*, 111 Cal. App. 3d 443, 168 Cal. Rptr. 722 (1980).

36. *Cleary v. American Airlines, Inc., supra.*

37. *Pugh v. See's Candies, Inc.*, 116 Cal. App. 3d 311, 171 Cal. Rptr. 917 (1981).

38. *Toussaint v. Blue Cross & Blue Shield of Michigan*, 408 Mich. 579, 292 N.W. 2d 880 (1980).

39. *Weiner v. McGraw-Hill, Inc.*, 57 N.W. 2d 458 (1982).

40. *Grouse v. Group Health Plan, Inc.*, 306 N.W. 2d 114 (Minn. 1981).

41. *M.B.M. Company, Inc. v. Counce*, 596 S.W. 2d 681 (Ark. 1980); *Bodewig v. K-Mart, Inc.*, 635 P.2d 657 (Or. App. 1981).

42. *Chamberlain v. Bissell, Inc.*, 31 EPD Para. 33,367 (W.D. Mich, 1982).

66

Alabama
Labor Laws

[66.01] LABOR RELATIONS LAWS

Collective bargaining rights of firefighters: Although Alabama has no labor relations act comparable to the federal "Taft-Hartley Act," there is a law permitting the right of firefighters to self-organization.[1]

Right-to-work statute: Alabama has enacted a right-to-work statute, pursuant to the authority of Section 14(b) of the Labor Management Relations Act.[2] Employers are forbidden to require any person to become or remain a member of any labor union or labor organization,[3] or to pay any dues, fees, or other charges of any kind to any labor union or organization, as a condition of employment or continuation of employment.[4]

[66.02] STRIKES, PICKETING, AND BOYCOTT LAWS

Conspiracy to interfere with business: Alabama has a statute that forbids two or more persons, without a just cause or legal excuse for doing so, to conspire for the purpose of preventing any other persons, firms, corporations, or associations of persons from carrying on any lawful business.[5] (However, in view of a U.S. Supreme Court decision[6] and the provisions of the Norris-LaGuardia Act,[7] the applicability of this statute in labor disputes is probably limited to acts of violence, threats, mass picketing, and other injurious conduct occurring during strikes, boycotts, or other pickets.)

Interference with employment relationship: Sections 27-7-9 of the Alabama Code prohibits any person or firm to attempt to interfere with the lawful employment of another.

[66.03] MEDIATION AND ARBITRATION LAWS

Section 25-7-50 of the Alabama Code provides for the submission of grievances or labor disputes between employers and employees to a local board of arbitrators for hearing and settlement. The statute further establishes the procedures to select arbitrators and to conduct the hearing.[8]

[66.04] REGULATION OF UNION ACTIVITIES

The regulation of union activities in Alabama is controlled by the Bradford Act, codified in Sections 25-7-1, *et seq.* of the Alabama Code. Among other things, the Bradford Act requires unions to file copies of contributions, by-laws, and amendments thereto, as well as annual financial reports, with the Alabama Department of Labor. The Bradford Act also protects the right of labor unions to adopt and use union labels for the purpose of designating and distinguishing products and goods produced by union labor.

[66.05] REGULATION OF EMPLOYMENT PRACTICES

Jury duty: Section 12-16-8 of the Alabama Code requires employers to excuse employees from work for the day or days required of them to serve as a juror in any Alabama Court. It also requires an employer to pay such employees their usual compensation during such periods, less the fee or compensation they received as jury pay.[9]

Blacklisting: Section 13A-11-123 of the Alabama Code forbids blacklisting. The statute forbids the maintenance of a blacklist and the use by any means to attempt to prevent any person from receiving employment from whomsoever he or she so desires. Anyone violating this statute is guilty of a misdemeanor.

Resident workmen requirements: Section 39-3-2 of the Alabama Code requires all public works within the state, including municipalities, to employ only employees who have actually resided in the state for at least two years prior to employment, unless no qualified employees can be found within the state for such job openings.

[66.06] WAGE AND HOUR LAWS

Child labor: With few exceptions, employment of children under 14 years of age is forbidden by Alabama laws.[10] The statute also limits the hours and occupations for employees under 16 years of age.[11] In addition, children under 18 years of age are restricted from certain specified occupations.[12] The statute requires age and employment certificates for many minor employees as a prerequisite to their employment.[13]

Voting: The Alabama statutes provide that employees are entitled to vote free of intimidation from their employers.[14]

Wage claims: Section 25-3-2 of the Alabama Code charges the commissioner of the Department of Labor with the duty of investigating and attempting to adjust wage claims in an equitable manner.

[66.07] SAFETY AND HEALTH LAWS

The Alabama statutes require employers to provide a safe work environment for employees, furnish and use safety devices and safeguards, adopt and use methods and processes reasonably adequate to render such employment and places where employment is performed reasonably safe, and do everything reasonably possible to protect life, health, and safety of their employees.[15]

[66.08] UNEMPLOYMENT COMPENSATION LAWS

Unemployment compensation benefits are available to Alabama employees who satisfy certain basic requirements such as

- being capable of performing work
- filing a proper and timely claim
- registering for work with the state agency and regularly reporting to the agency
- satisfying the waiting requirements of the Act, etc.[16]

A claimant may be disqualified from receiving benefits for a variety of reasons specified in the statute such as

- leaving his or her employment voluntarily without good cause connected to such work
- being discharged for dishonest or criminal acts committed in connection with the work
- failing to either apply for or accept available, suitable work without sufficient justification, or
- failing to work due to sickness or disability, etc.[17]

[66.09] WORKERS' COMPENSATION LAWS

The workers' compensation laws of Alabama are found in Sections 25-5-1, *et seq.* of the Alabama Code. The statute provides a schedule of compensation benefits to be awarded to employees who suffer injury or death as a result of an accident arising out of and in the course of their employment.[18]

Benefits and payments are paid to employees in accordance with established schedules, the amount and duration of which are dependent upon the gravity of the injury or occupational disease, and whether the disability is temporary or permanent and/or partial or total. Alabama law forbids discharge of an employee because he or she has filed a workers' compensation claim.[19]

[66.10] EMPLOYMENT-AT-WILL DEVELOPMENTS

Alabama courts have recognized certain exceptions to the employment-at-will doctrine.

"**Independent consideration**" **exception:** Alabama courts have held a contract for "permanent" employment to be outside the employment-at-will rule whenever an employee provides consideration, independent of the regular employment services to be performed.[20]

Implied contract exception: Although recent Alabama cases[21] have not recognized an implied contract flowing from a personnel policy as an exception to the at-will principle, a 1931 Alabama case suggested that a statement in an employer's personnel policy that employees were employed for an indefinite period might constitute an enforceable contract.[22]

Intentional infliction of emotional distress exception: The Alabama Supreme Court has held actionable a wrongful discharge case in which the plaintiff was continuously harassed on the job due to her pregnancy and suffered a miscarriage one week following her termination, the court ruling that such outrageous discharge falls outside the employment-at-will principle in Alabama.[23]

NOTES TO CHAPTER 66

1. See Code of Alabama, Sections 11-43-143 and 11-43-144.
2. See Code of Alabama, Section 25-7-30, *et seq.*
3. Code of Alabama, Section 25-7-32.
4. Code of Alabama, Section 25-7-34.
5. Code of Alabama, Section 13A-11-122.
6. *Garner v. Teamsters Union*, 346 U.S. 485 (1953).
7. The Norris-LaGuardia Act is discussed in Chapter 29.
8. Code of Alabama, Section 25-7-50, *et seq.*
9. Code of Alabama, Section 12-16-8.
10. Code of Alabama, Section 25-8-5.
11. Code of Alabama, Sections 25-8-4 and 25-8-2.
12. Code of Alabama, Sections 25-8-2 and 25-8-11.
13. Code of Alabama, Sections 25-8-13 and 25-8-14.
14. Code of Alabama, Sections 17-23-10 and 17-23-11.
15. Code of Alabama, Section 25-1-1.
16. Code of Alabama, Section 25-4-77.
17. Code of Alabama, Section 25-4-78.
18. Code of Alabama, Section 25-5-51.
19. Code of Alabama, Section 25-5-51.
20. *Scott v. Lane*, 409 S.2d 791 (Ala. 1982).
21. See, for example: *White v. Chelsea Industries, Inc.*, 425 S.2d 1090 (Ala. 1983).
22. *Peters v. Alabama Power Co.*, No. 82-248 (Ala. S.Ct. 1931).
23. *Rice v. United Ins. Co. of America*, Case No. 83-84 (Ala. S.Ct., 1984).

67

Alaska
Labor Laws

[67.01] LABOR RELATIONS LAWS

Public employment relations act: Section 23.40.070, *et seq.*, of the Alaska Statutes sets forth the Public Employment Relations Act which protects the right of public employees to self-organize.[1] The statute further establishes procedures for conducting representation elections, processing unfair labor practices against employee organizations and public employers, mediation and arbitration, and other guidelines regarding public employee bargaining rights.[2]

Teacher's collective bargaining rights: Section 14.20.550, *et seq.*, of the Alaska Statutes establishes a teacher's collective bargaining law which, among other things, requires each city, borough, or regional school board to negotiate with its certificated employees in good faith on matters pertaining to their employment and the fulfillment of their professional duties. The statute establishes procedures relative to representation elections, mediation, and grievances involving certificated teachers.[3]

Nonright-to-work policy: Union security (union shop) clauses are permissible in the state of Alaska inasmuch as Alaska has not adopted a right-to-work statute as permitted by Section 14(b) of the Labor-Management Relations Act.

[67.02] STRIKES, PICKETING, AND BOYCOTT LAWS

Riots: Alaskan statutes prohibit any use of force or violence, or any threat to use force or violence, if accompanied by immediate power of execution by three or more persons acting together without authority of law.[4]

Unlawful assembly: The statute also forbids three or more persons to assemble with intent to do an unlawful act.[5]

[67.03] MEDIATION AND ARBITRATION LAWS

Section 09.43.010 of the Alaska Statutes recognizes and validates the right of two or more parties to agree to submit an existing controversy to arbitration. However, the provisions of this statute do not apply to a collective bargaining contract unless such an express agreement to arbitrate is incorporated into the contract by reference or its application is provided by a specific statute.[6]

[67.04] REGULATION OF UNION ACTIVITIES

The state of Alaska requires unions that have no locals within the state to register with its Department of Labor and to comply with all regulations in connection therewith, in order to have standing in its courts to enforce the provisions of a collective bargaining contract.[7] Alaskan labor laws permit unions to adopt and use labels, trademarks, designs, etc., for the purpose of making known merchandise and goods produced by union labor.[8] The statute forbids counterfeiting or imitating such labels.[9]

[67.05] REGULATION OF EMPLOYMENT PRACTICES

Anti-discrimination laws: Section 18.80.220 of the Alaska Statutes prohibits discrimination in employment by reason of race, religion, color, national origin, age, physical handicap, sex, marital status, changes in marital status, pregnancy or parenthood, except for a bona fide occupational qualification.

Polygraph restrictions: Section 23.10.37 of the Alaska Statutes forbids a person to require an applicant or employee to submit to a polygraph or other lie detecting device as a condition of applying for employment or as a condition of continuing employment.

False representations to procure employees: Alaskan statutes prohibit any person doing business in the state to induce an individual to change from one employment to another, or to bring an individual into the state, by means of false pretense concerning the kind and character of the work to be done, or the amount and character of compensation to be paid, or the nature of working conditions of his or her employment.[10]

Equal pay: Alaskan statutes require equal pay for equal work between male and female employees.[11]

[67.06] WAGE AND HOUR LAWS

Child labor: Alaskan statutes place certain restrictions on the employment of children under 16 years of age.[12] The statutes also limit children under 18 years of age to nonhazardous jobs.[13] Children under 17 years of age must receive a written permit from the State Department of Labor in order to work, except for parent-related employment.[14]

Hourly rate of pay: Section 23.10.065 of the Alaska Statutes requires employers to pay employees not less than fifty cents per hour greater than the prevailing federal minimum wage and prohibits employers from applying tips or gratuities bestowed upon employees as a credit toward payment of such minimum hourly wage rate.

Payment of wages upon termination: Alaskan employers are required to pay employees all wages, salaries, or other compensation due them within three working days after termination, regardless of the cause for termination.[15]

Voting time: Section 15.56.100 of the Alaska Statutes requires employers to allow employees who do not have time to vote outside normal working hours, sufficient time (two consecutive hours) off work to do so.

Garnishment: Section 47.23.070(d) of the Alaska Statutes forbids the termination of an employee because his or her wages are subject to an assignment order to pay child support.

[67.07] SAFETY AND HEALTH LAWS

General provisions: Alaskan statutes require employers to do everything necessary to protect the life, health, and safety of employees within their employment, including the duty to comply with all occupational safety and health standards, and furnish to employees a place of employment free from recognized hazards determined to cause or likely to cause death or serious physical harm to the employees.[16]

Toxic substances—right to know: Alaskan statutes require employers to conduct educational programs for employees who are assigned to perform work involving a toxic substance.[17] The statutes also require a display of information designed to properly inform employees about toxic substances within their work areas.[18] Employees are to be furnished a copy of the most recent OSHA Form 20 (or equivalent information) as to toxic substances to which they may be exposed, provided employees request such information.[19]

[67.08] UNEMPLOYMENT COMPENSATION LAWS

The Alaskan statutory law requiring and regulating unemployment compensation benefits to employees so qualfying are set out in Section 23.20.350 of the Alaskan statutes.

[67.09] WORKERS' COMPENSATION LAWS

The Alaskan Workers' Compensation laws are codified in Sections 23.30.005, *et seq.*, of the Alaska Statutes. The statutes provide disability benefits to employees injured on the job, subject to specified qualifications and limitations.[20]

Benefits and payments are paid to employees in accordance with established schedules, the amounts and duration of which are dependent upon the gravity of the injury or disease and whether the disability is temporary or permanent and/or partial or total. The statute also prescribes coverage for certain occupational diseases as well as sets up a second injury fund program.[21]

[67.10]   EMPLOYMENT-AT-WILL DEVELOPMENTS

Alaskan courts have recognized certain exceptions to the employment-at-will rule.

Covenant of good faith and fair dealing exception: Alaskan courts have held that at-will relationships contain an implied covenant of good faith and fair dealing and that an employer is obligated to discharge employees in good faith; otherwise, an action might lie outside the at-will principle.[22]

"Permanent employment" exception: Alaskan courts have also held that a contract for employment "until retirement" constitutes an agreement for a definite period of time and is outside the at-will doctrine, the court ruling that a termination of the subject employee must be supported by good cause.[23]

NOTES TO CHAPTER 67

1. Alaska Statutes, Section 23.40.080.
2. See Alaska Statutes, Section 23.40.70 through 23.40.220.
3. See Alaska Statutes, Section 14.20.550 through 14.20.610.
4. Alaska Statutes, Section 11.45.020.
5. Alaska Statutes, Section 11.45.020.
6. Alaska Statutes, Section 09.43.010.
7. Alaska Statutes, Section 23.40.20.
8. Alaska Public Acts, S.B. 123, Section 1 (L. 1959).
9. Alaska Public Acts, S.B. 123, Section 1 (L. 1959).
10. Alaska Statutes, Section 23.10.015.
11. Alaska Statutes, Section 18.80.220.
12. Alaska Statutes, Section 23.10.340.
13. Alaska Statutes, Section 23.10.350.
14. Alaska Statutes, Section 23.10.332.
15. Alaska Statutes, Section 23.05.140.
16. Alaska Statutes, Section 18.60.075.
17. Alaska Statutes, Section 18.60.066.

18. Alaska Statutes, Section 18.60.068.

19. Alaska Statutes, Section 18.60.067.

20. Alaska Statutes, Section 23.30.005, *et seq.*

21. Alaska Statutes, Section 23.30.040.

22. *Mitford v. Lasala*, 666 P.2d 1000 (Alaska, 1983).

23. *Eales v. Tanana Valley Medical Surgical Group, Inc.*, 663 P.2d 958 (Alaska, 1983).

68

Arizona
Labor Laws

[68.01] LABOR RELATIONS LAWS

Collective bargaining rights of agricultural employees: Arizona has within its statutory provisions a law protecting the right of agricultural employees to self-organization and to join or refrain from joining labor unions.[1] The Arizona Agricultural Employment Relations Act prohibits certain unfair labor practices by both agricultural employers and unions.[2] It also established procedures and guidelines for processing representation petitions and conducting representation elections.[3]

Right-to-work law: The Arizona revised statutes provide no person shall be denied the opportunity to obtain or retain employment because of nonmembership in a labor union.[4]

"Yellow-dog" contracts: Section 23-1342 of the Arizona Revised Statutes prohibits employers from requiring an employee to promise not to join, become, or remain a member of any labor organization as a condition of employment, or to promise to withdraw from employment upon joining or becoming a member of a labor union.

[68.02] STRIKES, PICKETING, AND BOYCOTT LAWS

Anti-injunction statute: The Arizona statutory laws forbid the issuance of a restraining order or injunction involving a labor dispute, unless such an injunction is necessary to prevent irreparable injury to property.[5]

Unlawful assembly: Section 13-2902 of the Arizona Revised Statutes makes it a misdemeanor for two or more persons to assemble with the intent of engaging in conduct constituting a riot.

Secondary boycotts: Section 23-1322 of the Arizona Revised Statutes makes is unlawful for a union to engage in secondary boycotts.

[68.03] MEDIATION AND ARBITRATION LAWS

Although the Arizona statutes recognize the validity and enforceability of a written agreement to arbitrate a controversy, the statutes do not extend to, nor apply to, collective bargaining contracts in respect to terms or conditions of employment.[6]

[68.04] REGULATION OF UNION ACTIVITIES

The counterfeiting, imitating, or improper use of union labels constitutes a misdemeanor under Section 44-1453 of the Arizona Revised Statutes. The

Arizona labor laws make it unlawful for a labor union that is organized or doing business in the state to make any contribution of money or anything of value for the purpose of influencing a political election.[7]

[68.05] REGULATION OF EMPLOYMENT PRACTICES

Anti-discrimination laws: Section 41-1463 of the Arizona Revised Statutes makes it unlawful for an employer, employment agency, or a labor union to discriminate in employment because of race, color, religion, sex, age, or national origin.

Jury duty: Arizona employers are forbidden to dismiss or, in any other manner, penalize an employee by reason of his or her jury service.[8] However, the statute does not require an employer to compensate an employee when absent from employment because of jury duty.[9]

Blacklisting: The Arizona Constitution prohibits employers from exchanging, soliciting, or distributing any labor blacklist.[10]

Employment under false pretenses: Section 23-201 of the Arizona Revised Statutes forbids any employer from hiring an individual on the pretense that he or she has adequate funds to compensate the employee for services performed, if the employer does not have such funds. Section 23-202 of the Arizona Revised Statutes forbids the extortion of job applicants in any manner.

Protection of employee's political and voting freedom: Section 16-1012 of the Alaska Revised Statutes makes it unlawful for an employer to interfere with an employee's political or voting privileges.

Employee right of access to consumer reports: Any employer using a consumer report prepared by a consumer reporting agency in an employment decision, must disclose the name and address of the agency to the affected applicant or employee upon written request.[11]

National Guard member protection: Sections 26-167 and 26-168 of the Arizona Revised Statutes protect the right of National Guard members to take leaves of absence from their employment to attend military camp, maneuvers, or drills and prohibit an employer from discriminating against National Guard members by reason of such leaves.

Equal pay: Arizona employers are required to pay equal pay for equal work without regard to sex.[12]

[68.06] WAGE AND HOUR LAWS

Child labor: The Arizona statutes restrict the employment of children under ages 16 and 18 to certain categories of work.[13]

Payment of wages: Employers in Arizona must establish paydays for their employees not more than 16 days apart.[14]

Payment upon termination: Whenever an employee is discharged, his or her employer is required to pay accrued wages by the end of the next regular pay period or within three days of termination, whichever is the earlier. Whenever an employee quits his or her employment, wages are due no later than the next regular payday.[15]

Voting time: Section 16-897 of the Arizona Revised Statutes provides that an employee must be given time off from his or her job, up to three consecutive hours, for voting purposes.

[68.07] SAFETY AND HEALTH LAWS

The Arizona Safety and Health Act requires employers to furnish their employees a place of employment free from recognized hazards and to comply with the occupational safety and health standards, as well as all rules and regulations, issued pursuant to the provisions of the Act.[16]

[68.08] UNEMPLOYMENT COMPENSATION LAWS

The Arizona unemployment compensation laws are found in Section 23-601, et seq., of the Arizona Revised Statutes. The statute provides for compensation benefits to employees who qualify under the provisions of its guidelines and regulations.[17] The statute also establishes grounds for denying benefits.[18]

[68.09] WORKERS' COMPENSATION LAWS

The Arizona workers' compensation statutes are found at Section 23-901, et seq., of the Arizona Revised Statutes. The statute applies to every employer within the state, excluding employers of domestic servants.[19] Compensation benefits are paid to qualified recipients based upon a specified schedule.[20]

[68.10] EMPLOYMENT-AT-WILL DEVELOPMENTS

The Arizona courts have subscribed to some limited exceptions to the employment-at-will principle.

Public policy exception: An Arizona court of appeals has permitted a cause of action in a case where an employee was discharged for refusing to cover up a company theft.[21]

Implied contract exception: The Arizona Supreme Court has ruled that it will recognize, as actionable, any wrongful discharge that is in violation of a public policy or that contravenes implied statements contained in an employee handbook or policy manual.[22]

NOTES TO CHAPTER 68

1. Arizona Revised Statutes, Section 23-1381, *et seq.*
2. Arizona Revised Statutes, Section 23-1385.
3. Arizona Revised Statutes, Sections 23-1386 and 23-1389.
4. Arizona Revised Statutes, Section 23-1301, *et seq.*
5. Arizona Revised Statutes, Section 23-1393.
6. Arizona Revised Statutes, Section 12-1517 (although such agreements are recognized by the federal labor policy).
7. Arizona Revised Statutes, Section 16-471.
8. Arizona Revised Statutes, Section 21-236.
9. Arizona Revised Statutes, Section 21-236.
10. Arizona Constitution, Article 18, Section 8.
11. Arizona Revised Statutes, Section 44-1693.
12. Arizona Revised Statutes, Sections 23-340 and 23-341.
13. Arizona Revised Statutes, Sections 23-231 and 23-233.
14. Arizona Revised Statutes, Section 23-351.
15. Arizona Revised Statutes, Section 23-353.
16. Arizona Revised Statutes, Sections 23-403 and 23-404.
17. See generally Arizona Revised Statutes, Section 23-601, *et seq.*
18. See generally Arizona Revised Statutes, Sections 23-771 and 23-776.
19. Arizona Revised Statutes, Section 23-902.
20. See, for example, Arizona Revised Statutes, Section 23-1044 through 23-1046.
21. *Vermillon v. AAA Pro Moving & Storage*, Case No. 2, CA-CIV 5297 (Ariz. Ct. of App., 1985).
22. *Wagenseller v. Scottsdale Memorial Hosp.*, Case No. 17646-PR (Ariz. S.Ct., 1985).

69

Arkansas
Labor Laws

[69.01] LABOR RELATIONS LAWS

Right-to-work law: The Arkansas statutes provide that no person shall be denied employment because of failure or refusal to join or affiliate with a labor union, nor shall any person, unless he or she voluntarily consents in writing, be compelled to pay dues, or any other monetary consideration to any labor organization as a prerequisite to, or condition of, continuance of employment.[1]

Collective bargaining policy: Although Arkansas has no law comparable to the Labor Management Relations Act, Section 81-201 of the Arkansas Statutes declares it to be a public policy of the state for organized labor to be free to bargain collectively and unorganized labor to be free to bargain individually. The state Attorney General has issued an opinion that a public employer, although not required to do so, may engage in collective bargaining with his or her employees, so long as any agreements reached pursuant thereto do not purport to delegate away powers which the public employer is required to exercise by virtue of the law.[2]

[69.02] STRIKES, PICKETING, AND BOYCOTT LAWS

Interference with lawful employment: The Arkansas statutory laws make it unlawful for any person to use violence or threats to prevent or attempt to prevent any person from engaging in any lawful vocation within the state.[3]

Interference with railroad trains during picketing: Sections 81-214 of the Arkansas Statutes make it unlawful for anyone to interfere with railroad operations as a result of a labor dispute.

[69.03] MEDIATION AND ARBITRATION LAWS

Section 81-107 of the Arkansas Statutes empowers the Arkansas Commissioner of Labor to intervene in any labor dispute in a conciliatory or mediatory capacity upon written invitation by either party to the controversy and to promote the voluntary arbitration thereof.

[69.04] REGULATION OF UNION ACTIVITIES

The Arkansas statutes require anyone soliciting advertising in the name of, on behalf of, or claiming to represent a bona fide labor organization, to file with the Arkansas Secretary of State a bond in the amount of $5,000 as

494

surety of performance on any contracts entered into by the person on behalf of such labor organization.[4]

[69.05] REGULATION OF EMPLOYMENT PRACTICES

Anti-discrimination laws: Section 6-1506 of the Arkansas Statutes makes it unlawful for state contractors to discriminate in employment on the basis of race, color, creed, national origin, or ancestry. Section 81-405 forbids sexual harassment within an employer's work place.

Interference with employment: Section 81-210 of the Arkansas Statutes prohibits any person to interfere with, entice away, knowingly employ, or induce a worker who has contracted an employment agreement with another person for a specified period of time to leave such employment prior to the expiration of the contract, without the consent of the other employer.

Blacklisting: Arkansas statutes make it unlawful for anyone to attempt to blacklist another for the purpose of preventing such person from securing employment or for the purpose of causing such person to be discharged from his or her employment.[5]

Wrongful discharge: An employee whose employment is for a definite term and who is discharged by his or her employer for any reason other than good cause prior to the expiration of the fixed term, may bring an action against such employer for damages sustained, including any unpaid wages.[6]

Jury service: Arkansas employers are required to excuse from work those employees who are called to jury service and are prohibited from penalizing such employees in any manner as a result of such absence.[7]

Discrimination against political and voting activities: Arkansas statutes make it unlawful for anyone to threaten to discharge, or discharge, an employee as a means to attempt to influence the political vote of such employee.[8]

Protection of public employees: Public employers are forbidden to discriminate in employment against an employee because of his or her membership in the General Assembly, service as an election official, service upon a jury, service as an elected official of any office not otherwise prohibited by the Arkansas Constitution, or in the performance of his or her duties as required by the state laws.[9] A state employee shall not be denied retention in employment or any promotion or other incident or advantage of employment or transferred involuntarily to another position because he or she is a member of a reserve component of the Armed Services of the United States.[10]

Medical examination payments: Section 81-212 of the Arkansas Statutes require employers to pay the cost of medical examinations that are required of applicants and employees.

Equal pay: The Arkansas labor laws prohibit discrimination in payment of wages as between sexes for comparable work, except as specified in the statute.[11]

[69.06]   WAGE AND HOUR LAWS

Child labor: The Arkansas statutes restrict the employment of children under 14 years of age to jobs controlled by parents or guardians, and then only during school vacations.[12] Children under 16 years of age may not be employed in jobs of a hazardous nature.[13] Employment certificates are required for employment of children under 16 years of age.[14]

Payment of wages upon termination: Employees who are discharged or refused further employment may request payment of any wages due and must be paid by the employer within seven days from discharge or termination.[15]

Access to medical reports: An Arkansas employer may not require an applicant or employee to take a medical examination as a condition of employment, or as a condition of continued employment, without furnishing a copy of the medical examiner's report to the employee at no cost to the employee.[16]

Voting time: Arkansas laws provide that employees of mines, mills, shops, and factories are entitled to vote in general elections.[17]

Medical insurance continuance: Arkansas statutes provide that terminating employees must be provided an option to convert a group health insurance policy to his or her individual coverage.[18]

[69.07]   SAFETY AND HEALTH LAWS

The Arkansas statutes require employers within the state to furnish a safe place to work for their employees.[19] Section 81-108 of the Arkansas Statutes also requires Arkansas employers to comply with the health and safety standards established by the state.

[69.08]   UNEMPLOYMENT COMPENSATION LAWS

The Arkansas unemployment compensation laws are found in Section 81.1101, *et seq.*, of the Arkansas Statutes. Benefits are payable to employees provided they meet the qualifying criteria outlined in the statute.[20]

[69.09] WORKERS' COMPENSATION LAWS

The Arkansas workers' compensation laws are found in Section 81-1301, *et seq.*, of the Arkansas Statutes. Benefits and payments are paid to employees in accordance with established schedules, the amounts and duration of which are dependent upon the gravity of the injury or occupational disease and whether the disability is temporary or permanent and/or partial or total.

[69.10] EMPLOYMENT-AT-WILL DEVELOPMENTS

The Arkansas courts have recognized certain exceptions to the employment-at-will doctrine.

Public policy exception: An Arkansas court has held that the discharge of a female employee for refusing to sleep with her supervisor is so repugnant to the public policy against prostitution that an action will lie for wrongful discharge, irrespective of the at-will doctrine.[21]

Intentional infliction of emotional distress exception: Although an Arkansas court dismissed a wrongful discharge action on the theory of intentional infliction of emotional distress, the court remanded the case to the trial court on the issue of whether the employer's postdischarge action in forcing the employee to submit to a lie detector test was so extreme and outrageous to make the employer liable for damages under the emotional distress theory.[22]

NOTES TO CHAPTER 69

1. Arkansas Statutes, Section 81-202.
2. See Arkansas Attorney General Opinion No. 77-99.
3. Arkansas Statutes, Section 81-206.
4. Arkansas Statutes, Section 71-201.
5. Arkansas Statutes, Section 81-211.
6. Arkansas Statutes, Section 81-310.
7. Arkansas Statutes, Section 39-103.
8. Arkansas Statutes, Section 3-1105(o).
9. Arkansas Public Acts, No. 46, Section 1 (L. 1961).
10. Arkansas Public Acts, No. 406, Section 2 (L. 1973).
11. Arkansas Statutes, Section 81-624.
12. Arkansas Statutes, Section 81-701.
13. Arkansas Statutes, Sections 81-702 and 81-703.
14. See Arkansas Statutes, Section 81-708 through 81-711.
15. Arkansas Statutes, Section 81-308.

16. Arkansas Statutes, Section 81-212.

17. Arkansas Statutes, Section 3-1602.

18. Arkansas Public Laws, Acts 8115; 854 (L. 1985).

19. Arkansas Statutes, Section 81-108.

20. See, for example: Arkansas Statutes, Section 81-1105, *et seq.*

21. *Lucas v. Brown & Root,* 736 F.2d 1202 (CA-8, 1984).

22. *M.B.M. Co., Inc. v. Counce*, 268 Ark. 269, 596 S.W.2d 681 (1980).

70

California
Labor Laws

Collective bargaining rights of public employees: Public employees in the state of California have the right to form, join, and participate in the activities of employee organizations of their own choosing for the purpose of representation in all matters of employer-employee relations.[1] The California statute permits an "agency shop" whenever properly negotiated[2] and requires public agencies to "meet and confer" in good faith with recognized employee organizations who represent an appropriate unit of public employees.[3]

Collective bargaining rights of agricultural employees:[4] California law provides agricultural employees with the right to self-organize, to assist labor organizations, and to bargain collectively through representatives of their own choosing.[5] Elections are provided by the statute to determine whether an appropriate unit of agricultural employees desire a petitioning union.[6] Procedures to process unfair labor practice complaints are also provided by the statute.[7]

Higher education employees' bargaining rights: Employees of the University of California, Hastings College of Law, and the California State University and Colleges are given the right to bargain collectively through representatives of their choosing by virtue of the California Higher Education Employees Relations Act.[8]

Public school employees' bargaining rights: Section 3540 of the California Government Code extends the legislation enacted to govern employer-employee relations of other public employees to public school employees.[9]

Firefighter's bargaining rights: Section 1960, *et seq.*, of the California Labor Code permits firefighters within the state the right of self-organization and the right to join and assist labor unions.

Nonright-to-work policy: Union security (union shop) clauses are permissible in the state of California inasmuch as California has not adopted a right-to-work statute as permitted by Section 14(b) of the Labor-Management Relations Act.

"Yellow-dog" contracts: Section 920, *et seq.*, of the California Labor Code makes it unlawful for anyone to coerce or compel any person to enter into an agreement not to join or become a member of any labor organization as a condition of employment.

[70.02] STRIKES, PICKETING, AND BOYCOTT LAWS

Striker replacements and strikebreakers: Employers and/or their agents are required to plainly and explicitly mention in advertisements or solicitations for employment applicants that a strike, lockout, or other labor disturbance exists, if that be the case.[10] California statutory laws make it unlawful for any employer to willingly and knowingly utilize any professional strikebreaker to replace an employee or employees involved in a strike or lockout at a place of business within the state.[11] California statutes prohibit any public entity to permit any peace officers to be employed by any private employer as a security guard during a strike, lockout, or picketing in the jurisdiction in which the peace officer is regularly employed.[12] Concealed weapons are forbidden to be carried by individuals participating in a labor dispute.[13]

Jurisdictional strikes: Jurisdictional strikes are unlawful under the California Labor Code and subject to injunctive relief.[14]

Unlawful assembly: California statutes forbid two or more persons to assemble together to do an unlawful act or to do a lawful act in a violent, boisterous, or tumultuous manner.[15]

Anti-injunction statutes: California statutes prohibit injunctive relief to curtail peaceful picketing except under specified conditions.[16]

[70.03] MEDIATION AND ARBITRATION LAWS

Section 1280, *et seq.,* of the California Civil Code provides that written agreements to submit an existing controversy to arbitration is valid, enforceable, and irrevocable, except upon such grounds as exist for the revocation of any such contract.

[70.04] REGULATION OF UNION ACTIVITIES

Employment agencies in California are required to notify applicants of the existence of any labor contract at the prospective employer's facility and whether union membership is required under such labor contract.[17] Employment agencies must also notify applicants of any labor dispute in existence.[18] California statutes make it unlawful for anyone to misuse or forge a union label.[19] The misuse of a union card is also forbidden by California law.[20]

[70.05] REGULATION OF EMPLOYMENT PRACTICES

Anti-discrimination laws: California law forbids employers to discriminate in the employment or in selection of a training program for reason of race, religion, creed, color, national origin, ancestry, physical handicap, or sex.[21] Age discrimination in employment,[22] sexual harassment within the work place,[23] or pregnancy discrimination is also forbidden.[24]

Protection of political freedom: California employers are forbidden to attempt to coerce or influence political decisions of their employees by threat of discharge, etc.[25]

Registration of employment applications: Employers must file, in the office of the California Division of Labor Law Enforcement, a copy of their application form, provided applicants are required to sign such a form upon applying for a job.[26]

Jury duty: No employer shall discharge or in any manner discriminate against an employee in his or her employment for taking time off to serve on an inquest jury or trial jury, provided reasonable notice is given to the employer by the employee.[27]

Sterilization: California statutes make it an unlawful employment practice for an employer to require an employee to be sterilized as a condition of employment.[28]

Investigative consumer reports: Upon a timely request, an investigative consumer reporting agency must disclose to an applicant or employee any investigative consumer report prepared on the applicant or employee which the investigative consumer reporting agency has furnished for employment purposes.[29]

Arrest record: With limited exceptions, no public or private employers in the state of California are permitted to ask applicants for employment to disclose, through written form or verbally, information concerning an arrest or detention that did not result in a conviction.[30]

Access to personnel records: California statutes provide that every employer shall, at reasonable times and intervals, and upon proper application of an employee, permit such employee to inspect such personnel files that are used or have been used to determine the employee's qualification for employment, promotion, additional compensation, termination, or other disciplinary action.[31]

Confidentiality of medical information: With limited exception, a California employer may not disclose medical information that the employer possesses pertaining to his or her employees without the employee having signed a proper authorization permitting such use or disclosure.[32]

Employment under false pretense: California labor laws forbid any person to employ another through or by means of such false representations as the type of work involved, the existence or nonexistence of a labor dispute, length of service, etc.[33]

Polygraph restrictions: No California employer may demand or require any applicant for employment or any employee to submit to or take a polygraph, lie detector, or similar test or examination as a condition of employment or continued employment, excepting the use of such tests in certain state agencies or subdivisions thereof.[34]

California employers are also forbidden to use any system that examines or records in any manner, voice prints or other voice stress patterns of an applicant or employee without his or her written consent.[35] The provisions of these statutes do not apply to peace officers.[36]

Protection of military personnel: Section 394 of the California Military and Veterans Code prohibits the discharge of any employee who is called upon to perform military service. The statute also requires employers to grant military leaves of absence to any employee who is a member of the reserve forces of the United States and who is engaged in military duty ordered for purposes of military training, drill, encampment, and the like.[37]

Blacklisting, photographing, and fingerprinting: Any person who, by any misrepresentation, prevents or attempts to prevent an employee who has been terminated from obtaining employment elsewhere is guilty of a misdemeanor under Section 1050 of the California Labor Code. Photographing and fingerprinting employees, except for an employer's own use, are forbidden in California.[38]

Whistle-blowing statute: California law forbids an employer to retaliate against an employee for disclosing a violation of state or federal law to appropriate government agencies.[39]

Cancer recovery: California employers are forbidden to discriminate in employment against former cancer patients.[40]

Alcoholic rehabilitation: Private employers in California are required to make reasonable accommodations for employees who desire to enter and participate in alcoholic rehabilitation programs.[41]

Plant closures: The California Employee Ownership Act provides assistance for possible employee ownership of a business that is closing.

Medical examination payments: Section 222.5 of the California Labor Code requires employers to pay the cost associated with any pre-employment or other such medical examinations of their prospective and regular employees.

Equal pay: Section 1197 of the California Labor Code requires employers to pay female employees the same wage rate as paid male employees in the same establishment for the same quantity and quality of work.

[70.06] WAGE AND HOUR LAWS

Child labor: California statutes normally limit employment of children to ages 16 years and up.[42] The Industrial Welfare Commissioner's written consent is required to employ minors under 16 years of age in the theater and related arts.[43]

Hours of work: With limited exceptions, California employers are prohibited from working employees more than six days out of seven.[44]

Payment of wages: Employers are required to pay wages at least twice a month on regular paydays, excepting wages of executive, administrative, and professional employees who must be paid their wages no less than once a month on or before the twenty-sixth day.[45]

Payment upon termination: With limited exceptions, employees who quit without notice are to be paid their wages within seventy-two hours; employees who are discharged are due their wages immediately.[46]

Garnishment: Section 2929 of the California Labor Code forbids discharge of an employee because of garnishments pertaining to any one judgment.

Medical insurance conversion: Section 1373.6 of the California Health and Safety Code provides that terminating employees are to be given an opportunity to convert group health plans into individual coverage.

Voting time: California employees who do not have sufficient time in which to vote must be permitted sufficient time off work by their employer, either at the beginning or ending of the shift, for that purpose.[47]

Anti-reprisal statute: Retaliation against an employee who files a complaint against an employer alleging wage and hour violations is forbidden in California.[48]

[70.07] SAFETY AND HEALTH LAWS

General provisions: California statutes require employers to furnish a safe and healthful place of employment for their employees to work.[49] Employers are forbidden to discharge or in any other manner discriminate against employees who file complaints relating to hazardous substances, etc.[50]

Toxic substances—right to know: California law requires a manufacturer or user of a hazardous substance to make available to employees who might be exposed to such products a material safety data sheet regarding any toxic substances contained therein.[51] Employee inquiries regarding toxic substances must be answered by the employer within fifteen days.[52]

[70.08] UNEMPLOYMENT COMPENSATION LAWS

The California Unemployment Insurance Compensation Laws are found in the California Unemployment Compensation Insurance Code.[53] Under the California Unemployment Insurance Code, weekly benefits are provided for persons unable to work because of nonindustrial disability resulting from illness or injury as well as benefits received during unemployment.[54]

[70.09] WORKERS' COMPENSATION LAWS

The California Workers' Compensation Laws provide comprehensive workers' compensation and insurance to employees who suffer injury or occupational disease, arising out of and sustained in the course and scope of their employment.[55]

Benefits and payments are paid to employees in accordance with established schedules, the amounts and duration of which are dependent upon the gravity of the injury or disease and whether the disability is temporary or permanent and/or partial or total. Employers are prohibited from discharging or taking other adverse action against an employee as a result of his or her having filed a workers' compensation claim.[56]

[70.10] EMPLOYMENT-AT-WILL DEVELOPMENTS

California courts have been most active in recognizing exceptions to the employment-at-will doctrine.

Implied contract exception: California courts have sustained a cause of action in which promises were made through a personnel handbook that an employee would not be discharged until given a fair chance to perform, the court recognizing that a handbook may constitute an implied-in-fact employment contract.[57]

Convenant of good faith and fair dealing exception: A California appellate court has recognized that an employer may have an implied obligation to deal fairly with an employee and not act arbitrarily in a disharge matter.[58]

"Independent consideration" exception: Whenever an employer promises not to terminate an employee except for good cause or when services are performed in addition to regular employment services, such employee will not be viewed as an employee-at-will and may be discharged only for cause.[59]

Public policy exception: California courts have sustained actions where employees have been discharged for refusing to violate the public policy.[60]

NOTES TO CHAPTER 70

1. California Government Code, Section 3502.
2. California Government Code, Section 3502.5.
3. California Government Code, Section 3505.
4. See California Labor Code, Section 1152, *et seq.*
5. California Labor Code, Sections 1152-1154.
6. California Labor Code, Section 1156, *et seq.*
7. California Labor Code, Section 1160.
8. See California Government Code, Section 3560, *et seq.*
9. See a discussion of the California law regulating the Collective Bargaining Rights of Public Employees at [70.01].
10. California Labor Code, Sections 973-974.
11. California Labor Code, Section 1134.
12. California Labor Code, Sections 1112-1113.
13. California Penal Code, Section 12590(a)(1).
14. California Labor Code, Sections 1115-1116.
15. California Penal Code, Section 407.
16. See California Civil Procedure Code, Section 527, *et seq.*
17. California Business and Professions Code, Section 9972.
18. California Business and Professions Code, Section 9988.
19. California Labor Code, Section 1010, *et seq.*
20. California Labor Code, Section 1017.
21. California Government Code, Section 12940, *et seq.*
22. California Government Code, Section 12941, *et seq.*
23. California Government Code, Section 12940(i).
24. California Government Code, Sections 12943 and 12945.
25. California Labor Code, Section 1101, *et seq.*
26. California Labor Code, Section 430, *et seq.*
27. California Labor Code, Section 230.
28. California Government Code, Section 12945.5.
29. California Civil Code, Section 1786.
30. California Labor Code, Section 432.7.
31. California Labor Code, Section 1198.5.
32. California Civil Code, Section 56.20.
33. California Labor Code, Section 970.
34. California Labor Code, Section 432.2.
35. California Penal Code, Section 637.
36. California Penal Code, Section 637.

37. California Military and Veterans Code, Section 394.

38. California Labor Code, Section 1051.

39. California Government Code, Section 10545.

40. California Government Code, Section 12926.

41. California Labor Code, Section 1025, *et seq.*

42. California Labor Code, Section 1290.

43. California Labor Code, Section 1308.

44. California Labor Code, Section 552, *et seq.*

45. California Labor Code, Sections 204-210.

46. California Labor Code, Sections 201-203.

47. California Elections Code, Section 14350.

48. California Labor Code, Section 98.6.

49. California Labor Code, Section 6400, *et seq.*

50. California Labor Code, Section 6399.7.

51. California Labor Code, Section 6399, *et seq.*

52. California Labor Code, Section 6399, *et seq.*

53. California Unemployment Ins. Code, Section 1, *et seq.*

54. California Unemployment Ins. Code, Section 2601, *et seq.*

55. California Labor Code, Section 3201, *et seq.*

56. California Labor Code, Section 132a.

57. *Walker v. Northern San Diego County Hosp. Dist.*, 135 Cal. App. 3d. 896, 185 Cal. Rptr. 617 (1982).

58. *Pugh v. See's Candies, Inc.*, 116 Cal. App. 3d 311, 171 Cal. Rptr. 917 (1981), See also: *Cancellier v. Federated Dept. Stores*, 672 F.2d 1312 (CA-9, 1982).

59. *Alvarez v. Dart Industries, Inc.*, 55 Cal. App. 3d 91, 127 Cal. Rptr. 222 (1976).

60. *Tameny v. Atlantic Richfield Co.*, 27 Cal. 3d 167, 610 P.2d 1330, 164 Cal. Rptr. 839 (1980); *Petermann v. International Brotherhood of Teamsters*, 174 Cal. App. 2d 184, 344 P.2d 25 (1959); *Crossen v. Foremost McKesson, Inc.*, 537 F. Supp. 1076 (ND Cal., 1982).

71

Colorado
Labor Laws

[71.01] LABOR RELATIONS LAWS

Collective bargaining laws: Section 8-13-101, *et seq.*, of the Colorado Revised Statutes provides that employers with eight or more employees, other than employers and employees specifically exempted, and excluding state and subdivisions, must recognize and bargain in good faith with unions properly certified as representatives of their employees. Section 80-3-106, *et seq.*, of the Colorado Revised Statutes accords all employees in the state the right of self-organization and prohibits any employer, or employer's agent, to interfere with such right.

Nonright-to-work policy: Union security (union shop) clauses are permissible in the state of Colorado inasmuch as Colorado has not adopted a right-to-work statute as permitted by Section 14(b) of the Labor Management Relations Act.

"Yellow-dog" contracts: Colorado statutes make it unlawful for anyone to coerce or compel any person to enter into an agreement not to join or become a member of any labor union as a condition of employment.[1]

[71.02] STRIKES, PICKETING, AND BOYCOTT LAWS

Prohibition of injunctions to restrain strikes: Colorado statutes restrict the issuance of injunctions to restrain peaceful picketing and boycotts.[2]

Interference with employment: Colorado statutes make it unlawful for anyone to attempt to prevent any person from engaging in any lawful occupation.[3]

Unlawful assembly: Section 18-9-108 of the Colorado Revised Statutes prohibits two or more persons to assemble together to do an unlawful act.

Secondary boycotts: Colorado statutes forbid secondary boycott activity[4] and also make it unlawful to print or circulate boycott pamphlets.[5]

Striker replacements: Colorado statutes require employment agencies to notify applicants of any existing strike or lockout prior to sending such an applicant to a prospective employer experiencing such labor conditions.[6] Section 8-2-104, *et seq.*, of the Colorado Revised Statutes requires advertisements and solicitations for employment applicants to state any existence of a strike, lockout, or other labor trouble at the place of the proposed employment.

Strikebreakers: Section 8-2-104 of the Colorado Revised Statutes makes it unlawful for an employer to utilize professional strikebreakers to replace employees involved in a labor dispute.

[71.03] MEDIATION AND ARBITRATION LAWS

Colorado has adopted the Uniform Arbitration Act recognizing any written agreement to submit an existing controversy to arbitration as valid, enforceable, and irrevocable, excepting such grounds as exist at law or equity for the revocation thereof.[7]

Section 8-3-113 of the Colorado Revised Statutes provides for mediation of labor disputes by mediators appointed by the Colorado Industrial Commission. In the event mediation fails to resolve a labor dispute, the statute requires the Industrial Commission to encourage the parties to submit their differences to a board of arbitration.[8]

[71.04] REGULATION OF UNION ACTIVITIES

The Colorado Trademark Act protects the right of a union label from misuse upon proper registration with the Colorado Secretary of State.[9]

[71.05] REGULATION OF EMPLOYMENT PRACTICES

Anti-discrimination laws: Section 24-34-402 of the Colorado Revised Statutes prohibits discrimination in the employment of an individual by reason of race, creed, color, sex, national origin, ancestry, or handicap. Age discrimination in employment is also forbidden in Colorado.[10]

Employment under false pretenses: Colorado employers are forbidden to obtain the labor or services of another through the intentional use of false pretenses.[11]

Protection of political freedom: Colorado labor laws make it unlawful for an employer to attempt to prevent employees from engaging or participating in politics or from becoming candidates for public office.[12]

Military leaves of absence: Colorado National Guard members are entitled to leaves of absence from their employment up to fifteen days in any one calendar year to receive military training without loss of seniority or classifications.[13]

Jury duty: Colorado employers are forbidden to discharge or otherwise discriminate against an employee who serves on jury duty.[14]

Blacklisting: Colorado employers are prohibited from maintaining a blacklist or notifying any other employer that any worker has been blacklisted by such employer for the purpose of preventing such worker from receiving employment.[15]

Medical examination payments: Colorado employers who require applicants or employees to undergo physical examinations as a condition of potential employment or as a condition of continued employment must pay for such examinations.[16]

Equal pay: Colorado employers are required to pay equal wages for comparable work, regardless of sex.[17]

[71.06]   WAGE AND HOUR LAWS

Child labor: The Colorado Youth Employment Opportunity Act governs employment of children.[18] Children 18 years or under are prohibited from working certain enumerated hazardous jobs.[19] The statute requires certain permits and proof of age certificates for certain age groups among minors.[20]

Payment of wages: The Colorado statutes require all wages, other than those relating to termination of employment, to be paid at least monthly and no later than ten days following the close of a pay period, unless the employer and employee mutually agree otherwise.[21]

Payment upon termination: Colorado employees who are discharged are to be paid their wages immediately; employees who quit without notice must be paid their remaining wages no later than the next regular pay day.[22]

Voting time: Employers are required to excuse an employee for a period not exceeding two hours between the time of opening and time of closing of election polls whenever such an employee does not have at least three hours or more between the time of opening and time of closing of polls away from his or her employment in which to vote.[23] Although the statute requires an employer to pay the employee his or her usual wages for the period of time absent, the employer may specify the two-hour period at the beginning or end of his or her shift during which time the employee may be absent.[24]

Garnishments: Section 5-5-106, *et seq.,* of the Colorado Revised Statutes forbids the discharge of an employee because of a garnishment against wages to pay off a judgment arising out of a consumer credit sale, lease, or loan.

[71.07] SAFETY AND HEALTH LAWS

Section 8-11-101, *et seq.,* of the Colorado Revised Statutes sets forth the Colorado Occupational Safety and Health Act. The statute requires Colorado employers to furnish places of employment that are free from recognized safety hazards and to comply with the safety and health standards, rules, and regulations promulgated by the Occupational Safety and Health Standards Board.[25]

[71.08] UNEMPLOYMENT COMPENSATION LAWS

The Colorado Employment Security Act covers full-time employees who qualify under the provisions of the statute.[26] The statute establishes criteria to qualify and disqualify recipients for benefits.[27]

[71.09] WORKERS' COMPENSATION LAWS

Section 8-40-101, *et seq.,* of the Colorado Revised Statutes sets forth the Colorado Workmen's Compensation Act. The statute provides disability and death benefits to employees injured on the job, or who suffer occupational diseases as a result of their job, subject to specified qualifications and limitations.[28]

[71.10] EMPLOYMENT-AT-WILL DEVELOPMENTS

Colorado has not adopted exceptions to the historic employment-at-will doctrine, as of this writing. Some Colorado courts have implied they might do so in the future, however, given justifiable facts and circumstances. For example, Colorado courts have not ruled out the possibility of recognizing an exception to the at-will rule should an employee be discharged for performing a statutory duty, such as serving on a jury.[29] Arguably, an employer's personnel policy manual has been recognized as constituting an employment agreement, creating rights in employees not to be ''bumped'' improperly during lay-off.[30]

NOTES TO CHAPTER 71

1. Colorado Revised Statutes, Section 8-3-108.
2. Colorado Revised Statutes, Section 8-3-118.
3. Colorado Revised Statutes, Section 8-2-101, *et seq.*

4. Colorado Revised Statutes, Section 8-3-108(g).

5. Colorado Revised Statutes, Section 8-2-112.

6. Colorado Revised Statutes, Section 12-24-109.

7. Colorado Revised Statutes, Section 8-3-12, *et seq.*

8. Colorado Revised Statutes, Section 8-3-113.

9. Colorado Revised Statutes, Section 7-70-101, *et seq.*

10. Colorado Revised Statutes, Section 8-2-116.

11. Colorado Revised Statutes, Section 8-2-104, *et seq.*

12. Colorado Revised Statutes, Section 1-13-719.

13. Colorado Revised Statutes, Section 28-3-609, *et seq.*

14. Colorado Revised Statutes, Section 13-71-118.

15. Colorado Revised Statutes, Section 8-2-111.

16. Colorado Revised Statutes, Section 8-2-118.

17. Colorado Revised Statutes, Section 8-5-101, *et seq.*

18. Colorado Revised Statutes, Section 8-12-101, *et seq.*

19. Colorado Revised Statutes, Section 8-12-110.

20. Colorado Revised Statutes, Section 8-12-111 through 8-12-113.

21. Colorado Revised Statutes, Section 8-4-105 and Section 8-4-106.

22. Colorado Revised Statutes, Section 8-4-104.

23. Colorado Revised Statutes, Section 31-10-603.

24. Colorado Revised Statutes, Section 31-10-603.

25. Colorado Revised Statutes, Section 8-11-108.

26. Colorado Revised Statutes, Section 8-70-103, *et seq.*

27. Colorado Revised Statutes, Section 8-70-101, *et seq.*

28. Colorado Revised Statutes, Section 8-40-101, *et seq.*

29. See *Lampe v. Presbyterian Medical Center,* 41 Colo. App. 465, 590 P.2d 513 (1978); *Rawson v. Sears, Roebuck & Co.,* 530 F.Supp. 776 (D. Colo. 1982).

30. *Brooks v. Trans World Airlines, Inc.,* 574 F.Supp. 805 (D. Colo. 1983).

72

Connecticut Labor Laws

[72.01] LABOR RELATIONS LAWS

Connecticut Labor Relations Act: Section 31-101, *et seq.*, of the Connecticut General Statutes establishes the Connecticut Labor Relations Law which, among other things, guarantees employees within the state, self-organizational rights and the right to join or refrain from union activities. The Connecticut Labor Relations Law extends and applies to all employers within the state but does not include any person engaged in farming or any person subject to the provisions of the National Labor Relations Act, unless the National Labor Relations Board has declined to assert jurisdiction over such persons.[1]

State employees' bargaining rights: Section 5-270, *et seq.*, of the Connecticut General Statutes grants to state employees the right to organize and bargain collectively. The statute provides that state employees shall have the right of self-organization, to form, join, or assist any employee organization, to bargain collectively through representatives of their own choosing on questions of wages, hours and other conditions of employment, except as prohibited in Subsection D of Section 5-272 of the statute.[2]

Municipal employees' bargaining rights: Section 7-467, *et seq.*, of the Connecticut General Statutes provides collective bargaining rights to Connecticut municipal employees.

Teachers' bargaining rights: Section 10-153 of the Connecticut General Statutes provides that members of the teaching profession shall have the right to form, join, or assist, or refuse to form, join, or assist any organization for professional or economic improvements and to negotiate in good faith through representatives of their own choosing with respect to salaries and other conditions of employment.

Nonright-to-work policy: Union security (union shop) clauses are permissible in the state of Connecticut inasmuch as Connecticut has not adopted a right-to-work statute pursuant to Section 14(b) of the Labor Management Relations Act.

"Yellow-dog" contracts: Connecticut statutes make it unlawful for anyone to coerce or compel any person to enter into an agreement not to join or become a member of any labor union as a condition of employment.[3]

[72.02] STRIKES, PICKETING, AND BOYCOTT LAWS

Limitation of anti-strike injunctions: Section 31-113 of the Connecticut General Statutes prohibits courts within the state to issue restraining orders or injunctions in any case involving or growing out of any labor dispute other than for the purpose of curtailing violence, threats, and mass picketing.

Unlawful assembly: Connecticut statutes make it unlawful for persons to assemble with intent to do any unlawful act.[4]

Striker replacements: Section 31-121 of the Connecticut General Statutes prohibits any employer, or his or her agents, to solicit persons to replace employees, or fill the positions made vacant as the result of a strike, lockout, or other labor dispute, by means of newspaper advertisements, posters, oral or written communications, or otherwise, unless such solicitations state plainly and specifically that a strike, lockout, or other labor dispute exists.

Strikebreakers: Connecticut labor laws make it unlawful for any employer to utilize professional strikebreakers to replace an employee involved in a strike or lockout through the use of misrepresentation, threats, or force.[5]

Use of municipal police officers during strike: The Connecticut statutes prohibit any employer, except the state or political subdivision thereof, or an employee organization involved in a labor dispute, to hire any member of a municipal police department in the town in which the labor dispute is taking place for protection or other duties related to the labor dispute.[6]

[72.03] MEDIATION AND ARBITRATION LAWS

Connecticut has adopted the Uniform Arbitration Act recognizing any written agreement to submit an existing controversy to arbitration as valid, enforceable, and irrevocable, except on such grounds as exist at law or equity for the revocation thereof.[7]

[72.04] REGULATION OF UNION ACTIVITIES

Connecticut statutes require labor organizations to file with the Secretary of State and make available to its members a written report containing pertinent information as required within the provisions of the statute.[8]

[72.05] REGULATION OF EMPLOYMENT PRACTICES

Anti-discrimination laws: Connecticut labor laws prohibit discrimination in employment on the basis of race, marital status, age, sex, physical disability, mental retardation, or religion.[9]

Inquiries regarding arrest record: Connecticut labor laws limit inquiries concerning the arrest record of an applicant if used in the employment decision-making process.[10]

Employment of illegal aliens: Connecticut employers are prohibited from employing aliens who are not entitled to lawful residence in the United States.[11]

Polygraphs prohibited: The Connecticut statutes prohibit any employer or employment agency to require any person to submit to or take a polygraph examination as a condition of obtaining employment or of continuing employment.[12]

Electronic surveillance forbidden: Connecticut employers are prohibited from operating any electronic surveillance device for the purpose of recording or monitoring the activities of their employees in areas designated for the health or personal comfort of the employees or for the safeguarding of their possessions, such as rest rooms, locker rooms, or lounges.[13]

Protection of political freedom: Section 9-365 of the Connecticut General Statutes prohibits employers from attempting to influence the vote of any employee by threats, promises, or dismissals.

Jury duty: Connecticut employers are forbidden to deprive any employee of his or her employment because the employee receives a summons to serve on a jury within the state.[14]

Witness duty: Connecticut statutes also provide that an employer shall not deprive an employee of his or her employment because the employee obeys a legal subpoena to appear before any court of the state as a witness in any criminal proceeding.[15]

Military leaves of absence: Connecticut employees who are required to attend military reserve of National Guard meetings or drills during regular working hours shall be permitted a leave of absence for such purpose and during such duration from their employers.[16]

Access to personnel records: Connecticut statutes require employers, within a reasonable time after receipt of a written request from an employee, to permit such employee to inspect his or her personnel file if such a file exists.[17] Employers are also required to permit employees to inspect medical records pertaining to them should such records exist.[18]

Whistle-blowing statute: Connecticut labor laws forbid an employer to discharge or otherwise penalize any employee because the employee reports a violation of a state or federal law.[19]

Blacklisting: Section 31-51 of the Connecticut General Statutes prohibits employers from blacklisting any former employee in an attempt to interfere with his or her prospective employment.

Plant closures: Whenever a Connecticut employer with 100 or more employees closes operations or relocates, the employer must pay in full for the continuation of existing health insurance for a period of ninety days.[20]

Equal pay: Connecticut statutes require equal pay for comparable work.[21]

[72.06] WAGE AND HOUR LAWS

Child labor: Connecticut statutes provide that minors may not be employed in occupations that are pronounced hazardous by the State Department of Health or the Department of Labor, unless the child is at least 16 years of age. Connecticut statutes provide that minors under 16 years of age must obtain a certificate from the State Board of Education before engaging in employment, and the employer of such minor must possess such a certificate.[22]

Hours of work: Connecticut statutes provide that eight hours of labor in any one day is a legal day's work unless otherwise agreed between the employer and employee.[23]

Payment of wages: Connecticut statutes provide that all wages shall be paid by cash or negotiable check and that all monies due employees are payable on a regular weekly payday, designated in advance.[24] The statute further provides that the end of a pay period shall not be more than eight days before the designated payday.[25]

Payment upon termination: In the event the employee leaves voluntarily, he or she must be paid, in full, no later than the next regular payday; in the event the employee is discharged, he or she must be paid on the next business day after discharge, should the employee so request.[26]

Garnishments: Connecticut statutes forbid the discharge of an employee because of garnishment orders against wages, unless garnishments exceed seven in any one calendar year.[27]

Medical insurance conversion: Section 38-262(d) of the Connecticut General Statutes provides that terminating employees are to be given an opportunity, at their own expense, to convert group health plans into individual coverage.

[72.07] SAFETY AND HEALTH LAWS

General provisions: Section 31-370 of the Connecticut General Statutes requires employers to maintain a place of employment that is free from recognized hazards that are causing or likely to cause death or serious physical harm to such employees.

Toxic substances—right to know: Connecticut statutes require employers that use or produce certain specified toxic chemicals to notify current and prospective employees about the hazards of such chemicals.[28]

[72.08] UNEMPLOYMENT COMPENSATION LAWS

The Connecticut Unemployment Compensation laws are found in Section 31-222, *et seq.*, of the Connecticut General Statutes. The statute provides for compensation benefits to unemployed workers who qualify under the provisions of the guidelines and regulations therein.

[72.09] WORKERS' COMPENSATION LAWS

The Workers' Compensation Laws of Connecticut are found in Section 31-275, *et seq.*, of the Connecticut General Statutes. The statute provides a schedule of compensation benefits to be awarded to employees who suffer injury as a result of an accident arising out of and in the course of their employment.[29]

[72.10] EMPLOYMENT AT-WILL DEVELOPMENTS

Connecticut courts have recognized certain exceptions to the at-will principle.

Violation of public policy: The Connecticut Supreme Court has held that a discharge might be unlawful if occurring as a result of the employee refusing to violate some public policy.[30]

Convenant of good faith and fair dealing: Connecticut courts imply a covenant of good faith and fair dealing in the employer/employee relationship, prohibiting discharges with malice or in bad faith.[31]

"Independent consideration" exception: Connecticut courts also recognize a lifetime employment relationship if the employee has given special consideration independent of what is required in the performance of his or her regular duties.[32]

NOTES TO CHAPTER 72

1. Connecticut General Statutes, Section 31-101.
2. Connecticut General Statutes, Section 5-271.
3. Connecticut General Statutes, Section 31-90.
4. Connecticut General Statutes, Section 53a-177.
5. Connecticut General Statutes, Section 31-121, *et seq.*
6. Connecticut Public Acts, No. 77 (L. 1981).
7. Connecticut General Statutes, Section 52-408, *et seq.*
8. Connecticut General Statutes, Section 31-77.
9. Connecticut General Statutes, Section 46a-51, *et seq.*

10. Connecticut General Statutes, Section 31-51(i).

11. Connecticut General Statutes, Section 31-51(k).

12. Connecticut General Statutes, Section 31-51(g).

13. Connecticut General Statutes, Section 31-48(b).

14. Connecticut General Statutes, Section 51-247(a).

15. Connecticut General Statutes, Section 54-85(b).

16. Connecticut General Statutes, Section 27-33, *et seq.*

17. Connecticut General Statutes, Section 31-128a, *et seq.*

18. See Connecticut General Statutes, Section 31-128a, *et seq.*

19. Connecticut Public Acts, No. 289 (L.1982).

20. Connecticut Public Acts, No. 451 (L. 1983).

21. Connecticut General Statutes, Section 31-75.

22. Connecticut General Statutes, Sections 10-189 and 10-193.

23. Connecticut General Statutes, Section 31-21.

24. Connecticut General Statutes, Section 31-71a, *et seq.*

25. Connecticut General Statutes, Section 31-71a, *et seq.*

26. Connecticut General Statutes, Section 31-71c.

27. Connecticut Public Laws, No. 83-581 (L. 1983.)

28. Connecticut General Statutes, Section 31-40j, *et seq.*

29. Connecticut General Statutes, Section 31-284.

30. *Sheets v. Teddy's Frosted Foods, Inc.,* 179 Conn. 471, 472 A.2d 385 (1980).

31. *Magnan v. Anaconda Industries, Inc.,* 37 Conn. Super. 38 (1980).

32. *Fisher v. Jackson,* 142 Conn. 734, 118 A.2d 316 (1955).

73

Delaware
Labor Laws

[73.01] LABOR RELATIONS LAWS

Public employees' bargaining rights: Section 19-1301 of the Delaware Code established the right of public employees to bargain collectively with their employer. The statute, among other things, provides a method of conducting representation elections to determine bargaining representatives.[1]

School employees' bargaining rights: Section 14-4001, *et seq.*, of the Delaware Code established the Delaware Public School Employment Relations Act.[2] The statute grants to school employees the right to self-organization and to form, join, or assist any employee organization.[3]

Nonright-to-work policy: Union security (union shop) clauses are permissible in the state of Delaware inasmuch as Delaware has not enacted a right-to-work statute pursuant to Section 14(b) of the Labor Management Relations Act.

[73.02] STRIKES, PICKETING, AND BOYCOTT LAWS

Unlawful assembly: Delaware statutes make it unlawful for persons to meet together and attempt to commit violence or injury to any person or property of any person.[4]

Strikebreakers: Delaware laws make it unlawful for any person not directly involved in a labor dispute to recruit any person for employment when the purpose of such recruitment is to have such person take the place in employment of employees in an industry where a labor strike or a lockout exists.[5] The statute does not apply to the state or federal employment services.[6]

[73.03] MEDIATION AND ARBITRATION LAWS

Although the state of Delaware has enacted the Uniform Arbitration Act,[7] the statute expressly excludes labor contracts.

[73.04] REGULATION OF UNION ACTIVITIES

Delaware statutes provide that a labor union, the principles and activities of which are not repugnant to federal or state laws, may register a facsimile, duplicate or description of its name, badge, motto, button, decoration, charm, emblem, rosette, or other insignia.[8] Delaware statutes make it unlawful for any person or corporation to knowingly counterfeit or imitate a union label or insignia.[9]

[73.05]   REGULATION OF EMPLOYMENT PRACTICES

Anti-discrimination laws: Section 19-711, *et seq.*, of the Delaware Code prohibits discrimination in the employment of any individual on the basis of race, color, age, religion, sex, or national origin.

Polygraph restrictions: Delaware statutes prohibit any person from requiring, requesting, or suggesting that a prospective employee, or employees, take a polygraph, lie detector, or similar test or examination as a condition of employment or continuation of employment.[10]

Employment of illegal aliens: Delaware employers are forbidden to employ an alien who is not entitled to lawful residence of the United States, if such employment would have an adverse effect on lawful resident workers.[11]

Protection of political freedom: Delaware employers are prohibited from interfering with an employee's right to vote or from taking adverse action in the employment rights of any employee because such employee has exercised his or her right to vote.[12]

National guard members: Members of the reserve components of the armed forces must be granted leaves of absence to attend military training, etc. and reinstated without loss of entitlements upon their return.[13]

Whistle-blowing statute: State employees may not be discharged or otherwise discriminated against in retaliation for their reporting a violation, or suspected violation, of a federal or state law to the Delaware auditor of accounts.[14]

Access to personnel records: Delaware employers are required to permit employees to inspect their personnel records, upon proper request, and at reasonable times. Should an employee disagree with information contained in such records, he or she may file a protest to the employer and ask for removal of that portion with which issue is taken. If the employee and the employer cannot agree upon removal or correction of the material or information in question, the employee's written protest to such materials or information shall be maintained as part of the personnel records.[15]

[73.06]   WAGE AND HOUR LAWS

Child labor: Delaware statutes provide that children under 16 years of age are restricted to work in only certain jobs.[16] Children between 14 and 16 years of age must possess general employment certificates in order to work at all jobs not specifically forbidden to such age group.[17] Employers are required to maintain employment certificates for children under 16 years of age and certificates of age for children between 16 and 18 years of age.[18]

Payment of wages: Delaware employers are required to pay their employees accrued wages at least once a month and on regular paydays designated in advance.[19] The statute also provides that the end of the pay period shall be no more than seven days before the payday.[20]

Payment on termination: Whenever a Delaware employee is discharged, his or her employer is required to pay all due wages at the time of discharge.[21] Whenever an employee resigns, his or her wages are payable no later than the next regular payday, unless the employee gives at least a day's notice of his or her resignation, in which event, his or her wages are due on the day of resignation.[22]

Garnishments: Section 1-3509 of the Delaware Code forbids an employer to discharge an employee because his or her wages are subjected to garnishment orders.

[73.07] SAFETY AND HEALTH LAWS

General provisions: Delaware statutes require employers to furnish a safe work place with proper sanitation safeguards and protective devices to protect life and limb of the worker.[23]

Toxic substances—right to know: Delaware employers are required to provide, at least annually, education and training for employees using or handling hazardous chemicals regarding potential daners of such chemicals.[24]

[73.08] UNEMPLOYMENT COMPENSATION LAWS

The Delaware unemployment compensation laws govern the eligibility requirements of recipients of unemployment compensation benfits.[25] The Delaware unemployment compensation laws are found in Delaware Code, Section 19-3301, *et seq.*

[73.09] WORKERS' COMPENSATION LAWS

Delaware's workers' compensation statute provides for a schedule of benefits to be paid to employees injured while in the course and scope of their employment.[26] The statute also covers occupational diseases.[27] Benefits and payments are paid to employees in accordance with established schedules; the amounts and duration of which are dependent upon the gravity of the injury or disease and whether the disability is temporary or permanent and/or partial or total.

[73.10]   EMPLOYMENT-AT-WILL DEVELOPMENTS

Delaware courts have refused, as of this writing, to judicially erode the employment-at-will principle, rejecting specifically, that personnel policy provisions that promise job security may be construed as implied employment contracts for a specific term.[28]

NOTES TO CHAPTER 73

1. Delaware Code, Sections 19-1305 through 19-1308.
2. Delaware Code, Section 14-4001, *et seq.*
3. Delaware Code, Section 14-4003.
4. Delaware Code, Section 11-1302, *et seq.*
5. Delaware Code, Section 19-704.
6. Delaware Code, Section 19-703.
7. Delaware Public Acts, S.B. No. 425 (L. 1972).
8. Delaware Code, Section 6-3331.
9. Delaware Code, Section 6-3305.
10. Delaware Code, Section 19-704.
11. Delaware Code, Section 19-705.
12. Delaware Code, Section 15-5302.
13. Delaware Code, Section 20-905.
14. Delaware Code, Section 29-5115.
15. Delaware Public Acts, Chapter 473 (L. 1984).
16. Delaware Code, Section 19-512.
17. Delaware Code, Section 19-542.
18. Delaware Code, Section 19-541.
19. Delaware Code, Section 19-1102.
20. Delaware Code, Section 19-1102.
21. Delaware Code, Section 19-1103.
22. Delaware Code, Section 19-1103.
23. Delaware Code, Section 19-106.
24. Delaware Public Laws, S.B. 436 (L. 1984).
25. Delaware Code, Section 19-3301, *et seq.*
26. Delaware Code, Section 19-2101, *et seq.*
27. Delaware Code, Section 19-2301, *et seq.*
28. *Heideck v. Kent General Hospital, Inc.*, 446 A.2d 1095 (Del. 1982).

74

District of Columbia
Labor Laws

[74.01] LABOR RELATIONS LAWS

Public employees' bargaining rights: The District of Columbia Government Comprehensive Merit Personnel Act established a Labor Management Relations program for employees of the District of Columbia.[1] The statute accords employees of the District of Columbia the right to form, join, and assist a labor organization or to refrain from such activity and to engage in collective bargaining through representatives of their own choosing, without fear of penalty or reprisal.[2] The District of Columbia Labor Management Relations Program enumerates conduct that constitutes unfair labor practices as well as preserves certain management prerogatives to government employers.[3] The statute provides that it shall be unlawful for any District of Columbia employee or labor union to participate in, authorize, or ratify a strike against the District.[4]

Nonright-to-work policy: Union security (union shop) clauses are permissible in the district of Columbia.

[74.02] STRIKES, PICKETING, AND BOYCOTT LAWS

Unlawful assembly: Section 22-1107 of the Code of the District of Columbia makes it unlawful for any persons to congregate or assemble for the purpose of engaging in disorderly conduct.

Threats of violence: District of Columbia statutory laws forbid anyone to threaten bodily harm to another.[5]

[74.03] MEDIATION AND ARBITRATION

The District of Columbia has adopted the Uniform Arbitration Act recognizing any written agreement to submit an existing controversy to arbitration as valid, enforceable, and irrevocable, excepting such grounds as exist at law or equity for the revocation thereof.[6]

[74.04] REGULATION OF UNION ACTIVITIES

No provisions are noted for this subheading.

[74.05] REGULATION OF EMPLOYMENT PRACTICES

Anti-discrimination laws: Section 1-2512, *et seq.*, of the Code of the District of Columbia prohibits discrimination in employment on the basis of race, color, religion, national origin, sex, age, marital status, personal appearance, sexual orientation, physical handicap, student status, family responsibilities, or political affiliation. Discrimination in employment with respect to pregnancy is also forbidden.[7]

Access to personnel records: Section 3105 of the District of Columbia Comprehensive Merit Personnel Act provides that the official personnel record of a District of Columbia employee shall be disclosed to the employee upon proper request and at reasonable times, excepting confidential and other specified information. The statute also permits the employee the right to present information immediately germane to any information contained in his or her official personnel record and seek to have irrelevant, immaterial, or untimely information removed from the record.

Polygraph restrictions: No District of Columbia employer or prospective employer is permitted to accept or use the results of any lie detector, polygraph, or similar test or examination in connection with the employment, application, or consideration of an individual, or have administered such a test or examination to a prospective employee in connection therewith.[8]

[74.06] WAGE AND HOUR LAWS

Child labor: The District of Columbia statutes provide that children under 14 years of age may not be employed in gainful employment, except in the home or on a farm, or in the distribution of newspapers outside school hours if 10 years of age or over.[9] The statute also places certain enumerated limitations on children in age groups 16 to 18.[10] Children under 18 years of age must obtain work permits in order to engage in gainful employment.[11]

Payment of wages: District of Columbia employers are required to pay all wages earned to employees at least twice during each calendar month, on regular paydays designated in advance, with no more than ten working days to elapse between the end of a pay period covered and the regular payday designated by the employer.[12]

Payment upon termination: As a general statutory requirement, the District of Columbia Code requires that discharged employees be paid wages earned not later than the day following discharge and that employees not under written contract who voluntarily resign be paid wages due upon the next regular payday or within seven days from the day of quitting, whichever is earlier.[13]

[74.07] SAFETY AND HEALTH LAWS

District of Columbia employers are required to furnish an employment environment to their employees that is free of hazards and dangerous conditions and to adopt and use practices, means, methods, operations, and processes that are reasonably safe and adequate to render such employment reasonably safe.[14]

[74.08] UNEMPLOYMENT COMPENSATION LAWS

The District of Columbia unemployment compensation laws are found at Section 46-101, *et seq.*, of the District of Columbia Code. The statute provides certain enumerated benefits for individuals qualifying under its provisions. Benefits are available to pregnant employees who are otherwise eligible under the Act in that pregnancy creates no presumption of inability to work.[15] Aliens who are not lawfully admitted for permanent residence are ineligible to receive benefits.[16]

[74.09] WORKERS' COMPENSATION LAWS

The provisions of the Longshoremen and Harbor Workers' Compensation Act[17] are applicable to job-related injuries and deaths of District of Columbia employees. However, compensation for disability or death resulting from a job-related injury is governed by the District of Columbia Workers' Compensation Act[18] which parallels the provisions of the Longshoremen and Harbor Compensation Act, except as enumerated therein.

[74.10] EMPLOYMENT-AT-WILL DEVELOPMENTS

The District of Columbia courts have been reluctant to recognize judicial exceptions to the employment-at-will doctrine, holding that unless employment contracts are for a specific period they are terminable at the will of either the employee or employer.[19] However, a 1941 District of Columbia case suggested that a "permanent" employment arrangement might be considered an exception to the at-will rule.[20] Similarly, a District of Columbia court held in a 1984 case that a partially disabled employee may maintain a cause of action based on an alleged breach of an oral lifetime contract of employment despite receiving workers' compensation benefits.[21]

NOTES TO CHAPTER 74

1. D.C. Code, Section 1-618.1, *et seq.*
2. D.C. Code, Section 1-618.6.

3. D.C. Code, Section 1-618.4.

4. D.C. Code, Section 1-618.5.

5. D.C. Code, Section 22-507.

6. D.C. Code, Section 16-4301, *et seq.*

7. D.C. Code, Sections 1-2502(17), 1-2512.

8. D.C. Code, Section 36-801, *et seq.*

9. D.C. Code, Section 36-501.

10. D.C. Code, Section 36-502.

11. D.C. Code, Section 36-507, *et seq.*

12. D.C. Code, Section 36-102.

13. D.C. Code, Section 36-103.

14. D.C. Code, Section 36-228.

15. D.C. Code, Section 46-101, *et seq.*

16. D.C. Code, Section 46-110.

17. The Longshoremen and Harbor Workers' Compensation Act is discussed in Chapter 62.

18. D.C. Code, Section 36-301, *et seq.*

19. *Prouty v. National R.R. Passenger Corp.*, 572 F.Supp. 200 (D. D.C. 1982).

20. *Littel v. Evening Star Newspaper Co.*, 120 F.2d 36 (D.C. Cir. 1941).

21. *Kitzmiller v. Washington Post*, 115 LRRM 3015 (D. D.C. 1984).

75

Florida
Labor Laws

[75.01] LABOR RELATIONS ACTS

Employees' rights of self-organization: Section 447.03 of the Florida Statutes provides that Florida employees shall have the right to self-organization, to form, join, or assist labor unions or to refrain from such activity and that such employees shall also have the right to bargain collectively through representatives of their own choosing and to engage in concerted activities for the purpose of collective bargaining or other mutual aid or protection.

Public employees' bargaining rights: Specifically, Florida statutes provide that public employees shall have the right of self-organization and the right to join and assist labor unions, or to refrain from union activities.[1] The statute prohibits certain conduct of both public employers and labor organizations, the violations of which constitute unfair labor practices.[2] The Florida Public Employees Relations Act also provides for an election process to determine bargaining representatives, establishes registration requirements for labor organizations, and forbids strikes.[3]

Right-to-work statute: The Florida Constitution prohibits the denial of employment to anyone on account of membership or nonmembership in a labor union or organization.[4]

[75.02] STRIKES, PICKETING, AND BOYCOTT LAWS

Regulation of strike activity: Florida statutes make it unlawful for any person to

- picket beyond the area of the industry or employment within which a labor dispute arises
- engage in picketing by force and violence, or to picket in such a manner as to prevent ingress or egress to and from any premises, or to picket other than in a reasonable and peaceable manner
- coerce or intimidate any employee in the employment of his or her legal rights or to coerce or intimidate any elected or appointed public official, or to intimidate the family, picket the domicile, or injure the person or property of such employee or public official or his or her family[5]

Unlawful assembly: Florida laws prohibit three or more persons from meeting together to commit a breach of the peace, or to do any unlawful act.[6]

534

Striker replacements: Section 449.07 of the Florida Statutes makes it unlawful for private employment agencies to send any applicant to any place where a strike is in active progress, without first notifying the applicant of such conditions.

[75.03] MEDIATION AND ARBITRATION LAWS

The Florida Arbitration Act recognizes written agreements between two parties to submit any controversy between them to arbitration as valid, enforceable, and irrevocable, without regard to the justiciable character of the controversy.[7] Section 453.01, *et seq.*, of the Florida Statutes established the Public Utility Arbitration Act, the declared purpose of the Act being to facilitate the prompt, peaceful, and just settlement of labor disputes between public utility employers and their employees that cause or threaten to cause an interruption in the supply of services necessary to the health, safety, and well-being of the citizens of Florida.

[75.04] REGULATION OF UNION ACTIVITIES

Section 447.01, *et seq.*, of the Florida Statutes established the Florida Union Regulation Law. Among other things, the statute requires labor unions to file certain reports, union business agents to obtain a license or permit to operate, and labor organizations to keep accurate records.

The Florida Union Regulation Law also forbids anyone to conduct a "strike vote" without a secret ballot election; charge, receive or obtain any union dues, assessments or other charges in excess of, or not authorized by, the constitution or bylaws of such union; to solicit membership for or to act as a representative of an existing labor organization without authority from such union; to seize or occupy property unlawfully during the existence of a labor dispute; or to cause any work stoppage by reason of any jurisdictional dispute.[8] The Florida statutes prohibit anyone from making or using any counterfeited union label.[9]

[75.05] REGULATION OF EMPLOYMENT PRACTICES

Anti-discrimination laws: Florida statutory laws prohibit discrimination in employment on the basis of race, color, religion, sex, national origin, age, handicap, or marital status.[10] Employment discrimination because of a sickle cell trait is also forbidden.[11]

Jury duty: Section 40.271 of the Florida Statutes forbids the dismissal of an employee because of his or her having served on a grand or petit jury in the state.

Employment of illegal aliens: Florida employers are prohibited from recruiting or hiring aliens not duly authorized to work by the immigration laws or by the Attorney General of the United States.[12]

Protection of political freedom: Florida statutes make it unlawful for any person to discriminate against employees for exercising their right to vote as they choose in any state, county, or municipal election.[13]

Protection of National Guard members: Florida statutes forbid employers to discharge, reprimand, or in any manner penalize a Florida National Guard member because of absence due to active duty in the National Guard.[14]

Blacklisting: Florida statutes make it unlawful for two or more persons to agree to conspire together for the purpose of preventing any person from procuring employment elsewhere.[15]

Equal pay: Florida employers are forbidden to discriminate in the payment of wages on the basis of sex.[16]

[75.06] WAGE AND HOUR LAWS

Child labor: Florida statutes restrict the employment of certain age groups of children, such as the following:

- Children under 10 years of age are prohibited from selling or distributing newspapers, etc.[17]
- Children under 12 years are prohibited from employment, with limited exceptions.[18]
- Children under 16 years of age are prohibited from working in certain enumerated "hazardous duty" jobs.[19]
- Children under 18 years of age are prohibited from employment in any establishment selling alcoholic beverages (with limited exceptions).[20]

Payment of wages: Generally, wages are payable on demand by negotiable instrument or in cash, without discount.[21]

Medical insurance conversion: Section 627.6675 of the Florida Statutes provides that terminating employees must be given an opportunity to convert their insurance coverage under a group health plan to an individual plan, provided certain qualifications are met.

[75.07] SAFETY AND HEALTH LAWS

General provisions: Florida health and safety laws require employers within the state to furnish safe employment for employees, and to furnish and use safety devices and safeguards, adopt and use methods and processes reasonably adequate to render such employment and place of employment safe, and do every other thing reasonably necessary to protect life, health, and safety of employees.[22]

Toxic substances—right to know: Employers manufacturing or using hazardous chemicals in their work place must post certain notices to employees about potential dangers of such chemicals and provide certain education and training to employees regarding such substances.[23]

[75.08] UNEMPLOYMENT COMPENSATION LAWS

Florida Unemployment Compensation Laws provide for benefits to be paid to certain qualified individuals who are presently out of work due to reduction in force, layoff conditions, and so forth.[24]

[75.09] WORKERS' COMPENSATION LAWS

The Florida Workers' Compensation Laws are found in Sections 440.01, *et seq.*, of the Florida Statutes and provide certain scheduled benefits to employees who suffer job-related injuries and occupational diseases. The law forbids an employer to retaliate against an employee who files a workers' compensation claim.[25]

[75.10] EMPLOYMENT-AT-WILL DEVELOPMENTS

Florida courts have recognized limited exceptions to the employment-at-will doctrine, although the doctrine is yet rigidly applied in most wrongful discharge actions.[26]

Public policy exception: Florida courts have held that a discharge of an employee in retaliation of the employee's filing a worker's compensation claim was repugnant to public policy, sufficient to remove the employee's employment status from the at-will rule.[27]

''Independent consideration'' exception: In a wrongful discharge case involving an employee who sold his business to the employer in return for guaranteed permanent employment, a Florida court held that the employee had provided consideration independent of performing regular employment services and that an action for breach of employment contract was justifiable.[28]

NOTES TO CHAPTER 75

1. Florida Statutes, Section 447.209, *et seq.*

2. Florida Statutes, Section 447.501.

3. See generally Florida Statutes, Section 447.201, *et seq.*

4. Florida Revised Constitution, Section 6, Art. 1.

5. Florida Statutes, Section 447.09(11) through (13).

6. Florida Statutes, Section 870.01, *et seq.*

7. Florida Statutes, Section 682.02.

8. Florida Statutes, Section 447.09

9. Florida Statutes, Section 506.06.

10. Florida Statutes, Section 760.01, *et seq.*

11. Florida Statutes, Section 448.075.

12. Florida Statutes, Section 448.09.

13. Florida Statutes, Section 104.081.

14. Florida Statutes, Section 250.48.

15. Florida Statutes, Section 448.045

16. Florida Statutes, Section 448.07.

17. Florida Statutes, Section 450.021.

18. Florida Statutes, Section 450.021.

19. Florida Statutes, Section 450.061.

20. Florida Statutes, Section 450.021.

21. Florida Statutes, Section 532.01.

22. Florida Statutes, Section 440.56.

23. Florida Public Laws, Chapters 84-223 (L. 1984).

24. Florida Statutes, Section 443.011, *et seq.*

25. Florida Statutes, Section 440.205.

26. See, for example: *Muller v. Stromberg Carlson Corp.*, 427 So.2d 266 (2d Dist. Ct. Fla. App. 1983).

27. *Smith v. Piezo Technology*, 427 So.2d 182 (Fla. 1983).

28. *Chatelier v. Robertson*, 118 So.2d 241 (2d Dist. Ct. Fla. App. 1960).

76

Georgia
Labor Laws

[76.01] LABOR RELATIONS LAWS

Firefighters' bargaining rights: The Georgia Firefighter's Mediation Act provides that firefighters within the state shall have the right to bargain collectively with their respective corporate authorities. The statute also provides a mediation process to resolve labor disputes.[1]

Right-to-work statute: Section 34-6-23 of the Georgia Code Annotated makes it unlawful for any employer to require an individual to become or remain a member of a labor union as a condition of employment.

[76.02] STRIKES, PICKETING, AND BOYCOTT LAWS

Anti-picketing statute: Section 34-6-2 of the Georgia Code Annotated forbids anyone to prevent, or attempt to prevent, any individual from quitting or continuing in the employment of, or from accepting or refusing employment by any employer, or from entering or leaving any place of employment of such employer.

Unlawful assembly: Georgia statutes make it unlawful for any two or more persons to assemble at or near any place where a labor dispute exists and attempt to prevent any person from engaging in any lawful vocation.[2]

Interference with employment rights: Georgia statutes forbid any person to attempt to prevent anyone from engaging in, remaining in, or performing the business, labor, or duties of any lawful employment or occupation.[3]

Mass picketing prohibited: Georgia laws also make it unlawful for any person to engage in mass picketing at or near any place where a labor dispute exists in such a manner as to obstruct or interfere with ingress or egress.[4]

Prohibition against public employee strikes: Georgia statutory laws prohibit state employees or officials from promoting, encouraging or participating in a strike.[5]

[76.03] MEDIATION AND ARBITRATION LAWS

Section 9-9-30, *et seq.*, of the Georgia Code Annotated provides the right of parties disagreeing over controversies to submit the matters to third parties for a determination on the issues involved. Section 34-2-6 of the Georgia Code Annotated empowers the state Commissioner of Labor to promote the voluntary arbitration, mediation, and conciliation of disputes between employers and employees and to do everything in his or her power to avoid strikes, picketing, lockouts, boycotts, etc.

[76.04] REGULATION OF UNION ACTIVITIES

Georgia statutes make it unlawful for any person or corporation to counterfeit or imitate a union label.[6] Georgia laws make unlawful contracts between employers and labor unions which limit the use of "piggyback" conveyances in the transporting of goods and products.[7]

[76.05] REGULATION OF EMPLOYMENT PRACTICES

Anti-discrimination laws (public sector): Section 45-19-29 of the Georgia Code Annotated makes it unlawful for public sector employers to discriminate in employment on the basis of race, color, religion, national origin, sex, handicap, or age. Age discrimination in employment[8] and employment against the physically handicapped[9] by single employers are also forbidden.

Unlawful enticement of employees: Georgia employers are prohibited by Section 60-9904, *et seq.*, of the Georgia Code from attempting to entice employees who are under contract to another away from such employment during the term of service.

Forged letters of reference restrictions: Georgia statutes make it unlawful for any person to forge any letter or certificate of employment reference.[10]

Lie detector restrictions: Georgia statutes prohibit polygraph examiners from inquiring into such areas as religious beliefs or affiliations, racial matters, political beliefs, or affiliations regarding a labor union, during pre-employment or periodic employment examinations.[11]

Military leave (public employees): Georgia statutes require state agencies to grant up to thirty days' leave of absence per year to state employees for the purpose of military training or other duty, without loss of entitlements.[12]

Equal pay: Georgia employers are forbidden to discriminate on the basis of sex by paying wages to employees of one sex at a rate less than that paid to employees of the opposite sex for equal work.[13]

[76.06] WAGE AND HOUR LAWS

Child labor: Georgia wage and hour laws regulate the rights and restrictions of certain age groups of children to engage in gainful employment.[14]

Garnishments: Section 18-4-7 of the Georgia Code forbids the discharge of an employee because his or her wages have been subjected to garnishments for any one indebtedness.

Terms of employment: Section 34-7-1 of the Georgia Code Annotated provides that whenever the employer and employee agree to stipulated wages for a fixed period, that the employment of the employee is for that fixed period of time. The statute also provides, however, that should anything in the agreement between the employer and the employee evidence the employment was for a longer term, the mere reservation of wages for a shorter term would not control. Otherwise, an indefinite hiring may be terminated at will by either party.

Voting time: Georgia statutes require employers to permit employees to leave work for a period not exceeding two hours as shall be necessary in order to vote in political elections within the state, provided such employees' hours of work do not commence at least two hours after the opening of the election polls or do not end at least two hours before the closing of the polls. [15]

Payment of wages: Georgia employers are required to pay wages to nonsupervisory employees at least twice a month on regularly designated paydays except those employees in farming, sawmill, and turpentine industries. [16]

[76.07] SAFETY AND HEALTH LAWS

Section 34-2-10 of the Georgia Code Annotated requires employers within the state to furnish employment that shall be reasonably safe for employees, to furnish and use safety devices and safeguards, to adopt and use methods and processes reasonably adequate to render employment and the place of employment reasonably safe, and to do every other thing reasonably necessary to protect the life, health, and safety of employees.

[76.08] UNEMPLOYMENT COMPENSATION LAWS

The Georgia unemployment compensation laws are governed by section 34-8-1, *et seq.*, of the Georgia Code Annotated. Benefits are payable to out-of-work employees provided they meet enumerated requirements such as proper and timely filing, availability for work, waiting for the prescribed period of time, etc. [17]

[76.09] WORKERS' COMPENSATION LAWS

The Georgia Workers' Compensation Laws are found at Section 34-9-1, *et seq.*, of the Georgia Code Annotated. The statute provides certain scheduled benefits to employees who suffer job-related injuries and certain occupational diseases.[18]

[76.10] EMPLOYMENT-AT-WILL DEVELOPMENTS

Georgia courts have steadfastly refused to recognize such deviations from the employment-at-will doctrine as public policy exceptions,[19] implied contract exceptions, etc., as of this writing.[20]

Some inroads have been made in the tort exception to the at-will rule, however. For example, a Georgia court permitted a cause of action where it was alleged that an employer negligently allowed a supervisor to sexually harass an employee.[21]

A Georgia Court of Appeals held an employee may recover for mental anguish where the employer had deliberately, maliciously, and falsely accused the employee of stealing.[22]

Another intentional tort claim was held actionable where an employer detained and questioned an employee for some five hours, preventing her from taking needed medication.[23]

Moreover, as discussed at [76.06], an employee's term of employment will be construed to be the same period of time as is designated for his or her pay periods, whether daily, weekly, monthly, or annually.

NOTES TO CHAPTER 76

1. Georgia Public Acts, H.B. 569 (L. 1971).
2. Georgia Code Annotated, Section 16-11-30, *et seq.*
3. Georgia Code Annotated, Section 34-6-4.
4. Georgia Code Annotated, Section 34-6-5.
5. Georgia Code Annotated, Section 45-19-1, *et seq.*
6. Georgia Code Annotated, Section 10-1-451.
7. Georgia Code Annatated, Section 34-6-8.
8. Georgia Code Annotated, Section 34-1-2.
9. Georgia Code Annotated, Section 34-6A-4.
10. Georgia Code Annotated, Section 34-10-14.
11. Georgia Code Annotated, Section 43-36-14.
12. Georgia Code Annotated, Section 38-2-279.
13. Georgia Code Annotated, Section 45-19-29.
14. See, Georgia Child Labor Regulations, Section 300-7-1, *et seq.*
15. Georgia Code Annotated, Section 21-2-404.
16. Georgia Code Annotated, Section 34-7-2.
17. Georgia Code Annotated, Section 34-8-1, *et seq.*

18. Georgia Code Annotated, Section 34-9-1, *et seq.*

19. See, for example: *Troy v. Interfinancial, Inc.,* 320 S.E.2d 872 (Ga. Ct. of App., 1984).

20. *Nelson v. M & M Products Co.,* 168 Ga. App. 280, 308 S.E.2d 607 (Ga. Ct. of App., 1983).

21. *Cox v. Brazo,* 303 S.E.2d 71 (Ga. Ct. of App., 1983).

22. *Beavers v. Johnson,* 145 S.E.2d 776 (Ga. Ct. of App., 1965).

23. *Smith v. Rich's, Inc.,* 104 Ga. App. 883, 123 S.E.2d 316 (Ga. Ct. of App., 1961).

77

Hawaii
Labor Laws

Hawaii Employment Relations Act: Section 377-1, *et seq.,* of the Hawaii Revised Statutes provides that Hawaii employers, other than employers and employees specifically exempted, and excluding the state and subdivisions thereof, must recognize and bargain in good faith with unions properly certified as representatives of their employees.

Public employees' bargaining rights: Hawaii statutes provide that public employees shall have the right of self-organization and the right to join and assist labor unions, or to refrain from union activities, except under conditions requiring the payment of union dues.[1] Section 89-5 of the Hawaii Revised Statutes established the Hawaii Public Employment Relations Board whose function is to administer and enforce the provisions and requirements of the Act. The Act provides for an election process to determine bargaining representatives,[2] establishes procedures to determine bargaining units,[3] and forbids strikes.[4]

Nonright-to-work policy: Union security (union shop) clauses are permissible in the state of Hawaii inasmuch as Hawaii has not adopted a right-to-work statute as permitted by Section 14(b) of the Labor Management Relations Act.

[77.02]   STRIKES, PICKETING, AND BOYCOTT LAWS

Unlawful assembly: Section 711-1104 of the Hawaii Revised Statutes makes it unlawful for a person to assemble with five or more persons with an intent to engage in a riot.

Picketing of residence or dwelling: Hawaii statutory laws forbid anyone to engage in picketing before or about the residence or dwelling place of another individual.[5]

Strike vote: Section 372-6(5) of the Hawaii Revised Statutes makes it an unfair labor practice to picket or engage in a work stoppage unless a majority of the employees in the bargaining unit have voted by secret ballot to call a strike.

Striker replacements and strikebreakers: Section 379-3 of the Hawaii Revised Statutes requires advertisements and solicitations for employment applicants to state any existence of a strike, lockout, or other labor trouble at the place of the proposed employment. Hawaii statutes make it unlawful for any employer to utilize professional strikebreakers to replace an employee involved in a strike or lockout through the use of misrepresentations, threats, or force.[6]

Anti-injunction laws: Hawaii statutory laws restrict the power of Hawaii courts to issue injunctions against peaceable picketing and legally protected strike activity.[7]

Interference with ingress or egress: Section 711-1105 of the Hawaii Revised Statutes makes it unlawful for anyone, not having a legal privilege to do so, to obstruct highways or public passages.

Restrictions in stevedore strikes: Section 382-1, *et seq.*, of the Hawaii Revised Statutes provides that under certain strike conditions in the stevedoring industry, the governor of Hawaii is empowered to declare an emergency and seize and operate the plants and facilities of the stevedoring company experiencing such labor dispute.

[77.03]   MEDIATION AND ARBITRATION LAWS

The Hawaii Public Utility Labor Act declares it a public policy to prevent or promptly and orderly settle a labor dispute affecting public utilities.[8] To further the purpose of the act, public utilities and their employees, including employees' representatives, have the duty to use the processes of conference and collective bargaining in the settlement of all disputes between them without resorting to lockout or strike.[9]

[77.04]   REGULATION OF UNION ACTIVITIES

Hawaii statutes forbid any person to adopt or use a union label without authorization by the subject union.[10] Section 337-14 of the Hawaii Revised Statutes requires labor unions operating within the state to register with the Hawaii Employment Relations Board. Section 377-10 of the Hawaii Revised Statutes requires labor unions to furnish certain financial statements to their members on an annual basis.

[77.05]   REGULATION OF EMPLOYMENT PRACTICES

Anti-discrimination laws: Hawaii statutory laws prohibit discrimination in employment whenever based on race, sex, age, religion, ancestry, physical handicap, or criminal record not having substantial relationship to the job requirements.[11]

Unlawful enticement: Hawaii laws forbid any person, by promise of employment without the state, to induce or entice any employee who has contracted to serve his or her employer for a specific length of time, to leave the service of the employer during that time.[12]

Jury pay: Hawaii employers, having twenty-five employees or more, are required to pay employees who serve on a jury or a public board, compensation in an amount equal to the difference between the remuneration such employee would receive for such service on a jury or public board, and his or her regular wages.[13]

Polygraph restrictions: Hawaii statutes make it unlawful for employers to require an employee to submit to a polygraph or lie detector test as a condition of employment or continued employment.[14]

Witness appearances: Hawaii laws prohibit an employer from depriving an employee of his or her employment, or threatening to do so, because the employee receives a summons, serves as a witness, or attends court as a prospective witness.[15]

Criminal and arrest records (state employees): The state of Hawaii and its political subdivisions are forbidden to use, distribute, or disseminate arrest and related records in connection with any employment decision of their employees.[16] The statute also provides that no person shall be disqualified from employment by the state of Hawaii or any of its protected subdivisions solely by reason of a conviction of a crime.

Military leave: Section 79-23 of the Hawaii Revised Statutes requires the state and its political subdivisions to re-employ military personnel upon their return from military service to their former or similar positions, if still qualified to perform them, without loss of seniority or other employment status or pay. Hawaii statutes provide that every employee of a private employer who is a member of a National Guard shall be entitled to absent himself or herself from employment duties while engaged in the performance of National Guard Service and return to his or her position without loss of seniority, status, or pay.[17]

Equal pay: Section 387-4 of the Hawaii Revised Statutes makes it unlawful to discriminate in payment of wages on the basis of race, religion, or sex.

[77.06] WAGE AND HOUR LAWS

Child labor: Secton 390-1, *et seq.*, of the Hawaii Revised Statutes sets certain restrictions on the employment of children within the state.

Voting time: Hawaii statutes provide that employees shall be excused from employment up to two consecutive hours to exercise voting privileges provided such employees do not have two consecutive hours outside of work hours to cast their votes.[18]

Payment of wages: Section 388-2 of the Hawaii Revised Statutes requires Hawaii employers, excluding state agencies, to pay employees their wages no less than twice during a month and no later than fifteen days from the established pay period.

Payment upon termination: Hawaii employers are required to pay discharged employees their wages in full at time of discharge, or no later than the following day where extreme conditions prevent such.[19] An employee who voluntarily resigns his or her job is due accrued wages no later than the next regular payday.[20]

Garnishments: Section 378-32(1) of the Hawaii Revised Statutes makes it unlawful to discharge an employee because the employee's wages have been subjected to a garnishment.

[77.07]   SAFETY AND HEALTH LAWS

General provisions: Hawaii health and safety laws require employers within the state to furnish safe employment for employees, and to furnish and use safety devices and safeguards, adopt and use methods and processes reasonably adequate to render such employment and place of employment safe, and do every other thing reasonably necessary to protect life, health, and safety of employees.[21] Section 396-8(e)(1) of the Hawaii Revised Statutes makes it unlawful to discriminate against any employee by reason of the employee's refusal to operate any unsafe machine or equipment, to engage in unsafe practices in violation of the Hawaii Occupational Safety and Health Act (HOSHA) or because of the employee's filing of a complaint to exercise his or her rights under HOSHA.

Toxic substances—right to know: Hawaii statutes require employers who use or manufacture hazardous chemicals and toxic materials to provide prompt information to employees when they have been or are being exposed to toxic materials and harmful physical agents in concentrations above certain enumerated levels.[22]

[77.08]   UNEMPLOYMENT COMPENSATION LAWS

The Hawaii unemployment compensation laws govern, among other things, the eligibility requirements of recipients of unemployment compensation benefits.[23]

[77.09]   WORKERS' COMPENSATION LAWS

Section 386-10, *et seq.*, of the Hawaii Revised Statutes sets forth the Hawaii Workmen's Compensation Act. The statute provides disability benefits to employees injured on the job or who suffer occupational diseases as a result of their job, subject to specified qualifications and limitations.[24] Hawaii statutes make it unlawful to discharge an employee because he or she has suffered a work-related injury.[25]

[77.10] EMPLOYMENT-AT-WILL DEVELOPMENTS

Hawaii courts have continued to apply the general rule that an employee can be terminated at the will of the employer in the absence of written contract or statute that provides otherwise.[26] Some exceptions have been noted, however.

Public policy exception: Hawaii courts will recognize an exception to the at-will rule where an employee is discharged for refusing to commit an unlawful act or for exercising a lawful right.[27]

Promissory estoppel exception: Hawaii courts have also sustained causes of action where a prospective employee relied on an employer's promise of definite employment.[28]

NOTES TO CHAPTER 77

1. Hawaii Revised Statutes, Section 89-3.
2. Hawaii Revised Statutes, Sections 89-7 and 89-8.
3. Hawaii Revised Statutes, Section 89-6.
4. Hawaii Revised Statutes, Section 89-12.
5. Hawaii Revised Statutes, Section 379-A-1.
6. Hawaii Revised Statutes, Section 379-2.
7. Hawaii Revised Statutes, Section 380-1, *et seq.*
8. Hawaii Public Acts, No. 146 (L. 1949).
9. Hawaii Public Acts, No. 146, Section 4163 (L. 1949).
10. Hawaii Revised Statutes, Section 482-4.
11. Hawaii Revised Statutes, Section 378-1, *et seq.*
12. Hawaii Public Acts, Chapter 70 (L. 1911).
13. Hawaii Revised Statutes, Section 612-25. See also: Sections 95-26 and 79-14.
14. Hawaii Revised Statutes, Section 378-21.
15. Hawaii Public Acts, No. 621 (L. 1978).
16. Hawaii Revised Statutes, Section 378-2.
17. Hawaii Revised Statutes, Section 121-43.
18. Hawaii Revised Statutes, Section 11-95.
19. Hawaii Revised Statutes, Section 388-3(a).
20. Hawaii Revised Statutes, Section 388-3(b).
21. Hawaii Revised Statutes, Section 396-6(a) and (c).

22. Hawaii Revised Statutes, Section 396-7.

23. Hawaii Revised Statutes, Section 383-1, *et seq.*

24. Hawaii Revised Statutes, Section 386-1, *et seq.*

25. Hawaii Revised Statutes, Section 378-32(2).

26. *Lim v. Motor Supply Co.*, 45 Hawaii 111, 364 P.2d 38 (1961).

27. *Parnar v. Americana Hotels, Inc.*, 652 P.2d 625 (Hawaii, 1982).

28. *Ravelo v. County of Hawaii*, 66 Hawaii 197, 658 P.2d 883 (1983).

78

Idaho
Labor Laws

[78.01] LABOR RELATIONS LAWS

Agricultural employees' bargaining rights: Idaho has within its statutory provisions a law protecting the right of agricultural employees to self-organization and to join or refrain from joining labor unions.[1]

Teachers' bargaining rights: Section 33-1271 of the Idaho Code provides that the board of trustees of each school district is empowered to, and shall, upon its own initiative or upon the request of a local education organization, enter into a negotiation agreement with professional employees in good faith on those matters specified in any negotiation agreement between the local board of trustees and the local education organization. Should such parties be unable to come to an agreement upon items subject to negotiation, a process of mediation is provided.[2]

Municipal employees' and firefighters' bargaining rights: The Idaho Code accords collective bargaining rights and the right of self-organization to firefighters within the state.[3] Municipalities of the state of Idaho have the power to enter into collective bargaining contracts with their employees, or their employees' bargaining representative, under the authority of Section 50-901 of the Idaho Code, according to an opinion of the Idaho Attorney General in 1959.

Right-to-work statute: Idaho law provides that no person shall be denied employment because of a failure or refusal to join a labor union or pay union dues.[4]

"Yellow-dog" contracts: Section 44-901 of the Idaho Code makes it unlawful for anyone to coerce or compel any person to enter into an agreement not to join or become a member of any labor organization as a condition of employment.

[78.02] STRIKES, PICKETING, AND BOYCOTT LAWS

Anti-injunction laws: Idaho laws restrict the power of Idaho courts to issue injunctions against peaceable picketing and legally protected strike activity.[5]

Unlawful assembly: Section 18-6402 of the Idaho Code prohibits two or more persons to assemble together to do an unlawful act.

Strikebreakers: Section 18-712 of the Idaho Code permits a civil action against any person or entity who knowingly brings into the state of Idaho, an armed or unarmed police force, detective agency or force, or armed or unarmed body of men for the suppression of domestic violence.

[78.03] MEDIATION AND ARBITRATION LAWS

Idaho statutes recognize any written agreement to submit an existing controversy to arbitration as valid and enforceable.[6] Section 44-106 of the Idaho Code empowers the state Commissioner of Labor, or a mediator in his or her behalf, to mediate and attempt to conciliate labor disputes upon requests of any party to such controversy.

[78.04] REGULATION OF UNION ACTIVITIES

Idaho statutes make it unlawful for anyone to misuse or forge a union label or other union insignia, or to misrepresent that employment of union labor went into the production or manufacture of goods or services.[7]

[78.05] REGULATION OF EMPLOYMENT PRACTICES

Anti-discrimination laws: Idaho statutory laws prohibit discrimination in employment on the basis of race, color, religion, sex, national origin, or age.[8]

Freedom of political activities: Section 18-2319 of the Idaho Code makes it unlawful for any person to attempt to influence the vote of any elector by discharging him or her from employment.

Jury or witness duty: Idaho employers are forbidden to attempt to deprive any employee of his or her employment because such employee receives a summons, responds thereto, serves a juror, or attends court for prospective jury service.[9]

Employment under false pretense: Section 18-3101 of the Idaho Code prohibits any person to obtain the labor or service of another by any false or fraudulent representations or pretense.

National Guard duty: Idaho law provides that any employee is entitled to military leave up to fifteen days to attend military training and must be restored to his or her former job upon return without loss of any job entitlements.[10]

Polygraph restrictions: No employer shall demand or require any applicant for employment or any employee to submit to or take a polygraph, lie detector, or similar tests or examinations as a condition of employment or continued employment, excepting the use of such tests in certain state agencies or subdivisions thereof.[11]

Equal pay: Section 44-1702 of the Idaho Code prohibits employers to discriminate on the basis of pay by paying wages to employees of one sex less than that paid to employees of the opposite sex for comparable work.

[78.06] WAGE AND HOUR LAWS

Child labor: Idaho child labor laws are covered in the Idaho Code, Section 44-1301, *et seq.* Children 12 years or older may be employed in certain jobs during regular school vacations.[12] Children 16 years or older may be employed in certain limited jobs even during a school term, provided certain qualifications are met.[13] Children of certain age groups are prohibited by Idaho laws to work in certain hazardous occupations.[14]

Payment of wages: Idaho employers are required to pay all wages due employees at least once per month and on regular paydays designated in advance.[15] The statute further requires that the end of the designated pay period be no more than seven days before regular payday.[16]

Payment upon termination: Section 45-606 of the Idaho Code requires employers to pay discharged or laid off employees within 48 hours of discharge or layoff.

Garnishments: Section 28-35-106 of the Idaho Code forbids the discharge of an employee because of a garnishment order arising out of a regulated credit transaction.

[78.07] SAFETY AND HEALTH LAWS

Section 44-104 of the Idaho Code requires Idaho employers to provide a safe work place for employees. Section 72-1101 of the Idaho Code authorizes the Idaho Industrial Board to prevent employment of workers in unsafe places and to require employers to adopt reasonable minimum safety standards.

[78.08] UNEMPLOYMENT COMPENSATION LAWS

The Idaho unemployment compensation laws govern, among other things, the eligibility requirements of recipients of unemployment compensation benefits.[17]

[78.09] WORKERS' COMPENSATION LAWS

Section 72-101, *et seq.,* of the Idaho Code sets forth the Idaho Workmen's Compensation Act. The statute provides disability benefits to employees injured on the job or who suffer occupational diseases as a result of their job, subject to specified qualifications and limitations.[18]

[78.10] EMPLOYMENT-AT-WILL DEVELOPMENTS

The Idaho courts have permitted a limited encroachment upon the employment-at-will doctrine as of this writing.

Implied contract exception: The Idaho Supreme Court has held that it will recognize, as an exception to the at-will doctrine, an implied employment contract flowing from job security statements contained in a personnel policy handbook.[19]

Fraud: An Idaho Court of Appeals has sustained a cause of action where employees were fraudulently induced to accept work that replaced striking employees under the guise that the work would be permanent, only to be terminated when striking employees were later reinstated to their regular jobs.[20]

NOTES TO CHAPTER 78

1. Idaho Code, Section 22-4101, *et seq.*
2. Idaho Code, Section 33-1274.
3. Idaho Code, Section 44-1801, *et seq.*
4. Idaho Code, Section 44-2001, *et seq.*
5. Idaho Code, Section 44-701, *et seq.*
6. Idaho Code, Section 7-901, *et seq.*
7. Idaho Code, Section 44-601, *et seq.*
8. Idaho Code, Section 67-5909, *et seq.*
9. Idaho Code, Section 2-218.
10. Idaho Code, Section 46-224.
11. Idaho Code, Section 44-903.
12. Idaho Code, Section 44-1301.
13. Idaho Code, Section 44-1302.
14. Idaho Code, Section 44-1301, *et seq.*
15. Idaho Code, Section 45-610.
16. Idaho Code, Section 45-610.
17. Idaho Code, Section 72-1361, *et seq.*
18. Idaho Code, Section 72-101, *et seq.*
19. *MacNeil v. Minidoka Memorial Hospital*, 701 P.2d 208 (Idaho S.Ct., 1985).
20. *Verway v. Blinkcoe Packing Co.*, Case No. 15189 (Idaho Ct. of App., 1985).

79

Illinois
Labor Laws

[79.01] LABOR RELATIONS LAWS

Public employees' bargaining rights: Illinois public employees are provided the right of self-organization and the right to join and assist labor unions, or to refrain from union activities.[1]

Illinois Executive Order No. 6 of 1973 created the Illinois Office of Collective Bargaining, whose function is to administer and enforce the provisions and requirements of the Order.

Bargaining rights of teachers: Illinois statutes provide that educational employees shall have the right to organize, form, join, or assist in employee organizations or engage in lawful concerted activities for the purpose of collective bargaining.[2]

Nonright-to-work policy: Union security (union shop) clauses are permissible in the state of Illinois inasmuch as Illinois has not adopted a right-to-work statute as permitted in Section 14(b) of the Labor Management Relations Act.

"Yellow-dog" contracts: Illinois laws make it unlawful for anyone to coerce or compel any person to enter into an agreement not to join or become a member of any labor organization as a condition of employment.[3]

[79.02] STRIKES, PICKETING, AND BOYCOTT LAWS

Interference with employment: Chapter 38, Section 12.6, of the Illinois Revised Statutes makes it unlawful for anyone to use force, threats, or other means of coercion to prevent any person from engaging in the lawful occupation of his or her choice.

Unlawful assembly: Illinois statutes prohibit two or more persons to assemble together to do an unlawful act.[4]

Striker replacements: Illinois statutes require advertisements for employment applicants to state any existence of a strike, lockout, or other labor trouble at the place of the proposed employment.[5]

Strikebreakers: Illinois statutes make it unlawful for any employer to utilize professional strikebreakers to replace an employee involved in a strike or lockout.[6]

Anti-injunction statute: Illinois statutes restrict courts within the state from issuing injunctions or restraining orders that limit or restrain peaceable picketing or other legally protected strike activity.[7]

Picketing of residence or dwelling: Illinois statutory laws forbid anyone to engage in picketing before or about the residence or dwelling of anyone, except when the residence or dwelling is used as a business.[8]

Inciting strikes: Illinois laws make it unlawful for the holder of a private detective license or certificate to knowingly incite, encourage, or aid in the indictment or encouragement of any person or persons who have become a party to strike.[9]

Restriction of railroad picketing: Chapter 114, Section 101, *et seq.*, of the Illinois Revised Statutes prohibits persons from willfully and maliciously impeding or obstructing railroad operations.

[79.03]   MEDIATION AND ARBITRATION LAWS

Illinois has adopted the Uniform Arbitration Act recognizing any written agreement to submit an existing controversy to arbitration as valid, enforceable, and irrevocable, excepting such grounds as exist at law or equity for the revocation thereof.[10] Chapter 10, Section 20, *et seq.*, of the Illinois Revised Statutes provides that labor controversies between employers and employees within the state may be submitted to the Illinois Department of Labor for an investigation of the cause and advice to the parties of its recommendations to resolve the dispute.

[79.04]   REGULATION OF UNION ACTIVITIES

Illinois statutes make it unlawful for any person to attempt to extort money or other property from any employer as a consideration for the withholding, settling, or terminating of any dispute or controversy relating to the handling, delivery, or use of materials or supplies.[11] Illinois statutes make unlawful agreements that restrict the transportation of goods by "piggyback" conveyances.[12]

[79.05]   REGULATION OF EMPLOYMENT PRACTICES

Anti-discrimination laws: Chapter 68, Section 1-102, *et seq.*, of the Illinois Revised Statutes prohibits discrimination in the employment of an individual by reason of race, religion, color, sex, national origin, ancestry, handicap, age, marital status, or unfavorable military discharge, except in cases involving dishonorable discharges.

Military personnel leaves: Illinois statutory laws require private sector employers to re-employ military personnel upon their return from military service to their former or similar position, provided such individuals are still qualified to perform the requirements of the job.[13]

Arrest records: Illinois statutes forbid an inquiry into the arrest record of an applicant for employment.[14]

Jury and witness duty: Illinois employers are required to excuse employees who have been selected to serve on a jury or to appear as a witness in a legal matter.[15]

Whistle-blowing statute (public employees): Illinois law forbids any public employer to take disciplinary action against any public employee for the disclosure of information that the employee reasonably believes evidences a violation of any law, rule, regulation, or mismanagement, a gross waste of funds, an abuse of authority or a substantial and specific danger to public health or safety, if the disclosure is not otherwise specifically prohibited by law.[16]

Polygraph restrictions: Chapter 111, Section 2415.1, of the Illinois Revised Statutes forbids pre-employment or periodic employment polygraph examinations to inquire into certain beliefs and affiliations in relation to religion, unions, racial feelings, politics, etc.

Access to personnel records: Illinois employers must permit their employees to inspect their personnel records at least twice a year, upon request and at reasonable times.[17] Where an employee disagrees with any information contained in his or her personnel record, a request for correction may be filed with the employer and, if the employer does not make such correction, the request for correction will remain a part of the employee's personnel file.[18]

Medical examination payments: Chapter 48, Section 172d, of the Illinois Revised Statutes requires employers to pay the cost of any pre-employment or similar medical examinations required of applicants and employees.

Equal pay: Chapter 48, Section 4(a), of the Illinois Revised Statutes forbids sex and handicap discrimination in wage payment for jobs requiring equal skill, effort, and responsibility and performed under similar working conditions.

[79.06] WAGE AND HOUR LAWS

Child labor: Chapter 48, Section 31, *et seq.*, of the Illinois Revised Statutes governs the Illinois child labor laws.

Payment of wages: Illinois wage and hour laws require employers to pay employee wages earned at least semimonthly.[19]

Payment on termination: Illinois employers are required to pay employees in full, at the time of their separation, if at all possible, but in no case later than the next regularly scheduled payday.[20]

Garnishments: Chapter 110, Section 12-818, of the Illinois Revised Statutes forbids the discharge of an employee because of garnishments for any one indebtedness.

[79.07] SAFETY AND HEALTH LAWS

General provisions: Illinois health and safety laws require employers within the state to furnish safe employment for employees, and to furnish and use safety devices and safeguards, adopt and use methods and processes reasonably adequate to render such employment and place of employment safe, and do every other thing reasonably necessary to protect the life, health, and safety of employees.[21]

Toxic substances—right to know: Chapter 48, Section 1401, *et seq.*, of the Illinois Revised Statutes provides that an employee may refuse to work with a hazardous chemical or toxic substance if such employee has inquired of his or her employer regarding the toxic substances and has not received the information requested within a specified time frame.

[79.08] UNEMPLOYMENT COMPENSATION LAWS

The Illinois unemployment compensation laws govern, among other things, the eligibility requirements of recipients to unemployment compensation benefits.[22] Benefits are generally provided to employees who

- have properly registered for work at an unemployment office
- have properly applied for unemployment benefits
- are able to work, available for work, and actively seeking work
- are not otherwise disqualified under other provisions of the act[23]

[79.09] WORKERS' COMPENSATION LAWS

Chapter 48, Sections 138, *et seq.*, of the Illinois Revised Statutes sets forth the Illinois Workmen's Compensation Act. The statute provides disability and death benefits to, or on behalf of, employees injured on the job or who suffer occupational diseases as a result of their job, subject to specified qualifications and limitations.[24] The statute also forbids a discharge of an employee for filing a worker's compensation action.[25]

[79.10] EMPLOYMENT-AT-WILL DEVELOPMENTS

The Illinois courts have recognized at least three exceptions to the employment-at-will rule, as of this writing.

Public policy exception: An Illinois court has ruled that an employee may recover in an action where he or she was discharged for exercising a lawful right, such as processing a worker's compensation claim[26] or for whistle-blowing activities.[27]

"Independent consideration" exception: An Illinois court has ruled that an employee who foregoes a job offer with another employer in reliance on a promise of employment until retirement may not be discharged without cause.[28]

Intentional infliction of emotional distress exception: An Illinois Court of Appeals has ruled that where an employer's conduct is so outrageous as to go beyond all possible bounds of decency resulting in severe emotional distress to an employee, an action will lie for damages to redress such wrongdoing.[29]

NOTES TO CHAPTER 79

1. Illinois Executive Order No. 6 of 1973.
2. Illinois Public Acts, No. 1014 (L. 1984).
3. Illinois Revised Statutes, Ch. 48, Section 2b.
4. Illinois Revised Statutes, Ch. 38, Section 25.1.
5. Illinois Revised Statutes, Ch. 48, Section 2d.
6. Illinois Revised Statutes, Ch. 48, Section 2f.
7. Illinois Revised Statutes, Ch. 48, Section 2a.
8. Illinois Revised Statutes, Ch. 38, Section 21.1-1.
9. Illinois Revised Statutes, Ch. 38, Section 201.11.
10. Illinois Revised Statutes, Ch. 10, Section 101, *et seq.*
11. Illinois Revised Statutes, Ch. 38, Section 242.
12. Illinois Public Acts, S.B. 192 (L. 1961).
13. Illinois Revised Statutes, Ch. 126 1/2, Section 31, *et seq.*
14. Illinois Revised Statutes, Ch. 48, Section 2-103.
15. Illinois Revised Statutes, Ch. 78, Section 4.1.
16. Illinois Public Acts, No. 82-734 (L. 1981).
17. Illinois Revised Statutes, Ch. 48, Section 2001.
18. Illinois Revised Statutes, Ch. 48, Section 2001, *et seq.*
19. Illinois Revised Statutes, Ch. 48, Section 39m.
20. Illinois Revised Statutes, Ch. 48, Section 39m.
21. Illinois Revised Statutes, Ch. 48, Section 137.3.
22. Illinois Revised Statutes, Ch. 48, Section 300, *et seq.*
23. Illinois Revised Statutes, Ch. 48, Section 401, *et seq.*
24. Illinois Revised Statutes, Ch. 48, Section 138, *et seq.*

25. Illinois Revised Statutes, Ch. 48, Section 138h.

26. *Kelsay v. Motorola, Inc.*, 74 Ill. 2d 172, 384 N.E.2d 353 (1978).

27. *Palmateer v. International Harvester*, 85 Ill. App. 2d 124, 421 N.E.2d 876 (1981).

28. *Martin v. Federated Life Insurance Co.*, 109 Ill. App. 3d 596, 440 N.E.2d 998 (1982).

29. *Harris v. First Federal Savings & Loan Assn. of Chicago*, 473 N.E.2d 457 (Ill. Ct. of App., 1984).

80

Indiana
Labor Laws

[80.01] LABOR RELATIONS LAWS

Teachers' bargaining rights: Indiana statutes provide that certificated school employees shall have the right of self-organization and the right to join and assist employee organizations.[1] The statute prohibits certain conduct of both school employers and employee organizations, the violation of which constitutes unfair labor practices.[2] The statute also provides for an election process to determine bargaining representatives, establishes standards for determining bargaining units,[3] and forbids strikes.[4]

Right to organize: Indiana laws provide that no worker or group of workers who shall have a legal residence in the state shall be denied the right to organize into a local union or association.[5]

Nonright-to-work policy: Union security (union shop) clauses are permissible in the state of Indiana inasmuch as Indiana has not chosen to enact a right-to-work statute as permitted by Section 14(b) of the Labor Management Relations Act.

"Yellow-dog" contracts: Section 35-15-3-1 of the Indiana Code Annotated makes it unlawful for anyone to coerce or compel any person to enter into an agreement not to join or become a member of any labor organization as a condition of employment.

[80.02] STRIKES, PICKETING, AND BOYCOTT LAWS

Anti-injunction statute: Section 22-6-1, *et seq.*, of the Indiana Code Annotated restricts the power of Indiana courts to issue injunctions against peaceable picketing and legally protected strike activity.

Striker replacements: Section 25-16-1-12 of the Indiana Code Annotated requires employment agencies to notify applicants of any existing strikes or lockouts prior to referring such applicants to a prospective employer experiencing such labor conditions.

Unlawful interference with employment: Section 35-15-4-2 of the Indiana Code Annotated makes it unlawful for any person to attempt to prevent any person from engaging in any lawful employment within the state of Indiana.

[80.03] MEDIATION AND ARBITRATION LAWS

Written agreements to submit an existing controversy to arbitration are valid, enforceable, and irrevocable in the state of Indiana, excepting such grounds as exist at law or equity for the revocation thereof.[6] Section 22-1-1-8 of the Indiana Code Annotated provides for a mediation and conciliation process to resolve labor disputes through the offices of the Indiana Commissioner of Labor.

[80.04] REGULATION OF UNION ACTIVITIES

Section 23-116 of the Indiana Code Annotated outlaws contracts, combinations in the form of trusts or otherwise, or conspiracies in the restraint of trade within the state.

[80.05] REGULATION OF EMPLOYMENT PRACTICES

Anti-discrimination laws: Section 22-9-1-2, *et seq.*, of the Indiana Code Annotated prohibits discrimination in the employment of an individual by reason of race, religion, color, sex, national origin, ancestry, age, or handicap.

Freedom of political activities: Section 3-4-7-3 of the Indiana Code Annotated makes it unlawful for any employer to threaten to withhold the wages of, or to dismiss from service, any employee for the purpose of influencing the employee's vote in a political election.

Service letter: Indiana employers are required by Section 22-6-3-1 of the Indiana Code Annotated to give to employees who quit, or who are discharged, a letter setting forth the nature and character of service rendered by the employee and the duration thereof, and truly state for what cause, if any, such employee quit or was discharged, provided the employee requests such a service letter.

Whistle-blowing statute: Indiana law forbids the discharge of an employee for reporting a violation of a state or federal law or misuse of public resources.[7]

Military personnel leaves: Section 10-5-9-1 of the Indiana Code Annotated requires Indiana employers to re-employ military personnel upon their return from military service to their former or similar positions, without loss of seniority or other employment status or pay. Indiana statutes provide that every employee who is a reserve member of the Armed Forces of the United States shall be entitled to be absent from his or her employment duties, for a period not to exceed fifteen days, while engaged in the performance of military service.[8]

Blacklisting: Indiana employers are prohibited from maintaining a blacklist or notifying any other employer that any worker has been blacklisted for the purpose of preventing such worker from receiving employment.[9]

Jury service: Indiana laws prohibit an employer from attempting to deprive an employee of his or her employment because the employee receives a summons, serves as a juror, or attends court as a prospective juror.[10]

Equal pay: Section 22-2-2-4 of the Indiana Code Annotated makes it unlawful to discriminate in payment of wages on the basis of sex.

[80.06] WAGE AND HOUR LAWS

Child labor: Section 20-8-1-4-1, *et seq.,* of the Indiana Code Annotated governs the occupations in which children may work. For example, children under 14 years of age may work only in jobs such as farm or domestic helpers, golf caddies or newspaper carriers.[11] Children under 12 years of age are permitted to work only as farm labor.[12] Children under age 17 are prohibited from working in certain hazardous jobs.[13]

Voting time: Section 3-1-21-7 of the Indiana Code Annotated provides that Indiana employees in manufacturing and related jobs are entitled to be excused from their employment, for a period of up to four hours, to vote in a federal, state, or local election.

Payment of wages: Indiana statutes provide that employees in manufacturing and related jobs are required to be paid every two weeks, unless a contract between the employer and the employees provides for the payment of wages on a weekly basis.[14]

Payment upon termination: Indiana employers are required to pay discharged employees no later than the next regular payday.[15] An employee who voluntarily resigns his or her job is due full wages no later than the next regular payday.[16]

Garnishments: Section 24-4.5-5-106 of the Indiana Code Annotated forbids the discharge of an employee because of garnishment of wages.

[80.07] SAFETY AND HEALTH LAWS

Indiana statutes require employers to furnish a safe and healthful place of employment for their employees to work.[17] Employers are required to furnish and use safety devices and safeguards and to adopt and use practices, methods, operations, and processes that are reasonably adequate to render a safe and healthful work environment.[18]

[80.08] UNEMPLOYMENT COMPENSATION LAWS

The Indiana Unemployment Compensation laws provide certain benefits to unemployed workers who qualify under the Act.[19] Unemployed workers are eligible to receive benefits only if they are able to work, available for work, and make efforts to obtain employment.[20]

[80.09] WORKERS' COMPENSATION LAWS

The Indiana Workmen's Compensation Act is found in Section 22-3-2-1, *et seq.*, of the Indiana Code Annotated. The statute generally governs the payment of workers' compensation benefits to employees incurring job-related injuries or death.[21] A companion statute provides for compensation benefits for death or injury to health by reason of certain diseases contracted in the course of employment.[22]

[80.10] EMPLOYMENT-AT-WILL DEVELOPMENTS

Indiana courts have recognized certain exceptions to the employment-at-will principle, as noted below.

Public policy exception: Indiana courts have found retaliatory discharges for filing a workers' compensation claim with respect to an otherwise at-will employee to be illegal.[23] Indiana courts have also recognized the public policy exception to the at-will rule in a case involving a discharge for refusal to participate in anti-competitive practices.[24]

Promissory estoppel exception: Indiana courts have suggested that reliance upon the promise of a new job, and incurring moving expenses to the new job, might justify an exception to the at-will rule when the employee is thereafter discharged without just cause.[25]

NOTES TO CHAPTER 80

1. Indiana Statutes, Section 20-7.5-1-1.
2. Indiana Statutes, Section 20-7.5-1-7.
3. Indiana Statutes, Section 20-7.5-1-10.
4. Indiana Statutes, Section 20-7.5-1-14.
5. Indiana Public Acts, Senate Bill No. 251 (1957).
6. Indiana Code Annotated, Section 34-4-1-1.
7. Indiana Code Annotated, Section 4-15-10-4.
8. Indiana Code Annotated, Section 10-5-9-2.
9. Indiana Code Annotated, Section 22-5-3-2.
10. Indiana Code Annotated, Section 35-44-3-10.
11. Indiana Code Annotated, Section 20-8.1-4-21.
12. Indiana Code Annotated, Section 20-8.1-4-21.
13. Indiana Code Annotated, Section 20-8.1-4-27.

14. Indiana Code Annotated, Section 22-2-4-1.

15. Indiana Code Annotated, Section 22-2-5-1.

16. Indiana Code Annotated, Section 22-2-5-1.

17. Indiana Code Annotated, Section 22-8-1.1-1.

18. Indiana Code Annotated, Section 22-8-1.1-4.

19. Indiana Code Annotated, Section 22-4-14-1, *et seq.*

20. Indiana Code Annotated, Section 22-5-14-3.

21. Indiana Code Annotated, Section 22-3-2-1, *et seq.*

22. Indiana Code Annotated, Section 22-3-7-1, *et seq.*

23. *Frampton v. Central Indiana Gas Co.*, 297 N.E.2d 425 (Ind. 1973).

24. *Perry v. Hartz Mountain Corp.*, 537 F.Supp. 1387 (S.D. Ind. 1982).

25. *Eby v. York Division, Borg Warner*, 455 N.E.2d 623 (Ind. App. 1983); *Pepsi-Cola General Bottlers, Inc. v. Woods*, 440 N.E.2d 696 (Ind. App. 1982).

81

Iowa
Labor Laws

[81.01] LABOR RELATIONS LAWS

Public employees' bargaining rights: Iowa statutes provide that public employees shall have the right of self-organization and the right to join and assist labor unions, or to refrain from union activities.[1] The statute reserves certain enumerated management rights to public employers.[2] It also prohibits certain conduct of public employers as well as labor organizations, the violation of which constitutes unfair labor practices.[3] The Iowa Public Employment Relations Act also provides for an election process to determine bargaining representatives[4] and forbids strikes.[5]

Right-to-work statute: Iowa statutes declare it to be the policy of the state that no person within its boundaries, except railroad employees, shall be deprived of the right to work at his or her chosen occupation for any employer because of membership in, affiliation with, withdrawal or expulsion from, or refusal to join, any labor union.[6]

[81.02] STRIKES, PICKETING AND BOYCOTT LAWS

Unlawful assembly: Iowa laws forbid three or more persons to assemble together to do an unlawful act.[7]

Secondary boycotts: Iowa statutes forbid anyone to cause or threaten to cause injury to one not a party to a particular labor dispute.[8]

Jurisdictional disputes: Chapter 732.3 of the Iowa Public Acts of 1947 makes it unlawful for any labor union to cause a work stoppage because of a dispute between labor unions with respect to jurisdiction over certain jobs.

Strikebreakers: Iowa statutes make it unlawful for any employer to utilize professional strikebreakers to replace employees involved in a strike or lockout at a place of business within the state.[9]

[81.03] MEDIATION AND ARBITRATION LAWS

The state of Iowa recognizes any written agreement to submit an existing controversy to arbitration as valid, enforceable, and irrevocable, excepting such grounds as exist at law or equity for the revocation thereof.[10] Iowa laws also provide that parties to a labor dispute, or the labor commissioner, after investigation thereto, may make written application to the governor of Iowa for the appointment of a Board of Arbitration and Conciliation, to which board such dispute may be deferred under the provisions of the act.[11]

[81.04] REGULATION OF UNION ACTIVITY

Iowa statutes make it unlawful for anyone to misuse or forge a union label.[12] Chapter 509, Section 1(4), of the Iowa Code places certain requirements and restrictions on group insurance policies issued to a labor union to insure its members for the benefit of persons other than the union or any of its officials, representatives, or agents.

[81.05] REGULATION OF EMPLOYMENT PRACTICES

Anti-discrimination statutes: Section 601A.6 of the Code of Iowa makes it an unfair employment practice to discriminate against anyone in employment because of age, race, creed, color, sex, national origin, religion, or disability.

Military leaves of absence: Employees who are duly qualified members of the Iowa National Guard are entitled to leaves of absence from their employment in order to perform military duty and training, and their employers are required to honor their employment rights to seniority and classification upon their return.[13]

Drunk driving rehabilitation: Iowa law prohibits the discharge of an employee by reason of the employee being ordered by court to attend a course for drunk drivers.[14]

Blacklisting: Iowa employers are prohibited from maintaining a blacklist or notifying any other employer that any worker has been blacklisted for the purpose of preventing such worker from receiving employment.[15]

Whistle-blowing statute (public employees): Iowa law provides that employees employed under the Iowa Merit Employment Commission may not be discharged for disclosure of information to appropriate authorities regarding violations of law, abuse of public funds, mismanagement, etc., believed to exist in his or her work place.[16]

Polygraph restrictions: No employer shall demand or require any applicant for employment or any employee to submit to a polygraph, lie detector, or similar test or examination as a condition of employment or continued employment in the state of Iowa.[17]

Comparable work law (public employees): Iowa law provides that there shall be no discrimination in compensation for comparable work among state employees.[18]

[81.06]   WAGE AND HOUR LAWS

Child labor: Iowa statutes provide that children 10 years or over may be employed in street occupations such as peddling, bootblacking, and distributing newspapers.[19] Children at least 14 years of age may work in any nonhazardous job, except in street trade occupations and migratory labor occupations enumerated in the statute.[20] The Iowa laws also restrict children 16 years of age or under, as well as those 18 years of age or under, to certain nonhazardous occupations.[21]

Voting time: Chapter 49, Section 109, of the Iowa Code requires Iowa employers to excuse employees from their employment up to three consecutive hours to provide them an opportunity to vote in political elections.

Payment of wages: Chapter 91A, Section 3(1), of the Iowa Code requires Iowa employers to pay employees their wages at least in monthly, semimonthly, or biweekly installments on regular paydays.

Payment upon termination: Iowa employers are required to pay discharged or suspended employees their wages in full not later than the next regular payday.[22]

Garnishments: Chapter 642, Section 21, of the Iowa Code forbids the discharge of an employee because of wage garnishments.

[81.07]   SAFETY AND HEALTH LAWS

General provisions: Iowa statutes require employers to furnish a safe and healthful place of employment for their employees to work. Employers are required to furnish and use safety devices and safeguards and to adopt and use practices, methods, operations, and processes that are reasonably adequate to render a safe and healthful work environment.[23]

Toxic substances—right to know: Iowa law requires disclosure of various information relating to hazardous chemicals by employers to employees who may be exposed and adversely affected by such chemical or toxic substances in his or her work area.[24]

[81.08]   UNEMPLOYMENT COMPENSATION LAWS

The Iowa unemployment compensation laws are found in Chapter 96, Section 1, *et seq.*, of the Iowa Code and govern, among other things, the eligibility requirements of recipients of unemployment compensation benefits.

[81.09] WORKERS' COMPENSATION LAWS

The Iowa Workmen's Compensation Act provides compensation for injuries to employees in the course of, and arising out of, their employment.[25] Benefits and payments are paid to employees in accordance with established schedules, the amounts and duration of which are dependent upon the gravity of the injury or disease and when the disability is temporary or permanent and/or partial or total.

[81.10] EMPLOYMENT-AT-WILL DEVELOPMENTS

Iowa courts have been reluctant to recognize judicial exceptions to the employment-at-will doctrine, specifically rejecting an implied employment contract for job security, as contained in a personnel policy manual.[26] The courts have not recognized a public policy exception to the at-will rule, either, as of this writing, but one court has suggested it might do so in the future, given appropriate facts and circumstances.[27] The Iowa courts have specifically adopted some limited judicial exceptions to the at-will principle, as noted below.

Covenant of good faith and fair dealing exception: An Iowa court has held actionable a case in which an employee was discharged because of his age on the theory that the employer's covenant of good faith and fair dealing to the employee had been breached.[28]

"Independent consideration" exception: An Iowa court has held that whenever an employee furnishes consideration independent of his or her regular employment services, such as terminating other employment to accept an offer of permanent employment, the employee will be considered to be more than merely at-will, requiring just cause for his or her dismissal.[29]

NOTES TO CHAPTER 81

1. Code of Iowa, Section 20.8.
2. Code of Iowa, Section 20.7.
3. Code of Iowa, Section 20.10.
4. Code of Iowa, Section 20.15.
5. Code of Iowa, Section 20.12.
6. Code of Iowa, Section 731.1.
7. Code of Iowa, Section 723.2.
8. Code of Iowa, Section 732.1.
9. Code of Iowa, Section 732.6.

10. Code of Iowa, Section 679.1, *et seq.*

11. Code of Iowa, Section 90.1.

12. Code of Iowa, Section 548.10.

13. Code of Iowa, Section 29A.43.

14. Code of Iowa, Section 321.283(8).

15. Code of Iowa, Section 730.2.

16. Code of Iowa, Section 19A.19.

17. Code of Iowa, Section 730.4(2).

18. Code of Iowa, Section 79.18.

19. Iowa Public Acts, Section 2.1, H.B. 1251 (1970).

20. Iowa Public Acts, Section 4, H.B. 1251 (1970).

21. Iowa Public Acts, Section 5, H.B. 1251 (1970).

22. Code of Iowa, Section 91A.4.

23. Code of Iowa, Section 88.4.

24. Code of Iowa, Section 455D.1.

25. Code of Iowa, Section 85.1, *et seq.*

26. *Allen v. Highway Equipment Co.*, 239 N.W.2d 135 (Iowa S.Ct., 1976).

27. *Abrisz v. Pulley Freight Lines, Inc.*, 270 N.W.2d 454 (Iowa S.Ct., 1978).

28. *High v. Sperry Corp.*, 581 F.Supp. 1246 (S.D. Iowa, 1984).

29. *Collins v. Parsons College*, 203 N.W.2d 594 (Iowa, 1973).

82

Kansas
Labor Laws

[82.01] LABOR RELATIONS LAWS

Kansas LMRA: Section 44-801, *et seq.*, of the Kansas Statutes Annotated sets forth the Kansas "little Taft-Hartley" law. This statute provides that employees shall have the right to self-organization to form, join, or assist labor organizations and to bargain collectively through representatives of their own choosing.

Agricultural employees' bargaining rights: Kansas has within its statutory provisions a law protecting the right of agricultural employees to self-organization and to join or refrain from joining labor unions.[1]

Teachers' bargaining rights: Section 72-5411, *et seq.*, of the Kansas Statutes Annotated established the Kansas Professional Negotiations Act. This statute provides that public schoolteachers shall have the right of self-organization and the right to join and assist professional employees' organizations, or to refrain from such activities.[2] The statute prohibits certain conduct of both public school boards and labor organizations, the violation of which constitutes unfair labor practices.[3]

Public employees' bargaining rights: The Kansas Public Employer–Employee Relations Act establishes a framework of employer–employee relations by providing a method for collective bargaining between public employers and certain public employees.[4]

Right-to-work statute: Kansas statutes prohibit the denial of employment to anyone on account of membership or nonmembership in a labor union or organization.[5]

[82.02] STRIKES, PICKETING, AND BOYCOTT LAWS

Anti-injunction laws: Kansas laws restrict the power of Kansas courts to issue injunctions against peaceable picketing and legally protected strike activity.[6]

Unlawful assembly: Section 21-1001 of the Kansas Statutes Annotated prohibits three or more persons to assemble together to do an unlawful act.

Interference with railroads: Section 21-1901 of the Kansas Statutes Annotated makes it unlawful for a locomotive engineer to willfully or maliciously abandon his locomotive. The statute also makes it unlawful for any person to otherwise interfere with or obstruct the regular operation of a railroad company.[7]

Strikebreakers: Kansas statutes forbid any person to bring into the state of Kansas any other person or association of persons for the purpose of discharging the duties devolving upon sheriffs, police officers, or other peace officers in the protection or preservation of public or private property.[8]

Secondary boycotts and jurisdictional disputes: Section 44.809(a) of the Kansas Statutes Annotated declares it to be unlawful and against public policy for anyone to engage in secondary boycotts or jurisdictional disputes.

[82.03] MEDIATION AND ARBITRATION LAWS

Section 5-201, *et seq.*, of the Kansas Statutes Annotated provides that all persons who shall have any controversy may submit such controversy to the arbitration of any person or persons, to be mutually agreed upon by the parties, and may make such submission a rule of any record in the state. The Kansas Compulsory Arbitration and Mediation Act provides for compulsory arbitration of labor disputes in certain industries affecting the public interest of the state, such as labor disputes involving public utilities.[9] Section 21-712 of the Kansas Statutes Annotated makes it a misdemeanor for anyone to attempt to influence an arbitrator improperly.

[82.04] REGULATION OF UNION ACTIVITIES

Kansas statutes make it unlawful for anyone to misuse or forge a union label or other union insignia, or to misrepresent that employment of union labor went into the production or manufacture of goods or services.[10] Section 44-805 of the Kansas Statutes Annotated requires labor unions with at least 100 members who operate within the state to file copies of their constitution and certain annual reports with appropriate state officials. Kansas statutes forbid a union to charge, receive, or retain any union dues, assessments, or other charges in excess of, or not authorized by, the union's constitution and bylaws.[11]

[82.05] REGULATION OF EMPLOYMENT PRACTICES

Anti-discrimination laws: Kansas statutes prohibit discrimination in the employment of an individual by reason of race, religion, color, sex, national origin, ancestry, or handicap.[12]

Protection of political freedom: Kansas labor laws make it unlawful for any employer within the state to attempt to influence the political vote of an employee or control such employee as to how he or she shall vote by offering any award or threatening his or her discharge from employment.[13]

Service letter: Section 44-808(3) of the Kansas Statutes Annotated requires employers to furnish, upon a written request of any employee whose services have been terminated, a service letter setting forth the tenure of employment, occupational classification, and wage rate paid the employee.

Hiring of illegal aliens: Kansas statutes forbid any Kansas employer to knowingly employ any alien illegally within the territory of the United States.[14]

Whistle-blowing statute (state employees): State agencies are forbidden to discharge or otherwise discriminate against any employee for reporting any violation of state or federal laws, rules, or regulations.[15]

Blacklisting: Kansas employers are prohibited from maintaining a blacklist or notifying any other employer that any worker has been blacklisted for the purpose of preventing such worker from receiving employment elsewhere.[16]

Equal pay: Kansas law makes it unlawful to discriminate in payment of wages on the basis of sex by paying female employees at a rate less than that paid male employees for the same quality and quantity of the same work classification, except for variations in pay based upon seniority, merit systems, or other such factors.[17]

[82.06] WAGE AND HOUR LAWS

Child labor: Section 38-601, *et seq.,* of the Kansas Statutes Annotated regulates the employment of children. The statute exempts several enumerated jobs from its regulation of child labor, thus permitting the right of children to work in certain limited jobs.[18]

Voting time: Kansas statutes provide that an employee eligible and duly registered to vote at a primary, general, or special election shall be excused from his or her employment not exceeding two consecutive hours, to exercise such voting privilege, provided such employee does not have two consecutive hours between the time of opening and closing of polls when he or she is not working for the employer.[19]

Payment of wages: Section 44-314 of the Kansas Statutes Annotated requires Kansas employers to pay employees their wages no less than twice during a month and no later than fifteen days from the established pay period.

Payment upon termination: Kansas employers are required to pay discharged employees, and employees who voluntarily resign their jobs, their full wages no later than the next regular payday.[20]

Garnishments: Section 60-2311(a) of the Kansas Statutes Annotated forbids discharge of an employee because of a garnishment order against his or her wages.

Medical insurance conversion: Provided certain requirements are met, group health plans may be converted to individual coverage by terminating employees, as is more fully discussed in Section 40-2209 of the Kansas Statutes Annotated.

[82.07] SAFETY AND HEALTH LAWS

Section 44-636 of the Kansas Statutes Annotated empowers the Kansas Secretary of Human Resources to enter and inspect places of business and to examine employee work areas for dangerous and unsanitary conditions. The statute also provides that employers are to be notified of any hazardous or unsanitary condition by the Department of Human Resources, whenever such circumstances exist, and be given up to sixty days in which to correct the hazardous or unsanitary condition.[21]

[82.08] UNEMPLOYMENT COMPENSATION LAWS

The Kansas unemployment compensation laws are found at Kansas Statutes Annotated, Section 44-701, *et seq.*, and govern the eligibility requirements of recipients of unemployment compensation benefits.

[82.09] WORKERS' COMPENSATION LAWS

The Kansas Workmen's Compensation Act is found in Section 44-501, *et seq.*, of the Kansas Statutes Annotated and is administered by the State Director of Workers' Compensation. The act provides for certain enumerated benefits for accidental injury or death arising out of and in the course of employment.[22]

[82.10] EMPLOYMENT-AT-WILL DEVELOPMENTS

Kansas courts have recognized some limited exceptions to the at-will principle, as discussed below.

Public policy exception: An employee who is discharged for refusal to withdraw a worker's compensation claim may recover damages in tort for wrongful discharge in the state of Kansas.[23]

Promissory estoppel exception: Kansas courts have given some deference to the promissory estoppel exception to the at-will rule, holding that an employee may recover moving expenses where he or she detrimentally relied upon a prospective employer's promise of a job.[24]

Implied contract exception: Kansas courts have generally refused to recognize an implied employment contract flowing from an employee personnel policy.[25] However, in one Kansas case, the court held a breach of contract action may be maintained by an employee who alleged dismissal in violation of a personnel policy statement that prohibited termination for minor contractual violations unless previous warnings were given.[26]

NOTES TO CHAPTER 82

1. Kansas Statutes Annotated, Section 44-818, *et seq.*
2. Kansas Statutes Annotated, Section 72-5414.
3. Kansas Statutes Annotated, Section 72-5430.
4. Kansas Statutes Annotated, Section 75-4321, *et seq.*
5. Kansas Statutes Annotated, Section 44-831.
6. Kansas Statutes Annotated, Section 60-904, *et seq.*
7. Kansas Statutes Annotated, Section 21-1901, *et seq.*
8. Kansas Statutes Annotated, Section 21-1616, *et seq.*
9. Kansas Statutes Annotated, Section 44-603.
10. Kansas Statutes Annotated, Section 81-105, *et seq.*
11. Kansas Statutes Annotated, Section 44-809(6).
12. Kansas Statutes Annotated, Section 44-1001, *et seq.*
13. Kansas Statutes Annotated, Section 25-418.
14. Kansas Statutes Annotated, Section 21-4409.
15. Kansas Public Laws, H.B. 2621 (L. 1984).
16. Kansas Statutes Annotated, Section 44-118.
17. Kansas Statutes Annotated, Section 44-1210(b).
18. Kansas Statutes Annotated, Section 38-614.
19. Kansas Statutes Annotated, Section 25-418.
20. Kansas Statutes Annotated, Section 44-315(a).
21. Kansas Statutes Annotated, Section 44-636.
22. Kansas Statutes Annotated, Section 44-501.
23. *Murphy v. City of Topeka-Shawnee County Dept.*, 630 P.2d 186 (Kan., 1981).
24. *Lorson v. Falcon Coach, Inc.*, 522 P.2d 449 (Kan. 1974).
25. *Owens v. City of Derby*, 586 F.Supp. 37 (D. Kan. 1984).
26. *Rouse v. People's National Gas Co.*, 116 LRRM 2875 (D. Kan., 1984).

83

Kentucky
Labor Laws

[83.01] LABOR RELATIONS LAWS

Employees' right of self-organization: Section 336.130 of the Kentucky Revised Statutes provides that Kentucky employees shall have the right to self-organization and to form, join, or assist labor unions, and such employees shall also have the right to bargain collectively through representatives of their own choosing.

Firefighters and police officers: Kentucky statutes bestow upon firefighters of a city containing a population of at least 300,000 the right of self-organization and the right to form, join, or assist labor unions.[1] Kentucky laws provide also that county police officers shall have the right to bargain collectively in any county that has a populaton of 300,000 or more and that has adopted the merit system for its police force.[2] Strikes by members of any such bargaining unit are prohibited.[3]

Nonright-to-work policy: Union security (union shop) clauses are permissible in the state of Kentucky inasmuch as Kentucky has not chosen to enact a right-to-work statute as permitted by Section 14(b) of the Labor Management Relations Act.

[83.02] STRIKES, PICKETING, AND BOYCOTT LAWS

Unlawful assembly: Section 437.010 of the Kentucky Revised Statutes makes it unlawful to have breaches of peace, riots, or illegal assemblages.

Striker replacements: Kentucky statutes require employment agencies to notify applicants of any existing strikes or lockouts prior to referring such applicants to a prospective employer experiencing such labor conditions.[4]

Interference with transportation: Section 433.370 of the Kentucky Revised Statutes makes it unlawful for anyone to interfere with the transportation of freight or passengers within the state.

[83.03] MEDIATION AND ARBITRATION LAWS

Section 417.010 of the Kentucky Revised Statutes permits the submission of controversies to one or more arbitrators for decision whenever the parties have so contracted by written agreement. Section 336.140 of the Kentucky Revised Statutes empowers the State Commissioner of Industrial Relations to inquire into the cause of a labor dispute and attempt to mediate differences and to effect an amicable settlement of strikes and lockouts.

[83.04] REGULATION OF UNION ACTIVITIES

Kentucky statutes make it unlawful for any national or international labor organization having 100 or more members in good standing who reside or work in Kentucky, not to have at all times one or more duly chartered and established local or subsidiary organizations in the state.[5] Kentucky statutes make it unlawful for anyone to misuse or forge a union label or other union insignia.[6] Kentucky laws make it unlawful for anyone to enter into agreements that limit transportation of goods by ''piggyback'' conveyances.[7]

[83.05] REGULATION OF EMPLOYMENT PRACTICES

Anti-discrimination laws: Section 344.040 of the Kentucky Revised Statutes forbids discrimination in employment on the basis of race, color, religion, national origin, sex, or age. Section 207.130 of the Kentucky Revised Statutes prohibits discrimination in employment because of handicap. Pregnancy discrimination in employment is forbidden by Section 344.030 of the Kentucky Revised Statutes.

Jury duty: Kentucky laws prohibit an employer from attempting to deprive an employee of his or her employment because the employee receives a summons, responds thereto, serves as a juror, or attends court for prospective jury service.[8]

Unlawful enticement: Kentucky laws forbid anyone to induce or entice any person, who has contracted to serve his or her employer for a specific length of time, to leave the service of his or her employer during such term, without the employer's consent.[9]

Protection of political activities: Kentucky statutes forbid employers to interfere with the voting rights of their employees.[10]

Employment of convicted persons: Kentucky laws provide that no person shall be disqualified from public employment, nor shall a person be disqualified from pursuing, practicing, or engaging in any occupation, solely because of a prior conviction of a crime, unless the crime is one limited to convictions for felonies, high misdemeanors, or crimes involving moral turpitude.[11]

National Guard members: Section 38.460 of the Kentucky Revised Statutes makes it unlawful for any person to willfully deprive a member of the National Guard of his or her employment.

Equal pay: Section 337.423 of the Kentucky Revised Statutes makes it unlawful to discriminate in the payment of wages based on sex.

[83.06] WAGE AND HOUR LAWS

Child labor: Section 339.210, *et seq.*, of the Kentucky Revised Statutes regulate the employment of minors. Children under 18 years of age must possess a general, special or vacation employment certificate to work in jobs not enumerated above.[12] Employment is prohibited in any occupation which the Kentucky Commissioner of Labor has determined to be hazardous or injurious to the life, health, safety, or welfare of a minor.[13]

Voting time: Kentucky statutes provide that employees shall be excused from their employment, not to exceed four consecutive hours between the time of opening and closing of the polls, to exercise their voting privileges, without liability to deduction from usual wages, and no employer shall discharge or threaten to discharge such employees for exercising such rights.[14]

Payment of wages: Section 337.020 of the Kentucky Revised Statutes requires Kentucky employers to pay employees their wages no less than twice during a month.

Payment upon termination: Kentucky employers are required to pay discharged employees and employees who voluntarily resign, their full wages no later than the next regular payday, or within 14 days following their termination.[15]

Garnishments: Section 427.140 of the Kentucky Revised Statutes forbids the discharge of an employee because his or her wages have been subjected to garnishments for any one indebtedness.

Medical insurance conversion: Section 304.18-110 of the Kentucky Revised Statutes provides that employees must be permitted to convert group health plans into individual coverage upon termination of employment, provided certain requirements are met.

[83.07] SAFETY AND HEALTH LAWS

Kentucky laws require employers within the state to furnish safe employment for employees, and to furnish and use safety devices and safeguards, adopt and use methods and processes reasonably adequate to render such employment and place of employment safe and do every other thing reasonably necessary to protect the life, health, and safety of employees.[16]

[83.08] UNEMPLOYMENT COMPENSATION LAWS

The Kentucky unemployment compensation laws govern the eligibility requirements of recipients of employment compensation benefits.[17]

[83.09] WORKERS' COMPENSATION LAWS

The Kentucky Workers' Compensation Act provides for compensation benefits for job-related injuries, occupational diseases, and deaths.[18] The act is mandatory for those employers not specifically excluded from its requirements and employees are considered to have accepted coverage under the act unless they specifically elect not be be covered or are otherwise exempt from coverage.[19]

[83.10] EMPLOYMENT-AT-WILL DEVELOPMENTS

Kentucky courts have recognized some limited exceptions to the employment-at-will doctrine, as discussed below.

Public policy exception: An employee who is dismissed from employment for pursuing a workers' compensation claim may recover damages, in tort, for wrongful discharge.[20]

Implied contract exception; Personnel policies that assure employees that they will not be discharged except for cause creates an implied employment contract for a definite term.[21]

Presumption of term exception: An oral contract for a yearly salary raises an inference of a year-to-year employment contract during which period an employee may not be lawfully discharged except for just cause.[22]

NOTES TO CHAPTER 83

1. Kentucky Revised Statutes, Section 345.010, *et seq.*
2. Kentucky Public Acts, H.B. 217 (L. 1972).
3. Kentucky Public Acts, H.B. 217 (L.1972).
4. Kentucky Revised Statutes, Section 340.050.
5. Kentucky Revised Statutes, Section 336.170.
6. Kentucky Revised Statutes, Section 365.120.
7. Kentucky Public Acts, H.B. 362 (1962).
8. Kentucky Public Acts, H.B. 23-X (L. 1976).
9. Kentucky Revised Statutes, Section 433.310.

10. Kentucky Revised Statutes, Section 121.310.

11. Kentucky Public Acts, H.B. 100 (1978); see also Kentucky Revised Statutes, Section 335B.2(1).

12. Kentucky Revised Statutes, Section 339.280.

13. Kentucky Revised Statutes, Section 339.230.

14. Kentucky Revised Statutes, Section 118.035.

15. Kentucky Revised Statutes, Section 337.055.

16. Kentucky Revised Statutes, Section 338.031.

17. Kentucky Revised Statutes, Section 341.350, *et seq.*

18. Kentucky Revised Statutes, Section 342.001, *et seq.*

19. Kentucky Revised Statutes, Section 342.630; 342.650.

20. *Firestone Textile Co. Division v. Meadows*, 666 S.W.2d 730 (Ky., 1983).

21. *Shah v. American Synthetic Rubber Corp.*, 655 S.W.2d 489 (Ky., 1983).

22. *Moore v. Young Women's Christian Ass'n*, Case No. 84-CA-1508-MR (Ky., Ct. of App., 1985).

84

Louisiana
Labor Laws

[84.01] LABOR RELATIONS LAWS

General right to organize: Section 23:822 of the Louisiana Revised Statutes provides that Louisiana employees shall have the right to self-organization, to form, join, or assist labor unions.

Public transit employees' bargaining rights: Louisiana statutes accord to public transit employees the right of self-organization; to form, join, or assist labor organizations; to bargain collectively through representatives of their own choosing; and to engage in other concerted activities for the purpose of collective bargaining or other mutual aid or protection.[1] The statute also requires that labor disputes arising between municipalities and collective bargaining representatives of public transit employees shall be resolved through arbitration.[2]

Right-to-work statute: Louisiana laws prohibit the denial of employment to anyone on account of membership or nonmembership in a labor union or organization.[3]

"Yellow-dog" contracts: Section 23:823 of the Louisiana Revised Statutes makes it unlawful for anyone to coerce or compel any person to enter into an agreement not to join or become a member of any labor organization as a condition of employment.

[84.02] STRIKES, PICKETING, AND BOYCOTT LAWS

Anti-injunction laws: Section 23:841 of the Louisiana Revised Statutes limits the authority of Louisiana courts to issue injunctions and restraining orders in connection with labor disputes.

Strikebreakers: Louisiana laws make it unlawful to bring into the state professional strikebreakers if for the purpose of obstructing or interfering with peaceable picketing.[4] The Louisiana statutes forbid any person not directly involved in a labor dispute to hire any person with the purpose of employing such person to take the place of a striking employee.[5]

Obstruction of commerce or passageways: Louisiana statutes make it unlawful for any person to willfully obstruct the normal use of any public highway or passageway or entrances to public buildings and other public structures.[6]

Picketing of courts: Section 14:401 of the Louisiana Revised Statutes makes it unlawful for anyone to obstruct the administration of justice by picketing in or near a building or residence occupied by a judge, juror, witness, or court officer as a means to influence such person.

[84.03] MEDIATION AND ARBITRATION LAWS

Louisiana statutes require the State Commissioner of Labor to promote the voluntary conciliation of disputes between employers and employees.[7]

[84.04] REGULATION OF UNION ACTIVITIES

Louisiana statutes make it unlawful for anyone to misuse or forge a union label or other union insignia.[8]

[84.05] REGULATION OF EMPLOYMENT PRACTICES

Anti-discrimination laws: Louisiana statutes prohibit discrimination in employment based on race, color, religion, sex, or national origin.[9] Age[10] and handicap[11] discrimination in employment are also prohibited employment practices.

Hiring of illegal aliens: Section 23:992 of the Louisiana Revised Statutes forbids any person to knowingly employ within the state of Louisiana an alien who is not entitled to lawful residence in the United States, except where aliens are employed in the production of raw agricultural crops and related jobs.

Whistle-blowing statutes (environmental conditions): Louisiana employees are protected against discharge and other forms of retaliation whenever they report or complain about possible environmental violations.[12]

Reemployment rights of veterans: Section 29:28 of the Louisiana Revised Statutes requires employers to reemploy returning military personnel to their former or similar positions without loss of seniority, employment status, or pay.

Protection of political activities: Louisiana employers with twenty or more employees are forbidden to attempt to influence or interfere with the voting and political rights of their employees.[13]

Jury duty: Louisiana statutes prohibit the discharge of an employee because he or she serves on a jury.[14]

Prior criminal convictions: Section 37:2950 of the Louisiana Revised Statutes prohibits an employer to disqualify a person from a job opportunity because of a prior criminal record, except when the conviction is of a felony offense or of such a nature that relates to the position sought.

Access to medical records: Louisiana employees have the right of access to any medical report or examination, as required by the employer.[15]

Medical examination payments: Section 23:897 of the Louisiana Revised Statutes requires employers to pay all medical costs incurred as a result of pre-employment or other such medical examinations required of applicants of employees.

[84.06]   WAGE AND HOUR LAWS

Child labor: The child labor provisions of the Louisiana statutes are inapplicable to children employed in agriculture, domestic services in private homes, or employment or training related to the curriculum while attending business or vocational-technical schools approved by the State Board of Elementary and Secondary Education or the Advisory Commission on Proprietary Schools, or employed in federally funded youth training programs.[16] Children who are not apprentices may not work in specified places, or in any occupation dangerous to life or limb or injurious to health or morals.[17]

Payment of wages: Section 23:633 of the Louisiana Revised Statutes requires Louisiana employers with ten or more employees in manufacturing or related jobs, to pay employees their wages as often as once every two weeks or twice during each calendar month, and no later than ten days from the established pay period.

Payment upon termination: Louisiana employers are required to pay discharged employees and employees who voluntarily resign their jobs full wages not later than three days following their discharge or termination.[18]

Garnishments: Section 23:731(c) of the Louisiana Revised Statutes forbids the discharge of an employee because of a garnishment of one indebtedness.

[84.07]   SAFETY AND HEALTH LAWS

General provisions: Section 23:8 of the Louisiana Revised Statutes empowers the State Commissioner of Labor to prescribe reasonable rules and regulations for use of safety devices and other guards for prevention of accidents and industrial or occupational diseases in places of employment.

Toxic substances—right to know: Louisiana laws require employers to provide employees access to records regarding their exposure to toxic substances, etc.[19]

[84.08] UNEMPLOYMENT COMPENSATION LAWS

The Louisiana unemployment compensation laws govern the eligibility requirements of recipients of unemployment compensation benefits.[20] Section 23:1600, *et seq.*, of the Louisiana Revised Statutes enumerates requirements and disqualifications of the state unemployment compensation laws.

[84.09] WORKERS' COMPENSATION LAWS

The Louisiana Workmen's Compensation Act provides disability benefits to employees injured on the job or who suffer certain occupational diseases as a result of their job, subject to specified qualifications and limitations.[21] Section 23:1361 of the Louisiana Revised Statutes prohibits the termination of an employee for filing a workers' compensation claim.

[84.10] EMPLOYMENT-AT-WILL DEVELOPMENTS

Louisiana courts have refused to recognize some of the developing exceptions to the employment-at-will doctrine and, as of this writing, have specifically rejected the public policy[22] and implied contracts[23] exceptions to the at-will rule.

NOTES TO CHAPTER 84

1. Louisiana Public Acts, No. 127, Section 4 (1964).
2. Louisiana Public Acts, No. 127, Section 5 (1964).
3. Louisiana Revised Statutes, Section 23:983.
4. Louisiana Revised Statutes, Section 23:898.
5. Louisiana Revised Statutes, Section 23:901.
6. Louisiana Revised Statutes, Section 14:100.
7. Louisiana Revised Statutes, Section 23:6.
8. Louisiana Revised Statutes, Section 51:211, *et seq.*
9. Louisiana Revised Statutes, Section 23:1006.
10. Louisiana Revised Statutes, Section 23:973.
11. Louisiana Revised Statutes, Section 46:2254(1).
12. Louisiana Revised Statutes, Section 30:1074.1.
13. Louisiana Revised Statutes, Section 23:962.
14. Louisiana Revised Statutes, Section 23:965.
15. Louisiana Revised Statutes, Section 23:1125.
16. Louisiana Revised Statutes, Section 23:151, *et seq.*

17. Louisiana Revised Statutes, Section 23:161.
18. Louisiana Revised Statutes, Section 23:631, *et seq.*
19. Louisiana Revised Statutes, Section 23:1126.
20. Louisiana Revised Statutes, Section 23:1600, *et seq.*
21. Louisiana Revised Statutes, Section 23:1021, *et seq.*
22. *Gil v. Metal Service Corp.,* 412 So.2d 706 (La. Ct. of App., 1982).
23. *Williams v. Delta Haven, Inc.,* 416 So.2d 637 (La. Ct. of App., 1982).

85

Maine
Labor Laws

State employees' bargaining rights: Maine statutes accord state employees the right to join labor organizations and to be represented by such organizations in collective bargaining.[1] The statute prohibits certain conduct of public employers and state employees.[2] The statute also prescribes guidelines to determine appropriate bargaining units and bargaining agents,[3] as well as a process for resolving labor disputes.[4]

Public employees' bargaining rights: Maine statutes provide that public employees shall have the right of self-organization and the right to join and assist labor unions, or to refrain from union activities.[5] The statute prohibits certain conduct of both public employers and labor organizations, the violation of which constitutes unfair labor practices.[6]

University employees' bargaining rights: The University of Maine Labor Relations Act is found at Title 26, Section 10.21, *et seq.,* of the Maine Revised Statutes Annotated. The statute extends collective bargaining rights to university employees, establishes guidelines to determine appropriate bargaining units and collective bargaining representatives, as well as prescribes certain prohibited conduct by university employers and employees and their bargaining representatives.[7]

Bargaining rights of judicial employees: Maine statutes provide that judicial employees within the state shall have the right of self-organization to join, form, and participate in the activities of organizations of their own choosing for the purpose of collective bargaining.[8]

General right to organize statute: Title 26, Section 911, of the Maine Revised Statutes Annotated provides that employees within the state shall have full freedom of association, self-organization, and designation of representatives of their own choosing, for the purpose of negotiating the terms and conditions of their employment or other mutual aid or protection.

Nonright-to-work policy: Union security (union shop) clauses are permissible in the state of Maine inasmuch as Maine has not chosen to enact a right-to-work statute as permitted by Section 14(b) of the Labor Management Relations Act.

[85.02] STRIKES, PICKETING, AND BOYCOTT LAWS

Anti-injunction laws: Maine laws restrict the power of Maine courts to issue injunctions against peaceable picketing and legally protected strike activity.[9]

Unlawful assembly: Title 17, Section 3352, of the Maine Revised Statutes Annotated prohibits three or more persons to assemble together to do an unlawful act.

Interference with railroads: Title 17, Section 3605, of the Maine Revised Statutes Annotated makes it unlawful for any person to interfere with the regular operation of a railroad company in furtherance of a labor dispute.

Strikebreakers: Maine statutes prohibit the recruitment and furnishing of professional strikebreakers to replace employees involved in labor strikes or lockouts.[10]

Striker replacements: Title 26, Section 921 of the Maine Revised Statutes Annotated requires advertisements and solicitations for employment applicants to state the existence of any strike, lockout, or other labor trouble at the place of the proposed employment.

Mass picketing: Maine labor laws make it unlawful for any person to attempt to prevent the delivery to any public, commercial, or industrial enterprise of any supplies or services through the use of mass picketing, force, coercion, or physical obstruction.[11]

Cancellation of health insurance during strike: Maine statutes forbid an employer to cancel any policy or group health insurance, issued to employees pursuant to Title 24-A, Section 2894, of the Maine Revised Statutes Annotated, during which time a strike is in existence, unless such employer notifies the striking employees that the policy is to be cancelled.[12]

Interference with public utilities' employment: Maine statutes make it unlawful to interfere with employment relating to a public utility company.[13]

[85.03]   MEDIATION AND ARBITRATION LAWS

Maine has adopted the Uniform Arbitration Act which recognizes any written agreement to submit an existing controversy to arbitration as valid, enforceable, and irrevocable, excepting such grounds as exist at law or equity for the revocation thereof.[14] Title 26, Section 891, of the Maine Revised Statutes Annotated provides for the establishment of a panel of mediators for the resolution of disputes between public employers and their employees.

[85.04]   REGULATION OF UNION ACTIVITIES

Maine statutes make it unlawful for anyone to misuse or forge a union label or other union insignia, or to misrepresent that employment of union labor went into the production or manufacture of goods or services.[15]

[85.05] REGULATION OF EMPLOYMENT PRACTICES

Anti-discrimination laws: Maine statutory laws prohibit discrimination in employment on the basis of race, color, sex, age, religion, ancestry, or physical or mental handicap.[16] Pregnancy discrimination in employment is also forbidden in the state of Maine.[17]

Blacklisting: Maine employers are prohibited from maintaining a blacklist or notifying any other employer that any worker has been blacklisted by such employer for the purpose of preventing such worker from receiving employment.[18]

Polygraph restrictions: No employer shall require any applicant for employment or any employee to submit to a polygraph, lie detector, or similar test or examination as a condition of employment or continued employment, excepting the use of such tests in certain state agencies or subdivisions thereof.[19]

National Guard members: Maine statutory laws forbid any person to willfully deprive a member of the National Guard or other authorized state military forces of his or her employment.[20]

Military leaves of absence: Employees who are reserve members of the U.S. Armed Forces are entitled to leaves of absence from their employment up to seventeen days in any one calendar year to receive military training and their employers are required to honor their employment rights to seniority and classification upon their return.[21]

Hiring of illegal aliens: Maine statutes make it unlawful for an employer to knowingly employ an alien who has not been lawfully admitted to the United States for permanent residence, unless the employment is authorized by the United States Immigration and Naturalization Service.[22]

Plant closures: Any person employing at any time in the preceding twelve-month period 100 or more employees, who proposes to relocate any industrial or commercial facility or part thereof outside the state of Maine, shall notify his or her employees and the municipal officers of the municipality where the plant is located of the proposed relocation not less than sixty days prior to the relocation.[23] With limited exceptions, as enumerated in the Act, any employer who relocates such an establishment shall be liable to his or her employees for severance pay at the rate of one week's pay for each year of employment.[24]

Disclosure of consumer reports: Title 10, Section 1320, of the Maine Revised Statutes Annotated requires any employer using information provided by a consumer reporting agency for employment purposes to disclose, in writing, certain information to a rejected applicant.

Access to employment records: Title 26, Section 631, of the Maine Revised Statutes Annotated requires employers to provide an employee, or his or her duly authorized representative, with an opportunity to review his or her personnel file, upon written request and at reasonable times.

Whistle-blowing statute: Maine statutes make it unlawful for employers to discharge or otherwise discriminate against an employee for reporting suspected violations of a federal, state, or local law or regulation.[25]

Service letter: Maine laws provide that an employer must provide a terminated employee written reasons for the termination of his or her employment, upon written request from the employee asking for such information.[26]

Comparable pay: Maine statutes prohibit an employer from discriminating on the basis of sex by paying wages to one employee at a rate less than the rate of pay he or she pays another of the opposite sex for comparable work on jobs which have comparable requirements relating to skill, effort, working conditions, and responsibility.[27]

Medical examination payments: Title 26, Section 592, of the Maine Revised Statutes Annotated requires employers to make payment for the cost of any pre-employment medical examinations.

[85.06] WAGE AND HOUR LAWS

Child labor: Maine child labor laws regulate minimum age requirements for children to engage in certain occupations.[28]

Payment of wages: Maine statutes require employers to pay to employees, on a weekly basis, wages earned within eight days of date of payment.[29]

Payment upon termination: Maine wage and hour laws provide that an employee leaving employment shall be paid in full within a reasonable time after demand at the employer's office where payrolls are kept and wages are paid.

[85.07] SAFETY AND HEALTH LAWS

General provisions: Title 26, Section 561, *et seq.,* of the Maine Revised Statutes Annotated subject all Maine employers, except owners of farms and private residences, commercial fishing operations, the federal government and activities regulated by the Interstate Commerce Commission, to comply with safety rules and regulations formulated by the State Board of Occupational Safety and Health.

Toxic substances—right to know: Maine statutes require all employers to provide information to employees regarding toxic substances within the work place, including the institution of an annual education program about hazardous chemicals, etc.[30]

[85.08] UNEMPLOYMENT COMPENSATION LAWS

The Maine unemployment compensation laws provide benefits to unemployed individuals who are eligible under the requirements of the act and otherwise not disqualified.[31]

[85.09] WORKERS' COMPENSATION LAWS

The Maine Workmen's Compensation Act provides disability benefits to employees who suffer job-related injuries, or certain enumerated occupational diseases, subject to specified qualifications and limitations.[32]

[85.10] EMPLOYMENT-AT-WILL DEVELOPMENTS

Maine courts have been reluctant to subscribe to some of the developing exceptions to the employment-at-will principle.[33] For example, the public policy exception to the at-will rule has been rejected by the Maine courts.[34] The Maine courts have recognized the implied contract exception to the employment-at-will rule, however. In a 1984 case, a Maine court held that an employer's promise not to discharge an employee in bad faith and without just cause in exchange of the employee's promise to work full time created an implied employment contract.[35]

NOTES TO CHAPTER 85

1. Maine Revised Statutes Annotated, Title 26, Section 979.
2. Maine Revised Statutes Annotated, Title 26, Section 979.
3. Maine Revised Statutes Annotated, Title 26, Section 979-E and F.
4. Maine Revised Statutes Annotated, Title 26, Section 979-K.
5. Maine Revised Statutes Annotated, Title 26, Section 963, *et seq.*
6. Maine Revised Statutes Annotated, Title 26, Section 964.
7. Maine Revised Statutes Annotated, Title 26, Section 1021, *et seq.*
8. Maine Public Acts, Chapter 702 (L. 1984).
9. Maine Public Acts, Chapter 620 (L. 1972).
10. Maine Revised Statutes Annotated, Title 26, Section 851.

11. Maine Revised Statutes Annotated, Title 17, Section 3606.
12. Maine Revised Statutes Annotated, Title 26, Section 634.
13. Maine Revised Statutes Annotated, Title 17, Section 3601.
14. Maine Revised Statutes Annotated, Title 14, Section 1151, *et seq.*
15. Maine Revised Statutes Annotated, Title 16, Section 1341.
16. Maine Revised Statutes Annotated, Title 5, Section 4571, *et seq.*
17. Maine Revised Statutes Annotated, Title 5, Section 4572-A.
18. Maine Revised Statutes Annotated, Title 17, Section 401.
19. Maine Revised Statutes Annotated, Title 32, Section 7166.
20. Maine Revised Statutes Annotated, Title 26, Section 811.
21. Maine Revised Statutes Annotated, Title 26, Section 811.
22. Maine Revised Statutes Annotated, Title 26, Section 871.
23. Maine Revised Statutes Annotated, Title 26, Section 625 B(6).
24. Maine Revised Statutes Annotated, Title 26, Section 625 B(2).
25. Maine Revised Statutes Annotated, Title 26, Section 831, *et seq.*
26. Maine Revised Statutes Annotated, Title 26, Section 630.
27. Maine Revised Statutes Annotated, Title 26, Section 628.
28. Maine Revised Statutes Annotated, Title 26, Section 711, *et seq.*
29. Maine Revised Statutes Annotated, Title 26, Section 621.
30. Maine Revised Statutes Annotated, Title 26, Section 1701, *et seq.*
31. Maine Revised Statutes Annotated, Title 26, Section 1192.
32. Maine Revised Statutes Annotated, Title 39, Section 1, *et seq.*
33. *Merrill v. Western Union Tele. Co.*, 2 A.847 (Maine, 1886).
34. *MacDonald v. Eastern Fine Paper Inc.*, 485 A.2d 228 (Maine, 1984).
35. *Larrabee v. Penobscot Frozen Foods, Inc.*, 486 A.2d 97 (Maine, 1984).

86

Maryland
Labor Laws

[86.01] LABOR RELATIONS LAWS

General right to organize: Maryland statutes provide that employees within the state shall have full freedom of association, self-organization, and designation of representatives of their choosing, for the purpose of negotiating the terms and conditions of their employment or other mutual aid or protection.[1]

Teachers' bargaining rights: Article 77, Section 160, *et seq.*, of the Maryland Annotated Code extends bargaining rights to certificated employees of public schools and sets out guidelines to determine appropriate bargaining units, provides procedures and methods to determine bargaining representatives, specifies the nature and duty of public school boards to bargain, permits resolution of grievances by binding arbitration, prescribes permissible and impermissible union conduct, and forbids strikes.

Public school employees' bargaining rights: Maryland statutes also accord bargaining rights to noncertificated public school employees and permits certain boards of education within the state to negotiate with bargaining representatives of such employees.[2]

Nonright-to-work policy: Union security (union shop) clauses are permissible in the state of Maryland inasmuch as Maryland has not chosen to enact a right-to-work statute as permitted by Section 14(b) of the Labor Management Relations Act.

"Yellow-dog" contracts: Maryland statutes make it unlawful for anyone to coerce or compel any person to enter into an agreement not to join or become a member of any labor organization as a condition of employment.[3]

[86.02] STRIKES, PICKETING, AND BOYCOTT LAWS

Anti-injunction laws: Maryland statutory laws limit the power of Maryland courts to issue injunctions against conduct growing out of labor disputes.[4]

Sit-down strikes: Article 27, Section 552, of the Maryland Annotated Code makes it unlawful for any employee or former employee to participate in sit-down strikes.

Strikebreakers: Maryland statutes make it unlawful for any employer to utilize professional strikebreakers to replace an employee involved in a strike or lockout.[5]

[86.03] MEDIATION AND ARBITRATION LAWS

Article 89, Section 3, *et seq.*, of the Maryland Code Annotated provides that upon proper information that a dispute has arisen between an employer and its employees which may result in a strike or lockout, the Commissioner of Labor, or his or her designee, may investigate the dispute and seek to mediate it. Maryland statutes provide that employees of the executive branch of the state government, except those specifically excluded by the Act, may present grievances, free from interference, coercion, restraint, discrimination, or reprisal.[6] A similar procedure is also provided for classified employees of the University of Maryland.[7]

[86.04] REGULATION OF UNION ACTIVITIES

Maryland statutes make it unlawful for anyone to misuse or forge a union label.[8] Article 100, Section 66, of the Maryland Annotated Code provides that no labor organization or officer or member thereof, shall be liable for the unlawful acts of individual officers, members, or agents, except upon proof by the weight of the evidence, and without the aid of any presumptions of law or fact.

[86.05] REGULATION OF EMPLOYMENT PRACTICES

Anti-discrimination laws: Maryland statutes prohibit discrimination in the employment of an individual by reason of race, color, religion, sex, age, national origin, marital status, or physical or mental handicap.[9]

Polygraph restrictions: No Maryland employer shall require any applicant for employment or any employee to submit to a polygraph, lie detector, or similar test or examination as a condition of employment or continued employment.[10]

Discrimination against volunteer public service forbidden: Maryland employers are also forbidden to discharge an employee by reason of the employee's participation in civil defense, civil air patrol, volunteer rescue squad, or volunteer fire department activities that occur in response to a state-declared emergency.[11]

Reemployment rights of military personnel: Maryland statutes require employers to reemploy military personnel upon their return from military service to their former or similar positions without loss of seniority or status.[12]

Whistle-blowing statute (public employees): Maryland law forbids any appointing public authority to take disciplinary action against any employee for the disclosure of information that the employee reasonably believes evidences a violation of any law, rule, or regulation or misman-agement, a gross waste of funds, an abuse of authority, or a substantial and specific danger to public health or safety, if the disclosure is not specifically prohibited by law.[13]

Arrest records: Maryland employers are forbidden to require an ap-plicant to disclose information concerning arrest records.[14]

Medical records: Maryland statutes also prohibit employers from re-quiring applicants to answer questions pertaining to any physical, psycho-logical, or psychiatric illness, disability, handicap, or treatment that has no bearing on the applicant's fitness or capacity to perform the job.[15] Article 4, Section 303, of the Maryland Annotated Code provides that employees shall be permitted access to their medical records.

Jury duty: Maryland employers are forbidden to discharge or other-wise discriminate against an employee for his or her responding to a sum-mons or attending court as a juror.[16]

Comparable pay: Maryland law forbids pay differentials for employ-ees of opposite sexes for work of comparable character.[17]

[86.06] WAGE AND HOUR LAWS

Child labor: Article 100, Section 4, *et seq.,* of the Maryland Annotated Code regulates the employment of child labor within the state. For example, children under 18 years of age may not engage in employment unless they possess a valid work permit.[18]

Voting time: Maryland statutes provide that an employee eligible and duly registered to vote at a primary, general, or special election shall be excused from his or her employment not exceeding two consecutive hours, to exercise such voting privilege, provided the employee does not have two hours outside work time to cast his or her vote.[19]

Payment of wages: Article 100, Section 94, of the Maryland Anno-tated Code requires Maryland employers to pay employees their wages not less than twice during a month or once every two weeks.

Payment upon termination: Maryland employers are required to pay dismissed employees their wages in full, prior to termination.[20]

Garnishments: Article 15, Section 606, of the Maryland Annotated Code forbids the discharge of an employee because of the garnishment of his or her wages for any one indebtedness within a calendar year.

Medical insurance conversion: Article 95A, Section 5A, of the Mary-land Annotated Code provides that employees who are terminated must be notified of their right to convert group hospital and medical insurance coverage to their own individual coverage, provided certain requirements are met.

[86.07] SAFETY AND HEALTH LAWS

Maryland employers are required to furnish their employees with a place of employment that is free from recognized hazards that are causing or are likely to cause death or serious physical harm to their employees.[21]

[86.08] UNEMPLOYMENT COMPENSATION LAWS

Article 95A, Section 1, *et seq.,* of the Maryland Annotated Code provides that unemployed workers may be eligible to receive unemployment benefits provided they satisfy the eligibility requirements of the act and are not otherwise disqualified.

[86.09] WORKERS' COMPENSATION LAWS

Maryland's Workmen's Compensation Act provides disability benefits to employees who suffer on-the-job injuries or certain specified occupational diseases, subject to certain qualifications and limitations.[22] Benefits and payments are paid to employees in accordance with established schedules, the amounts and duration of which are dependent upon the gravity of the injury or disease and whether the disability is temporary or permanent and/or partial or total.

[86.10] EMPLOYMENT-AT-WILL DEVELOPMENTS

Maryland courts have suggested they will permit certain exceptions to the employment-at-will doctrine, provided certain elements are met.

Public policy exception: The Maryland Court of Appeals has ruled that it will recognize a cause of action for abusive discharge of an at-will employee when the motive for the discharge violates some clear mandate of public policy.[23]

Intentional infliction of emotional distress exception: The Maryland Court of Appeals has recognized the tort of intentional infliction of emotional distress in an employment case, holding that an employee may recover under such theory provided (1) the employer's conduct was intentional or reckless, (2) the conduct was extreme and outrageous, (3) there was causal connection between the conduct and the emotional distress, and (4) the emotional distress was severe.[24] (However, this theory has not been used in Maryland with respect to a wrongful discharge case, as of this writing.)

Implied contract exception: A Maryland Court has ruled that an employer must follow the counseling and termination procedures contained in a personnel policy handbook in order to effectuate a lawful termination.[25]

NOTES TO CHAPTER 86

1. Annotated Code of Maryland, Art. 100, Section 63.
2. Annotated Code of Maryland, Art. 77, Section 160A, *et seq.*
3. Annotated Code of Maryland, Art. 100, Section 64.
4. Annotated Code of Maryland, Art. 100, Sections 70 and 71.
5. Annotated Code of Maryland, Art. 100, Section 51A.
6. Annotated Code of Maryland, Art. 64A, Section 52, *et seq.*
7. Maryland Public Acts, Chapter 723 (L. 1978).
8. Annotated Code of Maryland, Art. 27, Section 187.
9. Annotated Code of Maryland, Art. 49B, Section 16.
10. Annotated Code of Maryland, Art. 100, Section 95.
11. Annotated Code of Maryland, Art. 100, Section 109.
12. Annotated Code of Maryland, Art. 65, Section 32A.
13. Annotated Code of Maryland, Art. 64A, Section 12(G).
14. Annotated Code of Maryland, Art. 27, Section 740(a).
15. Annotated Code of Maryland, Art. 100, Section 95A.
16. Maryland Courts and Judicial Proceedings Code Annotated, Section 8-105.
17. Annotated Code of Maryland, Art. 100, Section 55A.
18. Annotated Code of Maryland, Art. 100, Section 23(a)-(6).
19. Annotated Code of Maryland, Art. 33, Section 24-26.
20. Annotated Code of Maryland, Art. 100, Section 94E.
21. Annotated Code of Maryland, Art. 89, Section 32A.
22. Annotated Code of Maryland, Art. 101, Section 36, *et seq.*
23. *Adler v. American Standard Corp.*, 538 F.Supp. 572 (D.Md., 1982); *Adler v. American Standard Corp.*, 432 A.2d 464 (Md. Ct. of App., 1981).
24. *Harris v. Jones*, 380 A.2d 611 (Md. Ct. of App., 1977).
25. *Staggs v. Blue Cross of Maryland, Inc.*, Case No. 538 (Md. Ct. of Sp. App., 1985).

87

Massachusetts Labor Laws

Massachusetts Labor Relations Law: Chapter 150A, Section 1, *et seq.*, of the Massachusetts General Laws provides that Massachusetts employers must recognize and bargain in good faith with unions properly certified as representatives of their employees. Employees are provided the right of self-organization and the right to join or refrain from union activities.[1] The statute also provides for the machinery to conduct representation elections and procedures to process unfair labor practice charges against employers and labor organizations.[2]

Housing employees' bargaining rights: Chapter 121B, Section 29, of the Massachusetts General Laws extends to housing authority employees the right to bargain collectively through representatives of their choosing and requires Housing Authorities within the state to bargain collectively with labor organizations representing their employees.

Public employees' bargaining rights: Massachusetts statutes provide that public employees shall have the right of self-organization and the right to join and assist labor unions, or to refrain from union activities.[3] The statute prohibits certain conduct of both public employers and labor organizations, the violation of which constitutes unfair labor practices.[4] The Massachusetts Public Employees Relations Act also sets forth an election process to determine bargaining representatives, establishes registration requirements for labor organizations, forbids strikes, and provides a method for final and binding arbitration.[5]

State employees' grievance rights: Chapter 30, Section 53, of the Massachusetts General Laws empowers and requires the State Director of Personnel and Standardization to make rules and regulations providing an informal procedure for the prompt disposition of a grievance of any employee of the Commonwealth of Massachusetts.

Prohibition against pay-offs: Massachusetts laws prohibit the payment of money or any other thing of value to encourage or discourage employees in exercising their self-organizational and collective bargaining rights.[6]

Collective bargaining successor clauses: Chapter 149, Section 179C, of the Massachusetts General Laws provides that successor clauses in collective bargaining contracts shall be binding upon and enforceable against any employer who succeeds to the contracting employer's business until the expiration date of the agreement stated in the contract.

Nonright-to-work policy: Union security (union shop) clauses are permissible in the state of Massachusetts inasmuch as Massachusetts has not chosen to enact a right-to-work statute as permitted by Section 14(b) of the Labor Management Relations Act.

"Yellow-dog" contracts: Chapter 149, Section 20A, of the Massachusetts General Laws makes it unlawful for anyone to coerce or compel any person to enter into an agreement not to join or become a member of any labor organization as a condition of employment.

[87.02]   STRIKES, PICKETING, AND BOYCOTT LAWS

Anti-injunction act: Massachusetts statutes forbid the issuance of any restraining order or injunction in a labor dispute except under specifically enumerated conditions, as noted in the statute.[7]

Unlawful secondary boycotts: Chapter 149, Sections 20C(d) and (f), of the Massachusetts General Laws forbids any unlawful secondary boycotts.

Unlawful assembly: Massachusetts statutes make it unlawful whenever twelve or more persons armed with clubs or other dangerous weapons, or whenever thirty or more persons, whether armed or unarmed, assemble in a riotous and tumultuous manner and do not immediately and peaceably disperse when commanded to do so by peace officers.[8]

Unlawful interference with employment: Massachusetts statutes make it unlawful for any person to seek to prevent any person from engaging in any lawful employment within the state.[9]

Picketing of courts: Massachusetts statutes make it unlawful for anyone to obstruct or impede the administration of justice by picketing in or near a building or residence occupied by a judge, juror, witness, or court official.[10]

Declaration of emergency during transit strikes: The governor of Massachusetts is empowered to declare that an emergency exists and take possession of and operate a transit line and its facilities in order to safeguard the public health, safety, and welfare in the event there exists a transit strike that threatens the availability of essential services, endangers health, safety, and the welfare of the community and continues in violation of a court injunction.[11]

Strikebreakers: Massachusetts laws require the registration of labor replacements or strikebreakers from outside the Commonwealth.[12] Chapter 802, Section 22A, of the Massachusetts General Laws makes it unlawful for any employer to utilize professional strikebreakers to replace an employee or employees involved in a strike or lockout.

Striker replacements: Massachusetts statutes require advertisements and solicitations for employment applicants to state the existence of any strike, lockout, or other labor trouble at the place of the proposed employment.[13]

Use of police officers and firefighters during strike: Massachusetts laws prohibit auxiliary police personnel, who were originally organized by civil defense agencies under state or federal civil defense laws, to be used or called up for service in any labor dispute.[14] Chapter 48, Section 88, of the Massachusetts General Laws forbids firefighters to perform the duties of police officers in connection with any industrial or labor dispute.

[87.03] MEDIATION AND CONCILIATION LAWS

Chapter 150, Sections 1–10, of the Massachusetts General Laws establishes procedures for the conciliation and arbitration of industrial and labor disputes by the Massachusetts Board of Conciliation and Arbitration.

Chapter 150B, Sections 1–7, of the Massachusetts General Laws sets forth guidelines and procedures for the peaceful settlement of industrial and labor disputes that threaten substantial interruption of the distribution of food, fuel, water, electric light and power, gas, and hospital and medical services essential to the public health and safety. Massachusetts statutes also provide procedures relating to arbitration involving employees of police and fire departments.[15] Chapter 161A, Section 19, of the Massachusetts General Laws establishes arbitration procedures to resolve labor disputes between employee organizations and the Massachusetts Bay Transportation Authority.

[87.04] REGULATION OF UNION ACTIVITIES

Chapter 612, Sections 1–5, of the Massachusetts General Laws requires labor unions to file registration and financial statements with the Commissioner of Labor and Industries. Massachusetts statutes make it unlawful for anyone to misuse or forge a union label or union name.[16] Chapter 149, Section 150B, of the Massachusetts General Laws forbids a labor union to require any person, as a condition of securing or continuing employment, to pay any fee or assessment not authorized by its constitution and bylaws. Massachusetts statutes provide certain enumerated procedures and guidelines for the administration and regulation of employee health, welfare, and retirement trust funds.[17]

[87.05] REGULATION OF EMPLOYMENT PRACTICES

Anti-discrimination laws: Chapter 151B, Section 4, of the Massachusetts General Laws prohibits discrimination in the employment of an individual by reason of race, religion, creed, color, sex, national origin, or ancestry. Discrimination in employment because of age[18] or handicap[19] is likewise prohibited in Massachusetts.

Freedom of political activities: Chapter 56, Section 33, of the Massachusetts General Laws makes it unlawful for any employer to threaten to withhold the wages of, or to dismiss from service, any employee for the purpose of influencing the employee's vote in a political election.

Jury duty: Massachusetts employers are forbidden to attempt to deprive any employee of his or her employment.[20]

Military leaves of absence: Employees who are members of a ready reserve of the armed forces are entitled to leaves of absence from their employment up to seventeen days in any one calendar year in order to receive military training, and their employers are required to honor their employment rights to seniority and classification upon their return.[21]

Employment under false pretense: Massachusetts labor laws forbid any person to employ another through or by means of false or fraudulent representations.[22]

Polygraph restrictions: No Massachusetts employer shall require any applicant for employment, or any employee, to submit to a polygraph, lie detector, or similar test or examination as a condition of employment or continued employment, excepting the use of such tests administered by law enforcement agencies.[23]

Medical examination reports: Massachusetts statutes provide that any employer who requires a physical examination of an employee must furnish to him or her a copy of the medical report of said examination, upon request.[24]

Arrest records: Chapter 276, Section 100A, of the Massachusetts General Laws provides that an application for employment, used by an employer, which seeks information concerning prior arrests or convictions, shall contain language informing the applicant of his or her right to answer ''no record'' if a prior arrest did not result in a conviction or a conviction record resulting from an arrest has been expunged.

Hiring of illegal aliens: Massachusetts law forbids an employer to knowingly employ any alien in the state who has not been admitted to the United States for permanent residence, except those who are admitted under a work permit, or through the authorization of the Attorney General of the United States.[25]

Disclosure of consumer reports: Consumer reporting agencies are required to disclose to applicants and employees information in their files that had previously been furnished to the prospective employer or employers, concerning a background investigation and used by such employer in an employment decision upon request and proper identification of such applicants or employees.[26]

Political influence relating to public utilities employees: Chapter 271, Section 40, of the Massachusetts General Laws prohibits the use of political influence in connection with the employment rights of public utilities employees.

Plant closures: Massachusetts law provides that employers must continue health benefits for ninety days after the closing of a plant. Also, employers who seek financial assistance from certain state programs are required to make a good faith effort to notify their employees, in advance, of a plant closing.[27]

Equal pay: Chapter 149, Section 105A, of the Massachusetts General Laws makes it unlawful to discriminate in the payment of wages on the basis of sex.

[87.06] WAGE AND HOUR LAWS

Child labor: The Massachusetts child labor laws specify minimum age requirements in order for minors to engage in certain occupations.[28]

Voting time: Massachusetts statutes provide that an employee eligible and duly registered to vote in an election shall be excused from his employment for the first two hours after the opening of the polls.[29]

Payment of wages: Chapter 149, Section 148, of the Massachusetts General Laws requires Massachusetts employers, not specifically exempted, to pay employees their wages on a weekly basis.

Payment upon termination: Massachusetts employers are required to pay discharged employees their wages in full on the day of discharge.[30] An employee who voluntarily resigns his or her job is due full wages no later than the next regular payday.[31]

Medical insurance continuance: Chapter 175, Section 110G, of the Massachusetts General Laws requires employers to notify employees who are involuntarily laid off of their right to retain medical coverage for thirty-nine weeks or until they receive coverage under a new plan, at the employee's own expense for any premiums due for such continued coverage.

[87.07] SAFETY AND HEALTH LAWS

General provisions: Chapter 149, Sections 6–8, of the Massachusetts General Laws requires the Department of Labor and Industries to investigate places of employment and determine what suitable safety devices or other reasonable means or requirements for prevention of accidents and occupational diseases shall be adopted.

Toxic substances—right to know: Massachusetts statutes provide that employers must furnish certain training and information to employees who are exposed to toxic substances and chemicals regarding the properties and potential dangers of such substances. Massachusetts law also provides that an employee's treating physician may have access to an employee's medical records and documents regarding toxic chemicals, etc.[32]

[87.08] UNEMPLOYMENT COMPENSATION LAWS

Massachusetts unemployment compensation laws govern the eligibility requirements of recipients of unemployment compensation benefits.[33] Benefits are generally provided to unemployed workers who

- have properly registered for work at an unemployment office
- have properly applied for unemployment benefits
- are able to work, available for work, and actively seeking work
- are not otherwise disqualified under other provisions of the Act[34]

[87.09] WORKERS' COMPENSATION LAWS

The Massachusetts Workmen's Compensation Act provides disability benefits to employees who sustain job-related injuries or death or who suffer certain enumerated occupational diseases as a result of their job, subject to specific qualifications and limitations.[35] Whenever an employer and employee accept and comply with the requirements of the statute, all other rights and remedies, statutory or common law, on account of personal injuries or death are surrendered.[36]

[87.10] EMPLOYMENT-AT-WILL DEVELOPMENTS

Massachusetts courts have recognized several exceptions to the employment-at-will principle.

Public policy exception: An employee discharged in contravention of a public policy may recover damages against his or her employer.[37]

Implied contract exception: A personnel manual's promise of job security may create an implied employment contract, precluding an employer from discharging an employee except for cause.[38]

Covenant of good faith and fair dealing exception: A Massachusetts court has ruled that an employer may be liable for a bad faith discharge of an at-will employee, under certain circumstances.[39]

Intentional infliction of emotional distress exception: Massachusetts courts have recognized the outrageous conduct exception to the at-will rule if it can be shown that management's conduct toward an employee was so outrageous and extreme as to go beyond all bounds of decency and so atrocious as to be utterly intolerable in a civilized community.[40]

NOTES TO CHAPTER 87

1. Massachusetts General Laws, Chapter 150A, Section 3.
2. Massachusetts General Laws, Chapter 150A, Section 1, *et seq.*
3. Massachusetts General Laws, Chapter 150E, Section 2.
4. Massachusetts General Laws, Chapter 150E, Section 10.
5. Massachusetts General Laws, Chapter 150E, Section 1, *et seq.*
6. Massachusetts General Laws, Chapter 149, Section 20D.
7. Massachusetts General Laws, Chapter 214, Section 6.
8. Massachusetts General Laws, Chapter 269, Section 1.
9. Massachusetts General Laws, Chapter 149, Sections 19 and 18.
10. Massachusetts General Laws, Chapter 268, Section 13a.
11. Massachusetts General Laws, Chapter 544, Section 19A.
12. Massachusetts General Laws, Chapter 150D, Section 1, *et seq.*
13. Massachusetts General Laws, Chapter 149, Section 22.
14. Massachusetts General Laws, Chapter 149, Section 23B.
15. Massachusetts Public Acts, Chapter 154, (L-1979).
16. Massachusetts General Laws, Chapter 110, Sections 7–11 and Chapter 266, Section 71A.
17. Massachusetts General Laws, Chapter 151D, Section 1, *et seq.*
18. Massachusetts General Laws, Chapter 149, Section 24A.
19. Massachusetts General Laws, Chapter 149, Section 24K.
20. Massachusetts General Laws, Chapter 234A, Section 61.
21. Massachusetts General Laws, Chapter 149, Section 52A.
22. Massachusetts General Laws, Chapter 149, Section 21.

23. Massachusetts General Laws, Chapter 149, Section 19B.

24. Massachusetts General Laws, Chapter 149, Section 19A.

25. Massachusetts General Laws, Chapter 149, Section 19C.

26. Massachusetts General Laws, Chapter 93, Section 56.

27. Massachusetts Public Laws, H.6120 (1984).

28. Massachusetts General Laws, Chapter 149, Section 56, *et seq.*

29. Massachusetts General Laws, Chapter 149, Section 178.

30. Massachusetts General Laws, Chapter 149, Section 148.

31. Massachusetts General Laws, Chapter 149, Section 148.

32. Massachusetts General Laws, Chapter 111F, Section 1, *et seq.*

33. Massachusetts General Laws, Chapter 151A, Section 1, *et seq.*

34. Massachusetts General Laws, Chapter 151A, Section 24, *et seq.*

35. Massachusetts General Laws, Chapter 152, Section 1, *et seq.*

36. Massachusetts General Laws, Chapter 152, Section 25A.

37. *McKinney v. National Dairy Council,* 491 F.Supp. 1108 (D. Mass., 1980).

38. *Garrity v. Valley View Nursing Home, Inc.,* 406 N.E.2d 423 (Mass. Ct. of App., 1980).

39. *Fortune v. National Cash Register Co.,* 364 N.E.2d 1251 (Mass., 1977).

40. *Agis v. Howard Johnson Co.,* 355 N.E.2d 315 (Mass., 1976).

88

Michigan
Labor Laws

623

Public employees' bargaining rights: Michigan statutes provide that public employees shall have the right of self-organization and the right to join and assist labor unions, or to refrain from union activities.[1] The statute prohibits certain conduct of both public employers and labor organizations, the violation of which constitutes unlawful interference.[2] The Michigan Public Employment Relations Act also provides for an election process to determine bargaining representatives, establishes requirements to determine appropriate bargaining units, provides mediation of grievances, and forbids strikes.[3]

Michigan LMRA (Bonnie-Tripp Act): Michigan's little "Taft-Hartley" law, the Bonnie-Tripp Act, provides that it shall be lawful for Michigan employees to organize together or to form, join, or assist in labor organization; to engage in lawful concerted activities for the purpose of collective negotiation or other mutual aid and protection; or to negotiate or bargain collectively with their employers through representatives of their own choosing.[4] The statute creates the Employment Relations Commission within the State Department of Labor to administer the Act.[5] The statute also prescribes guidelines to determine appropriate bargaining units, a process to conduct representation elections, to mediate and conciliate labor disputes, and specifies conduct that will constitute unlawful labor practices.[6]

Police officers' and firefighters' labor disputes: Michigan statutes provide that whenever, in the course of mediation of a public police or fire department employees' dispute, a dispute has not been resolved to the agreement of both parties within thirty days of the submission of the dispute to mediation, or within mutually extended periods, the employees or employer may initiate binding arbitration through the procedures outlined in the Act.[7]

Nonright-to-work policy: Union security (union shop) clauses are permissible in the state of Michigan inasmuch as Michigan has not chosen to enact a right-to-work statute as permitted by Section 14(b) of the Labor Management Relations Act.

[88.02] STRIKES, PICKETING, AND BOYCOTT LAWS

Unlawful coercion: Section 423.17 of the Michigan Compiled Laws makes it unlawful for any employee to attempt to force any person to become or remain a member of a labor organization or to refrain from engaging in employment of his or her choice.[8]

Sit-down strikes: Section 423.15 of the Michigan Compiled Laws makes it unlawful for any person to participate in a sit-down strike and withhold possession of property against the will of the owner or other lawful possessor thereof.

Unlawful picketing: Section 423.9f of the Michigan Compiled Laws forbids any person to engage in mass picketing that obstructs ingress or egress to or from any place of employment or that interferes with free and uninterrupted use of public roads, streets, highways, railroads, airports, or other ways of travel or conveyance. The statute also forbids picketing in or near a private residence.

Unlawful assembly: Michigan laws make it unlawful for persons to assemble for unlawful purposes or to refuse or neglect to obey a command to depart from a place of riotous or unlawful assembly.[9]

Interference with transportation: Michigan statutes forbid any person, without lawful authority, to stop or hinder the operation of any vehicle transporting farm or commercial products within the state of Michigan.[10]

Strikebreakers and replacements: Michigan laws prohibit the recruitment of or advertising for employees to replace employees engaged in a labor dispute without stating that the employment offered is in place of striking employees.[11] Professional strikebreaking is also forbidden by this statute.

[88.03]   MEDIATION AND CONCILIATION LAWS

Section 423.9d of the Michigan Compiled Laws provides that any labor dispute, other than a representation question, may lawfully be submitted to voluntary arbitration in accordance with the procedures provided therein. Section 423.231, *et seq.,* of the Michigan Compiled Laws provide a process of mediation and binding arbitration to resolve labor disputes between public police and fire department employees and their employers. Michigan laws also provide for the compulsory arbitration of labor disputes involving state police troopers and sergeants.[12]

[88.04]   REGULATION OF UNION ACTIVITIES

Michigan laws provide that any ten or more residents of the state may incorporate themselves for the establishment of a trade union or other labor organization, provided they meet the conditions and requirements of the Act.[13] Michigan laws make it unlawful for anyone to misuse or forge a union label or other union insignia.[14]

[88.05]   REGULATION OF EMPLOYMENT PRACTICES

Anti-discrimination laws: Michigan laws prohibit discrimination in the employment of an individual by reason of race, color, religion, sex, age, national origin, marital status, height, or weight.[15] The Michigan statutes also forbid discrimination in employment because of handicap.[16]

Freedom of political activities: Michigan statutes make it unlawful for any person to attempt to influence the vote of any elector by promising or giving such voter money or valuable consideration as an inducement.[17]

Jury duty: Michigan employers are forbidden to attempt to deprive any employee of his or her employment because such employee is summoned for jury duty, serves as a juror, or attends court for prospective jury service.[18]

Polygraph restrictions: No Michigan employer shall require any applicant for employment or any employee to submit to a polygraph, lie detector, or similar test or examination as a condition of employment or continued employment, except for use of such tests in certain state agencies or subdivisions thereof.[19]

Whistle-blowing statute: Michigan law forbids any employer within the state to take disciplinary action against an employee because he or she reports, or is about to report, a violation or suspected violation of a law, regulation, or rule promulgated pursuant to the law of Michigan.[20]

Reemployment rights of military personnel: Michigan laws require Michigan employers to reemploy military personnel upon their return from military service to their former or similar positions without loss of seniority, status, or pay.[21]

Arrest records: Michigan employers are prohibited from using arrest records in employment decisions.[22]

Access to personnel records: Michigan employers, upon written request, are required to provide an employee with an opportunity to review periodically, at reasonable intervals, his or her personnel record, if such a record is maintained by the employer.[23] The statute also provides that the employee is entitled to obtain a copy of the information contained in the personnel file, if he or she so requests. In the event of disagreement over information contained in the personnel record, the statute provides that the employee may submit a written statement of such and place it in the file.[24]

Wage disclosure protection: Section 408.483 of the Michigan Compiled Laws forbids an employer to discharge or discipline an employee for disclosing his or her wages to another person or employee.

Wage evasion: An employer that consistently discharges employees within ten weeks of their employment and replaces them with other employees, without work stoppage, is presumed to have taken such action to evade payment of wage rates and commits an unlawful act, punishable as a misdemeanor.[25]

Equal pay: Section 408.397 of the Michigan Compiled Laws makes it unlawful to discriminate in the payment of wages on the basis of sex.

[88.06] WAGE AND HOUR LAWS

Child labor: The Michigan child labor laws found at Section 409.01, *et seq.*, of the Michigan Compiled Laws limit and restrict the employment of children.

Payment of wages: Section 408.472 of the Michigan Compiled Laws requires Michigan employers (excluding employers of individuals harvesting crops by hand) to pay employees, on or before the first day of each calendar month, wages earned during the first fifteen days of the preceding calendar month; and, on or before the fifteenth day of each calendar month, wages earned during the preceding calendar month from the sixteenth day through the last day.

Payment upon termination: Michigan employers are required to pay discharged employees their wages in full as soon as they can be determined.[26] An employee who voluntarily resigns his or her job is also due full wages as soon as the amount can be determined.[27]

Garnishment: Section 600.4015 of the Michigan Compiled Laws forbids discharge because of one or more garnishment actions brought against an employee.

[88.07] SAFETY AND HEALTH LAWS

General provisions: Michigan occupational safety and health laws require employers to furnish a safe and healthful place of employment for their employees to work. Employers are required to furnish and use safety devices and safeguards and to adopt and use practices, methods, operations, and processes that are reasonably adequate to render a safe and healthful work environment.[28]

Toxic substances—right to know: Michigan employers who use or manufacture hazardous chemicals or toxic substances are required to provide notice postings to employees containing the trade and chemical names of each hazardous substance, its toxic properties, and procedures to follow in the event of a spillage or overexposure.[29]

[88.08] UNEMPLOYMENT COMPENSATION LAWS

Michigan unemployment compensation laws which govern the eligibility requirements of recipients of unemployment compensation benefits are found at Section 421.1, *et seq.*, of the Michigan Compiled Laws.

[88.09] WORKERS' COMPENSATION LAWS

Michigan statutes provide disability benefits to employees who sustain job-related injuries or death or who suffer occupational diseases as a result of their job, subject to specified qualifications and limitations.[30] Benefits and payments are paid to employees in accordance with established schedules, the amounts and duration of which are dependent upon the gravity of the injury or disease and whether the disability is temporary or permanent and/or partial or total.

[88.10] EMPLOYMENT-AT-WILL DEVELOPMENTS

Michigan courts have been most suspect of the historic employment-at-will rule and have recognized many exceptions to it in recent years.

Public policy exception: The discharge of an employee for having filed a worker's compensation claim violates public policy in the state of Michigan, giving rise to a cause of action for wrongful discharge.[31]

Negligent discharge exception: The failure to inform an employee that his or her job is in jeopardy at a performance evaluation, when shortly thereafter the employee is discharged, may give rise to a wrongful discharge action on the theory of negligence.[32]

Intentional infliction of emotional distress exception: Although no recovery has been permitted under the theory as of this writing, a Michigan court has indirectly recognized the intentional infliction of emotional distress exception to the at-will rule in cases where the stress inflicted is so severe that no reasonable person could be expected to endure it.[33]

Implied contract exception: Michigan courts were some of the first to recognize that an implied employment contract might be created through the language of a personnel policy that promises job security and assures that no employee will be discharged except for cause.[34]

NOTES TO CHAPTER 88

1. Michigan Compiled Laws, Section 423.209.
2. Michigan Compiled Laws, Section 423.210.

3. Michigan Compiled Laws, Section 423.201, *et seq.*

4. Michigan Compiled Laws Annotated, Section 423.8.

5. Michigan Compiled Laws Annotated, Section 423.3.

6. Michigan Compiled Laws Annotated, Section 423.1, *et seq.*

7. Michigan Compiled Laws, Section 423.231, *et seq.*

8. Michigan Compiled Laws, Section 28-584.

9. Michigan Compiled Laws, Section 28-79.

10. Michigan Compiled Laws, Section 28-655.

11. Michigan Statutes Annotated, Section 17-456(1).

12. Michigan Public Acts, No. 17 (1980), Section 1-16.

13. Michigan Compiled Laws, Section 454.71, *et seq.*

14. Michigan Compiled Laws, Section 750.265a.

15. Michigan Compiled Laws, Section 37.2202.

16. Michigan Compiled Laws, Section 37.1101, *et seq.*

17. Michigan Statutes Annotated, Section 6.1931.

18. Michigan Compiled Laws, Section 600.1348(1).

19. Michigan Compiled Laws, Section 37.201, *et seq.*

20. Michigan Compiled Laws Annotated, Section 15.362.

21. Michigan Compiled Laws Annotated, Section 32.271, *et seq.*

22. Michigan Compiled Laws, Section 37.2205a.

23. Michigan Compiled Laws Annotated, Section 423.501, *et seq.*

24. Michigan Compiled Laws Annotated, Section 423.501, *et seq.*

25. Michigan Compiled Laws, Section 408.396.

26. Michigan Compiled Laws, Section 408.475.

27. Michigan Compiled Laws, Section 408.475.

28. Michigan Compiled Laws, Section 408.1011.

29. Michigan Compiled Laws, Section 408.1001, *et seq.*

30. Michigan Compiled Laws, Section 411.1, *et seq.*

31. *Sventko v. Kroger Co.,* 245 N.W.2d 151 (Mich., 1976).

32. *Chamberlain v. Bissell, Inc.,* 547 F.Supp. 1067 (WD Mich., 1982).

33. See *Novesel v. Sears, Roebuck & Co.,* 495 F.Supp. 344 (ED Mich., 1980).

34. See, for example: *Toussaint v. Blue Cross & Blue Shield of Michigan,* 292 N.W.2d 880 (Mich. S.Ct., 1980).

89

Minnesota
Labor Laws

Minnesota Labor Relations Act: Section 179.01 of the Minnesota Statutes provides that Minnesota employers, other than employers specifically exempted, and excluding the state and subdivisions thereof, must recognize and bargain in good faith with unions properly certified as representatives of their employees. Employees are provided the right of self-organization and the right to join, or refrain from, union activities.[1] The statute also provides for the machinery to conduct representation elections and the procedures to process unfair labor practice charges against employers and labor organizations.[2]

Public employees' bargaining rights: Minnesota statutes provide that public employees shall have the right of self-organization and the right to join and assist labor unions or to refrain from union activities.[3] The statute prohibits certain conduct of both public employers and labor organizations, the violation of which constitutes unfair labor practices.[4] The Minnesota Public Employment Relations Act also provides for an election process to determine bargaining representatives, establishes registration requirements for labor organizations, and forbids strikes.[5]

Nonright-to work policy: Union security (union shop) clauses are permissible in the state of Minnesota inasmuch as Minnesota has not adopted a right-to-work statute as permitted by Section 14(b) of the Labor Management Relations Act.

"Yellow-dog" contracts: Section 179.60 of the Minnesota Statutes makes it unlawful for anyone to attempt to force any person to enter into an agreement not to join or become a member of any labor organization as a condition of employment.

[89.02] STRIKES, PICKETING, AND BOYCOTT LAWS

Anti-injunction statute: Section 185.02 of the Minnesota Statutes prohibits the issuance of restraining orders and injunctions in cases involving labor disputes, except under specifically enumerated conditions as outlined in the statute.

Unlawful assembly: Minnesota statutes make it unlawful when three or more persons assemble together and disturb the public peace by an intentional act of unlawful force or violence without lawful purpose, and refuse to leave when so directed by a law enforcement officer.[6]

Striker replacements: Section 184.38(10) of the Minnesota Statutes requires employment agencies to state in any advertisement, proposal, or contract for employment, the existence of any strike or lockout at the place of the proposed employment, if they have knowledge of such.

False advertisements and representations in hiring: Section 181.64 of the Minnesota Statutes makes it unlawful for any person to attempt to induce an employee from his or her place of employment through false representations or fail to state in any advertisement, proposal, or contract for employment the existence of any strike or lockout at the place of the proposed employment.

Use of police officers limited during strikes: Minnesota laws forbid the employment of members of the Bureau of Criminal Apprehension to render police service in connection with labor strikes, lockouts, or other labor disputes.[7]

Use of licensed private detectives during strikes: Section 326.337 of the Minnesota Statutes limits the participation and involvement of private detectives in a strike, lockout, or labor dispute.

Striker employment protection: Minnesota statutes forbid any person or firm to attempt to prevent any person from obtaining or retaining employment by reason of his or her having engaged in a labor dispute.[8] Section 181.53 of the Minnesota Statutes prohibits any employer to require any written statements from an applicant as to his or her participation in a strike as a condition of employment or continued employment.

Secondary boycotts: Minnesota statutes forbid anyone to cause or conspire to cause injury to one not a party to a particular labor dispute.[9]

[89.03] MEDIATION AND ARBITRATION LAWS

Minnesota has adopted the Uniform Arbitration Act recognizing any written agreement to submit an existing controversy to arbitration as valid, enforceable, and irrevocable, except for such grounds as exist at law or equity for the revocation thereof.[10] Section 179.06 of the Minnesota Statutes provides a method of conciliation as a means to settle labor disputes within the state.

Section 179.07 of the Minnesota Statutes empowers the governor to appoint a commission to conduct a hearing and make a report to the governor's office on the issues of a labor dispute in an industry, business, or institution affected with a public interest. The Minnesota Public Employment Relations Act establishes procedures for adjusting grievances and disputes involving public employees and employee organizations.[11]

[89.04] REGULATION OF UNION ACTIVITIES

Section 333.41 of the Minnesota Statutes makes it unlawful for anyone to misuse or forge a union label or other union insignia. Section 179.21 of the Minnesota Statutes requires labor unions to furnish certain financial statements to their members on an annual basis. Minnesota statutes make it unlawful for any employee or labor organization to compel or attempt to compel any person to join or refrain from joining any labor organization or any strike against his will by unlawful interference, threats, or force.[12]

[89.05] REGULATION OF EMPLOYMENT PRACTICES

Anti-discrimination laws: Section 363.01, *et seq.,* of the Minnesota Statutes prohibit discrimination in the employment of an individual by reason of race, religion, creed, color, sex, national origin, marital status, disability, status with regard to public assistance, or age.

Protection of political freedom: Minnesota laws make it unlawful for any person or firm to interfere with the voting privileges of any employee.[13] Section 3.083 of the Minnesota Statutes protects the right of employees, who are also legislators, to make political statements without fear of reprisal from their employers.

Blacklisting: Minnesota employers are prohibited from maintaining a blacklist or notifying any other employer that any worker has been blacklisted by such employer for the purpose of preventing such worker from receiving employment.[14]

Employment under false pretense: Minnesota labor laws forbid any person to employ another through or by means of false representations.[15]

Polygraph restrictions: Minnesota employers are forbidden to require any applicant for employment or any employee to submit to a polygraph, lie detector, or similar test or examination to test his or her honesty.[16]

National Guard members: Section 192.34 of the Minnesota Statutes provides that no employer shall discharge any person from employment because of being an officer or enlisted person of the military forces of the state, attempt to prevent such employee from performing any military service that he or she may be called upon to perform by proper authority, or attempt to dissuade any person from military enlistment.

Equal pay: Minnesota law requires employers to pay female employees the same wage as that paid to male employees for work requiring equal skill, effort, and responsibility and performed under similar working conditions.[17]

Criminal and arrest records: The state of Minnesota and its political subdivisions are forbidden to use, distribute, or disseminate arrest records or related records in connection with any employment decision where such records did not result in convictions or, if resulted in convictions, such convictions involved misdemeanors.[18]

Jury duty: Minnesota statutes provide that an employer shall not attempt to deprive an employee of his or her employment because the employee receives a summons, responds thereto, serves as a juror, or attends court for prospective jury service.[19]

Mandatory insurance participation restricted: Section 61A.091 of the Minnesota Statutes forbids employers to require employees to participate in employer-sponsored insurance plans as a condition of employment, unless the employer pays the full cost of the plan, where at least five or more employees are employed.

Pre-employment medical exams: Minnesota employers may require applicants for employment to undergo physical examination provided an offer of employment has been made, the offer is conditioned upon the applicant meeting the physical and mental requirements of the job, the medical examination is limited to job-related abilities, and that such examinations are required of all applicants on a nondiscriminatory basis.[20]

Maternity leaves: Minnesota statutes require employers to provide maternity leaves for adoptive mothers and fathers on the same basis as are provided biological parents.[21]

[89.06] WAGE AND HOUR LAWS

Child labor: The Minnesota Child Labor Standards Act prescribes certain minimum age requirements for children to engage in occupations within the state.[22]

Voting time: Minnesota statutes provide that an employee eligible and duly registered to vote in any statewide general election shall be excused from his or her employment during the forenoon of election day to exercise such voting privilege without penalty or deduction from wages.[23]

Garnishment: Section 571.61 of the Minnesota Statutes forbids the discharge of an employee on the basis that his or her wages have been subjected to garnishment.

Medical coverage continuance: Section 62A.17 of the Minnesota Statutes requires employers to notify terminated employees of their right to continue health insurance coverage at their own expense.

[89.07] SAFETY AND HEALTH LAWS

General provisions: Section 182.653 of the Minnesota Statutes provides that Minnesota employers shall furnish employees a place of employment free from recognized hazards that are causing or are likely to cause death or serious injury to such employees.

Toxic substances—right to know: Section 182.65, *et seq.*, of the Minnesota Statutes requires employers who use or manufacture hazardous substances to provide certain information and education to employees regarding potential hazards and properties of such substances.

[89.08] UNEMPLOYMENT COMPENSATION LAWS

The Minnesota Unemployment Compensation Act provides certain benefits for unemployed workers, provided they register for work at the unemployment office, submit timely and proper claims, be able and available for work, wait the one-week waiting period, and have fifteen or more credit weeks in nonseasonal employment at 30 percent of statewide average weekly wage and not be otherwise disqualified.[24]

[89.09] WORKERS' COMPENSATION LAWS

The Minnesota Workers' Compensation Act provides compensation for personal injury or death caused by accident arising out of and in the course of employment, unless injury was intentionally self-inflicted or caused by drunkenness.[25] Certain enumerated occupational diseases are considered to be personal injuries and fall within the coverage of the statute.[26]

[89.10] EMPLOYMENT-AT-WILL DEVELOPMENTS

Minnesota courts have recognized certain judicial exceptions to the employment-at-will rule, as noted below.

Promissory estoppel exception: Where an employee relies upon an offer of employment from a defendant, resigns his position from his previous employment and rejects an offer of employment from another employer, only to learn that the defendant has reneged on the offer, the employee may recover from the defendant on the theory of promissory estoppel.[27]

Implied contract exception: Where an employer discharges an employee and fails to follow the termination procedures enumerated in an employee handbook, the employee may have a cause of action for wrongful discharge under the theory that the employer breached his or her implied contractual duties that were created through the language of the hand-book.[28]

"Independent consideration" exception: Minnesota courts have held that an employee's at-will employment status may be modified where he or she provides consideration in addition to normal employment duties, such as transferring stock to an employer as partial consideration for the job.[29]

Intentional infliction of emotional distress exception: A Minnesota court has recognized the tort of intentional infliction of emotional distress as an exception to the at-will doctrine in cases where the facts surrounding the claim demonstrate egregious conduct on the part of the employer.[30]

Covenant of good faith and fair dealing exception: One Minnesota court has suggested that the implied covenant of good faith and fair dealing exception to the at-will rule may be asserted as a proper cause of action in certain cases, although the court rejected the theory as being applicable to the particular case in question.[31]

NOTES TO CHAPTER 89

1. Minnesota Statutes, Section 179.10.
2. Minnesota Statutes, Section 179.01, *et seq.*
3. Minnesota Statutes, Section 179A.06.
4. Minnesota Statutes, Section 179A.06.
5. Minnesota Statutes, Section 179A.01, *et seq.*
6. Minnesota Statutes, Section 609.715.
7. Minnesota Statutes, Section 299C.03.
8. Minnesota Statutes, Section 181.52.
9. Minnesota Statutes, Section 179.40, *et seq.*
10. Minnesota Statutes, Section 572.08, *et seq.*
11. Minnesota Statutes, Section 179.61, *et seq.*
12. Minnesota Statutes, Section 179.11.
13. Minnesota Statutes, Section 210.12.
14. Minnesota Statutes, Section 179.12.
15. Minnesota Statutes, Section 181.64.
16. Minnesota Statutes, Section 181.75.
17. Minnesota Statutes, Section 181.66–71.
18. Minnesota Statutes, Section 364.04.
19. Minnesota Public Acts, Chapter 286 (L. 1977).
20. Minnesota Statutes, Section 363.02.

21. Minnesota Statutes, Section 181.92.
22. Minnesota Statutes, Section 181A.05, *et seq.*
23. Minnesota Statutes, Section 204C.04.
24. Minnesota Statutes, Section 268.07–09.
25. Minnesota Statutes, Section 176.021, *et seq.*
26. Minnesota Statutes, Section 176.66.
27. *Grouse v. Group Health Plan, Inc.*, 306 N.W.2d 114 (Minn., 1981).
28. *Pine River State Bank v. Mettille,* 333 N.W.2d 622 (Minn., 1983).
29. *Bussard v. College of St. Thomas, Inc.,* 200 N.W.2d 155 (Minn., 1972).
30. *Hubbard v. United Press International, Inc.,* 330 N.W.2d 428 (Minn., 1983).
31. *Eklund v. Vincent Brass & Aluminum Co.,* 351 N.W.2d 371 (Minn., 1984).

90

Mississippi
Labor Laws

[90.01] LABOR RELATIONS LAWS

Union telegraphers' rights: Mississippi statutes make it unlawful for any telegraph company, telephone company, telegraph press association, railroad company, or any leased wire firm or private individual doing business in the state and employing telegraphers to discharge or otherwise discriminate against any such telegrapher because of such telegrapher's affiliation with or membership in any lawful organization or trade or labor union of telegraphers.[1]

Right-to-work statute: Section 71-1-47 of the Mississippi Code provides that no person shall be required by an employer to become or remain a member of any labor union as a condition of employment or be required to pay any dues, fees, or other charges of any kind to any labor union as a condition of employment. The statute does not apply to any employer or employee under the jurisdiction of the Federal Railway Labor Act.[2]

"Yellow-dog" contracts: Section 6984.5(1)(d) of the Mississippi Code makes it unlawful for anyone to attempt to coerce any person to enter into an agreement not to join or become a member of any labor organization as a condition of employment.

[90.02] STRIKES, PICKETING, AND BOYCOTT LAWS

Interference with employment: Mississippi statutes make it unlawful for two or more persons to conspire, by threats, or other means of coercion, to prevent any person from engaging in any lawful occupation at any place he or she sees fit.[3]

Unlawful assembly: Section 219-25-67 of the Mississippi Code prohibits riots, routs, affrays, and unlawful assemblages.

Interference with business: Mississippi laws make it unlawful for any person to interfere with the lawful employment of another.[4]

Interference with transportation: Section 97-25-43 of the Mississippi Code makes it unlawful for two or more persons to interfere with or obstruct the regular operation of a railroad company, public service corporation, public utility, or other corporation carrying passengers and property for hire.

Restriction of railroad picketing: Mississippi statutes forbid any person to willfully and maliciously impede or obstruct the regular operation and conduct of the business of any railroad company.[5]

Use of highway patrol during strikes: Section 45-3-21 of the Mississippi Code provides that state highway patrolmen are not to be ordered or required to be used in any strike, lockout, or other labor controversy to supplant or displace the peace officers of the state, except that said patrolmen shall have the power to arrest, without warrant, any person or persons committing or attempting to commit a breach of peace or a felony on a state highway.

Use of violence or threats forbidden: Mississippi statutes make it unlawful for any person, by force or threats, to attempt to prevent any person from engaging in any lawful vocation within the state.[6]

[90.03] MEDIATION AND CONCILIATION LAWS

Section 11-15-1 of the Mississippi Code provides that all persons, except infants and persons of unsound mind, may submit to the decision of one or more arbitrators any controversy existing between them that might be the subject to an action, and may, in such submission, agree that the court having jurisdiction of the subject matter shall render judgment on the award made pursuant to such submission.

[90.04] REGULATION OF UNION ACTIVITIES

Mississippi statutes make it unlawful for anyone to misuse or forge a union label or other union insignia.[7] Mississippi laws forbid any agreement or arrangement whereby a carrier or shipper of property agrees to pay a charge other than transportation charges for services actually performed to any organization, individual, or corporation.[8]

Mississippi statutes provide that no person who is an alien or who is or has been a member of the Communist Party or who has been convicted of, or served any part of a prison term resulting from his or her conviction of, robbery, bribery, extortion, embezzlement, grand larceny, burglary, arson, violation of narcotics laws, murder, rape, assault with intent to kill, or conspiracy to commit any such crimes, shall serve (1) as an officer, director, trustee, or member of any executive board or similar governing body, business agent, manager, organizer, or other employee (other than an employee performing exclusively clerical or custodial duties) of any labor organization, or as a manager, or any person occupying a bargaining position with industry; or (2) as a labor relations consultant either of a labor organization or of an employer or both, or as an officer, director, agent, or employee (other than as an employee performing exclusively clerical or custodial duties) of any group or association of employers dealing with any labor organization, during or for five years after the termination of his membership in the Communist Party, or for five years after such conviction.[9]

[90.05]   REGULATION OF EMPLOYMENT PRACTICES

Anti-discrimination laws (state employees): Mississippi fair employment practices statutes apply only to state employees and forbid discrimination in employment on the basis of political affiliation, race, national origin, sex, religious creed, age, or disability.[10]

Jury duty: Section 13-5-23 of the Mississippi Code makes it unlawful for an employer to attempt to persuade any juror to avoid jury service, or to intimidate or threaten any juror in any respect.

Protection of military personnel: Section 33-1-15 of the Mississippi Code prohibits the discharge of any employee who is called upon to perform military service. The statute also requires employers to reinstate reserve members of the armed forces to their previous positions upon their return from service.[11]

Unlawful enticement: Mississippi laws forbid any person to entice any employee who has contracted to serve his or her employer for a specific length of time, to leave the service of such employer during that time.[12]

Protection of political activities: Mississippi laws forbid any employer to interfere with the voting privileges of its employees.[13]

[90.06]   WAGE AND HOUR LAWS

Child labor: Section 71-1-1, *et seq.,* of the Mississippi Code establishes certain minimum age requirements for children to work.

Payment of wages: Section 71-1-35 of the Mississippi Code requires manufacturing employers of fifty or more employees to pay employees their wages no less than twice during a month and no later than ten days from the established pay period.

[90.07]   SAFETY AND HEALTH LAWS

Section 75-37-1, *et seq.,* of the Mississippi Code establishes certain safety and sanitation standards for Mississippi employers. For example, Mississippi manufacturing plants must be supplied with ample water and adequate toilets so located as to be readily accessible to employees.[14]

[90.08]   UNEMPLOYMENT COMPENSATION LAWS

The Mississippi unemployment compensation laws govern, among other things, the eligibility requirements of recipients of unemployment compensation benefits.[15] Benefits are generally provided to unemployed workers who

- have properly registered for work at an unemployment office
- have properly applied for unemployment benefits
- are able to work, available for work, and actively seeking work
- have been unemployed for at least one week
- are not otherwise disqualified under other provisions of the Act[16]

[90.09] WORKERS' COMPENSATION LAWS

The Mississippi Workmen's Compensation Act provides disability benefits to employees injured on the job or who suffer occupational diseases as a result of their job, subject to specified qualifications and limitations.[17] Benefits and payments are paid to employees in accordance with established schedules, the amounts and duration of which are dependent upon the gravity of the injury or disease and whether the disability is temporary or permanent and/or partial or total.

[90.10] EMPLOYMENT-AT-WILL DEVELOPMENTS

Mississippi courts have adhered to the employment-at-will doctrine rather rigidly. However, several cases suggest that some judicial exceptions might be recognized in the future.

Implied contract exception: Where an employer's personnel handbook sets out conditions of employment and limits termination to specifically listed violations, the handbook modifies the at-will status of the employees affected and precludes termination for any reason other than those listed.[18]

"Independent consideration" exception: A limitation on an employer's right to terminate at-will may arise when the employee has supplied additional consideration for the position independent of his or her regular employment duties.[19]

Intentional tort exception: Mississippi courts may permit a cause of action for wrongful discharge on the theory that an employer has committed an intentional tort, such as for discharging an employee because of his having filed a suit against the employer under the Jones Act.[20]

NOTES TO CHAPTER 90

1. Mississippi Code, Section 77-9-725, *et seq.*
2. Mississippi Code, Section 71-1-47.

3. Mississippi Code, Section 97-1-1, *et seq.*

4. Mississippi Code, Section 97-23-83.

5. Mississippi Code, Section 77-9-236.

6. Mississippi Code, Section 97-23-39.

7. Mississippi Code, Section 97-21-53.

8. Mississippi Public Acts, H.B. 123 (L. 1962).

9. Mississippi Code, Section 71-1-49.

10. Mississippi Code, Section 25-9-103.

11. Mississippi Code, Section 33-1-19.

12. Mississippi Code, Section 97-23-29.

13. Mississippi Code, Section 23-3-29.

14. Mississippi Code, Section 75-37-19.

15. Mississippi Code, Section 71-5-1, *et seq.*

16. Mississippi Code, Section 71-5-511.

17. Mississippi Code, Section 71-3-1, *et seq.*

18. *Conley v. Board of Trustees,* 707 F.2d 175 (CA-5, 1983).

19. *McGlohn v. Gulf and S.I.R.R.,* 174 So. 250 (Miss., 1937); *Sartin v. City of Columbus Utilities Commission,* 421 F.Supp. 393 (N.D. Miss., 1976).

20. *Smith v. Atlas Off-Shore Boat Service,* 653 F.2d 1057 (CA-5, 1981); See also: *Moeller v. Fuselier, Ott & McKee,* 115 LRRM 2600 (Miss., 1984).

91

Missouri
Labor Laws

[91.01] LABOR RELATIONS LAWS

General right to organize: Article 1, Section 29, of the Missouri Constitution provides that employees within the state shall have the right to organize and bargain collectively through representatives of their own choosing.

Public employees' bargaining rights: Missouri statutes accord all public employees within the state, except police, deputy sheriffs, Missouri State Highway Patrolmen, and Missouri National Guard, the right to form and join labor organizations and to present proposals to any public body relative to salaries and other conditions of employment through representatives of their own choosing.[1] The statute excludes collective bargaining rights to all teachers of all Missouri schools, colleges, and universities.[2] The Missouri Board of Mediation is empowered by the statute to resolve issues with respect to appropriateness of bargaining units and majority representative status involving public employees.[3] The statute does not grant a right of public employees to strike.[4]

Nonright-to-work policy: Union security (union shop) clauses are permissible in the state of Missouri inasmuch as Missouri has not adopted a right-to-work statute pursuant to Section 14(b) of the Labor Management Relations Act.

[91.02] STRIKES, PICKETING, AND BOYCOTT LAWS

Interference with employment: Missouri statutes make it unlawful for anyone to use force, threats, or coercion to prevent any person from engaging in any lawful occupation of his or her choice.[5]

Unlawful assembly: Section 562.150 of the Missouri Revised Statutes prohibits three or more persons to assemble together to do an unlawful act.

Importation of private detectives during strikes: Missouri statutes forbid any person to bring into the state any other person for the purpose of discharging the duties devolving upon sheriffs, police officers, or other peace officers in the protection or preservation of public or private property.[6]

Restriction of railroad picketing: Section 560.315 of the Missouri Revised Statutes forbids any person to impede or obstruct the regular operation of any railroad company.

Illegal seizure of property: Section 560.435 of the Missouri Revised Statutes forbids any person to take or keep possession of any real property by actual force or violence, without the authority of law.

[91.03] MEDIATION AND ARBITRATION LAWS

The Missouri Utility Disputes Mediation Act provides for the mediation of labor disputes in public utilities through the services of the State Board of Mediation.[7] The statute also provides for the seizure and public operation of utilities to ensure continuous operation of such services whenever labor disputes create an emergency condition as determined by the governor of the state.[8] Section 435.010, *et seq.,* of the Missouri Revised Statutes provides that all persons who shall have any controversy, may submit such controversy to the arbitration of any person, to be mutually agreed upon by the parties, and may make such submission a rule of any record in the state.

[91.04] REGULATION OF UNION ACTIVITIES

Section 416.031 of the Missouri Revised Statutes outlaws contracts, combinations in the form of trust or otherwise, or conspiracies in restraint of trade within the state.

[91.05] REGULATIONS OF EMPLOYMENT PRACTICES

Anti-discrimination laws: Section 296.010, *et seq.,* of the Missouri Revised Statutes prohibits discrimination in the employment of an individual by reason of race, creed, color, religion, sex, national origin, ancestry, or handicap.

Protection of political freedom: Missouri labor laws make it unlawful for any employer within the state to attempt to prevent its employees from engaging or participating in politics or from becoming candidates for public office.[9] The statute also makes it unlawful for an employer to discharge or otherwise discriminate against any employee because of his or her political opinions or persuasion.[10]

Service letter: Missouri employers are required by Section 290.140 of the Missouri Revised Statutes to provide employees who quit, or who are discharged, a letter setting forth the nature and character of service rendered by the employee and the duration thereof, and truly state for what cause, if any, such employee quit or was discharged, provided the employee requests such a service letter.

Employment rights of military: Section 41.730 of the Missouri Revised Statutes provides that no employer shall discharge any person from employment because of being a member of the organized militia of the state, attempt to prevent him or her from performing any militia service or attempt to dissuade any person from military enlistment.

Wage reduction: Missouri employers are required to give thirty days' written notice of any wage reductions, stating the amount of the reduction and the classifications of employees affected.[11]

Equal pay: Missouri statutes make it unlawful to discriminate in payment of wages on the basis of sex by paying female employees at a rate less than that paid male employees for similar or equal work.[12]

[91.06] WAGE AND HOUR LAWS

Child labor: Missouri child labor laws specify minimum age requirements as conditions to working in certain jobs within the state.[13]

Voting time: Missouri statutes provide that an employee eligible and duly registered to vote in state or local elections shall be excused from his or her employment not exceeding three consecutive hours, to exercise such voting privilege, provided such employee does not have three consecutive hours between the time of opening and closing of the polls when he or she is not working for the employer.[14]

Payment of wages: Section 290.090 of the Missouri Revised Statutes requires manufacturing employers to pay employees their full wages at least once in every fifteen days.

Payment upon termination: Missouri employers are required to pay discharged employees their wages on the day of discharge.[15]

Garnishments: Section 525.030 of the Missouri Revised Statutes forbids discharge on the basis of garnishment for any one indebtedness.

Medical coverage continuance: Section 376.397 of the Missouri Revised Statutes requires employers to notify terminated employees of their right to continue medical insurance coverage at their own expense.

[91.07] SAFETY AND HEALTH LAWS

Missouri safety laws are found at Section 291.010, *et seq.*, of the Missouri Revised Statutes. Section 291.130 of the Missouri Revised Statutes provides that the Director of Industrial Inspections shall appoint assistants and inspectors of buildings and shops, investigate all accidents requiring physical rehabilitation, and make recommendations to employers regarding safety matters.

[91.08] UNEMPLOYMENT COMPENSATION LAWS

The Missouri unemployment compensation laws may be found at Section 288.01, *et seq.*, of the Missouri Revised Statutes. The law governs the eligibility requirements of recipients of unemployment compensation benefits.[16]

[91.09] WORKERS' COMPENSATION LAWS

Section 287.010, *et seq.*, of the Missouri Revised Statutes sets forth the Missouri Workmen's Compensation Act. The statute provides disability benefits to employees injured on the job or who suffer occupational diseases as a result of their job, subject to specified qualifications and limitations.[17] Benefits and payments are paid to employees in accordance with established schedules, the amounts and duration of which are dependent upon the gravity of the injury or disease and whether the disability is temporary or permanent and/or partial or total. Missouri employers are forbidden to discharge or otherwise discriminate against employees for having filed a worker's compensation claim.[18]

[91.10] EMPLOYMENT-AT-WILL DEVELOPMENTS

Missouri courts have recognized limited exceptions to the at-will rule, as noted below.

   Public policy exception: Where employees have been discharged in retaliation for filing a worker's compensation claim, a cause of action may lie based on the public policy exception to the at-will principle.[19]

   Intentional infliction of emotional distress exception: An employee may recover damages against his or her employer based on the theory of intentional infliction of emotional distress, such as where an employee was trapped on an elevator for a prolonged period of time and unable to take needed medication.[20]

   Implied contract exception: The Missouri Supreme Court has ruled that an employer's personnel manual might create an implied employment contract if such handbook communicated job security to employees upon which assurances terminated employees relied.[21]

NOTES TO CHAPTER 91

   1. Missouri Revised Statutes, Section 105.510, *et seq.*
   2. Missouri Revised Statutes, Section 105.510.
   3. Missouri Revised Statutes, Section 105.530.

4. Missouri Revised Statutes, Section 105.540.
5. Missouri Revised Statutes, Section 559.460.
6. Missouri Revised Statutes, Section 562.200.
7. Missouri Revised Statutes, Section 295.010, *et seq.*
8. Missouri Revised Statutes, Section 295.180.
9. Missouri Revised Statutes, Section 15.020(7).
10. Missouri Revised Statutes, Section 115.635(b).
11. Missouri Revised Statutes, Section 296.100.
12. Missouri Revised Statutes, Section 290.400, *et seq.*
13. Missouri Revised Statutes, Section 294.011, *et seq.*
14. Missouri Revised Statutes, Section 115.639.
15. Missouri Revised Statutes, Section 290.110.
16. Missouri Revised Statutes, Section 288.040.
17. Missouri Revised Statutes, Section 287.010, *et seq.*
18. Missouri Revised Statutes, Section 287.780.
19. *Arie v. Intertherm, Inc.,* 648 S.W.2d 142 (Mo. App., 1983).
20. *Bass v. Nooney Co.,* 644 S.W.2d 765 (Mo. S.Ct., 1983).
21. *Arie v. Intertherm, Inc.,* 648 S.W.2d 142 (Mo. App., 1983); *Hinkeldey v. Cities Service Oil Co.,* 470 S.W.2d 494 (Mo., 1971). See also: *Enyeart v. Shelter Mutual Ins. Co.,* Case No. 36426 (Mo. Ct. of App., 1985).

92

Montana
Labor Laws

[92.01] LABOR RELATIONS LAWS

Public employees' bargaining rights: Montana statutes provide that public employees shall have the right of self-organization and the right to join and assist labor unions, or to refrain from union activities.[1]

Nurses' bargaining rights: Section 39-32-101, *et seq.*, of the Montana Code Annotated extends collective bargaining rights to nurses at public and private health-care facilities.

Nonright-to-work policy: Union security (union shop) clauses are permissible in the state of Montana inasmuch as Montana has not adopted a right-to-work statute pursuant to Section 14(b) of the Labor Management Relations Act.

[92.02] STRIKES, PICKETING, AND BOYCOTT LAWS

Anti-injunction statutes: Montana statutes restrict the power of courts within the state to issue injunctions or restraining orders with regard to labor disputes.[2]

Unlawful assembly: Section 45-8-103 of the Montana Code Annotated makes it unlawful to commit the offense of riot or disturb the peace by engaging in an act of violence as part of an assemblage of five or more persons.

Strikebreakers: Section 39-33-201, *et seq.*, of the Montana Code Annotated makes it unlawful for any employer to utilize professional strikebreakers to replace an employee involved in a strike or lockout at a place of business within the state, through the use of misrepresentations, threats, or force.

Striker replacements: Section 39-2-303, *et seq.*, of the Montana Code Annotated requires advertisements and solicitations for employment applicants to state the existence of any strike, lockout, or other labor trouble occurring at the place of the proposed employment.

Sit-down strikes: Section 45-6-203 of the Montana Code Annotated forbids any employee, or former employee, to remain upon the premises of his or her employer after a notice to leave, when the purpose of such refusal to leave is to deprive the employer of the substantial possession of such premises.

Importation of private detectives during strikes: Montana statutes forbid any person to bring into the state any individual for the purpose of discharging the duties devolving upon sheriffs, police officers, or other peace officers in the protection or preservation of public or private property.[3]

[92.03]   MEDIATION AND CONCILIATION LAWS

Section 27-4-101, *et seq.,* of the Montana Code Annotated provides that persons capable of contracting may submit to arbitration any controversy which might be the subject of a civil action between them. The statute also provides that it may be stipulated in the submission that it be entered as an order of the district court.[4] Section 39-34-101 of the Montana Code Annotated provides that if an impasse is reached in the course of collective bargaining between a public employer and a firefighters' exclusive representative, and if the procedures for mediation and fact-finding have been exhausted, either party or both jointly may petition the board for final and binding arbitration.

Section 2-18-1001 of the Montana Code Annotated states that an employee of the Department of Highways, aggrieved by a serious matter of his or her employment based upon work conditions, supervision, or the result of an administrative action, is entitled to a hearing before the Board of Personnel Appeals for resolution of the grievance. Section 2-18-1011, *et seq.,* of the Montana Code Annotated specifies that public employees, or their representatives, are entitled to file grievances with the State Board of Personnel Appeals and to be heard under the provisions of a grievance procedure to be prescribed by the Personnel Appeals Board.

[92.04]   REGULATION OF UNION ACTIVITIES

Section 39-33-101 of the Montana Code Annotated makes it unlawful for any union or union member to interfere with the rights of sole proprietors or members of a partnership to do any work in their places of business.

[92.05]   REGULATION OF EMPLOYMENT PRACTICES

Anti-discrimination laws: Montana statutes prohibit discrimination in the employment of an individual by reason of race, creed, color, religion, sex, marital status, national origin, ancestry, age, or handicap.[5]

Hiring of illegal aliens: Montana statutes make it unlawful for any Montana employer knowingly to employ an alien who is not lawfully authorized to accept employment.[6]

Polygraph restrictions: No Montana employer shall require any applicant for employment or an employee to submit to a polygraph, lie detector, or similar test or examination as a condition of employment or continued employment.[7]

Blacklisting: Montana employers are prohibited from maintaining a blacklist or notifying any other employer of a blacklist of any employee or former employee.[8]

Service letter: Montana employers are required by Section 39-2-801 of the Montana Code Annotated to provide a terminated employee a letter setting forth the cause, if any, for which such employee was discharged, provided the employee requests such a service letter.

Unlawful enticement: Section 39-2-303 of the Montana Code Annotated provides no person or firm shall attempt to induce an employee of another person or firm to change employment through means of deception, misrepresentation, or false advertising concerning the kind or character of the work, the sanitary or other conditions of employment, or as to the existence of a strike or other trouble pending between the employer and its employees, at the time of, or immediately prior to, such agreement.

Comparable pay: Section 39-3-104 of the Montana Code Annotated provides that private or public persons or firms may not employ women at wages less than those paid men for comparable service in the occupation.

[92.06] WAGE AND HOUR LAWS

Child labor: Children within the state of Montana below 16 years of age are not permitted to work in any mine; mill; smelter; workshop; factory; steam, electric, hydraulic, or compressed-air railroad; or passenger or freight elevator; or where any machinery is operated; or for any telegraph, telephone, or messenger company; or in any occupation not here enumerated, known to be dangerous or unhealthful or which may be in any way detrimental to a minor's morals.[9] Montana employers who employ children 16 years of age must possess age certificates issued by the Commissioner of Labor and Industry, showing such age.[10]

Payment of wages: Section 39-3-204 of the Montana Code Annotated provides that Montana employers, except those specifically excluded, shall not withhold any wages earned or upaid more than ten business days after they become due and payable.

Payment upon termination: Montana employers are required to pay separated employees their wages within three days, except for employees of the state, who must be paid on the next regular payday, or fifteen days from the date of separation, whichever occurs first.[11]

Garnishments: Section 39-2-302 of the Montana Code Annotated forbids the discharge of an employee because of an attachment or garnishment of his or her wages.

[92.07] SAFETY AND HEALTH LAWS

Section 50-71-202, *et seq.*, of the Montana Code Annotated outlines safety in the work-place requirements within the state. Montana statutes provide that the State Board of Health shall limit the levels, concentrations, or quantities or emissions of various pollutants from any source necessary to prevent, abate, or control occupational disease.[12]

[92.08] UNEMPLOYMENT COMPENSATION LAWS

The Montana Unemployment laws provide that unemployment benefits are payable to individuals who are, or who become unemployed, provided certain eligibility requirements are met.[13] Recipients may become disqualified for continuation of benefits by failure to apply for or accept suitable work, or to return to customary occupation.[14]

[92.09] WORKERS' COMPENSATION LAWS

Section 39-71-101, *et seq.*, of the Montana Code Annotated sets forth the Montana Workmen's Compensation Act. The statute provides disability benefits to employees injured on the job, subject to specified qualifications and limitations.[15]

[92.10] EMPLOYMENT-AT-WILL DEVELOPMENTS

Montana courts have permitted certain judicial exceptions to the at-will rule, irrespective of Section 39-2-503 of the Montana Code Annotated which codified the employment-at-will doctrine into state law.

Covenant of good faith and fair dealing exception: Montana courts recognize that there is an implied covenant by an employer to deal fairly with an employee and an employer may breach such covenant by discharging an employee in bad faith and without warning or hearing.[16]

Public policy exception: Public policy exceptions to the at-will principle are recognized by Montana courts in discharge cases involving the refusal to commit perjury, refusal to engage in sexual relations with a supervisor, assertion of a worker's compensation claim, etc.[17]

NOTES TO CHAPTER 92

1. Montana Code Annotated, Section 39-31-201.
2. Montana Code Annotated, Section 27-19-103.
3. Montana Code Annotated, Section 45-8-106.

4. Montana Code Annotated, Sections 47-5-102 and 47-5-103.

5. Montana Code Annotated, Section 49-1-102, *et seq.*

6. Montana Code Annotated, Section 39-2-305.

7. Montana Code Annotated, Section 39-2-304.

8. Montana Code Annotated, Section 39-2-802, *et seq.*

9. Montana Code Annotated, Section 41-2-101.

10. Montana Code Annotated, Section 41-2-113.

11. Montana Code Annotated, Section 39-3-205.

12. Montana Code Annotated, Section 50-70-113.

13. Montana Code Annotated, Section 39-51-2103, *et seq.*

14. Montana Code Annotated, Section 39-51-2103.

15. Montana Code Annotated, Section 39-71-701, *et seq.*

16. *Gates v. Life of Montana Insurance Co.,* 668 P.2d 213 (Mont. S.Ct., 1983).

17. See statement of legal principle in *Keneally v. Orgain,* 606 P.2d 127 (Mont., 1980).

93

Nebraska
Labor Laws

Teachers' bargaining rights: The Nebraska Teachers' Negotiations Act provides that certificated public school employees shall have the right to form, join, and participate in the activities of organizations of their choosing for the purpose of representation on all matters of employment relations, but no certificated public school employee shall be compelled to join such an organization and individual employees shall have the right to individually represent themselves in their employment relations.[1] The statute further provides that school boards and other boards of education within the state shall meet and confer with the representatives of an organization of certificated school employees whenever a majority of the members of such boards decide to recognize such employee organization.[2] The statute provides that unresolved labor disputes between such parties be referred to a fact-finding board who shall hear and review the matters relating to the dispute and shall thereafter render a report and make recommendations to settle the dispute, which recommendations shall receive the good faith considerations from both parties.[3]

Public employees' bargaining rights: Section 48-801, *et seq.,* of the Revised Statutes of Nebraska created the Commission of Industrial Relations to settle labor disputes affecting public utilities. The statute also extended collective bargaining rights to public employees and empowered the Nebraska Commission of Industrial Relations to determine questions of representation for purposes of collective bargaining for and on behalf of employees, and to make rules and regulations for the conduct of representation elections.[4]

Right-to-work statute: Section 48-217 of the Revised Statutes of Nebraska forbids any person to deny employment to another because of membership in or affiliation with, or resignation or expulsion from a labor organization or because of refusal to join, affiliate with, or pay a fee, to a labor organization.

[93.02]   STRIKES, PICKETING, AND BOYCOTT LAWS

Destruction of property: Section 25-580 of the Revised Statutes of Nebraska forbids any person to maliciously destroy or injure any property or product of another.

Unlawful interference with employment: Nebraska laws make it unlawful for any person or firm to interfere with any other person in the exercise of his or her lawful right to work or to pursue any lawful employment.[5]

Mass picketing: Nebraska statutes forbid any form of picketing in which there are more than two pickets at any one time within either 50 feet of any entrance to the premises being picketed or within 50 feet of any other picket or pickets, or in which pickets constitute an obstacle to the free ingress or egress to and from the premises being picketed or in any way obstruct public roads or passageways.[6]

Secondary boycotts: Nebraska law makes it unlawful for any person to engage in a secondary boycott within the state.[7]

[92.03] MEDIATION AND CONCILIATION LAWS

Section 25-2103 of the Revised Statutes of Nebraska provides that all controversies that might be the subject of civil actions may be submitted to the decision of one or more arbitrators. Nebraska statutes also provide for compulsory arbitration to resolve labor disputes involving public utilities.[8]

[92.04] REGULATION OF UNION ACTIVITIES

Nebraska statutes make unlawful any agreement that limits the conveyance of goods and products by ''piggyback'' conveyances.[9] Section 28-548 of the Revised Statutes of Nebraska makes it unlawful for any officer, agent, or attorney of any voluntary association or labor organization to embezzle or otherwise fraudulently take any money, goods, funds or property belonging to any such voluntary association or labor organization. Section 4-106 of the Revised Statutes of Nebraska makes it unlawful for any alien to be elected to or hold any office in a labor or educational organization in the state of Nebraska.

[93.05] REGULATION OF EMPLOYMENT PRACTICES

Anti-discrimination laws: Nebraska statutes prohibit discrimination in the employment of an individual by reason of race, religion, color, sex, age, national origin, marital status, or handicap.[10]

Protection of political freedom: Nebraska labor laws make it unlawful for any employer to interfere with the voting privileges of his or her employees.[11]

Medical examinations and coverage continuance: Nebraska statutes make it unlawful for any employer to require an applicant for employment to pay the cost of a medical examination required by the employer as a condition of his or her employment.[12] Section 44-1633 of the Revised Statutes of Nebraska provides that employees terminated involuntarily for reasons other than misconduct are entitled to continue certain medical insurance from the employer up to a maximum period of six months, provided certain requirements are met.

Polygraph restrictions: No Nebraska employer shall require any applicant for employment, or any employee, to submit to a polygraph, lie detector, or similar test or examination as a condition of employment or continued employment, unless such employment involves public law enforcement.[13]

Military leaves of absence: Nebraska laws provide that Nebraska employees shall be entitled to absent themselves from their employment duties while engaged in the performance of military service with the armed forces of the United States.[14]

Jury duty: Nebraska statutes provide that any person who is summoned to serve on jury duty shall not be subject to discharge from employment, loss of pay, loss of sick leave, loss of vacation time, or any other form of penalty, as a result of his or her absence from employment, upon giving reasonable notice to the employer of such summons.[15] The statute further provides that any person who is summoned to serve on jury duty shall be excused, upon request, from any shift work for those days required to serve as a juror, without loss of pay.[16]

Service letter: Nebraska laws require public service corporations and contractors doing business within the state of Nebraska to issue to a former employee a service letter that sets forth the nature of the service rendered by him to the corporation or contractor and the duration of employment, and truly state in such letter the cause for which such employee was discharged or quit, provided the former employee requests such a letter.[17]

Equal pay: Section 48-1221 of the Revised Statutes of Nebraska forbids employers with twenty-five or more employees to discriminate in wages between employees on the basis of sex for equal work on jobs requiring equal skill, effort, and responsibility.

[93.06] WAGE AND HOUR LAWS

Child labor: Nebraska child labor laws require employment certificates, as a condition to employment, for children between 14 and 16 in any mercantile institution, store, office, hotel, laundry, manufacturing establishment, bowling alley, elevator, factory or workshop, restaurant, drive-in theater, concert hall, or place of amusement.[18] The statute also provides that employment certificates for children under 14 years of age will be issued only for work connected with an employment program supervised by a school in which such children are enrolled.[19]

Voting time: Nebraska statutes provide that an employee eligible and duly registered to vote at a statewide or local election shall be excused from employment not exceeding two consecutive hours to exercise such voting privilege, without any reduction of pay for such absence.[20]

Payment of wages: Nebraska laws require employees to be paid on regular paydays designated by the employer or as mutually agreed upon by the employer and employees or the employees' representatives.[21]

Payment upon termination: Nebraska employers are required to pay separated employees their wages no later than the next regular payday or within two weeks of termination, whichever is sooner.[22]

Garnishments: Section 25-1558(b) of the Revised Statutes of Nebraska forbids discharge of an employee for garnishment for any one indebtedness.

[93.07] SAFETY AND HEALTH LAWS

Safety in the work-place requirements are found at Section 48-401, *et seq.,* of the Revised Statutes of Nebraska. Section 48-404 of the Revised Statutes of Nebraska requires factories, mills, workshops, and mechanical establishments to keep their places of business in an acceptable sanitary condition.

[93.08] UNEMPLOYMENT COMPENSATION LAWS

The Nebraska unemployment compensation laws are found at Section 24-601, *et seq.,* of the Revised Statutes of Nebraska and govern, among other things, the eligibility requirements of recipients of unemployment compensation benefits.

[93.09] WORKERS' COMPENSATION LAWS

Section 48-101, *et seq.,* of the Revised Statutes of Nebraska sets forth the Nebraska Workmen's Compensation Act. The statute provides for disability benefits to employees injured on the job or who suffer occupational diseases as a result of their job, subject to specified qualifications and limitations.[23]

[93.10] EMPLOYMENT-AT-WILL DEVELOPMENTS

Nebraska courts have given little deference to some of the developing judicial exceptions to the employment-at-will doctrine.[24] However, a few Nebraska courts have implied that they might be less than sympathetic to strict adherence to the at-will doctrine in certain cases in the future. For example, one Nebraska court held that an at-will employee may have a cause of action for wrongful discharge where a personnel handbook enumerates procedures limiting the right of the employer to discharge employees.[25]

NOTES TO CHAPTER 93

1. Revised Statutes of Nebraska, Section 79-1288.
2. Revised Statutes of Nebraska, Section 79-1290.
3. Revised Statutes of Nebraska, Section 79-1293.
4. Revised Statutes of Nebraska, Section 48-838.
5. Nebraska Public Acts, L.B. 38 (L. 1977), Section 301.
6. Ibid., Section 302.
7. Revised Statutes of Nebraska, Section 48-901, *et seq.*
8. Revised Statutes of Nebraska, Section 43-801, *et seq.*
9. Nebraska Public Acts, L.B. 672 (L. 1963).
10. Revised Statutes of Nebraska, Section 48-1001, *et seq.*
11. Revised Statutes of Nebraska, Section 32-1223.
12. Revised Statutes of Nebraska, Section 48-221.
13. Nebraska Public Acts, L.B. 485 (L. 1980).
14. Revised Statutes of Nebraska, Section 55-161.
15. Revised Statutes of Nebraska, Section 25-1640.
16. Revised Statutes of Nebraska, Section 25-1640.
17. Revised Statutes of Nebraska, Section 48-211.
18. Revised Statutes of Nebraska, Section 48-304.
19. Revised Statutes of Nebraska, Section 48-302, 303.
20. Revised Statutes of Nebraska, Section 32-1046.
21. Revised Statutes of Nebraska, Section 48-1230.
22. Revised Statutes of Nebraska, Section 48-1231.
23. Revised Statutes of Nebraska, Section 48-101, *et seq.*
24. See, for example: *Mau v. Omaha Nat'l Bank,* 299 N.W.2d 147 (Neb., 1980).
25. *Morris v. Lutheran Medical Center,* 340 N.W.2d 388 (Neb., 1983); see also *Corso v. Creighton University,* 731 F.2d 529 (CA-8, 1984).

94

Nevada
Labor Laws

[94.01] LABOR RELATIONS LAWS

General right to organize: Section 614.090 of the Nevada Revised Statutes provides that employees within the state shall have full freedom of association, self-organization, and designation of representatives of their own choosing, for the purpose of negotiating the terms and conditions of their employment or other mutual aid or protection, free from interference, restraint, coercion by their employers, or other persons.[1]

Municipal employees' bargaining rights: Nevada statutes provide that employees of local governments shall have the right of self-organization and the right to join and assist labor unions, or to refrain from union activities.[2] Section 288.080, *et seq.,* of the Nevada Revised Statutes established the Local Government Employee-Management Relations Board, whose function is to administer and enforce the provisions and requirements of the act. The statute prohibits certain conduct of both public employers and labor organizations, the violation of which constitutes unfair labor practices.[3] The statute provides for an election process to determine bargaining representatives, establishes registration requirements for labor organizations, and forbids strikes.[4]

Right-to-work statute: The Nevada statutes prohibit the denial of employment to anyone on account of membership or nonmembership in a labor union or organization.[5]

"Yellow-dog" contracts: Section 613.130 of the Nevada Revised Statutes makes it unlawful for anyone to compel any person to enter into an agreement not to join or become a member of any labor organization as a condition of employment.

[94.02] STRIKES, PICKETING, AND BOYCOTT LAWS

Interference with employment: Nevada statutes make it unlawful for anyone to attempt to prevent any person from engaging in any lawful occupation.[6]

Breach of employment contracts: Section 613.100 of the Nevada Revised Statutes makes it unlawful for any person to willfully or maliciously break a contract of service or employment, knowing or having reasonable cause to believe that the consequence of his or her breach will endanger human life, cause grievous bodily injury, or expose valuable property to destruction or serious injury.

Strike notices: Nevada statutes require employment agencies to notify applicants of any existing strike or lockout prior to sending such an applicant to a prospective employer experiencing such labor conditions.[7] Section 614.120 of the Nevada Revised Statutes makes it unlawful for any person or firm to issue or circulate any printed or written notice that a strike exists unless such notice shall contain the signatures of at least three persons who, at the time of signing said circulars, were residents and citizens of the state for a period of six months.

[94.03] MEDIATION AND CONCILIATION LAWS

Nevada has adopted the Uniform Arbitration Act recognizing any written agreement to submit an existing controversy to arbitration as valid, enforceable, and irrevocable, except on such grounds as exist at law or equity for the revocation thereof.[8] Section 614.010 of the Nevada Revised Statutes provides for mediation of labor disputes within the state. In the event mediation fails to resolve a labor dispute, the statute provides for a method of submitting the differences of the parties to arbitration.[9]

[94.04] REGULATION OF UNION ACTIVITIES

Nevada statutes make it unlawful for anyone to misuse or forge a union label or other union insignia, or to falsely misrepresent that employment of union labor went into the production or manufacture of goods or services.[10] Section 613.125 of the Nevada Revised Statutes makes it unlawful for an employer to agree to make payments to a health or welfare fund or other such plans for the benefit of an employee, or agree to enter into a collective bargaining agreement providing for such payments, and thereafter renege on such commitment. Section 614.140 of the Nevada Revised Statutes makes it unlawful to bribe union representatives for the purpose of attempting to induce such representatives to cause or prevent labor strikes.

[94.05] REGULATION OF EMPLOYMENT PRACTICES

Anti-discrimination statutes: Section 613.310, *et seq.,* of the Nevada Revised Statutes prohibits discrimination in the employment of an individual by reason of race, religion, color, sex, age, national origin, or handicap.

Polygraph restrictions: Nevada employers are forbidden to require any applicant for employment or any employee to submit to a polygraph, lie detector, or similar test or examination unless certain safeguards are provided such applicant or employee as enumerated in the statute.[11]

Protection of political freedom: Nevada labor laws make it unlawful for any employer to forbid or attempt to prevent his or her employees from engaging or participating in politics or from becoming candidates for public office.[12]

Employment under false pretense: Section 613.090 of the Nevada Revised Statutes provides that it shall be unlawful for any person to obtain employment by a forged letter, certificate of recommendation, or union card. Nevada labor laws also forbid any person to employ another through false representations.[13]

Jury and witness duty: Nevada employers are forbidden to discharge or otherwise discriminate against an employee because of jury[14] or witness[15] duty.

Blacklisting: Nevada employers are prohibited from maintaining a blacklist or notifying any other employer that they have blacklisted an employee or former employee.[16]

Service letter: Section 613.240 of the Nevada Revised Statutes requires Nevada employers to provide terminated employees a letter stating truthfully the reason for termination, if such employees timely request such information.

Discharge of volunteer firefighters: Nevada law forbids the discharge of a person who serves as a volunteer firefighter because of his or her firefighter duties.[17]

Restrictions on detectives and "spotters": Section 613.160 of the Nevada Revised Statutes makes it unlawful to discharge or discipline an employee as a result of a report from a detective or "spotter" unless the employee is accorded a hearing, upon request, and given an opportunity to confront such detective or "spotter" and present his or her defenses to any allegations contained in such report.

Equal pay: Section 608.017 of the Nevada Revised Statutes makes it unlawful to discriminate in payment of wages on the basis of sex.

[94.06] WAGE AND HOUR LAWS

Child labor: Section 609.220, *et seq.*, of the Nevada Revised Statutes governs the employment of minors. Nevada laws forbid the employment of a child under 14 years of age without the written permit of the district court judge of the county wherein such minor may live, except for certain farm work and housework.

Voting time: Nevada statutes provide that an employee eligible and duly registered to vote in an election shall be excused from his or her employment not exceeding one hour, if living within two miles of a polling place, two hours if living between two and ten miles of a polling place, and three hours if living more than ten miles of a polling place, without any reduction of pay or reprisals for such absence.[18]

Payment of wages: Employees in Nevada are to be paid at least semimonthly with the requirement that wages earned before the first of any month must be paid by 8:00 A.M. on the fifteenth of the following month, and wages earned before the sixteenth of the month must be paid by 8:00 A.M. of the last day of the month.[19]

Payment upon termination: Nevada employers must pay discharged employees their full wages due immediately and must pay the full wages due to employees who voluntarily quit within twenty-four hours, after demand.[20]

[94.07] SAFETY AND HEALTH LAWS

General provisions: Section 618.375, *et seq.,* of the Nevada Revised Statutes provides that employers are required to furnish and use safety devices and safeguards and to adopt and use practices, methods, operations, and processes that are reasonably adequate to render a safe and healthful work environment.

Toxic substances—right to know: Section 668.380 of the Nevada Revised Statutes requires employers to notify employees promptly of their exposure to any toxic substances in concentrations or at levels exceeding certain standards. Section 618.370 of the Nevada Revised Statutes requires employers to provide employees access to any records, in the employer's possession, which indicate the employee's exposure to toxic substances or materials.

[94.08] UNEMPLOYMENT COMPENSATION LAWS

The Nevada unemployment compensation laws are set forth in Section 612.010, *et seq.,* of the Nevada Revised Statutes and govern the eligibility requirements of recipients of unemployment compensation benefits.

[94.09] WORKERS' COMPENSATION LAWS

The Nevada Industrial Insurance System provides disability benefits to employees injured on the job, subject to specified qualifications and limitations.[21] Benefits and payments are paid to employees in accordance with established schedules, the amounts and duration of which are dependent upon the gravity of the injury or disease and whether the disability is temporary or permanent and/or partial or total.

[94.10] EMPLOYMENT-AT-WILL DEVELOPMENTS

Nevada courts have recognized certain judicial exceptions to the employment-at-will rule.

Public policy exception: Nevada courts have held that a discharge in retaliation for the filing of a worker's compensation claim is a violation of public policy and actionable in tort.[22]

Implied contract exception: A Nevada court has ruled that an employer is bound by the termination procedures in an employment handbook and an employee may not be terminated unless such procedures are followed.[23]

NOTES TO CHAPTER 94

1. Nevada Revised Statutes, Section 614.100.
2. Nevada Revised Statutes, Section 288.140.
3. Nevada Revised Statutes, Section 288.270.
4. Nevada Revised Statutes, Section 288.010, *et seq.*
5. Nevada Revised Statutes, Section 613.230, *et seq.*
6. Nevada Revised Statutes, Section 100.48.
7. Nevada Revised Statutes, Section 611.290.
8. Nevada Revised Statutes, Section 38.035, *et seq.*
9. Nevada Revised Statutes, Section 614.020.
10. Nevada Revised Statutes, Section 205.205.
11. Nevada Public Acts, Chapter 676 (L. 1981).
12. Nevada Revised Statutes, Section 613.040.
13. Nevada Revised Statutes, Section 613.010.
14. Nevada Public Acts, Chapter 150 (L. 1977).
15. Nevada Revised Statutes, Section 50.070.
16. Nevada Revised Statutes, Section 613.210, *et seq.*
17. Nevada Public Acts, Chapter 381 (L. 1983).
18. Nevada Revised Statutes, Section 293.463.
19. Nevada Revised Statutes, Section 608.060.
20. Nevada Revised Statutes, Sections 608.020 and 608.030.
21. Nevada Revised Statutes, Section 616.570, *et seq.*
22. *Hansen v. Harrah's,* 675 P.2d 394 (Nev. S.Ct., 1984).
23. *Southwest Gas Corp. v. Ahmad,* 668 P.2d 261 (Nev. S.Ct., 1983).

95

New Hampshire
Labor Laws

[95.01] LABOR RELATIONS LAWS

State employees' bargaining rights: Chapter 273-A:1, *et seq.,* of the New Hampshire Revised Statutes sets forth the New Hampshire Public Employees Relations Act. The act establishes a framework of employer-employee relations by providing a uniform and orderly method for collective bargaining between public employers and certain public employees.[1]

Municipal employees' bargaining rights: New Hampshire laws provide that municipalities may recognize unions of employees and collectively bargain with such unions.[2]

Nonright-to-work policy: Union security (union shop) clauses are permissible in the state of New Hampshire inasmuch as New Hampshire has not adopted a right-to-work statute pursuant to Section 14(b) of the Labor Management Relations Act.

"Yellow-dog" contracts: New Hampshire laws make it unlawful for anyone to coerce or compel any person to enter into an agreement not to join or become a member of any labor organization as a condition of employment.[3]

[95.02] STRIKES, PICKETING, AND BOYCOTT LAWS

Unlawful assembly: Chapter 644:1 of the New Hampshire Revised Statutes prohibits two or more persons to assemble together to do an unlawful act.

Striker replacements: New Hampshire statutes require advertisements and solicitations for employment applicants to state the existence of a strike, lockout, or other labor trouble at the place of the proposed employment.[4]

Strikebreakers: Chapter 275-A:2 of the New Hampshire Revised Statutes makes it unlawful for any employer to utilize professional strikebreakers to replace an employee involved in a strike or lockout at a place of business within the state.

Restrictions on use of National Guard in strikes: New Hampshire statutes forbid the ordering of the State National Guard into a community where a strike or lockout exists unless the governor has investigated the need for such action through the local public authorities and employer and employee representatives of the industries involved in such labor dispute.[5]

[95.03] MEDIATION AND CONCILIATION LAWS

New Hampshire has adopted the General Arbitration Act, recognizing any written agreement to submit an existing controversy to arbitration as valid, enforceable, and irrevocable, except on such grounds as exist at law or equity for the revocation thereof.[6] Chapter 210:12, *et seq.*, of the New Hampshire Revised Statutes established a State Board of Conciliation and Arbitration whose function is to resolve labor disputes and controversies within the state.

[95.04] REGULATION OF UNION ACTIVITIES

New Hampshire statutes make it unlawful for anyone to misuse or forge a union label or other union insignia.[7] Chapter 664:1, *et seq.*, of the New Hampshire Revised Statutes forbids employers and labor organizations to make certain political contributions to support political parties, causes, or candidates.

[95.05] REGULATION OF EMPLOYMENT PRACTICES

Anti-discrimination laws: New Hampshire law forbids employers to discriminate in employment by reason of race, religion, creed, color, national origin, age, ancestry, marital status, physical or mental handicap, or sex.[8]

Employment of aliens: New Hampshire laws prohibit the employment of any alien not entitled to lawful residence in the United States, unless such alien is authorized to work by U.S. authorities.[9]

Freedom of expression (state employees): Chapter 98-E:2 of the New Hampshire Revised Statutes makes it unlawful for any person to interfere in any way with the right of freedom of speech, full criticism, or disclosure by any state employee.

Protection of military personnel: Chapter 110-B:65 of the New Hampshire Revised Statutes prohibits the discharge of any employee who is called upon to perform military service. New Hampshire laws require the state and its political subdivisions to take necessary action to secure the employment of veterans.[10]

Unlawful procurement of employees: Chapter 275:7 of the New Hampshire Revised Statutes provides that no person shall be required to pay money for securing employment except payment of money to employment agencies.

Access to personnel records: Chapter 275:56 of the New Hampshire Revised Statutes requires employers to permit employees access to their personnel records. Employees may submit a written statement as to any information in the file with which they disagree and make such written statement a part of the personnel record.

Consumer reporting agency requirements: New Hampshire statutes provide that whenever employment is denied to an individual because of information contained in a consumer report, the prospective employer or user of such information is required to inform the rejected applicant of such report and supply the name and address of the consumer reporting agency making the report to such applicant.[11]

Equal pay: New Hampshire statutes make it unlawful to discriminate in payment of wages on the basis of sex by paying female employees at a rate less than that paid male employees for similar or equal work.[12]

[95.06]   WAGE AND HOUR LAWS

Child labor: New Hampshire child labor laws set minimum age requirements for children to be employed in certain jobs and occupations. New Hampshire statutes provide that no child shall be permitted to work without an employment certificate, except in the performance of work for his or her parents, grandparents or guardians, or at work defined as casual or as farm labor.[13]

Payment of wages: Chapter 275:43 of the New Hampshire Revised Statutes requires New Hampshire employers to pay employees their wages weekly and no later than eight days from the established pay period.

Payment upon termination: New Hampshire employers are required to pay discharged employees their wages in full within seventy-two hours from time of discharge.[14] An employee who voluntarily resigns his or her job is due full wages no later than the next regular payday, unless other arrangements are made.[15]

Medical examinations and insurance coverage continuance: Chapter 275:3 of the New Hampshire Revised Statutes requires employers to pay for any pre-employment medical examinations of prospective employees. Chapter 500:3 of the New Hampshire revised statutes requires employers to notify terminated employees that they may continue medical coverage for a certain period provided they pay the premiums of such coverage.

[95.07]   SAFETY AND HEALTH LAWS

General provisions: Chapter 277:11 of the New Hampshire Revised Statutes provides that whenever the nature or condition of employment or machinery is such as to render work dangerous to the safety and health of employees, that safeguards, safety devices, appliances, and lighting facilities must be provided and maintained. The statute requires employers covered under its provisions to do such things as are necessary and practicable to lessen dangers of employment.[16]

Toxic substances—right to know: Chapter 277-A:1, *et seq.,* of the New Hampshire Revised Statutes provides that employers who use or manufacture toxic substances in the work place must maintain material substance data sheets (MSDS) regarding toxic substances and make such documents available to employees, post certain required notices with respect to hazardous substances, and conduct educational programs for all employees routinely exposed to toxic substances.

[95.08] UNEMPLOYMENT COMPENSATION LAWS

The New Hampshire unemployment compensation laws are found at Chapter 282-A:1, *et seq.,* of the New Hampshire Revised Statutes and govern the eligibility requirements of recipients of unemployment compensation benefits.

[95.09] WORKERS' COMPENSATION LAWS

The New Hampshire Workmen's Compensation Act provides disability to employees injured on the job or who suffer occupational diseases as a result of their job, subject to specified qualifications and limitations.[17] Benefits and payments are paid to employees in accordance with established schedules, the amounts and duration of which are dependent upon the gravity of the injury or disease and whether the disability is temporary or permanent and/or partial or total.

[95.10] EMPLOYMENT-AT-WILL DEVELOPMENTS

New Hampshire courts have recognized several judicial exceptions to the employment-at-will principle.

Covenant of good faith and fair dealing exception: A New Hampshire court held that an employer breached the implied covenant of good faith and fair dealing to an employee when the employee was discharged for refusing the sexual advances of a supervisor.[18]

Public policy exception: New Hampshire courts have ruled that employers may not lawfully discharge employees in contravention of some public policy.[19]

"Independent consideration" exception: An employee who has a long record of good employment and relocated his or her family at the employer's request may be regarded by the court as more than an at-will employee.[20]

NOTES TO CHAPTER 95

1. New Hampshire Revised Statutes, Chapter 273-A:1, *et seq.*
2. New Hampshire Public Acts, Chapter 255 (L. 1955).
3. New Hampshire Revised Statutes, Chapter 275:2.
4. New Hampshire Revised Statutes, Chapter 275-A:2.
5. New Hampshire Revised Statutes, Chapter 111:1.
6. New Hampshire Revised Statutes, Chapter 542:1.
7. New Hampshire Revised Statutes, Chapter 207:1-7.
8. New Hampshire Revised Statutes, Chapter 354-A:1, *et seq.*
9. New Hampshire Revised Statutes, Chapter 275-A:4-5.
10. New Hampshire Public Acts, Chapter 434 (L. 1981).
11. New Hampshire Revised Statutes, Chapter 359-B:3.
12. New Hampshire Revised Statutes, Chapter 275:36-41.
13. New Hampshire Revised Statutes, Chapter 276A:4.
14. New Hampshire Revised Statutes, Chapter 277:44(I).
15. New Hampshire Revised Statutes, Chapter 277:44(II).
16. New Hampshire Revised Statutes, Chapter 277:12.
17. New Hampshire Revised Statutes, Chapter 281-A:1, *et seq.*
18. *Monge v. Beebe Rubber Co.,* 316 A.2d 549 (N.H., 1974).
19. *Cloutier v. Great Atlantic and Pacific Tea Co.,* 436 A.2d 1140 (N.H., 1980).
20. *Foley v. Community Oil Co.,* 64 F.R.D. 561 (D. N.H., 1974).

96

New Jersey
Labor Laws

General right to organize: Article I, Para. 19, of the 1947 New Jersey Constitution provides that employees in private employment shall have the right to organize and bargain collectively, and persons in public employment shall have the right to organize, present to and make known to the state, or any of its political subdivisions or agencies, their grievances and proposals through representatives of their own choosing.

Public Utility Labor Disputes Act: New Jersey statutes provide that the state may seize and operate public utilities whenever the public interests are threatened by strikes, lockouts, and other labor disputes.[1] The statute also provides for certain compulsory arbitration of labor disputes and for penalties and injunctive relief for violations of the requirements and provisions of the act.[2]

State employees' bargaining rights: Section 34:13A-1, *et seq.,* of the New Jersey Statutes Annotated provides a uniform basis for recognizing the right of state employees to join labor organizations and to be represented by such organizations in collective bargaining. Section 34:13A-5.4 of the statute prohibits certain conduct of public employees and state employees. The statute also prescribes guidelines to determine appropriate bargaining units and bargaining agents, as well as a process for resolving labor disputes.[3]

Nonright-to-work policy: Union security (union shop) clauses are permissible in the state of New Jersey inasmuch as New Jersey has not adopted a right-to-work statute pursuant to Section 14(b) of the Labor Management Relations Act.

"Yellow-dog" contracts: Section 34:12-2 of the New Jersey Statutes Annotated makes it unlawful for anyone to coerce or compel any person to enter into an agreement not to join or become a member of any labor organization as a condition of employment.

[96.02] STRIKES, PICKETING, AND BOYCOTT LAWS

Anti-injunction laws: New Jersey laws limit the power of New Jersey courts to issue injunctions against picketing and strike activity, unless certain guidelines and procedures are met.[4]

Unlawful assembly: Section 2A:126-4 of the New Jersey Statutes Annotated forbids an assembly of twelve or more armed persons for unlawful purposes.

Restriction of railroad picketing: Section 48:12-164, *et seq.,* of the New Jersey Statutes Annotated forbids the malicious obstruction of railroad operations.

Striker replacements: Section 30:8-40 of the New Jersey Statutes Annotated forbids the employment of prisoners to replace stirking employees. Section 34:8-25 of the New Jersey Statutes Annotated limits temporary help agencies in sending out employees to replace striking or locked-out employees.

[96.03] MEDIATION AND CONCILIATION LAWS

New Jersey has adopted a General Arbitration Act recognizing any written agreement to submit an existing controversy to arbitration as valid, enforceable, and irrevocable, excepting such grounds as exist at law or equity for the revocation thereof.[5] Section 34:13-1, *et seq.,* of the New Jersey Statutes Annotated provides for compulsory arbitration of labor disputes involving public fire or police departments.

[96.04] REGULATION OF UNION ACTIVITIES

New Jersey statutes make it unlawful for anyone to misuse or forge a union label or other union insignia.[6] New Jersey statutes provide that any part of any agreement which requires a carrier or shipper to pay a levied charge that is not a part of the direct cost of transportation shall be unlawful.[7]

[96.05] REGULATION OF EMPLOYMENT PRACTICES

Anti-discrimination laws: Section 10:5-1, *et seq.,* of the New Jersey Statutes Annotated prohibits discrimination in the employment of an individual by reason of race, religion, color, sex, age, national origin, nationality, ancestry, marital status, handicap, liability for military service, or atypical blood trait.

Protection of political freedom: New Jersey labor laws make it unlawful for any employer within the state to attempt to interfere with the voting rights of his or her employees.[8]

Reemployment rights of military personnel: New Jersey statutory laws require employers to reemploy military personnel upon their return from military service to their former or similar positions provided such individuals are still qualified to perform the requirements of the job.[9]

Polygraph restrictions: New Jersey statutes forbid New Jersey employers to require any applicant for employment or any employee to submit to a polygraph, lie detector, or similar test or examination as a condition of employment or continued employment.[10]

Jury duty (public employees): Section 2A:69-5 of the New Jersey Statutes Annotated provides that state, county, municipal, and mass transit employees must be excused from work for jury duty and paid the difference between jury pay and their usual compensation.

Convictions: Section 2C:52-1, *et seq.,* of the New Jersey Statutes Annotated forbids discrimination in employment because of an individual's conviction if the conviction has been expunged from the person's record by court order.

Medical coverage continuance: Section 17B:27-51.12 of the New Jersey Statutes Annotated requires employers to give certain terminated employees three months notice of their right to continue group medical insurance, obligating such employees to make a written election of such continuance and to assume payments of the premiums relating to the coverage.

Authorization of state employees' union dues deduction: New Jersey statutes provide that a state employee may authorize the appropriate dispersing officer to have any deductions made from his or her compensation for the purpose of paying dues to a bona fide employee organization duly certified as their bargaining representative.[11]

Equal pay: Section 34:11-56.2 of the New Jersey Statutes Annotated forbids employers to discriminate in rates of pay to any employee because of sex, except for differentials based on factors other than sex.

[96.06]   WAGE AND HOUR LAWS

Child labor: New Jersey laws regulate the employment of children in gainful occupations and specify certain minimum age requirements in order for a child to work.[12] The statute also requires employment certificates for children under 18 in any gainful occupations, except children over 16 are permitted to work in agricultural pursuits or as newspaper carriers, and in agricultural and domestic service for their parents or guardians as long as such work is performed outside regular school hours.[13]

Payment of wages: Section 34:11-4.2 of the New Jersey Statutes Annotated requires New Jersey employers to pay employees their wages no less than twice during a month or on regular paydays designated in advance.

Payment upon termination: New Jersey employers are required to pay terminated employees their wages in full no later than the next regular payday.[14]

Garnishment: Section 2A:170-90.4 of the New Jersey Statutes Annotated forbids discharge or discipline of an employee because of a garnishment of his or her wages.

[96.07] SAFETY AND HEALTH LAWS

General provisions: New Jersey laws require employers within the state to furnish a place of employment reasonably safe and healthful for employees.[15]

Toxic substances—right to know: Section 34:5A-1, *et seq.*, of the New Jersey Statutes Annotated requires employers to maintain certain records, post certain notices, provide educational training, and allow employees access to records regarding toxic substances used or manufactured in the work place.

[96.08] UNEMPLOYMENT COMPENSATION LAWS

The New Jersey unemployment compensation laws are found at Section 43:21-1, *et seq.*, of the New Jersey Statutes Annotated and govern, among other things, the eligibility requirements of recipients of unemployment compensation benefits.

[96.09] WORKERS' COMPENSATION LAWS

Section 34:15-1, *et seq.*, of the New Jersey Statutes Annotated sets forth the New Jersey Workers' Compensation Act. Benefits and payments are paid to employees in accordance with established schedules, the amounts and duration of which are dependent upon the gravity of the injury or disease and whether the disability is temporary or permanent and/or partial or total.

[96.10] EMPLOYMENT-AT-WILL DEVELOPMENTS

New Jersey courts have recognized certain judicial exceptions to the employment-at-will doctrine.

Public policy exception: A wrongful discharge lawsuit is actionable in New Jersey when an employee has been discharged for having filed a worker's compensation claim, such termination being in contravention of public policy.[16]

Implied contract exception: New Jersey courts have ruled that the language from a personnel policy that promises job security to employees might create an implied employment contract, thereby prohibiting the employer to discharge an employee without just cause.[17]

NOTES TO CHAPTER 96

1. New Jersey Statutes Annotated, Section 34:13B-13.
2. New Jersey Statutes Annotated, Section 34:13B-1.
3. New Jersey Statutes Annotated, Section 34:13A-1, *et seq.*
4. New Jersey Statutes Annotated, Section 2A:15-51, *et seq.*
5. New Jersey Statutes Annotated, Section 2A:24-1, *et seq.*
6. New Jersey Statutes Annotated, Section 56:2-1, *et seq.*
7. New Jersey Public Acts, Chapter 246 (L. 1962, 1963).
8. New Jersey Statutes Annotated, Section 19:34-27.
9. New Jersey Statutes Annotated, Section 10:5-5(g); 10:5-12.
10. New Jersey Statutes Annotated, Section 2C:40A-1.
11. New Jersey Statutes Annotated, Section 52:14-15.9C.
12. New Jersey Statutes Annotated, Section 34:2-21.
13. New Jersey Statutes Annotated, Section 34:2-3, 8, 11 and 15.
14. New Jersey Statutes Annotated, Section 34:11-4.3.
15. New Jersey Statutes Annotated, Section 34:6A-3.
16. *Lalley v. Copygraphics,* 428 A.2d 1317 (N.J., 1981).
17. *Wooley v. Hoffman-LaRoche, Inc.,* Case No. A-98-82 (N.J. S.Ct., 1985).

97

New Mexico
Labor Laws

[97.01] LABOR RELATIONS LAWS

State employees' bargaining rights: New Mexico regulations provide that individuals in the classified service of the state shall have the right to join and assist labor unions, or to refrain from union activities, free and without fear of penalty or reprisal.[1] The Labor Management Relations Regulations prohibit certain conduct of both public employers and labor organizations, the violation of which constitutes unfair labor practices.[2] The regulations also provide for an election process to determine bargaining representatives, establish guidelines to determine appropriate bargaining units, and forbid strikes.[3]

Nonright-to-work policy: Union security (union shop) clauses are permissible in the state of New Mexico inasmuch as New Mexico has not chosen to enact a right-to-work statute pursuant to Section 14(b) of the Labor Management Relations Act.

"Yellow-dog" contracts: New Mexico statutes make it unlawful for anyone to coerce or compel any person to enter into an agreement not to join or become a member of any labor organization as a condition of employment.[4]

[97.02] STRIKES, PICKETING AND BOYCOTT LAWS

Anti-injunction statute: Section 59-2-1, *et seq.*, of the New Mexico Statutes restricts New Mexico courts in issuing restraining orders and injunctions in any case involving or growing out of a labor dispute unless certain procedural safeguards and requirements are met.

Unlawful assembly: Section 41-1210 of the New Mexico Statutes prohibits three or more persons assembling together to do an unlawful act.

Interference with ingress or egress: Section 50-2-2(b) of the New Mexico Statutes makes it unlawful for anyone, not having a legal privilege to do so, to knowingly or recklessly obstruct any highway or public passage.

[97.03] MEDIATION AND ARBITRATION LAWS

New Mexico has adopted the Uniform Arbitration Act, recognizing any written agreement to submit an existing controversy to arbitration as valid, enforceable, and irrevocable, excepting such grounds as exist at law or equity for the revocation thereof.[5]

[97.04] REGULATION OF UNION ACTIVITIES

New Mexico statutes make it unlawful for anyone to misuse or forge a union label or other union insignia.[6] New Mexico statutes make it unlawful for any person to give money or other things of value to a union representative in an attempt to induce such representative to cause or prevent a strike.[7]

[97.05] REGULATION OF EMPLOYMENT PRACTICES

Anti-discrimination laws: New Mexico statutes prohibit discrimination in the employment of an individual by reason of race, age, color, religion, national origin, ancestry, sex, or physical or mental handicap.[8]

Protection of political freedom: New Mexico labor laws make it unlawful for any employer within the state to interfere with the voting rights and privileges of his or her employees.[9]

Reemployment rights of military personnel: New Mexico statutes require employers within the state to reemploy military personnel upon their return from military service to their former or similar positions without loss of seniority or other employment status or pay.[10]

Jury duty: New Mexico law provides that employers are forbidden to attempt to deprive an employee of his or her employment by reason of his or her receiving a summons to serve as a juror or attend court as a juror or prospective juror.[11]

Blacklisting: New Mexico employers are prohibited from maintaining a blacklist or notifying any other employer that they maintain a blacklist for the purpose of preventing an employee or former employee from receiving employment.[12]

Arrest records (public employees): Public employees in the state of New Mexico are protected against discrimination in employment because of an arrest record not followed by a valid conviction.[13]

Credit bureau requirements: New Mexico statutes require credit bureaus which furnish information pertaining to personnel investigations to adopt rigid safeguards in order that the specialized information developed in the course of such investigations other than credit information shall be maintained separately and shall not be incorporated in credit reports.[14]

[97.06] WAGE AND HOUR LAWS

Child labor: New Mexico child labor laws provide that no child between 14 and 16 years of age shall be employed in any gainful occupation during the regular school term unless such child possesses a permit certificate.[15]

Voting time: New Mexico statutes provide that an employee registered to vote in any election shall be excused from his or her employment, not exceeding two consecutive hours, to exercise such voting privileges, provided such employee does not have two consecutive hours between the time of opening and closing of polls when he or she is not working for the employer.[16]

Payment of wages: Section 50-4-2 of the New Mexico Statutes requires New Mexico employers to pay employees their wages not more than sixteen days apart, on designated paydays announced in advance.

Payment upon termination: New Mexico employers are required to pay discharged employees their wages in full no later than five days following discharge, if their wages are a fixed and definite amount.[17] An employee who voluntarily resigns his or her job is due full wages no later than the next regular payday.[18]

[97.07] SAFETY AND HEALTH LAWS

General provisions: New Mexico Health and Safety laws require employers within the state to furnish safe employment for employees, and to furnish and use safety devices and safeguards, adopt and use methods and processes reasonably adequate to render such employment and place of employment safe, and do every other thing reasonably necessary to protect life, health, and safety of employees.[19]

Toxic substances—right to know: Section 50-9-1, *et seq.,* of the New Mexico Statutes provides that employers shall furnish certain information and notices to employees who may be exposed to toxic substances in the work place.

[97.08] UNEMPLOYMENT COMPENSATION LAWS

The New Mexico unemployment compensation laws are found in Section 51-1-4B, *et seq.,* of the New Mexico Statutes. The statute governs the eligibility requirements of recipients.

[97.09] WORKERS' COMPENSATION LAWS

Section 52-1-8, *et seq.,* of the New Mexico Statutes sets forth the New Mexico Workmen's Compensation Act. The statute provides disability benefits to employees injured on the job, subject to specified qualifications and limitations.[20] Whenever an employer and employee accept and comply with the requirements of the statute, all other rights and remedies, statutory or common law, on account of personal injuries or death are surrendered.[21]

[97.10] EMPLOYMENT-AT-WILL DEVELOPMENTS

New Mexico courts have recognized certain exceptions to the employment-at-will rule, as noted below.

Public policy exception: New Mexico courts have recognized the public policy exception to the at-will rule where it can be shown that an employee was discharged for failure to perform an act condemned by public policy.[22]

Implied contract exception: New Mexico courts have held that a personnel policy manual's promise of job security may constitute an employment contract, forbidding discharge without cause.[23]

NOTES TO CHAPTER 97

1. New Mexico Labor-Management Relations Regulations, Section 3.
2. New Mexico Labor-Management Relations Regulations, Section 16.
3. New Mexico Labor-Management Relations Regulations, Section 1, *et seq.*
4. New Mexico Public Acts, S.B. 402 (L., 1967).
5. New Mexico Statutes, Section 44-7-1.
6. New Mexico Statutes, Section 52-201, *et seq.*
7. New Mexico Statutes, Section 50-2-3.
8. New Mexico Statutes, Section 28-1-1, *et seq.*
9. New Mexico Statutes, Section 3-10-11.
10. New Mexico Statutes, Section 28-15-1, *et seq.*
11. New Mexico Statutes, Section 38-5-18.
12. New Mexico Statutes, Section 30-13-3.
13. New Mexico Statutes, Section 28-2-3(B).
14. New Mexico Statutes, Section 56-3-5.
15. New Mexico Statutes, Section 50-6-2.
16. New Mexico Statutes, Section 1-12-42.
17. New Mexico Statutes, Section 50-4-4.
18. New Mexico Statutes, Section 50-4-5.
19. New Mexico Statutes, Section 52-1-8.
20. New Mexico Statutes, Section 52-1-9, *et seq.*
21. New Mexico Statutes, Section 52-1-8, *et seq.*
22. *Vigil v. Arzola,* 687 P.2d 1038. (N.M. S.Ct., 1984).
23. *Forrester v. Parker,* 606 P.2d 191 (N.M. S.Ct., 1980).

98

New York
Labor Laws

New York State Labor Relations Act: New York statutes provide that New York employers must recognize and bargain in good faith with unions properly certified as representatives of their employees.[1] The statute provides for the machinery to conduct representation elections and procedures to process unfair labor practice charges against employers and labor organizations.[2]

General right to organize: Article 1, Section 17, of the New York Constitution provides that employees within the state shall have the right to organize and bargain collectively through representatives of their own choosing.

Port Authority employees' benefits: New York laws provide that employees of the New York Port Authority shall be extended the benefits of representation and negotiation.[3]

Public employees' bargaining rights: New York statutes provide that public employees shall have the right of self-organization and the right to join and assist labor unions, or to refrain from union activities.[4] The statute prohibits certain conduct of both public employers and labor organization, the violation of which constitutes unfair labor practices.[5] The statute also provides for an election process to determine bargaining representatives and forbids strikes.[6]

Labor and Management Improper Practices Act: Section 720, *et seq.,* of the New York Labor and Management Improper Practices Act declares it to be the public policy of the state of New York that employers, employer organizations, labor relations consultants, and other such persons shall not participate in violations of fiduciary obligations of officers and agents of labor organizations.

Nonright-to-work policy: Union security (union shop) clauses are permissible in the state of New York inasmuch as New York has not adopted a right-to-work statute pursuant to Section 14(b) of the Labor Management Relations Act.

''Yellow-dog'' contracts: New York laws make it unlawful for anyone to coerce or compel any person to enter into an agreement not to join or become a member of any labor organization as a condition of employment.[7]

[98.02]   STRIKES, PICKETING, AND BOYCOTT LAWS

Anti-injunction statute: Section 807, *et seq.,* of the New York Anti-Injunction Act restricts the power of New York courts to issue injunctions and restraining orders in cases involving labor disputes.

Interference with employment: New York statutes make it unlawful for two or more persons to conspire, by use of force or other means, to prevent any person from engaging in any lawful occupation of his or her trade or calling.[8]

Use of detectives during strikes: New York statutes limit the use of private detectives in strikes.[9]

[98.03]   MEDIATION AND ARBITRATION LAWS

Section 7501 of the State Civil Practice Law provides that a written agreement to submit any controversy to arbitration is enforceable without regard to the justiciable character of the controversy and confers jurisdiction on the courts of the state to enforce it and to enter judgment on any such arbitration award. The New York Labor Mediation Act establishes and prescribes the powers and duties of the State Board of Mediation which function is to attempt to resolve labor disputes within the state.[10] Section 601, *et seq.,* of the General Municipal Law of the state statutes provides a grievance process for the settlement of certain differences between public employees and their employers. The Penal Code of the New York Statutes makes it unlawful for an arbitrator to misuse or abuse his or her duty to render a fair and impartial decision in an arbitration hearing.[11] The State Penal Code also makes it unlawful for anyone to attempt to improperly influence or intimidate an arbitrator within the state.[12]

[98.04]   REGULATION OF UNION ACTIVITIES

New York statutes make it unlawful for anyone to misuse or forge a union label or other union insignia.[13] New York labor laws make it unlawful for any person to misrepresent that he or she is a member of a labor union that does not exist within the state, or in any other way misrepresent himself or herself in connection with union affairs.[14] Section 726 of the New York Labor and Management Improper Practices Act requires labor unions to furnish certain financial statements to their members on an annual basis.

Section 37, *et seq.,* of the New York Mitchell–Hollinger Law establishes certain regulations and requirements in the supervision and management of employee welfare funds to protect the rights of employees and their families.[15]

New York statutes provide for the authorization of an interstate compact with the state of New Jersey to establish a system of registration and regulation of longshoremen in an effort to eliminate certain criminal and corrupt practices in the handling of waterfront freight in the Port of New York and to also regulate the employment of waterfront labor.[16]

[98.05] REGULATION OF EMPLOYMENT PRACTICES

Anti-discrimination laws: New York statutes prohibit discrimination in the employment of an individual by reason of age, race, creed, color, sex, national origin, marital status, or disability.[17]

Employment agency requirements: New York laws forbid employment agencies to send or cause to be sent, any person to any employer where the employment agency knows that the prospective employer is in violation of state or federal laws governing minimum wages, child labor, or compulsory education or involved in a labor dispute without notifying the applicant of such fact.[18]

Psychogalvanic stress evaluation exams: New York statutes forbid employers to demand or require any employee or prospective employee to submit to a psychogalvanic stress evaluation examination (voice stress test) as a condition of employment or continued employment.[19]

Misrepresentation of employment opportunities: Section 396-1 of the New York General Business Laws of the state statutes forbids any person to misrepresent in advertisement, or otherwise, that a job opening is at a fixed salary whenever such employment is actually on a commission basis.

Arrest and conviction records: Sections 296(15) and (16) of the New York Executive Laws makes it unlawful for any person or firm to make any inquiry about a conviction or any arrest of any person in connection with the licensing, employment, or providing of credit or insurance to such individual, unless there is a direct relationship between the conviction and the job or the employment of the individual would involve an unreasonable risk to property or to the safety and welfare of others.

Fingerprinting limitations: New York statutes prohibit any person from requiring an applicant or employee to be fingerprinted as a condition of securing or retaining employment, unless otherwise required or permitted by statutory authority.[20]

Disclosure of consumer reports: Section 380(a), *et seq.*, of the New York General Business Laws requires consumer reporting agencies to furnish, disclose, and maintain certain information previously provided to an employer in connection with recruiting and selection practices.

Jury and witness duty: New York employers are forbidden to attempt to deprive any employee of his or her employment because such employee receives a summons, responds thereto, serves as a juror[21] or witness or attends[22] court for prospective jury or witness service.

Importation of migratory farm labor: New York statutes require employers who bring into the state five or more out-of-state migrant farm or food processing workers who are residents of the United States, to register with the Industrial Commissioner and submit such facts on wages, housing, working conditions, and such other information as the Commissioner may prescribe.[23]

Whistle-blowing statutes: New York law forbids any employer within the state, with certain exceptions, to take disciplinary action against any employee for the disclosure of information which the employee reasonably believes evidences a violation of any law, rule, or regulation, or creates a substantial and specific danger to public health or safety, if the disclosure is not specifically prohibited by law.[24]

Protection of railroad employees: Section 54-b of the New York Railroad Laws generally forbids a railroad company to reduce wages, seniority, vacation rights, etc., of its employees unless otherwise agreed to between a railroad and the organization certified to represent such employees.

Protection of military personnel: Section 318 of the New York Military Laws prohibits the discharge or discrimination in employment of any employee who is called upon to perform military service.

Blacklisting: New York employers are prohibited from maintaining a blacklist or notifying any other employer of the blacklisting of an employee or former employee for the purpose of preventing such worker from receiving employment.[25]

Medical examination payments: Section 201b of the New York Labor Laws requires employers to pay for the cost of pre-employment medical examinations.

Eavesdropping on union activities: Section 704 of the New York Labor Laws forbids eavesdropping with respect to organized labor activities.

Equal pay: Section 194 of the New York Labor Laws makes it unlawful to discriminate in payment of wages on the basis of sex.

[98.06] WAGE AND HOUR LAWS

Child labor: New York state labor laws regulate the employment of children in gainful occupations. New York statutes forbid children under 14 years of age to be employed in or with any trade, business, or service when attendance is required by the education law or is in violation of the certificating provisions of the education law, except children in certain age brackets under 14 years of age may be employed as child performers, newspaper carriers, or in domestic or agricultural work if performed under the supervision of parents or guardians during nonschool hours.[26] Children 14 or 15 years of age are similarly limited in employment,[27] as well as those in the age group 16 and 17 years of age.[28]

Voting time: New York statutes provide that an employee eligible and duly registered to vote in an election shall be excused from his or her employment for at least two consecutive hours, without loss of pay, to exercise such voting privileges, provided such employee does not have two consecutive hours between the time of opening and closing of polls when he or she is not working for the employer.[29]

Payment upon termination: New York employers are required to pay terminated employees their earned wages no later than the next regular payday.[30]

Garnishments: Section 5252 of the New York Civil Practice Law and Rules provides that no employer may discharge or lay off an employee because of one or more wage assignments.

Medical insurance continuance: Section 162(5)(a) of the New York Insurance Laws require employers to notify terminated employees of their right to convert the employer's medical group insurance policy into individual coverage, provided certain conditions are met, such as the assumption of payments for premiums by the terminated employee.

[98.07] SAFETY AND HEALTH LAWS

General provisions: The New York Commissioner of Labor shall by rule adopt, amend, or repeal safety and health standards that provide reasonable and adequate protection of lives, safety, or health of employees and of persons lawfully frequenting places of employment.[31]

Toxic substances—right to know: Section 875, *et seq.,* of the New York Toxic Substance Law requires New York employers to provide certain education and training to the employees who might be exposed to toxic substances in the work place. It also requires employers to post notices and furnish certain information to employees regarding toxic substances.

[98.08] UNEMPLOYMENT COMPENSATION LAWS

The New York unemployment compensation laws govern, among other things, the eligibility requirements of recipients of unemployment compensation benefits.[32] For example, employees who participate in labor strikes in New York may nonetheless be entitled to unemployment compensation benefits.[33] (Most other state unemployment compensation laws do not permit strike participants to draw unemployment compensation benefits, unless extenuating circumstances prevail such as a lockout.)

[98.09] WORKERS' COMPENSATION LAWS

The New York Workers' Compensation Act provides disability benefits to employees injured on the job or who suffer occupational diseases as a result of their job, subject to specified qualifications and limitations.[34] Whenever an employer and employee accept and comply with the requirements of the statute, all other rights and remedies, statutory or common law, on account of personal injuries or death are surrendered.[35] Section 120 of the New York Workers' Compensation Act forbids termination of an employee because of his or her filing a worker's compensation claim.

[98.10] EMPLOYMENT-AT-WILL DEVELOPMENTS

The New York courts have recognized some exceptions to the employment-at-will doctrine, within certain guidelines.

Implied contract exception: New York courts have recognized a cause of action for breach of an employment contract where an employment application expressly incorporates a just cause requirement from the employer's personnel handbook.[36]

Promissory estoppel exception: A New York court denied summary judgment in a case where the plaintiff accepted a written job offer, stating annual salary, vacation benefits, and so forth, but, prior to the starting date, the defendant withdrew the offer. The court ruled that the facts alleged created an issue as to whether proposed employment was for a fixed duration.[37]

NOTES TO CHAPTER 98

1. Consolidated Laws of New York, Labor Laws, Section 700, *et seq.*
2. Consolidated Laws of New York, Labor Laws, Section 700, *et seq.*
3. New York Public Acts, Chapter 1203 (L. 1971).
4. Consolidated Laws of New York, Civil Service Laws, Section 202.
5. Consolidated Laws of New York, Civil Service Laws, Section 209.

6. Consolidated Laws of New York, Civil Service Laws, Section 200, *et seq.*

7. New York Public Acts, Chapter 11 (L. 1935).

8. Consolidated Laws of New York, Penal Code, Section 580.

9. Consolidated Laws of New York, General Business Law, Section 84.

10. Consolidated Laws of New York, Labor Laws, Section 751, *et seq.*

11. Consolidated Laws of New York, Penal Code, Section 373.

12. Consolidated Laws of New York, Penal Code, Sections 376 and 860.

13. Consolidated Laws of New York, Labor Laws, Section 209.

14. Consolidated Laws of New York, Labor Laws, Section 209-a.

15. Consolidated Laws of New York, Insurance and Banking Laws, Section 37, *et seq.*

16. Consolidated Laws of New York, Unconsolidated Laws, Section 9801, *et seq.*

17. Consolidated Laws of New York, Executive Laws, Section 291, *et seq.*

18. Consolidated Laws of New York, General Business Laws, Section 187.

19. Consolidated Laws of New York, Labor Laws, Section 733, *et seq.*

20. Consolidated Laws of New York, Labor Laws, Section 201-a.

21. Consolidated Laws of New York, Judiciary Law, Section 519.

22. Consolidated Laws of New York, Penal Code, Section 215.11.

23. Consolidated Laws of New York, Labor Laws, Section 212a.

24. Consolidated Laws of New York, Labor Laws, Section 740.

25. Consolidated Laws of New York, Labor Laws, Section 704(2).

26. Consolidated Laws of New York, Labor Laws, Section 130.

27. Consolidated Laws of New York, Labor Laws, Section 131(4).

28. Consolidated Laws of New York, Labor Laws, Section 3215(4).

29. Consolidated Laws of New York, Election Laws, Section 3.110.

30. Consolidated Laws of New York, Labor Laws, Section 191(3).

31. Consolidated Laws of New York, Labor Laws, Section 28(2)(a).

32. Consolidated Laws of New York, Labor Laws, Section 591, *et seq.*

33. See Consolidated Laws of New York, Labor Laws, Section 591, *et seq.*

34. Consolidated Laws of New York, Workers' Compensation Law, Section 1, *et seq.*

35. Consolidated Laws of New York, Workers' Compensation Law, Sections 10 and 11.

36. *Weiner v. McGraw-Hill,* 443 N.E.2d 441 (N.Y., 1982); as limited by certain requirements therein.

37. *Myers v. Coradian Corp.,* 459 N.Y.S.2d 929 (1983).

99

North Carolina Labor Laws

[99.01] LABOR RELATIONS LAWS

Ban against joining unions (public employees): North Carolina laws forbid employees of the state, and its subdivisions, to become members of trade or labor unions. The statute declares that any labor agreement between municipalities and labor unions shall be deemed null and void and unenforceable.[1]

Right-to-work statute: North Carolina laws prohibit the denial of employment to anyone on account of membership or nonmembership in a labor union or organization.[2]

[99.02] STRIKES, PICKETING, AND BOYCOTT LAWS

Unlawful assembly: Section 15-30 of the General Statutes of North Carolina requires every person present at any riot, affray, or other breach of the peace to endeavor to suppress and prevent the same.

Possession of weapons on picket lines: Section 14-277.2 of the General Statutes of North Carolina makes it unlawful for any person to be in possession of an armed weapon while participating in a strike.

Public employee strikes prohibited: North Carolina laws provide that strikes by public employees are illegal and against the public policy of the state.[3]

[99.03] MEDIATION AND ARBITRATION LAWS

Section 95-32, *et seq.*, of the General Statutes of North Carolina establishes a State Conciliation Service in the Department of Labor which purpose is to provide for the mediation and conciliation of labor disputes. In addition, North Carolina has adopted the Uniform Arbitration Act, recognizing any written agreement to submit an existing controversy to arbitration as valid, enforceable, and irrevocable, excepting such grounds as exist at law or equity for the revocation thereof.[4]

[99.04] REGULATION OF UNION ACTIVITIES

North Carolina statutes forbid agreements in which carriers or shippers are required to pay a levied charge that is not a part of the direct cost of transportation.[5] North Carolina laws make it unlawful for any person to counterfeit or misuse a union label or insignia.[6]

[99.05] REGULATION OF EMPLOYMENT PRACTICES

Anti-discrimination laws: North Carolina laws prohibit discrimination in employment against any individual because of race, religion, color, national origin, age, sex, or handicap.[7] Discrimination in employment because of a sickle cell trait is also forbidden by Section 95-28 of the North Carolina General Statutes.

Re-employment rights of military personnel: Section 127A-201, *et seq.,* of the General Statutes of North Carolina requires employers to re-employ National Guard members upon their return from military service to their former or similar positions, without loss of seniority, status, or pay.

Blacklisting: North Carolina employers are prohibited from maintaining a blacklist or notifying any other employer that any individual has been blacklisted for the purpose of preventing such worker from receiving employment.[8]

Unlawful enticement: North Carolina laws forbid any person to induce or entice an employee of another to leave such employment prior to the expiration of the employment term.[9] Section 14-349 of the General Statutes of North Carolina makes it unlawful for any person to induce any seaman, in the employment of any domestic or foreign vessel, in any of the ports of North Carolina, to leave any such vessel before his or her term of service expires.

Fraudulent receipt of wage advancement: Section 14-104 of the General Statutes of North Carolina makes it unlawful for any person to receive advanced payments for wages based on fraudulent misrepresentations that such individual will perform certain work for the employer.

Medical examination payment: Section 14-357.1 of the General Statutes of North Carolina requires employers to pay for any pre-employment medical examination required of a prospective employee.

[99.06] WAGE AND HOUR LAWS

Child labor: North Carolina child labor laws regulate the employment of children and specify minimum age requirements that must be met as a condition to employment.[10] Employment certificates are required for all employment of children under 18 years of age, except in jobs specifically exempted by the statute.[11]

Payment of wages: Section 95-25.6 of the General Statutes of North Carolina requires employers to pay employees all wages and tips accrued on regular paydays.

Payment upon termination: North Carolina statutes require employers to pay employees whose employment is discontinued for any reason all wages due on or before the next regular payday.[12]

[99.07] SAFETY AND HEALTH LAWS

General provisions: North Carolina health and safety laws require employers to furnish to employees conditions and places of employment free from recognized hazards that are causing or are likely to cause serious injury, physical harm, or death to such employees.[13] The statute also provides that North Carolina employers must comply with all occupational safety and health standards, rules, regulations, and orders that are issued pursuant to the Act.[14]

Toxic substances—right to know: Section 95-143 of the General Statutes of North Carolina requires employers to promptly notify employees who have been (or are being) exposed to toxic substances in concentrations exceeding standards promulgated under the North Carolina Occupational Safety and Health Act, and inform such employees what corrective action, if any, should be taken.

[99.08] UNEMPLOYMENT COMPENSATION LAWS

The North Carolina unemployment compensation laws are set forth in Section 96-13, *et seq.,* of the General Statutes of North Carolina and govern, among other things, the eligibility requirements of recipients of unemployment compensation benefits.

[99.09] WORKERS' COMPENSATION LAWS

Section 97-1, *et seq.,* of the General Statutes of North Carolina sets forth the North Carolina Workers' Compensation Act. The statute provides disability benefits to employees injured on the job or who suffer occupational diseases as a result of their job, subject to specified qualifications and limitations.[15] Section 97-6.1 of the General Statutes of North Carolina makes it unlawful to discharge or otherwise discriminate against an employee in retaliation for filing a workers' compensation claim.

[99.10] EMPLOYMENT-AT-WILL DEVELOPMENTS

The North Carolina courts have been most reluctant to depart from the historic employment-at-will rule.[16] However, in a 1922 North Carolina case, a state court held that employers are contractually obligated to provide employment benefits which have been established for employees,[17] implying a theoretical departure from the employment-at-will rule. Moreover, other cases in North Carolina suggest a further erosion of the at-will doctrine, as noted below.

Implied contract exception: In another North Carolina case, a court held that where there is a business usage that demonstrates the employer and employee intended the employment to continue for a definite term, the at-will relationship is modified, precluding the discharge of the employee prior to the expiration of the fixed term, except for cause.[18]

Public policy exception: A North Carolina Court of Appeals has ruled that it will recognize a cause of action in a wrongful discharge claim where an employee is dismissed for refusing to violate a state law, since such discharge would contravene the public policy of the state.[19]

NOTES TO CHAPTER 99

1. General Statutes of North Carolina, Section 95-98.
2. General Statutes of North Carolina, Section 97-78, *et seq.*
3. General Statutes of North Carolina, Section 95-98.1.
4. General Statutes of North Carolina, Section 95-36.1, *et seq.*
5. General Statutes of North Carolina, Section 95-101.2.
6. General Statutes of North Carolina, Sections 80-8 and 80-9.
7. General Statutes of North Carolina, Section 143-422.1.
8. General Statutes of North Carolina, Sections 14-355 and 14-356.
9. General Statutes of North Carolina, Section 14-347.
10. General Statutes of North Carolina, Section 95-25.
11. General Statutes of North Carolina, Sections 95-25.5(a) and (d).
12. General Statutes of North Carolina, Section 95.25.7.
13. General Statutes of North Carolina, Section 95-129(1).
14. General Statutes of North Carolina, Section 95-129(2).
15. General Statutes of North Carolina, Section 97-1, *et seq.*
16. *Brooks v. Carolina Tel. and Tel. Co.,* 290 S.E.2d 370 (N.C., 1982).
17. *Roberts v. Mays Mills, Inc.,* 114 S.E. 530 (N.C., 1922).
18. *Still v. Lance,* 182 S.E.2d 403 (N.C. S.Ct., 1971); see also: *Sides v. Duke Hospital,* Case No. 83145C1308 (N.C. Ct. of App., 1985).
19. *Sides v. Duke Hospital, supra.*

100

North Dakota
Labor Laws

[100.01]   LABOR RELATIONS LAWS

North Dakota Labor Management Relations Act: North Dakota statutes provide that North Dakota employers must recognize and bargain in good faith with unions properly certified as representatives of their employees.[1]

Teachers' bargaining rights: North Dakota statutes extend organization, representation, and collective bargaining rights to certificated employees of the public schools in the state.[2]

Court enforcement of collective bargaining contracts: North Dakota laws provide that an executed contract entered into between an employer and a labor union may be enforced by either party by an action commenced in a district court of the state.[3]

Public policy regarding bargaining rights: Section 34-09-01 of the North Dakota Century Code declares it to be a public policy of the state that a worker shall be free to obtain employment whenever possible without interference or hindrance in any way and shall also have the right of association and organization with his or her fellow employees and the right to designate a representative of one's choice.

Right-to-work statute: North Dakota laws prohibit the denial of employment to anyone on account of membership or nonmembership in a labor union or organization.[4]

"Yellow-dog" contracts: The North Dakota statutes make agreements not to join or become a member of any labor organization as a condition of employment unenforceable in the state courts.[5]

[100.02]   STRIKES, PICKETING, AND BOYCOTT LAWS

Anti-injunction statute: North Dakota statutes restrict state courts in the issuance of injunctions and restraining orders in cases involving labor disputes.[6]

Stranger picketing: Section 34-09-12 of the North Dakota Century Code makes it unlawful for any person other than an employee of the establishment against which a strike is called, or a local resident member of the union representing the employees in such establishment, to picket in aid of such strike.

Secondary boycotts: Section 34-09-13 of the North Dakota Century Code forbids secondary boycotting and sympathy strikes.

Unlawful assembly: North Dakota laws prohibit three or more persons to assemble with intent to do an unlawful act.[7]

Striker replacement notices: North Dakota statutes forbid employment agencies to fail to state in any advertisement, proposal, or contract for employment, the existence of a strike or lockout at the place of proposed employment, if such employment agency has knowledge that such conditions exist.[8]

Unlawful interference with employment: North Dakota statutes make it unlawful for any person to attempt to prevent any individual from engaging in any lawful employment within the state.[9]

Public utility strikes: Section 37-01-06, *et seq.,* of the North Dakota Century Code provides that the governor of the state may commandeer and take control over coal mines and public utilities in strikes or lockouts that threaten to endanger the life and property of the people of the state.

[100.03] MEDIATION AND ARBITRATION LAWS

Section 34-11-01 of the North Dakota Century Code provides for the prevention and settlement of labor disputes through mediation and conciliation. The statute provides for the establishment of a Labor Dispute Board, whose function is to attempt to mediate and conciliate labor disputes within the state.[10] North Dakota statutes also provide for a mediation process to resolve labor disputes involving public employers and employees.[11] The statute establishes a Mediation Board and empowers the Board to hold hearings and to issue recommendations to resolve state employer-employee labor disputes.[12]

Section 32-29-01 of the North Dakota Century Code provides that persons capable of contracting may submit to the decision of one or more arbitrators any controversy that might be the subject of a civil action between them, except the question of title to real property in fee or for life.

[100.04] REGULATION OF UNION ACTIVITIES

North Dakota laws make it unlawful for any person to wear or use a union label or emblem without being entitled to do so by the rules of the union.[13] North Dakota statutes provide that no person who has been convicted of any crime involving moral turpitude or of a felony, excepting traffic violations, shall serve in any official capacity or as any officer in any labor union, nor shall such an individual be qualified to act as bargaining agent or representative for employees in the state.[14]

[100.05] REGULATION OF EMPLOYMENT PRACTICES

Anti-discrimination laws: North Dakota statutory laws prohibit discrimination in employment whenever based on race, color, sex, age, religion, mental or physical disability, marital status, receipt of public assistance, or national origin.[15]

Rights of military personnel (public employees): Section 37-01-25.1 of the North Dakota Century Code requires the state and its political subdivisions to reemploy military personnel upon their return from military service.

Blacklisting: North Dakota employers are prohibited from maintaining a blacklist or notifying any other employer of such blacklist for the purpose of preventing such worker from receiving employment.[16]

Jury duty: North Dakota laws prohibit an employer from depriving an employee of his or her employment, or threatening to do so, because the employee receives a summons, responds thereto, serves as a juror, or attends court as a prospective juror.[17]

Fraudulent receipt of wage advancements: Section 34-01-10 of the North Dakota Century Code forbids the taking of advanced wages through misrepresentation.

Protection of political activities (public employees): Section 39-01-04 of the North Dakota Century Code forbids public employees to engage in political activities while on duty or in uniform.

Medical examination payments: Section 34-01-15 of the North Dakota Century Code requires employers to pay for medical examinations required of employees or prospective employees.

Polygraph requirements: Although North Dakota statutes do not outlaw polygraph examinations in connection with the selection or separation of employment, the polygraph examiner is required, upon written request of the examinee, to make known the results of the exam to the person so examined.[18]

Equal pay: Section 34-06.1-03 of the North Dakota Century Code forbids any employer within the state to discriminate between employees on the basis of sex, by paying wages to an employee at a rate less than that paid to employees of the opposite sex for comparable work on jobs.

[100.06] WAGE AND HOUR LAWS

Child labor: The North Dakota Commissioner of Labor is empowered to ascertain and declare standards of condition of labor for children in any occupations and may prepare rules and regulations in connection there-with.[19]

Payment of wages: Section 34-14-02 of the North Dakota Century Code requires North Dakota employers to pay employees their wages no less than twice during a month or on regular agreed upon paydays designated in advance.

Payment upon termination: North Dakota employers are required to pay discharged employees their wages within twenty-four hours at the employer's place of business, or by certified mail within fifteen days of discharge.[20] An employee not under written contract, who voluntarily resigns his job, is due his or her full wages no later than the next regular payday.[21]

Garnishments: Section 32-09.1-18 of the North Dakota Century Code forbids discharge because of garnishments.

[100.07] SAFETY AND HEALTH LAWS

The North Dakota Workmen's Compensation Bureau is empowered to issue and enforce all necessary and proper rules and safety regulations.[22]

[100.08] UNEMPLOYMENT COMPENSATION LAWS

North Dakota unemployment compensation benefits are generally provided to unemployed workers who

- have properly registered for work at an unemployment office
- have properly applied for unemployment benefits
- are able to work, available for work, and actively seeking work
- are not otherwise disqualified under other provisions of the Act[23]

[100.09] WORKERS' COMPENSATION LAWS

Section 65-01-01, *et seq.,* of the North Dakota statutes sets forth the North Dakota Workmen's Compensation Act. The statute provides disability benefits to employees injured on the job or who suffer occupational diseases as a result of their job, subject to specified qualifications and limitations.[24]

[100.10] EMPLOYMENT-AT-WILL DEVELOPMENTS

The North Dakota courts have been reluctant to recognize some of the developing judicial exceptions to the at-will doctrine.[25] Some North Dakota

courts have permitted limited exceptions to the employment-at-will rule,
however. One court held that a company's personnel handbook that prom-
ised payments for accrued vacation benefits may have created an implied
employment contract between the parties.[26]

NOTES TO CHAPTER 100

1. North Dakota Century Code, Section 34-12-01, *et seq.*
2. North Dakota Century Code, Section 15-38.01-07.
3. North Dakota Century Code, Section 34-09-08.
4. North Dakota Century Code, Section 34-01-14.
5. North Dakota Century Code, Section 34-08-04.
6. North Dakota Century Code, Section 34-08-03.
7. North Dakota Century Code, Section 12-19-06.
8. North Dakota Public Acts, Chapter 255, Section 10 (L. 1963).
9. North Dakota Century Code, Section 34-01-04, *et seq.*
10. North Dakota Century Code, Section 34-11-01, *et seq.*
11. North Dakota Century Code, Section 34-11-01, *et seq.*
12. North Dakota Century Code, Section 34-11-03.
13. North Dakota Century Code, Section 12-38-19.
14. North Dakota Century Code, Section 34-01-16.
15. North Dakota Century Code, Section 14-02.4-03.
16. North Dakota Century Code, Section 34-12-03.
17. North Dakota Public Acts, S.B. 2320 (L. 1971).
18. North Dakota Century Code, Section 41-31-03.
19. North Dakota Century Code, Section 34-07-03, *et seq.*
20. North Dakota Century Code, Section 34-14-03(1).
21. North Dakota Century Code, Section 34-14-03(2).
22. North Dakota Century Code, Section 65-03-01.
23. North Dakota Century Code, Section 52-06-01, *et seq.*
24. North Dakota Century Code, Section 65-05-01, *et seq.*
25. *Wood v. Buchanan,* 5 N.W.2d 680 (N.D., 1942).
26. *Aasmundstad v. Dickenson State College,* 337 N.W.2d 792 (N.D., 1983).

101
Ohio
Labor Laws

Public employees' bargaining rights: Ohio statutes provide that public employees shall have the right of self-organization and the right to join and assist labor unions, or to refrain from union activities.[1] The statute prohibits certain conduct of both public employers and labor organizations, the violation of which constitutes unfair labor practices.[2] The Ohio State Employment Relations Act also provides for an election process to determine bargaining representatives, and establishes guidelines to determine appropriate bargaining units.[3]

Public utility bargaining: Section 717.03 of the Ohio Statutes provides that public utility successors may contract with a predecessor union on the terms and conditions that previously existed.

Successor employers bargaining: Ohio statutes provide that whenever a collective bargaining agreement between an employer and a labor union contains a successor clause, such clause is binding upon and enforceable against any successor employer who succeeds to the contracting employer's business, but for no longer than a three-year period.[4]

Nonright-to-work policy: Union security (union shop) clauses are permissible in the state of Ohio inasmuch as Ohio has not adopted a right-to-work statute pursuant to Section 14(b) of the Labor Management Relations Act.

"Yellow-dog" contract: Section 4113.02 of the Ohio Statutes makes it unlawful for anyone to coerce or compel any person to enter into an agreement not to join or become a member of any labor organization as a condition of employment.

[101.02] STRIKES, PICKETING, AND BOYCOTT LAWS

Unlawful assembly: Ohio statutes provide that no one shall assemble with two or more other persons to do an unlawful act with force and violence.[5]

Striker replacements: Section 4143.12 of the Ohio Statutes requires employment agencies to notify applicants of any existing strike or lockout prior to sending such an applicant to a prospective employer experiencing such labor conditions.

Injury to person or property: Ohio statutes forbid any person to maliciously or intentionally damage or injure any person, public or private property.[6]

[101.03] MEDIATION AND ARBITRATION LAWS

Ohio has adopted a General Arbitration Act recognizing any written agreement to submit an existing controversy to arbitration as valid, enforceable, and irrevocable, excepting such grounds as exist at law or equity for the revocation thereof.[7] Section 4129.01, *et seq.*, of the Ohio Statutes provides that the Ohio Industrial Commission will visit the locality of any labor dispute, investigate the matter, and make recommendations to the parties to resolve the controversy. In the event such efforts fail to resolve a labor dispute, the statute requires the Industrial Commission to encourage the parties to submit their differences to arbitration.[8] The statute also specifies the procedures for processing such an arbitration case.[9]

[101.04] REGULATION OF UNION ACTIVITIES

Ohio statutes make it unlawful for anyone to misuse or forge a union label or other union insignia.[10]

[101.05] REGULATION OF EMPLOYMENT PRACTICES

Anti-discrimination laws: Ohio statutory laws prohibit discrimination in employment whenever based on race, color, sex, age, religion, national origin, ancestry, or handicap.[11]

Arrest records: Section 2953.42 of the Ohio Statutes provides that no applicant for emplyment shall be questioned with respect to any arrest record that has been expunged.

Conviction records: An applicant may not lawfully be questioned about a conviction record, unless the question bears a direct and substantial relationship to the job being sought.[12]

Access to medical records: Ohio statutes require employers in the state to make available medical records to such employees, upon proper written request.[13]

Jury and witness duty: Section 2313.18 of the Ohio Statutes forbids any employer to discharge or otherwise discriminate against any permanent employee who is summoned to serve as a juror or witness[14] if the employee gives reasonable notice to the employer of the summons prior to the commencement of the employee's service as a juror or witness and if the employee is absent from employment because of the actual service.

Military leaves of absence: Ohio employees who are reserve members of the armed forces of the United States are entitled to leaves of absence from their employment up to fifteen days in any one calendar year to receive military training, and their employers are required to honor their employment rights to seniority and classification upon their return.[15]

Use of railroad "spotters": Ohio statutes require railroad companies, employing detectives ("spotters") for the purpose of investigating, obtaining and reporting information concerning their employees, to permit an employee an opportunity to confront his or her accuser concerning a question of honesty or integrity prior to discharge.[16]

Protection of political activities: Section 3599.06 of the Ohio Statutes forbids employers to discharge an employee for taking a reasonable amount of time to vote on election day or for exercising other voting and political rights.

Blacklisting: Section 1331.03 of the Ohio Statutes forbids blacklisting an individual for the purpose of interfering with his or her employment opportunities.

Medical examination payments: Section 4113.21 of the Ohio Statutes requires employers to pay the cost of medical examinations that are required of employees or applicants as a condition of employment or continued employment.

Service letter (railroad employees): Section 4973.03 of the Ohio Statutes requires an employer to furnish a railroad employee a service letter stating the reason for discharge, provided the employee requests such information.

Equal pay: Secton 4111.17 of the Ohio Statutes forbids Ohio employers to discriminate in the payment of wages on the basis of sex.

[101.06]   WAGE AND HOUR LAWS

Child labor: Section 4109.01 of the Ohio Statutes regulates the employment of children and specifies certain minimum age requirements with respect thereto. The Ohio child labor laws also require the issuance of age and schooling certificates before children of certain ages are permitted to work in gainful occupations.[17]

Payment of wages: Ohio statutes require Ohio employers to pay wages earned in the first fifteen days of the month by the first of the following month, and wages earned in the second half of the month by the fifteenth of the following month.[18]

Garnishments: Section 2716.05 of the Ohio Statutes forbids the discharge of an employee because his or her wages were subject to a single garnishment within a one-year period.

Notice of medical insurance continuance: Section 1737.30 of the Ohio Statutes requires an employer to notify a terminated employee of his or her right to convert group health insurance to the employee's individual policy, assuming certain conditions are met, such as the employee paying the premiums for such insurance coverage.

[101.07]   SAFETY AND HEALTH LAWS

Ohio health and safety laws require employers within the state to furnish safe employment for employees, and to furnish and use safety devices and safeguards, adopt and use methods and processes reasonably adequate to render such employment and place of employment safe, and do every other thing reasonably necessary to protect the life, health, and safety of employees.[19]

[101.08]   UNEMPLOYMENT COMPENSATION LAWS

The Ohio unemployment compensation laws are set forth in Section 4141.01, *et seq.*, of the Ohio Statutes and govern the eligibility requirements of recipients of unemployment compensation benefits.[20]

[101.09]   WORKERS' COMPENSATION LAWS

Section 4121.01, *et seq.*, of the Ohio Statutes sets forth the Ohio Workers' Compensation Act. The statute provides disability benefits to employees injured on the job, or who suffer occupational diseases as a result of their job, subject to specified qualifications and limitations.[21] Section 4123.90 of the Ohio Statutes forbids the discharge of an employee for having filed a workers' compensation claim.

[101.10]   EMPLOYMENT-AT-WILL DEVELOPMENTS

Ohio courts have continued to uphold the employment-at-will doctrine,[22] permitting only a few judicial exceptions, as noted below.

Implied contract exception: Several lower Ohio courts have ruled that job security assurances contained in an employee personnel handbook may create an implied employment contract, foreclosing a discharge not in keeping with policies and procedures of such handbook.[23]

Promissory estoppel exception: One Ohio court has recognized the promissory estoppel exception to the at-will rule with regard to an employee's reliance on promises of job security contained in a personnel policy manual.[24]

Public policy exception: Although Ohio courts have ruled rather consistently that they do not recognize the public policy exception to the at-will rule, a federal district court, interpreting Ohio law, held that an action would lie on public policy theory where an employee was discharged for refusing to commit perjury.[25]

NOTES TO CHAPTER 101

1. Ohio Statutes, Section 4117.03.
2. Ohio Statutes, Section 4117.11.
3. Ohio Statutes, Section 4117.01, *et seq.*
4. Ohio Statutes, Section 4113.30.
5. Ohio Statutes, Section 3761.13.
6. Ohio Statutes, Section 2901.07.
7. Ohio Statutes, Section 2711.01, *et seq.*
8. Ohio Statutes, Section 4129.02.
9. Ohio Statutes, Section 4129.03, *et seq.*
10. Ohio Statutes, Section 2911.27.
11. Ohio Statutes, Section 4112.02.
12. Ohio Statutes, Section 2953.32.
13. Ohio Statutes, Section 4113.23.
14. Ohio Statutes, Section 2313.18.
15. Ohio Statutes, Section 5903.061.
16. Ohio Statutes, Section 4999.17.
17. Ohio Statutes, Sections 3331.01; 4109.01.
18. Ohio Statutes, Section 4113.15(A).
19. Ohio Statutes, Section 4101.11.
20. Ohio Statutes, Section 4141.29, *et seq.*
21. Ohio Statutes, Section 4123.54.
22. *Henkel v. Educational Research Council of America*, 344 N.E.2d 118 (Ohio, 1976).
23. See, for example: *Day v. Good Samaritan Hospital*, Case No. 8062 (2nd App. Dist. of Ohio, 1983).
24. *Jones v. East Center for Community Mental Health*, Case No. L-83-280 (6th App. Dist. of Ohio, 1984).
25. *Merkel v. Scovill, Inc.*, 570 F. Supp. 133 (S.D. Ohio, 1983).

102

Oklahoma
Labor Laws

Collective bargaining laws: The Oklahoma statutes accord collective bargaining rights to police officers and firefighters within the state.[1] Title 70, Section 509.1, *et seq.*, of the Oklahoma Statutes Annotated established a framework for negotiation between school employees and employing school districts. This statute also specifies negotiation guidelines, provides for a three-member committee to resolve impasses, and nullifies recognition of any representative of professional or nonprofessional employees who engage in a strike.[2]

Nonright-to-work policy: Union security (union shop) clauses are permissible in the state of Oklahoma inasmuch as Oklahoma has not adopted a right-to-work statute pursuant to Section 14(b) of the Labor Management Relations Act.

[102.02] STRIKES, PICKETING, AND BOYCOTT LAWS

Unlawful assembly: Oklahoma statutes make it unlawful whenever three or more persons, acting together, make any attempt to do any act toward the commission of an act that would be a riot if actually committed.[3]

Use of prisoners during strike: Title 57, Section 543.1, of the Oklahoma Statutes Annotated prohibits the hiring of inmates to replace any employee engaged in a strike, negotiation, or arbitration growing out of a labor dispute.

Use of detectives during strike: Oklahoma statutes make it unlawful for any person to hire private detective agencies to come into the state armed with deadly weapons of any kind without a permit, in writing, from the governor.[4]

Strikebreakers: Title 40, Section 199.1, of the Oklahoma Statutes Annotated makes it unlawful for any employer to utilize professional strikebreakers to replace an employee or employees involved in a strike or lockout at a place of business within the state.

Strike replacement notices: Oklahoma statutes require advertisements and solicitations for employment applicants to state any existence of a strike, lockout, or other labor trouble at the place of the proposed employment.[5]

Seizure of property: Title 21, Section 1351, of the Oklahoma Statutes Annotated makes it unlawful for anyone to use or detain any lands or possessions of another, except in circumstances permitted by law.

Unlawful interference with employment: Oklahoma laws forbid any person or firm to attempt to prevent anyone employed by another from continuing or performing his or her work or from accepting any new work.[6]

[102.03] MEDIATION AND ARBITRATION LAWS

Article 9, Section 42, of the Oklahoma Constitution provides that every license issued or charter granted to a mining or public service corporation, foreign or domestic, shall contain a stipulation that such' corporation will submit any difference it may have with employees in reference to labor, to arbitration, as shall be provided by law. Oklahoma laws empower the State Board of Barber Examiners to act as mediators and arbitrators in any controversy or dispute that may arise among or between barbers and or their employees.[7]

Oklahoma statutes empower the State Dry Cleaners Board to serve as mediators and arbitrators in any controversy or dispute involving dry cleaner owners, employers, employees, or operators as between themselves or that may arise between themselves as groups.[8]

Title 21, Section 383, of the Oklahoma Statutes Annotated makes it unlawful to bribe, or attempt to bribe, arbitrators in the state. Title 47, Section 176, of the Oklahoma Statutes Annotated provides for revocation of motor carrier certificates and permits when such carriers are unable to provide transportation services due to unresolved labor problems.

[102.04] REGULATION OF UNION ACTIVITIES

Oklahoma statutes make it unlawful for anyone to misuse or forge a union label or other union insignia.[9]

[102.05] REGULATION OF EMPLOYMENT PRACTICES

Anti-discrimination laws: Oklahoma statutes forbid discrimination in employment against individuals on the basis of race, color, religion, sex, national origin, or handicap.[10]

Employment under false pretense: Title 40, Section 167, of the Oklahoma Statutes Annotated forbids any person to employ another through false representations.

Protection of political freedom: Oklahoma labor laws make it unlawful for any employer within the state to interfere with the voting rights and privileges of his or her employees.[11]

Leaves of absence for political activities (railroad employees): Title 40, Section 185, *et seq.*, of the Oklahoma Statutes Annotated provides that all railroad companies within the state are required to grant leaves of absence to employees who desire to run for or seek public office, or who are required to serve in any government position or who have been elected or appointed to public office.

Jury service: Oklahoma statutes forbid any person to discharge or otherwise discriminate against an employee because of his or her absence from work by reason of having been required to serve on a jury within the state.[12]

National Guard members: Title 44, Section 208, of the Oklahoma Statutes Annotated prohibits the discharge of any employee required to take a leave of absence to perform military training or service.

Freedom of expression (state employees): Oklahoma laws provide that no supervisor or appointing authority of any state agency shall prohibit employees of such agency from discussing the operations of the agency with any member of the Legislature.[13]

Service letter (public sevice employees): Oklahoma public service employers are required by Title 40, Section 171, of the Oklahoma Statutes Annotated to give to terminated employees a letter setting forth the nature and character of service rendered by the employee, the duration thereof, and truly state for what cause, if any, such employee quit or was discharged, provided the employee requests such a service letter.

Blacklisting: Oklahoma employers are prohibited from maintaining a blacklist or notifying any other employer that any worker has been blacklisted by such employer for the purpose of preventing such worker from receiving employment.[14]

Medical examinations: Title 40, Section 191, *et seq.*, of the Oklahoma Statutes Annotated requires employers to pay the costs of medical examinations required of applicants and employees and obligates employers to provide a copy of such medical reports to the employee.

Equal pay: Oklahoma statutes make it unlawful for an employer to pay female employees at rates less than those received by employees of the opposite sex for work on jobs that are comparable as to skill, effort, and responsibility.[15]

[102.06] WAGE AND HOUR LAWS

Child labor: Oklahoma laws provide that no child under 14 years of age may work in any factory, theater, bowling alley, pool hall, or steam laundry, except nonresidents in theater performances when accompanied by or in custody of parent, guardian, or teacher.[16] Children under 16 years of age are similarly limited in performing gainful employment without age and schooling certificates.[17]

Voting time: Oklahoma statutes provide that an employee, eligible and registered to vote in any election, shall be excused from his or her employment not exceeding two consecutive hours without loss of pay to exercise such voting privileges, provided such employee does not have two consecutive hours between the time of opening and closing of polls when he or she is not working for the employer.[18]

Payment of wages: Title 40, Section 165, of the Oklahoma Statutes Annotated requires Oklahoma employers to pay employees their wages not less than twice during a month on regular paydays designated in advance.

Payment upon termination: Oklahoma employers are required to pay terminated employees their earned wages no later than the next regular payday.[19]

Garnishments: Oklahoma employers are forbidden to discharge employees because of garnishments being placed against their wages, unless the employer is served to collect one or more judgments against the employee within a one-year period.[20]

[102.07] SAFETY AND HEALTH LAWS

Title 40, Section 403(1), *et seq.*, of the Oklahoma Statutes Annotated requires employers to furnish a safe and healthful place of employment for their employees to work.

[102.08] UNEMPLOYMENT COMPENSATION LAWS

The Oklahoma unemployment compensation laws are set forth in Title 40, Section 2-201, *et seq.*, of the Oklahoma Statutes Annotated and govern, among other things, the eligibility requirements of recipients of unemployment compensation benefits.

[102.09] WORKERS' COMPENSATION LAWS

The Oklahoma Workers' Compensation Act provides disability benefits to employees injured on the job or who suffer occupational diseases as a result of their job, subject to specified qualifications and limitations.[21] Title 85, Section 5, of the Oklahoma Statutes Annotated forbids discharge of an employee in retaliation of his or her filing a workers' compensation claim.

[102.10] EMPLOYMENT-AT-WILL DEVELOPMENTS

General rule: Oklahoma courts continue to recognize the employment-at-will doctrine as the general rule of law on the subject,[22] permitting only limited exceptions, as of this writing.

Implied contract exception: Oklahoma courts have held that an employee handbook may give rise to an implied employment contract, prohibiting a discharge unless such termination conforms with the procedures and policies contained in the handbook.[23] The Oklahoma Supreme Court has also recognized the implied covenant of good faith and fair dealing exceptions to the at-will doctrine.[24]

NOTES TO CHAPTER 102

1. Oklahoma Statutes Annotated, 11:51-101.
2. Oklahoma Statutes Annotated, 70:509.1, *et seq.*
3. Oklahoma Statutes Annotated, 21:1311, *et seq.*
4. Oklahoma Statutes Annotated, 40:169.
5. Oklahoma Statutes Annotated, 40:169.
6. Oklahoma Statutes Annotated, 21:837 and 21:838.
7. Oklahoma Statutes Annotated, 59:94(C).
8. Oklahoma Statutes Annotated, 59:743(C).
9. Oklahoma Statutes Annotated, 78:9, *et seq.*
10. Oklahoma Statutes Annotated, 25:1302.
11. Oklahoma Statutes Annotated, 26:440.
12. Oklahoma Statutes Annotated, 38:34.
13. See Oklahoma Public Acts, H.B. 1128 (L. 1981).
14. Oklahoma Statutes Annotated, 40:172.
15. Oklahoma Statutes Annotated, 40:198.1.
16. Oklahoma Statutes Annotated, 40:71.
17. Oklahoma Statutes Annotated, 40:74 through 77.
18. Oklahoma Statutes Annotated, 26:7-101.
19. Oklahoma Statutes Annotated, 26:165.3.
20. Oklahoma Statutes Annotated, 14A:5-106.
21. Oklahoma Statutes Annotated, 85:1, *et seq.*
22. *Foster v. Atlas Life Ins. Co.*, 6 P.2d 805 (Okla., 1931).
23. *Vinyard v. King*, 728 F.2d 428 (CA-10, 1984); *Langdon v. Saga Corp.*, 569 P.2d 524 (Okla. App., 1976).
24. *Hall v. Farmers Ins. Exchange*, Case no. 59584 (Okla. S. Ct., 1985).

103

Oregon
Labor Laws

[103.01] LABOR RELATIONS LAWS

Labor Peace Act: Section 663.005, *et seq.*, of the Oregon Revised Statutes provides that Oregon employers, unless otherwise exempt, must recognize and bargain in good faith with unions properly certified as representatives of their employees. The statute provides for the machinery to conduct representation elections and procedures to process unfair labor practice charges against employers and labor organizations.[1]

Nurses' bargaining rights: Section 662.705 of the Oregon Revised Statutes extends collective bargaining rights to professional and practical nurses in private health-care facilities, establishes guidelines to determine appropriate bargaining units and bargaining representatives for such employees, as well as prescribes certain prohibited conduct by health-care employers, nurses, and their bargaining representatives.

Public employees' bargaining rights: Oregon statutes provide that public employees shall have the right of self-organization and the right to join and assist labor unions, or to refrain from union activities.[2] The statute prohibits certain conduct of both public employers and labor organizations, the violation of which constitutes unfair labor practices.[3] The Oregon Public Employees Relations Act also provides for an election process to determine bargaining representatives, establishes requirements for determining bargaining units, forbids strikes, and provides for mediation and binding arbitration to resolve labor disputes.[4]

Nonright-to-work policy: Union security (union shop) clauses are permissible in the state of Oregon inasmuch as Oregon has not chosen to enact a right-to-work statute pursuant to Section 14(b) of the Labor Management Relations Act.

"Yellow-dog" contracts: Section 662.030 of the Oregon Revised Statutes declares an agreement not to join or become a member of any labor organization as a condition of employment to be contrary to public policy and unenforceable.

[103.02] STRIKES, PICKETING, AND BOYCOTT LAWS

Anti-injunction laws: Oregon statutory laws restrict the power of Oregon courts to issue injunctions against peaceable picketing and legally protected strike activity.[5]

Secondary boycotts and hot cargo clauses forbidden: Section 662.210, *et seq.*, of Oregon Revised Statutes makes it unlawful for anyone to engage in secondary boycotts or refuse to handle "hot cargo."

Unlawful interference with employment: Oregon statutes make it unlawful for any person to attempt to prevent any person from engaging in any lawful employment within the state.[6]

Unlawful assembly: Section 23-801 of the Oregon Revised Statutes prohibits three or more persons to assemble together to do an unlawful act.

Picketing of farms: Oregon statutes make it unlawful for any person to picket any farm, ranch, or orchard where perishable agricultural crops are produced, while such crops are being harvested, unless such picketer has been a regular employee on such farm, ranch, or orchard prior to the commencement of the picketing.[7]

Striker replacements: Oregon statutes require employment agencies to notify applicants of any existing strike or lockout prior to sending such an applicant to a prospective employer experiencing such labor conditions.[8] Section 659.210, *et seq.*, of the Oregon Revised Statutes forbids deceptive advertising for employment and requires advertisements and solicitations for employment applicants to state any existence of a strike, lockout, or other labor trouble at the place of the proposed employment.

Strikebreakers: Oregon revised statutes make it unlawful for any employer to utilize professional strikebreakers to replace an employee involved in a strike or lockout at a place of business within the state.[9]

[103.03] MEDIATION AND ARBITRATION LAWS

Section 662.405 of the Oregon Revised Statutes established a State Conciliation Service in the Bureau of Labor. The statute provides that the State Conciliation Service shall serve to prevent labor disputes and strikes by attempting to procure settlement of issues between employers and employees through conciliation, mediation, and voluntary arbitration.

[103.04] REGULATION OF UNION ACTIVITIES

Oregon statutes make it unlawful for anyone to misuse or forge a union label or other union insignia.[10] Oregon statutes forbid a union to charge, receive, or retain any union dues, assessments, or other charges not properly authorized.[11] Section 661.040 of the Oregon Revised Statutes requires labor unions to permit members to inspect certain financial records of the union at all reasonable times.

[103.05]   REGULATION OF EMPLOYMENT PRACTICES

Anti-discrimination laws: Section 659-030, *et seq.*, of the Oregon Revised Statutes prohibits discrimination in the employment of an individual by reason of race, religion, color, sex, national origin, marital status, or age. Oregon statutes also prohibit discrimination in employment against the physically or mentally handicapped.[12]

Polygraph restrictions: No Oregon employer shall demand or require any applicant for employment, or any employee, to submit to a polygraph, lie detector, breathalyzer, or similar test or examination as a condition of employment or continued employment.[13]

Jury service: Oregon employers are forbidden to deprive, or attempt to deprive, any employee of employment because such employee receives a summons, responds thereto, serves as a juror, or attends court for prospective jury service.[14]

Access to personnel records: Oregon statutes provide that every employer shall, at reasonable times and intervals, and upon proper application of an employee, permit such employee to inspect such personnel files which are used, or have been used, to determine the employee's qualification for employment, promotion, additional compensation, termination, or other disciplinary action.[15]

Whistle-blowing statute (public employees): Oregon law forbids any public employer to take disciplinary action against any employee for the disclosure of information which the employee reasonably believes evidences a violation of any law, rule, or other improper action on the part of a superior officer.[16]

Employment under false pretense: Section 659.260 of the Oregon Revised Statutes forbids employers within the state to falsely advertise wages to be paid, work to be performed, or working conditions where such advertising is used to solicit prospective employees.

Fraudulent receipt of wage advances: Section 659.250 of the Oregon Revised Statutes forbids any person to accept or receive advanced wages for labor to be performed with the intent of defrauding the prospective employer out of said wages by nonperformance.

Blacklisting: Oregon employers are prohibited from maintaining a blacklist or notifying other employers that they maintain a blacklist of any employee, or former employee, for the purpose of preventing such worker from receiving employment.[17]

National Guard duty (public employees): Section 408.210, *et seq.*, of the Oregon Revised Statutes requires public employers to permit leaves of absence for employees who are members of the National Guard for training purposes and other military services, and thereafter, restore the individual to his or her regular employment.

Anti-nepotism discrimination: Section 659.340 of the Oregon Revised Statutes forbids the rejection or termination in employment of an individual because another family member is currently employed by the employer.

Medical examinations: Oregon statutes make it unlawful for an employer to discharge an employee for nonpayment of any medical examination or cost of a health certificate.[18]

Prior testimony: Section 659.270 of the Oregon Revised Statutes makes it unlawful to discriminate in employment against anyone because of his or her previous testimony before the state legislature.

Juvenile record: Oregon statutes forbid discrimination in employment of any individual because of a juvenile record that has been expunged.[19]

[103.06] WAGE AND HOUR LAWS

Child labor: Oregon statutes regulate the employment of children in gainful occupations and specify certain minimum age requirements in connection therewith. Unless otherwise permitted by law, rule, or regulations, children between 14 and 17 years of age must obtain a work permit and age statement prior to securing employment.[20]

Payment of wages: Section 652.120 of the Oregon Revised Statutes requires Oregon employers to pay employees their wages due at least once every thirty-five days; however, an employer is not prevented from maintaining paydays at more frequent intervals.

Payment upon termination: Oregon employers are required to pay discharged employees their earned wages immediately after discharge.[21]

Garnishments: Section 23.185(5) of the Oregon Revised Statutes forbids the discharge of an employee because of a garnishment of his or her wages.

Medical insurance conversion: Section 743.850 of the Oregon Revised Statutes requires employers to notify terminating employees of their right to convert group medical insurance coverage to individual coverage, at the employee's expense.

[103.07] SAFETY AND HEALTH LAWS

Oregon health and safety laws require employers within the state to furnish safe employment for employees, and to furnish and use safety devices and safeguards, adopt and use methods and processes reasonably adequate to render such employment and place of employment safe, and do every other thing reasonably necessary to protect life, health, and safety of employees.[22]

[103.08] UNEMPLOYMENT COMPENSATION LAWS

The Oregon unemployment compensation laws are set forth in Section 657.005, *et seq.*, of the Oregon Revised Statutes which govern, among other things, the eligibility requirements of recipients of unemployment compensation benefits.

[103.09] WORKERS' COMPENSATION LAWS

The Oregon Workers' Compensation Act provides disability benefits to employees injured on the job or who suffer occupational diseases as a result of their job, subject to specified qualifications and limitations.[23] Section 659.410, *et seq.*, of the Oregon Revised Statutes makes it unlawful to discharge or otherwise discriminate against an employee for filing a workers' compensation claim.

[103.10] EMPLOYMENT-AT-WILL DEVELOPMENTS

Oregon courts have recognized several exceptions to the employment-at-will principle.

Implied contract exception: Oregon courts have ruled that an employee handbook may create an implied employment contract and that a discharge is lawful only to the degree that it conforms to procedures enumerated in such handbook.[24]

Public policy exception: Oregon courts consistently hold that an employee may recover damages for unlawful discharge when he or she is terminated for exercising some legal right or fulfilling a societal obligation, such as serving on a jury.[25]

Intentional infliction of emotional distress exception: Oregon courts have also held that an employee may recover damages for an outrageous discharge such as the dismissal of an employee who was induced to sign a false confession for stealing.[26]

NOTES TO CHAPTER 103

1. Oregon Revised Statutes, Section 663.005, *et seq.*
2. Oregon Revised Statutes, Section 243.662.

3. Oregon Revised Statutes, Section 243.672.

4. Oregon Revised Statutes, Section 243.650, *et seq.*

5. Oregon Revised Statutes, Section 662.010, *et seq.*

6. Oregon Revised Statutes, Section 659.240.

7. Oregon Public Acts, Chapter 543 (L. 1963).

8. Oregon Revised Statutes, Section 658.225.

9. Oregon Public Acts, Chapter 645 (L. 1975).

10. Oregon Revised Statutes, Section 661.210, *et seq.*

11. Oregon Revised Statutes, Section 661.040(1).

12. Oregon Revised Statutes, Section 659.425.

13. Oregon Revised Statutes, Section 659.227.

14. Oregon Public Acts, Chapter 160 (L. 1975).

15. Oregon Revised Statutes, Section 652.750.

16. Oregon Revised Statutes, Section 240.3165.

17. Oregon Revised Statutes, Section 659.230.

18. Oregon Revised Statutes, Section 659.330.

19. Oregon Revised Statutes, Section 659.030(a).

20. Oregon Wage and Hour Commission Rules, OAR 21-215(1).

21. Oregon Revised Statutes, Section 652.140(1).

22. Oregon Revised Statutes, Section 654.010.

23. Oregon Revised Statutes, Section 656.001, *et seq.*

24. *Fleming v. Kids and Kin Head Start*, 693 P.2d 1363 (Ore. S.Ct., 1985).

25. *Nees v. Hocks*, 536 P.2d 512 (Ore. S.Ct., 1975).

26. *Smithson v. Nordstrom, Inc.*, 664 P.2d 1119 (Ore Ct. of App., 1983).

104

Pennsylvania
Labor Laws

General right to organize: Pennsylvania statutes make it lawful for all classes of mechanics, journeymen, tradesmen, and laborers to form societies and associations for their mutual aid, benefit, and protection and to peaceably meet, discuss, and establish all necessary bylaws, rules, and regulations to carry out the same, except that this provision is inapplicable to the counties of Clearfield and Centre.[1]

Pennsylvania Labor Relations Act: Title 43, Section 211.1, *et seq.*, of the Pennsylvania Statutes provides that employers must recognize and bargain in good faith with unions properly certified as representatives of their employees. The statute provides for the machinery to conduct representation elections and procedures to process unfair labor practice charges against employers and labor organizations.[2]

Public employees' bargaining rights: Pennsylvania statutes provide that public employees shall have the right of self-organization and the right to join and assist labor unions, or to refrain from union activities.[3] The Pennsylvania Public Employees Relations Act provides for an election process to determine bargaining representatives, establishes guidelines to determine appropriate bargaining units, and limits strikes and picketing.[4]

Public transit employees' bargaining rights: Pennsylvania statutes accord to public transit employees the right of self-organization to form, join, or assist labor organizations, to bargain collectively through representatives of their own choosing, and to engage in other concerted activities for the purpose of collective bargaining or other mutual aid or protection.[5]

Firefighters' and police officers' bargaining rights: Pennsylvania statutes provide that police officers and firefighters employed by a political commonwealth or its subdivisions shall have the right to bargain collectively with their public employers.[6]

Nonright-to-work policy: Union security (union shop) clauses are permissible in the state of Pennsylvania inasmuch as Pennsylvania has not adopted a right-to-work statute pursuant to Section 14(b) of the Labor Management Relations Act.

"Yellow-dog" contracts: Pennsylvania laws make it unlawful for anyone to coerce or compel any person to enter into an agreement not to join or become a member of any labor organization as a condition of employment.[7]

[104.02] STRIKES, PICKETING, AND BOYCOTT LAWS

      Anti-injunction laws: Pennsylvania statutory laws restrict the power of Pennsylvania courts to issue injunctions against peaceable picketing and legally protected strike activity.[8]

      Striker replacements: Pennsylvania statutes require employment agencies to notify an applicant of any existing strike or lockout prior to sending such an applicant to a prospective employer experiencing such labor conditions.[9] Pennsylvania statutes also require employer advertisements and solicitations for employment applicants to state the existence of a strike, lockout or other labor trouble at the place of the proposed employment.[10]

      Strikebreakers: Pennsylvania laws make it unlawful for any employer to utilize professional strikebreakers in a labor dispute.[11]

      Right to strike: Title 43, Section 199, of the Pennsylvania Statutes makes it lawful for employees to participate in work stoppages.

      Interference with railroads: Pennsylvania statutes make it unlawful for railroad employees, in furtherance of a strike, to willfully or maliciously abandon a locomotive.[12] The statute also makes it unlawful for any person to otherwise interfere with or obstruct the regular operation of a railroad company.[13]

[104.03] MEDIATION AND ARBITRATION LAWS

Pennsylvania has adopted the Uniform Arbitration Act, recognizing any written agreement to submit an existing controversy to arbitration as valid, enforceable, and irrevocable, except on such grounds as exist at law or equity for the revocation thereof.[14] Title 43, Section 211.31, *et seq.,* of the Pennsylvania Statutes provides for mediation of labor disputes through representatives of the State Department of Labor and Industry. Title 43, Section 213.1, of the Pennsylvania Statutes provides for the mediation and compulsory arbitration of public utility disputes.

[104.04] REGULATION OF UNION ACTIVITIES

Pennsylvania statutes make it unlawful for anyone to misuse or forge a union label[15] or other union insignia. Pennsylvania Statutes forbid corporations and unincorporated associations, and officers and agents thereof, to contribute money or gifts to political candidates.[16]

[104.05] REGULATION OF EMPLOYMENT PRACTICES

Anti-discrimination laws: Pennsylvania statutes prohibit discrimination in the employment of an individual by reason of race, creed, religion, color, sex, age, national origin, ancestry, or handicap.[17] Title 43, Section 955(k), of the Pennsylvania Statutes forbids discharge of an employee because he or she has only a GED certificate instead of a high school diploma.

Arrest records: Pennsylvania laws provide that misdemeanor convictions and arrests for offenses that do not relate to the applicant's suitability for employment in the position for which he or she has applied shall not be considered by the employer.[18]

Polygraph restrictions: No Pennsylvania employer shall require any applicant for employment, or any employee, to submit to polygraph, or similar tests or examinations as a condition of employment or continued employment.[19]

Voice stress analyzers: Pennsylvania statutes make it a misdemeanor for anyone to use any system that examines or records in any manner voice prints or other voice stress patterns of another person to determine the truth or falsity of statements made by such other person without his or her express consent.[20]

Employment under false pretenses: Title 18, Section 4856, of the Pennsylvania Statutes makes it unlawful for anyone to obtain employment under false pretenses.

Interference with employment: Title 18, Section 4670, of the Pennsylvania Statutes makes it unlawful for any person or firm to threaten any employee with the loss of employment for failing or refusing to sign any petition which such employee has been solicited or requested to sign.

Protection of political freedom: Pennsylvania employers are forbidden to coerce or influence or attempt to influence the political decisions of their employees through or by means of threat of discharge or loss of employment.[21]

Jury service: Pennsylvania laws prohibit an employer from attempting to deprive an employee of his or her employment because the employee receives a summons to serve as a juror, serves as a juror, or attends court as a prospective juror.[22]

Protection of volunteer firefighters: Pennsylvania statutes forbid employers to terminate an employee who is a volunteer firefighter and, in the line of duty, has responded to a call prior to the time he or she was due to report for work.[23]

Access to personnel records: Pennsylvania statutes provide that every employer shall, at reasonable times and intervals, and upon proper application of an employee, permit such employee to inspect his or her personnel files.[24]

Medical examination payments: Title 43, Section 1002, of the Pennsylvania Statutes requires employers to pay any medical costs incurred as a result of pre-employment physical examinations or other such examinations required of applicants or employees.

Equal pay: Pennsylvania statutes forbid employers to discriminate on the basis of sex by paying wages to employees of one sex at a rate less than those paid to employees of the opposite sex for work under comparable conditions requiring comparable skills, effort, and responsibility.[25]

[104.06] WAGE AND HOUR LAWS

Child labor: Pennsylvania laws regulate the employment of children and specify minimum age requirements in connection therewith. Employment certificates are required of children under 18 years of age who are employed during public school hours.[26]

Payment of wages: Pennsylvania wage and hour laws provide that wages shall be due employees within standard time lapses customary in trade or within fifteen days from end of established pay period, in absence of written provisions.[27]

Payment on termination: Pennsylvania employers are required to pay terminated employees their earned wages in full no later than the next regular payday on which wages would otherwise be due and payable.[28]

Medical insurance continuance: Title 40, Section 756.2, of the Pennsylvania Statutes requires employers to notify terminating employees of their right to convert their group medical insurance to an individual coverage, provided certain conditions are met, such as the assumption of payment for premiums by the terminating employee.

[104.07] HEALTH AND SAFETY LAWS

Title 43, Section 9, *et seq.,* of the Pennsylvania Statutes establishes certain safety and sanitation standards for Pennsylvania employers.

[104.08] UNEMPLOYMENT COMPENSATION LAWS

Title 43, Section 751, *et seq.,* of the Pennsylvania Statutes establishes guidelines to govern the eligibility requirements of recipients of unemployment compensation benefits.[29]

[104.09] WORKERS' COMPENSATION LAWS

The Pennsylvania Workers' Compensation Act provides disability benefits to employees injured on the job or who suffer occupational diseases as a result of their job, subject to specified qualifications and limitations.[30]

[104.10] EMPLOYMENT-AT-WILL DEVELOPMENTS

Pennsylvania courts have recognized certain limited exceptions to the employment-at-will rule, as noted below.

Public policy exception: Pennsylvania courts recognize causes of action for wrongful discharge when employees are terminated for refusal to violate some public policy.[31]

"Independent consideration" exception: Pennsylvania courts have ruled that when an employee gives an employer consideration in addition to normal employment services, that the employee's at-will status may be modified, requiring just cause as a condition to discharge.[32]

Intentional infliction of emotional distress exception: A federal district court, applying Pennsylvania law, has recognized that a forced resignation of an employee by an employer to avoid a sexual harassment claim is so outrageous that a cause of action may lie for intentional infliction of emotional distress.[33]

NOTES TO CHAPTER 104

1. Pennsylvania Statutes, Title 43, Section 191.
2. Pennsylvania Statutes, Title 43, Section 211.1, *et seq.*
3. Pennsylvania Public Employee Relations Act, Section 401.
4. Pennsylvania Public Employee Relations Act, Section 101, *et seq.*
5. Pennsylvania Public Laws, Act 288 (L. 1967).
6. Pennsylvania Public Laws, Act 111 (L. 1968).
7. Pennsylvania Statutes, Title 18, Section 4669.
8. Pennsylvania Statutes, Title 43, Section 206a, *et seq.*
9. Pennsylvania Statutes, Title 43, Section 23.
10. Pennsylvania Public Laws, Act 187 (L. 1972).
11. Pennsylvania Public Laws, Act 187 (L. 1972).
12. Pennsylvania Public Laws, Act 872 (L. 1939).
13. Pennsylvania Statutes, Title 18, Section 4664, and Title 18, Section 4921.
14. Pennsylvania Statutes, Title 42, Section 7303.
15. Pennsylvania Statutes, Title 73, Section 105.

16. Pennsylvania Statutes, Title 25, Section 3225.

17. Pennsylvania Statutes, Title 43, Section 955.

18. Pennsylvania Public Laws, H.B. 2095 (L. 1978).

19. Pennsylvania Statutes, Title 18, Section 7321.

20. Pennsylvania Statutes, Title 18, Section 7507.

21. Pennsylvania Statutes, Title 25, Section 3547.

22. Pennsylvania Public Laws, Act 17 (L. 1978).

23. Pennsylvania Public Laws, Act 83 (L. 1977).

24. Pennsylvania Public Laws, Act 286 (L. 1978).

25. Pennsylvania Public Laws, Act 694 (L. 1968).

26. Pennsylvania Statutes, Title 24, Section 13-1391.

27. Pennsylvania Public Laws, Act 329 (L. 1961).

28. Pennsylvania Public Laws, Act 329 (L. 1961).

29. Pennsylvania Statutes, Title 43, Section 751, *et seq.*

30. Pennsylvania Statutes, Title 77, Section 1, *et seq.*

31. *McNulty v. Borden, Inc.,* 474 F.Supp. 1111 (E.D. Pa., 1979).

32. *Cory v. SmithKline Beckman Corp.,* 116 LRRM 3361 (E.D. Pa., 1984).

33. *Shaffer v. National Can Corp.,* 565 F.Supp. 909 (E.D. Pa., 1983).

105

Rhode Island
Labor Laws

Rhode Island State Labor Relations Act: Section 28-7-1, *et seq.,* of the Rhode Island General Laws provides that Rhode Island employers, unless otherwise exempted, must recognize and bargain in good faith with unions properly certified as representatives of their employees.

Public employees' bargaining rights: Section 36-11-1, *et seq.,* of the Rhode Island General Laws established a framework of employer-employee relations by providing a uniform and orderly method for collective bargaining between public employers and certain public employees. The statute also prohibits discrimination because of employee membership in a labor organization and sets out guidelines for binding arbitration to resolve public employment labor disputes.[1]

Municipal employees' bargaining rights: Rhode Island statutes provide that municipal employees shall have the right to form, join, or assist labor unions and shall also have the right to bargain collectively through representatives of their own choosing with municipal employers.[2]

Teachers' bargaining rights: Section 28-9.3-1, *et seq.,* of the Rhode Island General Laws established the right of teachers in the state to organize and bargain collectively. The statute provides that unresolved collective bargaining issues are to be submitted to mediation or arbitration.[3]

Firefighters' and police officers' bargaining rights: The Rhode Island statutes accord collective bargaining rights and the right of self-organization to firefighters[4] and police officers within the state.[5]

State police officers' bargaining rights: Section 28-9.5-1, *et seq.,* of the Rhode Island General Laws accords state police the right to bargain collectively with the state of Rhode Island as well as provides binding arbitration to resolve collective bargaining issues.

Nonright-to-work policy: Union security (union shop) clauses are permissible in the state of Rhode Island inasmuch as Rhode Island has not adopted a right-to-work statute pursuant to Section 14(b) of the Labor Management Relations Act.

"Yellow-dog" contracts: Section 28–7–13 of the Rhode Island General Laws makes it unlawful for anyone to coerce or compel any person to enter into an agreement not to join or become a member of any labor organization as a condition of employment.

[105.02] STRIKES, PICKETING, AND BOYCOTT LAWS

Anti-injunction laws: Rhode Island statutory laws restrict the power of Rhode Island courts to issue injunctions against peaceable picketing and legally protected strike activity.[6]

Unlawful assembly: Rhode Island statutes provide for dispersal of unlawful assemblies of twelve or more armed persons or thirty or more riotously assembled persons, upon command of any law enforcement officer.[7]

Interference with employment: Rhode Island statutes make it unlawful for anyone to attempt to prevent any person from engaging in any lawful occupation at any place he or she sees fit.[8]

Interference with railroads: Section 11-36-3 of the Rhode Island General Laws makes it unlawful for anyone to interfere with railway employees while in discharge of their duties.

Use of tear gas prohibited during strikes: Rhode Island statutes prohibit the use of tear gas, or similar substances, except as may be used by peace officers in the enforcement of their duty.[9]

Strikebreakers and replacement notices: Rhode Island statutory laws make it unlawful for any employer to utilize professional strikebreakers to replace employees involved in a strike.[10] Rhode Island employers are required to explicitly mention in advertisements or solicitations for employment applicants the existence of any strike, lockout, or other labor dispute at their place of business.[11]

[105.03] MEDIATION AND ARBITRATION LAWS

Section 28-9-1 of the Rhode Island General Laws provides that a provision in a written contract between an employer and an association of employees or labor union, or between an association of employers and an association of employees, or labor unions, to settle any controversy by arbitration shall be valid, irrevocable, and enforceable, except upon such grounds as exist in law or in equity.

[105.04] REGULATION OF UNION ACTIVITIES

Section 11-14-5 of the Rhode Island General Laws makes it unlawful for anyone to use or display the label or logo of the American Federation of Musicians without the written permission and/or authorization of the federation.

[105.05] REGULATION OF EMPLOYMENT PRACTICES

Anti-discrimination laws: Rhode Island statutes prohibit discrimination in the employment of an individual by reason of race, color, religion, sex, age, national origin, ancestry, or handicap.[12]

Polygraph restrictions: Rhode Island employers are forbidden to require any applicant for employment or any employee to submit to a polygraph or similar test or examination as a condition of employment or continued employment.[13]

Arrest Records: Section 28-5-7 of the Rhode Island General Laws makes it an unlawful employment practice for any employer to include on any application for employment an inquiry with respect to an applicant's arrest record.

Medical examinations payments: Rhode Island statutes provide that whenever an employer shall require an applicant to take a physical examination prior to employment, the cost of such an examination is to be paid by the employer, whether or not the applicant is hired.[14]

Protection of political freedom: Rhode Island employers are forbidden to attempt to influence the political decisions of their employees by threat of discharge or loss of employment.[15]

Confidentiality of medical information: Section 5-37.3-4(a) of the Rhode Island General Laws provides that, unless otherwise permitted by statute, a Rhode Island employer may not disclose medical information pertaining to an employee without the written consent of such employee.[16]

Reemployment rights of military personnel: Section 30-11-2, *et seq.*, of the Rhode Island General Laws requires employers to reemploy military personnel upon their return from military service.

Jury duty: Section 9-9-28 of the Rhode Island General Laws forbids the discharge of an employee because he or she has been called to serve on a jury.

Whistle-blowing statute (public employees): Section 3 of the Rhode Island Whistle-Blowers's Protection Act forbids discharge or discrimination against a public employee because such employee reports to a public body a believed violation of some law, regulation, or rule promulgated under the laws of the state.

Equal pay: Section 28-6-17 of the Rhode Island General Laws requires employers to pay female employees the same wage rate as paid male employees for equal or comparable work.

[105.06] WAGE AND HOUR LAWS

Child labor: Rhode Island statutes prescribe certain minimum age requirements that must be met before children within such age groups may work in gainful employment.[17]

Payment of wages: Section 28-14-2 of the Rhode Island General Laws requires Rhode Island employers, unless otherwise excluded, to pay employees all wages due on a weekly basis.

Payment upon termination: Rhode Island employers are required to pay terminated employees all wages due within twenty-four hours of time of separation.[18]

Garnishments: Section 15-13-3.1 of the Rhode Island General Laws forbids discharge of an employee because his or her wages have been garnished for child support.

Medical insurance continuance: Section 27-19.1-1 of the Rhode Island General Laws requires employers to allow involuntary layoff employees to continue in a group medical plan, provided the employee assumes the payment of premiums for such insurance coverage.

[105.07] HEALTH AND SAFETY LAWS

General provisions: Rhode Island statutes require employers to furnish a safe and healthful place of employment for their employees to work.[19]

Toxic substances—right to know: Section 28-21-1, *et seq.,* of the Rhode Island General Laws requires employers who manufacture or use toxic substances within their work place to provide training about such substances to employees who may be adversely affected if overexposed to such agents.

[105.08] UNEMPLOYMENT COMPENSATION LAWS

The Rhode Island unemployment compensation laws govern the distribution of unemployment benefits to unemployed workers.[20] As contrasted to most other states, Rhode Island permits striking employees to receive unemployment compensation.[21]

[105.09] WORKERS' COMPENSATION LAWS

The Rhode Island Workers' Compensation Act provides disability benefits to employees injured on the job or who suffer occupational diseases as a result of their job, subject to specified qualifications and limitations.[22]

[105.10] EMPLOYMENT–AT–WILL DEVELOPMENTS

Rhode Island courts have consistently refused to recognize some of the developing exceptions to the employment-at-will doctrine, as of this writing. Additional consideration, aside from the performance of regular employment duties, is necessary to remove an employee from at-will status.[23]

NOTES TO CHAPTER 105

1. Rhode Island General Laws, Section 36-11-1, *et seq.*
2. Rhode Island General Laws, Section 28-9.4-1, *et seq.*
3. Rhode Island General Laws, Section 28-9.3-9.
4. Rhode Island General Laws, Section 28-9.1-2, *et seq.*
5. Rhode Island General Laws, Section 28-9.2-2, *et seq.*
6. Rhode Island General Laws, Section 28-10-2, *et seq.*
7. Rhode Island General Laws, Section 11-38-1.
8. Rhode Island General Laws, Section 11-11-4.
9. Rhode Island General Laws, Sections 28-10-7 and 28-10-8.
10. Rhode Island General Laws, Section 28-10-10, *et seq.*
11. Rhode Island General Laws, Section 28-10-13.
12. Rhode Island General Laws, Section 28-5-7, *et seq.*
13. Rhode Island General Laws, Section 28-6.1-1.
14. Rhode Island General Laws, Section 28-6.2-1.
15. Rhode Island General Laws, Section 17-23-5.
16. Rhode Island Public Laws, Chapter 119 (L. 1968).
17. Rhode Island General Laws, Section 28-3-1, *et seq.*
18. Rhode Island General Laws, Section 28-14-4.
19. Rhode Island General Laws, Section 28-20-8(a).
20. Rhode Island General Laws, Section 28-44-1, *et seq.*
21. Rhode Island General Laws, Section 28-44-1, *et seq.*
22. Rhode Island General Laws, Section 28-33-1, *et seq.*
23. *Lamoureax v. Burrillville Racing Ass'n.*, 161 A.2d 213 (R.I., 1960).

106

South Carolina
Labor Laws

[106.01] LABOR RELATIONS LAWS

Grievance procedures: South Carolina laws established a State Employee Grievance Committee to serve as an administrative hearing body for state employee grievances.[1] South Carolina laws also authorize the establishment of procedures to resolve grievances of county and municipal employees relating to their employment.[2]

Right-to-work statute: Section 41-7-10 of the South Carolina Code of Laws prohibits the denial of employment to anyone on account of membership or nonmembership in a labor union or organization.

"Yellow-dog" contracts: Section 41-7-30(2) of the South Carolina Code of Laws makes it unlawful for anyone to coerce or compel any person to enter into an agreement not to join or become a member of any labor organization as a condition of employment.

[106.02] STRIKES, PICKETING, AND BOYCOTT LAWS

Unlawful assembly against political beliefs: South Carolina statutes make it unlawful for two or more persons to conspire against another with intent to injure his or her person or property because of the political opinions by the latter.[3]

Striker replacements: South Carolina statutes require employment agencies to notify applicants of any existing strike or lockout prior to sending such an applicant to a prospective employer experiencing such labor conditions.[4]

Use of detectives during strikes: South Carolina laws limit the use of private detectives in a strike situation except upon the application of the General Assembly or the Executive of the State.[5]

[106.03] MEDIATION AND ARBITRATION LAWS

Section 41-17-10, *et seq.,* of the South Carolina Code of Laws provides that the Commissioner of Labor shall investigate industrial labor disputes arising between employers and employees, attempt to ascertain the cause of such dispute, make a finding of fact in respect thereto, and endeavor to effect a settlement of such labor controversy between the parties. The South Carolina Constitution provides that the General Assembly of the state shall pass laws allowing differences to be decided by arbitrators, who shall be appointed by parties who choose to settle their controversies in such a man-ner.[6]

[106.04] REGULATION OF UNION ACTIVITIES

South Carolina statutes make is unlawful for anyone to misuse or forge a union label or other union insignia.[7] Section 41-1-60 of the South Carolina Code of Laws makes unlawful agreements which limit the transportation of goods or products by "piggyback" conveyances.

[106.05] REGULATION OF EMPLOYMENT PRACTICES

Anti-discrimination laws: South Carolina statutes prohibit discrim-ination in the employment of an individual by reason of race, religion, color, creed, sex, national origin, age, or handicap.[8]

Protection of political freedom: South Carolina statutes forbid the discharge of any person in an attempt to influence his or her vote or political decision or because of his or her political beliefs.[9]

Reemployment rights of military personnel: South Carolina laws require employers to reemploy South Carolina National Guard members upon their return from military service to their former or similar position.[10]

Discrimination against union members: Section 41-1-20 of the South Carolina Code of Laws makes it unlawful for anyone to discharge or dis-criminate in the payment of wages against any person because of his or her membership in a labor union.

Plant closings: Section 41-1-40 of the South Carolina Code of Laws requires employers to give advanced notice to their employees of any pend-ing shutdown if such employers require from their employees notice of the intent and time an employee desires to quit.

Voice stress analyzers: Section 40-53-40 of the South Carolina Code of Laws forbids the use of voice stress analyzers.

[106.06] WAGE AND HOUR LAWS

Child labor: South Carolina statutes regulate the employment of chil-dren and specify minimum age requirements in connection therewith.[11]

Payment on termination: South Carolina employers are required to pay discharged employees all wages earned within forty-eight hours of dis-charge or the next regular payday, which shall not exceed thirty days after notice is given.[12]

Garnishments: South Carolina statutes make unlawful the discharge of an employee because of garnishment proceedings against his or her wages.[13]

Medical insurance conversion: Section 38-35-946 of the South Carolina Code of Laws requires employers to notify terminating employees of their right to convert group medical insurance to individual coverage, provided the employee in question makes all payments for premiums in connection therewith.

[106.07] SAFETY AND HEALTH LAWS

General provisions: South Carolina health and safety laws require employers within the state to furnish safe employment for employees, and to furnish and use safety devices and safeguards, adopt and use methods and processes reasonably adequate to render such employment and place of employment safe, and do every other thing reasonably necessary to protect the life, health, and safety of employees.[14]

Toxic substances—right to know: Section 41-15-210, *et seq.*, of the South Carolina Code of Laws requires employers who use or manufacture toxic substances to notify employees who have been exposed to such substances in concentrations or at levels exceeding certain prescribed standards of such exposure.

[106.08] UNEMPLOYMENT COMPENSATION LAWS

The South Carolina Unemployment Compensation laws are set forth in Section 41-27-10 of the South Carolina Code of Laws and govern, among other things, the eligibility requirements of recipients of unemployment compensation benefits.

[106.09] WORKERS' COMPENSATION LAWS

Section 42-1-10, *et seq.*, of the South Carolina Code of Laws sets forth the South Carolina Workmen's Compensation Act. The statute provides disability benefits to employees injured on the job or who suffer occupational diseases as a result of their job, subject to specified qualifications and limitations.[15]

[106.10] EMPLOYMENT–AT–WILL DEVELOPMENTS

South Carolina courts continue to apply the employment-at-will rule in discharge matters.[16] However, in one case, the South Carolina Supreme Court ruled that an employee who had been discharged immediately after taking a lie detector test, suggesting that he had been terminated for wrongful conduct, stated a cause of action for defamation against the employer.[17] In another case, the South Carolina Supreme Court recognized a public policy exception to the employment-at-will doctrine, where an employee was discharged for honoring a subpoena to appear at a state employment security commission hearing.[18]

NOTES TO CHAPTER 106

1. South Carolina Public Laws, H.B. 2626 (L. 1982).
2. Code of Laws of South Carolina, Section 8-17-110.
3. Code of Laws of South Carolina, Section 16-101.
4. Code of Laws of South Carolina, Section 41-25-50(c).
5. Article 8, Section 9, of the South Carolina Constitution.
6. Article 6, Section 1, of the South Carolina Constitution.
7. Code of Laws of South Carolina, Section 39-15-110, *et seq.*
8. Code of Laws of South Carolina, Sections 1-13-80 and 43-33-550.
9. Code of Laws of South Carolina, Section 16-17-560.
10. Code of Laws of South Carolina, Section 25-1-2310.
11. Code of Laws of South Carolina, Section 41-13-110, *et seq.*
12. Code of Laws of South Carolina, Section 41-11-170.
13. Code of Laws of South Carolina, Section 37-5-106.
14. Code of Laws of South Carolina, Section 41-15-80.
15. Code of Laws of South Carolina, Section 42-1-10, *et seq.*
16. *Todd v. South Carolina Farm Bureau Mut. Ins. Co.,* 278 S.E.2d 607 (S.C., 1981).
17. *Tyler v. Macks Stores of South Carolina, Inc.,* 272 S.E.2d 633 (S.C. S.Ct., 1980).
18. *Ludwick v. This Minute of Carolina, Inc.,* Case no. 22408 (S.C. S.Ct., 1985).

107

South Dakota
Labor Laws

[107.01] LABOR RELATIONS LAWS

South Dakota Labor Relations Act: South Dakota laws provide that South Dakota employers, unless otherwise excluded, are required to recognize and bargain with unions properly certified as representatives of their employees.[1] The statute also provides for the machinery to conduct representation elections and procedures to process unfair labor practice charges against employers and labor organizations.[2]

Public employees' bargaining rights: South Dakota laws establish a framework of employer-employee relations by providing a uniform and orderly method for collective bargaining between public employers and certain public employees. The statute also establishes guidelines to process representation petitions for elections, forbids certain unfair labor practices, and prohibits strikes by public employees.[3]

Right-to-work statute: South Dakota statutes prohibit the denial of employment to anyone on account of membership or nonmembership in a labor union or organization.[4]

[107.02] STRIKES, PICKETING, AND BOYCOTT LAWS

Unlawful assembly: South Dakota laws make it unlawful whenever three or more persons assemble with intent to do an unlawful act.[5]

Unlawful interference with employment: South Dakota statutes make it unlawful for any person or firm to attempt to prevent anyone from engaging in any lawful employment within the state.[6]

Unlawful picketing: South Dakota laws make it unlawful for anyone to picket another in his or her work or employment by force, threats, violence, or intimidation or in such a manner as to obstruct or interfere with the free use of public streets, sidewalks, or public ways.[7]

Strike notice: South Dakota statutes provide that an employer, or his or her employees, may file at a public employment office a signed statement with regard to a strike or lockout affecting their trade.[8]

[107.03] MEDIATION AND ARBITRATION LAWS

Section 1 of the South Dakota Uniform Arbitration Act provides that any written agreement to submit an existing controversy to arbitration shall be recognized as valid, enforceable, and irrevocable, except on such grounds as exist at law or equity for the revocation thereof. South Dakota statutes require the Commissioner of Labor, when so requested by either party, to provide the voluntary conciliation of labor disputes between employers and employees.[9]

[107.04] REGULATION OF UNION ACTIVITIES

South Dakota statutes make it unlawful for anyone to misuse or forge a union label or other union insignia.[10] South Dakota laws require labor unions operating within the state to file certain financial statements with the South Dakota Secretary of State upon notification of and order of the State Commissioner of Labor.[11] South Dakota's Union Regulation Act forbids any person to solicit or accept money or gratuities for services rendered to any employer of the class mentioned in the statute by reason of his or her labor union connections or associations.[12]

[107.05] REGULATION OF EMPLOYMENT PRACTICES

Anti-discrimination laws: Section 20-13-1, *et seq.*, of the South Dakota Codified Laws forbids discrimination in employment on the basis of race, creed, religion, sex, ancestry, or national origin.

Protection of political freedom: South Dakota laws forbid employers to attempt to coerce or influence the voting and political decisions of their employees through threats of discharge or other such reprisals.[13]

Jury duty: Section 16-13-41.1 of the South Dakota Codified Laws prohibits an employer from attempting to deprive an employee of his or her employment because the employee serves as a juror or attends court as a prospective juror.

Access to personnel records (state employees): South Dakota statutes provide that the State Personnel Commissioner shall, at reasonable times and intervals, and upon proper application of employees, permit State Career Service Employees to inspect their personnel records.[14]

Military duty: Section 33-17-15 of the South Dakota Codified Laws requires South Dakota employers to reinstate returning military employees to their former or similar positions without loss of seniority, status, or pay.

Medical examination payments: Section 60-11-2 of the South Dakota Codified Laws requires employers to pay the costs of any medical examinations required of applicants or employees in connection with their employment or prospective employment.

Equal pay: South Dakota laws make it unlawful to discriminate in payment of wages on the basis of sex.[15]

[107.06] WAGE AND HOUR LAWS

Child labor: South Dakota labor laws regulate the employment of children in gainful occupations and specify minimum age requirements in connection therewith.[16] Employment certificates are required of children under 16 years of age in any factory, workshop, mine, or mercantile establishment.[17]

Voting time: Section 12-3-5 of the South Dakota Codified Laws provides that an employee eligible and registered to vote in a public election shall be excused from his or her employment not exceeding two consecutive hours, without loss of pay, to exercise such voting privileges, provided such employee does not have two consecutive hours between the time of opening and closing of polls when he or she is not working for the employer.

Payment of wages: South Dakota employers are required to pay employees their wages no less than once a month, or on regularly agreed upon days designated in advance.[18]

Payment upon termination: South Dakota employers are required to pay terminated employees earned wages within five days of separation. Employees who quit their employment must be paid all accrued wages no later than the next regular payday.[19]

[107.07] SAFETY AND HEALTH LAWS

Section 60-12-7, *et seq.*, of the South Dakota Statutes provides that every factory, mill, or workshop shall be kept clean, be properly ventilated, and at all times be kept in a sanitary condition.

[107.08] UNEMPLOYMENT COMPENSATION LAWS

The South Dakota unemployment compensation laws are set forth in 61-6-20, *et seq.*, of the South Dakota Codified Laws and govern, among other things, the eligibility requirements of recipients to unemployment compensation benefits.

[107.09] WORKERS' COMPENSATION LAWS

The South Dakota Workers' Compensation Act provides disability benefits to employees injured on the job or who suffer occupational diseases as a result of their job, subject to specified qualifications and limitations.[20] Benefits and payments are paid to employees in accordance with established schedules, the amounts and duration of which are dependent upon the gravity of the injury or disease and whether the disability is temporary or permanent and/or partial or total.

[107.10] EMPLOYMENT-AT-WILL DEVELOPMENTS

South Dakota courts have permitted some limited exceptions to the employment-at-will principle, as discussed below.

Implied contract exception: South Dakota courts have ruled that termination guidelines contained in an employee handbook create an implied contractual agreement that an employee must be discharged in conformity with such guidelines, the absence of which may sustain a cause of action for wrongful discharge.[21]

Presumption of term exception: South Dakota laws provide that the length of time adopted for wages and salary (weekly, monthly, annually) will be relevant in the determination of the term of employment between an employer and employee but should not serve as a sole presumption that the term of employment is for such period.[22] (Previous South Dakota statutes provided that an employee is presumed to be hired for such length of service as the parties adopt for payment of wages and salary.)

NOTES TO CHAPTER 107

1. South Dakota Compiled Laws, 60-9A-1, *et seq.*
2. South Dakota Compiled Laws, 60-9A-7 & 12.
3. South Dakota Compiled Laws, Section 3-18-1, *et seq.*
4. South Dakota Compiled Laws, Section 60-8-3, *et seq.*
5. South Dakota Compiled Laws, Section 22-10-1, *et seq.*
6. South Dakota Compiled Laws, Section 60-8-1.
7. South Dakota Compiled Laws, Section 60-10-9.
8. South Dakota Compiled Laws, Section 60-6-19 & 20.
9. South Dakota Compiled Laws, Section 60-10-1.
10. South Dakota Compiled Laws, Section 37-6-2.
11. South Dakota Compiled Laws, Section 60-9-6.
12. South Dakota Compiled Laws, Section 60-9-8.
13. South Dakota Compiled Laws, Section 12-26-13.
14. South Dakota Compiled Laws, Section 3-6A-31.
15. South Dakota Compiled Laws, Section 60-12-15.
16. South Dakota Compiled Laws, Section 60-12-2, *et seq.*

17. South Dakota Compiled Laws, Section 60-12-4.

18. South Dakota Compiled Laws, Section 60-11-9.

19. South Dakota Compiled Laws, Section 60-11-10.

20. South Dakota Compiled Laws, Section 62-5-1, *et seq.*

21. *Osterkamp v. Alkota Manufacturing, Inc.,* 332 N.W.2d 275 (S.D., 1983).

22. South Dakota Public Laws, S.B. 263 (L., 1985).

108

Tennessee
Labor Laws

[108.01]   LABOR RELATIONS LAWS

Professional Negotiations Act: Section 49-5-601, *et seq.*, of the Tennessee Code Annotated sets forth the Tennessee Professional Negotiations Act. The act establishes a framework of employer–employee relations by providing a method for collective bargaining between certificated school employees and boards of education.[1] It also establishes guidelines to process representation petitions for elections, makes unlawful certain unfair labor practices, and forbids strikes.[2]

Public transit employees' bargaining rights: Tennessee statutes empower municipalities, counties, and transit authorities to make fair and equitable arrangements for the protection of employees of existing public transportation systems.[3] The statute provides that such protection of public transit employees may include such provisions as may be necessary for the preservation of rights, privileges, and benefits under existing collective bargaining agreements, the continuation of collective bargaining rights, protection of certain individual rights, assurances of employment to employees of acquired mass transportation systems, and training and retraining programs.[4]

Collective bargaining sunshine laws: Section 8-44-201 of the Tennessee Code Annotated provides that labor negotiations between representatives of public employees unions or professional associations and representatives of a local or state governmental entity shall be open to the public.

Right-to-work statute: Tennessee laws prohibit the denial of employment to anyone because of membership or nonmembership in a labor union or organization.[5]

[108.02]   STRIKES, PICKETING, AND BOYCOTT LAWS

Use of armed guards during strikes: Tennessee statutes make it unlawful for any person to hire armed guards for any kind of purpose without a permit from the governor of the state, provided that nothing contained in the statute shall be construed to interfere with the right of any person to guard or protect his or her private property or private interests, as is now provided by law.[6]

"Sit-down" strikes: Section 50-1-303 of the Tennessee Code Annotated makes it unlawful for employees to cease work and refuse to leave the employer's premises within a reasonable time thereafter.

Strike replacement notices: Tennessee statutes require employment agencies within the state to notify an applicant of an existing strike or lockout prior to sending such an applicant to a prospective employer experiencing such labor conditions.[7] Section 50-1-102(a) of the Tennessee Code Annotated requires advertisements and solicitations for employment applicants to state the existence of a strike, lockout, or other labor trouble at the place of the proposed employment.

Unlawful inducement for employment: Tennessee statutes make it unlawful for any person or firm to attempt to induce an employee of another to breach his or her current employment obligations.[8]

[108.03] MEDIATION AND ARBITRATION LAWS

Section 29-5-101, *et seq.,* of the Tennessee Code Annotated comprises the Tennessee General Arbitration Act. The statute provides that all causes of action within the state, whether there be a lawsuit pending or not, may be submitted to the decision of one or more arbitrators, except where one of the parties to the controversy is an infant or of unsound mind or where claims relative to an estate in real property are in dispute.[9]

[108.04] REGULATION OF UNION ACTIVITIES

Tennessee law makes it unlawful for any person to misuse or counterfeit a union label or union insignia.[10]

[108.05] REGULATION OF EMPLOYMENT PRACTICES

Anti-discrimination laws: Tennessee laws forbid discrimination in employment on the basis of race, creed, color, religion, sex, age, or national origin,[11] and physical or mental handicap.[12]

Freedom of political activities: Section 2-19-34 of the Tennessee Code Annotated makes it unlawful for any person to attempt to influence the vote of any elector by discharging or threatening to discharge him or her from employment.

Jury service: Tennessee employers are forbidden to deprive any employee of his or her employment because of jury service. Employers are required to pay the difference between jury pay and regular wages.[13]

Unlawful enticement: Tennessee laws forbid any person or firm to induce or entice away employees under contract or in the employment of another before the expiration of the term of employment.[14]

Selection of physician: Section 50-1-302(a) of the Tennessee Code Annotated prohibits any employer to dictate, or interfere with, an employee's right to select his or her own family physician.

Access to personnel records (state employees): Tennessee laws provide that any state employee is entitled to have access, at any reasonable time, to his or her personnel files.[15] Superintendents of public schools have the duty to grant any certificated employee access, at any reasonable time, to his or her personnel files.[16]

Military duty: Section 58-1-604 of the Tennessee Code Annotated makes it unlawful to discharge or to refuse to reinstate a member of the National Guard because of military training or service.

Medical examination payments: Section 50-1-302 of the Tennessee Code Annotated requires employers to pay for the costs of any pre-employment medical examinations.

Equal pay: Section 50-2-202 of the Tennessee Code Annotated makes it unlawful to discriminate in payment of wages on the basis of sex.

[108.06]   WAGE AND HOUR LAWS

Child labor: The Tennessee child labor laws regulate the employment of children and specify minimum age requirements in connection therewith.[17]

Voting time: Tennessee statutes provide that an employee, eligible and registered to vote at public elections, shall be excused from his or her employment not exceeding three consecutive hours, without loss of pay, to exercise such voting privileges, provided such employee does not have three consecutive hours between the time of opening and closing of the polls when he or she is not working for the employer.[18]

Payment of wages: Section 50-2-103(a) of the Tennessee Code Annotated requires private employers with five or more workers to pay employees not later than the twentieth day of the month those wages earned prior to the first day of the same month and not later than the fifth day of the month those wages earned prior to the sixteenth day of the preceding month.

Medical coverage conversion: Section 56-7-1501 of the Tennessee Code Annotated provides that terminating employees are to be permitted to convert employer group medical insurance coverage to their own individual coverage, provided such employees assume payment of the premiums thereof.

Wage assignments for child support: Section 50-2-105 of the Tennessee Code Annotated forbids the discharge of an employee because his or her wages have been subjected to a wage assignment to pay child support.

[108.07]   HEALTH AND SAFETY LAWS

General provisions: Section 50-3-105 of the Tennessee Code Annotated requires employers within the state to furnish employees a place of employment free from recognized hazards and to comply with regulations and standards promulgated under the act.

Toxic substances—right to know: Tennessee statutes require employers to provide certain training and education to employees who may be exposed to hazardous substances as well as to inform employees about the properties of such substances, etc.[19]

[108.08]   UNEMPLOYMENT COMPENSATION LAWS

Tennessee statutes generally provide that unemployment benefits are available to unemployed workers who

- have properly registered for work at an unemployment office
- have properly applied for unemployment benefits
- are able to work, available for work, and actively seeking work
- have satisfied their required base period, and
- are not otherwise disqualified under other provisions of the Act[20]

[108.09]   WORKERS' COMPENSATION LAWS

The Tennessee Workers' Compensation Act provides disability benefits to employees injured on the job or who suffer occupational diseases as a result of their job, subject to specified qualifications and limitations.[21]

[108.10]   EMPLOYMENT–AT–WILL DEVELOPMENTS

General rule: Tennessee courts have continued to adhere to the employment-at-will principle,[22] although some erosion of the doctrine has occurred.

Public policy exception: The Tennessee Supreme Court has ruled that the discharge of an employee for filing a workers' compensation claim is a violation of public policy and such an employee may recover punitive damages for wrongful dismissal.[23]

Implied contract exception: Although the Tennessee courts have not officially recognized the implied contract exception to the at-will rule, as of this writing,[24] one Tennessee court has suggested, by implication, that an employee handbook could give rise to an implied employment contract, under certain conditions.[25]

NOTES TO CHAPTER 108

1. Tennessee Code Annotated, Section 49-5-601, *et seq.*
2. Tennessee Code Annotated, Section 49-5-601, *et seq.*
3. Tennessee Code Annotated, Section 7-56-102.
4. Tennessee Code Annotated, Section 7-56-102.
5. Tennessee Code Annotated, Section 50-1-201.
6. Tennessee Code Annotated, Section 50-1-102(d), (e).
7. Tennessee Code Annotated, Section 50-8-111.
8. Tennessee Code Annotated, Section 47-1706.
9. Tennessee Code Annotated, Section 29-5-101.
10. Tennessee Code Annotated, Section 47-25-407, *et seq.*
11. Tennessee Code Annotated, Section 4-21-105, *et seq.*
12. Tennessee Code Annotated, Section 8-50-103.
13. Tennessee Code Annotated, Section 22-4-108.
14. Tennessee Code Annotated, Section 50-1-101(a).
15. Tennessee Code Annotated, Section 8-50-108.
16. Tennessee Code Annotated, Section 49-224.
17. Tennessee Code Annotated, Section 50-5-103, *et seq.*
18. Tennessee Code Annotated, Section 2-1-108, *et seq.*
19. Tennessee Public Laws, Ch. 417 (L. 1985).
20. Tennessee Code Annotated, Section 50-7-301, *et seq.*
21. Tennessee Code Annotated, Section 50-6-101, *et seq.*
22. *Whittaker v. Care-More, Inc.,* 621 S.W.2d 395 (Tenn. App., 1981).
23. *Clanton v. Cain-Sloan Co.,* 117 LRRM 2789 (Tenn., 1984).
24. See, for example: *Gee v. Federal Express Corp.,* 710 F.2d 1181 (CA-6, 1983), applying Tennessee law.
25. *Hamby v. Genesco,* 627 S.W.2d 373 (Tenn. App., 1981).

109

Texas Labor Laws

[109.01]   LABOR RELATIONS LAWS

Fire and Police Employee Relations Act: Texas statutes accord collective bargaining rights to firefighters and police officers within the state. The statute provides for impasse guidelines, voluntary mediation, and prohibitions against police and firefighter strikes.[1]

General right to organize: Texas statutes provide that it shall be lawful for employees within the state to form trade unions in their respective pursuits and employments.[2]

Right-to-work statute: Texas statutes prohibit the denial of employment to anyone because of membership or nonmembership in a labor union or organization.[3]

[109.02]   STRIKES, PICKETING, AND BOYCOTT LAWS

Secondary boycotts: Section 1 of Article 5154F of the Texas Statutes makes it unlawful for anyone to establish or participate in a secondary boycott.

Employment of armed detectives: Texas statutes forbid the employment of nonresident armed detectives.[4]

Public employee strikes: Section 3 of Article 5154c of the Texas Statutes declares it to be against public policy for public employees to engage in strikes against the state of Texas or any political subdivision thereof.

Strikes against public utilities: Texas laws make it unlawful for any person to picket the premises of a public utility within the state with the intent to disrupt the service of such utility or to prevent the maintenance thereof.[5]

Mass picketing: Section 1 of Article 5154d of the Texas Statutes makes it unlawful for any person to engage in mass picketing.

Interference with employment: Texas statutes forbid any person or firm to interfere with the lawful employment of another.[6]

[109.03]   MEDIATION AND ARBITRATION LAWS

Texas laws provide that it shall be lawful to submit any labor controversy or dispute to a board of arbitrators who shall be empowered to hear, adjudicate, and determine the same, upon mutual consent of all parties to the grievance or dispute.[7] The Texas Labor Arbitration Act further specifies procedures and guidelines for such boards of arbitrators.[8]

[109.04] REGULATION OF UNION ACTIVITIES

Texas statutes make it unlawful for anyone to misuse or forge a union label or other union insignia.[9] Texas statutes make unlawful agreements that restrict the transportation of goods and products by ''piggyback'' conveyances.[10] Texas laws require every labor union operating within the state to file certain reports with the Secretary of Labor.[11] Section 10 of Article 5154a of the Texas Statutes requires a union to accord a fair hearing to its members prior to their expulsion. Texas statutes require all labor union organizers operating within the state to register with the Secretary of State before soliciting membership on behalf of their unions.[12]

Section 4b of Article 5154a of the Texas Statutes makes it unlawful for any labor union to make any financial contribution to any political party or to any persons running for political office as a part of the campaign expenses of such individual. Texas laws provide that a labor organization whose members strike against any person or firm shall be liable in damages for any loss resulting to such party in the event such strike is held to be a breach of contract by a court of competent jurisdiction.[13]

[109.05] REGULATION OF EMPLOYMENT PRACTICES

Anti-discrimination laws: Texas statutes prohibit discrimination in the employment of an individual by reason of race, religion, color, sex, age, handicap, or national origin.[14] Texas laws also forbid discrimination in employment against mentally retarded persons.[15]

Protection of military personnel: Texas laws prohibit any employer from terminating a permanent employee who is a member of the State Military Forces because the employee is ordered to active military duty.[16] Such employees are also entitled to reinstatement upon their return from such military duty.[17]

Jury service: Texas laws prohibit the discharge of an employee because of his or her jury service.[18]

Blacklisting: Texas employers are forbidden to maintain a blacklist or to notify any other employer that they have blacklisted an employee, or former employees, for the purpose of preventing such worker from receiving employment.[19]

Whistle-blowing statute (public employees): Section 16(a) of Article 6252 of the Texas Statutes forbids the discharge of a public employee for reporting suspected violations of laws to appropriate law enforcement authorities.

Voice stress analyzers: Section 4 of Article 4413 of the Texas Statutes forbids the use of voice stress analyzers and other such truth detection devices that do not record a visual cardiovascular and respiratory response.

Political activities: Texas laws make it unlawful to refuse to permit employees to attend local or state political conventions when they have been chosen as duly constituted delegates.[20]

Service letters: Article 5196 of the Texas Statutes requires employers to provide service letters to discharged employees, stating the true cause of discharge within ten days after demand for such service letter.

Equal pay (public employees): Texas statutes provide that there shall be no distinction in compensation on the basis of sex when performing public service for the state.[21]

[109.06]   WAGE AND HOUR LAWS

Child labor: Texas child labor laws regulate the employment of children in gainful occupations and specify minimum age requirements in connection therewith.[22]

Voting time: Texas laws require employers to permit an employee time off from employment to vote in a public election, and wages for such voting time may not be deducted from the employee's pay.[23]

Payment of wages: Texas employers shall pay those employees exempt from the overtime provisions of the Federal Fair Labor Standards Act earned wages not less than once per month, and all other employees earned wages no less than twice per month.[24]

Payment upon termination: Texas statutes require the payment to terminated nonrailroad employees all wages due within six days of demand by the separated employee.[25] Railroad employees who separate from a company must be paid within fifteen days of demand.[26]

Wage assignments: Texas laws make it unlawful to discharge or otherwise discriminate against an employee because of an assignment of wages.[27]

[109.07]   SAFETY AND HEALTH LAWS

Texas health and safety laws require employers within the state to furnish safe employment for employees, and to furnish and use safety devices and safeguards, adopt and use methods and processes reasonably adequate to render such employment and place of employment safe and do every other thing reasonably necessary to protect the life, health, and safety of employees.[28]

[109.08] UNEMPLOYMENT COMPENSATION LAWS

The Texas unemployment compensation laws make certain benefits available to unemployed workers who

- have properly registered for work at an unemployment office
- have properly applied for unemployment benefits
- are able to work, available for work, and actively seeking work, and
- are not otherwise disqualified under other provisions of the Act[29]

[109.09] WORKERS' COMPENSATION LAWS

The Texas Workers' Compensation Act generally provides disability benefits to employees injured on the job or who suffer certain occupational diseases as a result of their job, subject to specified qualifications and limitations.[30] Article 8307c of the Texas Statutes prohibits the discharge of an employee in retaliation of his or her filing a workers' compensation claim.

[109.10] EMPLOYMENT–AT–WILL DEVELOPMENTS

Texas courts have recognized some limited exceptions to the employment-at-will doctrine, as noted below.

Public policy exception: A Texas court has recognized a cause of action by an employee who was discharged for refusal to pump bilges of a vessel at a location where it was forbidden by law.[31]

Implied contract exception: Texas courts have generally refused to permit a cause of action based on the theory that the language in an employee handbook may constitute an implied employment contract. However, one court has held that an employee handbook that lists dischargeable offenses implies that discharge must be for just cause.[32] In another case, a Texas Court of Appeals ruled that supervisory statements that promise job security may create an implied employment contract, requiring just cause to discharge.[33]

NOTES TO CHAPTER 109

1. Texas Statutes, Article 5154(e)-1, Section 1, *et seq.*
2. Texas Public Laws, Article 5152, (P.L. 1899).

3. Vernon's Texas Statutes, Article 5207a, Section 2.

4. Texas Statutes, Article 5207.

5. Texas Statutes, Article 1446a, Section 3.

6. Texas Statutes, Article 5154d, Section 2.

7. Texas Public Laws, Article 239 (L. 1895).

8. Texas Public Laws, Article 239 (L. 1895).

9. Texas Public Laws, Article 1061 (L. 1895).

10. Texas Statutes, Article 1690e.

11. Texas Statutes, Article 5154a, Section 3.

12. Texas Statutes, Article 5154a, Section 5.

13. Texas Statutes, Article 5154b.

14. Texas Statutes, Article 5221K, Section 1, *et seq.*

15. Texas Statutes, Article 5547-300, Section 9.

16. Texas Statutes, Article 5765, Section 7A.

17. Texas Statutes, Article 5765, Section 7A.

18. Texas Statutes, Article 5207b.

19. Texas Statutes, Article 5196, *et seq.*

20. Texas Election Code, Article 13.34a.

21. Texas Statutes, Section 6825.

22. Texas Public Laws, Chapter 531 (L. 1981).

23. Texas Election Code, Section 15.14 of Title 9.

24. Texas Public Laws, H.B. 79 (L. 1983).

25. Texas Statutes, Articles 5156, 5157, & 5158.

26. Texas Statutes, Article 6431.

27. West's Texas Family Code, Section 14.091(i).

28. Texas Statutes, Article 5182a, Section 10.23.

29. Texas Statutes, Article 5221b, Section 2, *et seq.*

30. Texas Statutes, Article 8306, Section 1, *et seq.*

31. *Sabine Pilots, Inc. v. Hauck,* 687 S.W.2d 733 (Tex. Ct. App., 1985).

32. *Reynolds Mfg. Co. v. Mendoza,* 644 S.W.2d 536 (Tex. Ct. App., 1982).

33. *Johnson v. Ford Motor Co.,* 690 S.W.2d 90 (Tex. Ct. of App., 1985).

110

Utah
Labor Laws

[110.01] LABOR RELATIONS LAWS

Utah Labor Relations Act: Utah statutes provide for a uniform basis for recognizing the right of employees to join labor organizations and to be represented by such organizations in collective bargaining.[1] The Utah Labor Relations Act prohibits certain conduct on the part of employers, employees, and employee representatives.[2] The statute also prescribes guidelines to determine appropriate bargaining units and bargaining agents.[3]

Firefighters' bargaining rights: Section 34-20a-1 of the Utah Code Annotated provides for recognition of firefighters' rights to organize and specifies procedures to resolve labor disputes and collective bargaining issues.

Rights of labor: The Utah Constitution provides that the rights of labor shall have just protection through laws circulated to promote the industrial welfare of the state.[4]

Right-to-work law: Utah statutes prohibit the denial of employment to anyone because of membership or nonmembership in a labor union or organization.[5]

"Yellow-dog" contracts: Section 34-1-24 of the Utah Code Annotated makes it unlawful for anyone to coerce or compel any person to enter into an agreement not to join or become a member of any labor organization as a condition of employment.

[110.02] STRIKES, PICKETING, AND BOYCOTT LAWS

Anti-injunction statutes: Utah statutory laws restrict the power of Utah courts to issue injunctions against peaceable picketing and legally protected strike activity.[6]

Unlawful assembly: Section 76-9-101 of the Utah Code Annotated provides that any use of force or violence that disturbs the public peace is unlawful.

Interference with employment: Utah statutes make it unlawful for anyone to use force, threats, or other means of coercion or intimidation to prevent any person from engaging in any lawful occupation at any place he or she sees fit.[7]

Sabotage: Section 76-8-802 of the Utah Code Annotated makes it unlawful for anyone to maliciously or intentionally damage or injure another's real or personal property.

Employment of armed guards: The Utah Constitution forbids any person or firm to bring any armed persons into the state for the preservation of the peace, or the suppression of domestic troubles, without authority of law.[8]

Deputized employees during strikes: Section 34-19-12 of the Utah Code Annotated makes it unlawful to deputize employees of any employer whose employees are on strike for any purpose arising from or in connection with such strike.

[110.03] MEDIATION AND ARBITRATION LAWS

Utah laws provide that two or more parties may agree to submit to arbitration any controversy existing between them, which agreement to arbitrate such controversy shall be valid and enforceable, and no party shall have the right to revoke the submission of such matters to arbitration, except upon such grounds as exist at law and equity.[9] Section 35-1-16(5) of the Utah Code Annotated provides that it shall be the duty of the State Industrial Commission to promote the voluntary arbitration, mediation, and conciliation of labor disputes between employers and employees. Utah laws also provide a grievance procedure for state employees and establish guidelines for the appointment of a Grievance Hearing Examiner to hear and adjudicate grievance issues of state employees.[10]

[110.04] REGULATION OF UNION ACTIVITIES

Utah statutes make it unlawful for anyone to misuse or forge a union label or other union insignia.[11] Any individual who falsely alters, counterfeits, or forges any union card with intent to defraud another is guilty of a forgery.[12] Section 34-34-7 of the Utah Code Annotated makes it unlawful for any person to exact, by threat or coercion, any money, tribute, or support whatsoever from any person or to induce him or her by threats or coercion to join any organization.

[110.05] REGULATION OF EMPLOYMENT PRACTICES

Anti-discrimination laws: Section 35-35-6, *et seq.,* of the Utah Code Annotated prohibits discrimination in the employment of an individual by reason of race, religion, color, sex, national origin, ancestry, handicap, or age.

Protection of political freedom: Utah employers are forbidden to attempt to influence the political decisions of their employees by threat of discharge or loss of employment.[13]

Polygraph restrictions: No Utah employer shall demand any applicant for employment to take a lie detector test as a condition of employment, without the applicant's consent.[14]

Blacklisting: Utah employers are prohibited from maintaining a blacklist or notifying any other employer that any worker has been blacklisted for the purpose of preventing such worker from receiving employment.[15]

Access to personnel records (public employees): Utah statutes provide that the state of Utah shall, at reasonable times and intervals, and upon proper application of a state employee, permit such employee to inspect his or her personnel records.[16]

Military duty: Section 39–1–36 of the Utah Code Annotated forbids deprivation of employment because of National Guard duty.

Medical examination payments: Section 34-33-1 of the Utah Code Annotated requires employers to pay the cost of any pre-employment medical examination.

Equal pay: Section 34-35-6 of the Utah Code Annotated makes it an unfair employment practice to discriminate in matters of compensation against employees because of race, color, sex, religion, ancestry, or national origin.

[110.06] WAGE AND HOUR LAWS

Child labor: Utah's Uniform Child Labor Act regulates the employment of children and specifies minimum age requirements in connection therewith.[17]

Voting time: Utah statutes provide that an employee, eligible and registered to vote in a public election, shall be excused from his employment not exceeding two consecutive hours, to exercise such voting privileges.[18]

Payment of wages: Section 34-28-3 of the Utah Code Annotated requires employers to pay wages to employees at least twice each month on regular days, announced in advance.

Payment upon termination: Utah employers are required to pay discharged employees their earned wages within twenty-four hours.[19] An employee who voluntarily resigns his or her job is due earned wages no later than seventy-two hours thereafter.[20]

Garnishments: Section 70B-5-106 of the Utah Code Annotated makes unlawful any discharge by reason of an employee being subjected to garnishment for any one indebtedness.

[110.07] SAFETY AND HEALTH LAWS

Utah statutes require employers to furnish a safe and healthful place of employment for their employees to work and to furnish and use safety devices and safeguards and to adopt and use practices, methods, operations, and processes that are reasonably adequate to render a safe and healthful work environment.[21]

[110.08] UNEMPLOYMENT COMPENSATION LAWS

The Utah unemployment compensation laws are set forth in Section 35-4-1, *et seq.,* of the Utah Code Annotated and govern, among other things, the eligibility requirements of recipients of unemployment compensation benefits.

[110.09] WORKERS' COMPENSATION LAWS

Section 35-1-1, *et seq.,* of the Utah Code Annotated sets forth the Utah Workmen's Compensation Act. The statute provides disability benefits to employees injured on the job or who suffer occupational diseases as a result of their job, subject to specified qualifications and limitations.[22]

[110.10] EMPLOYMENT–AT–WILL DEVELOPMENTS

Utah courts have been most reluctant to recognize exceptions to the employment-at-will rule as of this writing. Thus, the general rule prevails in Utah that an employee-at-will may be terminated at any time for any cause.[23]

NOTES TO CHAPTER 110

1. Utah Code Annotated, Section 34-20-7.
2. Utah Code Annotated, Section 34-20-8.
3. Utah Code Annotated, Section 34-20-1, *et seq.*
4. Utah Constitution, Article XVI, Section 1.
5. Utah Code Annotated, Section 34-34-1, *et seq.*
6. Utah Code Annotated, Section 34-19-1.

7. Utah Code Annotated, Section 34-2-3.
8. Utah Constitution, Article XII, Section 16.
9. Utah Code Annotated, Section 78-31-1, *et seq.*
10. Utah Public Laws, S. B. 133 (L. 1977).
11. Utah Code Annotated, Section 76-10-1002.
12. Utah Code Annotated, Section 76-10-1002.
13. Utah Code Annotated, Sections 20-13-6 and 20-13-7.
14. Utah Code Annotated, Section 34-37-16.
15. Utah Code Annotated, Section 34-24-1.
16. Utah Code Annotated, Sections 67-18-1, 63-2-66.
17. Utah Code Annotated, Section 34-23-1, *et seq.*
18. Utah Code Annotated, Section 20-13-18.
19. Utah Code Annotated, Section 34-28-5(1).
20. Utah Code Annotated, Section 34-28-5(2).
21. Utah Code Annotated, Section 35-9-5.
22. Utah Code Annotated, Section 35-1-1, *et seq.*
23. *Bihlmaier v. Carson,* 630 P.2d 790 (Utah, 1979).

111

Vermont
Labor Laws

Vermont Labor Relations Law: Vermont statutes provide that employers with five or more employees, other than employers and employees specifically exempted, and excluding the state and subdivisions thereof, must recognize and bargain in good faith with unions properly certified as representatives of their employees.[1] The statute provides for the machinery to conduct representation elections and procedures to process unfair labor practice charges against employers and labor organizations.[2]

State employees' bargaining rights: Vermont statutes provide for a uniform basis for recognizing the right of state employees to join labor organizations and to be represented by such organizations in collective bargaining.[3] The statute prohibits certain conduct of public employers and state employees.[4] The statute also prescribes guidelines to determine appropriate bargaining units and bargaining agents, as well as a process for resolving labor disputes.[5]

Teachers' bargaining rights: Vermont statutes accord teachers the right to join, assist, or participate in any teachers' organization of their choosing.[6] The statute also requires good faith negotiations between school boards and the recognized teacher organization.[7]

Vermont Municipal Labor Relations Act: Title 21, Section 172, *et seq.,* of the Vermont Statutes Annotated provides that municipal employees shall have the right to form, join or assist employee organizations and bargain collectively.

Nonright-to-work policy: Union security (union shop) clauses are permissible in the state of Vermont inasmuch as Vermont has not adopted a right-to-work statute pursuant to Section 14(b) of the Labor Management Relations Act.

[111.02] STRIKES, PICKETING, AND BOYCOTT LAWS

Unlawful assembly: Vermont statutes make it unlawful for three or more persons to assemble to do an unlawful act against one's person or property or against the public interest, or to fail to disperse from a riot after being commanded to do so by a peace officer.[8]

Interference with employment: Title 13, Section 931, of the Vermont Statutes Annotated forbids anyone to threaten violence or injury to another person with intent to prevent his or her employment.

"**Sit-down**" **strikes:** Title 13, Section 933, of the Vermont Statutes Annotated makes it unlawful for three or more persons to conspire together with the intent to occupy the premises of an employer without the consent of the management thereof.

[111.03] MEDIATION AND ARBITRATION LAWS

Title 21, Section 521, *et seq.,* of the Vermont Statutes Annotated declares it to be the policy of the state to provide full and adequate facilities for the fair and efficient settlement of disputes between private employers and employees or their representatives. The statute created the State Board of Labor Mediation and Arbitration whose duty is to resolve labor disputes through the process of mediation and voluntary arbitration.[9]

[111.04] REGULATION OF UNION ACTIVITIES

Vermont statutes make it unlawful for anyone to misuse or forge a union label or other union insignia, or to misrepresent that employment of union labor went into the production or manufacture of goods or services.[10]

[111.05] REGULATION OF EMPLOYMENT PRACTICES

Anti-discrimination laws: Vermont statutes prohibit discrimination in the employment of an individual by reason of race, religion, color, sex, national origin, ancestry, handicap, age, or place of birth.[11]

Employment of aliens: Vermont laws forbid the employment of any alien not entitled to lawful residence in the United States unless the employer determines the alien possesses a proper certificate issued pursuant to the Federal Immigration and Naturalization Act.[12]

Jury or witness duty: Vermont employers are forbidden to deprive any employee of his or her employment because such employee receives a summons or subpoena to serve as a witness, responds thereto, serves as a juror, or attends court for prospective jury service.[13]

Military duty: Employees who are duly qualified members of the reserve components of the Armed Forces are entitled to leaves of absence from their employment up to fifteen days in any one calendar year to receive military training.[14]

Access to personnel records (public employees): Vermont statutes provide that all information in personnel files of an employee of any public agency shall be made available to such employee or his or her designated representative, upon proper request.[15]

Medical examination payments: Title 21, Section 301, of the Vermont Statutes Annotated requires employers to pay the cost of any medical examinations required of applicants or employees.

Political leaves of absence: Title 21, Section 496, of the Vermont Statutes Annotated requires employers to give unpaid leaves of absence to employees who serve in the state legislature, provided certain conditions are met.

Equal pay: Title 21, Section 495, of the Vermont Statutes Annotated makes it unlawful for any employer, employment agency, or labor organization to discriminate against any individual regarding rates of pay because of his or her race, color, religion, ancestry, national origin, sex, place of birth, age, or qualified handicap.

[111.06]   WAGE AND HOUR LAWS

Child labor: Vermont statutes regulate the employment of children in gainful occupations and specify minimum age requirements in connection therewith.[16]

Payment upon termination: Vermont employers are required to pay discharged employees their earned wages within seventy-two hours of discharge.[17] An employee who voluntarily resigns his or her job is due earned wages no later than the next regular payday.[18]

Garnishments: Title 12, Section 3172, of the Vermont Statutes Annotated forbids the discharge of any employee because of garnishments against his or her wages.

[111.07]   SAFETY AND HEALTH LAWS

Vermont employers are required to furnish their employees places of employment which are free from recognized hazards that are causing or are likely to cause death or physical harm to employees.[19]

[111.08]   UNEMPLOYMENT COMPENSATION LAWS

The Vermont unemployment compensation laws are set forth in Title 21, Section 1301, *et seq.,* of the Vermont Statutes Annotated and govern the eligibility requirements of recipients of unemployment compensation benefits.

[111.09] WORKERS' COMPENSATION LAWS

Title 21, Section 601, *et seq.*, of the Vermont Statutes Annotated sets forth the Vermont Workmen's Compensation Act. The statute provides disability benefits to employees injured on the job or who suffer certain occupational diseases as a result of their job, subject to specified qualifications and limitations.[20]

[111.10] EMPLOYMENT–AT–WILL DEVELOPMENTS

Vermont courts have not recognized any of the developing exceptions to the employment-at-will principle as of this writing. However, the Vermont Supreme Court has suggested that it may permit a cause of action in the future for discharges in violation of some compelling public policy.[21]

NOTES TO CHAPTER 111

1. Vermont Statutes Annotated, Title 21, Section 1501, *et seq.*
2. Vermont Statutes Annotated, Title 21, Section 1501, *et seq.*
3. Vermont Statutes Annotated, Title 27, Section 901, *et seq.*
4. Vermont Statutes Annotated, Title 27, Sections 961 and 962.
5. Vermont Statutes Annotated, Title 27, Section 901, *et seq.*
6. Vermont Public Laws, Chapter 57 (L. 1969).
7. Vermont Public Laws, Chapter 57 (L. 1969).
8. Vermont Statutes Annotated, Title 13, Section 902, *et seq.*
9. Vermont Statutes Annotated, Title 21, Section 521, *et seq.*
10. Vermont Statutes, Ch. 337, Section 7759.
11. Vermont Statutes Annotated, Title 21, Section 495.
12. Vermont Public Laws, Act 99 (L. 1977).
13. Vermont Public Laws, S.B. 98 (L. 1969).
14. Vermont Statutes Annotated, Title 21, Section 491, *et seq.*
15. Vermont Statutes Annotated, Title 1, Section 317(b)(7).
16. Vermont Statutes Annotated, Title 21, Section 431, *et seq.*
17. Vermont Statutes Annotated, Title 21, Section 342(c)(2).
18. Vermont Statutes Annotated, Title 21, Section 342(c)(1).
19. Vermont Statutes Annotated, Title 21, Section 223(a).
20. Vermont Statutes Annotated, Title 21, Section 618, *et seq.*
21. *Brower v. Holmes Transp., Inc.*, 435 A.2d 952 (Vermont, 1981); *Jones v. Keough*, 409 A.2d 581 (Vermont, 1979).

112

Virginia
Labor Laws

[112.01] LABOR RELATIONS LAWS

Right-to-work statute: Virginia statutes prohibit the denial of employment to anyone because of nonmembership in a labor union or organization.[1]

"Yellow-dog" contracts: Section 40.1-61 of the Code of Virginia makes it unlawful for anyone to compel any person to abstain or refrain from becoming a member of any labor organization as a condition of employment.

[112.02] STRIKES, PICKETING, AND BOYCOTT LAWS

Unlawful assembly: Section 18.1-254 of the Code of Virginia makes it unlawful for any person to behave in a riotous or disorderly manner in any street, highway, public building, or other such public place, or cause any unnecessary disturbance in any streetcar or other public conveyance.

Interference with employment: Virginia statutes make it unlawful for anyone to attempt to prevent any person from engaging in any lawful occupation at any place he or she sees fit.[2]

Interference with ingress or egress: Section 40.1-53 of the Code of Virginia makes it unlawful for anyone, not having a legal privilege to do so, to obstruct any public passageway.

Picketing of residence or dwelling: Virginia statutory laws forbid anyone to engage in picketing near or about the residence or dwelling place of another.[3]

Public employee strikes: Section 40.1-55 of the Code of Virginia forbids any public employee to engage in strike activity against a government entity.

Hospital strikes: Section 40.1-54(1) of the Code of Virginia declares it to be the public policy of the state that hospitals shall be free from strikes and work stoppages.[4]

Public Utilities Seizure Act: Section 56-509, *et seq.*, of the Code of Virginia specifies certain guidelines and controls in permitting the seizure of public utilities' properties during emergency conditions caused by a strike or work stoppage.

Coal Industry Seizure Act: Section 45.1-145, *et seq.*, of the Code of Virginia provides for the seizure of coal properties within the state whenever emergency conditions arise as a result of a strike or work stoppage.

787

[112.03] MEDIATION AND ARBITRATION LAWS

Section 8.01-577, *et seq.*, of the Code of Virginia provides that all persons who shall have any controversy may submit such controversy to the arbitration of any person to be mutually agreed upon by the parties and may make such submission a rule of any record in the state. Section 22.1-306, *et seq.*, of the Code of Virginia provides for a grievance procedure for regularly certified public school personnel. Similarly, Section 2.1-114.5:1 of the Code of Virginia sets forth a grievance procedure for all public employees.

[112.04] REGULATION OF UNION ACTIVITIES

Virginia statutes make it unlawful for anyone to misuse or forge a union label or other union insignia.[5] Section 40.1-76 of the Code of Virginia requires labor unions operating within the state to register every three years with the State Department of Labor and Industry. Virginia statutes declare void and unenforceable any contracts or agreements that require a shipper or carrier to pay a levied charge that is not a direct cost of transportation.[6]

[112.05] REGULATION OF EMPLOYMENT PRACTICES

Anti-discrimination laws (state employees): Section 2.1-376 of the Code of Virginia forbids discrimination in employment against any state employee or applicant because of race, color, religion, sex, or national origin by state agencies and government contractors.

Employment of aliens: Virginia laws forbid the employment of any alien not entitled to lawful residence in the United States, unless such alien possesses a permit to work, issued by the U.S. Department of Justice.[7]

Polygraph restrictions: Virginia employers are forbidden to require a prospective employee to answer questions in a polygraph test concerning his or her sexual activities, unless such activities led to a criminal conviction.[8]

Blacklisting: Virginia employers are prohibited from blacklisting employees for the purpose of preventing such employees from receiving employment with any other person.[9]

Medical examinations payments: Section 40.1-28 of the Code of Virginia makes it unlawful for any employer to require any employee or applicant to pay the cost of a medical examination or the cost of furnishing any medical records required by the employer as a condition of employment.

Arrest inquiries: Section 19.2-392.4 of the Code of Virginia forbids employers to require an applicant to disclose information concerning any arrest or criminal charge that has been expunged.

Jury duty: Virginia laws make it unlawful to discharge an employee because of his or her jury duty.[10]

Military duty: Section 44-98 of the Code of Virginia forbids an employer to interfere with the enlistment and membership rights of a National Guardsman. Section 44-93 of the Code of Virginia requires public sector employers to grant up to fifteen paid days of leave to National Guard members who are participating in annual training or duty.

Equal pay: Section 40.1-28.6 of the Code of Virginia makes it unlawful to discriminate in the payment of wages on the basis of sex.

[112.06] WAGE AND HOUR LAWS

Child labor: Virginia statutes regulate the employment of children in gainful occupations and specify certain minimum age requirements in connection therewith.[11] For example, children under 14 years of age are prohibited from being employed in streets or public places in connection with gainful employment.[12] Children under 16 years of age are restricted to certain jobs, as enumerated in the statute.[13]

Payment of wages: Section 40.1-29(b) of the Code of Virginia requires Virginia employers to pay hourly employees their earned wages no less than twice during a month.

Payment upon termination: Virginia employers are required to pay terminated employees all accrued wages no later than the next regular payday.[14]

Garnishments: Section 34-29(f) of the Code of Virginia forbids the discharge of an employee because his or her wages have been subjected to a single garnishment.

Medical insurance conversion: Virginia laws require employers to permit terminating employees to convert his or her insurance coverage under a group medical plan to individual coverage, provided certain conditions are met and the employee assumes the obligation to pay premiums for such insurance continuance.[15]

[112.07] SAFETY AND HEALTH LAWS

General provision: Section 40.1-51(a) of the Code of Virginia requires employers to furnish employees a safe place of employment free from recognized hazards that are causing or likely to cause death or physical harm to such employees.

Toxic substances—right to know: Section 40.1-51.1(c) of the Code of Virginia requires employers to inform employees of their potential exposure to toxic substances used or manufactured in the work place.

[112.08] UNEMPLOYMENT COMPENSATION LAWS

The Virginia Unemployment Compensation laws are set forth in Section 60.1-1, *et seq.*, of the Code of Virginia and govern, among other things, the eligibility requirements of recipients of unemployment compensation benefits.

[112.09] WORKERS' COMPENSATION LAWS

The Virginia Workmen's Compensation Act provides disability benefits to employees injured on the job or who suffer occupational diseases as a result of their jobs, subject to specified qualifications and limitations.[16] Virginia employers are forbidden to discharge employees for filing workers' compensation claims.[17]

[112.10] EMPLOYMENT–AT–WILL DEVELOPMENTS

The Virginia courts continue to recognize the employment-at-will principle, permitting but a few exceptions to it.

Public policy exception: A Virginia Court of Appeals has permitted a cause of action under the public policy exception to the at-will rule in a case where employees were allegedly discharged for failure to cooperate with the employer by claiming they were unduly pressured into voting for a merger in a shareholders meeting which, in turn, led to the merger being aborted.[18]

Implied contract exception: A federal court, applying Virginia laws, denied a partial summary judgment for the employer on a claim that the employer's policy of encouraging long-term employment and assurances of job security created an implied employment contract.[19]

Presumption of term exception: One Virginia court has ruled that an employee who receives compensation stated in annual terms is presumed to have an employment contract for one year, foreclosing discharge during such period except for just cause.[20]

NOTES TO CHAPTER 112

1. Code of Virginia, Section 40.1-60.

2. Code of Virginia, Section 40.1-53.

3. Virginia Public Laws, Chapter 711 (L. 1970).

4. See also Code of Virginia, Section 40.1-54(2). (However, this provision may well be in contravention of the Federal Labor-Management Relations Act and, thereby, pre-empted by it.)

5. Code of Virginia, Section 18.1-410.

6. Code of Virginia, Section 40.1-54.

7. Code of Virginia, Section 40.1-11.1.

8. Code of Virginia, Section 40.1-51.4:3.

9. Code of Virginia, Section 40.1-27.

10. Virginia Public Laws (L. 1985, C. 436).

11. Code of Virginia, Section 40.1-100, *et seq.*

12. Code of Virginia, Section 40.1-105, *et seq.*

13. Code of Virginia, Section 40.1-78, *et seq.*

14. Code of Virginia, Section 40.1-29(a).

15. Code of Virginia, Section 38.1-348.11.

16. Code of Virginia, Section 65.1-1, *et seq.*

17. Code of Virginia, Section 65.1-40.1.

18. *Bowman v. State Bank of Keysville,* 331 SE2d 799 (Va. Ct. of App. 1985).

19. *Frazier v. Colonial Williamsburg Foundation,* 574 F.Supp. 318 (E.D. Va., 1983).

20. *Hoffman Specialty Co. v. Pelouze,* 164 S.E. 397 (Va., 1932).

113

Washington
Labor Laws

General right to organize: Section 49.36.010 of the Revised Code of Washington makes it lawful for working men and women to organize themselves into labor unions.

Public employees' bargaining rights: Section 41.56.010, *et seq.*, of the Revised Code of Washington sets out the Washington Public Employment Relations Act. The act establishes a framework of employer–employee relations by providing a uniform and orderly method for collective bargaining between public employers and certain public employees.[1]

Educational Employment Relations Act: Section 41.59.010, *et seq.*, of the Revised Code of Washington prescribes collective bargaining rights of school employees of school districts within the state and establishes procedures in relation thereto.

Academic employees' bargaining rights: Washington statutes declare that academic employees in community college districts have the right to bargain collectively and that boards of trustees of such institutions shall negotiate agreements with duly recognized representatives of employee organizations.[2]

Higher education collective bargaining: Section 28B.16.100, *et seq.*, of the Revised Code of Washington accords classified personnel in institutions of higher education the right to bargain collectively.

Health-care collective bargaining: Washington laws provide that health-care employees shall have the right to organize and select collective bargaining representatives of their own choosing.[3] The statute specifies guidelines to conduct elections and process unfair labor practice charges.[4]

Marine employees' bargaining rights: Section 47.64.010, *et seq.*, of the Revised Code of Washington accords collective bargaining rights to marine employees and specifies procedures to safeguard such rights.

Port district employees' bargaining rights: Section 53.18.010, *et seq.*, of the Revised Code of Washington provides for collective bargaining between port districts and employee organizations.

Public utility employees' bargaining rights: Washington laws provide that public utility districts are authorized to enter into collective bargaining relations with their employees.[5]

Nonright-to-work policy: Union security (union shop) clauses are permissible in the state of Washington inasmuch as Washington has not adopted a right-to-work statute pursuant to Section 14(b) of the Labor Management Relations Act.

"Yellow-dog" contracts: Section 49.32.030 of the Revised Code of Washington makes it unlawful for anyone to coerce or compel any person to enter into an agreement not to join or become a member of any labor organization as a condition of employment.

[113.02] STRIKES, PICKETING, AND BOYCOTT LAWS

Anti-injunction statute: Section 49.32.011 of the Revised Code of Washington limits the power of courts to issue restraining orders and injunctions in a case involving a labor dispute, except in strict conformity with the provisions of the statute.

Injury to property: Section 9.05.060 of the Revised Code of Washington makes it unlawful for anyone to injure or destroy any property whatsoever, wherein persons are employed.

Interference with employment: Washington statutes make it unlawful for two or more persons to conspire to prevent another person from exercising any lawful trade or calling, or from doing any other lawful act.[6]

Unlawful assembly: Section 9.27.040 of the Revised Code of Washington forbids three or more persons to assemble together to do an unlawful act.

Unlawful breach of contract: Section 49.44.080 of the Revised Code of Washington makes it unlawful to willfully breach a contract of employment, the consequence of which will endanger human life, cause grievous bodily injury, or expose valuable property to destruction or serious injury.

"Sit-down" strikes: Section 9.05.070 of the Revised Code of Washington provides that it shall be unlawful for anyone to take or retain possession or control of any premises of an employer without permission or consent of the management thereof.

Strikebreakers: Section 49.44.100 makes it unlawful for any person or firm, not directly involved in a labor dispute, to recruit and bring into the state any professional strikebreakers to replace striking employees. Section 49.44.100 of the Revised Code of Washington is inapplicable to activities and services offered by or through the Washington Employment Security Department.[7]

[113.03] MEDIATION AND ARBITRATION LAWS

Washington statutes provide that any written agreement to submit an existing controversy to arbitration shall be valid, enforceable, and irrevocable, except on such grounds as exist at law or equity for the revocation thereof.[8] Section 49.08.010, *et seq.*, of the Revised Code of Washington provides for mediation and arbitration of labor disputes.

[113.04] REGULATION OF UNION ACTIVITIES

Washington statutes make it unlawful for anyone to misuse or forge a union label.[9] Section 49.44.030 of the Revised Code of Washington makes it unlawful for anyone to give or offer any compensation or gratuity to any union representative with intent to influence him or her to cause or to prevent a labor strike.

[113.05] REGULATION OF EMPLOYMENT PRACTICES

Anti-discrimination laws: Section 49.60.010, *et seq.,* of the Revised Code of Washington prohibits discrimination in the employment of an individual by reason of race, creed, color, sex, national origin, marital status, handicap, or age.

Military duty: Section 73.16.033 of the Revised Code of Washington requires employers to reemploy military personnel upon their return from military service and reinstate them to their former or similar positions without loss of seniority, status, or pay.

Polygraph restrictions: Washington employers are forbidden to require applicants and employees to submit to a lie detector or similar test or examination as a condition of employment or continued employment.[10]

Employment under false pretenses: Section 49.44.040 of the Revised Code of Washington makes it unlawful for anyone to obtain employment under false pretense.

Whistle-blowing statute (state employees): Washington statutes protect state employees from retaliation when they report what they believe to be a violation of any law, rule, or regulation of the state.[11]

Service letters: Washington laws require employers to furnish written statements to discharged employees which set forth the true reason for discharge within ten working days from an employee's request for such service letter.[12]

Blacklisting: Section 49.44.010 of the Revised Code of Washington forbids the blacklisting of employees, or former employees, in an attempt to prevent their employment elsewhere or to cause their discharge.

Equal pay: Section 49.12.175 of the Revised Code of Washington makes it unlawful to discriminate in payment of wages on the basis of sex.

[113.06] WAGE AND HOUR LAWS

Child labor: Washington statutes regulate the employment of children in gainful occupations and specify minimum age requirements in connection therewith.[13] Washington statutes provide that the State Industrial Welfare Committee has the responsibility of issuing employment certificates for children between the ages of 16 and 18.[14]

Payment upon termination: Washington employers are required to pay terminated employees their earned wages, in full, no later than the end of the established pay period.[15]

Garnishments: Section 7.33.160 of the Revised Code of Washington forbids the discharge of an employee because his or her wages have been subjected to three or less garnishments for separate debts within a one-year period.

[113.07] SAFETY AND HEALTH LAWS

General provisions: Washington statutes require employers within the state to furnish employees a place of employment free from recognized hazards that are causing or are likely to cause serious injury or death to such employees.[16]

Toxic substances—right to know: Washington statutes require employers to furnish employees a copy of a material safety data sheet and similar information for their work area, upon request from employees in such work areas.[17]

[113.08] UNEMPLOYMENT COMPENSATION LAWS

The Washington Unemployment Compensation laws are set forth in Section 50.20.001, *et seq.,* of the Revised Code of Washington and govern, among other things, the eligibility requirements of recipients of unemployment compensation benefits.

[113.09] WORKERS' COMPENSATION LAWS

The Washington Workers' Compensation Act provides disability benefits to employees injured on the job or who suffer occupational diseases as a result of their jobs, subject to specified qualifications and limitations.[18]

[113.10] EMPLOYMENT-AT-WILL DEVELOPMENTS

Washington courts have adopted several judicial exceptions to the employment-at-will principle, as noted below.

Public policy exception: Washington courts have ruled that where an employee is discharged in violation of some public policy, an action may lie in tort for wrongful discharge.[19]

Implied contract exception: The Washington Supreme Court has ruled that statements in an employee handbook may create an implied employment contract, foreclosing discharge unless the employer complies with the language of the handbook.[20]

Intentional infliction of emotional distress exception: Washington courts will permit a cause of action where an employer's discharge is so outrageous that it exceeds all reasonable bounds of decency and inflicts severe emotional distress upon the person so discharged.[21]

NOTES TO CHAPTER 113

1. Revised Code of Washington, Section 41.56.010, *et seq.*
2. Revised Code of Washington, Section 28.B.52.010, *et seq.*
3. Revised Code of Washington, Section 49.66.010, *et seq.*
4. Revised Code of Washington, Section 49.66.010, *et seq.*
5. Revised Code of Washington, Section 54.04.170, *et seq.*
6. Revised Code of Washington, Section 9.22.010.
7. Revised Code of Washington, Section 49.44.100.
8. Revised Code of Washington, Section 7.04.010.
9. Revised Code of Washington, Section 9.16.030.
10. Revised Code of Washington, Section 49.44.120.
11. Washington Public Laws, Chapter 208 (L. 1982).
12. WAC, Section 296–126–050.
13. Revised Code of Washington, Section 26.28.060, *et seq.*
14. Revised Code of Washington, Sections 26.28.060 and 49.12.12.
15. Revised Code of Washington, Section 49.48.010.
16. Washington Public Laws, S.B. 2386 (L. 1973).
17. Washington Public Laws, S.B. 4831, Section 15 (L. 1984).
18. Revised Code of Washington, Section 50.04.010, *et seq.*
19. *Thompson v. St. Regis Paper Co.,* 685 P.2d 1081 (Wash., 1984).
20. *Roberts v. Atlantic Richfield Co.,* 568 P.2d 764 (Wash., 1977).
21. *Contreras v. Crown Zellerbach Corp.,* 565 P.2d 1173 (Wash., 1977).

114

West Virginia
Labor Laws

[114.01] LABOR RELATIONS LAWS

West Virginia Labor Management Relations Act: Section 21-1A-1, *et seq.,* of the West Virginia Code provides that employers with fifteen or more employees, other than employers and employees specifically exempted, and excluding the state and subdivisions thereof, must recognize and bargain in good faith with unions properly certified as representatives of their employees. The statute also provides for the machinery to conduct representation elections, procedures to process unfair labor practice charges against employers and labor organizations, and a process to mediate labor disputes.[1]

Nonright-to-work policy: Union security (union shop) clauses are permissible in the state of West Virginia inasmuch as West Virginia has not adopted a right-to-work statute pursuant to Section 14(b) of the Labor Management Relations Act.

[114.02] STRIKES, PICKETING, AND BOYCOTT LAWS

Unlawful assembly: West Virginia statutes make it unlawful for any person to engage in a riot or unlawful assemblage.[2]

Use of out-of-state police: Section 61-6-11 of the West Virginia Code makes it unlawful for any person or firm to employ any person not a bona fide resident of the state to perform police duty or in any way to aid or assist in the execution of the laws of the state.

Interference with employment at mines: Section 22-2-77 of the West Virginia Code makes it unlawful for any person to attempt to prevent anyone from working in or about any mine who has the lawful right and desire to work therein.

[114.03] MEDIATION AND ARBITRATION LAWS

Section 55-10-1, *et seq.,* of the West Virginia Code provides that all persons who shall have any controversy, may submit such controversy to the arbitration of any person to be mutually agreed upon by the parties, and that such submission may be entered on record in any court. Section 21-1A-1 of the West Virginia Code provides that the West Virginia Commissioner of Labor, or his or her designee, may investigate and mediate labor disputes and shall arbitrate, or arrange for the selection of boards of arbitration on such terms as all of the parties to such dispute may agree upon.

[114.04] REGULATION OF UNION ACTIVITIES

Section 47-2-3 of the West Virginia Code makes it unlawful for anyone to misuse or forge a union label.

[114.05] REGULATION OF EMPLOYMENT PRACTICES

Anti-discrimination laws: Section 5-11-19, *et seq.,* of the West Virginia Code prohibits discrimination in the employment of an individual by reason of race, religion, color, sex, national origin, ancestry, blindness, age, or handicap.

Protection of political freedom: West Virginia employers are forbidden to attempt to influence or coerce the political and voting decisions of their employees through threats of discharge or other such reprisals.[3]

Employment under false pretense: West Virginia statutes forbid employment agencies to make any false statement to any person seeking employment in regard to any employment or the circumstances surrounding such employment.[4]

Jury duty: West Virginia employers are forbidden to attempt to deprive any employee of his or her employment because such employee serves as a juror or attends court for prospective jury service.[5]

Military duty: West Virginia laws require West Virginia employers to reemploy members of an organized militia and reinstate them to their former or similar position upon their return from military duty.[6]

Polygraph restrictions: West Virginia employers are prohibited from requiring applicants and employees to submit to a lie detector or similar test as a condition of employment or continued employment, except under certain conditions as enumerated in the statute.[7]

Medical examination payments: Section 21-3-17 of the West Virginia Code obligates employers to pay for the costs of any medical examinations required of applicants or employees.

Equal pay: West Virginia laws forbid employers to discriminate between sexes in payment of wages for comparable work.[8]

[114.06] WAGE AND HOUR LAWS

Child labor: West Virginia statutes regulate the employment of children in gainful occupations and specify certain minimum age requirements in connection therewith.[9]

Voting time: West Virginia statutes provide that an employee who is eligible and duly registered to vote at a primary, general, or special election shall be excused from his or her employment not exceeding three consecutive hours, without reduction in pay, to exercise such voting privileges, provided such employee does not have three consecutive hours between the time of opening and closing of polls when he or she is not working for the employer.[10]

Payment of wages: Section 21-5-3 of the West Virginia Code provides that all employers except railroad companies shall pay earned wages to employees at least once every two weeks unless otherwise provided by special agreement.

Payment upon termination: West Virginia employers are required to pay discharged employees their earned wages in full within seventy-two hours after termination.[11] An employee who voluntarily resigns his or her job is due accrued wages no later than the next regular payday.[12]

Garnishments: Section 46A-2-131 of the West Virginia Code forbids discharge of any employee because his or her wages have been subjected to garnishment orders.

Medical insurance conversion: Section 33-16A-1, *et seq.,* of the West Virginia Code requires employers to permit terminating employees to convert insurance coverage from a group medical plan to an individual plan, provided certain conditions and eligibility standards are met.

[114.07] SAFETY AND HEALTH LAWS

General provisions: West Virginia health and safety laws require employers within the state to furnish safe employment for employees, and to furnish and use safety devices and safeguards, adopt and use methods and processes reasonably adequate to render such employment safe, and do every other thing reasonably necessary to protect life, health, and safety of employees.[13]

Toxic substances—right to know: Employers who use or manufacture toxic chemicals must disclose to employees the hazards of such substances and post notices and provide other information and training as specified in the statute.[14]

[114.08] UNEMPLOYMENT COMPENSATION LAWS

The West Virginia Unemployment Compensation laws are set forth in Section 21A-1-1, *et seq.,* of the West Virginia Code and govern the eligibility requirements of recipients of unemployment compensation benefits.

[114.09] WORKERS' COMPENSATION LAWS

The West Virginia Workers' Compensation Act provides disability benefits to employees injured on the job or who suffer occupational diseases as a result of their job, subject to specified qualifications and limitations.[15] Section 23-5A-1 of the West Virginia Code forbids discharge or other discrimination in employment because of filing a workers' compensation claim.

[114.10] EMPLOYMENT–AT–WILL DEVELOPMENTS

West Virginia courts have recognized several judicial exceptions to the employment-at-will rule, as discussed below.

Public policy exception: The West Virginia Supreme Court has held actionable a case involving the discharge of an employee in retaliation of his efforts to get his employer to operate in compliance with state and federal banking laws. The court ruled that such discharge was in violation of public policy.[16]

Implied contract exception: A federal court of appeals, applying West Virginia law, has ruled that a personnel policy handbook may create an implied employment contract, prohibiting the discharge of an employee unless the employer complies with the guidelines in such handbook.[17]

Intentional infliction of emotional distress exception: West Virginia courts may permit recovery of damages in wrongful discharge claims involving wanton, willful, or malicious conduct on the part of the employer that causes severe emotional distress on the part of the employee.[18]

NOTES TO CHAPTER 114

1. West Virginia Code, Section 21-1A-1, *et seq.*
2. West Virginia Code, Section 61-6-6.
3. West Virginia Code, Section 3-9-15.
4. West Virginia Code, Section 21-2-6.
5. West Virginia Code, Section 52-3-1.
6. West Virginia Code, Section 15-1F-8.
7. West Virginia Code, Section 21-5-5b.
8. West Virginia Code, Section 21-5B-3.
9. West Virginia Code, Section 21-6-1, *et seq.*
10. West Virginia Code, Section 3-1-42.
11. West Virginia Code, Section 21-5-4(b).
12. West Virginia Code, Section 21-5-4(c).

13. West Virginia Code, Section 21-3-1.
14. West Virginia Code, Section 21-3-18.
15. West Virginia Code, Section 23-1-1, *et seq.*
16. *Harless v. First Nat'l Bank in Fairmont,* 246 S.E.2d 270 (W.Va., 1978).
17. *McMillion v. Appalachian Power Co.,* 701 F.2d 166 (CA-4, 1983).
18. *Harless v. First Nat'l Bank in Fairmont, supra.*

115

Wisconsin
Labor Laws

Employment Peace Act: Section 111.01, *et seq.,* of the Wisconsin Statutes provides that private employers, other than employers and employees specifically excluded, must recognize and bargain in good faith with unions properly certified as representatives of their employees. The statute provides for the machinery to conduct representation elections and procedures to process unfair labor practice charges against employers and labor organizations.[1]

Municipal employees' bargaining rights: Section 111.70, *et seq.,* of the Wisconsin Statutes accords collective bargaining rights to municipal employees and provides procedures to conduct elections to determine bargaining representatives and guidelines to process unfair labor practice cases.

State employees' bargaining rights: Wisconsin statutes provide that employees of the state of Wisconsin shall have the right to form, join, or assist labor organizations and to select representatives of their own choosing and that state agencies and departments have the duty to meet and negotiate with their employees' duly recognized bargaining representatives.[2]

Police officers' and firefighters' bargaining representatives: Section 111.77, *et seq.,* of the Wisconsin Statutes extends to municipal fire and police departments and their employees the duty to bargain collectively in good faith, including the duty to refrain from strikes and lockouts.

Nonright-to-work policy: Union security (union shop) clauses are permissible in the state of Wisconsin inasmuch as Wisconsin has not adopted a right-to-work statute pursuant to Section 14(b) of the Labor Management Relations Act.

"Yellow-dog" contracts: Wisconsin statutes make it unlawful for anyone to coerce or compel any person to enter into an agreement not to join or become a member of any labor organization as a condition of employment.[3]

[115.02]   STRIKES, PICKETING, AND BOYCOTT LAWS

Anti-injunction statutes: Wisconsin statutes limit the power of Wisconsin courts to issue injunctions in any case involving a labor dispute.[4]

Unlawful assembly: Section 347.02 of the Wisconsin Statutes forbids three or more persons to assemble together to do an unlawful act.

Interference with employment: Wisconsin statutes make it unlawful for anyone to attempt to prevent any person from engaging in any lawful occupation at any place he or she sees fit.[5]

Disorderly conduct: Section 348.5 of the Wisconsin Statutes makes it unlawful for any person to engage in any violent, abusive, loud, boisterous, vulgar, lewd, wanton, obscene, or otherwise disorderly conduct tending to create or provoke a breach of the peace.

Mass picketing: Section 111.06(2)(f) of the Wisconsin Statutes prohibits mass and obstructive picketing.

Strike vote: Section 111.06(2)(e) of the Wisconsin Statutes forbids picketing in a strike not authorized by the majority of employees concerned therewith.

"Sit-down" strikes: Section 111.06(2)(b) of the Wisconsin Statutes prohibits anyone from remaining on an employer's premises without the employer's permission.

Strikebreakers: Wisconsin statutes make it unlawful for any employer to utilize professional strikebreakers to replace an employee involved in a strike or lockout through the use of misrepresentations, threats, or force.[6]

Picketing of resident or dwelling: Wisconsin laws forbid anyone to engage in picketing near or about the residence or dwelling place of another individual.[7]

Secondary boycotts: Section 111.06(2)(g) of the Wisconsin Statutes makes it unlawful for anyone to engage in a secondary boycott.

[115.03] MEDIATION AND ARBITRATION LAWS

Wisconsin statutes provide that any written agreement to submit an existing controversy to arbitration shall be valid, enforceable, and irrevocable, except on such grounds as exist at law or equity for the revocation thereof.[8] Section 111.50, *et seq.,* of the Wisconsin Statutes provides that it shall be the duty of public utility employers and their employees to exert every reasonable effort to settle labor disputes by the making of agreements through collective bargaining and to prevent, if possible, the collective bargaining process from reaching a state of impasse and stalemate through conciliation and arbitration.

[115.04] REGULATION OF UNION ACTIVITIES

Wisconsin statutes make it unlawful for anyone to misuse or forge a union label or other union insignia.[9] Section 211.01, *et seq.,* of the Wisconsin Statutes provides for the registration and examination of employee welfare funds by the Wisconsin Insurance Commissioner. Wisconsin statutes require every representative of employees for collective bargaining to keep an adequate record of the union's financial transactions and to present each member a detailed written financial report thereof on an annual basis.[10]

[115.05] REGULATION OF EMPLOYMENT PRACTICES

Anti-discrimination laws: Wisconsin statutes prohibit discrimination in the employment of an individual by reason of age, race, creed, color, sex, marital status, national origin, ancestry, handicap, arrest record, conviction record, or sexual orientation.[11]

Polygraph restrictions: Wisconsin employers are forbidden to require any applicant or employee to submit to polygraph, voice stress analysis, or similar test, to test the honesty of such applicant or employee, without his or her consent.[12]

Protection of political freedom: Section 103.18 of the Wisconsin Statutes forbids employers to attempt to influence the political or voting decisions of their employees through the threat of discharge or other such reprisals.

Jury duty: Section 756.25 of the Wisconsin Statutes makes it unlawful for employers to attempt to deprive any employee of his or her employment because such employee serves as a juror or attends court for prospective jury service.

Arrest records: Wisconsin statutes make it unlawful to discriminate in employment against an individual because of any arrest record.[13]

Access to personnel records: Wisconsin statutes provide that employers shall, at reasonable times and intervals, and upon proper application of an employee, permit the employee to inspect his or her personnel files.[14]

Blacklisting: Wisconsin statutes forbid any two or more persons to maintain a blacklist of any individual for the purpose of preventing such person from receiving employment.[15]

Plant closure: Section 109.07 of the Wisconsin Statutes requires every employer employing 100 or more persons to give the State Department of Industry, Labor, and Human Relations at least sixty days' notice of any relocation of its operations.

Medical examination payments: Section 103.37 of the Wisconsin Statutes requires employers to pay all costs of medical examinations incurred as a result of requiring employees or applicants to undergo medical examinations.

Whistle-blowing statute (state employees): Section 230.80, *et seq.*, of the Wisconsin Statutes forbids discharge or discrimination against any state employee because he or she reports a suspected violation of some federal or state law, rule, or regulation to appropriate authorities.

Equal pay: Wisconsin statutes make it unlawful for any employer to discriminate in wages on the basis of sex, age, race, color, handicap, creed, national origin, or ancestry.[16]

[115.06]   WAGE AND HOUR LAWS

Child labor: Wisconsin statutes regulate the employment of children and specify minimum age requirements in connection therewith.[17] The Wisconsin child labor laws provide that children between 14 and 18 years of age may not be permitted to work in any gainful occupation during hours children are required to attend school.[18]

Voting time: Wisconsin statutes provide that an employee eligible and registered to vote in any public election shall be excused from his or her employment not exceeding three hours to exercise such voting privileges.[19]

Payment upon termination: Wisconsin employers are required to pay discharged employees, unless otherwise excluded, their wages in full within three days following termination.[20] An employee who voluntarily resigns his or her job is due all accrued wages within fifteen days of the date of termination.[21]

Garnishments: Section 812.235 of the Wisconsin Statutes forbid discharge of an employee because his or her wages have been subjected to garnishment for any one indebtedness.

Medical insurance conversion: Section 632.897 of the Wisconsin Statutes provides that terminating employees must be given the opportunity to convert group medical coverage to individual coverage, provided the employee assumes the payment of the premium of such policy and meets other eligibility criteria.

[115.07]   SAFETY AND HEALTH LAWS

General provision: Section 101.11, *et seq.*, of the Wisconsin Statutes requires employers to provide employees a safe work place and to furnish and use safety devices and safeguards to render such work place as safe as reasonably possible.

Toxic substances—right to know: Section 101.58, *et seq.*, of the Wisconsin Statutes requires employers who use or manufacture toxic substances to post signs in work areas that inform employees of the potential hazards and properties of such substances.

[115.08] UNEMPLOYMENT COMPENSATION LAWS

The Wisconsin unemployment compensation laws are set forth in Section 108.01, *et seq.,* of the Wisconsin Statutes and govern, among other things, the eligibility requirements of recipients of unemployment compensation benefits.

[115.09] WORKERS' COMPENSATION LAWS

Section 102.01, *et seq.,* of the Wisconsin Statutes sets forth the Wisconsin Workers' Compensation Act. The statute provides disability benefits to employees injured on the job or who suffer occupational diseases as a result of their jobs, subject to specified qualifications and limitations.[22]

[115.10] EMPLOYMENT–AT–WILL DEVELOPMENTS

Wisconsin courts have permitted some exceptions to the employment-at-will doctrine, as noted below.

Implied contract exception: Wisconsin courts have ruled that job security representations in an employee handbook may create an implied employment contract, requiring the employer to comply with all the terms contained therein, prior to a dismissal.[23]

Public policy exception: Wisconsin courts have ruled that where a discharge violates some constitutional or statutory provision, a cause of action will lie under the public policy exception to the at-will rule.[24]

NOTES TO CHAPTER 115

1. Wisconsin Statutes, Section 111.01, *et seq.*
2. Wisconsin Statutes, Section 111.80, *et seq.*
3. Wisconsin Statutes, Section 103.52.
4. Wisconsin Statutes, Section 103.56.
5. Wisconsin Statutes, Section 343.683.
6. Wisconsin Statutes, Section 348.472.
7. Wisconsin Statutes, Section 111.06(2)(a).
8. Wisconsin Statutes, Section 298.01.
9. Wisconsin Statutes, Section 132.19.

10. Wisconsin Statutes, Section 111.08.

11. Wisconsin Statutes, Section 111.321, *et seq.*

12. Wisconsin Statutes, Section 111.37.

13. Wisconsin Statutes, Section 111.31, 111.335.

14. Wisconsin Statutes, Section 103.13, *et seq.*

15. Wisconsin Statutes, Section 343.682.

16. Wisconsin Statutes, Section 111.36.

17. Wisconsin Statutes, Section 103.66, *et seq.*

18. Wisconsin Statutes, Section 103.78.

19. Wisconsin Statutes, Section 6.76.

20. Wisconsin Statutes, Section 109.03.

21. Wisconsin Statutes, Section 109.03.

22. Wisconsin Statutes, Section 102.01, *et seq.*

23. *Ferrero v. Voelsch,* 350 N.W.2d 735 (Wis. S.Ct., 1985).

24. *Ward v. Frito-Lay, Inc.,* 290 N.W.2d 536 (Wisconsin Ct. of App., 1980).

116

Wyoming Labor Laws

[116.01] LABOR RELATIONS LAWS

General right to organize: Section 27-7-101 of the Wyoming Statutes accords employees within the state the right to form, join, or assist labor unions as a matter of public policy.

Firefighters' bargaining rights: Wyoming statutes extend collective bargaining rights to firefighters and provide that such firefighters may bargain collectively with their respective cities, towns, or counties, by and through representatives of their own choosing as to wages, rates of pay, working conditions, and all other terms and conditions of employment.[1]

Right-to-work statute: The Wyoming statutes prohibit the denial of employment to anyone on account of nonmembership in a labor union or organization.[2]

"Yellow-dog" contracts: Section 27-245.3 of the Wyoming Statutes makes it unlawful for anyone to coerce or compel any person to enter into an agreement not to join or become a member of any labor organization as a condition of employment.

[116.02] STRIKES, PICKETING, AND BOYCOTT LAWS

Anti-injunction statute: Wyoming laws limit the power of courts to issue a restraining order or an injunction in any case involving any labor dispute.[3]

Unlawful assembly: Section 6-10-108 of the Wyoming Statutes prohibits three or more persons to assemble together to do an unlawful act.

Use of police during strikes: Wyoming laws provide that no armed police force or detective agency shall be brought into the state for the suppression of domestic violence, except upon proper application to the state legislature or executive branch.[4]

[116.03] MEDIATION AND ARBITRATION LAWS

Wyoming has adopted the Uniform Arbitration Act, recognizing any written agreement to submit an existing controversy to arbitration as valid, enforceable, and irrevocable, except on such grounds as exist at law or equity for the revocation thereof.[5] Article 19, Section 5, of the Wyoming Constitution authorizes the state legislature to establish courts of arbitration, whose duty is to hear and determine all differences and controversies between labor organizations and employers.

[116.04] REGULATION OF UNION ACTIVITIES

Wyoming statutes exempt union officers and members from liability for the unlawful acts of other officers or members in the absence of actual participation, authorization, or ratification.[6]

[116.05] REGULATION OF EMPLOYMENT PRACTICES

Anti-discrimination laws: Wyoming statutes prohibit discrimination in the employment of an individual by reason of sex, race, creed, color, national origin, or ancestry.[7]

Protection of political freedom: Wyoming labor laws make it unlawful for any employer within the state to attempt to prevent his or her employees from engaging or participating in politics, or from becoming candidates for public office.[8]

Jury service: Wyoming employers are forbidden to attempt to deprive any employee of his or her employment because such employee serves as a juror or attends court for prospective jury service.[9]

Military duty (public employees): Section 19-3-105(e) of the Wyoming Statutes forbids state agencies, cities, counties, or political subdivisions thereof, to discharge employees because of their membership in the National Guard.

Access to medical records: Section 27-11-113 of the Wyoming Statutes provides that an employee shall have access to his or her medical records when such records are a result of some physical examination required by the employer.

Equal pay: Section 27-4-301 of the Wyoming Statutes forbids employers to pay any female employee a salary or hourly wage rate less than that which is paid to male employees for equal or similar work.

[116.06] WAGE AND HOUR LAWS

Child labor: Wyoming statutes regulate the employment of children within the state and specify minimum age requirements in connection therewith.[10]

Voting time: Wyoming statutes provide that an employee eligible and duly registered to vote at a primary, general, or special election shall be excused from his or her employment to exercise such voting privilege.[11]

Payment on termination: Wyoming statutes provide that employees who are discharged from their employment must be paid within twenty-four hours of discharge.[12] Employers are required to pay employees who quit all accrued wages in full within seventy-two hours after separation from employment, except as otherwise provided.[13]

Garnishments: Section 40-14-506 of the Wyoming Statutes forbids discharge of an employee because his or her wages are being subjected to garnishment orders.

[116.07] SAFETY AND HEALTH LAWS

Section 27-11-105(a) of the Wyoming Statutes requires employers within the state to furnish their employees a place of employment free from recognized hazards that are causing or likely to cause death or serious physical harm.

[116.08] UNEMPLOYMENT COMPENSATION LAWS

Wyoming's unemployment compensation provisions are governed by Section 27-3-101, *et seq.,* of the Wyoming Statutes.

[116.09] WORKERS' COMPENSATION LAWS

Section 27-12-101, *et seq.,* of the Wyoming Statutes sets forth the Wyoming Workmen's Compensation Act. The statute generally provides for disability benefits to employees injured on the job or who suffer occupational diseases as a result of their jobs, subject to specified qualifications and limitations.[14]

[116.10] EMPLOYMENT–AT–WILL DEVELOPMENTS

Wyoming courts have strictly adhered to the employment-at-will doctrine, permitting no exceptions as of this writing. However, in keeping with rather pervasive trends in other states, the at-will doctrine is likely to erode in Wyoming in future years.

NOTES TO CHAPTER 116

1. Wyoming Statutes, Section 27-10-101, *et seq.*
2. Wyoming Statutes, Section 27-7-108.
3. Wyoming Statutes, Section 27-7-103.
4. Wyoming Constitution, Article 19, Section 6.
5. Wyoming Statutes, Section 1-36-103.
6. Wyoming Statutes, Section 27-7-245.

7. Wyoming Statutes, Section 27-9-105, *et seq.*
8. Wyoming Statutes, Section 22-341, *et seq.*
9. Wyoming Statutes, Section 1-11-401(a).
10. Wyoming Statutes, Section 27-6-107, *et seq.*
11. Wyoming Statutes, Section 22-2-111.
12. Wyoming Statutes, Section 27-4-104.
13. Wyoming Statutes, Section 27-4-104.
14. Wyoming Statutes, Section 27-12-401, *et seq.*

Index